COMPACT
WORLD
ATLAS

LONDON, NEW YORK, MUNICH,
MELBOURNE, DELHI

A DORLING KINDERSLEY PUBLISHING BOOK
www.dk.com

EDITOR-IN-CHIEF
Andrew Heritage

SENIOR MANAGING ART EDITOR
Philip Lord

SENIOR CARTOGRAPHIC MANAGER
David Roberts

SENIOR CARTOGRAPHC EDITOR
Simon Mumford

MANAGING EDITOR
Punita Singh

PROJECT LEADER
Uma Bhattacharya

PROJECT EDITORS
Debra Clapson, Razia Grover

PROJECT CARTOGRAPHER
Alok Pathak

PROJECT DESIGNERS
Rachana Bhattacharya, Karen Gregory, Sabyasachi Kundu

SYSTEMS COORDINATOR
Philip Rowles

PRODUCTION
Michelle Thomas

First American edition 2001
Published in the United States by Dorling Kindersley Publishing, Inc.,
375 Hudson Street,
New York, New York 10014
Copyright © 2001, 2002 Dorling Kindersley Limited
Reprinted 2002

A Penguin Company

A CIP catalog record for this book is available from the Library of Congress

ISBN 0-7894-7987-7

Reproduced by Mondadori, Italy

Printed and bound in Spain by Artes Gráficas Toledo

D.L. TO: 367 - 2002

This book is supported by a website. For the most up-to-date information, visit:
www.dk.com/world-desk-reference

KEY TO MAP SYMBOLS

PHYSICAL FEATURES

Elevation

- 4,000m/13,124ft
- 2,000m/6,562ft
- 1,000m/3,281ft
- 500m/1,640ft
- 250m/820ft
- 100m/328ft
- 0
- Below sea level

△	Mountain
▽	Depression
▲	Volcano
)(	Pass/tunnel
▨	Sandy desert

DRAINAGE FEATURES

———	Major perennial river
———	Minor perennial river
– – –	Seasonal river
———	Canal
❙	Waterfall
⬭	Perennial lake
⬭	Seasonal lake
▨	Wetland

ICE FEATURES

▨	Permanent ice cap/ice shelf
▲▲▲	Winter limit of pack ice
▲▲▲	Summer limit of pack ice

BORDERS

———	Full international border
– – – –	Disputed de facto border
· · · · ·	Territorial claim border
x—x—x	Cease-fire line
– – –	Undefined boundary
———	Internal administrative boundary

COMMUNICATIONS

———	Major road
———	Minor road
———	Rail
✈	International airport

SETTLEMENTS

◉	Over 500,000
◉	100,000 - 500,000
○	50,000 - 100,000
○	Less than 50,000
●	National capital
●	Internal administrative capital

MISCELLANEOUS FEATURES

+	Site of interest
␣␣␣	Ancient wall

GRATICULE FEATURES

———	Line of latitude/longitude/Equator
– – –	Tropic/Polar circle
25°	Degrees of latitude/longitude

NAMES

Physical features

Andes	
Sahara	Landscape features
Ardennes	
Land's End	Headland
Mont Blanc 4,807m	Elevation/volcano/pass
Blue Nile	River/canal/waterfall
Ross Ice Shelf	Ice feature
PACIFIC OCEAN	
Sulu Sea	Sea features
Palk Strait	
Chile Rise	Undersea feature

Regions

FRANCE	Country
JERSEY (to UK)	Dependent territory
KANSAS	Administrative region
Dordogne	Cultural region

Settlements

PARIS	Capital city
SAN JUAN	Dependent territory capital city
Chicago	
Kettering	Other settlements
Burke	

INSET MAP SYMBOLS

▭	Urban area
⬠	City
▭	Park
▪	Place of interest
▫	Suburb/district

CONTENTS

THE
WORLD ATLAS

NORTH &
CENTRAL AMERICA

SOUTH AMERICA

AFRICA

EUROPE

ABBREVIATIONS

AFGH.
Afghanistan

ALB.
Albania

AUT.
Austria

AZ. OR AZERB.
Azerbaijan

B. & H.
Bosnia &
Herzegovina

BELA.
Belarus

BELG.
Belgium

BOTS.
Botswana

BULG.
Bulgaria

CAMB.
Cambodia

C.A.R.
Central African
Republic

CRO.
Croatia

CZ. REP.
Czech Republic

DOM. REP.
Dominican
Republic

EST.
Estonia

EQ. GUINEA
Equatorial
Guinea

HUNG.
Hungary

KYRG.
Kyrgyzstan

LAT.
Latvia

LIECH.
Liechtenstein

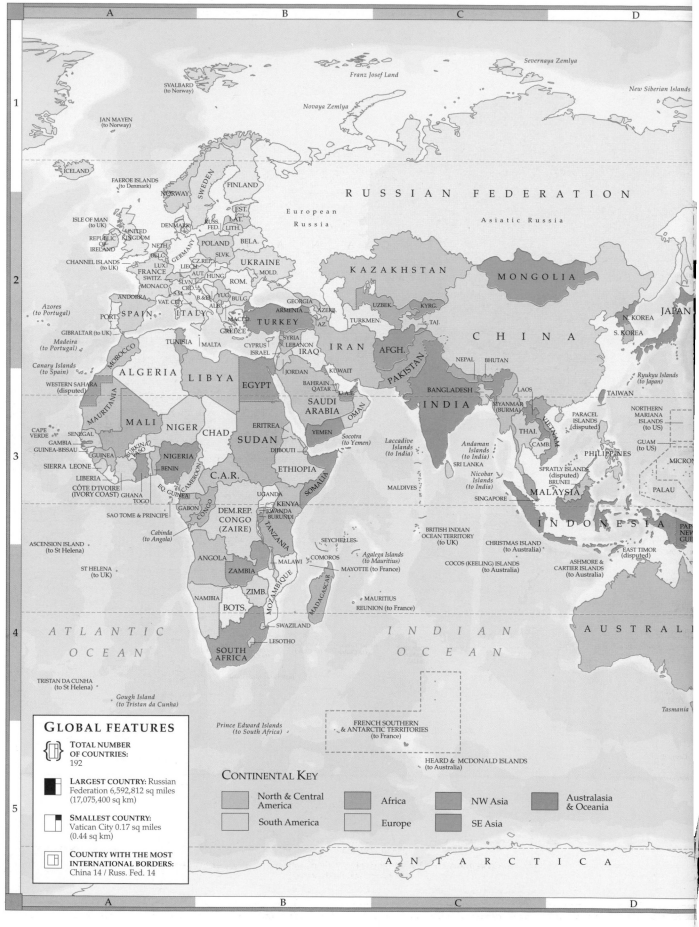

GLOBAL FEATURES

**TOTAL NUMBER
OF COUNTRIES:**
192

LARGEST COUNTRY: Russian
Federation 6,592,812 sq miles
(17,075,400 sq km)

SMALLEST COUNTRY:
Vatican City 0.17 sq miles
(0.44 sq km)

**COUNTRY WITH THE MOST
INTERNATIONAL BORDERS:**
China 14 / Russ. Fed. 14

CONTINENTAL KEY

North & Central America

South America

Africa

Europe

NW Asia

SE Asia

Australasia & Oceania

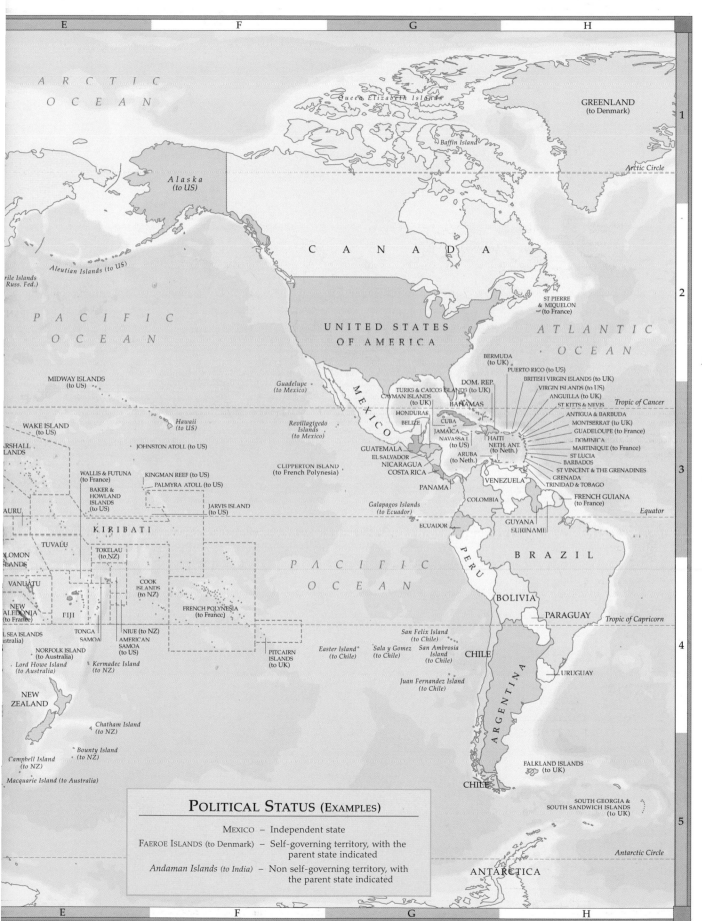

A R C T I C
O C E A N

Queen Elizabeth Islands

GREENLAND
(to Denmark)

1

Baffin Island

Arctic Circle

*Alaska
(to US)*

Aleutian Islands (to US)

*rile Islands
Russ. Fed.)*

C A N A D A

P A C I F I C
O C E A N

2

ST PIERRE
& MIQUELON
(to France)

A T L A N T I C
O C E A N

UNITED STATES
OF AMERICA

BERMUDA
(to UK)

MIDWAY ISLANDS
(to US)

PUERTO RICO (to US)
BRITISH VIRGIN ISLANDS (to UK)
VIRGIN ISLANDS (to US)
ANGUILLA (to UK)
ST KITTS & NEVIS

*Guadelupe
(to Mexico)*

DOM. REP.

TURKS & CAICOS ISLANDS (to UK)
CAYMAN ISLANDS
(to UK)

Tropic of Cancer

BAHAMAS

WAKE ISLAND
(to US)

*Hawaii
(to US)*

*Revillagigedo
Islands
(to Mexico)*

HONDURAS
BELIZE

CUBA

ANTIGUA & BARBUDA
MONTSERRAT (to UK)
GUADELOUPE (to France)
DOMINICA
MARTINIQUE (to France)
ST LUCIA
BARBADOS
ST VINCENT & THE GRENADINES
GRENADA
TRINIDAD & TOBAGO

ARSHALL
LANDS

JOHNSTON ATOLL (to US)

JAMAICA
NAVASSA I
(to US)

HAITI

NETH. ANT.
(to Neth.)

3

WALLIS & FUTUNA
(to France)

KINGMAN REEF (to US)
PALMYRA ATOLL (to US)

GUATEMALA
EL SALVADOR
NICARAGUA
COSTA RICA

ARUBA
(to Neth.)

*CLIPPERTON ISLAND
(to French Polynesia)*

AURU

BAKER &
HOWLAND
ISLANDS
(to US)

JARVIS ISLAND
(to US)

PANAMA

VENEZUELA

FRENCH GUIANA
(to France)

COLOMBIA

K I R I B A T I

*Galapagos Islands
(to Ecuador)*

GUYANA
SURINAME

Equator

TUVALU

ECUADOR

TOKELAU
(to NZ)

P A C I F I C

PERU

B R A Z I L

OLOMON
LANDS

O C E A N

VANUATU

COOK
ISLANDS
(to NZ)

FRENCH POLYNESIA
(to France)

BOLIVIA

NEW
ALEDONIA
(to France)

FIJI

PARAGUAY

Tropic of Capricorn

L SEA ISLANDS
ustralia)

TONGA
SAMOA

NIUE (to NZ)
AMERICAN
SAMOA
(to US)

*San Felix Island
(to Chile)*

NORFOLK ISLAND
(to Australia)

*Kermadec Island
(to NZ)*

PITCAIRN
ISLANDS
(to UK)

Easter Island
(to Chile)

*Sala y Gomez
(to Chile)*

*San Ambrosia
Island
(to Chile)*

CHILE

4

*Lord Howe Island
(to Australia)*

A R G E N T I N A

URUGUAY

NEW
ZEALAND

*Chatham Island
(to NZ)*

*Juan Fernandez Island
(to Chile)*

*Campbell Island
(to NZ)*

*Bounty Island
(to NZ)*

Macquarie Island (to Australia)

FALKLAND ISLANDS
(to UK)

CHILE

SOUTH GEORGIA &
SOUTH SANDWICH ISLANDS
(to UK)

5

Antarctic Circle

POLITICAL STATUS (EXAMPLES)

MEXICO – Independent state

FAEROE ISLANDS (to Denmark) – Self-governing territory, with the
parent state indicated

Andaman Islands (to India) – Non self-governing territory, with
the parent state indicated

ANTARCTICA

ABBREVIATIONS

LITH.
Lithuania

LUX.
Luxembourg

MACED.
Macedonia

MOLD.
Moldova

NETH.
Netherlands

NETH. ANT.
Netherland
Antilles

PORT.
Portugal

ROM.
Romania

RUSS. FED.
Russian
Federation

SLVK.
Slovakia

SLVN.
Slovenia

S. M.
San Marino

SWITZ.
Switzerland

TAJ.
Tajikistan

THAI.
Thailand

TURKMEN.
Turkmenistan

U. A. E.
United Arab
Emirates

UZBECK.
Uzbekistan

VAT. CITY
Vatican City

YUG.
Yugoslavia

ZIMB.
Zimbabwe

THE PHYSICAL WORLD

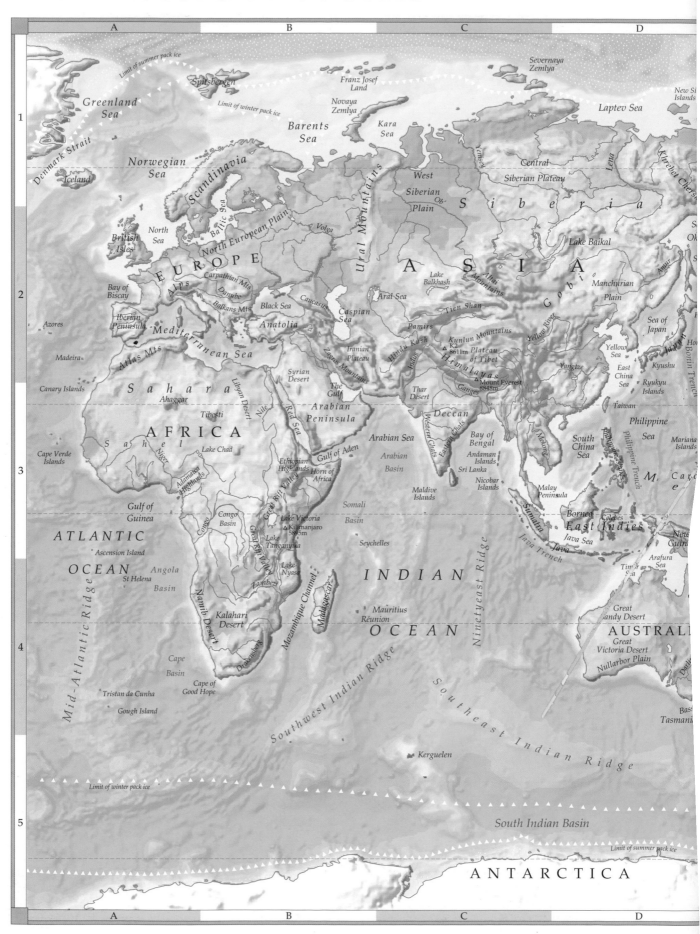

Greenland Sea

Spitsbergen

Limit of summer pack ice

Franz Josef Land

Novaya Zemlya

Severnaya Zemlya

New Si Islands

Laptev Sea

Limit of winter pack ice

Barents Sea

Kara Sea

Denmark Strait

Iceland

Norwegian Sea

Scandinavia

Baltic Sea

Yenisey

Central Siberian Plateau

Lena

Khrebet Chersk

British Isles

North Sea

North European Plain

Volga

Ural Mountains

West Siberian Plain

Ob

S i b e r i a

Si Ok

EUROPE

Alps

Carpathian Mts

Danube

Balkans Mts

A S I A

Lake Baikal

Amur

Manchurian Plain

Sea of Japan

Bay of Biscay

Black Sea

Caucasus

Aral Sea

Lake Balkhash

Altai Mountains

Gobi

Azores

Iberian Peninsula

Mediterranean Sea

Anatolia

Caspian Sea

Pamirs

Tien Shan

Yellow River

Yellow Sea

East China Sea

Kyushu

Ryukyu Islands

Bonin Islan

Madeira

Atlas Mts

Zagros Mountains

Iranian Plateau

Hindu Kush

Indus

Kunlun Mountains

K2 8611m

Plateau of Tibet

Himalayas

Mount Everest 8848m

Yangtze

Canary Islands

Sahara

Ahaggar

Libyan Desert

Nile

Syrian Desert

The Gulf

Arabian Peninsula

Thar Desert

Ganges

Deccan

Taiwan

Tibesti

Red Sea

AFRICA

Sahel

Niger

Lake Chad

Adamawa Highlands

Gulf of Aden

Ethiopian Highlands

Horn of Africa

Arabian Sea

Arabian Basin

Western Ghats

Eastern Ghats

Bay of Bengal

Andaman Islands

Sri Lanka

Mekong

Philippine Sea

Mariana Islands

M Ca e

South China Sea

Philippine Trench

Cape Verde Islands

Maldive Islands

Nicobar Islands

Malay Peninsula

Gulf of Guinea

Congo

Congo Basin

Great Rift Valley

Lake Victoria

Kilimanjaro 5895m

Somali Basin

Sumatra

Java Trench

Borneo

Celebes

East Indies

Java Sea

Java

New Guin

ATLANTIC

Ascension Island

OCEAN

Angola Basin

St Helena

Lake Tanganyika

Lake Nyasa

Zambezi

Seychelles

I N D I A N

Ninetyeast Ridge

Arafura Sea

Timor Sea

Namib Desert

Mozambique Channel

Madagascar

Mauritius

Réunion

O C E A N

Great Sandy Desert

AUSTRALI

Mid-Atlantic Ridge

Kalahari Desert

Drakensberg

Cape Basin

Great Victoria Desert

Nullarbor Plain

Darli

Tristan da Cunha

Cape of Good Hope

Gough Island

Southwest Indian Ridge

Southeast Indian Ridge

Bass

Tasmani

Limit of winter pack ice

Kerguelen

South Indian Basin

Limit of summer pack ice

A N T A R C T I C A

ARCTIC OCEAN

East Siberian Sea
Limit of summer pack ice
Chukchi Sea
Brooks Range
Bering Strait
Mount McKinley (Denali) 6194m
Limit of winter pack ice
Bering Sea
Aleutian Basin
Aleutian Islands
Aleutian Trench
Gulf of Alaska
Coast Mountains
Vancouver Island
Coast Ranges

Beaufort Sea
Mackenzie
Great Bear Lake
Great Slave Lake
Hudson Bay
Canadian Shield
Lake Winnipeg
Great Plains
Mississippi
Sierra Nevada
Sierra Madre Occidental
Sierra Madre Oriental
Gulf of Mexico
Yucatan Peninsula
Middle America Trench

Ellesmere Island
Queen Elizabeth Islands
Baffin Island
Baffin Bay
Greenland
Arctic Circle

NORTH AMERICA
Péninsula d'Ungava
Labrador Sea
Laurentian Mountains
Great Lakes
Appalachian Mts.
Grand Banks of Newfoundland
North American Basin
Mid-Atlantic Ridge
Tropic of Cancer

ATLANTIC OCEAN
West Indies
Greater Antilles
Caribbean Sea
Lesser Antilles

Northwest Pacific Basin
Emperor Seamounts
Mendocino Fracture Zone
Murray Fracture Zone
Hawaiian Islands
Hawaii
Central Pacific Basin
Marshall Islands
Micronesia
Line Islands
Phoenix Islands
Marquesas Islands
Tuamotu Islands
Samoa
Polynesia

PACIFIC OCEAN

East Pacific Rise
Peru Basin
Easter Island
Juan Fernandez Islands

Galapagos Islands
Equator
Guiana Highlands
Amazon
Amazon Basin
SOUTH AMERICA
Andes
Peru Chile Trench
Planalto de Mato Grosso
Brazilian Highlands
Brazil Basin
Tropic of Capricorn
Gran Chaco
Pantanal
Pampas
Cerro Aconcagua 6959m
Argentine Basin

Tasman Sea
South Island
North Island
New Zealand
Campbell Plateau
Vanuatu
Fiji
Tonga
Cook Islands
New Caledonia
Kermadec Trench
Coral Sea
Solomon Islands

Patagonia
Falkland Islands
Tierra del Fuego
Cape Horn
South Georgia
South Sandwich Islands
Drake Passage
Antarctic Peninsula
Limit of winter pack ice
Antarctic Circle

GLOBAL FEATURES

LARGEST CONTINENT:
Asia 17,521,750 sq miles
(45,381,300 sq km)

SMALLEST CONTINENT:
Australasia 3,376,700 sq miles
(8,745,750 sq km)

LARGEST LAKE: Caspian Sea,
Asia 143,243 sq miles
(371,000 sq km)

LONGEST RIVER:
Nile, Africa
4,160 miles (6,695 km)

HIGHEST POINT:
Mt. Everest, China/Nepal
29,030 ft (8,848 m)

ELEVATION

4000 m	13 124 ft
2000 m	6562 ft
1000 m	3281 ft
500 m	1640 ft
250 m	820 ft
100 m	328 ft
Sea Level	Sea Level
-250 m	-820 ft
-500 m	-1640 ft
-1000 m	-3281 ft
-2000 m	-6562 ft
-3000 m	-9843 ft
-4000 m	-13 124 ft

TIME ZONES

The numbers represented thus: +2/-2, indicate the number of hours ahead or behind GMT (Greenwich Mean Time) of each time zone.

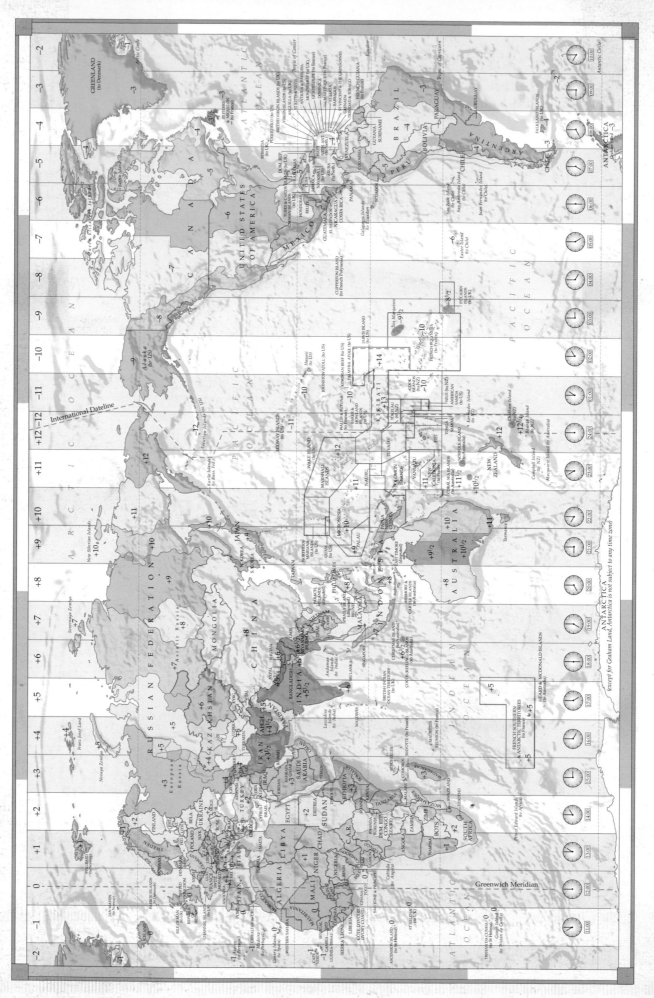

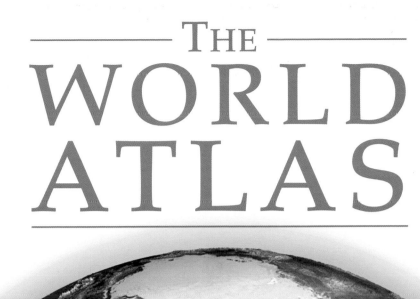

THE
WORLD
ATLAS

POPULATION

- ◉ Over 500,000
- ◉ 100,000 - 500,000
- ○ 50,000 - 100,000
- ○ Less than 50,000
- ● National capital

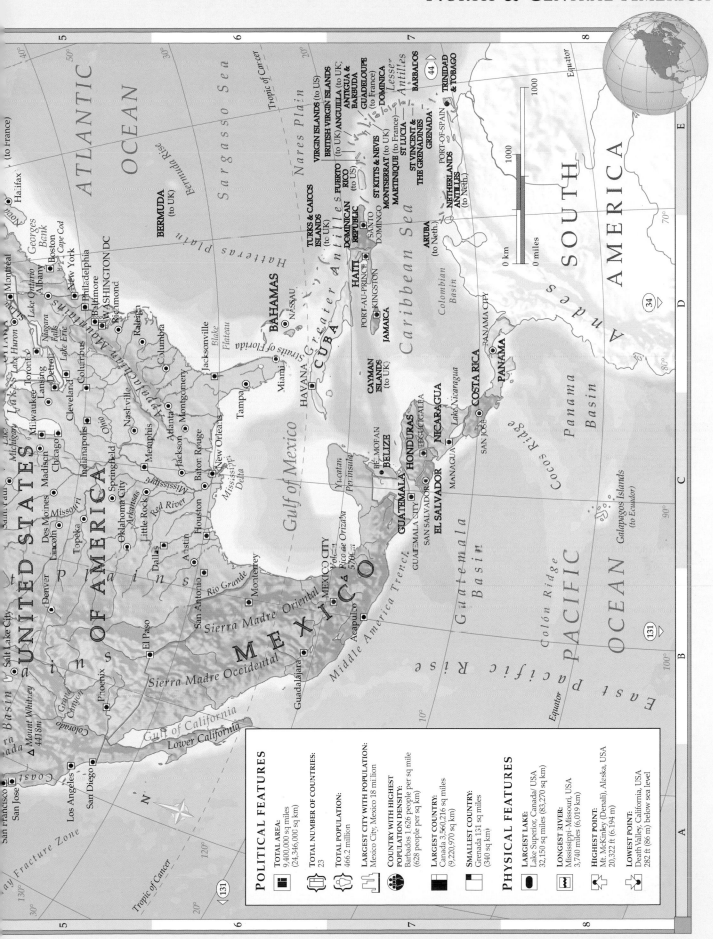

WESTERN CANADA & ALASKA

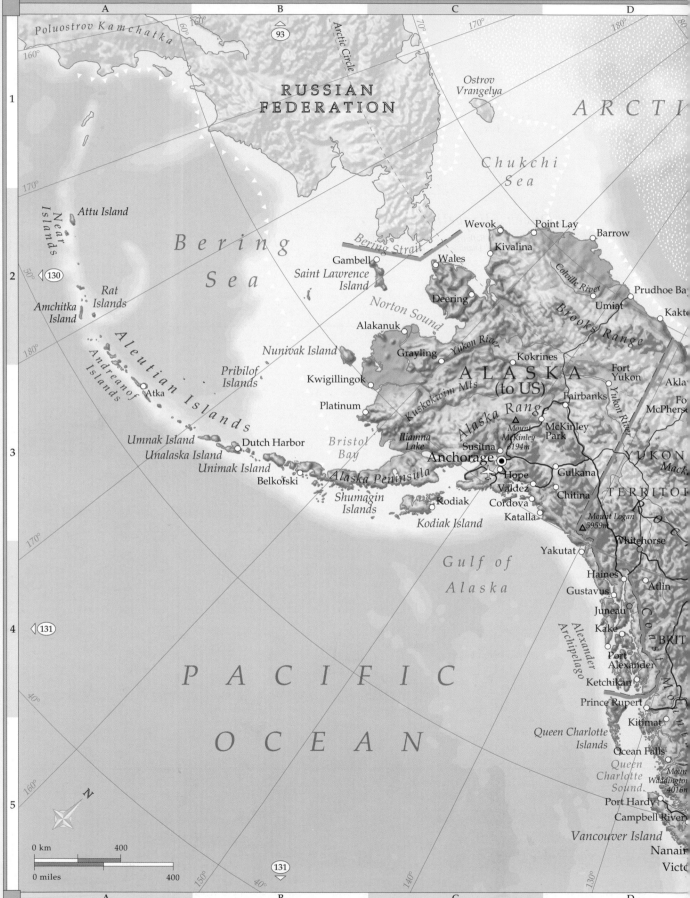

RUSSIAN FEDERATION

Poluostrov Kamchatka

Ostrov Vrangelya

ARCTI

Chukchi Sea

Bering Strait

Wevok
Point Lay
Barrow
Kivalina
Gambell
Wales
Deering
Coville River
Prudhoe Bay
Umiat
Kakte

Saint Lawrence Island

Norton Sound

Bering Sea

Near Islands

Attu Island

Rat Islands

Amchitka Island

Alakanuk
Grayling
Yukon River
Kokrines
Fort Yukon
Akla
Nunivak Island
ALASKA (to US)
Fairbanks
Fo McPhers
Brooks Range

Aleutian Islands

Andreanof Islands
Atka
Pribilof Islands
Kwigillingok
Platinum
Kuskokwim Mts
Alaska Range
△ *Mount McKinley 6194m*
McKinley Park
Yukon River

Umnak Island
Dutch Harbor
Unalaska Island
Unimak Island
Belkofski
Bristol Bay
Iliamna Lake
Susitna
Anchorage ●
Hope
Gulkana
YUKON
Mack.
TERRITOF
Alaska Peninsula
Valdez
Chitina
Shumagin Islands
Kodiak
Cordova
Katalla
△ *Mount Logan 5959m*
Kodiak Island

Yakutat
Whitehorse

Gulf of Alaska

Haines
Atlin
Gustavus
BRIT
Juneau
Kake
Alexander Archipelago
Port Alexander
Ketchikan
Prince Rupert
Coast Mountains
Kitimat
Queen Charlotte Islands
Ocean Falls
Queen Charlotte Sound
△ *Mount Waddington 4016m*
Port Hardy
Campbell River

PACIFIC OCEAN

Vancouver Island
Nanair
Victo

N

0 km   400
0 miles   400

93
130
131
131

ELEVATION

4000 m 13 124 ft	
2000 m 6562 ft	
1000 m 3281 ft	
500 m 1640 ft	
250 m 820 ft	
100 m 328 ft	
Sea Level	Sea Level
-250 m -820 ft	
-500 m -1640 ft	
-1000 m -3281 ft	
-2000 m -6562 ft	
-3000 m -9843 ft	
-4000 m -13 124 ft	

Eastern Canada

THE WORLD ATLAS

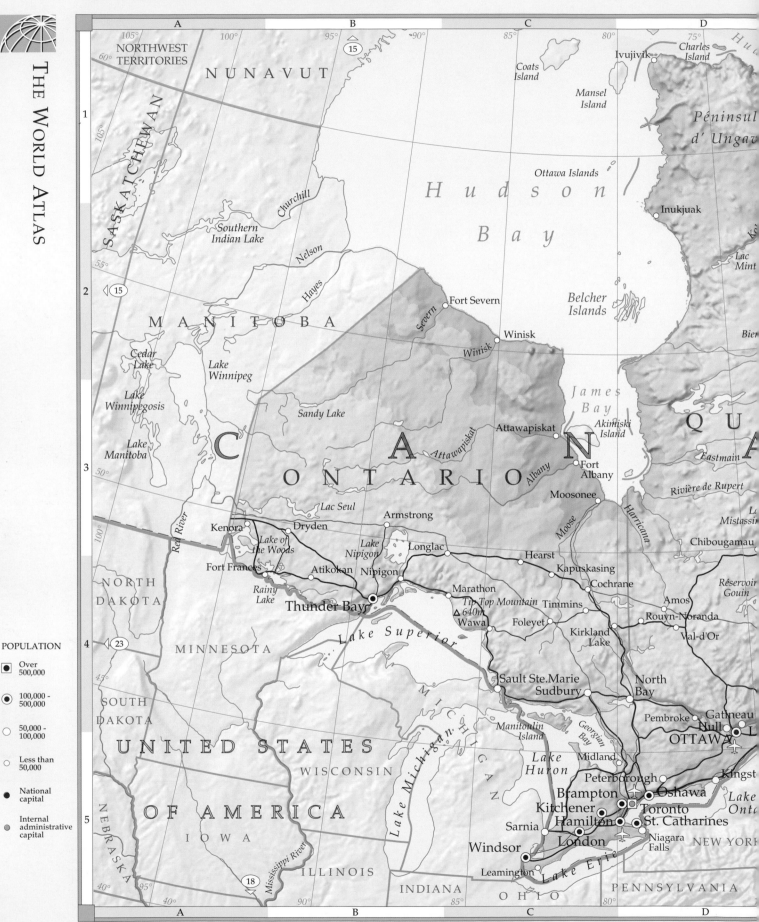

POPULATION

- ⊙ Over 500,000
- ◎ 100,000 – 500,000
- ○ 50,000 – 100,000
- ○ Less than 50,000
- ● National capital
- ● Internal administrative capital

NORTHWEST TERRITORIES

N U N A V U T

S A S K A T C H E W A N

Churchill

Southern Indian Lake

Nelson

Hayes

M A N I T O B A

Cedar Lake

Lake Winnipeg

Lake Winnipegosis

Lake Manitoba

Sandy Lake

C A N

O N T A R I O

Lac Seul

Kenora
Dryden
Armstrong
Lake Nipigon
Longlac

Fort Frances
Atikokan
Nipigon
Hearst
Kapuskasing
Cochrane

Rainy Lake

Thunder Bay

Marathon
Tip Top Mountain
△ 640m
Wawa

Timmins
Foleyet
Kirkland Lake

Amos
Rouyn-Noranda
Val-d'Or

Red River

N O R T H
D A K O T A

M I N N E S O T A

S O U T H
D A K O T A

U N I T E D   S T A T E S

W I S C O N S I N

O F   A M E R I C A

N E B R A S K A

I O W A

I L L I N O I S

I N D I A N A

Lake Superior

M I C H I G A N

Lake Michigan

Sault Ste.Marie
Sudbury

North Bay

Manitoulin Island

Georgian Bay

Lake Huron

Midland

Pembroke

Gatineau
Hull
OTTAWA
Kingston

Peterborough

Brampton
Kitchener
Hamilton
Sarnia
London
Windsor
Leamington

Oshawa
Toronto
St. Catharines
Niagara Falls

Lake Ontario

Lake Erie

O H I O

P E N N S Y L V A N I A

N E W   Y O R K

Mississippi River

HUDSON

Coats Island

Mansel Island

Ottawa Islands

H u d s o n

B a y

Ivujivik

Charles Island

Péninsula d' Ungava

Inukjuak

Fort Severn
Winisk
Winisk

Severn

J a m e s
B a y

Attawapiskat

Akimiski Island

Fort Albany

Moosonee

Attawapiskat

Albany

Moose

Harricana

Q U E

Eastmain

Rivière de Rupert

Chibougamau

Mistassini

Réservoir Gouin

Belcher Islands

Lac Mint

16

Baffin Island

Strait

Resolution Island

Button Islands

Akpatok Island

Ungava Bay

Kuujjuaq

Rivière à la Baleine

Nain

Caniapiscau

Hopedale

Makkovik

Cape Harrison

Labrador Sea

Schefferville

NEWFOUNDLAND

Cartwright

Smallwood Reservoir

Lake Melville

Churchill

St.Anthony

Réservoir de Caniapiscau

E C D A

Strait of Belle Isle

Gander

Grand Falls

St.John's

Havre-St-Pierre

Corner Brook

Newfoundland

Laurentian Mountains

Réservoir Manicouagan

Sept-Îles

Île d'Anticosti

Cape Race

Baie-Comeau

St.Lawrence

Gaspé

Gulf of St. Lawrence

Channel-Port aux Basques

Luc ean

Péninsule de Gaspé

Matane

Îles de la Madeleine

ST PIERRE & MIQUELON
(to France)

Chicoutimi

Rimouski

uière

Rivière-du-loup

PRINCE EDWARD ISLAND

Cabot Strait

a Tuque

Edmundston

Bathurst

Glace Bay

Charlesbourg

NEW BRUNSWICK

Charlottetown

Sydney

Cape Breton Island

Québec

Moncton

Amherst

Trois-Rivières

Oromocto

New Glasgow

St-Georges

Fredericton

Truro

Drummondville

NOVA SCOTIA

ontréal

Saint John

Bay of Fundy

Dartmouth

Sherbrooke

MAINE

Halifax

Sable Island

VERMONT

Liverpool

Yarmouth

NEW HAMPSHIRE

MASSACHUSETTS

Cape Cod

A T L A N T I C

CONNECTICUT

RHODE ISLAND

O C E A N

N

ELEVATION

4000 m
13 124 ft

2000 m
6562 ft

1000 m
3281 ft

500 m
1640 ft

250 m
820 ft

100 m
328 ft

Sea Level | Sea Level

-250 m
-820 ft

-500 m
-1640 ft

-1000 m
-3281 ft

-2000 m
-6562 ft

-3000 m
-9843 ft

-4000 m
-13 124 ft

0 km   400

0 miles   400

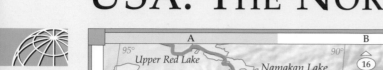

A   B   C   D

95°   90°   85°

Upper Red Lake
Lower Red Lake
Namakan Lake

16

1

CANADA

ONTARIO

Isle Royale

Lake Superior

Keweenaw Peninsula

MINNESOTA

Apostle Islands

Houghton

Superior

Ashland

Ironwood

Gogebic Range

Marquette

Mille Lacs Lake

Sault Sainte Marie

Saint Ignace

North Channel

Georgian

MICHIGAN

Woodruff

Iron Mountain

Escanaba

Saint Croix River

Rice Lake

Rhinelander

Cheboygan

Lake Huron

Ladysmith

Beaver Island

Petoskey

Alpena

2

45°

23

WISCONSIN

River Falls

Eau Claire

Wausau

Stevens Point

Green Bay

Traverse City

Roscommon

Beulah

Cadillac

Saginaw Bay

Mississippi River

Wisconsin Rapids

Appleton

Green Bay

Ludington

Midland

Bay City

Tomah

Oshkosh

Lake Winnebago

Muskegon

Mount Pleasant

Saginaw

La Crosse

Fond du Lac

Sheboygan

Wisconsin River

West Bend

Madison

Milwaukee

Grand Rapids

Flint

Port Huron

3

Waukesha

Racine

Wyoming

Lansing

Pontiac

Lake Saint Clair

Janesville

Kenosha

Kalamazoo

Livonia

Warren

Lake Erie

IOWA

Rockford

Waukegan

Ann Arbor

Detroit

Elgin

Evanston

Adrian

Toledo

Cleveland

Euclid

Sterling

Chicago

South Bend

Elkhart

War

Aurora

Gary

Bowling Green

Sandusky

Akron

Rock Island

Joliet

Valparaiso

Findlay

Youngstown

Ottawa

Kankakee

Fort Wayne

Van Wert

Mansfield

Canton

Galesburg

Wabash

Marion

Aliqu

4

40°

23

Peoria

Bloomington

Lafayette

Kokomo

Sidney

Delaware

Macomb

INDIANA

Anderson

Muncie

OHIO

Quincy

Pekin

Champaign

Carmel

Springfield

Zanesville

WE

Springfield

Decatur

Terre Haute

Indianapolis

Dayton

Columbus

VIRGIN

Jacksonville

Kettering

Wilmington

ILLINOIS

Columbus

Chillicothe

Athens

Clarksb

Alton

Effingham

Bloomington

Cincinnati

Parkersburg

East Saint Louis

Vincennes

Newport

Portsmouth

Ohio River

Belleville

Mount Vernon

New Albany

Louisville

Huntington

Charleston

MISSOURI

Carbondale

Evansville

Frankfort

Lexington

Saint Albans

Owensboro

Elizabethtown

Richmond

Beckley

Henderson

Green River

KENTUCKY

5

Ozark Plateau

Alton

Paducah

London

Pikeville

Bluef

Lake of the Ozarks

Hopkinsville

Bowling Green

Somerset

Middlesboro

Bristol

Pula

Kentucky Lake

Appalachi

ARKANSAS

20

TENNESSEE

90°   85°

A   B   C   D

POPULATION

- ◉ Over 500,000
- ◉ 100,000 – 500,000
- ○ 50,000 – 100,000
- ○ Less than 50,000
- ● National capital
- ● Internal administrative capital

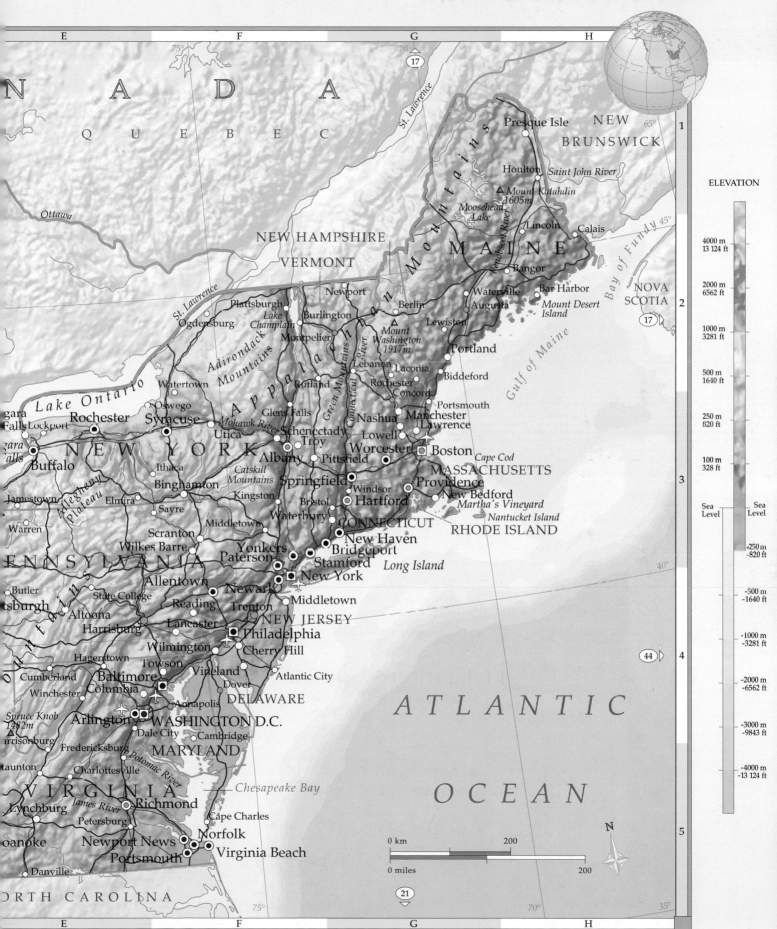

N A D A

Q U E B E C

C

Ottawa

St. Lawrence

St. Lawrence

Ogdensburg
Plattsburgh
Lake Champlain
Burlington

NEW HAMPSHIRE

VERMONT

Newport

Berlin

△ Mount Washington 1917m

Montpelier

Green Mountains

Connecticut River

Lebanon

Laconia

Rochester

Concord

Portsmouth

NEW BRUNSWICK

Presque Isle

Houlton
Saint John River
△ Mount Katahdin 1605m
Moosehead Lake
Penobscot River
Lincoln
Calais

M A I N E

Bangor

Waterville
Augusta
Lewiston

Bar Harbor
Mount Desert Island

Portland

Biddeford

Gulf of Maine

NOVA SCOTIA

Bay of Fundy

Adirondack Mountains

Appalachian Mountains

gara Falls
Lockport

gara alls

Rochester

Syracuse

Oswego

Watertown

Mohawk River

Utica

Glens Falls

NEW YORK

Schenectady

Troy

Albany

Ithaca

Buffalo

Binghamton

Catskill Mountains

Jamestown

Allegheny Plateau

Elmira

Sayre

Kingston

Warren

Rutland

Nashua
Lowell

Pittsfield

Springfield

Bristol

Windsor

Hartford

Waterbury

Manchester
Lawrence

Worcester

Boston

Providence

New Bedford

MASSACHUSETTS

Cape Cod

Martha's Vineyard
Nantucket Island

RHODE ISLAND

CONNECTICUT

New Haven

Bridgeport

Stamford

Long Island

Middletown

Scranton

Wilkes Barre

NNSYLVANIA

Butler

tsburgh

Altoona

Allentown

Paterson
Yonkers

Newark

New York

State College

Reading

Harrisburg

Lancaster

Middletown

Trenton

NEW JERSEY

Wilmington

Philadelphia

Cherry Hill

Vineland

Atlantic City

Hagerstown

Towson

Cumberland

Baltimore

Columbia

Dover

Winchester

Annapolis

DELAWARE

Spruce Knob 1282m △

Arlington

WASHINGTON D.C.

Dale City

Cambridge

arrisonburg

Fredericksburg

MARYLAND

Potomac River

Chesapeake Bay

ATLANTIC

OCEAN

Staunton

Charlottesville

VIRGINIA

James River

Richmond

Lynchburg

Petersburg

Cape Charles

oanoke

Newport News

Norfolk

Virginia Beach

Portsmouth

Danville

RTH CAROLINA

ELEVATION

4000 m
13 124 ft

2000 m
6562 ft

1000 m
3281 ft

500 m
1640 ft

250 m
820 ft

100 m
328 ft

Sea Level

Sea Level

-250 m
-820 ft

-500 m
-1640 ft

-1000 m
-3281 ft

-2000 m
-6562 ft

-3000 m
-9843 ft

-4000 m
-13 124 ft

0 km   200

0 miles   200

N

USA: THE SOUTHEAST

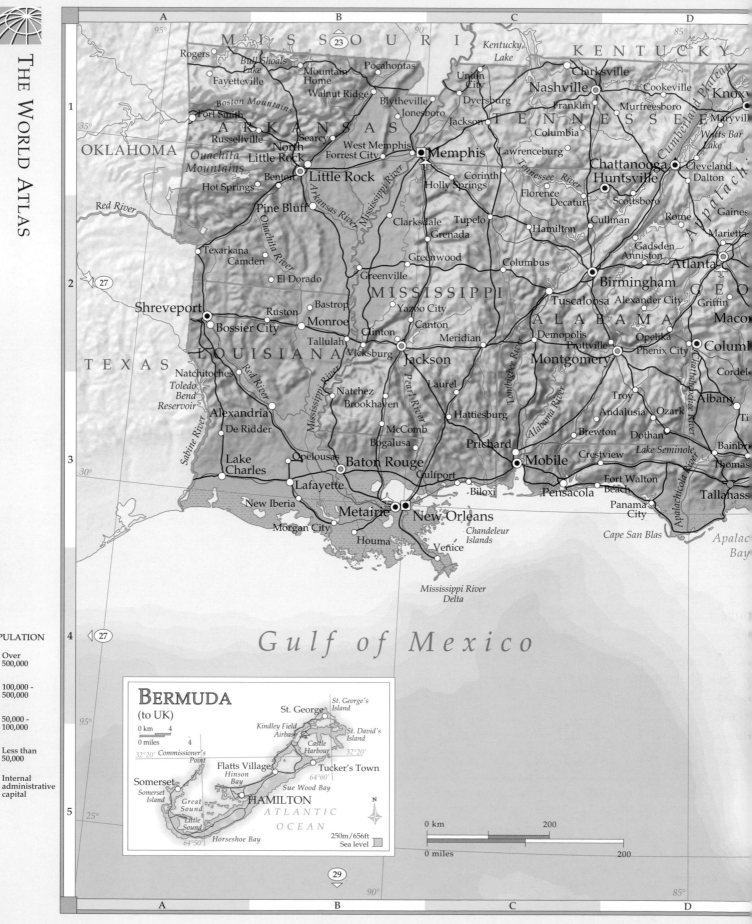

POPULATION

- ◉ Over 500,000
- ◉ 100,000 - 500,000
- ○ 50,000 - 100,000
- ○ Less than 50,000
- ● Internal administrative capital

BERMUDA
(to UK)

0 km 4
0 miles 4

Commissioner's Point

Somerset
Somerset Island

Flatts Village
Hinson Bay

Kindley Field Airbase

St. George
St. George's Island

Castle Harbour

St. David's Island

Tucker's Town

Sue Wood Bay

HAMILTON
Great Sound
Little Sound

ATLANTIC OCEAN

250m/656ft
Sea level

Horseshoe Bay

0 km 200
0 miles 200

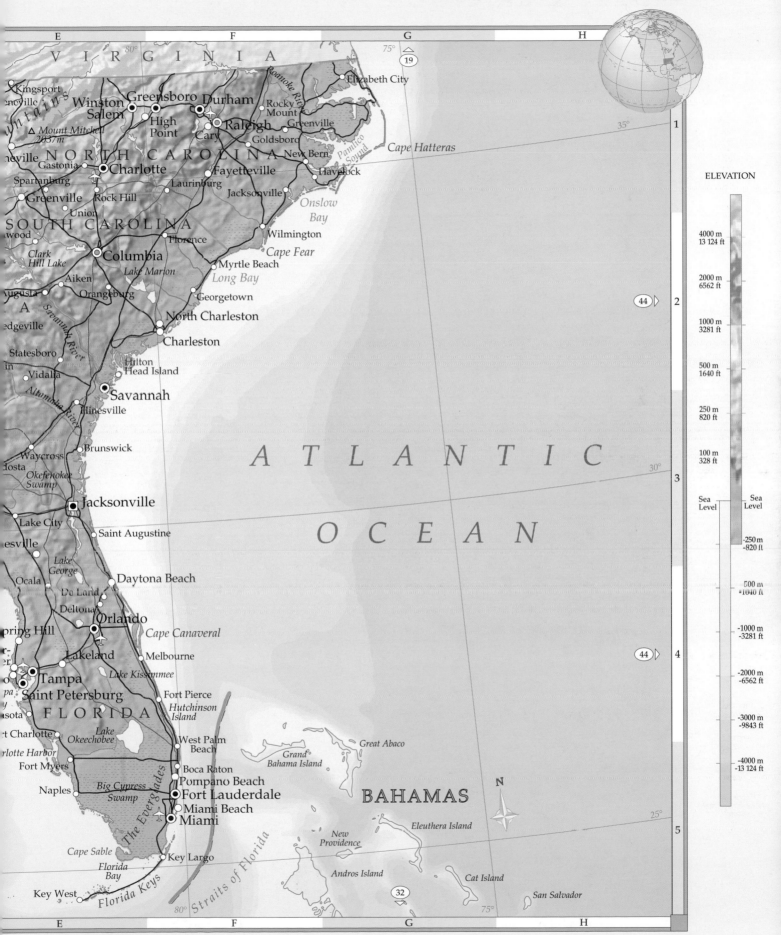

ELEVATION

4000 m
13 124 ft

2000 m
6562 ft

1000 m
3281 ft

500 m
1640 ft

250 m
820 ft

100 m
328 ft

Sea
Level

Sea
Level

-250 m
-820 ft

-500 m
-1640 ft

-1000 m
-3281 ft

-2000 m
-6562 ft

-3000 m
-9843 ft

-4000 m
-13 124 ft

E   F   G   H

VIRGINIA

Kingsport
eneville
Winston
Salem
Greensboro
Durham
High
Point
Cary
Raleigh
Rocky
Mount
Greenville
Elizabeth City
△ Mount Mitchell
2037m
NORTH CAROLINA
Goldsboro
New Bern
Havelock
Cape Hatteras
Roanoke River
Pamlico Sound
eville
Gastonia
Charlotte
Fayetteville
Laurinburg
Jacksonville
Spartanburg
Rock Hill
Onslow
Bay
Greenville
Union
SOUTH CAROLINA
Florence
Wilmington
Cape Fear
wood
Columbia
Myrtle Beach
Clark
Hill Lake
Aiken
Lake Marion
Long Bay
ugusta
Orangeburg
Georgetown
Savannah River
North Charleston
edgeville
Charleston
Statesboro
Hilton
Head Island
Vidalia
in
Altamaha River
Savannah
Hinesville
Waycross
Brunswick
osta
Okefenokee
Swamp
ATLANTIC
Jacksonville
Lake City
Saint Augustine
esville
OCEAN
Lake
George
Daytona Beach
Ocala
De Land
Deltona
Orlando
Cape Canaveral
pring Hill
Lakeland
Melbourne
Tampa
Lake Kissimmee
Saint Petersburg
FLORIDA
Fort Pierce
Hutchinson
Island
asota
Great Abaco
t Charlotte
Lake
Okeechobee
West Palm
Beach
Grand
Bahama Island
rlotte Harbor
Fort Myers
Boca Raton
Big Cypress
Swamp
Pompano Beach
Naples
Fort Lauderdale
BAHAMAS
The Everglades
Miami Beach
Miami
N
Cape Sable
Eleuthera Island
Florida
Bay
Key Largo
New
Providence
Key West
Florida Keys
Straits of Florida
Andros Island
Cat Island
San Salvador

1

2

3

4

5

19

44

44

32

E   F   G   H

USA: CENTRAL STATES

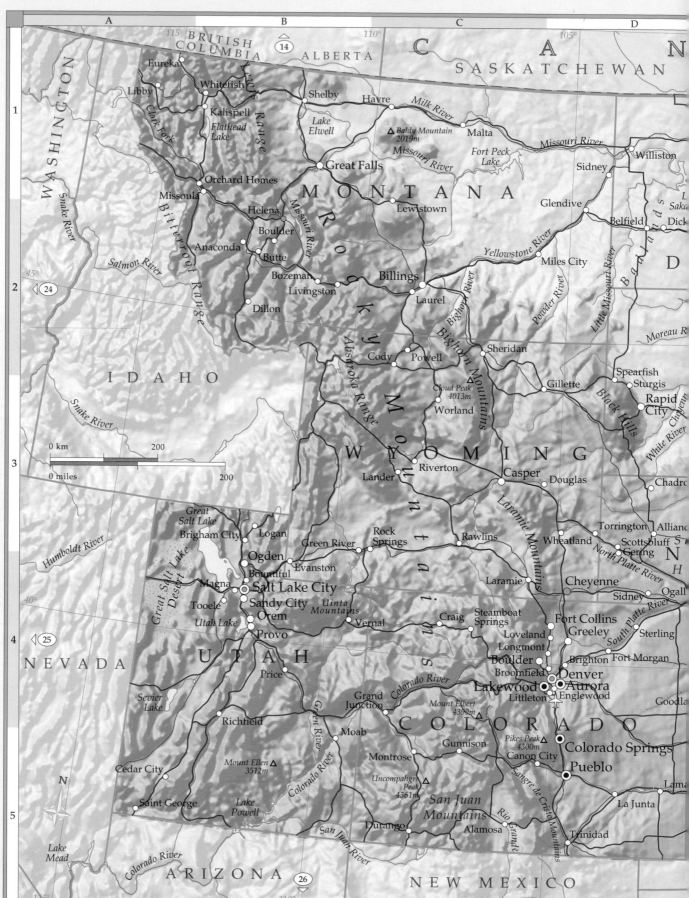

POPULATION

- ◉ Over 500,000
- ◉ 100,000 - 500,000
- ○ 50,000 - 100,000
- ○ Less than 50,000
- ● Internal administrative capital

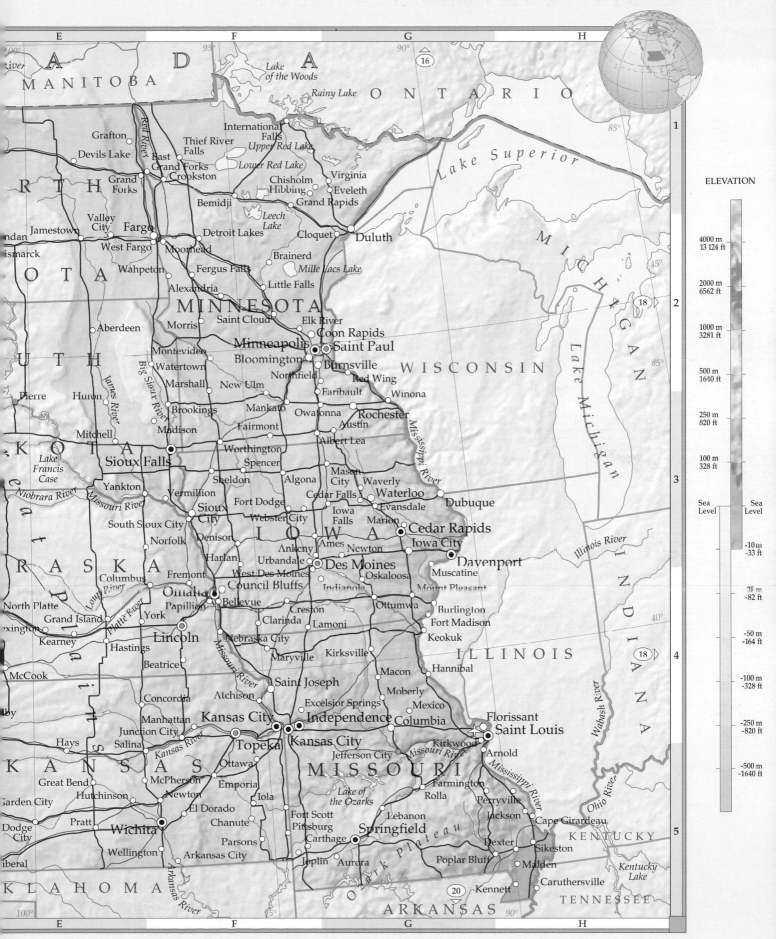

ELEVATION

4000 m
13 124 ft

2000 m
6562 ft

1000 m
3281 ft

500 m
1640 ft

250 m
820 ft

100 m
328 ft

Sea Level   Sea Level

-10 m
-33 ft

25 m
-82 ft

-50 m
-164 ft

-100 m
-328 ft

-250 m
-820 ft

-500 m
-1640 ft

USA: THE WEST

POPULATION

- ● Over 500,000
- ◉ 100,000 – 500,000
- ○ 50,000 – 100,000
- ○ Less than 50,000
- ● Internal administrative capital

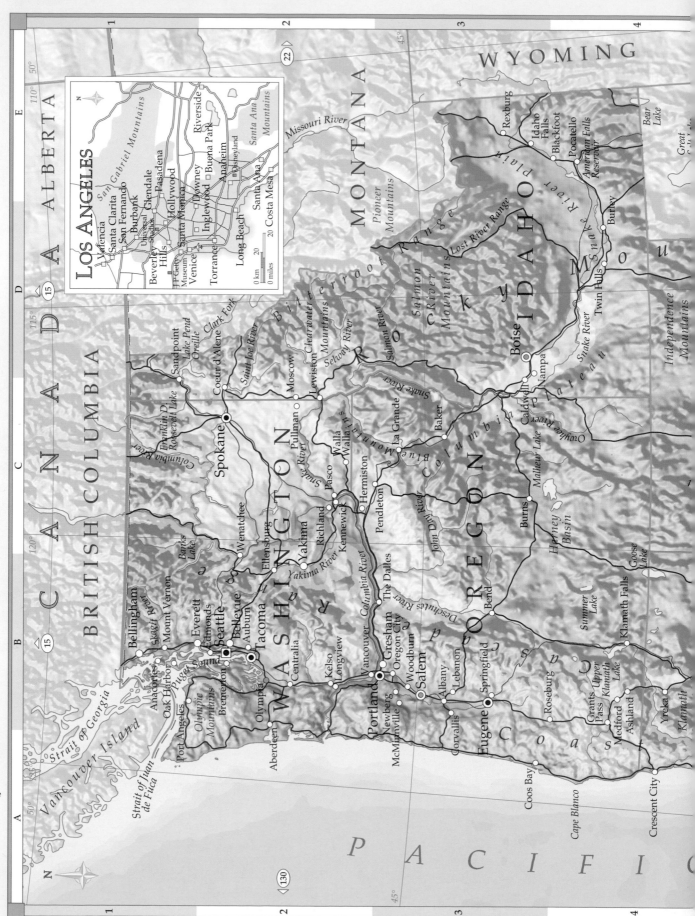

LOS ANGELES

Valencia
Santa Clarita
San Fernando
San Gabriel Mountains
Burbank
Universal Studios
Glendale
Pasadena
Hollywood
Beverley Hills
Santa Monica
J. Paul Getty Museum
Venice
Universal City
Downey
Inglewood
Anaheim
Buena Park
Disneyland
Santa Ana
Santa Ana Mountains
Riverside
Torrance
Long Beach
Costa Mesa

0 km 20
0 miles 20

CANADA
ALBERTA
BRITISH COLUMBIA
MONTANA
WYOMING
IDAHO
WASHINGTON
OREGON

ROCKY MOUNTAINS

Missouri River

Rexburg
Idaho Falls
Blackfoot
Pocatello
American Falls Reservoir
Bear Lake
Great

Pioneer Mountains
Lost River Range
Salmon River
Salmon River Mountains
Boise
Nampa
Caldwell
Twin Falls
Burley
Independence Mountains

Bitterroot Range
Clearwater Mountains
Selway River
Snake River
Owyhee River
Malheur Lake

Sandpoint
Lake Pend Oreille
Clark Fork
St. Joe River
Coeur d'Alene
Moscow
Pullman
Lewiston
La Grande
Baker

Columbia River
Blue Mountains
Umatilla Mountains

Franklin D. Roosevelt Lake
Spokane

Snake River
Pasco
Walla Walla
Hermiston
Pendleton
Burns
Harney Basin

Wenatchee
Ellensburg
Yakima
Richland
Kennewick

Banks Lake

Columbia River
Bend
Summer Lake
Klamath Falls
Goose Lake

John Day River
Deschutes River
The Dalles

Yakima River

Bellingham
Skagit River
Mount Vernon
Everett
Edmonds
Seattle
Bellevue
Auburn
Tacoma
Centralia

Anacortes
Oak Harbor
Port Angeles
Bremerton
Olympia
Aberdeen

Olympic Mountains
Puget Sound

Strait of Georgia
Vancouver Island
Strait of Juan de Fuca

Kelso
Longview
Vancouver
Gresham
Oregon City
Woodburn
Salem
Albany
Lebanon
Springfield
Eugene

Portland
Newberg
McMinnville
Corvallis

Coos Bay
Cape Blanco

Roseburg
Grants Pass
Medford
Ashland
Upper Klamath Lake
Klamath Falls
Yreka
Klamath
Crescent City

Coast Ranges
Cascade Range

PACIFIC

N
E
D
C
B
A

1 2 3 4

50°
110°
115°
120°
45°
45°
50°

22
15
15
130

ELEVATION

4000 m
13 124 ft

2000 m
6562 ft

1000 m
3281 ft

500 m
1640 ft

250 m
820 ft

100 m
328 ft

Sea Level | Sea Level

-250 m
-820 ft

-500 m
-1640 ft

-1000 m
-3281 ft

-2000 m
-6562 ft

-3000 m
-9843 ft

-4000 m
-13 124 ft

UTAH

ARIZONA

MEXICO

NEVADA

CALIFORNIA

Great Basin

Sierra Nevada

Central Valley

San Joaquin Valley

Sacramento Valley

Mojave Desert

Death Valley

Lake Powell
Grand Canyon
Colorado River
Lake Mead
Lake Mohave
Gila River
Colorado River

Las Vegas
Henderson
Alamo
Tonopah
Hawthorne

Reno
Sparks
Carson City
South Lake Tahoe
Lake Tahoe
Susanville
Chico
Yuba City
Woodland
Sacramento
Napa
Santa Rosa
Vallejo
Fairfield
Berkeley
Oakland
San Francisco
Palo Alto
Sunnyvale
San Jose
Stockton
Modesto
Manteca
Turlock
Madera
Fresno
Hanford
Visalia
Porterville
Delano
Bakersfield
Atascadero
Salinas
Gilroy
Santa Cruz
Monterey
San Luis Obispo
Santa Maria
Lompoc
Santa Barbara
Oxnard

Los Angeles
Pasadena
San Bernardino
Riverside
Santa Ana
Long Beach
Huntington Beach
Lancaster
Victorville
Barstow
Palm Springs
Escondido
Oceanside
Encinitas
Fallbrook
El Cajon
San Diego
Chula Vista
Lakeside
Brawley
El Centro
Blythe

Mount Whitney 4418m
Ridgecrest
Selma
Tulare Lake Bed

Mono Lake
Walker Lake
Pyramid Lake
Honey Lake
Eagle Lake
Carson Sink
Salton Sea

San Rafael Mountains
Santa Lucia Range
Monterey Bay
San Clemente Island
Santa Catalina Island
Santa Rosa Island
Channel Islands

Chocolate Mountains

OCEAN

PACIFIC OCEAN

HAWAII

Kauai
Lihue
Niihau
Oahu
Wahiawa
Honolulu
Kaneohe
Molokai
Maui
Wailuku
Hilo
Hawaii
Mauna Kea 4205m

2000m/6562ft
1000m/3281ft
500m/1640ft
200m/656ft
Sea level

0 km
0 miles

200
200

25

USA: THE SOUTHWEST

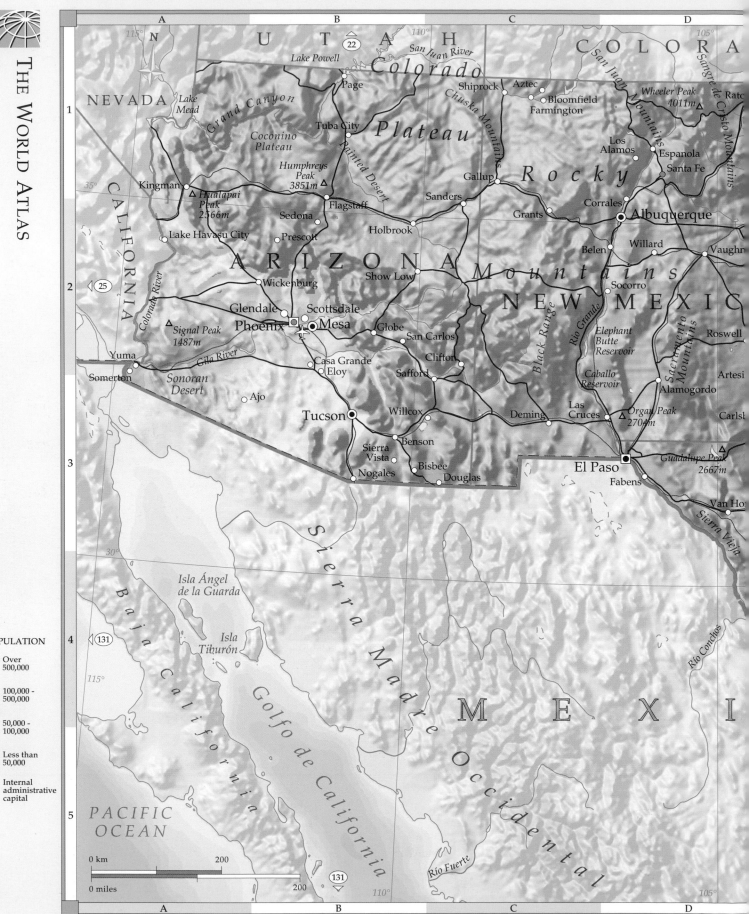

POPULATION

- ⊙ Over 500,000
- ◉ 100,000 – 500,000
- ○ 50,000 – 100,000
- ○ Less than 50,000
- ● Internal administrative capital

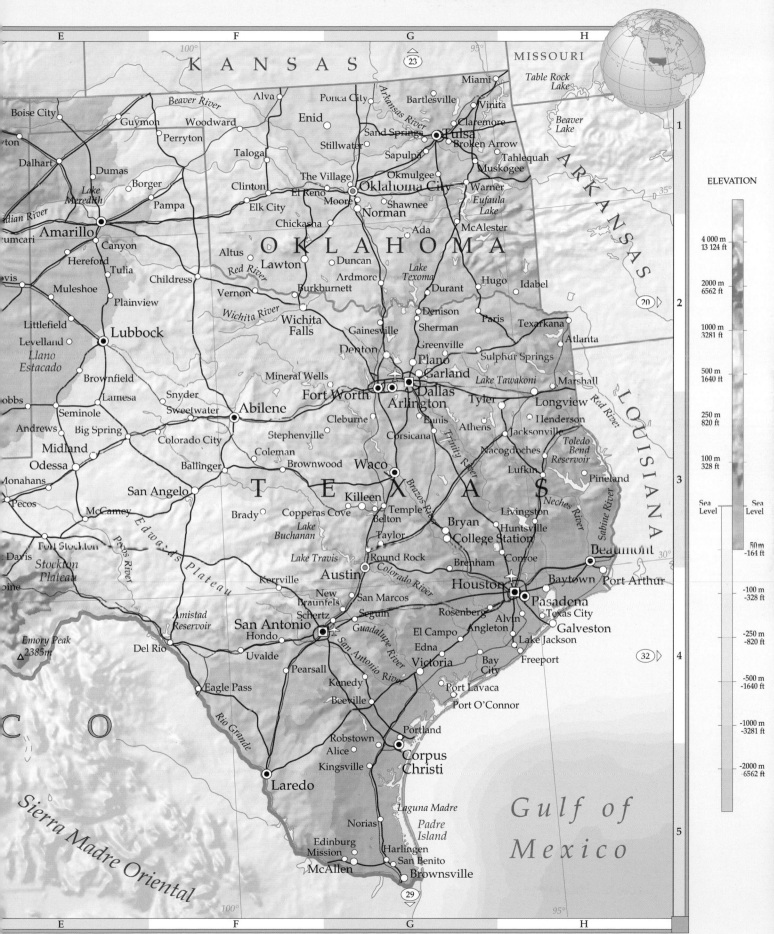

E   F   G   H

K A N S A S   MISSOURI

Table Rock Lake

Miami   *Beaver Lake*

Beaver River   Alva   Ponca City   Bartlesville   Vinita

Boise City   Guymon   Woodward   Enid   Claremore

...yton   Perryton   Sand Springs   Tulsa   Broken Arrow

Dalhart   Dumas   Stillwater   Sapulpa   Tahlequah

Borger   Clinton   The Village   Okmulgee   Muskogee

Lake Meredith   Pampa   El Reno   Oklahoma City   Warner

...dian River   Elk City   Moore   *Eufaula Lake*

Amarillo   Canyon   Shawnee

Chickasha   Norman   Ada   McAlester

Hereford   Tulia   O K L A H O M A

...avis   Muleshoe   Altus   Lawton   Duncan   Ardmore   Hugo   Idabel

Childress   *Red River*   *Lake Texoma*   Durant

Plainview   Vernon   Burkburnett   Denison   Paris   Texarkana

Littlefield   *Wichita River*   Wichita Falls   Gainesville   Sherman   Atlanta

Levelland   Lubbock   Greenville   Sulphur Springs

Llano Estacado   Denton   Plano   Garland

Brownfield   Mineral Wells   *Lake Tawakoni*   Marshall

...obbs   Lamesa   Snyder   Fort Worth   Dallas   Tyler   Longview

Seminole   Sweetwater   Abilene   Arlington   *Red River*

Andrews   Big Spring   Cleburne   Ennis   Henderson

Midland   Colorado City   Stephenville   Athens   Jacksonville

Odessa   Corsicana   Nacogdoches   *Toledo Bend Reservoir*

...onahans   Ballinger   Coleman   Brownwood   Waco   Lufkin   Pineland

Pecos   San Angelo   T   E   X   A   S   Livingston   *Neches River*   *Sabine River*

McCamey   Brady   Killeen   *Brazos R.*

Edwards Plateau   Copperas Cove   Temple   Bryan   Huntsville

...Davis   Fort Stockton   *Lake Buchanan*   Belton   College Station

Stockton Plateau   *Pecos River*   Taylor   Conroe   Beaumont

...oine   *Lake Travis*   Round Rock   Brenham   Port Arthur

Emory Peak △ 2385m   Kerrville   Austin   *Colorado River*   Houston   Baytown

New Braunfels   San Marcos   Rosenberg   Pasadena

Amistad Reservoir   Schertz   Seguin   Alvin   Texas City

Del Rio   San Antonio   Hondo   *Guadalupe River*   El Campo   Angleton   Galveston

Uvalde   Edna   *Lake Jackson*

Pearsall   *San Antonio River*   Victoria   Bay City   Freeport

Eagle Pass   Kenedy   Port Lavaca

Beeville   Port O'Connor

Rio Grande   Robstown   Portland

...C O   Alice   Corpus Christi

Kingsville

Laredo   *Laguna Madre*   G u l f   o f   M e x i c o

Norias   *Padre Island*

Sierra Madre Oriental   Edinburg   Mission   Harlingen

McAllen   San Benito   Brownsville

1

2

3

4

5

E   F   G   H

ELEVATION

4 000 m
13 124 ft

2000 m
6562 ft

1000 m
3281 ft

500 m
1640 ft

250 m
820 ft

100 m
328 ft

Sea Level   Sea Level

50 m
-164 ft

-100 m
-328 ft

-250 m
-820 ft

-500 m
-1640 ft

-1000 m
-3281 ft

-2000 m
-6562 ft

MEXICO

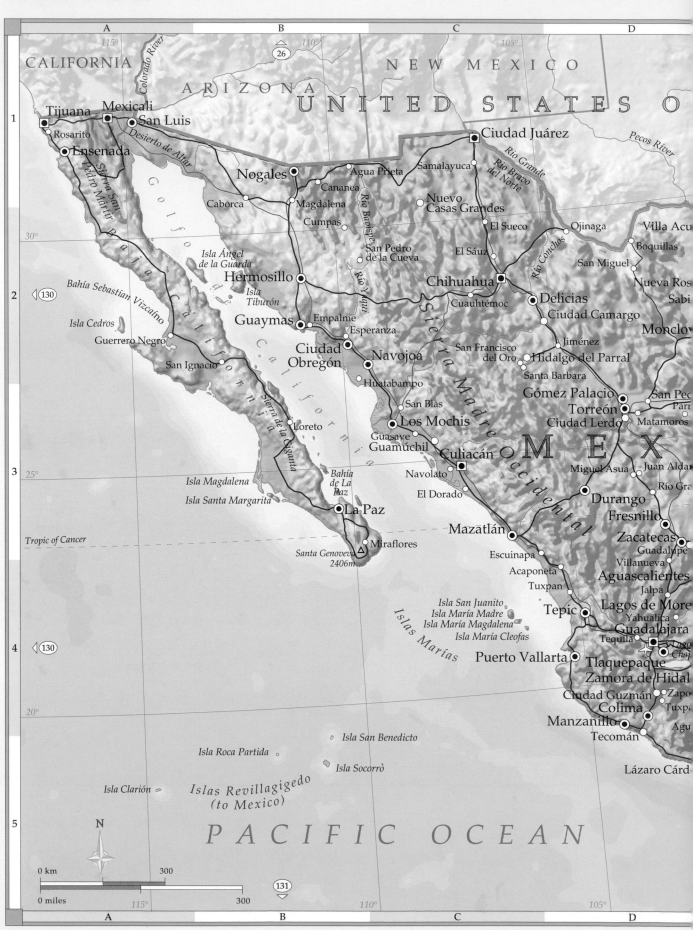

POPULATION

⬓	Over 500,000
⊙	100,000 – 500,000
○	50,000 – 100,000
○	Less than 50,000
●	National capital

CALIFORNIA

ARIZONA

NEW MEXICO

UNITED STATES O

Colorado River

Pecos River

115°

110°

105°

26

Tijuana
Rosarito
Mexicali
San Luis
Ensenada

Desierto de Altar

Ciudad Juárez

Rio Grande
Rio Bravo del Norte

Nogales
Agua Prieta
Samalayuca

Cananea
Caborca
Magdalena
Cumpas

Nuevo Casas Grandes

El Sueco
Ojinaga
Villa Acu

Río Bavispe

San Pedro de la Cueva
El Sáuz
San Miguel
Boquillas

30°

Isla Ángel de la Guarda

Golfo de

Baja California

Sierra San Pedro Mártir

Bahía Sebastián Vizcaíno

Isla Cedros

Hermosillo

Isla Tiburón

Río Yaqui

Chihuahua
Cuauhtémoc
Delicias
Ciudad Camargo

Nueva Ros
Sabi

Monclo

130°

Guaymas
Empalme
Esperanza

San Francisco del Oro
Jiménez
Hidalgo del Parral
Santa Barbara

Sierra Madre Occidental

Guerrero Negro
San Ignacio

Ciudad Obregón
Navojoa
Huatabampo

Gómez Palacio
Torreón
Ciudad Lerdo

San Pe
Parr
Matamoros

San Blas
Los Mochis
Guasave
Guamúchil

M E X

25°

Isla Magdalena
Isla Santa Margarita

Sierra de la Giganta

Loreto

Bahía de La Paz

Culiacán
Navolato
El Dorado

Miguel Asua
Juan Alda
Río Gra

Durango
Fresnillo

3

La Paz

Zacatecas
Guadalupe

Tropic of Cancer

Santa Genoveva 2406m
Miraflores

Mazatlán

Escuinapa

Villanueva
Aguascalientes
Jalpa

Acaponeta
Tuxpan

Lagos de More
Yahualica

Isla San Juanito
Isla María Madre
Isla María Magdalena
Isla María Cleofas

Islas Marías

Tepic
Tequila
Guadalajara

20°

Puerto Vallarta
Tlaquepaque
Zamora de Hidal

Ciudad Guzmán
Zapo
Colima
Tuxpa

Manzanillo
Tecomán
Agu

Isla San Benedicto

Isla Roca Partida

Isla Socorrò

Lázaro Cárd

Isla Clarión

Islas Revillagigedo
(to Mexico)

130°

N

PACIFIC OCEAN

0 km   300

0 miles   300

131

115°

110°

105°

28

ALABAMA
FLORIDA
MISSISSIPPI
LOUISIANA

M E R I C A

T E X A S

Brazos River
Red River
Sabine River
Mississippi River
Colorado River

Mississippi River Delta

dras Negras

Nuevo Laredo

Padre Island

Sabinas Hidalgo
Ciudad Miguel Alemán

Reynosa
Río Bravo
Matamoros

G u l f   o f

Monterrey
Montemorelos
llo
Linares

Laguna Madre

M e x i c o

Tropic of Cancer

Ciudad Victoria

Ciudad Mante

Río Lagartos
Tizimín
Cancún

Yucatan Channel

Progreso
Motul

Isla Cozumel

Ciudad Madero

Mérida

Umán
Pánuco
Tampico
uis
Ciudad Valles
sí

Ticul
Peto
Valladolid

Laguna de Tamiahua

Oxkutzcab
Teka

Felipe Carrillo Puerto

Verde
Dolores Hidalgo

Tamazunchale

Bahía de Campeche
Campeche

Yucatan Peninsula

Guanajuato
Tuxpan

Poza Rica

Champotón

Chetumal

apuato
Querétaro
Papantla

Tulancingo

Laguna de Términos

Fransisco Escárcega

Pachuca
Teziutlán
Xalapa

MÉXICO
(MEXICO CITY)
Perote
Veracruz

Frontera

Carmen

Villahermosa

BELIZE

elia
Tlaxcala

Comalcalco

Toluca
Cuernavaca
Puebla
Popocatépetl
5452m
Córdoba
San
Coatzacoalcos

Macuspana

Río Usumacinta

Gulf of Honduras

pan
Zacatepec
Tehuacán
Andrés
Tuxtla
Minatitlán

Teapa

Taxco
Cuautla

Tuxtepec

San Cristóbal
de Las Casas

a del rrillo
Iguala

Istmo de
Tehuantepec
Tuxtla

Chiapa de
Corzo
Comitán

Huajuapan

Chilpancingo

Oaxaca

Ocozocuautla
Matías Romero

sas

Tecpan

Sierra Madre del Sur

Ixtepec

Arriaga

Presa de la Angostura

Acapulco

Pinotepa Nacional
Tehuantepec
Juchitán
Salina Cruz

Pijijiapán

Miahuatlán

Escuintla

GUATEMALA
HONDURAS

Puerto Escondido
Puerto Angel

Golfo de Tehuantepec

Huixtla

Tapachula
Ciudad Hidalgo

EL SALVADOR

ELEVATION

4000 m
13 124 ft

2000 m
6562 ft

1000 m
3281 ft

500 m
1640 ft

250 m
820 ft

100 m
328 ft

Sea Level   Sea Level

m
-820 ft

-500 m
-1640 ft

-1000 m
-3281 ft

-2000 m
-6562 ft

-3000 m
-9843 ft

-4000 m
-13 124 ft

CENTRAL AMERICA

Yucatan Peninsula

MEXICO

GUATEMALA

Carmelita

Corozal
Caledonia
Orange Walk
San Pedro
Indian Church
Hill Bank
Belize City
Santa Elena
San Ignacio
BELMOPAN
Flores
San Benito
BELIZE
Dangriga
La Libertad
Río Usumacinta
Dolores
Maya
Mountains
Monkey River
Town
Sayaxché
San Luis
San Antonio
Roatán
Islas de la Bahía
Punta Gorda
Puerto Barrios
Gulf of Honduras
Iriona
Barillas
Chisec
Puerto Cortés
Trujillo
Limón
Brus Laguna
Tela
La Ceiba
Jacaltenango
Chajul
Cobán
Lago de
Izabal
Morales
San Pedro Sula
Tocoa
Savá
San Esteban
Huehuetenango
Nebaj
Salamá
Río Patuca
El Progreso
Santa Cruz del Quiché
Rabinal
Río Montagua
Gualán
Los Amates
Yoro
La Unión
Gualaco
Catacamas
San Marcos
Zacapa
HONDURAS
Quezaltenango
Chiquimula
Santa Rosa
de Copán
Siguatepeque
Campamento
Guaimaca
Bocay
CIUDAD DE GUATEMALA
(GUATEMALA CITY)
Juticalpa
Bonanz
Comayagua
Danlí
Jutiapa
La Esperanza
Jalapa
Siuna
Escuintla
Metapán
TEGUCIGALPA
Santa Ana
Chalatenango
Ocotal
San José
Ahuachapán
SAN SALVADOR
Somoto
Condega
La Sirer
Sonsonate
San Vicente
Esteli
Jinotega
La Unión
San Miguel
Choluteca
Sébaco
Matagalpa
EL SALVADOR
Usulután
Somotillo
Muy Muy
Ciudad Darío
NICARA
Gulf of Fonseca
Chinandega
Boaco
Corinto
Lago de Managua
Juigal
León
Tipitapa
MANAGUA
Masaya
Jinotepe
Granada
Nandaime
Lago de
Nicaragu
Belén
Rivas
Isla de
Ometepe
San Car
La Cruz
Upala
Golfo de
Papagayo
Liberia
Bag
Filadelfia
Nicoya
Puntaren
Península
de Nicoya

Sierra Madre

Río Choluteca

PACIFIC

OCEAN

POPULATION

- ⊡ Over
  500,000
- ◉ 100,000 –
  500,000
- ○ 50,000 –
  100,000
- ○ Less than
  50,000
- ● National
  capital

0 km   200

0 miles   200

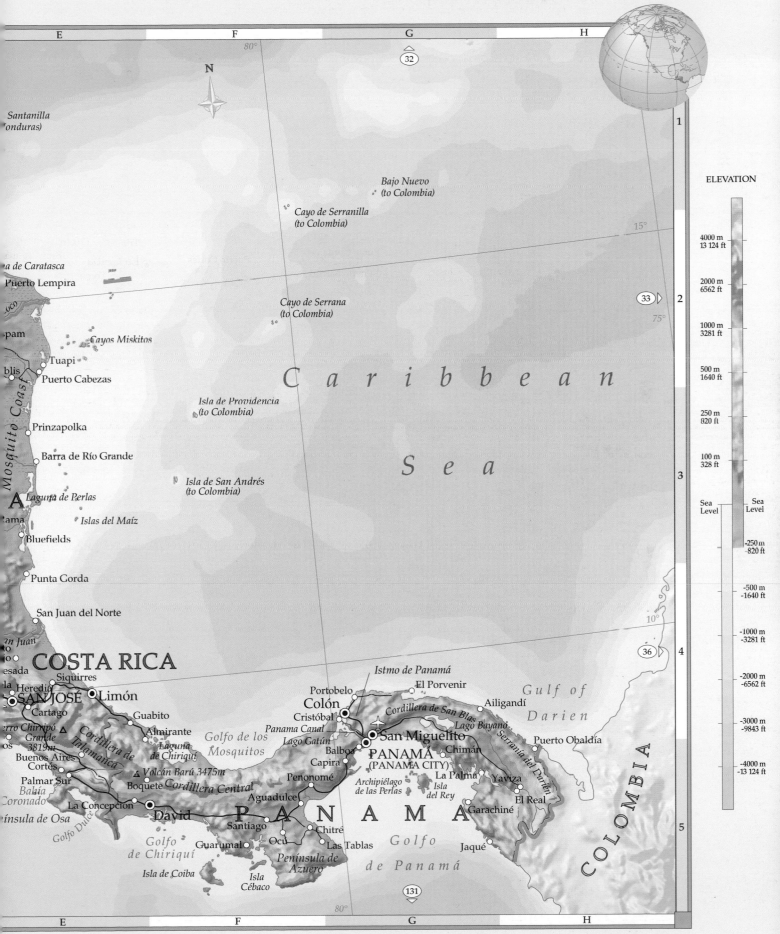

E   F   G   H

N

80°

32

ELEVATION

Santanilla
(Honduras)

Bajo Nuevo
(to Colombia)

Cayo de Serranilla
(to Colombia)

15°

1

4000 m
13 124 ft

ra de Caratasca

Puerto Lempira

33

75°

2000 m
6562 ft

2

Cayo de Serrana
(to Colombia)

pam

Cayos Miskitos

1000 m
3281 ft

blis

Tuapi

Puerto Cabezas

C a r i b b e a n

500 m
1640 ft

Isla de Providencia
(to Colombia)

Prinzapolka

S e a

250 m
820 ft

Barra de Río Grande

100 m
328 ft

Isla de San Andrés
(to Colombia)

A

Laguna de Perlas

3

Sea
Level

Sea
Level

ama

Islas del Maíz

Bluefields

-250 m
-820 ft

Punta Gorda

-500 m
-1640 ft

San Juan del Norte

10°

-1000 m
-3281 ft

an Juan
o

36

-2000 m
-6562 ft

4

COSTA RICA

Istmo de Panamá

El Porvenir

Gulf of

Siquirres

Portobelo

Ailigandí

Darien

Heredia

Colón

Cordillera de San Blas

-3000 m
-9843 ft

SAN JOSÉ   Limón

Cristóbal

Cartago

Panama Canal

Lago Bayano

Puerto Obaldía

Guabito

Golfo de los

Lago Gatún

San Miguelito

erro Chiripó

Almirante

Mosquitos

Balboa

PANAMÁ

Chimán

Grande

Laguna

(PANAMA CITY)

3819m

de Chiriquí

Capira

La Palma

os

Buenos Aires

Volcán Barú 3475m

Penonomé

Yaviza

Cortés

Cordillera Central

Archipiélago

Isla

Palmar Sur

Boquete

de las Perlas

del Rey

El Real

Bahía

La Concepción

Aguadulce

Garachiné

Coronado

David

P A N A M Á

nínsula de Osa

Santiago

Chitré

Golfo

Jaqué

Golfo Dulce

Golfo

Ocú

Guarumal

Las Tablas

de Panamá

de Chiriquí

Península de

Azuero

Isla de Coiba

Isla

Cébaco

131

80°

E   F   G   H

Mosquito Coast

COLOMBIA

Serranía del Darién

THE CARIBBEAN

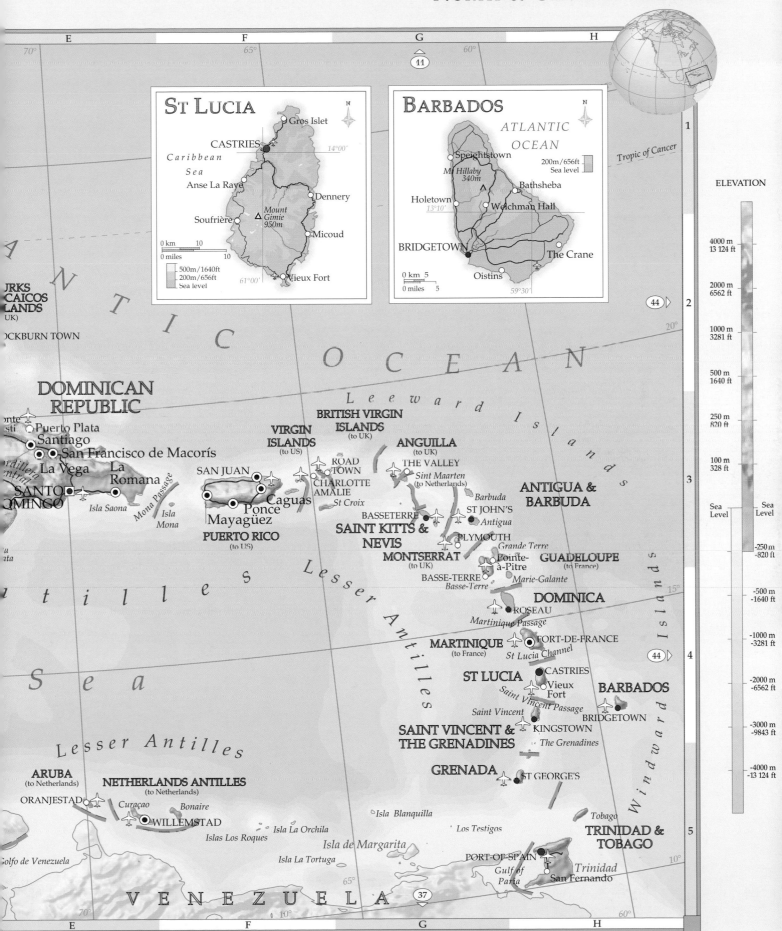

St Lucia

N

Gros Islet

CASTRIES

Caribbean Sea

14°00'

Anse La Raye

Dennery

Soufrière

△ Mount Gimie 950m

Micoud

0 km   10
0 miles   10

500m/1640ft
200m/656ft
Sea level

61°00'

Vieux Fort

Barbados

N

ATLANTIC OCEAN

Speightstown

Mt Hillaby 340m △

Bathsheba

Holetown

13°10'

Welchman Hall

200m/656ft
Sea level

BRIDGETOWN

0 km   5
0 miles   5

The Crane

Oistins

59°30'

11

44

ELEVATION

4000 m
13 124 ft

2000 m
6562 ft

1000 m
3281 ft

500 m
1640 ft

250 m
820 ft

100 m
328 ft

Sea Level   Sea Level

-250 m
-820 ft

-500 m
-1640 ft

-1000 m
-3281 ft

-2000 m
-6562 ft

-3000 m
-9843 ft

-4000 m
-13 124 ft

Tropic of Cancer

20°

ATLANTIC OCEAN

Leeward Islands

URKS
CAICOS
LANDS
(UK)

OCKBURN TOWN

DOMINICAN REPUBLIC

sti

Puerto Plata

Santiago

San Francisco de Macorís

La Vega

La Romana

SANTO
OMINGO

Isla Saona

Mona Passage

Isla Mona

VIRGIN ISLANDS (to US)

BRITISH VIRGIN ISLANDS (to UK)

SAN JUAN

ROAD TOWN

CHARLOTTE AMALIE

St Croix

Caguas

Ponce

Mayagüez

PUERTO RICO (to US)

ANGUILLA (to UK)

THE VALLEY

Sint Maarten (to Netherlands)

Barbuda

ANTIGUA & BARBUDA

BASSETERRE

St JOHN'S

Antigua

SAINT KITTS & NEVIS

PLYMOUTH

Grande Terre

MONTSERRAT (to UK)

Pointe-à-Pitre

GUADELOUPE (to France)

BASSE-TERRE

Basse-Terre

Marie-Galante

DOMINICA

ROSEAU

Martinique Passage

MARTINIQUE (to France)

FORT-DE-FRANCE

St Lucia Channel

ST LUCIA

CASTRIES

Vieux Fort

Saint Vincent Passage

BARBADOS

BRIDGETOWN

Saint Vincent

SAINT VINCENT & THE GRENADINES

KINGSTOWN

The Grenadines

GRENADA

ST GEORGE'S

Windward Islands

15°

Lesser Antilles

Lesser Antilles

Lesser Antilles

Sea

ARUBA (to Netherlands)

ORANJESTAD

NETHERLANDS ANTILLES (to Netherlands)

Curaçao

Bonaire

WILLEMSTAD

Islas Los Roques

Isla La Orchila

Isla Blanquilla

Los Testigos

Tobago

TRINIDAD & TOBAGO

Golfo de Venezuela

Isla La Tortuga

Isla de Margarita

PORT-OF-SPAIN

Gulf of Paria

Trinidad

San Fernando

10°

V E N E Z U E L A

65°

70°

10°

37

60°

44

33

SOUTH AMERICA

POPULATION

- ⊡ Over 500,000
- ⊙ 100,000 – 500,000
- ○ 50,000 – 100,000
- ○ Less than 50,000
- ● National capital

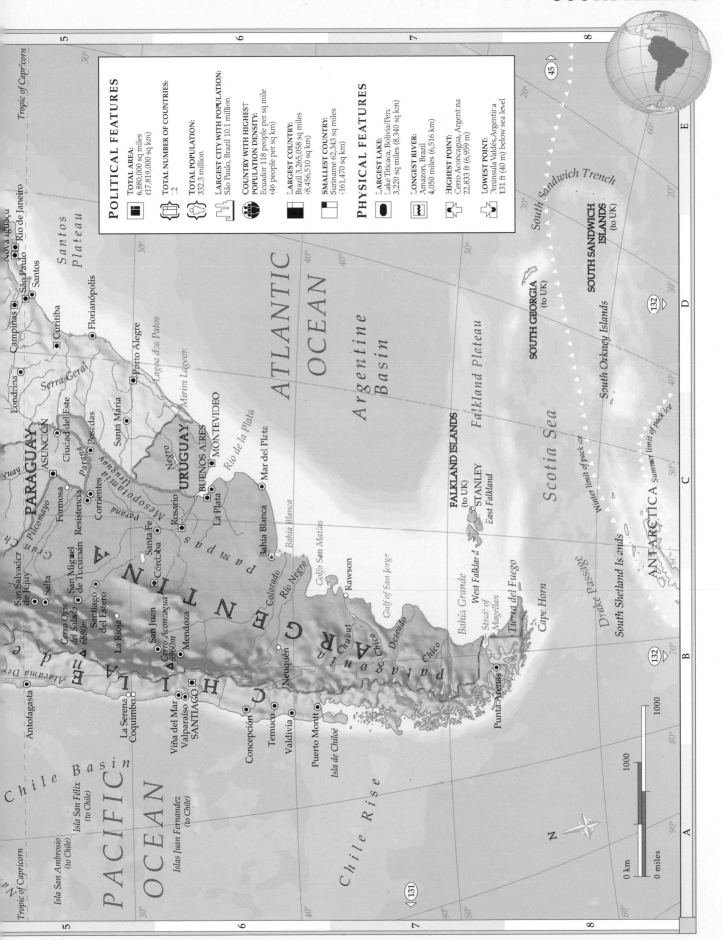

POPULATION

◙ Over 500,000

◉ 100,000 - 500,000

◎ 50,000 - 100,000

○ Less than 50,000

● National capital

ELEVATION

4000 m	13 124 ft
2000 m	6562 ft
1000 m	3281 ft
500 m	1640 ft
250 m	820 ft
100 m	328 ft
Sea Level	Sea Level
-250 m	-820 ft
-500 m	-1640 ft
-1000 m	-3281 ft
-2000 m	-6562 ft
-3000 m	-9843 ft
-4000 m	-13 124 ft

SAINT VINCENT & THE GRENADINES

BARBADOS

GRENADA

Isla Blanquilla

Isla de Margarita

Islas Los Testigos

Tobago

La Asunción

TRINIDAD & TOBAGO

Trinidad

tuga

orlamar

naná

Carúpano

Cariaco

Güiria

Gulf of Paria

The Serpent's Mouth

Puerto La Cruz

Barcelona

San Mateo

Maturín

Anaco

Cantaura

El Tigre

Tucupita

Ciudad Guayana

Río Orinoco

Upata

Ciudad Bolívar

Embalse de Guri

Matthews Ridge

Charity

Spring Garden

El Callao

Parika

Aurora

GEORGETOWN

El Dorado

Peters Mine

Bartica

New Amsterdam

Salto Angel

Rockstone

Nieuw Nickerie

Totness

PARAMARIBO

Nieuw Amsterdam

St-Laurent-du-Maroni

Kamarang

Linden

Sinnamary

Kourou

Mount Roraima 2810m

Chiyuni River

GUYANA

Orealla

Apoera

Kaaimanston

CAYENNE

Kurupukari

SURINAME

W. J. van Blommesteinmeer

Juliana Top 1230m

FRENCH GUIANA (to France)

Ouanary

St-Georges

Pakaraima Mountains

(Venezuela claims all of Guyana west of Essequibo River)

Lethem

Essequibo River

Courantyne River

Grand-Santi

Montagnes de la Trinité

Montagne Tortue

Camopi

Río Paragua

Río Caura

Río Caroni

uiana Highlands

Acarai Mountains

Tumuc Humac Mountains

(claimed by Suriname)

o Orinoco

(claimed by Suriname)

Equator

ATLANTIC OCEAN

Negro

BRAZIL

Amazon

Amazon

Amazon

Amazon

Río Purus

Río Tapajós

UELA

S

zon Basin

THE WORLD ATLAS

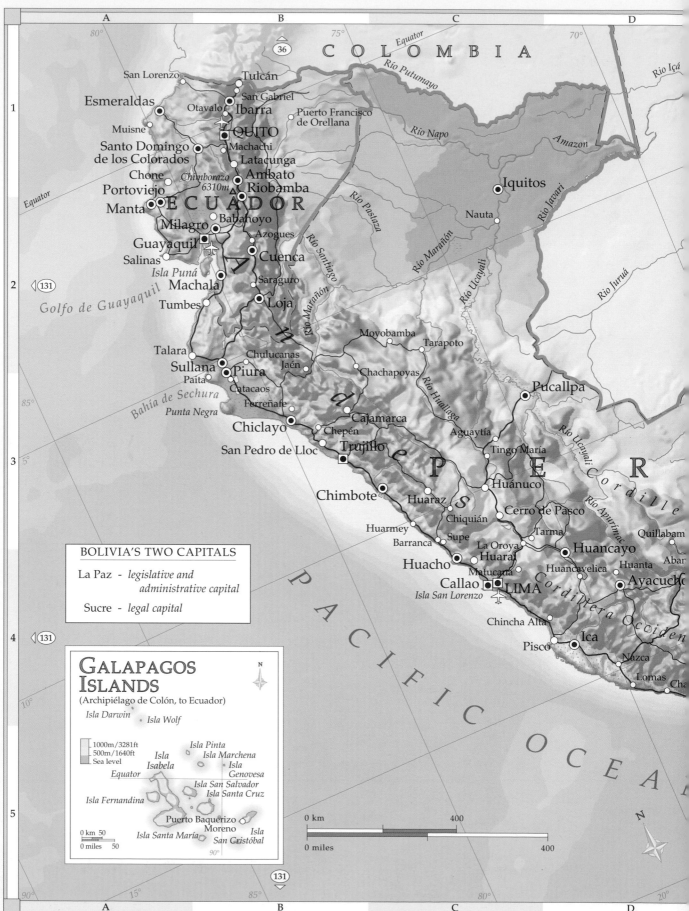

A   B   C   D

COLOMBIA

Equator

36

Río Putumayo

Río Içá

San Lorenzo

Tulcán

1

Esmeraldas

San Gabriel

Otavalo   Ibarra

Puerto Francisco de Orellana

Río Napo

Amazon

QUITO

Machachi

Santo Domingo de los Colorados

Latacunga

Iquitos

Equator

Chone

Chimborazo 6310m

Ambato

Riobamba

Río Pastaza

Portoviejo

ECUADOR

Nauta

Manta

Babahoyo

Milagro

Azogues

Río Santiago

Río Marañón

Río Javari

Guayaquil

Cuenca

Río Juruá

Salinas

2

Isla Puná

Saraguro

Machala

Loja

Golfo de Guayaquil

131

Tumbes

Río Marañón

Río Ucayali

Moyobamba

Tarapoto

Talara

Chulucanas

Jaén

Sullana

Piura

Paita

Chachapoyas

Pucallpa

Catacaos

Río Huallaga

Bahía de Sechura

Ferreñafe

Cajamarca

Río Ucayali

Punta Negra

Chiclayo

Chepén

Aguaytía

Cordillera

Río Apurímac

San Pedro de Lloc

Trujillo

Tingo María

3

Huánuco

Chimbote

Huaraz

Cerro de Pasco

Quillabam

Chiquián

Tarma

Huarmey

Barranca

Supe

La Oroya

Huancayo

Huanta

Abar

BOLIVIA'S TWO CAPITALS

Huaral

Huancavelica

Ayacuch

La Paz   -   *legislative and administrative capital*

Huacho

Matucana

Callao

LIMA

Sucre   -   *legal capital*

Isla San Lorenzo

4

131

Chincha Alta

GALAPAGOS ISLANDS

N

Pisco

Ica

(Archipiélago de Colón, to Ecuador)

Nazca

Isla Darwin

Isla Wolf

Lomas

Cha

1000m/3281ft

500m/1640ft

Sea level

Isla Pinta

Isla Marchena

Isla Isabela

Isla Genovesa

Equator

Isla San Salvador

Isla Santa Cruz

Isla Fernandina

5

Puerto Baquerizo Moreno

Isla Santa María

Isla San Cristóbal

0 km 50

0 miles 50

90°

PACIFIC OCEAN

0 km   400

0 miles   400

PERU

Cordillera Occiden

POPULATION

- Over 500,000
- 100,000 - 500,000
- 50,000 - 100,000
- Less than 50,000
- National capital

80°   75°   70°

85°   5°   10°   15°

90°   85°   80°   20°

131

E   F   G   H

65°   5°   60°   55°

Amazon

A m a z o n   B a s i n

Rio Madeira

Serra do Cachimbo

40

Rio São Manuel

10°

1

B   R   A   Z   I   L

41   2

Rio Purus

Rio Abunã

Fortaleza

Villa Bella

Chapada   dos   Parecis

15°

Rio Madre de Dios

Riberalta

Rio Guaporé

Rio Juruena

Cobija

Porvenir

Rio Beni

Magdalena

55°

Puerto
Maldonado

Santa Ana

Rio Mamoré

San Matías

3

Reyes

San Ignacio

Trinidad

Rio San Miguel

Concepción

Pantanal

Sicuani

B O L I V I A

oriental

Nevado Pupuya
△ 5818m

Moho

Puerto Acosta

Portachuelo

Montero
Warnes

San José

Puerto
Suárez

20°

yaviri

Juliaca

Achacachi

Buena Vista

Santa Cruz

Lake
Titicaca

Copacabana

Cochabamba

Puno

LA PAZ

Comarapa

C   h   a   c   o

Paraguay

41   4

vado Ampato
10m

Ilave

Viacha

Aiquile

Cordillera

△

Corocoro

Oruro

G

Volcán Misti
5822m

Huanuni

SUCRE

r

Nevado
Sajama
6520m

Uncía

Lagunillas

△

Arequipa

Challapata

a

Moquegua

Lago
Poopó

Potosí

Monteagudo

n

Altiplano

oriental

PARAGUAY

ollendo

Tacna

Ilo

Sabaya

Occidental

La Yarada

Uyuni

Cotagaita

San Lorenzo

C   H   I   L   E

Villa Martín

Desierto de Atacama

Tupiza

Tarija

25°

San Pablo

Villazón

Pilcomayo

Tropic of Capricorn

5

Tropic of Capricorn

A   R   G   E   N   T   I   N   A

42

70°   65°   60°

65°   25°   60°

E   F   G   H

ELEVATION

4000 m
13 124 ft

2000 m
6562 ft

1000 m
3281 ft

500 m
1640 ft

250 m
820 ft

100 m
328 ft

Sea
Level

Sea
Level

250 m
-820 ft

-500 m
-1640 ft

-1000 m
-3281 ft

-2000 m
-6562 ft

-3000 m
-9843 ft

-4000 m
-13 124 ft

BRAZIL

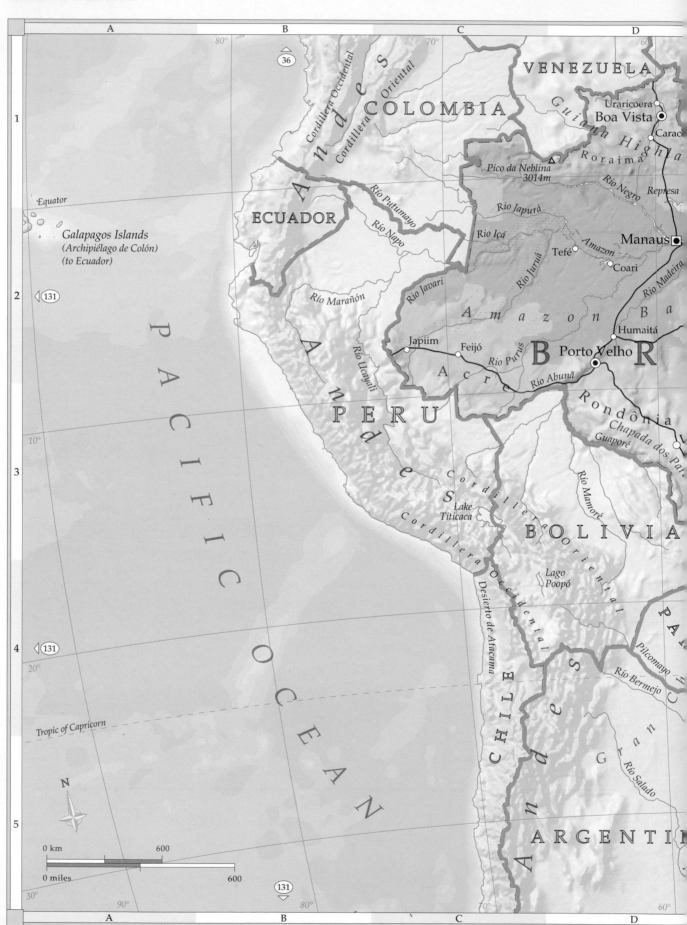

A   B   C   D

80°

70°

60°

1

VENEZUELA

Cordillera Occidental

Cordillera Oriental

COLOMBIA

Uraricoera

Boa Vista ⊙

Carac

Guiana Highla

Roraima

Equator

ECUADOR

Río Putumayo

Río Napo

Rio Japurá

Rio Içá

Rio Negro

Represa

Pico da Neblina
3014m △

Tefé

Coari

Amazon

Manaus ◉

Rio Madeira

*Galapagos Islands
(Archipiélago de Colón)
(to Ecuador)*

2

◁ 131

Río Marañón

Rio Javari

Rio Juruá

A   m   a   z   o   n

B

a

Humaitá

Río Ucayali

Japiim

Feijó

Rio Purus

A c r e

B **Porto Velho** ◉

R

Rio Abunã

Rondônia

Chapada dos Pa

Guaporé

PERU

A
n
d
e
s

PACIFIC

10°

3

Río Mamoré

Cordillera Oriental

Lake
Titicaca

Cordillera Occidental

B O L I V I A

*Lago
Poopó*

PA

A
n
d
e
s

Desierto de Atacama

4

◁ 131

20°

Pilcomayo

Río Bermejo

O C E A N

C H I L E

Tropic of Capricorn

A
n   a
n

G

Río Salado

N

5

A R G E N T I

0 km   600

0 miles   600

131

30°

90°

80°

70°

60°

A   B   C   D

ELEVATION

4000 m 13 124 ft	
2000 m 6562 ft	
1000 m 3281 ft	
500 m 1640 ft	
250 m 820 ft	
100 m 328 ft	
Sea Level	Sea Level
250 m -820 ft	
500 m -1640 ft	
-1000 m -3281 ft	
-2000 m -6562 ft	
-3000 m -9843 ft	
-4000 m -13 124 ft	

FRENCH GUIANA (to France)
INAME

Tumuc Humac Mountains

ATLANTIC OCEAN

Mouths of the Amazon

Equator

Amapá
Macapá
Ilha Caviana de Fora
Ilha de Marajó
Baía de Marajó
Belém
São Luís
Baía de São Marco
Parnaíba
Camocim
enquer
Amazon
Santarém
Altamira
Represa de Tucuruí
Bacabal
Piripiri
Fortaleza
Atol das Rocas
San Fernando de Noronha (to Brazil)
Itaituba
Imperatriz
Teresina
Mossoró
Açu
Cabo de São Roque
Rio Xingu
Marabá
Maranhão
Ceará
Floriano
Rio Grande do Norte
Natal
Carolina
Picos
Juazeiro do Norte
Balsas
Paraíba
João Pessoa
Serra do Cachimbo
Piauí
Pernambuco
Campina Grande
Recife
Juazeiro
Alagoas
Maceió
Serra Formosa
Represa de Sobradinho
Chapada Diamantina
Aracaju
Estância
Tocantins
Bahia
Feira de Santana
Salvador
Taguatinga
Baía de Todos os Santos
Cuiabá
Planalto
Itabuna
BRASÍLIA
Janaúba
Vitória da Conquista
Anápolis
Central
Canavieiras
Goiás
Montes Claros
Araçuaí
Jataí
Goiânia
Minas
Araguari
Gerais
ndonópolis
Mato Grosso do Sul
Governador Valadares
Espírito Santo
Uberlândia
Uberaba
Campo Grande
Belo Horizonte
Ribeirão Preto
Divinópolis
Vitória
quidauana
Juiz de Fora
Presidente Epitácio
Campos
Marília
Campinas
Londrina
Nova
Maringá
São Paulo
Iguaçu
Rio de Janeiro
Paraná
Santos
Represa de Itaipú
Ponta Grossa
Salto do Iguaçu
Rio Iguaçu
Curitiba
Joinville
Santa Catarina
Blumenau
Florianópolis
Passo Fundo
ta Maria
Canoas
Rio Grande
Porto Alegre
Bagé
Lagoa dos Patos
Rio Negro
Rio Grande
Mirim Lagoon
RUGUAY

Tropic of Capricorn

ATLANTIC OCEAN

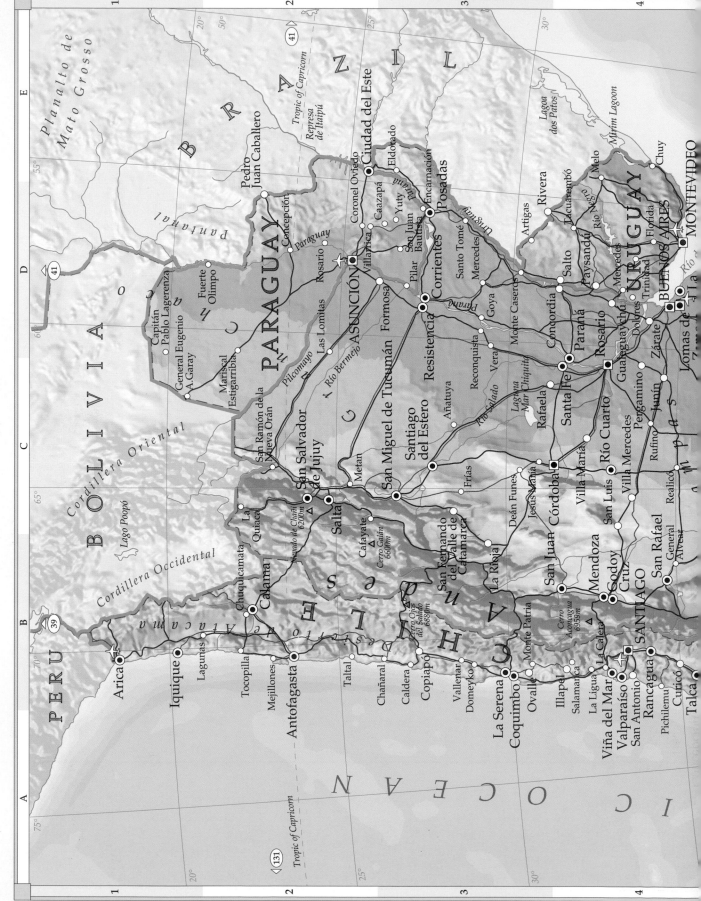

POPULATION

- ◉ Over 500,000
- ◉ 100,000 - 500,000
- ○ 50,000 - 100,000
- ○ Less than 50,000
- ● National capital

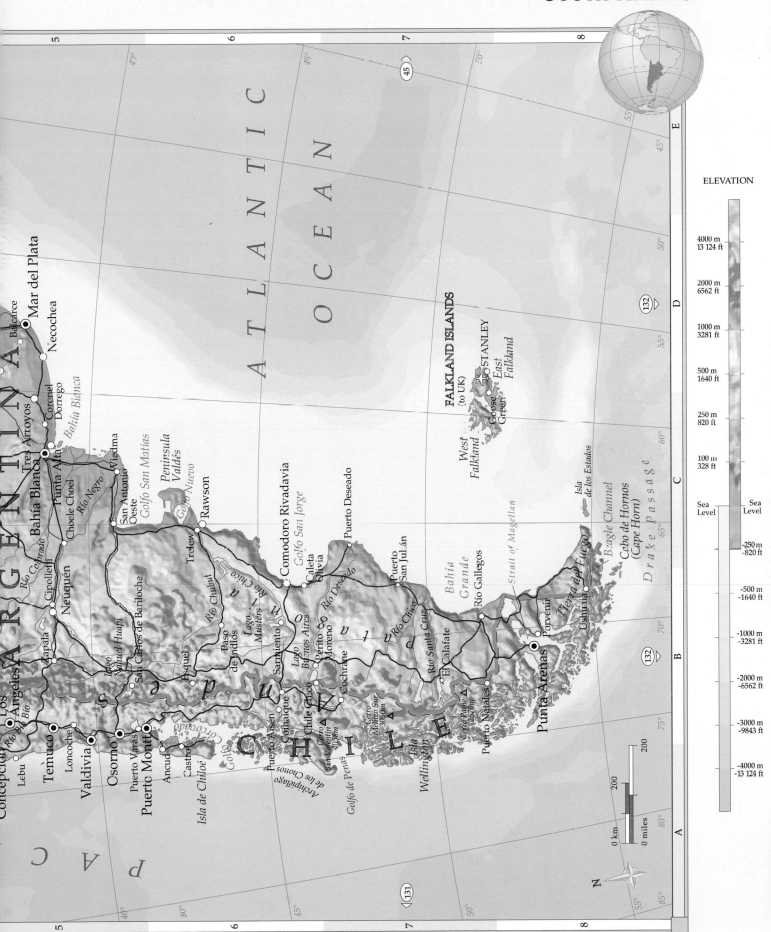

ELEVATION

4000 m	13 124 ft
2000 m	6562 ft
1000 m	3281 ft
500 m	1640 ft
250 m	820 ft
100 m	328 ft
Sea Level	Sea Level
−250 m	−820 ft
−500 m	−1640 ft
−1000 m	−3281 ft
−2000 m	−6562 ft
−3000 m	−9843 ft
−4000 m	−13 124 ft

ATLANTIC OCEAN

FALKLAND ISLANDS
(to UK)

STANLEY
East Falkland
Goose Green
West Falkland

ARGENTINA

Mar del Plata
Balcarce
Necochea
Coronel Dorrego
Bahía Blanca
Punta Alta
Tres Arroyos
Río Colorado
Cipolletti
Neuquén
Zapala
Viedma
San Antonio Oeste
Choele Choel
Río Negro
Peninsula Valdés
Golfo San Matías
Golfo Nuevo
Rawson
Trelew
Río Chubut
Comodoro Rivadavia
Golfo San Jorge
Caleta Olivia
Puerto Deseado
Río Deseado
Puerto San Julián
Río Chico
Bahía Grande
Río Santa Cruz
Río Chico
Río Gallegos
Isla de los Estados
Strait of Magellan
Tierra del Fuego
Ushuaia
Porvenir
Beagle Channel
Cabo de Hornos (Cape Horn)
Drake Passage

Concepción
Los Ángeles
Lebu
Río Bío Bío
Temuco
Loncoche
Valdivia
Osorno
Puerto Varas
Puerto Montt
Ancud
Castro
Isla de Chiloé
Golfo Corcovado
Archipiélago de los Chonos
Golfo de Penas
Isla Wellington

CHILE

San Carlos de Bariloche
Lago Nahuel Huapí
Esquel
Paso de Indios
Sarmiento
Lago Musters
Lago Buenos Aires
Perito Moreno
Cochrane
Coyhaique
Puerto Aisén
Chile Chico
Cerro San Valentín 4058 m
Cerro Macizo Sur 3050m
Cerro Paine 2670m
Puerto Natales
El Calafate
Punta Arenas

PACÍFIC

0 km   200
0 miles   200

131
132
132
45

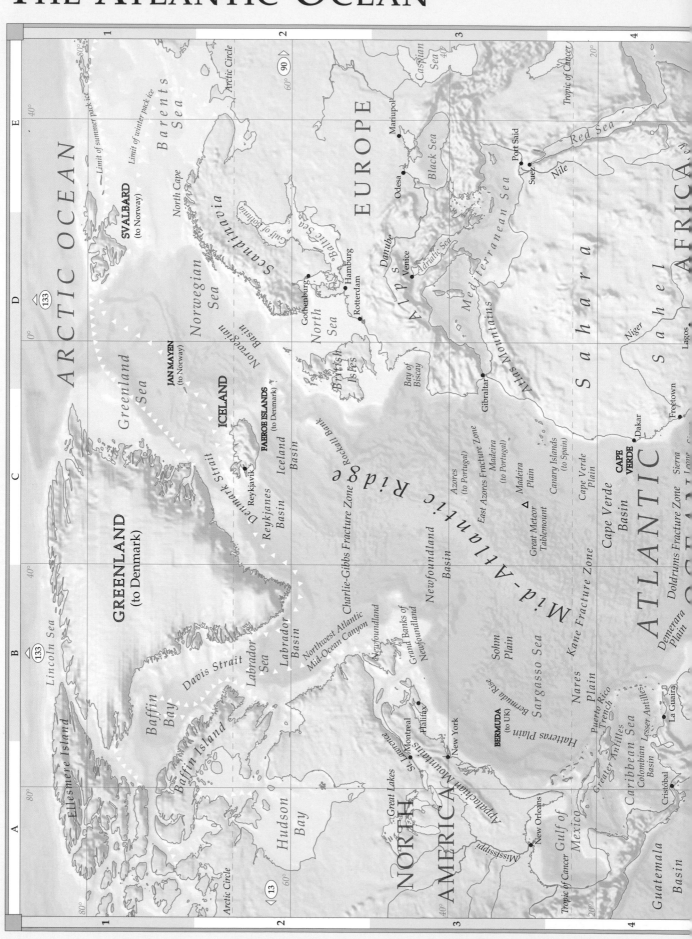

ARCTIC OCEAN

Limit of summer pack ice

Limit of winter pack ice

Arctic Circle

Barents Sea

SVALBARD (to Norway)

North Cape

Scandinavia

Gulf of Bothnia

Baltic Sea

EUROPE

Mariupol

Caspian Sea

Red Sea

Port Said

Suez

Nile

Odesa

Black Sea

Greenland Sea

JAN MAYEN (to Norway)

Norwegian Sea

Danube

Venice

Hamburg

Rotterdam

Adriatic Sea

Mediterranean Sea

Sahara

AFRICA

Gothenburg

North Sea

Alps

Atlas Mountains

Sahel

Niger

ICELAND

Norwegian Basin

British Isles

Gibraltar

Lagos

Denmark Strait

Reykjavik

FAROE ISLANDS (to Denmark)

Iceland Basin

Rockall Bank

Bay of Biscay

Azores (to Portugal)

East Azores Fracture Zone

Madeira (to Portugal)

Madeira Plain

Canary Islands (to Spain)

Cape Verde Plain

Dakar

Freetown

GREENLAND (to Denmark)

Reykjanes Basin

Mid-Atlantic Ridge

Great Meteor Tablemount

Cape Verde Basin

CAPE VERDE

ATLANTIC

Lincoln Sea

Labrador Sea

Labrador Basin

Charlie-Gibbs Fracture Zone

Northwest Atlantic Mid-Ocean Canyon

Newfoundland Basin

Kane Fracture Zone

Doldrums Fracture Zone

Demerara Plain

Sierra

Davis Strait

Baffin Bay

Baffin Island

Newfoundland

Grand Banks of Newfoundland

Sohm Plain

Sargasso Sea

Nares Plain

Puerto Rico Trench

Greater Antilles

Lesser Antilles

Colombian Basin

OCEAN

Ellesmere Island

Bermuda Rise

BERMUDA (to UK)

Hatteras Plain

New York

Halifax

Montreal

St. Lawrence

Caribbean Sea

La Guaira

Cristobal

Hudson Bay

Great Lakes

NORTH AMERICA

Appalachian Mountains

New Orleans

Gulf of Mexico

Mississippi

Tropic of Cancer

Guatemala Basin

Arctic Circle

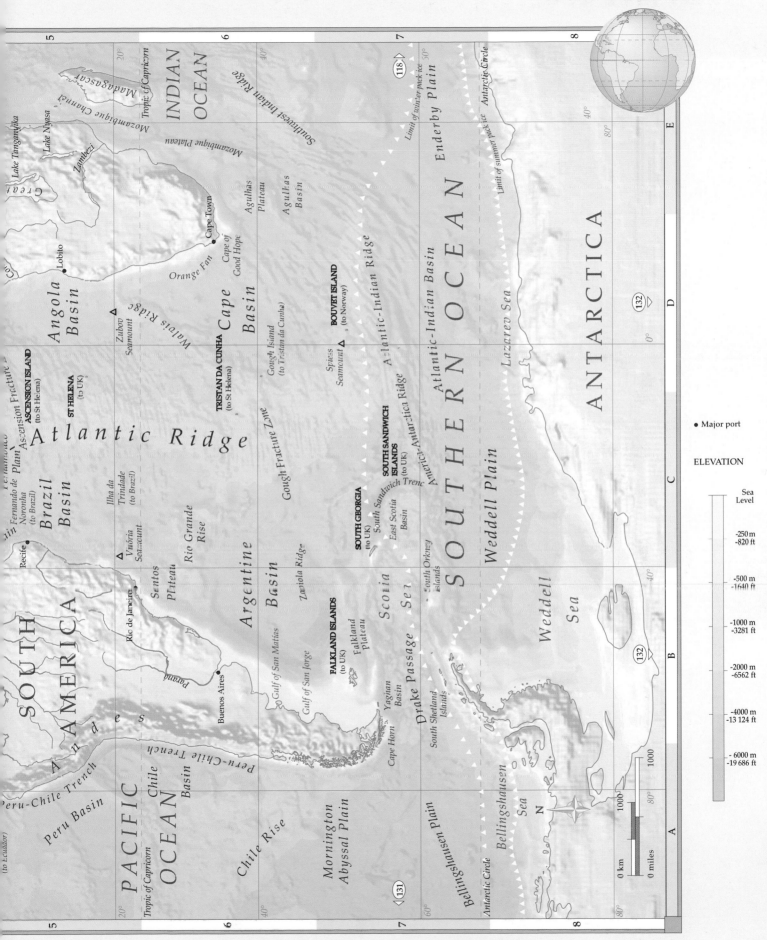

INDIAN OCEAN

Tropic of Capricorn

Madagascar

Lake Tanganyika
Lake Nyasa
Zambezi
Great

Mozambique Channel

Mozambique Plateau

Southwest Indian Ridge

Agulhas Plateau

Agulhas Basin

Cape Town
Cape of Good Hope
Orange Fan

Lobito

Angola Basin

Walvis Ridge

Zubov Seamount

Cape Basin

Gough Island
(to Tristan da Cunha)

Spiess Seamount

BOUVET ISLAND
(to Norway)

Atlantic-Indian Ridge

Enderby Plain

Limit of winter pack ice

Limit of summer pack ice

Antarctic Circle

Lazarev Sea

Atlantic-Indian Basin

SOUTHERN OCEAN

ANTARCTICA

118

132

132

Mid-Atlantic Ridge

ASCENSION ISLAND
(to UK)

ST HELENA
(to UK)

TRISTAN DA CUNHA
(to St Helena)

Gough Fracture Zone

America-Antarctica Ridge

SOUTH SANDWICH ISLANDS
(to UK)

South Sandwich Trench

SOUTH GEORGIA
(to UK)

East Scotia Basin

South Orkney Islands

Weddell Plain

Weddell Sea

Major port

ELEVATION

Ascension Fracture Zone

Fernando de Noronha
(to Brazil)

Ilha da Trindade
(to Brazil)

Brazil Basin

Recife

Vitória Seamount

Rio Grande Rise

Santos Plateau

Rio de Janeiro

Paraná

Buenos Aires

Argentine Basin

Zapiola Ridge

Gulf of San Matías

Gulf of San Jorge

FALKLAND ISLANDS
(to UK)

Falkland Plateau

Scotia Sea

Yaghan Basin

Drake Passage

Cape Horn

South Shetland Islands

Bellingshausen

Bellingshausen Plain

Bellingshausen Sea

N

SOUTH AMERICA

Andes

Peru-Chile Trench

Peru-Chile Trench

Chile Basin

Peru Basin

Chile Rise

Mornington Abyssal Plain

PACIFIC OCEAN

Tropic of Capricorn

Antarctic Circle

(to Ecuador)

131

Sea Level

-250 m
-820 ft

-500 m
-1640 ft

-1000 m
-3281 ft

-2000 m
-6562 ft

-4000 m
-13 124 ft

-6000 m
-19 686 ft

0 km   1000

0 miles   1000

AFRICA

PHYSICAL FEATURES

LARGEST LAKE: Lake Victoria, Uganda, Kenya, Tanzania, 26,828 sq miles (69,484 sq km)

LONGEST RIVER: Nile, Uganda/Sudan/Egypt 4,160 miles (6,695 km)

HIGHEST POINT: Kilimanjaro, Tanzania 19,341 ft (5,895 m)

LOWEST POINT: Lac' Assal, Djibouti 512 ft (156 m) below sea level

POLITICAL FEATURES

COUNTRY WITH HIGHEST POPULATION DENSITY: Mauritius 1,671 people per sq mile (645 people per sq km)

LARGEST COUNTRY: Sudan 917,373 sq miles (2,376,000 sq km)

SMALLEST COUNTRY: Seychelles 108 sq miles (280 sq km)

TOTAL AREA: 11,677,250 sq miles (30,244,050 sq km)

TOTAL NUMBER OF COUNTRIES: 53

TOTAL POPULATION: 776.5 million

LARGEST CITY WITH POPULATION: Cairo, Egypt 6.4 million

POPULATION

- ▣ Over 500,000
- ◉ 100,000 – 500,000
- ○ 50,000 – 100,000
- ○ Less than 50,000
- ● National capital

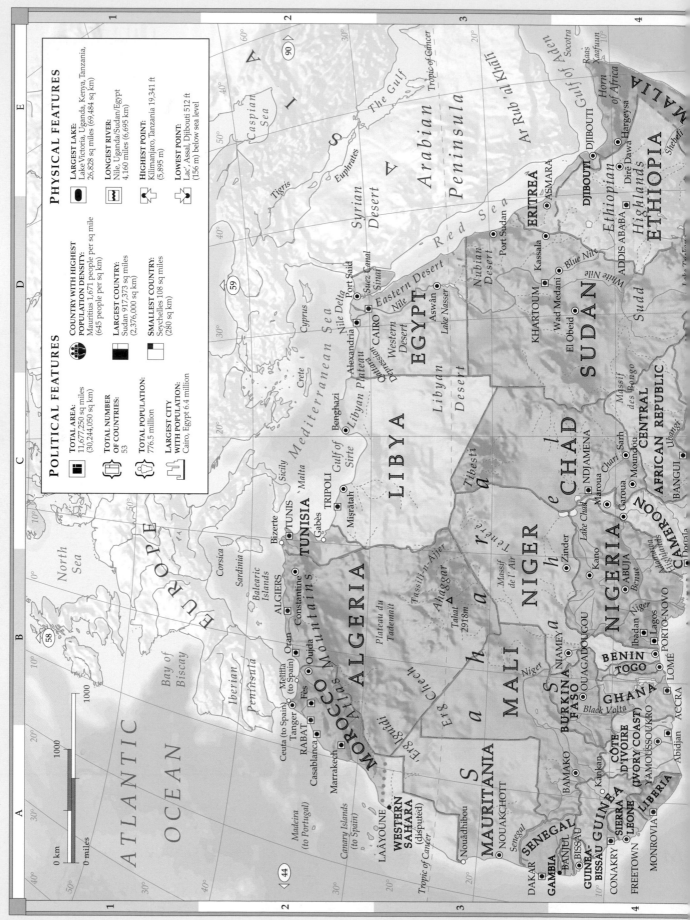

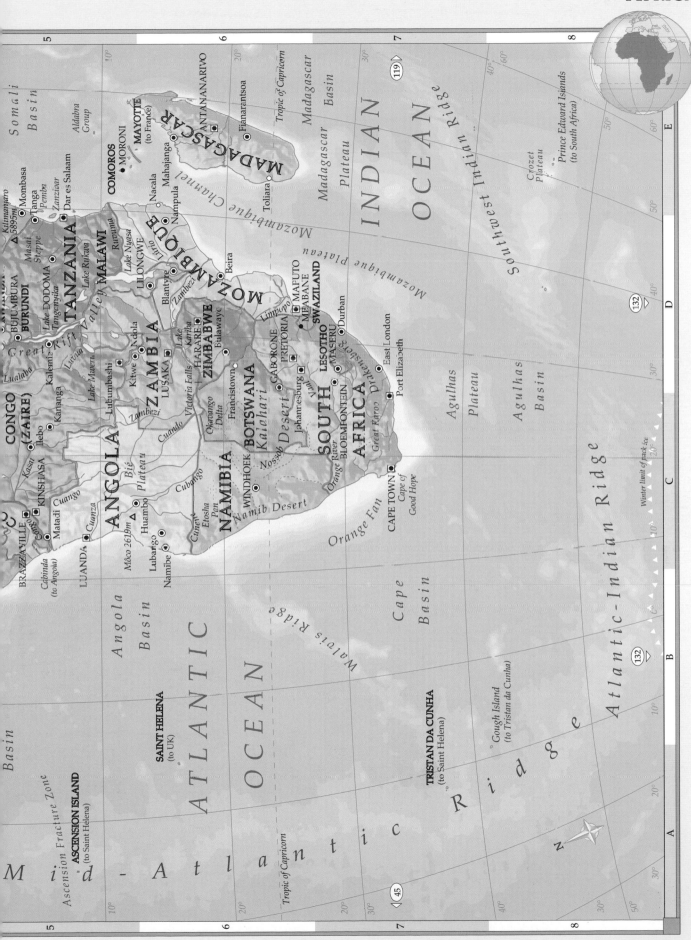

Somali Basin

Zanzibar

Kilimanjaro 5895m △

ALDABRA GROUP

COMOROS ● MORONI

MAYOTTE (to France)

ANTANANARIVO ◉

Fianarantsoa ●

Tropic of Capricorn

Madagascar Basin

MADAGASCAR

Mombasa

Tanga Pemba

Dar es Salaam

Nacala

Nampula

Masai Steppe

BURUNDI

BUJUMBURA ◉

TANZANIA

DODOMA ◉

Lake Rukwa

Lake Tanganyika

Lake Nyasa

Ruvuma

Lurio

MALAWI

LILONGWE ◉

Blantyre ●

Beira ●

Mahajanga

Toliara

INDIAN

OCEAN

Madagascar Plateau

Mozambique Channel

119

MOZAMBIQUE

Great Rift Valley

CONGO (ZAIRE)

Lualaba

Lake Mweru

Kalemie

Kananga

Lubumbashi

Kolwezi Ndola

ZAMBIA

LUSAKA ◉

Lake Kariba

Victoria Falls

ZIMBABWE

HARARE ◉

Bulawayo ●

Zambezi

MAPUTO ●

MBABANE ◉

SWAZILAND

PRETORIA ◉

Johannesburg ●

LESOTHO

MASERU ◉

Durban ●

East London ●

Port Elizabeth ●

Southwest Indian Ridge

132

Crozet Plateau

Prince Edward Islands (to South Africa)

Ilebo

KINSHASA ◉

Matadi

BRAZZAVILLE ◉

Congo

Cabinda (to Angola)

LUANDA ◉

ANGOLA

Môco 2619m △

Huambo △

Lubango ●

Namibe ●

Kasai

Cuango

Cuanza

Bié Plateau

Cubango

Cunene

Cuando

Okavango Delta

NAMIBIA

WINDHOEK ◉

Etosha Pan

Namib Desert

Nossob

Kalahari Desert

BOTSWANA

GABORONE ◉

Francistown ●

SOUTH AFRICA

BLOEMFONTEIN ◉

Great Karoo

Drakensberg

Orange River

Vaal

CAPE TOWN ● Cape of Good Hope

Agulhas Plateau

Agulhas Basin

Angola Basin

SAINT HELENA (to UK)

ASCENSION ISLAND (to Saint Helena)

Ascension Fracture Zone

ATLANTIC

OCEAN

Walvis Ridge

Orange Fan

Cape Basin

TRISTAN DA CUNHA (to Saint Helena)

Gough Island (to Tristan da Cunha)

Atlantic-Indian Ridge

132

Winter limit of pack ice

Mid-Atlantic Ridge

Tropic of Capricorn

45

N

NORTHWEST AFRICA

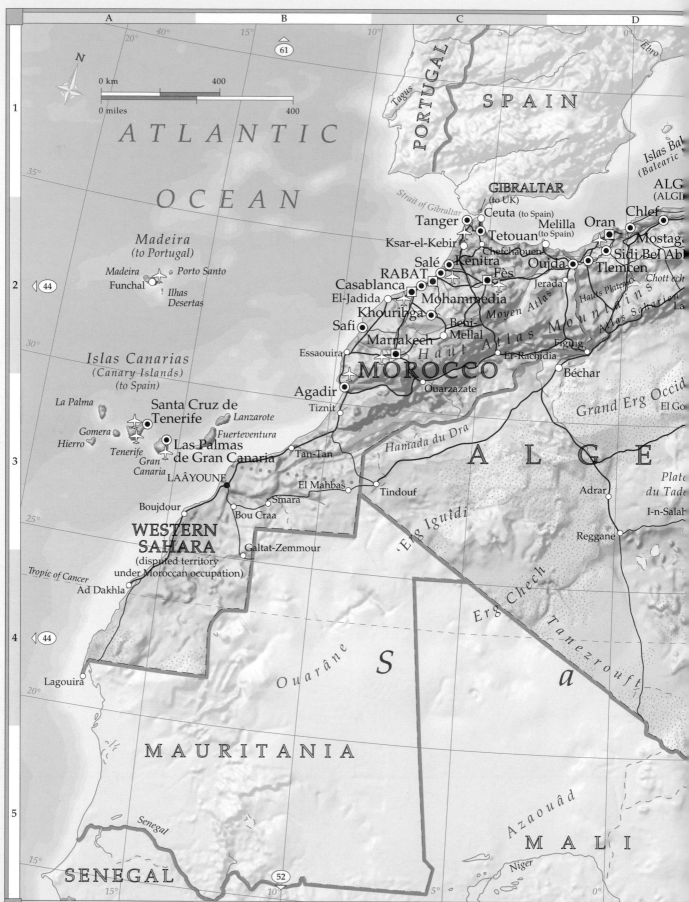

POPULATION

- ▣ Over 500,000
- ◉ 100,000 – 500,000
- ○ 50,000 – 100,000
- ∘ Less than 50,000
- ● National capital

ATLANTIC

OCEAN

Madeira
(to Portugal)

Madeira   • Porto Santo
Funchal
Ilhas
Desertas

Islas Canarias
(Canary Islands)
(to Spain)

La Palma
Gomera   Lanzarote
Hierro   Santa Cruz de
Tenerife   Fuerteventura
Tenerife
Gran
Canaria   Las Palmas
LAÂYOUNE   de Gran Canaria

Boujdour

WESTERN
SAHARA
(disputed territory
under Moroccan occupation)

Tropic of Cancer
Ad Dakhla

Lagouira

MAURITANIA

Ouarâne

SENEGAL

Senegal

PORTUGAL
SPAIN

Tagus

Islas Bal
(Balearic

Strait of Gibraltar

GIBRALTAR
(to UK)
Ceuta (to Spain)
Tanger
Ksar-el-Kebir   Tetouan
Chefchaouen   Melilla
                  (to Spain)
Salé   Kenitra
RABAT   Fès
Casablanca
El-Jadida   Mohammedia
Khouribga
Safi
          Beni-
          Mellal
Essaouira   Marrakech
          Haut
MOROCCO
          Ouarzazate

Tiznit

Tan-Tan

El Mahbas

Smara
Bou Craa

Galtat-Zemmour

Hamada du Dra

ALGE

Erg Iguîdi

Erg Chech

Tanezrouft

Azaouâd

Niger

MALI

Oran   Chlef
Mostag
Sidi Bel Ab
Oujda   Tlemcen
Jerada   Chott ech
          Hauts Plateau   Atlas Saharien
Moyen Atlas
Atlas Mountains
          Figuig
Er-Rachidia
          Béchar
Grand Erg Occid   El

Adrar

Reggane   Plate
du Tade
I-n-Salah

ALG
(ALGI)

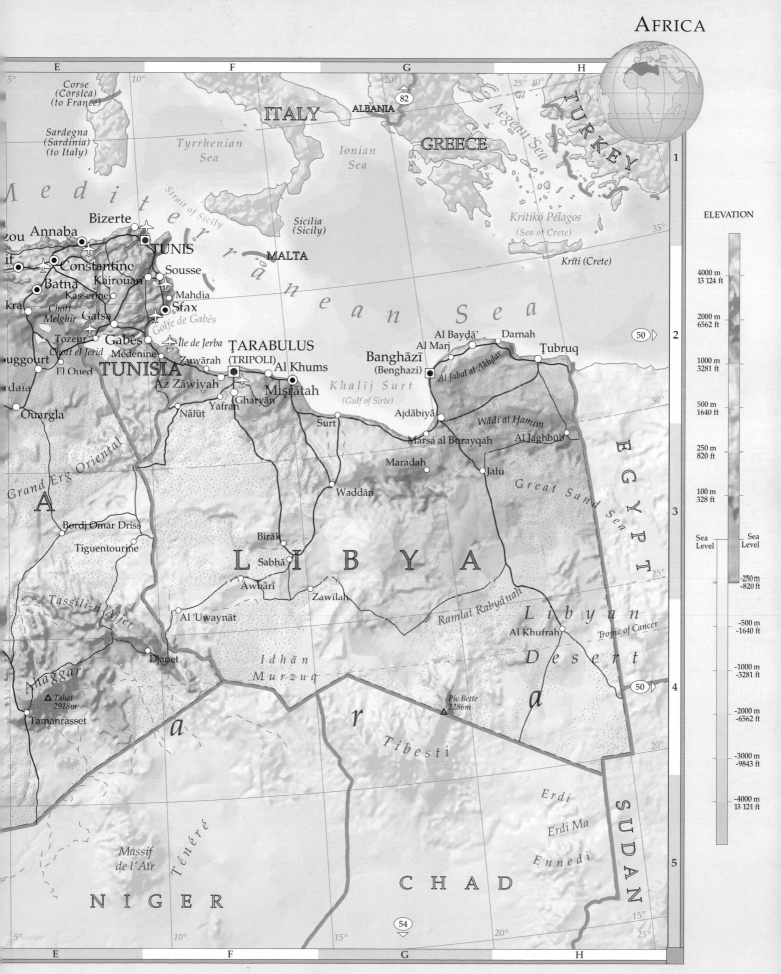

Corse
(Corsica)
(to France)

ITALY

ALBANIA

82

GREECE

Aegean Sea

TURKEY

Sardegna
(Sardinia)
(to Italy)

Tyrrhenian
Sea

Ionian
Sea

Kritikó Pélagos
(Sea of Crete)

1

zou

Bizerte

Mediterranean

Annaba

if

TUNIS

Sousse

Constantine

Kairouan

Sicilia
(Sicily)

MALTA

Kríti (Crete)

35°

Batna

Mahdia

Kasserine

Sea

kra

Gafsa

Sfax

Chott
Melghir

Golfe de Gabès

Al Baydā'

Darnah

Tozeur

Gabes

Al Marj

Ţubruq

50

2

uggourt

Chott el Jerid

Médenine

Île de Jerba

ṬARABULUS
(TRIPOLI)

Banghāzī
(Benghazi)

Al Jabal al Akhḍar

daïa

El Oued

TUNISIA

Zuwārah

Al Khums

Ouargla

Az Zāwiyah

Miṣrātah

Khalīj Surt
(Gulf of Sirte)

Ajdābiyā

Wādī al Ḥamīm

30°

Nālūt

Yafran

Gharyān

Surt

Marsa al Burayqah

Al Jaghbūb

Grand Erg Oriental

Maradah

Jalu

250 m
820 ft

A

Waddān

Great Sand Sea

EGYPT

3

Bordj Omar Driss

Birāk

L   I   B   Y   A

Tiguentourine

Sabhā

25°

Tassili-n'Ajjer

Awbārī

Zawīlah

Ramlat Rabyānah

Libyan

Al 'Uwaynāt

Al Khufrah

Tropic of Cancer

Djanet

Idhān
Murzuq

Desert

Ahaggar

a

△ Tahat
2918m

Pic Bette
△ 2286m

a

50

4

Tamanrasset

r

Tibesti

20°

Erdi

Massif
de l'Aïr

Ténéré

Erdi Ma

Ennedi

S U D A N

5

N   I   G   E   R

C   H   A   D

54

15°

5°

10°

15°

20°

25°

E

F

G

H

ELEVATION

4000 m
13 124 ft

2000 m
6562 ft

1000 m
3281 ft

500 m
1640 ft

250 m
820 ft

100 m
328 ft

Sea
Level

Sea
Level

-250 m
-820 ft

-500 m
-1640 ft

-1000 m
-3281 ft

-2000 m
-6562 ft

-3000 m
-9843 ft

-4000 m
13 124 ft

Strait of Sicily

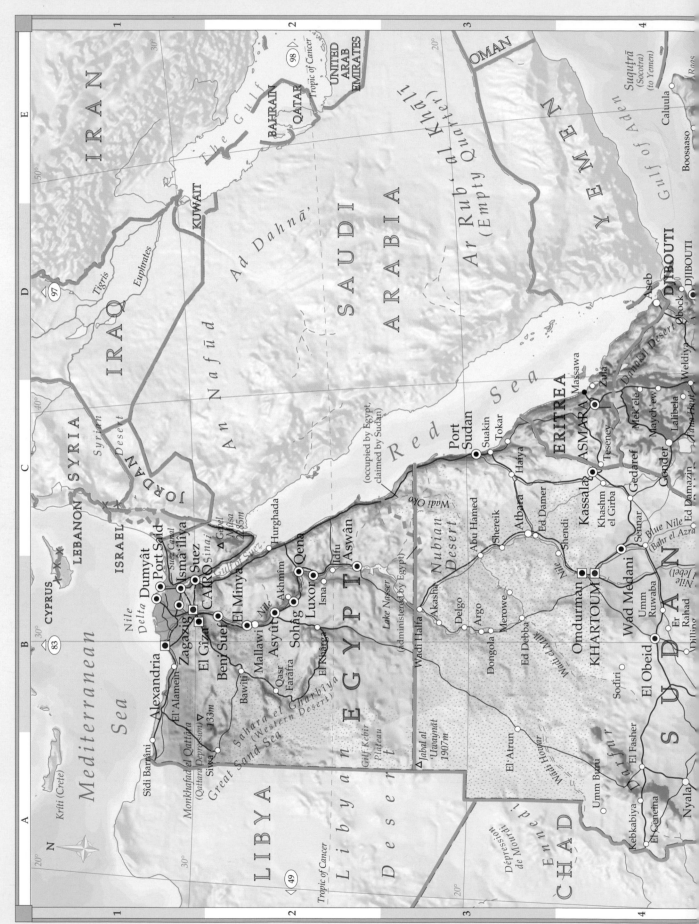

POPULATION

- ◉ Over 500,000
- ◉ 100,000 – 500,000
- ○ 50,000 – 100,000
- ○ Less than 50,000
- ● National capital

N

Kríti (Crete)

Mediterranean Sea

CYPRUS
LEBANON
SYRIA
ISRAEL
JORDAN

IRAN
IRAQ
Tigris
Euphrates
Syrian Desert

KUWAIT
The Gulf
BAHRAIN
QATAR
UNITED ARAB EMIRATES
Tropic of Cancer

OMAN

SAUDI ARABIA
An Nafūd
Ad Dahnā'

Ar Rub' al Khālī (Empty Quarter)
Ar Rub' al Khālī

YEMEN
Suquṭrā (Socotra) (to Yemen)
Calula
Ra'as
Boosaaso

Gulf of Aden

DJIBOUTI
DJIBOUTI
Obock
Aseb

Danakil Desert
Weldiya

Red Sea

Massawa
Zula
ERITREA
ASMARA
Mek'elē
Maych'ew
Lalibela
Āmba Ḥarēr

Port Sudan
Suakin
Tokar
Haiya
Teseney
Gedaref
Gonder
Ed Damazin

Alexandria
Sidi Barrāni
El Alamein
Port Said
Dumyât
Zagazig
Isma'iliya
Suez Canal
Suez
Gebel Mûsa 285m
Sinai
CAIRO
El Gîza
Nile Delta
Beni Suef
El Minya
Zagazig

Hurghada
Gulf of Suez

Qena
Idfu
Akhmîm
Luxor
Aswân
Isna
El Kharga
Sohâg
Asyût
Mallawi
Qasr Farâfra
Bawîti
El Kharga
Sahara el Gharbiya (Western Desert)

Monkhafad el Qattâra (Qattara Depression) -133m
Siwa

Great Sand Sea

Gulf Kebir Plateau
Jabal al 'Uwaynāt 1907m
El'Atrun

LIBYA
Libyan Desert
EGYPT
Tropic of Cancer

Lake Nasser
Wadi Halfa (administered by Egypt)
(occupied by Egypt, claimed by Sudan)
Wādī Oko

Nubian Desert
Akasha
Delgo
Abu Hamed
Shereik
Atbara
Ed Damer
Shendi
Argo
Dongola
Ed Debba
Merowe
Khashm el Girba
Kassala
Atbara
Nile

SUDAN
Omdurman
KHARTOUM
Wad Medani
Umm Ruwaba
Sennar
Blue Nile (Baḥr el Azra)
Wadi el Malik
Sodiri
El Obeid
Er Rahad
Dilling
Nile (Baḥr el Jebel)

Darfur
Umm Buru
Kebkabiya
El Fasher
El Geneina
Nyala

CHAD
Ennedi
Depression de Mourdi
Wādī Hogra

20°
30°
30°
20°
40°
50°
20°
30°
30°
20°

N 83
N 97
N 98
N 49

50

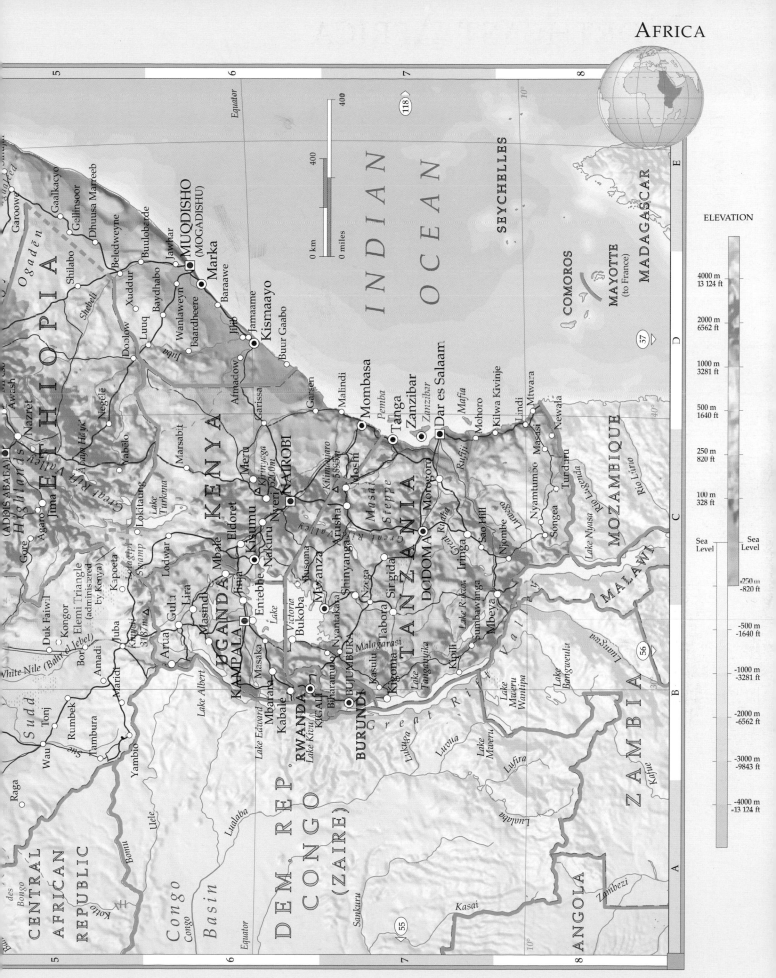

5   6   7   8

118

Equator

INDIAN

OCEAN

SEYCHELLES

COMOROS

MAYOTTE
(to France)

MADAGASCAR

400

400

0 km

0 miles

37

Garoowe

Gaalkacyo

Gellinsoor

Dhuusa Marreeb

Ogaden

Shilabo

Beledweyne

Xuddur

Buulobarde

Jawhar

MUQDISHO
(MOGADISHU)

Marka

Baraawe

ETHIOPIA
Highlands

Nazrēt

Jima

Agaro

Gore

Negēlē

Shebeli

Doolow

Baydhabo

Wanlaweyn

Jilib

Jamaame

Kismaayo

Buur Gaabo

Awash

(ADDIS ABABA)

Great Rift Valley

Aḍabā Hayk'

Kabelo

Luuq

Baardheere

Juba

Afmadow

Garissa

Garsen

Malindi

Mombasa

Pemba

Tanga

Zanzibar

Zanzibar

Dar es Salaam

Mafia

Mohoro

Kilwa Kivinje

Lindi

Mtwara

Newala

Masasi

MOZAMBIQUE

Lake Turkana

Marsabit

Meru

Kirinyaga
5200m

NAIROBI

Kilimanjaro
5895m

Moshi

Arusha

Masai
Steppe

Rufiji

KENYA

Eldoret

Nakuru

Nyeri

Kisumu

Mbale

Jinja

Musoma

Shinyanga

Nzega

Sirgida

DODOMA

Morogoro

Kilosa

Iringa

Sao Hill

Njombe

Songea

Turdiru

Nyamtumbo

Rio Lúrio

Lokitaung

Lodwar

Lira

Gulu

Masindi

Entebbe

KAMPALA

Lake Victoria

Bukoba

Mwanza

Nyankaka

Malagarasi

Tabora

Kasulu

Kigoma

Lake Tanganyika

Kipili

Sumbawanga

Mbeya

Lake Rukwa

Lake Nyasa

Luwegu

Songwe

Lake Rukwa

TANZANIA

Kapoeta

Shaml swamp

Lake Kyoga

UGANDA

Masaka

Mbarara

Kabale

RWANDA

KIGALI

BUJUMBURA

BURUNDI

Biharamulo

Nyakanazi

Great Rift Valley

Lukuga

Luvua

Lake Mweru
Wantipa

Lake Mweru

Lufira

Lake Bangweulu

Luapula

MALAWI

Duk Faiwl

Kongor

Elemi Triangle
(administered
by Kenya)

Juba

Kinyeti
3187 m

Arua

Lake Albert

Lake Edward

Lake Kivu

Sudd

White Nile (Bahr el Jebel)

Bor

Amadi

Maridi

Yambio

Tonj

Rumbek

Tambura

Wau

Raga

Uele

Uele

Bomu

Kotto

des
Bongo

CENTRAL
AFRICAN
REPUBLIC

Congo
Basin

Congo

Lualaba

Sankuru

Kasai

DEM. REP.
CONGO
(ZAIRE)

Equator

Lualaba

ANGOLA

ZAMBIA

Zambezi

Kafue

55

56

ELEVATION

4000 m
13 124 ft

2000 m
6562 ft

1000 m
3281 ft

500 m
1640 ft

250 m
820 ft

100 m
328 ft

Sea
Level

Sea
Level

-250 m
-820 ft

-500 m
-1640 ft

-1000 m
-3281 ft

-2000 m
-6562 ft

-3000 m
-9843 ft

-4000 m
-13 124 ft

5   6   7   8

E

D

C

B

A

10°

10°

30°

40°

WEST AFRICA

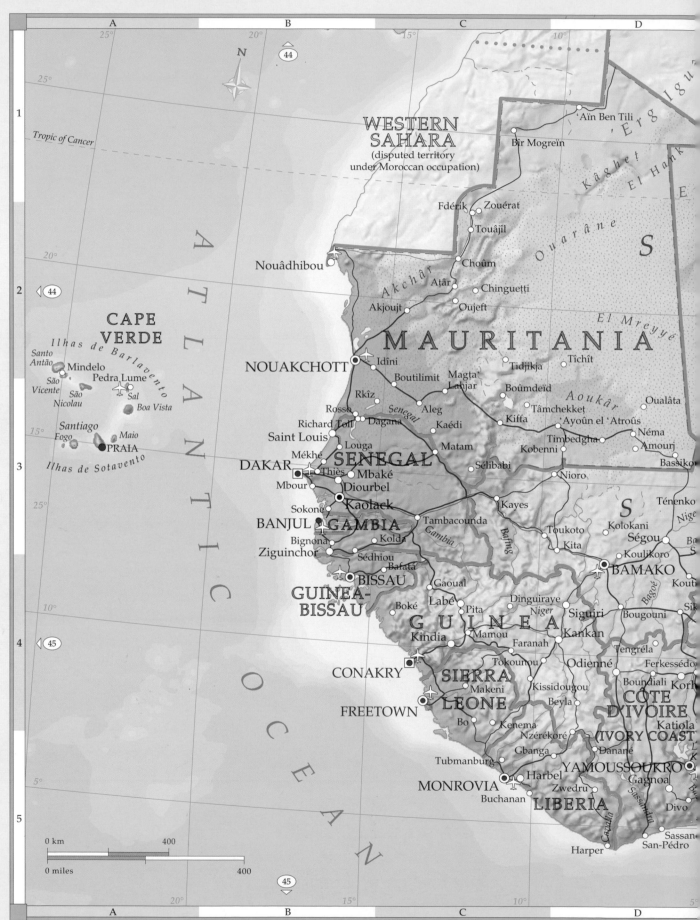

WESTERN SAHARA
(disputed territory under Moroccan occupation)

Aïn Ben Tili

Bîr Mogreïn

'Erg Iguı

Kâghet

El Hank

Fdérîk   Zouérat

Touâjîl

Ouarâne   S

Nouâdhibou

Choûm

Akchâr

Atâr   Chinguetti

Akjoujt   Oujeft   El Mreyyé

MAURITANIA

NOUAKCHOTT   Idîni

Boutilimit   Tidjikja   Tîchît

Rkîz   Magta Lahjar   Boûmdeïd   Aoukâr   Oualâta

Rosso   Aleg   Tâmchekket

Richard Toll Dagana   Kaédi   Kiffa   'Ayoûn el 'Atroûs   Néma

Saint Louis   Senegal   Amourj

Louga   Matam   Timbedgha   Bassikou

Mékhé   Sélibabi   Kobenni

DAKAR   SENEGAL   Nioro   S

Thiès Mbaké   Téneko

Mbour Diourbel   Kayes   Kolokani   Nigé

Kaolack   Koulikoro Ségou

Sokone   Tambacounda   Toukoto   Ba

BANJUL GAMBIA   Kita   BAMAKO

Bignona   Kolda   Gambia   Kout

Ziguinchor   Sédhiou   Bafing

Balala   Gaoual   Bagoé Sik

BISSAU   Labé   Dinguiraye   Niger Siguiri   Bougouni

GUINEA-   Boké   Pita   Mamou   Kankan   Tengréla

BISSAU   Kindia   GUINEA   Faranah   Odienné   Ferkessédo

CONAKRY   Tokounou   Kissidougou   Boundiali Korl

SIERRA   Makeni   Beyla   CÔTE
LEONE   D'IVOIRE

FREETOWN   Bo   Kenema   Katiola (IVORY COAST)

Nzérékoré   Gbanga   Danané   YAMOUSSOUKRO Gagnoa

Tubmanburg   Harbel   Divo

MONROVIA   Zwedru   Sassan

Buchanan   LIBERIA

Harper   San-Pédro

CAPE VERDE

Ilhas de Barlavento

Santo Antão   Mindelo
São Vicente   Pedra Lume
São Nicolau   Sal
Boa Vista

Santiago   Maio
Fogo

PRAIA

Ilhas de Sotavento

Tropic of Cancer

ATLANTIC OCEAN

Senegal

25°

20°

15°

25°

20°

15°

10°

5°

A B C D

POPULATION

- ● Over 500,000
- ◉ 100,000 - 500,000
- ○ 50,000 - 100,000
- ○ Less than 50,000
- ● National capital

0 km   400

0 miles   400

44

45

N

ELEVATION

4000 m 13 124 ft	
2000 m 6562 ft	
1000 m 3281 ft	
500 m 1640 ft	
250 m 820 ft	
100 m 328 ft	
Sea Level	Sea Level
-250 m -820 ft	
-500 m -1640 ft	
-1000 m -3281 ft	
-2000 m -6562 ft	
-3000 m -9843 ft	
-4000 m -13 124 ft	

LIBYA

ALGERIA

Tanezrouft

Tassili-n-Ajjer

S a h a r a

Ahaggar

Tibesti

Tropic of Cancer

Ténéré du Tafassâsset

Séguédine

a h a r a

Erg I-n-Sâkâne

Tessalit

Adrar des Ifôghas

Assamakka

Iferouâne

Massif de l'Aïr

Monts Bagzane 2022m

Ténéré

Grand Erg de Bilma

Araouane

Azaouâd

MALI

Tombouctou

Gao

NIGER

Agadez

Ngourti

oundam
Lac Niangay
Goundam
bine

Ansongo

Ménaka

Tahoua

Keïta

Dakoro

Dilia

Nguigmi

CHAD

Lake Chad

Hombori

Ayorou

Tillabéri

Birnin Konni

Maradi

Tessaoua

Zinder

Gouré

Ngourti

URKINA

Dogondoutchi

NIAMEY

Sokoto

Guidimouni

Hadejia

Nguru

Hadejia

Maiduguri

Kaya

OUAGADOUGOU

Sokoto

Gusau

Katsina

Kano

Potiskum

dougou

Fada-Ngourma

Koko

Zaria

Biu

FASO

Tenkodogo

Kandi

Yelwa

Kaduna

Bauchi

Kumo

o-Dioulasso

Bawku

Sansanné-Mango

Natitingou

Jos

Gombi

Bolgatanga

Oti

Jos Plateau

Shebshi Mountains

Yola

Wa

BENIN

NIGERIA

Yendi

Parakou

Minna

Jos

Lafia

Tamale

Sokodé

Ilorin

Jebba

ABUJA

Benue

Wukari

Goter Mountains

Adamawa Highlands

oukou

GHANA

Oyo

Ogbomosho

Niger

Lokoja

Makurdi

C.A.R.

unyani

Wenchi

Ibadan

Ede

Owo

Bonin City

Enugu

ngourou

Kumasi

Lake Volta

Abomey

PORTO-NOVO

Kpalimé

Cotonou

Lagos

Sapele

Onitsha

Calabar

Nsawam

LOMÉ

Warri

Owerri

Aba

Uyo

Asamankese

ACCRA

Port Harcourt

Djerem

Sanaga

CAMEROON

Aboisso

Cape Coast

Bight of Benin

Mouths of the Niger

djan

Sekondi-Takoradi

Gulf of Guinea

Isla de Bioco

EQUATORIAL GUINEA

Kainji Reservoir

Sokoto

Niger

Black Volta

White Volta

Volta

CENTRAL AFRICA

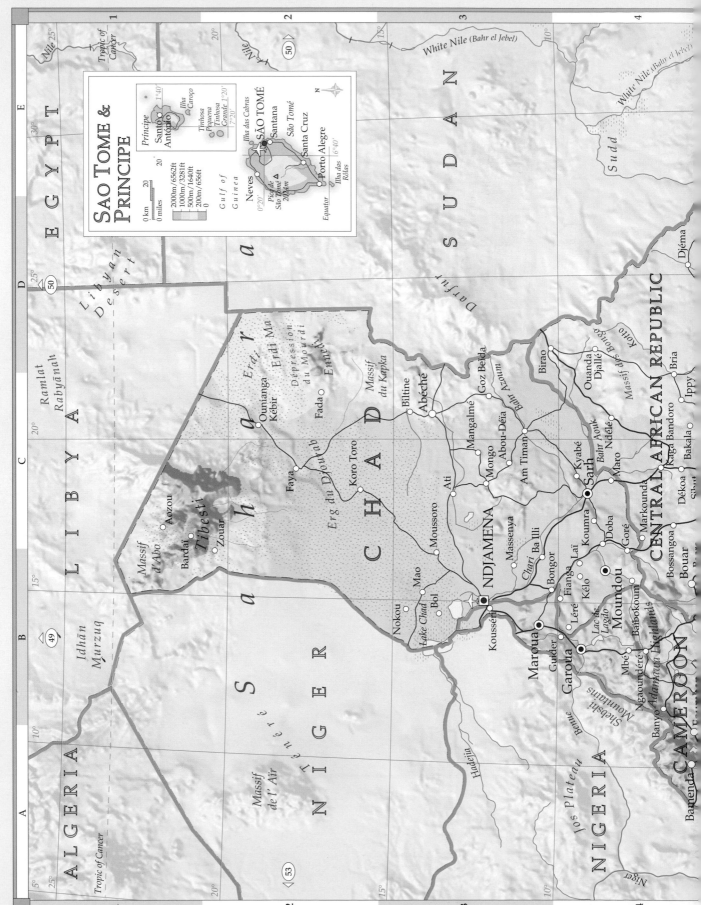

SAO TOME & PRINCIPE

Príncipe
Santo António

Ilha Caroço

Tinhosa Pequena
Tinhosa Grande

Ilha das Cabras
SÃO TOMÉ
Santana
São Tomé
Santa Cruz

Neves

Pico de São Tomé 2024m

Porto Alegre
Ilha das Rôlas

Equator

Gulf of Guinea

2000m/6562ft
1000m/3281ft
500m/1640ft
200m/656ft
0

0 km   20
0 miles   20

POPULATION

- Over 500,000
- 100,000 – 500,000
- 50,000 – 100,000
- Less than 50,000
- National capital

White Nile (Bahr el Jebel)

EGYPT

LIBYA

Nile

Tropic of Cancer

Ramlat Rabyānah

Libyan Desert

Idhān Murzuq

Massif de l'Aïr

Ténéré

NIGER

ALGERIA

Tropic of Cancer

Massif d'Abo
Aozou
Bardaï
Zouar
Tibesti
Erdi
Ounianga Kébir
Erdi Ma
Fada
Dépression du Mourdi
Ennedi

Sahara

Faya

Erg du Djourab

Koro Toro

Massif du Kapka
Biltine
Abéché

CHAD

Ati
Moussoro
Mongo
Abou-Déïa
Am Timan
Mangalmé

Goz Beïda

Bahr Azoum

Birao

Nokou
Lake Chad
Bol
Mao

NDJAMENA
Kousséri
Massenya
Chari Baguirmi
Bongor

Maroua
Guider
Garoua

NIGERIA

Benue
Jos Plateau

Hadejia

Niger

SUDAN

Darfur

Sudd

White Nile (Bahr el Jebel)

Kotto
Djéma

CENTRAL AFRICAN REPUBLIC

Massif des Bongo

Ouanda Djallé
Bria
Ippy
Bakala
Bamingui

Ndélé
Bahr Aouk
Sarh
Kyabé
Maro
Markounda
Bossangoa
Bouar

Doba
Goré
Koumra
Moundou
Kélo
Laï
Fianga
Léré
Lac de Lagdo
Mbé
Batbokoum
Ngaoundéré
Banyo
Adamawa Highlands

Shebshi Mountains

CAMEROON

Bamenda

ELEVATION

4000 m
13 124 ft

2000 m
6562 ft

1000 m
3281 ft

500 m
1640 ft

250 m
820 ft

100 m
328 ft

Sea Level — Sea Level

-250 m
-820 ft

-500 m
-1640 ft

-1000 m
-3281 ft

-2000 m
-6562 ft

-3000 m
-9843 ft

-4000 m
-13 124 ft

UGANDA
Great Rift Valley
Equator
Lake Victoria
Lake Albert
Ruwenzori
Lake Edward
Lake Kivu

TANZANIA
RWANDA
BURUNDI

Watsa
Is·ro
Mungbere
Beni
Betembo
Titule
Nia-Nia
Bunia
Goma
Bukavu
Kisangani
Yangambi
Lubutu
Lualaba
Lomami
Buta
Bumba
Isala
Gemena
Akula

DEM. REP. CONGO (ZAIRE)

Kalima
Kindu
Kibombo
Kasongo
Kongolo
Kalemie
Moba
Lake Tanganyika
Lake Mweru Wantipa
Lake Bangweulu
Luapula
Lake Mweru
Lac Upemba
Manono
Mulongo
Kabinda
Lubao
Gandajika
Kamina
Kasaji
Dilolo
Lufira
Kolwezi
Likasi
Kipushi
Lubumbashi

ZAMBIA
Zambezi
Kafue

Luanginga
Luangue-Bungo
Zambezi
Planalto do Bié

ANGOLA

Mbandaka
Boende
Ikela
Lodja
Lomela
Lac Mai-Ndombe
Lac Ntomba
Lukenie
Lukerie
Tshuapa
Sankuru
Lubefu
Mweka
Demba
Mbuji-Mayi
Mwene-Ditu
Lulua
Kasai
Lualaba

Kananga
Lusambo
Tshikapa
Mangai
Bandundu
Luluaburg
Kenge
Kikwit
Kwilu
Kasongo-Lunda
Kwango
Cuanza

Ilebo
Luebo

CONGO
Bumba
Congo
Lulonga
Ubangi (Oubangui)
Ubangi
Mpama
Batéké Plateaux
BRAZZAVILLE
KINSHASA
Mbanza-Ngungu
Matadi
Boma
Tshela
Sibiti
Dolisie
Pointe-Noire
Cabinda (to Angola)

Dongou
Impfondo
Epéna
Bétou
Makoua
Owando
Ngoko
Etoumbi
Sembé
Souanké
Bélinga
Ouesso
Gamboma
Djambala
Nkayi
Kibangou
Mossendjo
Ndindi
Setté Cama

GABON
LIBREVILLE
Mékambo
Lambaréné
Moanda
Koulamoutou
Franceville
Fougamou
Mouila
Ndendé
Omboué
Port-Gentil
Bitam
Oyem
Mitzic
Massif du Chaillu
Bonga
Bonda
N'djolé

Ngovi

CAMEROON
YAOUNDÉ
Sangmélima
Ebolowa
Edéa
Ambam
Kribi

EQUATORIAL GUINEA
MALABO
Bata
Cocobeach
Acalayong

SAO TOME & PRINCIPE
Isla de Bioco
Principe
São Tomé
SÃO TOMÉ
Equator

Gulf of Guinea

ATLANTIC OCEAN

N

0 km 400
0 miles 400

SOUTHERN AFRICA

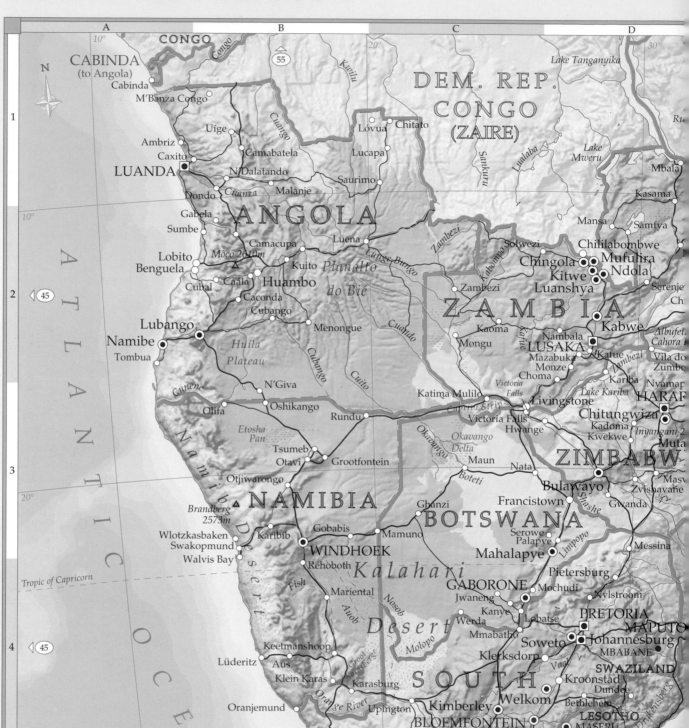

POPULATION

- ◉ Over 500,000
- ◉ 100,000 - 500,000
- ○ 50,000 - 100,000
- ○ Less than 50,000
- ● National capital

SOUTH AFRICA'S THREE CAPITALS

Pretoria - *administrative capital*

Cape Town - *legislative capital*

Bloemfontein - *judicial capital*

CONGO

CABINDA (to Angola)

Cabinda

M'Banza Congo

Uíge

Ambriz

Caxito

LUANDA

Dondo

N'Dalatando

Camabatela

Malanje

ANGOLA

Gabela

Sumbe

Camacupa

Lobito

Benguela

Môco 2610m

Kuito

Cubal

Caála

Huambo

Caconda

Cubango

Lubango

Namibe

Tombua

Menongue

Huíla Plateau

N'Giva

Olifa

Oshikango

Rundu

Cunene

Etosha Pan

Tsumeb

Otavi

Grootfontein

Otjiwarongo

Brandberg 2573m

NAMIBIA

Wlotzkasbaken

Karibib

Gobabis

Mamuno

Swakopmund

WINDHOEK

Walvis Bay

Rehoboth

Kalahari

Fish

Mariental

Nosob

Auob

Desert

Keetmanshoop

Lüderitz

Aus

Klein Karas

Karasburg

Oranjemund

Orange River

Upington

Prieska

DEM. REP. CONGO (ZAIRE)

Lake Tanganyika

Lóvua

Chitato

Lucapa

Saurimo

Congo

Kwilu

Cuango

Cuanza

Luena

Lunge-Bungo

Planalto do Bié

Zambezi

Cuando

Cubango

Cuito

Katima Mulilo

Caprivi Strip

Okavango

Okavango Delta

Maun

Ghanzi

BOTSWANA

Boteti

Nata

Sankuru

Lualaba

Lake Mweru

Mbala

Kasama

Mansa

Samfya

Solwezi

Chililabombwe

Chingola

Kitwe

Mufulira

Ndola

Luanshya

Serenje

ZAMBIA

Zambezi

Kaoma

Mongu

Kabwe

Nambala

LUSAKA

Mazabuka

Monze

Choma

Kafue

Katue

Victoria Falls

Livingstone

Victoria Falls

Hwange

Lake Kariba

Kariba

Kadoma

Kwekwe

ZIMBABWE

Bulawayo

Zvishavane

Gwanda

Francistown

Serowe

Palapye

Mahalapye

Limpopo

Shashe

Messina

Pietersburg

Nylstroom

GABORONE

Mochudi

Jwaneng

Kanye

Werda

Mmabatho

Lobatse

PRETORIA

Soweto

Johannesburg

Klerksdorp

SOUTH

Kimberley

BLOEMFONTEIN

De Aar

Colesberg

AFRICA

Welkom

Kroonstad

Dundee

Bethlehem

LESOTHO

MASERU

Pietermaritzburg

Durban

Kokstad

Umtata

Queenstown

Cradock

Mdantsane

East London

Port Alfred

MAPUTO

MBABANE

SWAZILAND

Vaal

Mansa

Albufeira Cahora

Vila do Zumbo

Zambezi

HARARE

Chitungwiza

Inyangani

Mutare

Masvingo

Prieska

Beaufort West

Great Karoo

Worcester

George

Mosselbaai

Bellville

CAPE TOWN

St Helena Bay

Cape of Good Hope

Uitenhage

Port Elizabeth

Gabela

10°

20°

30°

Tropic of Capricorn

ATLANTIC OCEAN

Namib Desert

Great Namaqualand

Molopo

Groot

Drakensberg

ANZANIA

MALAWI
Lake Nyasa
Mzuzu
Negomane
Rio Rovuma
Mocímboa da Praia
Rio Lugenda
Mucojo
Rio Messalo
ILONGWE
Pemba
Salima
Lúrio
Monkey Bay
Rio Lúrio
Nacala
Zomba
Lumbo
Blantyre
Nampula
Milange
Mocuba
Isanje
Quelimane

MOZAMBIQUE

moz
Beira
Machanga

Inhambane
Quissico
Xai

Mozambique Channel

SEYCHELLES

Amirante Islands
VICTORIA
Mahé
Inner Islands

Outer Islands

Aldabra Group

Farquhar Group

COMOROS
MORONI
Grande Comore
Anjouan
Mohéli
MAMOUDZOU
MAYOTTE
(to France)

Tanjona Bobaomby
Antsirañana

Ambanja
Maromokotro
2376m
Analalava
Sambava
Antsohihy
Antalaha
Mahajanga
Maroantsetra

Fenoarivo

Toamasina

ANTANANARIVO

Morondava
Betafo

Ambositra
Bemaraha
Mananjary
MAURITIUS
Makay
PORT LOUIS
Fianarantsoa
ST-DENIS
Manakara
Mangoky
Ihosy
RÉUNION
Toliara
Farafangana
(to France)

Vangaindrano

Mascarene Islands

Amboasary

Tanjona
Vohimena

M A D A G A S C A R

I N D I A N

O C E A N

40°
50°
10°
20°
30°
60°

Tropic of Capricorn

118
119
119
132

ELEVATION

4000 m	13 124 ft
2000 m	6562 ft
1000 m	3281 ft
500 m	1640 ft
250 m	820 ft
100 m	328 ft
Sea Level	Sea Level
	-250 m -820 ft
-500 m	-1640 ft
-1000 m	-3281 ft
-2000 m	-6562 ft
-3000 m	-9843 ft
-4000 m	-13 124 ft

0 km   400
0 miles   400

EUROPE

POLITICAL FEATURES

TOTAL AREA:
4,809,200 sq miles
(12,456,000 sq km)

TOTAL NUMBER OF COUNTRIES:
43

TOTAL POPULATION:
582.5 million

LARGEST CITY WITH POPULATION:
Moscow, European Russia 9 million

**COUNTRY WITH HIGHEST
POPULATION DENSITY:**
Monaco 42,503 people per sq mile
(16,410 people per sq km)

LARGEST COUNTRY:
European Russia 1,527,341 sq miles
(3,955,818 sq km)

SMALLEST COUNTRY:
Vatican City, Italy 0.17 sq miles
(0.44 sq km)

PHYSICAL FEATURES

LARGEST LAKE:
Ladoga, European Russia
7,100 sq miles (18,390 sq km)

LONGEST RIVER:
Volga, European Russia
2,290 miles (3,688 km)

HIGHEST POINT:
El'brus, Caucasus Mts, European Russia
18,510 ft (5,642 m)

LOWEST POINT:
Volga Delta, Caspian Sea, European
Russia 92 ft (28 m) below sea level

POPULATION

- ⦿ Over 500,000
- ◉ 100,000 - 500,000
- ○ 50,000 - 100,000
- ○ Less than 50,000
- ● National capital

ATLANTIC OCEAN

Azores-Biscay Rise

Charcot Seamounts

Iberian Plain

Horseshoe Seamounts

Madeira (to Portugal)

Canary Islands (to Spain)

Reykjanes Ridge

Iceland Basin

Hatton Ridge

Rockall Bank

Rockall Trough

Porcupine Plain

Biscay Plain

Bay of Biscay

Galicia Bank

Cordillera Cantábrica

Tagus Plain

Iberian Peninsula

Strait of Gibraltar

Atlas Mountains

AFRICA

REYKJAVÍK
ICELAND
Vatnajökull

Limit of winter pack ice
Arctic Circle

Norwegian Basin

Norwegian Sea

FAEROE ISLANDS (to Denmark)

Faeroe-Iceland Ridge

Faeroe-Shetland Trough

Shetland Islands

Trondheim

Bergen

OSLO

Stavanger

Orkney Islands

Outer Hebrides

British Isles

Ireland

Glasgow
Edinburgh
Belfast

REPUBLIC OF IRELAND
ISLE OF MAN (to UK)
DUBLIN
Liverpool
Manchester
UNITED KINGDOM
Britain
Birmingham

Cardiff
LONDON

Celtic Sea
Celtic Shelf

English Channel

CHANNEL IS. (to UK)
le Havre
Seine
Rennes
PARIS
Nantes
Loire
Orléans
FRANCE

North Sea

Gothenburg
Ålborg
Jönköp
Jylland
DENMARK
COPENH
Odense
Malm

Hamburg
NETHERLANDS
THE HAGUE
AMSTERDAM
Rotterdam
Hannover
Elbe
BELGIUM
BRUSSELS
Liège
BERLIN
Bonn
LUXEMBOURG
GERMANY
Wrocła
LUXEMBOURG
Frankfurt am Main
PRA
CZECH
REPUBL
Strasbourg
Rhine
Stuttgart
Munich
BRATIS
Zürich
LIECH.
VIENNA
BERN
SWITZERLAND
Salzburg
AUSTRIA
Innsbruck

Mont Blanc 4807m
Alps
SLOVENIA
Massif Central
Lyon
Milan
Venice
LJUBLJ
Z.
Rhône
Turin
Po
Trieste
CROA
Toulouse
Nice
Bologna
Pyrenees
Garonne
Bordeaux
Bilbao
ANDORRA
Marseille
MONACO
Pisa
SAN MARINO
BC
SARA
ITALY
Apennines
Mosta

A Coruña
Porto
PORTUGAL
Duero
Zaragoza
Ebro
MADRID
Tagus
SPAIN
Peninsula
Guadalquivir
Seville
Málaga
Barcelona
Valencia
Palma
Balearic Islands

Corsica
Sardinia
Algerian Basin
Tyrrhenian Sea
VATICAN CITY
ROME
Naples
Bari
Cagliari
Cosenza
Palermo
Mount Etna 3340m
Sicily
Catania
Mediterranea
Ion
Ba
MALTA
VALLETTA

LISBON

GIBRALTAR (to UK)
Ceuta (to Spain)
Melilla (to Spain)

N

0 km   500
0 miles   500

133
44
44
46

30° 20° 70° 10° 0°

60°
30°
20°
50°
40°
10°
30°
10° 30° 10°

Barents Sea

North Cape
Ostrov Kolguyev
Arctic Circle
Ural Mountains
Ob'
80°

1

Murmansk
Kola
Peninsula
Irtysh

FINLAND
White
Sea
Archangel
Northern Dvina
R U S S I A N

Gulf of Bothnia

Lake Onega
Perm'
90

F E D E R A T I O N
70°

Tampere
Lake Ladoga
Vologda
Ufa
50°

2

Turku HELSINKI
Saint Petersburg
Yaroslavl'
Kazan'

STOCKHOLM TALLINN
Nizhniy
Novgorod

ESTONIA

LATVIA
MOSCOW
Ul'yanovsk
Orenburg

RĪGA
Samara
Ural

LITHUANIA
KALININGRAD
(Russ Fed)
Kaliningrad
Vitsyebsk

Central
Russian
Upland
Volga Uplands
Volga
Aral Sea
Syr Darya

3

Bydgoszcz
VILNIUS

MINSK

WARSAW
Babruysk
Homyel'
Voronezh
Ural
Amu Darya

Brest
BELARUS
Pripet
Marshes
Don

Bug
Dnieper Lowlands
Kharkiv
Volgograd

POLAND
Kraków
KIEV
Dnieper
Astrakhan'

L'viv
Dniester
UKRAINE
Dnipropetrovs'k
Donets'k

SLOVAKIA
Carpathian Mountains
Chernivtsi
Rostov-na-Donu
Caspian Sea

40°

BUDAPEST
MOLDOVA
Stavropol'

4

HUNGARY
Cluj-Napoca
CHIŞINĂU
Sea of
Azov
90
60°

ROMANIA
Braşov
Odesa
Caucasus

BELGRADE
Crimea
El'brus 5642m

YUGO-
SLAVIA
Danube
BUCHAREST
Constanţa
Simferopol'
Black Sea

BULGARIA
Varna

Balkan Mountains
SOFIA
Burgas
TURKEY

MACED.
SKOPJE
TIRANA

ALBANIA
Pindus Mountains
Aegean
Sea
Anatolia
Zāgros Mountains

30°

5

GREECE ATHENS
Piraeus

Peloponnese

Ionian Sea
Irákleio
Cyprus
Tigris
Euphrates
96
50°

Crete

59

THE NORTH ATLANTIC

	A	B	C	D

1

Arctic Circle

Gulf of Boothia

Devon Island

Ellesmere Islan

Nares Strait

16

N U N A V U T

Hudson Bay

Southampton Island

Foxe Basin

Qaanaaq

Knud Rasmussen

Innaanganeq

Savissivik

Qimusseriarsuaq

2

16

C A N A D A

Baffin Island

Baffin Bay

Kullorsuaq

Péninsule d'Ungava

Hudson Strait

Upernavik

QUEBEC

Arnaud

Limit of summer pack ice

Uummannaq

Qeqertarsuaq

Qeqertarsuaq

Cumberland Sound

Davis Strait

Qeqertarsuup Tunua

G R E E N L A N D

(to Denmark)

3

Frobisher Bay

Sisimiut

Qasigiannguit

Ungava Bay

Kong Frederik IX Land

George

Maniitsoq

Kong Christian IX Land

Gunnbjørn

Mont Forel 3360m

3

NUUK

Ammassalik

4

17

Paamiut

Kong Frederik VI Kyst

Ivittuut

Denma

NEWFOUNDLAND

Labrador Sea

Qaqortoq

Nanortalik

Limit of winter pack ice

Reykjanes Basin

Nunap Isua (Kap Farvel)

5

ATLANTIC

OCEAN

0 km 400

0 miles 400

44

	A	B	C	D

E   F   G   H

1

ARCTIC

OCEAN

Lincoln
Sea

Kap Morris Jesup

*Wandel
Sea*

Zemlya
Frantsa-Iosifa

Independence Fjord

Nord

SVALBARD
(to Norway)

Kvitøya

Novaya
Zemlya

Nordaustlandet

Nordaustlandet

Kong Frederik VIII Land

Kong Karls Land

*Barents
Sea*

Spitsbergen

Barentsøya

2

LONGYEARBYEN

Edgeøya

Barentsberg

Storfjorden

88

*Greenland

Sea*

Christian X
Land

Limit of winter pack ice

Petermann Bjerg
2940m

Limit of summer pack ice

Daneborg

Bjørnøya
(to Norway)

Nordkapp
(North Cape)

3

FINLAND

Kong Oscar Fjord

Mohns Ridge

Ittoqqortoormiit

Kangertittivaq

Kangikajik

JAN MAYEN
(to Norway)

*Norwegian

Sea*

Arctic Circle

62

4

rait

Norwegian Basin

Vestfjorden

ICELAND

Siglufjördhur   Raufarhöfn
olungarvík

S
W
E
D
E
N

Húsavík

*Gulf
of
Bothnia*

ördhur

Akureyri

Seydhisfjördhur

Stykkishólmur

REYKJAVÍK

Neskaupstadhur

Vatnajökull

Seltoss

Djúpivogur

órlákshöfn

Hvannadalshnúkur
2119m

urtsey   Vestmannaeyjar

FAEROE ISLANDS
(to Denmark)

5

N O R W A Y

N

TÓRSHAVN

*Shetland
Islands*

63

E   F   G   H

ELEVATION

4000 m
13 124 ft

2000 m
6562 ft

1000 m
3281 ft

500 m
1640 ft

250 m
820 ft

100 m
328 ft

Sea
Level

Sea
Level

-250 m
-820 ft

-500 m
-1640 ft

-1000 m
-3281 ft

-2000 m
-6562 ft

-3000 m
-9843 ft

-4000 m
-13 124 ft

133

Scandinavia & Finland

POPULATION

	Over 500,000
	100,000 – 500,000
	50,000 – 100,000
	Less than 50,000
	National capital

ELEVATION

4 000 m	13 124 ft
2000 m	6562 ft
1000 m	3281 ft
500 m	1640 ft
250 m	820 ft
100 m	328 ft
Sea Level	Sea Level
-50 m	-164 ft
100 m	-328 ft
-250 m	-820 ft
-500 m	-1640 ft
-1000 m	-3281 ft
-2000 m	-6562 ft

RUSS. FED.

BELARUS

LATVIA

ESTONIA

LITHUANIA

KALININGRAD (to Russian Federation)

POLAND

GERMANY

NORWAY

DENMARK

Gulf of Finland

Gulf of Riga

Baltic Sea

Lake Peipus

Hiiumaa

Saaremaa

Neman

Western Dvina

Courland Lagoon

Gulf of Danzig

Wisła

Odra

Elbe

Weser

Ems

Ladozhskoye Ozero

HELSINKI

Espoo

Vantaa

Tampere

Turku (Åbo)

Pori

Rauma

Salo

Hanko (Hangö)

Kotka

Porvoo

Kouvola

Lahti

Hyvinkää

Hämeenlinna

Riihimäki

Nokia

Seinäjoki

Keuruu

Jyväskylä

Lappeenranta

Imatra

Varkaus

Hankasi

Joutseno

Saimaa

Pitkäranta

Niistijärvi

Närpiö

Närpes

Kankaanpää

STOCKHOLM

Uppsala

Norrtälje

Täby

Tierp

Gävle

Sandviken

Sala

Avesta

Falun

Borlänge

Ludvika

Leksand

Rättvik

Mora

Malung

Idre

Svg.

Sveg

Eslatan

Svensvik

Röros

Dombås

Lemunden

Hammerfest

Ange

Timrå

Kramfors

Härnösand

Sundsvall

Hudiksvall

Söderhamn

Bollnäs

Ljusnan

Nusdal

Västerås

Nora

Köping

Örebro

Karlstad

Filipstad

Säffle

Åmål

Säter

Hallsberg

Katrineholm

Södertälje

Flen

Eskilstuna

Nyköping

Norrköping

Linköping

Motala

Vadstena

Jönköping

Vänern

Vättern

Lidköping

Mariestad

Mjölby

Trollhättan

Uddevalla

Borås

Mölndal

Kungsbacka

Varberg

Ljungby

Halmstad

Laholm

Växjö

Göteborg (Gothenburg)

Kungälv

Strömstad

Fredrikstad

Moss

Sarpsborg

Halden

Mellerud

Grums

OSLO

Ski

Drammen

Sandvika

Lillestrøm

Kongsberg

Hønefoss

Hamar

Gjøvik

Lillehammer

Gol

Geilo

Eidfjord

Haugesund

Leirvik

Haukeligrend

Kristiansand

Likres

Evje

Moi

Arendal

Porsgrunn

Skien

Larvik

Horten

Tønsberg

Setesdal

Stavanger

Sandnes

Bergen

Hardangervidda

Hardanger

Jotunheimen

Galdhøpiggen 2469 m

Glittertind 2464 m

Glåma

Mjøsa

Andalsnes

Ringebu

Otta

Jostedalsbreen

Sognefjorden

Hermansverk

Hardangerfjorden

Florø

Aalesund

North Sea

Skagerrak

Kattegat

Gotland

Visby

Öland

Oskarshamn

Borgholm

Kalmar

Karlskrona

Kristianstad

Hanöbukten

Bornholm

Rønne

Helsingborg

Lund

Malmö

Trelleborg

Kristianssand

Ystad

Copenhagen (København)

Helsingør

Hillerød

Roskilde

Slagelse

Korsør

Nykøbing

Næstved

Falster

Møn

Lolland

Sjælland

Fyn

Odense

Svendborg

Nyborg

Kolding

Vejle

Fredericia

Storebælt

Århus

Randers

Viborg

Herning

Holstebro

Skagen

Frederikshavn

Hjørring

Ålborg

Esbjerg

Varde

Ringkøbing Fjord

Jylland

Himmelbjerg 173 m

Skive

Grenå

Rømø

Store Bælt

DENMARK

89

76

72

67

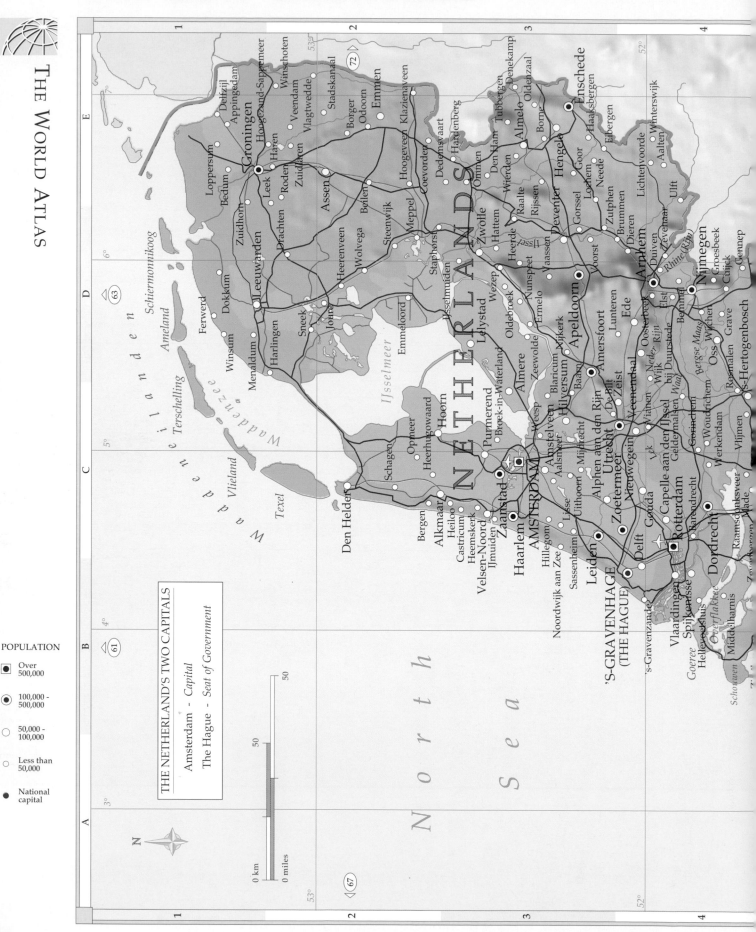

POPULATION

- ▣ Over 500,000
- ◉ 100,000 - 500,000
- ○ 50,000 - 100,000
- ∘ Less than 50,000
- ● National capital

THE NETHERLAND'S TWO CAPITALS

Amsterdam - *Capital*
The Hague - *Seat of Government*

N

0 km
0 miles
50
50

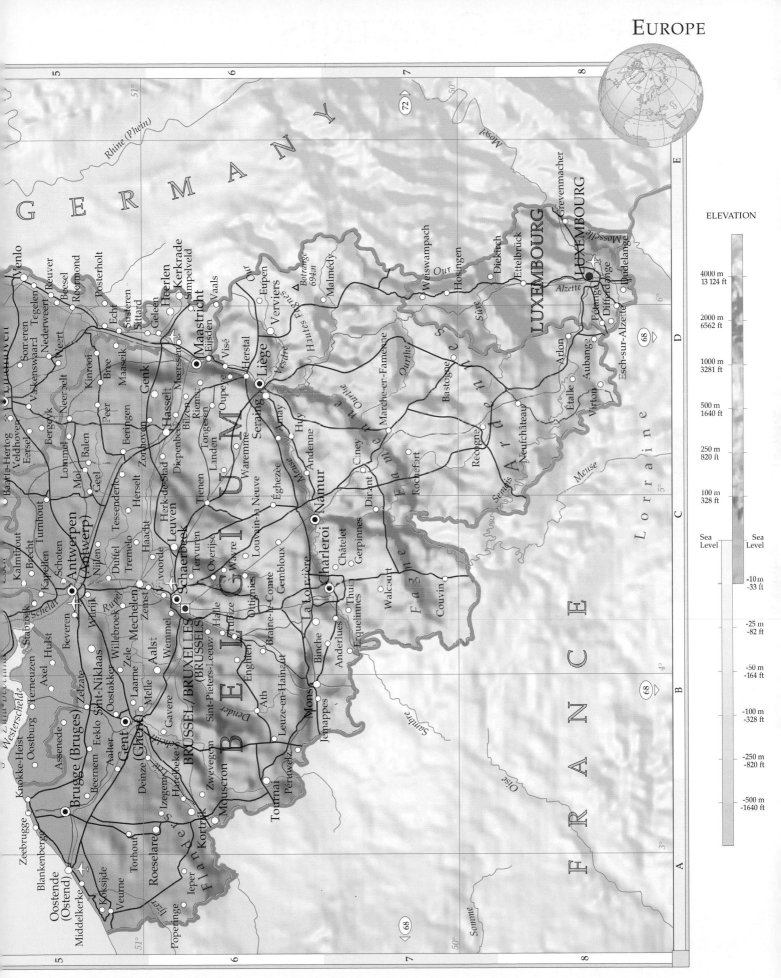

ELEVATION

4000 m
13 124 ft

2000 m
6562 ft

1000 m
3281 ft

500 m
1640 ft

250 m
820 ft

100 m
328 ft

| Sea Level | Sea Level |

-10 m
-33 ft

-25 m
-82 ft

-50 m
-164 ft

-100 m
-328 ft

-250 m
-820 ft

-500 m
-1640 ft

THE BRITISH ISLES

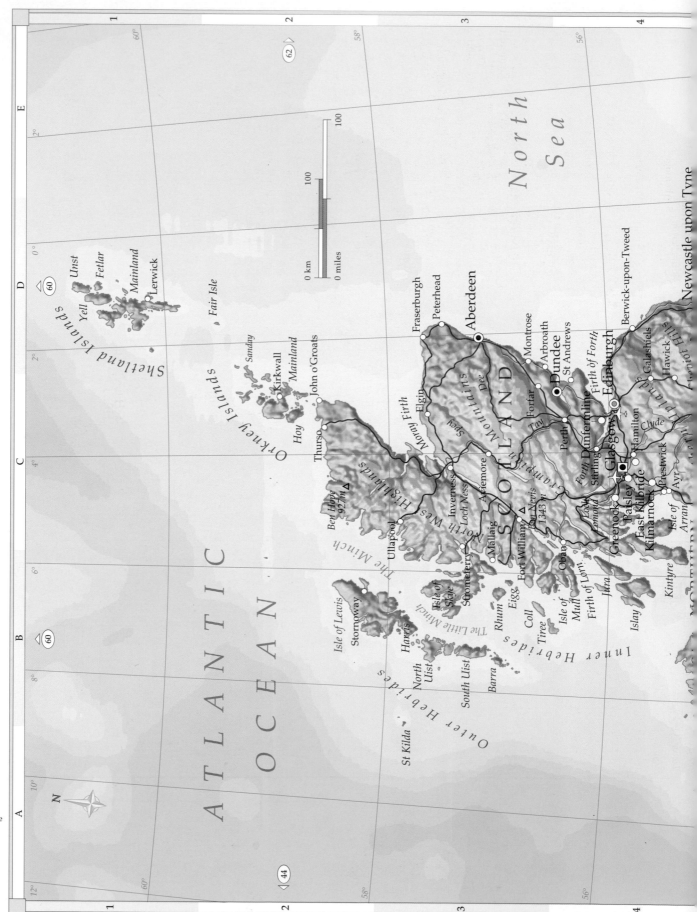

POPULATION

- Over 500,000
- 100,000 - 500,000
- 50,000 - 100,000
- Less than 50,000
- National capital
- Internal administrative capital

North Sea

ATLANTIC OCEAN

Shetland Islands
- Unst
- Yell
- Fetlar
- Mainland
- Lerwick

Fair Isle

Orkney Islands
- Sanday
- Kirkwall
- Mainland
- Hoy

John o'Groats
Thurso

Fraserburgh
Peterhead
Aberdeen

Elgin
Montrose
Arbroath
Dundee
St Andrews
Forfar

Moray Firth
Spey
Dee
Grampian Mountains
SCOTLAND
Tay
Perth

Inverness
Aviemore
Loch Ness
Ben Nevis 1343m
Fort William
Mallag
Stromeferry
Oban

Ullapool
Ben Hope 927m
Highlands
North West

The Minch

Isle of Lewis
Stornoway
Harris
North Uist
South Uist
Barra
Outer Hebrides
St Kilda

The Little Minch
Isle of Skye
Rhum
Eigg
Coll
Tiree
Isle of Mull
Firth of Lorn
Jura
Islay
Inner Hebrides
Kintyre

Loch Lomond
Stirling
Forth
Dunfermline
Firth of Forth
Edinburgh
Glasgow
Hamilton
Clyde
Greenock
Paisley
East Kilbride
Kilmarnock
Prestwick
Ayr
Isle of Arran

Berwick-upon-Tweed
Galashiels
Hawick
Newcastle upon Tyne

N

100 km
100 miles
0 km
0 miles

Map labels

UNITED KINGDOM

ENGLAND · **WALES** · **REPUBLIC OF IRELAND** · **IRELAND** · **Leinster** · **Munster** · **Connaught**

FRANCE

ISLE OF MAN (to UK) · DOUGLAS

CHANNEL ISLANDS (to UK) · Guernsey ST PETER PORT · ST HELIER · Jersey · Alderney · Sark

Seas and waters
Irish Sea · Celtic Sea · English Channel · Bristol Channel · Cardigan Bay · St George's Channel · Galway Bay · Bantry Bay · Dingle Bay · The Wash · Lyme Bay · Weymouth Bay · Lough Neagh · Lower Lough Erne · Upper Lough Erne · Lough Derg · Lough Corrib · Lough Ree

Places (England and Wales)
Whitby · Scarborough · Bridlington · Beverley · Kingston upon Hull · Grimsby · Skegness · Louth · Boston · Great Yarmouth · Lowestoft · King's Lynn · Norwich · Ipswich · Felixstowe · Harwich · Colchester · Southend-on-Sea · Margate · Canterbury · Dover · Folkestone · Hastings · Eastbourne · Brighton · Hove · Worthing · Crawley · Maidstone · London · Croydon · Watford · St Albans · Stevenage · Harlow · Bedford · Milton Keynes · Luton · Cambridge · Newmarket · Peterborough · Kettering · Northampton · Leicester · Nuneaton · Coventry · Birmingham · Wolverhampton · Kidderminster · Worcester · Gloucester · Cheltenham · Oxford · Swindon · Reading · Newbury · Andover · Winchester · Southampton · Portsmouth · Havant · Newport · Isle of Wight · Bournemouth · Poole · Weymouth · Dorchester · Yeovil · Taunton · Bridgwater · Exeter · Exmouth · Torquay · Plymouth · Saltash · Newquay · St Austell · Truro · Falmouth · Penzance · Land's End · Isles of Scilly · Bodmin · Bideford · Barnstaple · Ilfracombe · Newport · Cardiff · Swansea · Llanelli · Port Talbot · Carmarthen · Haverfordwest · Milford Haven · Fishguard · Aberystwyth · Tywyn · Barmouth · Bangor · Holyhead · Anglesey · Crewe · Stoke-on-Trent · Stafford · Shrewsbury · Chester · Birkenhead · Liverpool · Bolton · Preston · Blackpool · Lancaster · Barrow-in-Furness · Whitehaven · Manchester · Huddersfield · Bradford · Leeds · Castleford · Sheffield · Doncaster · Lincoln · Derby · Nottingham · York · Harrogate · Northallerton · Bristol · Bath · Weston-super-Mare · Salisbury · East Leigh · Guildford · Woking · Windsor

Places (Ireland and Northern)
Belfast · Omagh · Enniskillen · Sligo · Castlebar · Galway · Ennis · Limerick · Tralee · Killarney · Cork · Clonmel · Waterford · Kilkenny · Carlow · Wexford · Waterford · Athlone · Longford · Dundalk · Drogheda · Newry · Armagh · Dungannon · Downpatrick · Torr Head · DUBLIN · Dún Laoghaire · Lucan · Newbridge · Port Laoise · Tullamore

Rivers / physical
Ouse · Ribble · Mersey · Severn · Wye · Thames · Tamar · Avon · Blackwater · Shannon · Liffey · Barrow · Nore · Cotswold Hills · Brecon Beacons · Cambrian Mountains · Snowdonia · Dartmoor · Exmoor · Wicklow Mts · Leinster

Grid references
5 · 6 · 7 · 8 · 54° · 52° · 50° · 0° · 2° · 4° · 6° · 8° · 10°
A · B · C · D · E

(64) · (68) · (44)

Channel Tunnel · Seine

ELEVATION

4 000 m	13 124 ft
2000 m	6562 ft
1000 m	3281 ft
500 m	1640 ft
250 m	820 ft
100 m	328 ft
Sea Level	Sea Level
-50 m	-164 ft
-100 m	-328 ft
-250 m	-820 ft
-500 m	-1640 ft
-1000 m	-3281 ft
-2000 m	-6562 ft

LONDON (inset)

N

Watford · Enfield · Barnet · Edgware · Finchley · Wembley · Hampstead · Waltham Abbey · Dagenham · City · St Paul's Cathedral · Trafalgar Square · Houses of Parliament · Buckingham Palace · Greenwich · Dartford · Bexley · Bromley · Orpington · Wandsworth · Wimbledon · Kingston upon Thames · Richmond · Croydon · Epsom · Heathrow

M1 · M11 · M25 · M26 · M20 · M2 · M23 · M4 · M40 · A1 · A10 · A12 · A3 · A13 · A20

0 km · 10 · 0 miles · 10

Thames

■ Places of interest
□ Regions/suburbs

FRANCE, ANDORRA & MONACO

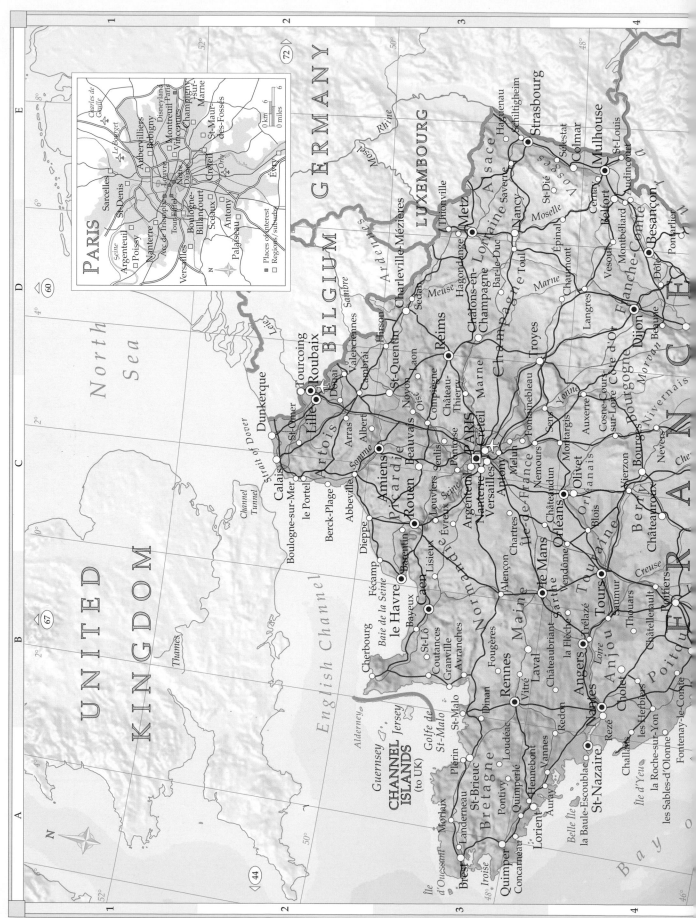

PARIS

Charles de Gaulle
Le Bourget
Sarcelles
St-Denis
Argenteuil
Poissy
Nanterre
Arc de Triomphe
Tour Eiffel
Louvre
Notre Dame
Versailles
Boulogne-Billancourt
Sceaux
Antony
Palaiseau
Aubervilliers
Bobigny
Disneyland
Montreuil Paris
Vincennes
Créteil
Orly
Évry
Champigny-sur-Marne
St-Maur-des-Fossés
Seine

Places of interest
Regions / suburbs

POPULATION

- Over 500,000
- 100,000 – 500,000
- 50,000 – 100,000
- Less than 50,000
- National capital

GERMANY
BELGIUM
LUXEMBOURG
UNITED KINGDOM

North Sea

Strait of Dover

English Channel

CHANNEL ISLANDS (to UK)

Guernsey
Jersey
Alderney

Bay of Biscay

Dunkerque
Calais
Boulogne-sur-Mer
le Portel
Berck-Plage
Abbeville
Dieppe
Fécamp
le Havre
Cherbourg
Bayeux
Caen
St-Lô
Coutances
Granville
Avranches
Fougères
Rennes
Dinan
St-Brieuc
St-Malo
Morlaix
Landerneau
Brest
Quimper
Concarneau
Lorient
Hennebont
Pontivy
Loudéac
Quimperlé
Auray
Vannes
Redon
St-Nazaire
Nantes
Rezé
Challans
Belle Île
Île d'Yeu
la Baule-Escoublac
les Sables-d'Olonne
la Roche-sur-Yon
Fontenay-le-Comte
Cholet
les Herbiers
Challans

Tourcoing
Roubaix
Lille
St-Omer
Douai
Valenciennes
Cambrai
Arras
Albert
Amiens
Beauvais
Louviers
Rouen
Évreux
Lisieux
Alençon
le Mans
Laval
Châteaubriant
Vitré
Angers
Trélazé
Saumur
Thouars
Châtellerault
Poitiers
la Flèche
Vendôme
Blois
Tours
Châteauroux
Châteaudun
Chartres
Dreux
Melun
Nemours
Montargis
Olivet
Orléans
Vierzon
Bourges
Nevers

St-Quentin
Laon
Noyon
Compiègne
Oise
Château-Thierry
Senlis
Pontoise
PARIS
Créteil
Argenteuil
Nanterre
Versailles
Antony
Fontainebleau
Sens
Yonne
Auxerre
Cosne-Cours-sur-Loire

Huson
Charleville-Mézières
Sedan
Ardennes
Sambre
Meuse
Reims
Châlons-en-Champagne
Bar-le-Duc
Toul
Troyes
Chaumont
Langres
Dijon
Beaune
Côte d'Or
Bourgogne
Morvan
Nivernais

Thionville
Hagondange
Metz
Nancy
Bar-le-Duc
Épinal
Moselle
Marne
Rhine
Mosel

Haguenau
Schiltigheim
Strasbourg
Sélestat
Colmar
St-Louis
Mulhouse
Audincourt
Belfort
Cernay
Vesoul
Montbéliard
Besançon
Dôle
Pontarlier
St-Dié
Alsace
Lorraine
Saverne
Vosges
Franche-Comté
Champagne

FRANCE

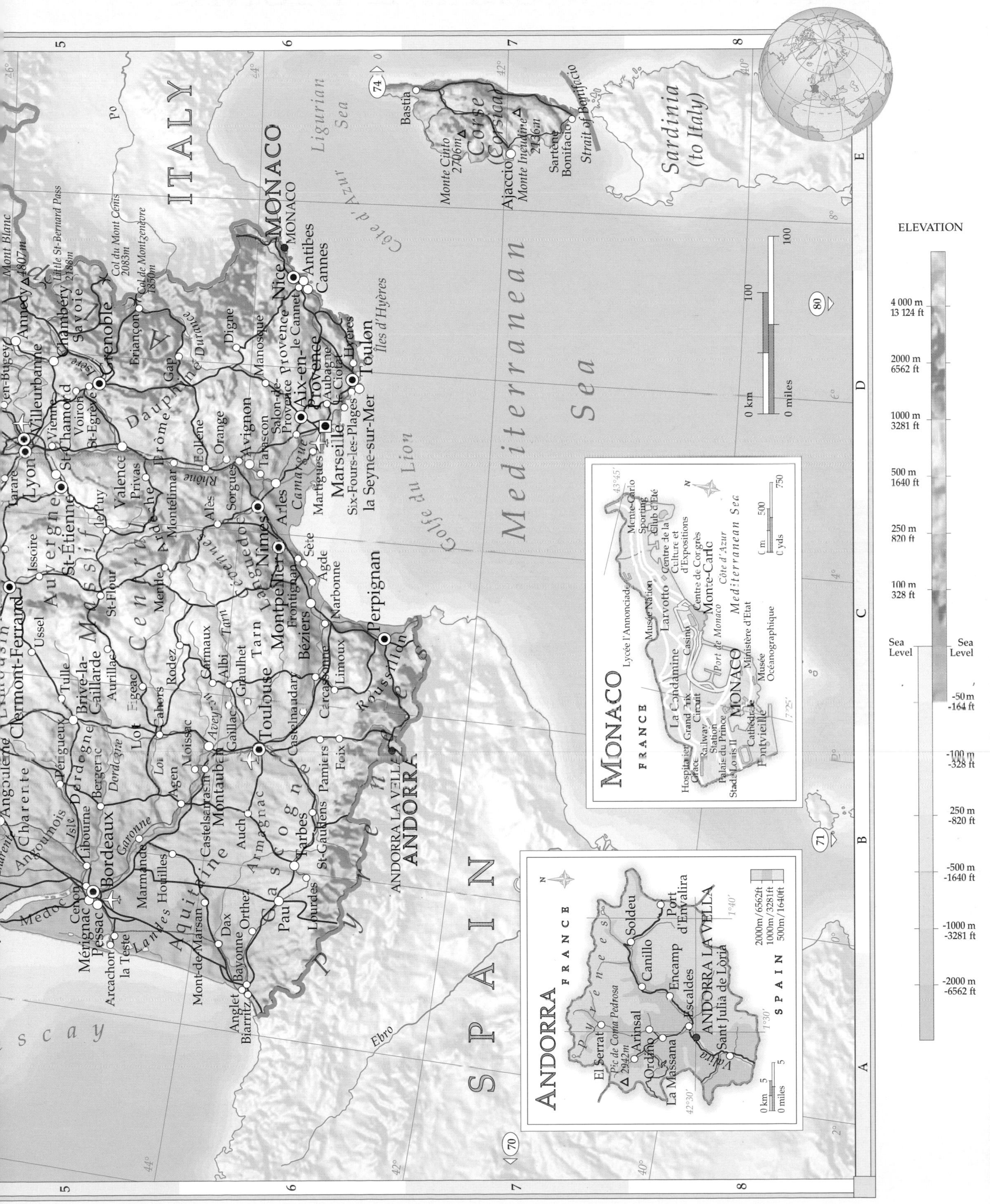

ITALY

Ligurian Sea

Côte d'Azur

Po

Mont Blanc 4807m
Little St-Bernard Pass
Col du Mont Cenis 2083m
Col de Montgenèvre 1850m
Annecy
Chambéry
Savoie
Voiron
Grenoble
St-Egrève
Briançon
Gap
Digne
Isère
Drôme
Dauphiné
Durance
Manosque
Aix-en-le-Cannet
Provence
Antibes
Cannes
MONACO
MONACO
Nice
Aubagne
Toulon
Hyères
Îles d'Hyères
la Seyne-sur-Mer
Six-Fours-les-Plages
Martigues
Marseille
Salon-de-Provence
Tarascon
Arles
Camargue
Sète
Golfe du Lion

Ébron-Bugey
Villeurbanne
Lyon
Tarare
Vienne
St-Chamond
St-Étienne
le Puy
Privas
Valence
Ardèche
Montélimar
Orange
Avignon
Sorgues
Bollène
Alès
Nîmes
Béziers
Frontignan
Narbonne

Issoire
Clermont-Ferrand
Ussel
Auvergne
St-Flour
Aurillac
Tulle
Brive-la-Gaillarde
Périgueux
Dordogne
Figeac
Aveyron
Rodez
Cahors
Massif
Central
Limousin
Albi
Carmaux
Gaillac
Graulhet
Castres
Mazamet
Castelnaudary
Carcassonne
Limoux
Foix
Pamiers

Angoulême
Charente
Libourne
Isle
Bergerac
Bordeaux
Garonne
Pessac
Mérignac
Cenon
Médoc
Arcachon
la Teste
Landes
Aquitaine
Dax
Mont-de-Marsan
Agen
Moissac
Montauban
Toulouse
Tarn
Languedoc
Roussillon
Perpignan
Gascogne
Armagnac
Auch
Tarbes
St-Gaudens
Lourdes
Pau
Orthez
Bayonne
Anglet
Biarritz
Marmande
Castelsarrasin

Pyrénées
Ébro

SPAIN

Bay of Biscay

ANDORRA LA VELLA
ANDORRA

Corse
(Corsica)
Monte Cinto 2706m
Monte Incudine 2136m
Bastia
Ajaccio
Sartène
Bonifacio
Strait of Bonifacio

Mediterranean Sea

Sardinia (to Italy)

ELEVATION

4 000 m	13 124 ft
2000 m	6562 ft
1000 m	3281 ft
500 m	1640 ft
250 m	820 ft
100 m	328 ft
Sea Level	Sea Level
-50 m	-164 ft
-100 m	-328 ft
250 m	-820 ft
-500 m	-1640 ft
-1000 m	-3281 ft
-2000 m	-6562 ft

MONACO
FRANCE

Monte-Carlo
Sporting Club d'Été
Larvotto
Centre de la Culture et d'Expositions
Musée National
Lycée l'Annonciade
La Condamine
Casino
Centre de Congrès
Monte-Carlo
Côte d'Azur
Port de Monaco
MONACO
Ministère d'Etat
Musée Océanographique
Cathédrale
Fontvieille
Hospital Grand Prix
Grace
Railway Station
Palais du Prince
Stade Louis II
Mediterranean Sea

ANDORRA
FRANCE

El Serrat
Soldeu
Port d'Envalira
Canillo
Encamp
Pic de Coma Pedrosa 2942m
Arinsal
Ordino
La Massana
Escaldes
ANDORRA LA VELLA
Sant Julià de Lòria
SPAIN
Pyrénées

2000m/6562ft
1000m/3281ft
500m/1640ft

SPAIN & PORTUGAL

POPULATION

- ◉ Over 500,000
- ◉ 100,000 - 500,000
- ○ 50,000 - 100,000
- ○ Less than 50,000
- ● National capital

AZORES (to Portugal)

Corvo
Flores
Faial
São Jorge
Pico
Graciosa
Terceira
São Miguel
Ponta Delgada
Santa Maria

0 km 100
0 miles 100

200m/656ft
Sea level

A · B · C · D

ATLANTIC OCEAN

Bay of Biscay

A Coruña (La Coruña)
Ferrol
Laracha
Betanzos
Santa Comba
Cabo Fisterra
Outes
Muros
Ribeira
Santiago
Lalín
O Carballiño
Pontevedra
Marín
Vigo
Ponteareas
Chantada
Monforte
Lugo
Galicia
Luarca
Pravia
Tineo
Avilés
Gijon (Xixon)
Villaviciosa
Oviedo
Mieres de Camino
Pola de Lena
Cabañaquinta
Asturias
Costa Verde
Santan...
Llanes
Torrelavega
Reinosa
Cordillera Cantábrica
Canta...
Ponferrada
León
Astorga
Benavente
Palencia
Ourense (Orense)
Xinzo de Limia
Castilla-León
Bu...
Ara... de D...
Ponté da Barca
Viana do Castelo
Braga
Guimarães
Vila Real
Bragança
Chaves
Embalse de Ricobayo
Zamora
Toro
Valladolid
Duero
Medina del Campo
Póvoa de Varzim
Vila do Conde
Matosinhos
Porto (Oporto)
Vila Nova de Gaia
Ovar
Albergaria-a-Velha
Aveiro
Ílhavo
Douro
Lamego
São João da Madeira
Viseu
Embalse de Almendra
Salamanca
Segov...
S P...
Coimbra
Figueira da Foz
Alto da Torre 1993m
Serra da Estrela
Guarda
Covilhã
Ciudad-Rodrigo
Béjar
Ávila
Sistema Central
Sierra de Gredos
MADRI...
Geta...
Leiria
PORTUGAL
Castelo Branco
Tomar
Abrantes
Tagus
Coria
Plasencia
Talavera de la Reina
Ara...
Toledo
Entroncamento
Caldas da Rainha
Peniche
Torres Vedras
Santarém
Coruche
Portalegre
Embalse de Alcántara
Cáceres
Embalse de Valdecañas
Herrera del Duque
Da...
Sintra
Cascais
LISBOA (LISBON)
Almada
Barreiro
Setúbal
Évora
Estremoz
Elvas
Serra d' Ossa
Guadiana
Mérida
Villanueva de la Serena
Don Benito
Castuera
Badajoz
Ciudad Real
Puertollano
Extremadura
Almendralejo
Villafranca de los Barros
Zafra
Alcácer do Sal
Baía de Setúbal
Azuaga
Pozoblanco
La Car...
Sines
Jeréz de los Caballeros
Beja
Cortegana
Sierra Morena
Córdoba
Montoro
Bujalance
Li...
Bail...
Ourique
Nerva
Guadalquivir
Palma del Río
Martos
Alcau...
Valverde del Camino
La Algaba
Carmona
Sevilla (Seville)
Ecija
Andaluc...
Lucena
Osuna
Giste...
Algarve
Ayamonte
Lepe
Isla Cristina
Dos Hermanas
Antequera
Archido...
Sie...
Portimão
Faro
Tavira
Olhão
Huelva
Las Cabezas de San Juan
Lebrija
Olvera
Álora
Gran...
Lagos
Cabo de São Vicente
Golfo de Cádiz
Sanlúcar de Barrameda
Ubrique
Ronda
Málag...
Com...
El Puerto de Santa María
Jeréz de la Frontera
Fuengirola
Cádiz
San Fernando
Vejer de la Frontera
Barbate de Franco
Marbella
Estepona
Costa de...
Costa de la Luz
Algeciras
GIBRALTAR (to UK)
Strait of Gibraltar
Ceuta (to Spain)
MOROCCO

E F G H

2° 0° 44° 2°

F R A N C E

△ 68

Bermeo
Zarautz
Eibar
Donostia-San Sebastián
Irún
Tolosa
Bergara
ís Vasco
Pamplona (Iruña)
ria-Gasteiz
Miranda de Ebro
grono
Navarra
Estella-Lizarra
Jaca
Monte Perdido △ 3348m
Pyrenees
ANDORRA
La Rioja
Arnedo
Calahorra
Huesca
La Seu d'Urgell
Berga
Ripoll
Figueres
Girona (Gerona)
Banyoles
Tudela
Ejea de los Caballeros
Barbastro
Manlleu
Tarazona
Soria
Monzón
Cataluña
Vic
Palafrugell
Palamós
urgo
Osma de
darrama
Zaragoza
Lleida (Lérida)
Balaguer
Cervera
Tárrega
Fraga
Sabadell
Terrassa
Mataró
Blanes
Arenys de Mar
Costa Brava

74 ▷

Calatayud
Aragón
Daroca
Alcañiz
Medinaceli
Vilafranca del Penedès
Valls
Barcelona
L'Hospitalet de Llobregat
Sitges
El Vendrell
Reus
Tarragona
Guadalajara
ala de Henares
jón de Ardoz
Teruel
Tortosa
Amposta
Sant Carles de la Ràpita
Vinaròs
Javalambre △ 2020m
Cuenca
Onda
Burriana
Castelló de la Plana
Ciutadella de Menorca
Menorca (Minorca)
Mahón
arancón
Vall d' Uxó
Sagunto
Burjassot
Golfo de Valencia
Pollença
Sa Pobla
Manacor
Felanitx
Palma
stilla-La Mancha
Mota del Cuervo
Campo de Criptana
Socuéllamos
Valencia
Catarroja
Sueca
Cullera
Gandía
Oliva
Llucmajor
Mallorca (Majorca)
Cabrera
Tomelloso
La Roda
Xàtiva
Denia
Eivissa (Ibiza)
Islas Baleares (Balearic Islands)
zanares
Solana
peñas
Albacete
Almansa
Onthyent
Alcoy
Eivissa
Villanueva de los Infantes
Villena
Benidorm
Formentera
Hellín
Jumilla
Elda
Villajoyosa
Beas de Segura
Moratalla
Monóvar
San Juan de Alicante
Cieza
Elche
Alicante
la
Cazorla
Mula
Callosa de Segura
Orihuela
Murcia
Murcia
ticos
Totana
La Unión
Huéscar
Lorca
Baza
Cartagena
Guadix
Aguilas
lhacén
1m
Mojácar
vada
Berja
Almería
Adra

75 ▷

M e d i t e r r a n e a n S e a

A L G E R I A

△ 49

Golfe du Lion

Costa del Azahar
País Valenciano
Torrente
Costa Blanca
Segura
Júcar

1
2
3
4
5

42° 40° 38° 36°

ELEVATION

4000 m
13 124 ft

2000 m
6562 ft

1000 m
3281 ft

500 m
1640 ft

250 m
820 ft

100 m
328 ft

Sea Level | Sea Level

-250 m
-820 ft

-500 m
-1640 ft

-1000 m
-3281 ft

-2000 m
-6562 ft

-3000 m
-9843 ft

-4000 m
-13 124 ft

GIBRALTAR (to UK)

5° 21'
SPAIN
N
Gibraltar Airport
North Mole
Gibraltar Harbour
Catalan Bay
Bay of Gibraltar
The Rock
Catalan Bay
36° 8'
Sandy Bay
Summit 426m △
Rosia
Rosia Bay
Buena Vista
Little Bay
Europa Point
Strait of Gibraltar

200m/656ft
Sea level
0 km   1
0 mile   1

71

LIECHTENSTEIN

AUSTRIA

SWITZERLAND

Ruggell
Mauren
Planken
Bendern
Schaan
VADUZ
Triesenberg
Triesen
Balzers

Rhine
Samīnatal
Alps

2000m / 6562ft
1000m / 3281ft
500m / 1640ft
250m / 820ft

0 km   4
0 miles   4

56°   54°   18°

SWEDEN

DENMARK

POLAND

GERMANY

NETHERLANDS

North Sea

Baltic Sea

Bornholm
(to Denmark)

Pomeranian
Bay

Oderhaff

Oder

Noteć

Jylland

Sjælland

Fyn

Falster

Kappeln
Schleswig
Flensburg
Rendsburg
Husum
Heide
Westerland

North Frisian Islands
(Nordfriesische Inseln)

Helgolander Bucht

Ostfriesische Inseln

Kiel
Eutin
Neumünster
Itzehoe
Elmshorn
Stade
Norderstedt
Hamburg
Rosengarten
Scheessel
Verden
Soltau
Celle

Sassnitz
Rügen
Bergen
Stralsund
Greifswald
Wolgast
Anklam
Demmin
Warnemünde
Rostock
Wismar
Teterow
Waren
Güstrow
Schwerin
Parchim
Neubrandenburg
Neustrelitz
Pasewalk
Prenzlau
Angermünde
Eberswalde-Finow
Bad Freienwalde
Frankfurt an der Oder
Eisenhüttenstadt
Guben
Cottbus
Finsterwalde
Hoyerswerda
Senftenberg
Görlitz
Bautzen
Döbeln
Riesa
Leipzig
Halle
Halle-Neustadt
Dessau
Bernburg
Torgau
Lübben
Lübbenau
Ludwigsfelde
BERLIN
Potsdam
Bernau
Oranienburg
Neuruppin
Wittstock
Müritz
Perleberg
Wittenberge
Ludwigslust
Lüchow-Dannenberg
Lüneburg
Uelzen
Salzwedel
Stendal
Brandenburg
Magdeburg
Schönebeck
Halberstadt
Wolfsburg
Braunschweig
Salzgitter
Seesen
Peine
Hannover
Hildesheim
Northeim
Göttingen
Eisleben
Nordhausen
Warburg
Kassel
Marsberg
Paderborn
Gütersloh
Bielefeld
Herford
Minden
Bassum
Diepholz
Osnabrück
Rheine
Nordhorn
Lingen
Ems
Meppen
Cloppenburg
Oldenburg
Delmenhorst
Bremen
Bremerhaven
Wilhelmshaven
Emden
Norden
Leer
Weener
Rhine
Bocholt
Recklinghausen
Essen
Duisburg
Krefeld
Düsseldorf
Leverkusen
Solingen
Wuppertal
Dortmund
Bochum
Hamm
Ahlen
Dülmen
Münster
Lübeck
Oldenburg
Pattgarden
Fehmarn
Kieler Bucht
Felmarn Belt
Mecklenburger Bucht
Weser
Aller
Elbe
Saale
Spree

Schleswig-Holstein

Niedersachsen

Ijsselmeer

POPULATION

Over 500,000

100,000 - 500,000

50,000 - 100,000

Less than 50,000

National capital

0 km   100
0 miles   100

N

8°   10°   12°   14°   16°   18°

56°   54°   52°

63

63

67

76

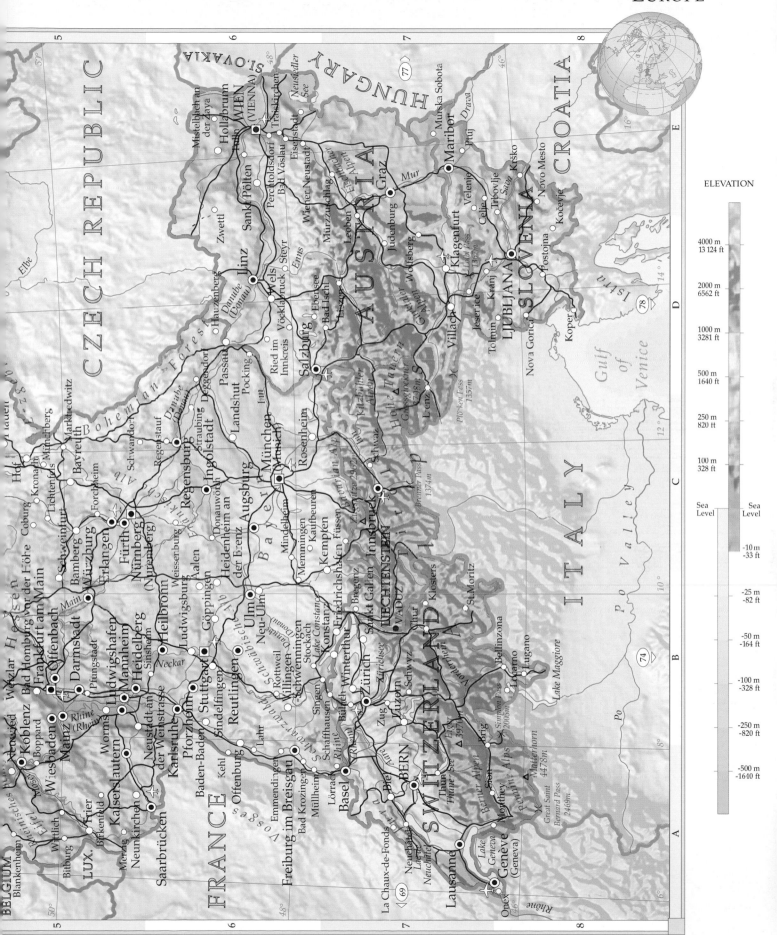

ELEVATION

4000 m
13 124 ft

2000 m
6562 ft

1000 m
3281 ft

500 m
1640 ft

250 m
820 ft

100 m
328 ft

Sea Level

Sea Level

-10 m
-33 ft

-25 m
-82 ft

-50 m
-164 ft

-100 m
-328 ft

-250 m
-820 ft

-500 m
-1640 ft

ITALY

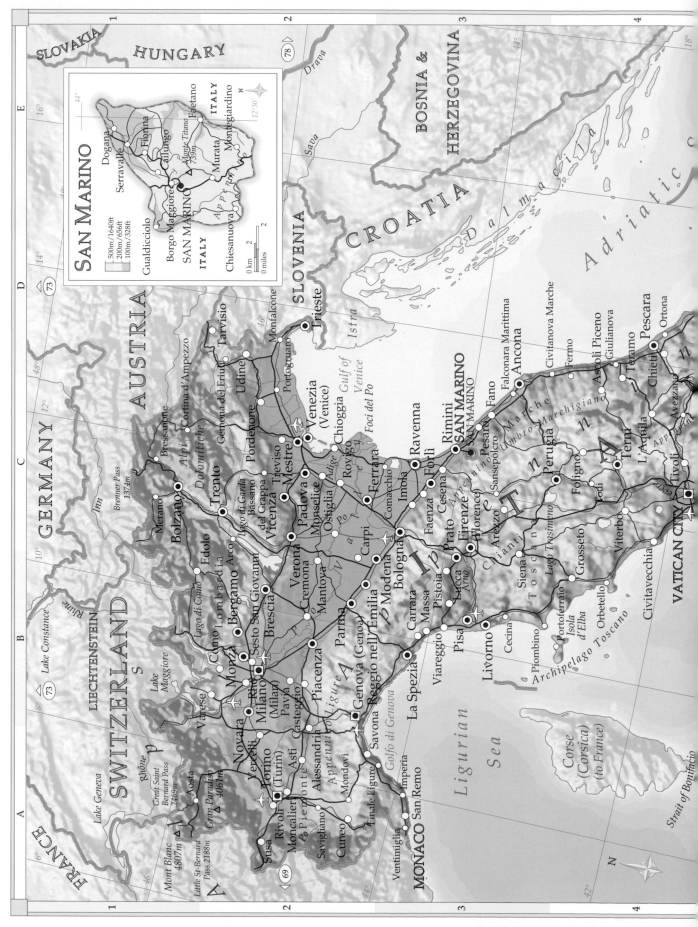

SAN MARINO

Dogana
Serravalle
Gualdicciolo
Borgo Maggiore
SAN MARINO
ITALY
Chiesanuova
Fiorina
Cailungo
Monte Titano 739m
Faetano
ITALY
Murata
Montegiardino

500m/1640ft
200m/656ft
100m/328ft

0 km 2
0 miles 2

POPULATION

■ Over 500,000

◉ 100,000 – 500,000

◯ 50,000 – 100,000

○ Less than 50,000

● National capital

SLOVAKIA
HUNGARY
Drava
BOSNIA & HERZEGOVINA
CROATIA
Sava
Dalmacija
Adriatic

AUSTRIA
GERMANY
SWITZERLAND
LIECHTENSTEIN
FRANCE

SLOVENIA
Trieste
Istra
Gulf of Venice

Tarvisio
Udine
Gemona del Friuli
Montfalcone
Portogruaro
Cortina d'Ampezzo
Bressanone
Merano
Bolzano
Alpi
Dolomitiche
Trento
Bremner Pass 1374m
Inn

Venezia (Venice)
Chioggia
Foci del Po
Treviso
Mestre
Pordenone
Bassano del Grappa
Vicenza
Padova
Mopaselice
Ostiglia
Adige
Rovigo
Ferrara
Comacchio
Ravenna
Imola
Forlì
Cesena
Rimini
SAN MARINO
Pesaro
Fano
Ancona
Falconara Marittima
Civitanova Marche
Fermo
Ascoli Piceno
Giulianova
Teramo
Pescara
Chieti
Ortona
Avezzano
L'Aquila
Terni
Foligno
Perugia
Umbro-Marchigiano
Marche
Appennino Marchigiano

Lago di Garda
Verona
Cremona
Mantova
Carpi
Modena
Bologna
Faenza
Prato
Firenze (Florence)
Arezzo
Lago Trasimeno
Toscana
Siena
Chianti
Grosseto
Orbetello
Civitavecchia
VATICAN CITY
Tivoli
Appennino
Todi
Viterbo

Como
Lago di Como
Bergamo
Sesto San Giovanni
Brescia
Edolo
Arco
Monza
Milano (Milan)
Pavia
Piacenza
Parma
Reggio nell'Emilia
Po
Lombardia
Varese
Lake Maggiore
Lago Maggiore
Novara
Vercelli
Rho
Casteggio
Alessandria
Asti
Savigliano
Cuneo
Mondovi
Finale Ligure
Savona
Genova (Genoa)
Golfo di Genova
La Spezia
Carrara
Massa
Lucca
Pistoia
Pisa
Arno
Viareggio
Livorno
Cecina
Piombino
Portoferraio
Isola d'Elba
Archipelago Toscano

Torino (Turin)
Rivoli
Moncalieri
Piemonte
Susa
Gran Paradiso 4061m
Aosta
Mont Blanc 4807m
Great Saint Bernard Pass 2469m
Little St-Bernard Pass 2188m
Rhône
Rhine
Lake Constance
Lake Geneva

Ventimiglia
San Remo
Imperia
MONACO
Ligurian Sea
Liguria

Corse (Corsica) (to France)
Strait of Bonifacio

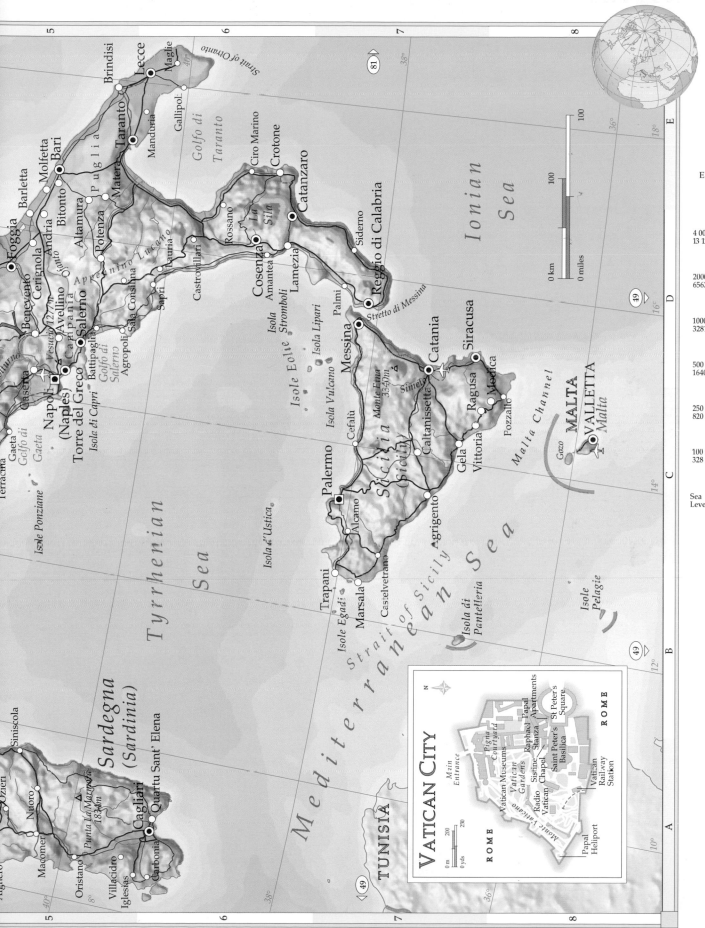

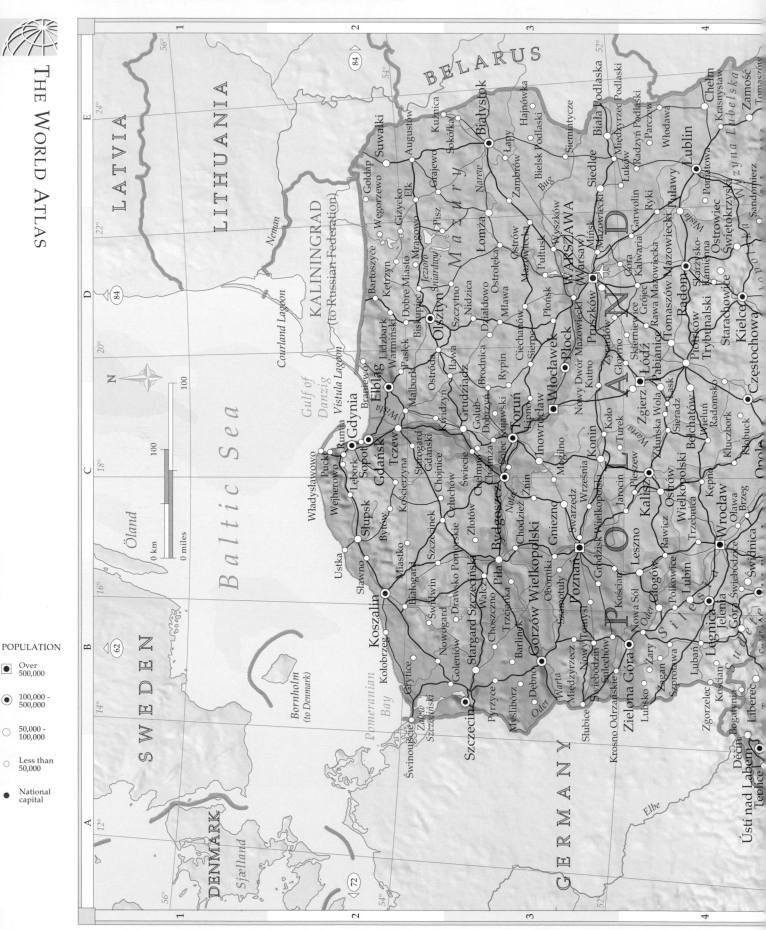

POPULATION

- Over 500,000
- 100,000 – 500,000
- 50,000 – 100,000
- Less than 50,000
- National capital

BELARUS

LATVIA

LITHUANIA

KALININGRAD
(to Russian Federation)

SWEDEN

DENMARK

GERMANY

P O L A N D

Baltic Sea

Gulf of Danzig

Courland Lagoon

Vistula Lagoon

Pomeranian Bay

Bornholm (to Denmark)

Öland

Sjælland

M a z u r y

S i l e s i a

W y ż y n a   L u b e l s k a

Neman

Oder

Elbe

Warta

Noteć

Suwałki
Gdynia
Sopot
Gdańsk
Tczew
Elbląg
Braniewo
Rumia
Puck
Władysławowo
Wejherowo
Lębork
Słupsk
Bytów
Kościerzyna
Starogard Gdański
Świecie
Chełmno
Chojnice
Człuchów
Szczecinek
Złotów
Miastko
Ustka
Sławno
Koszalin
Kołobrzeg
Gryfice
Świnoujście
Szczecin
Police
Goleniów
Nowogard
Stargard Szczeciński
Wałcz
Choszczno
Drawsko Pomorskie
Świdwin
Białogard
Pyrzyce
Myślibórz
Dębno
Barlinek
Gorzów Wielkopolski
Zielona Góra
Nowa Sól
Żary
Żagań
Szprotawa
Lubsko
Lubin
Głogów
Polkowice
Legnica
Jelenia Góra
Wrocław
Oława
Brzeg
Opole
Świebodzice
Świdnica
Kędzierzyn
Koźle
Racibórz
Krosno Odrzańskie
Gubin
Słubice
Sulechów
Świebodzin
Międzyrzecz
Nowy Tomyśl
Szamotuły
Oborniki
Poznań
Gniezno
Września
Środa Wielkopolska
Jarocin
Kalisz
Ostrów Wielkopolski
Leszno
Rawicz
Kościan
Pleszew
Krotoszyn
Kępno
Kluczbork
Kłobuck
Częstochowa
Radomsko
Wieluń
Bełchatów
Sieradz
Zduńska Wola
Łask
Pabianice
Zgierz
Łódź
Skierniewice
Tomaszów Mazowiecki
Piotrków Trybunalski
Starachowice
Skarżysko-Kamienna
Ostrowiec Świętokrzyski
Kielce
Sandomierz
Tarnobrzeg
Stalowa Wola
Kraśnik
Lublin
Puławy
Ryki
Dęblin
Garwolin
Radzyń Podlaski
Parczew
Włodawa
Chełm
Zamość
Krasnystaw
Biłgoraj
Lubartów
Świdnik
Mińsk Mazowiecki
Warszawa (Warsaw)
Pruszków
Piaseczno
Góra Kalwaria
Grójec
Grodzisk Mazowiecki
Żyrardów
Sochaczew
Łowicz
Kutno
Łęczyca
Gostynin
Płock
Włocławek
Nowy Dwór Mazowiecki
Legionowo
Wyszków
Pułtusk
Ostrów Mazowiecka
Ostrołęka
Maków Mazowiecki
Ciechanów
Płońsk
Sierpc
Rypin
Lipno
Toruń
Inowrocław
Żnin
Mogilno
Bydgoszcz
Chodzież
Piła
Trzcianka
Czarnków
Wągrowiec
Golub-Dobrzyń
Grudziądz
Chełmża
Wąbrzeźno
Brodnica
Działdowo
Mława
Nidzica
Szczytno
Dobre Miasto
Lidzbark Warmiński
Pasłęk
Morąg
Ostróda
Iława
Nowe Miasto
Lubawskie
Olsztyn
Bartoszyce
Kętrzyn
Giżycko
Mrągowo
Jezioro Śniardwy
Pisz
Ełk
Gołdap
Węgorzewo
Olecko
Augustów
Grajewo
Łomża
Zambrów
Kolno
Grajewo
Kuźnica
Sokółka
Białystok
Łapy
Bielsk Podlaski
Hajnówka
Siemiatycze
Wysokie Mazowieckie
Sokołów Podlaski
Węgrów
Siedlce
Łuków
Biała Podlaska
Międzyrzec Podlaski
Radzyń Podlaski
Mińsk

Wisła
Wisła
Warta
Narew
Bug

0 km 100
0 miles 100

UKRAINE

ROMANIA

SERBIA

YUGOSLAVIA

BOSNIA AND HERZEGOVINA

CROATIA

SLOVENIA

ITALY

AUSTRIA

Alps

SLOVAKIA

CZECH REPUBLIC

HUNGARY

Carpathian Mountains

Carpaţii Occidentali

Carpaţii Meridionali

Bohemia

Bohemian Forest

Moravia

Niedere Tauern

Great Hungarian Plain

Little Danube Alföld

Bakony

Mecsek

Papuk

Velebit

Vojvodina

Gulf of Venice

Adriatic Sea

Neusiedler See

Rivers / features:
Dniester, Tisza, Laborec, Hornád, Poprad, Váh, Nitra, Ipel', Hron, Morava, Danube, Drava, Mur, Mur, Mureş, Danube, Rába, Zala, Tisza, Berettyó, Drava

Cities (Hungary):
BUDAPEST, Debrecen, Miskolc, Nyíregyháza, Szeged, Pécs, Kecskemét, Szolnok, Békéscsaba, Hódmezővásárhely, Szombathely, Győr, Székesfehérvár, Veszprém, Tatabánya, Eger, Gyöngyös, Nagykőrös, Mezőtúr, Gyomaendrőd, Hajdúhadház, Nagykálló, Kisvárda, Sátoraljaújhely, Püspökladány, Fehérgyarmat, Berettyóújfalu, Makó, Túrkeve, Paks, Tolna, Szekszárd, Baja, Kalocsa, Dunaújváros, Komárom, Mosonmagyaróvár, Sopron, Pápa, Körmend, Zalaegerszeg, Keszthely, Lenti, Nagykanizsa, Kaposvár, Fonyód, Csurgó, Barcs, Siklós, Ózd, Sajószentpéter, Encs, Záhony

Cities (Slovakia):
BRATISLAVA, Košice, Prešov, Žilina, Martin, Trenčín, Nitra, Trnava, Banská Bystrica, Zvolen, Lučenec, Rožňava, Michalovce, Trebišov, Vranov nad Topľou, Bardejov, Ružomberok, Považská Bystrica, Rimavská Sobota, Topoľčany, Piešťany, Senica, Malacky, Pezinok, Senec, Galanta, Šurany, Komárno, Levice, Sereď, Zlaté Moravce, Čadca, Kysucké Nové Mesto, Svidník, Sniná, Nové Zámky, Šaľa, Velký Krtíš

Cities (Czech Republic):
Ostrava, Brno, Olomouc, Zlín, Přerov, Hranice, Frýdek-Místek, Opava, Nový Jičín, Kyjov, Hodonín, Znojmo, Břeclav, Vyškov, Prostějov, Boskovice, Blansko, Třebíč, Jihlava, Žďár, Humpolec, Pelhřimov, Tábor, Písek, Strakonice, Klatovy, Plzeň, Rokycany, Beroun, Kolín, Čáslav, Benešov, Prachatice, České Budějovice, Český Krumlov, Marianské Lázně, Tachov, Pardubice, Zábřeh, Šumperk

Cities (Poland):
POLSKA, Rzeszów, Tarnów, Nowy Sącz, Przemyśl, Jasło, Krosno, Sanok, Krynica, Limanowa, Rabka, Zakopane, Nowy Targ, Mszana Dolna, Wieliczka, Bielsko-Biała, Żywiec, Jastrzębie-Zdrój, Wodzisław Śląski, Ustrzyki Dolne, Lesko, Żory

Cities (Ukraine):
Užhorod, Mukačevo

Carpathian peaks/features: Rysy, Tatra Mts, Vysoké Tatry, Kékes 1014 m

ELEVATION

4000 m	13 124 ft
2000 m	6562 ft
1000 m	3281 ft
500 m	1640 ft
250 m	820 ft
100 m	328 ft
Sea Level	Sea Level
-10 m	-33 ft
-25 m	-82 ft
-50 m	-164 ft
-100 m	-328 ft
-250 m	-820 ft
-500 m	-1640 ft

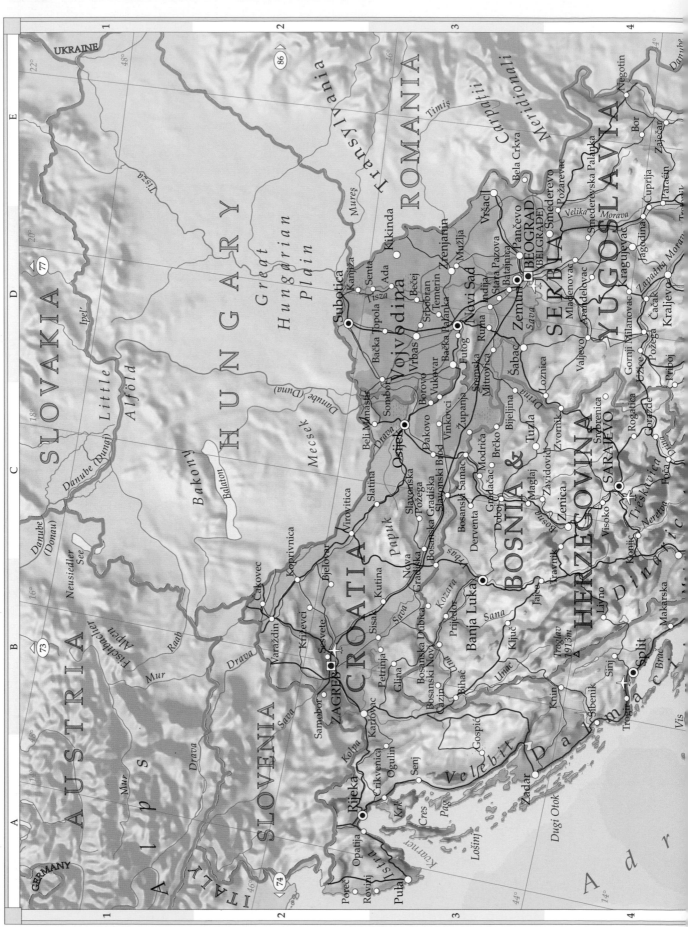

THE WORLD ATLAS

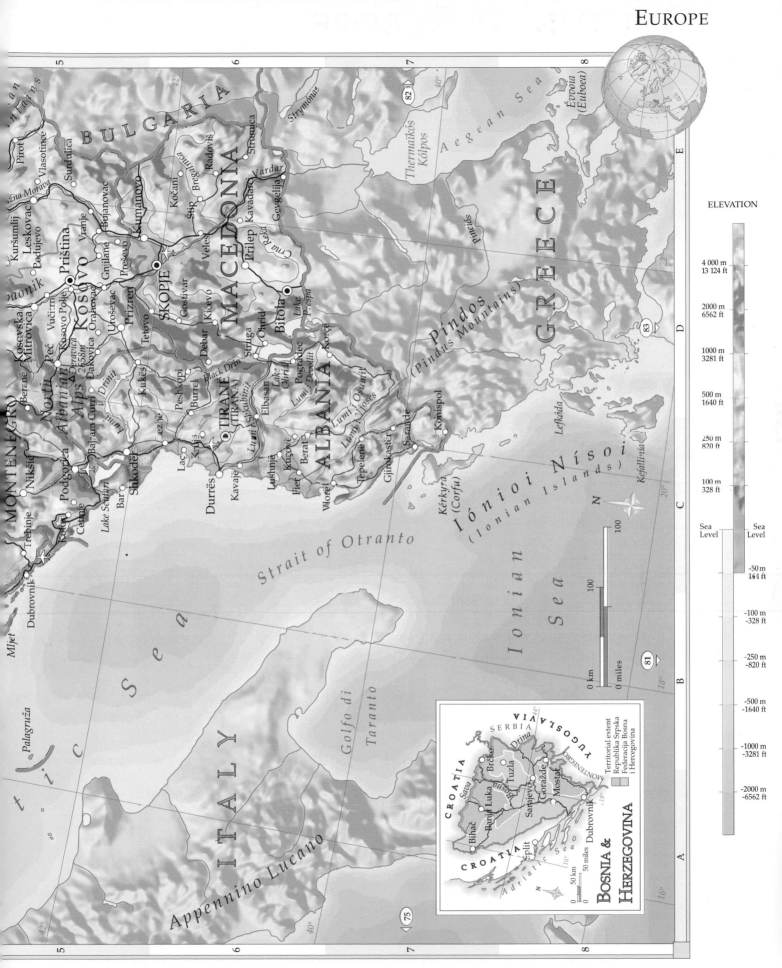

BULGARIA

MACEDONIA

GREECE

Aegean Sea

Thermaïkós Kólpos

Strymónas

Vardar

Strumica

Radoviš

Kočani

Štip

Bregalnica

Crna Reka

Kumanovo

SKOPJE

Veles

Gostivar

Kičevo

Prilep

Kavadarci

Gevgelija

Bitola

Lake Prespa

Ohrid

Struga

Pindos

(Pindus Mountains)

Piniós

Évvoia
(Euboea)

Pirot

Vlasotince

Surdulica

Vranje

Bujanovac

Preševo

Gnjilane

Leskovac

Podujevo

Kuršumlij

Južna Morava

PRIŠTINA

KOSOVO

Vučitrn

Uroševac

Prizren

Tetovo

Kosovska
Mitrovica

Peć

Koševska

Kosovo Polje

Vučitrn

Orahovac

Debar

Kopaonik

North
Albanian
Alps

Đakovica

Deravica
2658m

Kukës

i Drinit

Black Drim

Peshkopi

Burrel

Elbasan

Lumi i Shkumbinit

ALBANIA

Pogradec

Lake
Ohrid

Drejollit

Korçë

Lumi i Osumit

MONTENEGRO

Berane

Bajram Curri

Lumi i

Trebinje

Nikšić

PODGORICA

Cetinje

Kotor

Lake Scutari

Bar

Shkodër

Lac

Krujë

TIRANË
(TIRANA)

Lushnjë

Kavajë

Durrës

Fier

Kuçovë

Berat

Vlorë

Ishm

Lumi i Vjosës

Tepelenë

Gjirokastër

Sarandë

Konispol

Lefkáda

Kérkyra
(Corfu)

Iónioi Nísoi
(Ionian Islands)

Kefallinía

Mljet

Dubrovnik

A d r i a t i c   S e a

Palagruža

Strait of Otranto

I o n i a n   S e a

ITALY

Golfo di
Taranto

Appennino Lucano

N

N

0 km   100

0 miles   100

BOSNIA & HERZEGOVINA

YUGOSLAVIA

CROATIA

CROATIA

SERBIA

MONTENEGRO

Sava

Una

Bihać

Banja Luka

Brčko

Tuzla

Bosna

Vrbas

Sarajevo

Goražde

Mostar

Drina

Split

Dubrovnik

Adriatic Sea

0   50 km
0   50 miles

Territorial extent
Republika Srpska
Federacija Bosna
i Hercegovina

ELEVATION

4 000 m
13 124 ft

2000 m
6562 ft

1000 m
3281 ft

500 m
1640 ft

250 m
820 ft

100 m
328 ft

Sea
Level

Sea
Level

-50 m
164 ft

-100 m
-328 ft

-250 m
-820 ft

-500 m
-1640 ft

-1000 m
-3281 ft

-2000 m
-6562 ft

THE MEDITERRANEAN

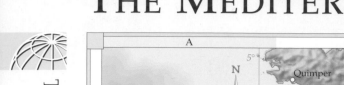

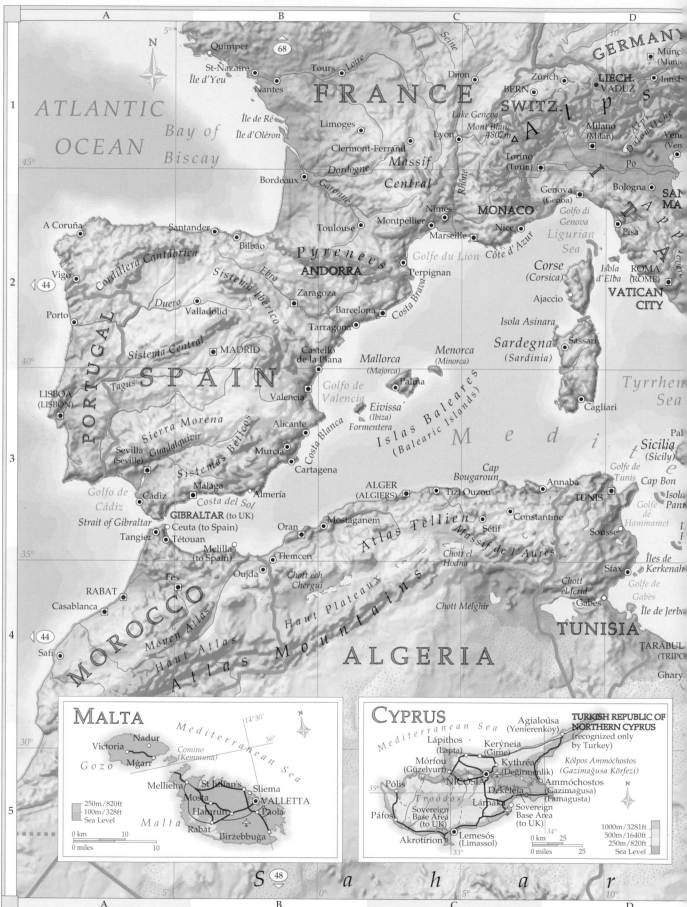

SLOVAKIA
WIEN
(VIENNA)
STRIA
Danube
BUDAPEST
Satu Mare
Tisza
Carpathian Mountains
Bălți
86 UKRAINE
MOLD.
CHIȘINĂU
Kakhovs'ka
Vodoskhovyshche
Dniester
Odesa
Berdyans'k
Sea of Azov
UBLJANA
HUNGARY
Great
Hungarian
Plain
Târgu Mureș
ROMANIA
ZAGREB
CROATIA
Novi Sad
Carpatii Meridonali
Galați
Krym's'kyy
Pivostrov
Kerch
RUSS.
FED.
BOSNIA
& HERZ.
N.
BEOGRAD
(BELGRADE)
BUCUREȘTI
(BUCHAREST)
Danube
Constanța
Sevastopol'
Novorossiysk
SARAJEVO
BULGARIA
Black Sea
YUGOSLAVIA
Balkan Mountains
Varna
Dalmacija
eka
Priština
SOFIYA
(SOFIA)
Burgas
ELEVATION
Adriatic Sea
ra
SKOPJE
TIRANË
(TIRANA)
MACED.
Rhodope
Mountains
Edirne
İstanbul
Boğazı
(Bosporus)
Zonguldak
Küre Dağları
Samsun
95
4000 m
13 124 ft
ALBANIA
Thessaloníki
(Salonica)
İstanbul
Marmara
Denizi
Bursa
ANKARA
Ordu
2000 m
6562 ft
Bari
Lecce
Pindus
(Pindus)
Mts.
Límnos
Balıkesir
TURKEY
Vesuvio 1277m
Napoli
(Naples)
Golfo di
Taranto
Strait of Otranto
Kérkyra
(Corfu)
Lárisa
Aegean
Sea
İzmir
Tuz
Gölü
Kayseri
1000 m
3281 ft
500 m
1640 ft
Ionian
osenza
Catanzaro
GREECE
Chíos
Sámos
Gaziantep
250 m
820 ft
Kefallinía
Sea
ATHÍNA
(ATHENS)
Dódekánisos
(Dodecanese)
Antalya
Toros Dağları
Adana
Euphrates
Monte Etna
3340m
Catania
Zákynthos
Kýthira
Kyklådes
(Cyclades)
Mirtóo
Pelagos
Antalya
Körfezi
İskenderun Körfezi
Ualab
(Aleppo)
100 m
328 ft
Siracusa
Kritikó Pélagos
(Sea of Crete)
Ródos
(Rhodes)
Kárpathos
NICOSIA
Sea
Level
Sea
Level
VALLETTA
Irákleio
Kríti
CYPRUS
Lárnaka
SYRIA
-250 m
ALTA
(Crete)
Lemesós
(Limassol)
LEBANON
-500 m
-1640 ft
n
BEYROUTH
(BEIRUT)
DIMASHQ
(DAMASCUS)
97
-1000 m
-3281 ft
e
Darnah
Hefa
-2000 m
-6562 ft
Mişrātah
Banghāzī
(Benghazi)
a
Ţubruq
ISRAEL
Tel Aviv-Yafo
JERUSALEM
Gaza
'AMMĀN
-3000 m
-9843 ft
Khalīj Surt
(Gulf of Sirte)
Sea
Alexandria
Nile
Delta
Port Said
Dead Sea
JORDAN
Surt
Libyan
Plateau
Suez
Canal
-4000 m
-13 124 ft
Ajdābiyā
Great Sand Sea
Monkhafad al Qattâra
(Qattara Depression)
CAIRO
Suez
Waddān
El Giza
Elat
Al 'Aqabah
SAUDI
ARABIA
LIBYA
0 km   400
Libyan
EGYPT
Sinai
Nile
Sahara el Sharqiya
(Eastern Desert)
Gulf of Suez
Red
Sea
0 miles   400
Desert
50

BULGARIA & GREECE

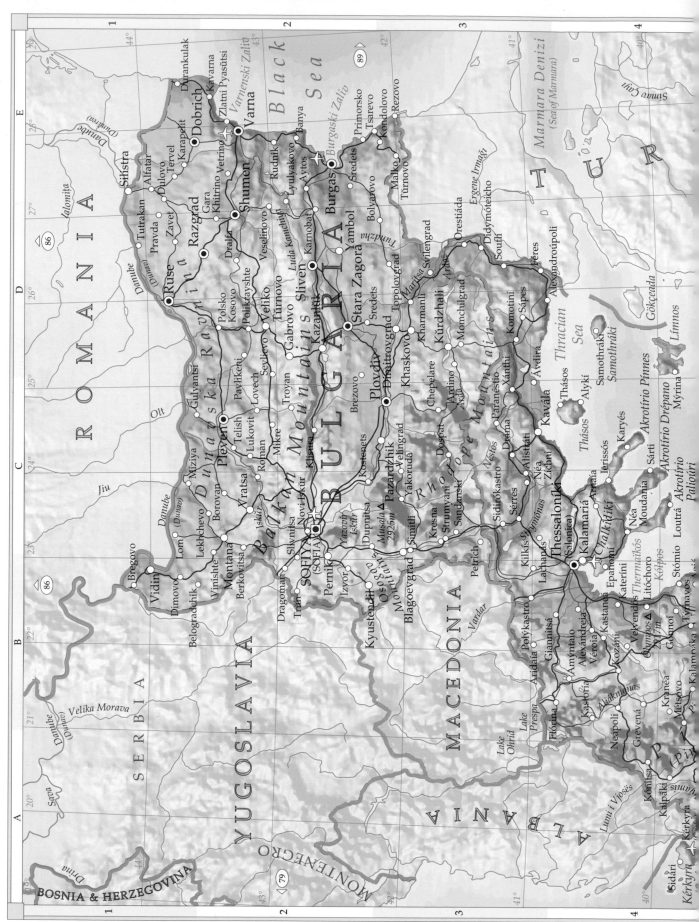

POPULATION

- ◼ Over 500,000
- ◉ 100,000 – 500,000
- ◯ 50,000 – 100,000
- ○ Less than 50,000
- ● National capital

T U R K E Y

Büyükmenderes Nehri
Gediz

5 · 6 · 7 · 8

39° · 38° · 37° · 36° · 35° · 34°

E · D · C · B · A

27° · 26° · 25° · 24° · 23° · 22° · 21° · 20°

Ródos (Rhodes)
Líndos
94

Kattaviá
Ródos (Rhodes)
Chálki
Kárpathos
Kárpathos

Kos
Nísyros
Tílos
Kásos
Saría

Sámos
Sámos
Thérma
Ikaría
Agia Marina
Kálimnos
Sýrna

Agathonísi
Arkoí
Léros
Léros
Astypálaia

Pátmos
Leipsoí

Dodekánisos (Dodecanese)

A e g e a n   S e a

Mytilíni
Lésvos (Lesbos)
Plomári
Chíos
Chíos
Psará
Antípsara

Amorgós
Amorgós
Akra Floúda
Anáfi

Náxos
Náxos
Íos
Íos
Thíra
Thíra
Thíra

Kritikó Pélagos (Sea of Crete)

Skiáthos
Skópelos
Strofyliá
Vólos
Skýros
Skýros
Kými
Kárystos
Kárystos

Andros
Andros
Tínos
Tínos
Sýros
Ermoúpoli
Kýthnos
Kýthnos
Kéa
Kéa

Kykládes (Cyclades)

Páros
Páros
Kástro
Sífnos
Sérifos
Mílos
Mílos
Eléganáres

Mýkonos

Neápoli
Sitéia
Agios Nikólaos
Ierápetra
Mýrtos
Zarós
Týmpáki
Gázios
Spíli
Lefká Orí
Dikti
Irákleio
Pánormos
Kríti (Crete)
Chaniá
Kastélli
Kántanos
Sfákia

Mediterranean Sea

Sourpi
Domokós
Lamía
Lidoríki
Karpenísi
Rentína
Árta
Préveza
Amfílochia
Thérmo
Neochóri
Katoúna
Vasilikí
Lefkáda
Lefkáda
Argostóli
Lixoúri
Kefallinía

Ágio Achaía
Káto Achaía
Lecháiná
Gastoúni
Pátra
Pýrgos
Kerí
Zákynthos
Zacháro
Lámpeia
Alfeiós
Kyparissía
Messíni
Pýlos
Koróni
Areópoli
Geroliménas

Agríni
Alivéri
Évvoia (Euboea)
Chalkída
Erétria
Marathónas
Keratéa
Lávrio
ATHÍNA (ATHENS)
Peiraiás (Piraeus)
Égina
Póros
Ermióni
Ýdra
Palaiá Epídavros
Nafplio
Árgos
Trípoli
Nemea
Korínthos (Corinth)
Korinthiakós Kólpos
Xylókastro
Kiáto
Sikyía
Alfeiós
Spárti
Kalamáta
Geráki
Gýtheio
Daimoniá
Neápoli

Pelopónnisos (Peloponnese)

Leonídi
Ka avás
Kýthira
Kýthira

Antikýthira
Potamós
Antikýthira

Mirtóo Pélagos

Lakonikós Kólpos

N
N í s o i (Ionian Islands)
Paxoí
Antipaxoi
Lefkáda

G R E E C E

Ionian Sea

81

ELEVATION

4 000 m / 13 124 ft
2000 m / 6562 ft
1000 m / 3281 ft
500 m / 1640 ft
250 m / 820 ft
100 m / 328 ft
Sea Level

Sea Level
-50 m / 164 ft
-100 m / -328 ft
-250 m / -820 ft
-500 m / -1640 ft
-1000 m / -3281 ft
-2000 m / -6562 ft

0 km
0 miles
100
100

N

THE WORLD ATLAS

SWEDEN

FINLAND

RUSSIAN FEDERATION

Gulf of Finland

Narva Bay

Narva Reservoir

Lake Peipus

Lake Pskov

Velikaya

ESTONIA

Sillamäe · Narva
Kohtla-Järve
Kunda
Rakvere · Tapa · Rakke
Loksa · Aegviidu · Raasiku
Maardu
TALLINN · Keila · Paide
Paldiski · Risti · Rapla
Haapsalu · Lihula · Pärnu-Jaagupi
Vormsi · Virtsu · Audru · Sindi
Kärdla · Emmaste · Orissaare · Kuressaare
Hiiumaa · Saaremaa
Väinameri · Suur Väin
Säära

Palamuse · Puurmani · Tartu
Kallaste · Vōnnu · Räpina
Otepää · Põlva · Vōru
Ape
Valga · Valka
Viljandi · Mōisaküla · Rōngu · Tōrva
Uulu · Kilingi-Nōmme · Staicele · Rūjiena
Smiltene
Pärnu
Ainaži · Aloja · Valmiera
Salacgrīva · Burtnieku Ezers · Cēsis
Gauja · Smiltene · Gaiziņa Kalns 311m · Munamägi 318m △
Alūksne · Balvi · Vilaka
Jaunpiebalga · Gulbene · Rugāji
Madona · Varakļāni · Lubāns · Rēzekne
Ludza · Malta
Spogi · Daugavpils
Plaviņas · Jēkabpils · Līvāni · Zilupe

Gulf of Riga
Ruhnu · Kihnu
Kolkasrags · Kolka · Roja · Mērsrags
Salacgrīva
SaulKrasti
Kandava · Tukums · Engure
RĪGA
Jūrmala
Mazirbe · Ugāle · Talsi · Kandava
Ventspils
Pāvilosta
Kuldīga · Saldus · Brocēni
Kurzeme
 Usmas Ezers · Engures Ezers · Durbe · Venta

LATVIA

Iecava · Bauska · Aizkraukle
Jelgava
Iecava
Dobele · Pasvalys · Nereta
Viesīte
Pakruojis
Radviliškis
Jonišķis · Papilė · Mažeikiai
Šiauliai
Panevēžys
Subačius · Obeliai · Zarasai
Biržai · Pasvalys · Anykščiai
Naujamiestis · Dotnuva · Jonava
Kupiškis · Rokiškis

LITHUANIA

Liepāja
Grobiņa
Rucava
Priekulė
Klaipėda
Kretinga · Gargždai
Neringa
Žemaičiu Aukštumas
Salantai · Skuodas · Plungė · Telšiai
Šiauliai · Raseiniai · Kelmė · Šilalė
Šilutė · Taurage · Neman · Jurbarkas · Skaudvilė
Neman
Courland Lagoon
KALININGRAD (to Russian Federation)
Zelenogradsk · Gvardeysk
Vilkaviškis · Gusev
Pionerskiy · Bagrationovsk · Mamonovo · Primorsk · Zheleznodoroznyy · Cherryakhovsk
Kaliningrad

Baltic Sea

Gotland
Öland
Gotska Sandön

Skiftet
Ālands Hav

POPULATION
- ◉ Over 500,000
- ◉ 100,000 – 500,000
- ○ 50,000 – 100,000
- ○ Less than 50,000
- ● National capital

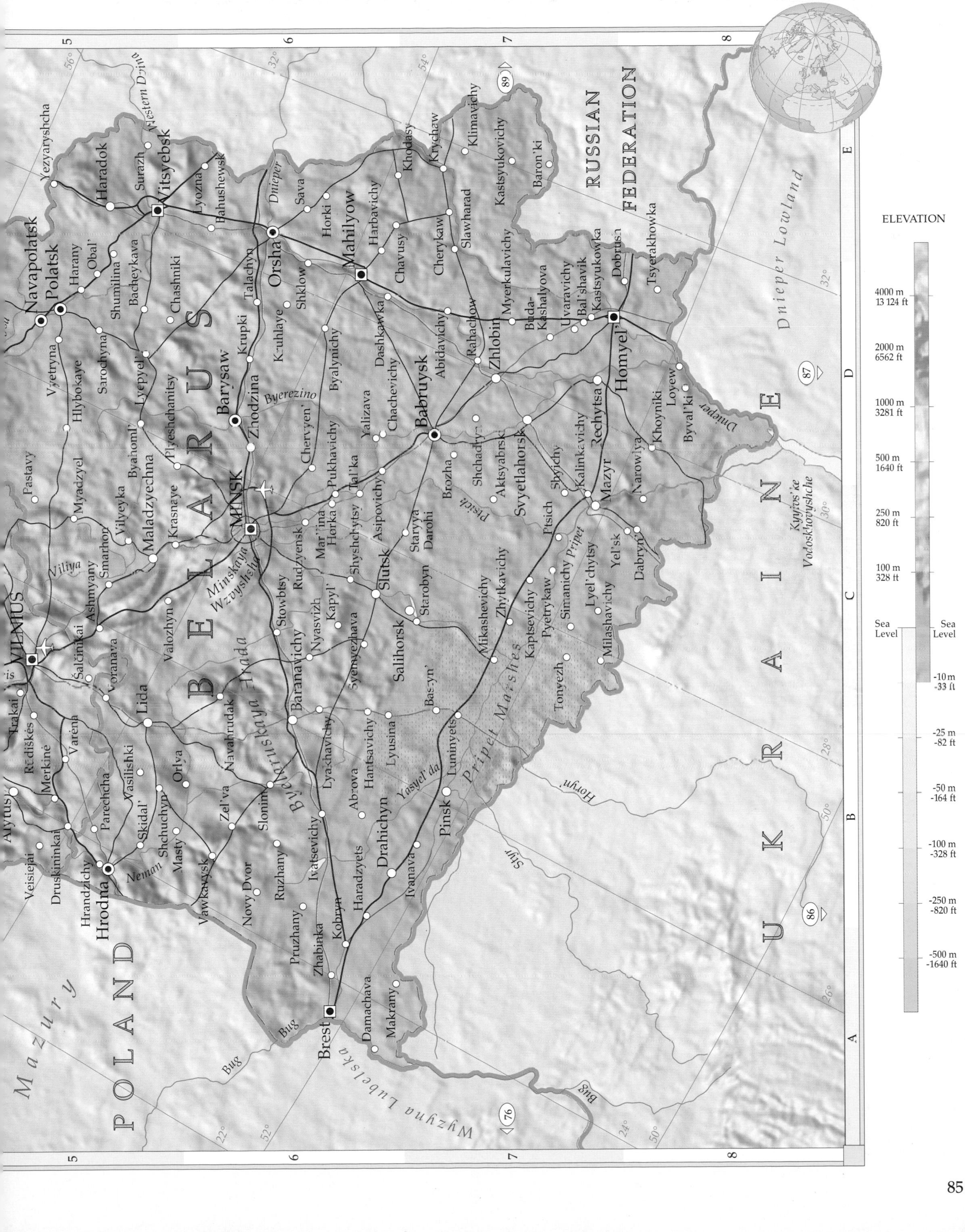

ELEVATION

4000 m	13 124 ft
2000 m	6562 ft
1000 m	3281 ft
500 m	1640 ft
250 m	820 ft
100 m	328 ft
Sea Level	Sea Level
-10 m	-33 ft
-25 m	-82 ft
-50 m	-164 ft
-100 m	-328 ft
-250 m	-820 ft
-500 m	-1640 ft

RUSSIAN FEDERATION

POLAND

UKRAINE

BELARUS

Dnieper Lowland

Pripet Marshes

Byelaruskaya Hrada

Minskaya Wzvyshsha

Mazury

Wyżyna Lubelska

Cities and places:
Vyezyaryshcha, Haradok, Surazh, Vitsyebsk, Lyozna, Bahushewsk, Navapolatsk, Polatsk, Harany, Obal', Shumilina, Bacheykava, Chashniki, Klimavichy, Krychaw, Khodasy, Slawharad, Kastsyukovichy, Baron'ki, Dnieper, Sava, Horki, Mahilyow, Cherykaw, Myerkulavichy, Budda-Kashalyova, Uvaravichy, Bal'shavik, Kastsyukowka, Dobrush, Tsyerakhowka, Harbavichy, Chavusy, Shklow, Orsha, Talachyn, Kruhlaye, Krupki, Byalynichy, Dashkawka, Rahachow, Zhlobin, Abidavichy, Babruysk, Brozha, Shchadryn, Aktsyabrsk, Svyetlahorsk, Rechytsa, Homyel, Khoyniki, Loyew, Byval'ki, Dnieper, Vyetryna, Hlybokaye, Sarochyna, Lyepyel', Byahoml', Plyeshchanitsy, Barysaw, Zhodzina, Byerezino, Cherven', Pukhavichy, Yalizava, Chachevichy, Kalinkavichy, Mazyr, Narowlya, Pastavy, Myadzyel, Smarhon', Krasnaye, Maladzyechna, Vilyeyka, MINSK, Mar'ina Horka, Asipovichy, Staryya Darohi, Ptsich, Skyichy, Simanichy Pripet, Lyel'chytsy, Yel'sk, Dabryn', Milashavichy, VILNIUS, Trakai, Ashmyany, Šalčininkai, Valozhyn, Rudzyensk, Shyshchytsy, Tal'ka, Slutsk, Starobyn, Mikashevichy, Zhytkavichy, Kaptsevichy, Pyetrykaw, Tonyezh, Luninyets, Rudziškės, Vorānava, Lida, Navahrudak, Stowbtsy, Nyasvizh, Kapyl', Zvyenyezhava, Salihorsk, Bas-yn', Lyusina, Alytus, Veisiejai, Merkinė, Varėna, Orlya, Zel'va, Lyakhavichy, Abrova, Hantsavichy, Drahichyn, Ivanava, Pinsk, Druskininkai, Hrandzichy, Hrodna, Neman, Vawkavysk, Novy Dvor, Ruzhany, Ivatsevichy, Pruzhany, Zhabinka, Kobryn, Haradzyets, Damachava, Makrany, Brest, Vasilishki, Skidal', Shchuchyn, Masty, Slonim, Baranavichy, Baranavichy

Bug, Neman, Viliya, Byerezino, Ptsich, Sluch, Horyn', Bug, Bug

UKRAINE, MOLDOVA & ROMANIA

E   32°   F   34°   G   36°   H   38°   40°

RUSSIAN
FEDERATION

Sred>nerusskaya
Vozvyshennost'

Don

ELEVATION

4 000 m
13 124 ft

2000 m
6562 ft

1000 m
3281 ft

500 m
1640 ft

250 m
820 ft

100 m
328 ft

Sea
Level

Sea
Level

-50 m
-164 ft

-100 m
-328 ft

-250 m
-820 ft

-500 m
-1640 ft

-1000 m
-3281 ft

-2000 m
-6562 ft

Dnieper
(Dnyapro)

Horodnya
Shostka
Shchors
Hlukhiv
Chernihiv   Krolevets'
Konotop
Nizhyn   Bakhmach
Oster   Nosivka   Romny   Sumy
Brovary   Pryluky   Pyryatyn   Lebedyn
Vasyl'kiv   Yahotyn   Psel   Okhtyrka   Zolochiv
tiv   Hrebinka   Lubny   Myrhorod   Derhachi
Kaniv   Lyubotyn   Kharkiv
ila Tserkva   Mereta
Bohuslav   Zolotonosha   Kup''yans'k
Horodyshche   Hlobyne   Poltava   Izyum   Kreminna   Starobil's'k
nyhorodka   Cherkasy   Kremenchuts'ke   Rubizhne
Smila   Vodoskhovyshche   Slov''yans'k   Syeverodonets'k
Shpola   Chyhyryn   Donets   Kramators'k   Lysychans'k
Tal'ne   Oleksandrivka   Svitlovods'k   Kremenchuk   Zolote
Mala Vyska   Znam''yanka   Dniprodzerzhyns'ke   Kostyantynivka   Luhans'k
Holovanivs'k   Oleksandriya   Vodoskhovyshche   Novomoskovs'k   Pavlohrad   Horlivka   Stakhanov
yanivka   Kirovohrad   Dniprodzerzhyns'k   Dnipropetrovs'k   Yenakiyeve   Krasnodon
Vil'shanka   Zhovti Vody   P''yatykhatky   Synel'nykove   Makiyivka   Krasnyy Luch
Pervomays'k   Dolyns'ka   Donets'k   Torez
ve Ozero   Arbyzynka   Bobrynets'   Kryvyy Rih   Pokrovs'ke
Novyy Buh   Inhulets'   Zaporizhzhya   Amvrosiyivka
Voznesens'k   Nikopol'   Orikhiv   Volnovakha   Dokuchayevs'k
Predennyy Buh   Ordzhonikidze   Marhanets'   Polohy   Don
Kam''yanka-Dniprovs'ka   Dniprorudne
l   Kakhovs'ka   Tokmak   Mariupol'   Novoazovs'k
a   Vodoskhovyshche   Molochans'k
c   Mykolayiv   Melitopol'   Gulf of Taganrog   Y'eya
k   Dnieper   Kakhovka   Berdyans'k
Zhovtneve   (Dnipro)   Akinovka   Prymors'k
S   Kherson   Low   RUSSIAN
Ochakiv   FEDERATION
Odesa   Hola Prystan'   Tsyurupyns'k   Novotroyits'ke
Illichivs'k   Chaplynka   Heniches'k   Sea of Azov
Kalanchak   Armyans'k
Karkinits'ka Zatoka   Krasnoperekops'k
Rozdol'ne   Kerch Strait
Krasnohvardiys'ke   Dzhankoy
Chornomors'ke   Zatoka   Kerch
Nyzhn'ohirs'kyy   Syvash   Kuban'
Yevpatoriya   Lenine
Saky   Kryms'kyy   Feodosiya
Simferopol'   Pivostriv
Bakhchysaray   Kryms'ki Hory
Sevastopol'   Alushta
Yalta
Alupka

Black Sea

0 km   100
0 miles   100

88

94

44°

E   32°   F   34°   G   36°   H   38°   40°

1   2   3   4   5

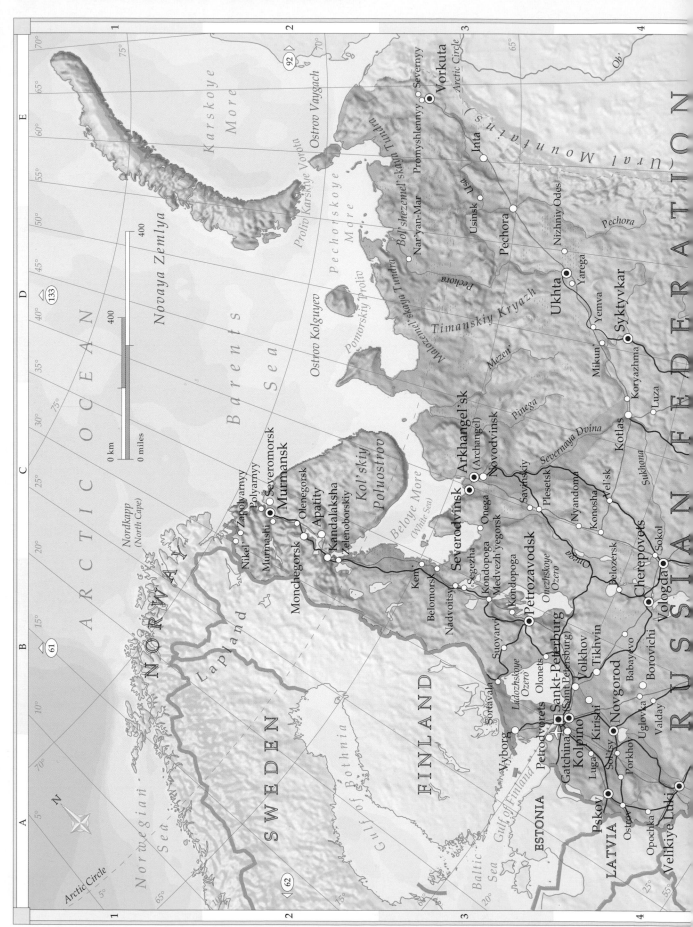

POPULATION

- ▣ Over 500,000
- ◉ 100,000 – 500,000
- ○ 50,000 – 100,000
- · Less than 50,000
- ● National capital

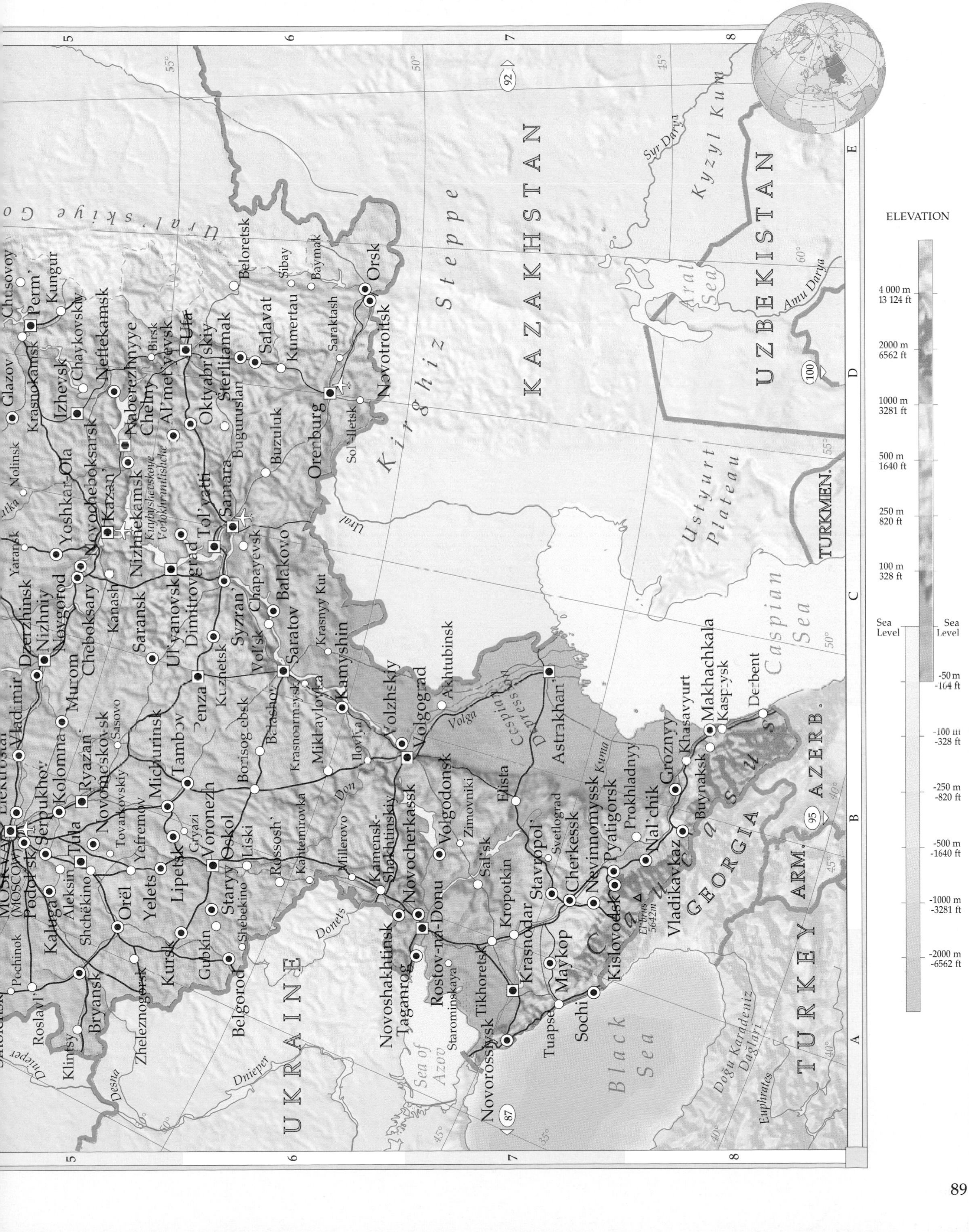

ELEVATION

Kyzyl Kum

Syr Darya

Aral Sea

Amu Darya

UZBEKISTAN

KAZAKHSTAN

Kirghiz Steppe

Ural'skiye Go

TURKMEN.

Ustyurt Plateau

Caspian Sea

Caspian Depression

Volga

Ural

4 000 m
13 124 ft

2000 m
6562 ft

1000 m
3281 ft

500 m
1640 ft

250 m
820 ft

100 m
328 ft

Sea Level

Sea Level

-50 m
-164 ft

-100 m
-328 ft

-250 m
-820 ft

-500 m
-1640 ft

-1000 m
-3281 ft

-2000 m
-6562 ft

Chusovoy
Perm'
Kungur
Glazov
Krasnokamsk
Izhevsk
Chaykovskiy
Neftekamsk
Nolinsk
Krasnoufimsk

Beloretsk
Sibay
Baymak
Orsk
Novotroitsk

Naberezhnyye Chelny
Birsk
Ufa
Salavat
Kumertau
Saraktash
Al'met'yevsk
Oktyabr'skiy
Sterlitamak
Buzuluk
Orenburg
Sol-Iletsk

Kazan'
Novocheboksarsk
Kinyushcheskoye Vodokhranilishche
Buguruslan

Yaransk
Yoshkar-Ola
Nizhnekamsk
Samara
Tol'yatti
Chapayevsk

Cheboksary
Nizhniy Novgorod
Dzerzhinsk
Saransk
Ul'yanovsk
Dimitrovgrad
Syzran'
Vol'sk
Balakovo
Krasnyy Kut
Kanash

Murom
Kuznetsk
Saratov
Kamyshin
Ramenskoye
Akhtubinsk

Vladimir
Kolomna
Ryazan'
Michurinsk
Tambov
Penza
Borisoglebsk
Balashov
Krasnoarmeysk
Mikhaylovka
Ilovlya
Volzhskiy
Volgograd

MOSKVA (MOSCOW)
Serpukhov
Novomoskovsk
Sasovo
Yefremov
Rossosh'
Kalemirovka
Millerovo
Kamensk-Shakhtinskiy
Volgodonsk
Zimovniki
Elista
Svetlograd

Tula
Aleksin
Shchëkino
Tovarkovsky
Oskol
Liski
Sal'sk
Stavropol'
Cherkessk
Nevinnomyssk
Pyatigorsk
Prokhladnyy
Groznyy
Khasavyurt
Makhachkala
Kaspiysk
Derbent

Podol'sk
Kaluga
Orël
Yelets
Lipetsk
Gryazi
Voronezh
Staryy Oskol
Shebekino
Novocherkassk
Rostov-na-Donu
Kropotkin
Krasnodar
Maykop
Kislovodsk
Nal'chik
Vladikavkaz
Buynaksk

Pochinok
Roslavl'
Bryansk
Shchëkino
Kursk
Gubkin
Belgorod
Novoshakhtinsk
Taganrog
Starominskaya
Tikhoretsk
Sochi
Tuapse

Klintsy
Zheleznogorsk
Donets
Novorossiysk
Dnieper
Desna

Elbrus 5642m

UKRAINE
GEORGIA
ARM.
AZERB.
TURKEY

Caucasus

Black Sea
Sea of Azov
Dniester

Dogu Karadeniz Daglari
Euphrates

Don
Kuma

92
100
95
87

55°
50°
45°
60°
55°
50°
45°
40°
35°
40°

5 6 7 8

NORTH & WEST ASIA

THE WORLD ATLAS

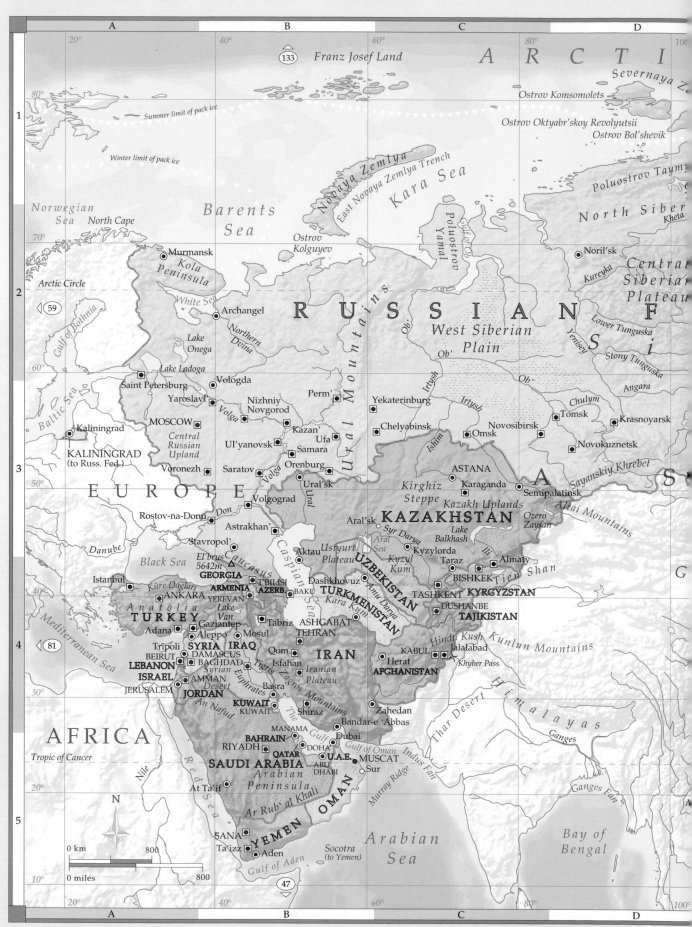

POPULATION

⊡ Over 500,000

◉ 100,000 – 500,000

○ 50,000 – 100,000

○ Less than 50,000

● National capital

A · B · C · D

133

Franz Josef Land

ARCTI

C

Severnaya Z

Ostrov Komsomolets

Ostrov Oktyabr'skoy Revolyutsii
Ostrov Bol'shevik

Poluostrov Taym

1

Summer limit of pack ice

Winter limit of pack ice

Novaya Zemlya

East Novaya Zemlya Trench

Kara Sea

North Siber

Kheta

Norwegian Sea   North Cape

Barents Sea

Ostrov Kolguyev

Poluostrov Yamal

Gulf of Ob

Central Siberian Plateau

Murmansk
Kola Peninsula

70°

2

Arctic Circle

59

White Sea

RUSSIAN F

Noril'sk

Kureyka

Archangel

Northern Dvina

West Siberian Plain

Ob'

Lower Tunguska

Yenisey

S

Stony Tunguska

i

Lake Onega

Ural Mountains

Ob'

Angara

60°

Lake Ladoga

Saint Petersburg

Vologda

Perm'

Yekaterinburg

Irtysh

Chulym

Tomsk

Krasnoyarsk

Yaroslavl

Nizhniy Novgorod

Ob'

Irtysh

Novosibirsk

Volga

Kazan'

Ufa

Chelyabinsk

Omsk

Novokuznetsk

MOSCOW

Ul'yanovsk

Ishim

Central Russian Upland

Samara

3

Voronezh

Saratov

Orenburg

ASTANA

Karaganda

Semipalatinsk

Sayanskiy Khrebet

A

S

50°

EUROPE

Volga

Ural'sk

Kirghiz Steppe

Kazakh Uplands

Ural

Volgograd

Aral'sk

KAZAKHSTAN

Ozero Zaysan

Altai Mountains

Rostov-na-Donu

Don

Astrakhan'

Syr Darya

Lake Balkhash

Ili

Stavropol'

Aktau

Ustyurt Plateau

Aral Sea

Kyzyl Kum

Kyzylorda

Taraz

Almaty

Black Sea

El'brus 5642m

Caucasus

Caspian Sea

UZBEKISTAN

BISHKEK

Tien Shan

G

Istanbul

T'BILISI

Dashkhovuz

Amu Darya

TASHKENT

KYRGYZSTAN

40°

Küre Dağları

GEORGIA

AZERB.

BAKU

TURKMENISTAN

DUSHANBE

ANKARA

ARMENIA

YEREVAN

Kara Kum

ASHGABAT

TAJIKISTAN

Anatolia

Lake Van

Tabriz

TEHRAN

Hindu Kush

Kunlun Mountains

TURKEY

Adana

Gaziantep

Mosul

KABUL

Jalalabad

Tripoli

SYRIA

IRAQ

Qom

IRAN

Herat

AFGHANISTAN

Khyber Pass

4

Aleppo

DAMASCUS

BAGHDAD

Isfahan

Iranian Plateau

Khyber Pass

Himalayas

BEIRUT

LEBANON

Syrian Desert

Tigris

ISRAEL

AMMAN

Euphrates

Basra

Zagros Mountains

Zahedan

81

Mediterranean Sea

JERUSALEM

JORDAN

KUWAIT

Shiraz

Bandar-e 'Abbas

Thar Desert

Ganges

30°

An Nafud

KUWAIT

The Gulf

MANAMA

Dubai

Gulf of Oman

Murray Ridge

Indus Fan

AFRICA

BAHRAIN

DOHA

U.A.E.

MUSCAT

Ganges Fan

Tropic of Cancer

RIYADH

QATAR

ABU DHABI

Sur

N

Nile

SAUDI ARABIA

Arabian Peninsula

OMAN

20°

Red Sea

At Ta'if

Bay of Bengal

5

Ar Rub' al Khali

Arabian Sea

0 km   800

SANA

YEMEN

Socotra (to Yemen)

0 miles   800

Ta'izz

Aden

Gulf of Aden

47

10°

20°   40°   60°   80°   100°

A · B · C · D

90

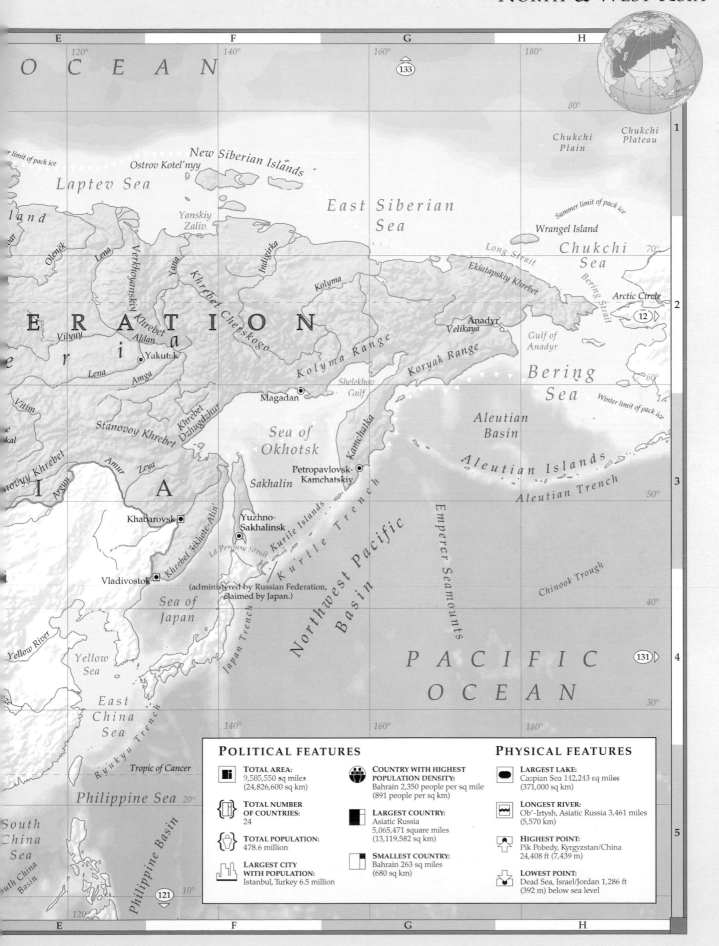

O C E A N

△
133

80°

Chukchi
Plain

Chukchi
Plateau

1

New Siberian Islands

Ostrov Kotel'nyy

Laptev Sea

_East Siberian
Sea_

Summer limit of pack ice

Wrangel Island

_Chukchi
Sea_

land

limit of pack ice

Yanskiy
Zaliv

Olenëk

Lena

Verkhoyanskiy

Indigirka

Long Strait

70°

Ekiatapskiy Khrebet

Bering Strait

Arctic Circle

12

2

E R A T I O N

Khrebet Cherskogo

Kolyma

Anadyr'
Velikaya

Gulf of
Anadyr

r i a

Vilyuy

Khrebet

Aldan

Yakutsk

Kolyma Range

Koryak Range

Bering
Sea

60°

Lena

Amga

Shelekhov
Gulf

Magadan

Aleutian
Basin

Winter limit of pack ice

Vitim

Stanovoy Khrebet

Khrebet Dzhugdzhur

_Sea of
Okhotsk_

Kamchatka

Aleutian Islands

50°

3

kal

ovyy Khrebet

Amur

Zeya

Petropavlovsk-
Kamchatskiy

Aleutian Trench

I A

Argun

Sakhalin

Kurile Islands

Kurile Trench

Emperor Seamounts

Khabarovsk

Yuzhno-
Sakhalinsk

_Northwest Pacific
Basin_

Chinook Trough

40°

131

Vladivostok

La Perouse Strait

Khrebet Sikhote-Alin'

(administered by Russian Federation,
claimed by Japan.)

_Sea of
Japan_

Japan Trench

Yellow River

_Yellow
Sea_

P A C I F I C

O C E A N

30°

E 120° F 140° G 160° H 180°

_East
China
Sea_

Tropic of Cancer

Ryukyu Trench

Philippine Sea 20°

South
China
Sea

Philippine Basin

South
China
Basin

121

10°

120°

POLITICAL FEATURES

TOTAL AREA:
9,585,550 sq miles
(24,826,600 sq km)

**TOTAL NUMBER
OF COUNTRIES:**
24

TOTAL POPULATION:
478.6 million

**LARGEST CITY
WITH POPULATION:**
Istanbul, Turkey 6.5 million

**COUNTRY WITH HIGHEST
POPULATION DENSITY:**
Bahrain 2,350 people per sq mile
(891 people per sq km)

LARGEST COUNTRY:
Asiatic Russia
5,065,471 square miles
(13,119,582 sq km)

SMALLEST COUNTRY:
Bahrain 263 sq miles
(680 sq km)

PHYSICAL FEATURES

LARGEST LAKE:
Caspian Sea 142,243 sq miles
(371,000 sq km)

LONGEST RIVER:
Ob'-Irtysh, Asiatic Russia 3,461 miles
(5,570 km)

HIGHEST POINT:
Pik Pobedy, Kyrgyzstan/China
24,408 ft (7,439 m)

LOWEST POINT:
Dead Sea, Israel/Jordan 1,286 ft
(392 m) below sea level

THE WORLD ATLAS

ELEVATION

4000 m
13 124 ft

2000 m
6562 ft

1000 m
3281 ft

500 m
1640 ft

250 m
820 ft

100 m
328 ft

Sea Level | Sea Level

-250 m
-820 ft

-500 m
-1640 ft

-1000 m
-3281 ft

-2000 m
-6562 ft

-3000 m
-9843 ft

-4000 m
-13 124 ft

ALASKA (to US)

Chukchi Sea

Bering Strait

Arctic Circle

Ostrov Vrangelya

Proliv Longa

Vostochno-Sibirskoye More

Bering Sea

Anadyrskiy Zaliv

Ekiatapskiy Khrebet

Anadyr'

Pevek

Anadyr

Koryakskoye Nagor'ye

OCEAN

Ostrov Komsomolets

Ostrov Oktyabr'skoy Revolyutsii

Severnaya Zemlya

Novosibirskiye Ostrova

Ostrova

Ostrov Novaya Sibir'

Ambarchik
Cherskiy

Ossora

Ostrov Karaginskiy

Ostrov Kotel'nyy

Ostrov Bol'shoy Lyakhovskiy

Alazeya

Indigirka

Kolyma

Zaliv Shelikhova

Ust'-Kamchatsk

Vulkan Klyucheyskaya Sopka 4750m

evik

Ostrov Taymyr

More Laptevykh

Ozero Taymyr

Ust'-Olenёk

Tiksi

Kazach'ye

Yana

Khrebet Cherskogo

Adycha

Susuman

Atka

Magadan

Atlasovo

Mil'kovo

Petropavlovsk-Kamchatskiy

Poluostrov Kamchatka

Sibirskaya Nizmennost'

Anabar

Olenёk

Khrebet Verkhoyanskiy

Lena

Aldan

Okhotsk

Okhotskoye More

Pervyy Kuril'skiy Proliv

Ostrov Paramushir

neta

Kotuy

Srednesibirskoye Ploskogor'ye

Olenёk

Vilyuy

Yakutsk

Amga

Aldan

Khrebet Dzhugdzhur

Shantarskiye Ostrova

Ostrov Sakhalin

Kuril'skiye Ostrova (Kurile Islands)

SIBIR (SIBERIA)

FEDERATION

Nyurba

Mirnyy

Suntar

Olekminsk

Lena

Lena

Olёkma

Amur

Neryungri

Tynda

Ostrov Sakhalin

Ostrov Urup

Ostrov Iturup

Kuril'sk

aya Tunguska

Chunya

ugara

Ust'-Ilimsk

Ust'-Kut

Bodaybo

Vitim

Skovorodino

Komsomol'sk-na-Amure

Amur

Khrebet Sikhote-Alin'

La Pérouse Strait

Yuzhno-Sakhalinsk

sk

Bratsk

Tulun

Ozero Baykal

Yablonovyy Khrebet

Svobodnyy

Khabarovsk

Birobidzhan

Khor

Bikin

(administered by Russian Federation, claimed by Japan)

n Sayan

Usol'ye-Sibirskoye

Angarsk

Chita

Shilka

Blagoveshchensk

Amur

Irkutsk

Ulan-Ude

Olovyannaya

Krasnokamensk

Zabaykal'sk

MONGOLIA

Kyakhta

CHINA

Ussuriysk

Vladivostok

Nakhodka

NORTH KOREA

Sea of Japan

JAPAN

POPULATION

- ◉ Over 500,000
- ◉ 100,000 – 500,000
- ○ 50,000 – 100,000
- ○ Less than 50,000
- ● National capital

ROMANIA

BULGARIA

UKRAINE

Black Sea

Kryms'kyy Pivostriv

Iacul Razim
Iacul Sinoie

Danube

Varnenski Zaliv

Burgaski Zaliv

Maritsa

Kırklareli
Edirne

Çorlu
Tekirdağ

İstanbul Boğazı (Bosporus)

Zonguldak
Devrek

Cide
İnebolu
Sinop
Gerze

Küre Dağları

Bartın
Kastamonu
Karabük
Kargı
Çerkeş

Bafra
Samsun

Çanik Dağları

İzmit
Adapazarı

İstanbul
Yalova
İznik Gölü
Bolu
Gerede
Çankırı
Merzifon
Çorum
Tokat

Bandırma
Bursa
Bilecik

Çanakkale

Balıkesir

Eskişehir
Bozüyük

ANKARA
Kalecik
Alaca

Yıldızeli

Çanakkale Boğazı (Dardanelles)

Edremit
Ayvalık

Kütahya

Polatlı
Kırıkkale
Sorgun

Şarkışla
Siv

Lésvos

Akhisar
Simav
Gediz

T   U   R   K

Hirfanlı Barajı
Boğazlıyan

Chíos

Manisa
Gediz Nehri
Uşak

Afyon

Kulu
Tuz Gölü

Bünyan
Hel

İzmir
Menemen

Cihanbeyli
Nevşehir
İncesu
Kayseri
Gürün

Ödemiş
Aydın
Nazilli
Dinar

Akşehir
Aksaray

Göksun
G   ü

Söke
Büyükmenderes Nehri

Alaşehir

Anatolia

Sámos

Denizli
Burdur
Isparta
Beyşehir Gölü

Konya
Niğde
Kahramanm

Milas
Tavas

Burdur Gölü
Süğla Gölü

Ereğli

Muğla

Karaman

Toros
Dağları
Gazi

Bodrum

Antalya

Ceyhan
Tarsus
Adana
Osmaniye

Dodekánisos (Dodecánese)

Marmaris

Dalaman
Fethiye
Kaş
Finike

Manavgat
Alanya
Mut

Mersin
İskenderun
Kilis

Kırıkhan

Antalya Körfezi

Silifke
Antakya

Ródos (Rhodes)

Anamur

Kárpathos

CYPRUS

TURKISH REPUBLIC OF NORTHERN CYPRUS
(recognised only by Turkey)

Orantes

LEBANON

MEDITERRANEAN Sea

0 km		200
0 miles		200

RUSSIAN
FEDERATION

Caucasus

Caspian Sea

Gagra
Gudaut'a
Sokhumi
Och'amch'ire
Abkhazia
Enguri
Mestia
Kazbek 5047m

K'ut'aisi
South Ossetia
GEORGIA
Samtredia
P'ot'i
Gori
Tsalka
T'BILISI
Rust'avi
Zaqatala
Xaçmaz
Quba
Siyäzän

K'obulet'i
Bat'umi
Hopa
Ajaria
Akhalts'ikhe
Lesser Caucasus
Kura
Şäki
Šamaxı
Sumqayıt

Trabzon
Of
Pazar
Rize
Artvin
Dağları
Çoruh Nehri
Gyumri
Vanadzor
Gäncä
Mingäçevir
Yevlax
BAKI
(BAKU)

resun
shane
Kars
Artik
Sevan
ARMENIA
AZERBAIJAN
Qazimämmäd
Ali-Bayramı

İspir
Sarıkamış
YEREVAN
Sevana Lich
Artashat
Nagornyy
Karabakh
Imişli
Biläsuvar

Erzincan
Tercan
Aşkale
Pasinler
Horasan
Aras
Büyükağrı Dağı (Mount Ararat)
5137m
AZERBAIJAN
Xankändi
Läňkäran

Erzurum
Ağrı
Doğubayazıt
Goris

Kemah
Patnos
Naxçıvan

Keban Barajı
Bingöl
Erciş
Muradiye

Flâzığ
Muş
Tatvan
Van Gölü
Van
Daryācheh-ye Orūmīyeh

Toroslar
Bitlis
Gevaş

Silvan
Siirt
IRAN

Diyarbakır
Batman
Şırnak
Kurdistan

Silverek
Mardin
Rishteh-ye Kühhä-ye Alborz (Elburz Mountains)

Viranşehir
Nusaybin

Şanlıurfa
Ceylanpınar

Al Jazīrah
Tigris

Euphrates

IRAQ

Jabal Bishrī

Buhayrat ath Tharthār

Kühhä-ye Zagros (Zagros Mountains)

RIA

ELEVATION

4 000 m 13 124 ft	
2000 m 6562 ft	
1000 m 3281 ft	
500 m 1640 ft	
250 m 820 ft	
100 m 328 ft	
Sea Level	Sea Level
	-50 m -164 ft
	-100 m -328 ft
	-250 m -820 ft
	-500 m -1640 ft
	-1000 m -3281 ft
	-2000 m -6562 ft

THE NEAR EAST

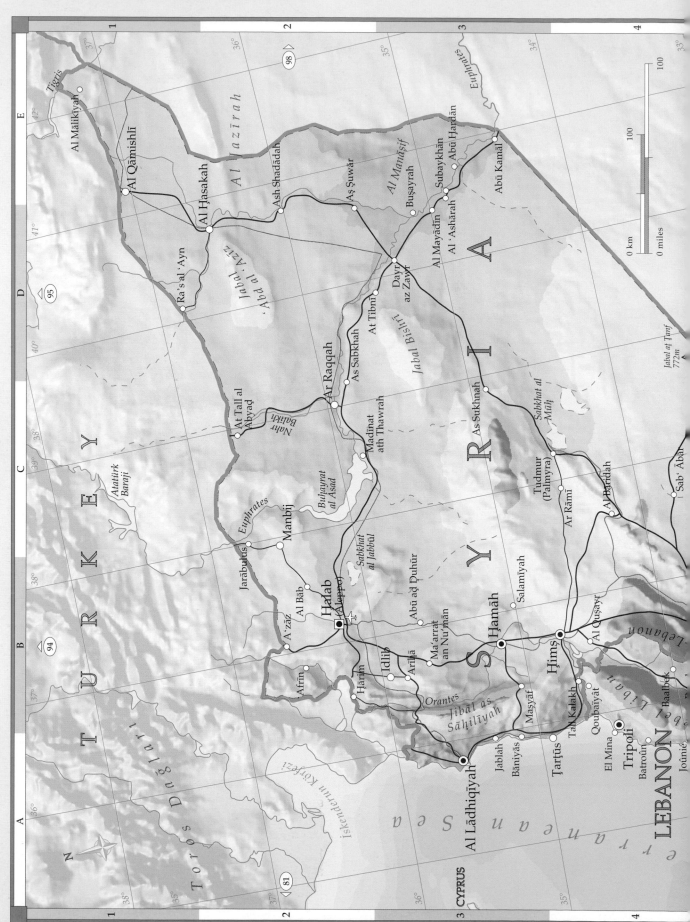

POPULATION

- ■ Over 500,000
- ◉ 100,000 – 500,000
- ○ 50,000 – 100,000
- ○ Less than 50,000
- ● National capital

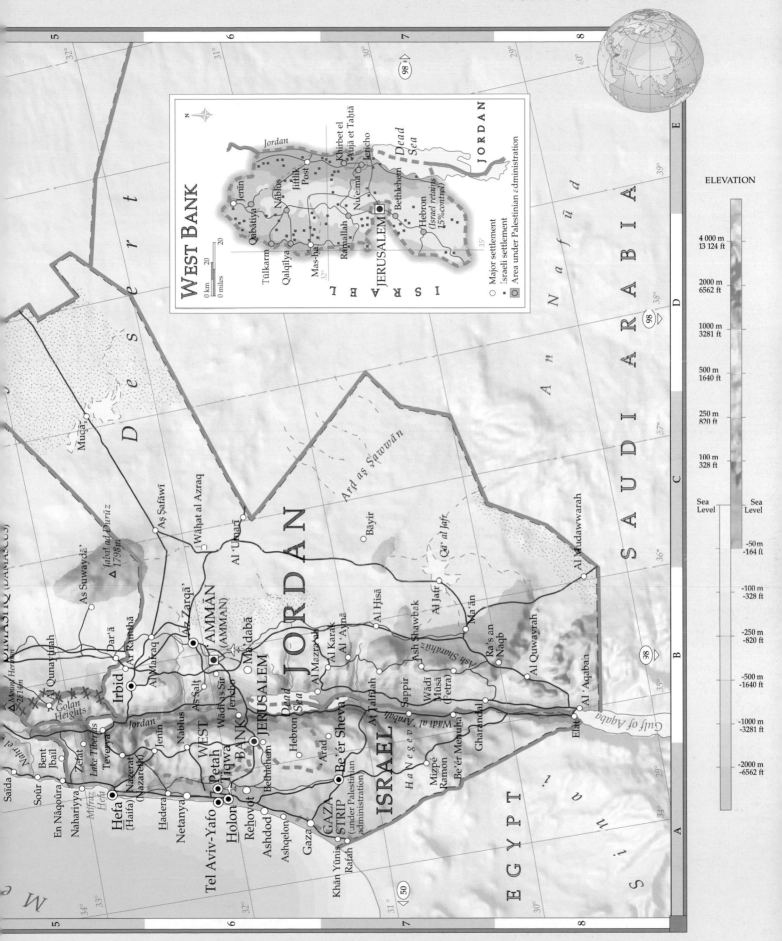

WEST BANK

N

Jordan

Khirbet el
'Auja et Tahtā
Jericho

Dead
Sea

JORDAN

Jenin

Jiftlik
Post

Nablus

Qabātiya

Nu'eima

Bethlehem

JERUSALEM

Hebron
(Israel retains
15% control)

Ramallah

Mas-ha

Tūlkarm

Qalqilya

ISRAEL

○ Major settlement
■ Israeli settlement
◎ Area under Palestinian administration

0 km   20   40
0 miles   20   40

JORDAN

SAUDI ARABIA

An Nafūd

DESERT

Muda'

As Suwaydā'

Jabal ad Durūz
1798m

Aş Şafāwī

Wāhat al Azraq

Al 'Umarī

Ard as Sawwān

Bāyir

Qa' al Jafr

Al Mudawwarah

Al Hisā

Al Jafr

Ma'ān

Al Quwayrah

Mount Hermon
2814m

Al Qunayţirah

Golan
Heights

DIMASHQ (DAMASCUS)

Nahr el...

Ṣaida

Şoūr

Bent
Jbail

En Nāqoūra

Nahariyya

Zefat

Mitraz
Ḥefa

Ḥefa
(Haifa)

Teverya

Lake Tiberias

Nazerat
(Nazareth)

Jordan

Dar'ā

Irbid

Al Mafraq

Az Zarqā'

AMMĀN
(AMMAN)

As Salt

Wādi as Sir

Mādabā

JORDAN

Al Karak

Al 'Aynā

Al Mazra'ah

Ash Shawbak

Ash Shārāhis

Ra's an
Naqb

Al 'Aqabah

Elāt

Gulf of Aqaba

Jenin

Nablus

WEST
BANK

JERUSALEM

Jericho

Dead
Sea

Bethlehem

Hebron

Arad

Be'ér Sheva'

Haderal

Netanya

Tel Aviv-Yafo

Holon

Reḥovot

Ashdod

Ashqelon

Gaza

GAZA
STRIP
(under Palestinian
administration)

Khān Yūnis

Rafah

ISRAEL

Hanegev

Mizpé
Ramon

Be'ér Menuha

Wādī al 'Arabā

At Talfilah

Sappir

Gharandal

Wādī
Mūsā
(Petra)

EGYPT

Sīnai

Petah
Tiqwa

At Ţalfīah

Hebron

Bethlehem

ELEVATION

4 000 m 13 124 ft	
2000 m 6562 ft	
1000 m 3281 ft	
500 m 1640 ft	
250 m 820 ft	
100 m 328 ft	
Sea Level	Sea Level
-50 m -164 ft	
-100 m -328 ft	
-250 m -820 ft	
-500 m -1640 ft	
-1000 m -3281 ft	
-2000 m -6562 ft	

THE MIDDLE EAST

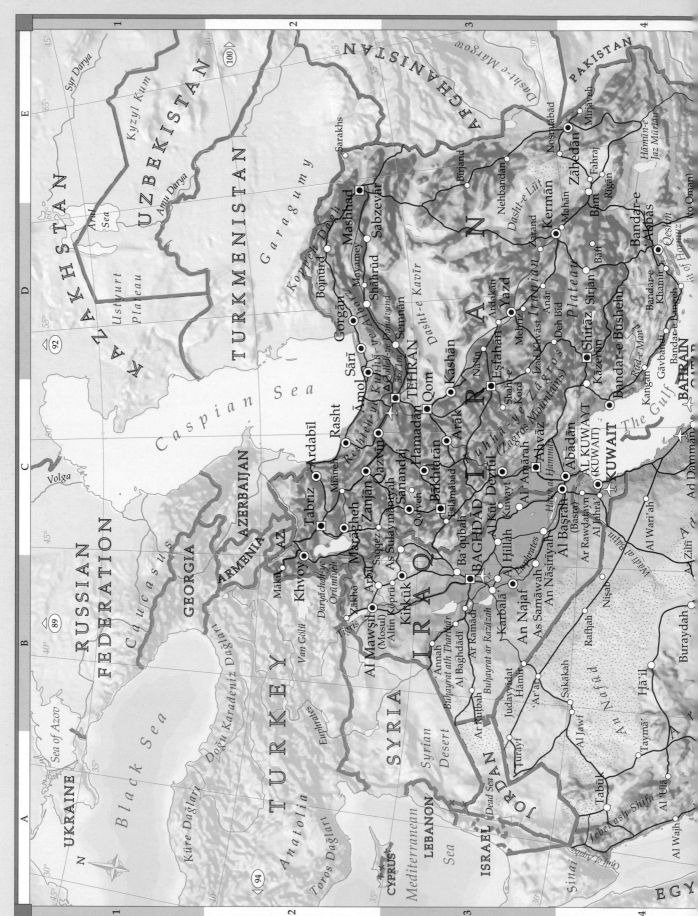

POPULATION

- ⊡ Over 500,000
- ⊙ 100,000 – 500,000
- ○ 50,000 – 100,000
- ○ Less than 50,000
- ● National capital

98

ELEVATION

4000 m
13 124 ft

2000 m
6562 ft

1000 m
3281 ft

500 m
1640 ft

250 m
820 ft

100 m
328 ft

Sea Level

Sea Level

-250 m
-820 ft

-500 m
-1640 ft

-1000 m
-3281 ft

-2000 m
-6562 ft

-3000 m
-9843 ft

-4000 m
-13 124 ft

INDIAN OCEAN

Arabian Sea

OMAN

Ṣūr
Ramlat
Al Waḥībah
Jazīrat Maṣīrah
Khalīj Maṣīrah
Al Chābah
Duqm
Ar Rusṭāq
Aṭ Ṭāʾiyah al Ghāṛbī
Laṭẖb al Chāṛbī

Ṣawqirah

Juzur al Ḥalānīyāt

UNITED ARAB EMIRATES
(ABŪ ẒABĪ)

SAUDI ARABIA

Ar Rubʿ al Khālī
(Empty Quarter)

P e n i n s u l a

Jabal Ṭuwayq
Laylā
(RIYADH)
As Sulayyil

Thamarīt
Ṣalālah

Damqawt

Al Mahrah

Sayḥūt

Suquṭrā
(Socotra)
(to Yemen)

Raas Xaafuun

YEMEN

Sanāw

Waḍīʿah

Tarīm
Sayʾūn
Ḥaḍramawt
Ash Shiḥr
Al Mukallā

Gulf of Aden

SOMALIA

Najrān
Tathlīth
Qalʿat Bīshah
Khamīs Mushayṭ
Saʿdah
Ramlat Dahm
Ramlat as Sabʿatayn
SANʿAʾ
(SANA)

Shuqrah
ʿAdan
(Aden)

Ogaden

Zahlīm
Turabah
Aṭ Ṭāʾif
Wādī Bīshah
Abhā
Ṣabyā
Jīzān
Zabīd
Taʿizz
Bab el Mandeb

Ḥarrat Rahaṭ
Al Bāḥah
Jazāʾir Farasān
Al Hudaydah
(Hodeida)

Al Līth
Makkah
(Mecca)
Jiddah
(Jedda)

DJIBOUTI

Red Sea

Nubian Desert

SUDAN

ERITREA

Danakil Desert

Ethiopian Highlands

Great Rift Valley

ETHIOPIA

99

CENTRAL ASIA

POPULATION

- ■ Over 500,000
- ◉ 100,000 - 500,000
- ○ 50,000 - 100,000
- ○ Less than 50,000
- ● National capital

0 km   200

0 miles   200

E   F   G   H

ELEVATION

KAZAKHSTAN

Ozero Balkhash

Peski Saryesik-Atyrau

Peski Taukum

Peski Moyynkum

Sur Darya

Borohoro Shan

Ili

93

1

4000 m
13 124 ft

BISHKEK
Kara-Balta   Tokmak   Tyup   Dzhergalan
Talas   Kemin   Ozero Issyk-Kul'   Karakol
Leninpol   Balykchy   Kyzyl-Suu
Gora Manas   Kadzhi-Say   Pik Pobedy
4482m   7439m

Kirghiz Range

TOSHKENT (TASHKENT)   Chirchiq   Tash-Kumyr   Kara-Say
Yangiyŭl   Angren   **Namangan**   Naryn   Karakol
Olmaliq   Dzhalal-Abad   Chatyr-Tash
Nurota   Bekobod   Qŭqon   Andijon
Langar   Guliston   Osh
darkŭl   Jizzakh   Khujand   Farghona   Kėk-Art
Jawoiy   Sulyukta
Kattaqŭrghon   Uroteppa   Khaydarkan   Sary-Tash
Samarqand   Zeravshan   Daroot-Korgon
Urgut   Qarokŭl
Kitob   Qarshi

KYRGYZSTAN

Khrebet Moldo-Too

Kokshaal-Tau

104

2

2000 m
6562 ft

1000 m
3281 ft

500 m
1640 ft

XINJIANG UYGUR ZIZHIQU

Taklimakan Shamo

40°

Gissar Range   Surkhob
DUSHANBE   Qullai Kommunizm 7495m
Norak   **TAJIKISTAN**   Qal'aikhum   Ghŭdara
Danghara   Murghob
Kŭlob   Bartang
Moskva   Dzhelandy
Farkhor   Khorugh   Qizilrabot
Dŭsti   Feyzābād
Kunduz   Ishkoshim
Khānābād   Baroghil Pass 3777m
Tāloqān

Denow
Dar'ya   Boysun
Qŭrghonteppa
Termiz   Jarqŭrghon
Balkh   Kholm
Mazār-e Sharif
Pol-e Khomri   Baghlān

C H I N A

(claimed by India)

AKSAI CHIN
(administered by China, claimed by India)

Aksai Chin

3

250 m
820 ft

100 m
328 ft

Sea Level   Sea Level

-10 m
-33 ft

Hindu Kush   Barīkowt
Chārīkār   Mahmūd-e Rāqi
KĀBUL   Asadābād
Maydān Shahr   Mehtarlām
  Jalālābād
Gardēz   Khyber Pass 1080m

Daryā-ye Kuhmard   Kūh-e Bābā

STAN   rūd

Karakoram Range

Indus

DEMCHOK/DÊMQOG
(administered by China, claimed by India)

104

4

-25 m
-82 ft

-50 m
-164 ft

Ghaznī
Khowst

-ye Arghandāb   Zarghūn Shahr
Kalāt

XIZANG ZIZHIQU (Tibet)

(administered by China, claimed by India)

35°

-100 m
-328 ft

-250 m
-820 ft

(A 'line of control' was agreed between India and Pakistan in 1972)

ndahār   Spīn Būldak
Toba Kākar Range

Indus

Ravi

Sulaimān Range

P A K I S T A N

Himalayas

I N D I A

NEPAL

30°

5

-500 m
-1640 ft

112

E   F   G   H

70°   75°   80°

POPULATION

- ◉ Over 500,000
- ◎ 100,000 – 500,000
- ○ 50,000 – 100,000
- ▫ Less than 50,000
- ● National capital

102

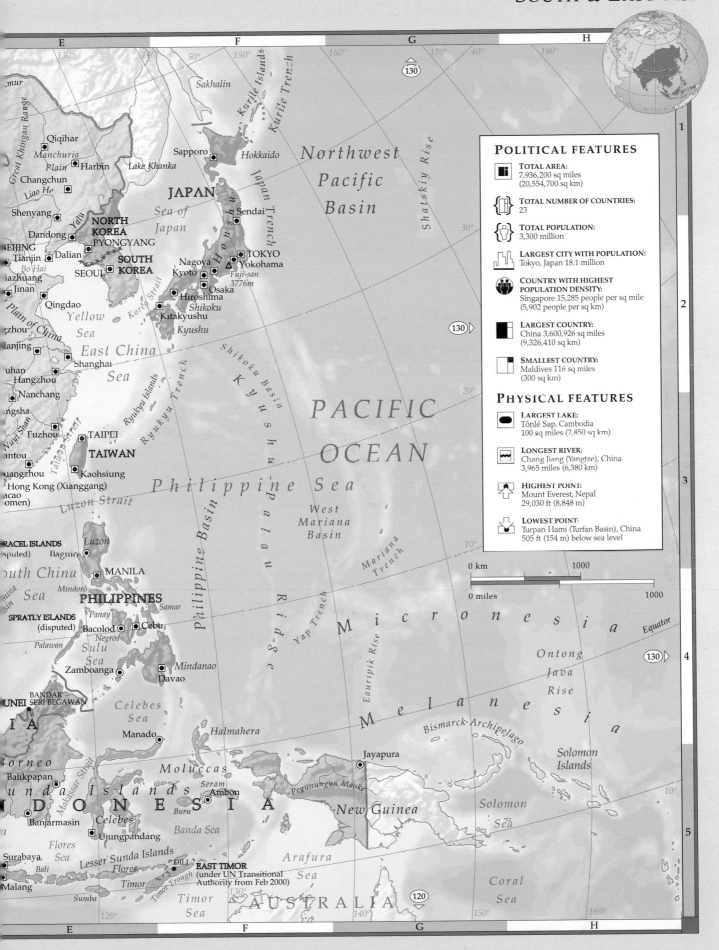

E F G H

130° 140° 50° 150° 160° 170° 40° 180°

130

mur

Qiqihar

Manchuria
Harbin   *Lake Khanka*

Great Khingan Range

Plain

Changchun

Liao He

Shenyang

Sakhalin

Kurile Islands

Kurile Trench

Sapporo   *Hokkaido*

JAPAN

Japan Trench

Northwest Pacific Basin

Shatskiy Rise

1

Yalu

BEIJING
Tianjin
Dalian
Dandong

NORTH KOREA
PYONGYANG

SOUTH KOREA
SEOUL

Bo Hai

Sea of Japan

Sendai

Honshu

□ TOKYO
Yokohama

Nagoya
Kyoto
Osaka

Fuji-san 3776m

30°

130 ▷

2

iazhuang
Jinan
Qingdao

Yellow Sea

Korea Strait

Hiroshima

Kitakyushu

Shikoku

Kyushu

POLITICAL FEATURES

TOTAL AREA:
7,936,200 sq miles
(20,554,700 sq km)

TOTAL NUMBER OF COUNTRIES:
23

TOTAL POPULATION:
3,300 million

LARGEST CITY WITH POPULATION:
Tokyo, Japan 18.1 million

COUNTRY WITH HIGHEST POPULATION DENSITY:
Singapore 15,285 people per sq mile
(5,902 people per sq km)

LARGEST COUNTRY:
China 3,600,926 sq miles
(9,326,410 sq km)

SMALLEST COUNTRY:
Maldives 116 sq miles
(300 sq km)

PHYSICAL FEATURES

LARGEST LAKE:
Tônlé Sap, Cambodia
100 sq miles (2,850 sq km)

LONGEST RIVER:
Chang Jiang (Yangtze), China
3,965 miles (6,380 km)

HIGHEST POINT:
Mount Everest, Nepal
29,030 ft (8,848 m)

LOWEST POINT:
Turpan Hami (Turfan Basin), China
505 ft (154 m) below sea level

zhou
anjing

Plain of China

uhan
Hangzhou
Nanchang

East China Sea

Shikoku Basin

Ryukyu Islands

Ryukyu Trench

K y u s h u

3

Nuyi Shan

ngsha

Fuzhou

TAIPEI

TAIWAN

Kaohsiung

Taiwan Strait

Philippine Sea

Philippine Basin

20°

Guangzhou

Hong Kong (Xianggang)
acao
omen)

Luzon Strait

West Mariana Basin

P a l a u   R i d g e

PACIFIC
OCEAN

0 km   1000

0 miles   1000

RACEL ISLANDS
puted)

Luzon

Baguio

Mariana Trench

10°

uth China
Sea

MANILA

Mindoro

PHILIPPINES

Panay   *Samar*

Yap Trench

M i c r o n e s i a

Equator

130 ▷

4

SPRATLY ISLANDS
(disputed)

Bacolod   Cebu

Negros

Palawan

Sulu Sea

Zamboanga

Mindanao

Davao

Eauripik Rise

Ontong Java Rise

UNEI
BANDAR
SERI BEGAWAN

Celebes Sea

Halmahera

M e l a n e s i a

Bismarck Archipelago

Solomon Islands

IA

Borneo

Manado

Balikpapan

Makassar Strait

Moluccas

Seram
Ambon
Buru

Jayapura

Pegunungan Maoke

New Guinea

Solomon Sea

10°

u n d a   I s l a n d s

N D O N E S I A

Banjarmasin

Celebes

Ujungpandang

Banda Sea

Arafura Sea

5

Flores Sea

Surabaya
Bali

Lesser Sunda Islands
Flores

DILI

EAST TIMOR
(under UN Transitional
Authority from Feb 2000)

Timor

Coral Sea

Malang

Sumba

Timor Trough

Timor Sea

120°

AUSTRALIA

130°

140°

120

150°

160°

E F G H

WESTERN CHINA & MONGOLIA

POPULATION

- ◉ Over 500,000
- ◉ 100,000 - 500,000
- ○ 50,000 - 100,000
- ○ Less than 50,000
- ● National capital
- ● Internal administrative capital

RUSS. FED.

zero Baykal

R A T I O N

Shilka

Ergun
Zuoqi   Jagdaqi

HEILONGJIANG

Lake
Khanka

Onon

Hailar
Manzhouli

Sühbaatar

Selenga

Darhan

Onon Gol   Choybalsan

Hulun
Nur

Da Hinggan Ling

JILIN

Erdenet

an

ULAANBAATAR
(ULAN BATOR)

Menengiyn
Tal

Hulingol

NEI MONGOL ZIZHIQU

Tongliao

Dzuunmod

Öndörhaan

Kerulen

Baruun-Urt

Liao He

O L I A

Xilinhot

LIAONING

Saynshand

Erenhot

Chifeng

NORTH
KOREA

Sea
of
Japan

Dalandzadgad

(Inner Mongolia)

Jining

Liaodong Wan

bi

n Nuruu

Lang Shan

Hohhot

BEIJING

Korea
Bay

SOUTH
KOREA

u Shan

Baotou

TIANJIN

Bo Hai

Huang He

Tengger
Shamo

Wuhai

Mu Us
Shamo

HEBEI

Yellow
Sea

JAPAN

NINGXIA
HUIZU
ZIZHIQU

Great Wall of China

SHANXI

SHANDONG

ning

N   A

SHAANXI

Huang He (Yellow River)

JIANGSU

GANSU

Han Shui

HENAN

ANHUI

SHANGHAI

East

SICHUAN

Chang Jiang (Yangtze)

HUBEI

ZHEJIANG

China

CHONGQING

JIANGXI

Sea

Nansei-shotō (to Japan)

HUNAN

YUNNAN

FUJIAN

Tropic of Cancer

GUIZHOU

TAIWAN

ELEVATION

4 000 m
13 124 ft

2000 m
6562 ft

1000 m
3281 ft

500 m
1640 ft

250 m
820 ft

100 m
328 ft

Sea
Level

Sea
Level

-50 m
-164 ft

-100 m
-328 ft

250 m
-820 ft

-500 m
-1640 ft

-1000 m
-3281 ft

-2000 m
-6562 ft

THE WORLD ATLAS

ELEVATION

4 000 m 13 124 ft	
2000 m 6562 ft	
1000 m 3281 ft	
500 m 1640 ft	
250 m 820 ft	
100 m 328 ft	
Sea Level	Sea Level
	-50 m -164 ft
-100 m -328 ft	
-250 m -820 ft	
-500 m -1640 ft	
-1000 m -3281 ft	
-2000 m -6562 ft	

East China Sea

Okinawa

Nansei-shoto (part of Japan)

Tropic of Cancer

PACIFIC OCEAN

TAIWAN

TAIPEI
Chilung
Taichung
Chiai
T'ainan
Kaohsiung

(China and Taiwan claim all of each other's territory)

Taiwan Strait

PHILIPPINES

Luzon Strait

SPRATLY ISLANDS
(disputed by China, Malaysia, Philippines, Taiwan and Vietnam)

Flat Island
Nanshan Island
Thitu Island
Loaita Island
Namyit Island
Len Dao
Spratly Island

South China Sea

PARACEL ISLANDS
(disputed by China, Taiwan and Vietnam)

Amphitrite Group
Crescent Group
Triton Island

Shanghai
Suzhou
Wuxi
Jiaxing
Ningbo
Hangzhou
Wenzhou
Jinhua
Shangrao
Fuzhou
Quanzhou
Yong'an
Xiamen
Shantou
Hong Kong (Xianggang)
Macao (Aomen)
Maoming
Zhanjiang
Haikou
Hainan Dao
HAINAN
Xuwen
Danzhou
Dongfang

Gulf of Tongking

VIETNAM

LAOS

THAILAND

CAMBODIA

Gulf of Thailand

Red River

Mekong

MYANMAR (BURMA)

Tropic of Cancer

Salween

INDIA

XIZANG ZIZHIQU (Tibet)

CHINA

Hengduan Shan

Jinsha Jiang

YUNNAN

Dali
Baoshan
Jinghong
Wuliang Shan
Kunming
Gejiu
Anshun
Guiyang
GUIZHOU
Zunyi
CHONGQING
Chongqing
Neijiang
Zigong
Leshan
Ya'an
Chengdu
Mianyang
Guangyuan
Sichuan Pendi
SICHUAN
Wanxian
Yichang
HUBEI
Xinyang
Hefei
ANHUI
Wuhu
Anqing
Huangshi
Jiujiang
Nanchang
JIANGXI
Lichuan
Jingdezhen
ZHEJIANG
Nanjing
Changsha
HUNAN
Yueyang
Dongting Hu
Xiangtan
Loudi
Hengyang
Shaoguan
GUANGDONG
Guangzhou
Dongguan
Jiangmen
Zhaoqing
Chenzhou
Ganzhou
Longyan
Zhangzhou
Liuzhou
GUANGXI ZHUANGZU ZIZHIQU
Nanning
Yulin
Beihai
Qinzhou
Suixi
Guilin
Quanzhou
Lengshuitan
Huaihua
Salween

Dongting Hu

Mekong

JAPAN

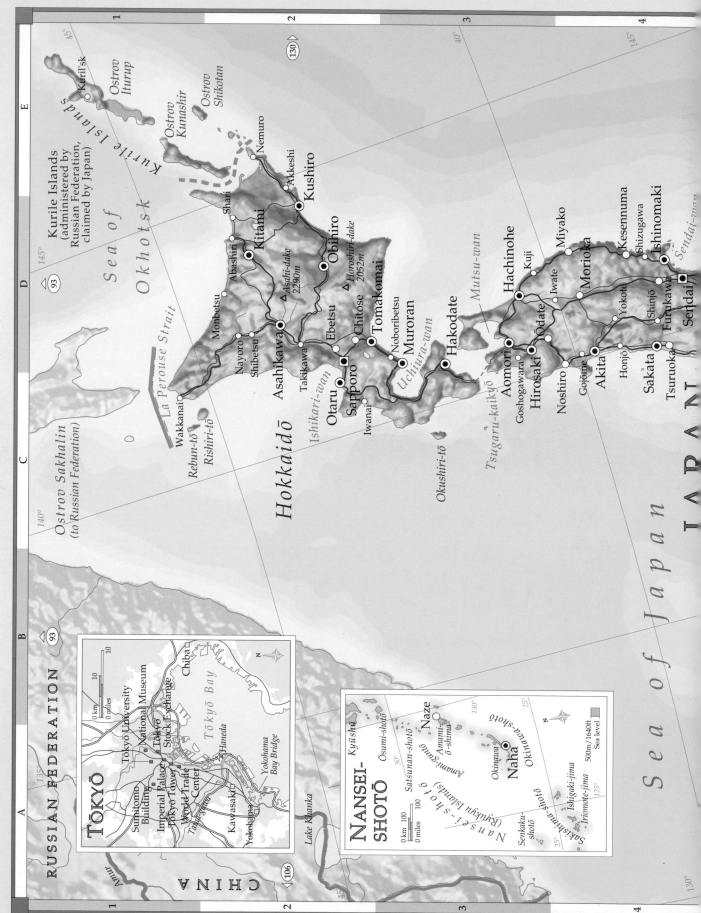

Kurile Islands (administered by Russian Federation, claimed by Japan)

Sea of Okhotsk

Ostrov Sakhalin (to Russian Federation)

Kuril'sk
Ostrov Iturup
Ostrov Kunashir
Ostrov Shikotan
Nemuro
Akkeshi
Shari
Kushiro
Kitami
Abashiri
Obihiro
Asahi-dake 2290m
Horoshiri-dake 2052m
Monbetsu
Tomakomai
Nayoro
Shibetsu
Asahikawa
Chitose
Ebetsu
Noboribetsu
Muroran
Hakodate
Takikawa
Otaru
Sapporo
Iwanai
Uchiura-wan
Wakkanai
Rebun-tō
Rishiri-tō
Ishikari-wan
Okushiri-tō
Tsugaru-kaikyō
La Perouse Strait

Hokkaidō

Mutsu-wan

Hachinohe
Kuji
Kesennuma
Miyako
Shizugawa
Ishinomaki
Morioka
Iwate
Yokota
Shinjō
Furukawa
Sendai
Odate
Hirosaki
Aomori
Goshogawara
Noshiro
Gojōme
Akita
Honjō
Sakata
Tsuruoka
Sendai-wan

JAPAN

Sea of Japan

CHINA

RUSSIAN FEDERATION

Amur
Lake Khanka

TŌKYŌ

Chiba
Tōkyō University
National Museum
Tōkyō
Stock Exchange
Sumitomo Building
Imperial Palace
Tōkyō Tower
World Trade Center
Yokohama
Bay Bridge
Kawasaki
Yokohama
Haneda
Tōkyō Bay

NANSEI-SHOTŌ

Kyūshū
Naze
Amami-ō-shima
Ōsumi-shotō
Satsunan-shotō
Amami-guntō
Okinawa
Naha
Okinawa-shotō
Nansei-shotō (Ryūkyū Islands)
Senkaku-shotō
Ishigaki-jima
Iriomote-jima
Sakishima-shotō

500m/1640ft
Sea level

Honshu

Iwaki
Hitachi
Utsunomiya
Mito
Ōyama
Chōshi
Kawagoe
Chiba
Kasumiga-ura
Yokohama
Bōsō-hantō

Mikuni-sanmyaku
Kawasaki
TŌKYŌ
Maebashi
Izu-hantō
Sagami-nada
Ō-shima
Nii-jima
Hachijō-jima

Takaoka
Nagano
Toyama
Matsumoto
Kōfu
Fujisan △ 3776 m
Fuji
Shizuoka
Toyota
Hamamatsu
Suruga-wan
Miyake-jima
Mikura-jima

Nagaoka
Jōetsu
Shinano-gawa
Itoigawa
Kanazawa
Komatsu
Fukui
Tsuruga
Hida-sammyaku
Gifu
Nakatsugawa
Ogaki
Nagoya
Okazaki
Tsu
Ise
Ise-wan
Owase
Owase
Shingū
Izu-shotō

Toyama-wan
Wakasa-wan
Biwa-ko
Kyōto
Ōtsu
Nara
Ōsaka
Wakayama
Gobō
Tanabe

Kyōto
Kōbe
Himeji
Akashi
Harima-nada
Kii-suidō
Shikoku

PACIFIC OCEAN

Tottori
Yonago
Matsue
Chūgoku-sanchi
Okayama
Kurashiki
Kure
Tokushima
Komatsujima
Miyama
Matsuyama
Kōchi
Tosa-wan
Nakamura
Sukumo

Oki-shotō
Dōgo
Dōzen
Liancourt Rocks (claimed by Japan & South Korea)

Gōtsu
Hamada
Masuda
Hiroshima
Iwakuni
Hōfu
Ube
Ōita
Iyo-nada
Bungo-suidō
Nobeoka
Kyūshū
Miyazaki
Miyakonojō
Shibushi-wan
Tanega-shima
Yaku-shima

Nagato
Yamaguchi
Shimonoseki
Kitakyūshū
Tsushima
Iki
Fukuoka
Kurume
Ōmuta
Kumamoto
Katsushiro
Sendai
Kagoshima
Kagoshima-wan
Osumi-shotō

N

SOUTH KOREA

Korea Strait
Kō-saki
Tsushima
Sasebo
Nagasaki
Amakusa-nada
Gotō-rettō
Koshikijima-rettō

East China Sea

⟨106⟩

ELEVATION

4000 m	13 124 ft
2000 m	6562 ft
1000 m	3281 ft
500 m	1640 ft
250 m	820 ft
100 m	328 ft
Sea Level	Sea Level
-250 m	-820 ft
-500 m	-1640 ft
-1000 m	-3281 ft
-2000 m	-6562 ft
-3000 m	-9843 ft
-4000 m	-13 124 ft

200
200
0 km
0 miles

SOUTH INDIA & SRI LANKA

THE WORLD ATLAS

Kalyān
Mumbai (Bombay)
Pune · Ahmadnagar · Nānded · Jagdalpur
Bārāmati · Nizāmābād · Karīmnagar
Solāpur · Vizianagaram
Sāngli · Secunderābād · Visākhapa
Kolhāpur · Gulbarga · Hyderābād · Rajahmu
Belgaum · Rāichūr · Kākin
Panaji · Gadag · Kurnool · Vijayawāda
Hubli · Nandyāl · Machilīpatn
Dāvangere · Tādpatri · Chīrāla
Shimoga · Anantapur · Ongole
Bhadrāvati · Kāvali
Udupi · Tumkūr · Nellore
Mangalore · Bangalore · Cuddapah
Kāsargod · Mandya · Vellore · Chennai (Madras)
Cannanore · Krishnagiri · Kānchīpuram
Mysore · Tiruppattūr · Pondicherry
Calicut · Erode · Salem · Neyveli
Coimbatore · Tamil Nādu
Trichūr · Tiruchchirāppalli
Ernākulam · Dindigul · Madurai
Cochin · Jaffna
Alleppey · Rājapālaiyam · SRI LANKA
Quilon · Mannar · Vavuniya · Trincomalee
Trivandrum · Tuticorin · Puttalam · Anurādhapura
Nāgercoil · Gulf of Mannar · Matale · Batticaloa
Negombo · Kandy
COLOMBO · Sri Jayawardanapu
Kalutara · Ratnapura
Galle
Matara

Arabian Sea

Amīndīvi Islands

Lakshadweep (Laccadive Islands) (to India)
Kavaratti Island
Kalpeni Island
Nine Degree Channel
Minicoy Island
Eight Degree Channel

MALDIVES

Ihavandippolhu Atoll
Faadhippolhu Atoll
Horsburgh Atoll
Male' Atoll
Ari Atoll · MALE'
Felidhu Atoll
Mulaku Atoll
Kolhumadulu Atoll
Hadhdhunmathi Atoll
North Huvadhu Atoll
South Huvadhu Atoll
Equator
Gan
Addu Atoll

Malabār Coast
Tungabhadra Reservoir
Godāvari
Krishna
Coromandel Coast
Palk Strait

INDIAN

POPULATION

- ◉ Over 500,000
- ◉ 100,000 – 500,000
- ○ 50,000 – 100,000
- ∘ Less than 50,000
- ● National capital

hmapur

Bay

of Bengal

MYANMAR
(BURMA)

THAILAND

Mouths of the Irrawaddy

114

115

North Andaman

Andaman Islands
(to India)

Middle Andaman

South Andaman

Port Blair

Andaman

Little Andaman

Sea

Mergui Archipelago

Isthmus
of Kra

Car Nicobar

Katchall Island

Nicobar Islands
(to India)

Little Nicobar

Great Nicobar

Indira Point

Strait of Malacca

Sumatera

INDONESIA

116

*Pulau
Simeulue*

Pulau Nias

O C E A N

Equator

ELEVATION

| 4000 m |
| 13 124 ft |
| 2000 m |
| 6562 ft |
| 1000 m |
| 3281 ft |
| 500 m |
| 1640 ft |
| 250 m |
| 820 ft |
| 100 m |
| 328 ft |
| Sea Level | Sea Level |
| 250 m |
| -820 ft |
| -500 m |
| -1640 ft |
| -1000 m |
| -3281 ft |
| -2000 m |
| -6562 ft |
| -3000 m |
| -9843 ft |
| -4000 m |
| 13 124 ft |

0 km   300

0 miles   300

119

85°   90°   95°

THE WORLD ATLAS

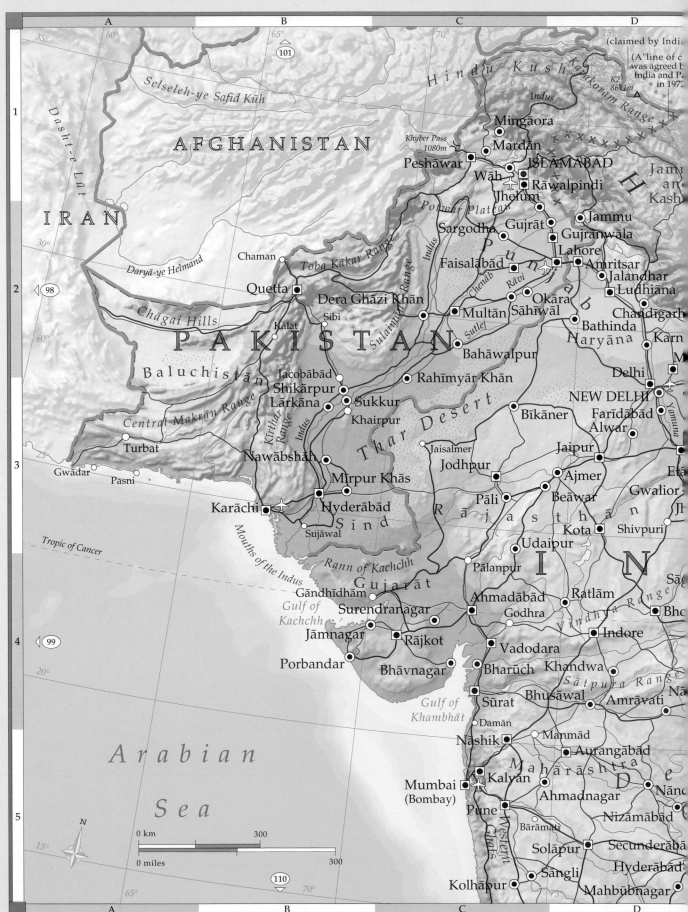

AFGHANISTAN

IRAN

Dasht-e Lūt

Selseleh-ye Safid Kūh

Khyber Pass
1080m

Mingaora
Mardān
Peshāwar
Wāh
ISLĀMĀBĀD
Rāwalpindi
Jhelum

Hindu Kush
Indus
Karakoram Range
K2
8611m

(claimed by Indi
(A "line of c
was agreed b
India and P
in 197:

Jam
an
Kash

Chaman
Toba Kākar Range
Quetta
Dera Ghāzi Khān
Sibi
Kālat

Daryā-ye Helmand

Chāgai Hills

PAKISTAN

Baluchistān

Central Makrān Range

Kīrthar Range

Turbat

Gwādar
Pasni

Jacobābād
Shikārpur
Lārkāna
Sukkur
Khairpur
Indus

Nawābshāh
Mīrpur Khās

Karāchi
Hyderābād
Sujāwal
Sind

Mouths of the Indus

Tropic of Cancer

Potwar Plateau
Sargodha
Faisalābād
Chenab
Rāvi
Multān
Sāhīwal
Okāra
Bahāwalpur
Sutlej

Punjab
Gujrāt
Gujrānwāla
Lahore
Amritsar
Jalandhar
Ludhiāna
Chandīgarh
Jammu

Haryāna
Karn

Rahīmyār Khān

Thar Desert

Bīkāner

Jaisalmer

Jodhpur

Pāli

Rā jasthā n

Delhi
NEW DELHI
Farīdābād
Alwar

Jaipur

Ajmer
Beāwar

Udaipur

Kota

Gwalior
Shivpuri

Et

Jh

Rann of Kachchh

Gujarāt

Gāndhīdhām
Surendranagar
Jāmnagar
Rājkot
Porbandar
Bhāvnagar

Gulf of
Kachchh

Ahmadābād
Godhra

Palanpur

Ratlām

I

N

Vindhya Range

Indore

Vadodara
Bharūch
Khandwa

Bhusāwal
Sūrat
Damān

Satpura Range

Amrāvati
Nā

Sā

Bhc

Gulf of
Khambhāt

Nāshik
Manmād
Aurangābād

Mumbai
(Bombay)
Kalyān
Pune

Ahmadnagar
Nizāmābād

Mahā rāshtra

D

Nanc

Bārāmati

Arabian

Sea

Solāpur
Sangli
Kolhāpur

Western Ghats

Secunderābā
Hyderābad
Mahbūbnagar

POPULATION

● Over
  500,000

◉ 100,000 -
  500,000

○ 50,000 -
  100,000

○ Less than
  50,000

● National
  capital

0 km   300

0 miles   300

N

101

98

99

110

35°
60°
65°
70°
75°

30°

60°

25°

20°

15°

65°
70°
75°

A   B   C   D

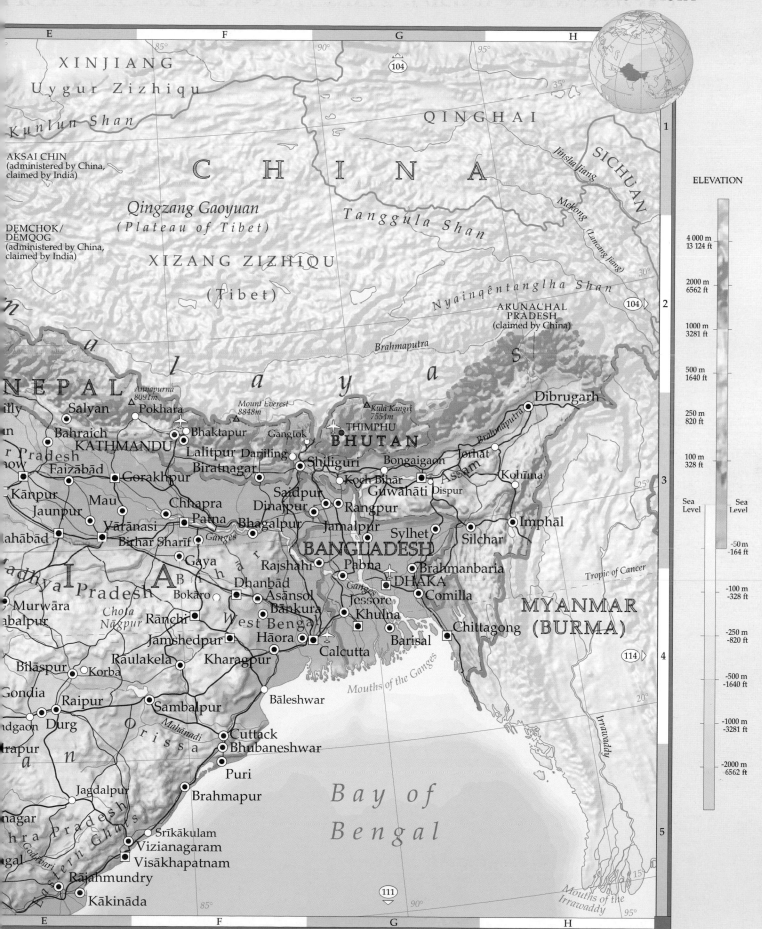

ELEVATION

4 000 m
13 124 ft

2000 m
6562 ft

1000 m
3281 ft

500 m
1640 ft

250 m
820 ft

100 m
328 ft

Sea Level | Sea Level

-50 m
-164 ft

-100 m
-328 ft

-250 m
-820 ft

-500 m
-1640 ft

-1000 m
-3281 ft

-2000 m
6562 ft

MAINLAND SOUTHEAST ASIA

POPULATION

- Over 500,000
- 100,000 – 500,000
- 50,000 – 100,000
- Less than 50,000
- National capital

Quy Nhơn
Play Cu
Tuy Hòa
Cam Ranh
Nha Trang
Đà Lạt
Phan Rang-Tháp Chàm
Phan Thiết
Biên Hòa
Hồ Chí Minh
Vũng Tàu
Mỹ Tho
Trà Vinh
Sóc Trăng
Bạc Liêu
Cà Mau
Rạch Giá
Cần Thơ
Long Xuyên
Châu Đốc
Côn Đảo

Mouths of the Mekong

Kepulauan Natuna
(to Indonesia)

South China Sea

Mali

CAMBODIA
PHNUM PENH
Kâmpóng Chhnăng
Kâmpóng Cham
Svay Riêng
Kâmpóng Spœ
Kâmpôt
Kâmpóng Saôm
Krâcheh
Trâpeăng Vêng
Stœ̆ng Trêng
Phumĭ Sâmraông
Tônlé Srêpŏk
Virôchey
Muang Không
Stœ̆ng Sên
Krâlănh
Mœ̆ng Roĕssei
Pôtĭsăt
Kâmpóng Thum
Kâmpóng Chhnăng
Krŏ̆ăchĕh Ŏdŏ̆ngk
Suông
Mekong
Pakxé
Champasak
Samakhixai
Pinum Đăngrêk
Surin
Buriram
Nakhon Ratchasima
Lop Buri
Sara Buri
KRUNG THEP (BANGKOK)
Samut Prakan
Chon Buri
Pattaya
Rayong
Bêtdâmbâng
Rêăng Kesei
Chanthaburi
Kc Chang
Phumĭ
Ayutthaya
Nakhon Pathom
Ratchaburi
Phetchaburi
Ao Krung Thep
Ban Hua Hin
Chumphon

Gulf of Thailand

Ko Chang

Srinagarind Reservoir

Phraya

MALAYSIA
Malay Peninsula

Tenasserim
Mergui
Mali Kyun
Kadan Kyun
Daung Kyun
Letsŏk-aw Kyun
Lanbi Kyun
Zadetkyi Kyun

Ye
Tavoy

Tenasserim Range

Isthmus of Kra

Rânong
Phang-Nga
Ko Phra Thong
Ko Phuket
Phuket
Ko Lanta
Ko Ta Ru Tao

Laang Suan
Sirat Thani
Sichon
Nakhon Si Thammarat
Pak Phanang
Ko Phangan
Ko Samui
Thung Song
Phatthalung
Thale Luang
Trang
Hat Yai
Yala
Songkhla
Pattani
Narathiwat

Pulau Pinang
Pulau Langkawi

Strait of Malacca

Sumatera (Sumatra)

INDONESIA

Andaman Sea

Mergui Archipelago

North Andaman
Andaman Islands (to India)
Middle Andaman
South Andaman
Little Andaman

Car Nicobar
Katchall Island
Nicobar Islands (to India)
Little Nicobar
Great Nicobar

Pulau Simeulue

INDIAN OCEAN

⟨117⟩
▷116
▷116
⟨111⟩

| 200 |
| 200 |
| 0 km |
| 0 miles |

ELEVATION

| 4 000 m / 13 124 ft |
| 2000 m / 6562 ft |
| 1000 m / 3281 ft |
| 500 m / 1640 ft |
| 250 m / 820 ft |
| 100 m / 328 ft |
| Sea Level — Sea Level |
| 50 m / -164 ft |
| -100 m / -328 ft |
| -250 m / -820 ft |
| -500 m / -1640 ft |
| -1000 m / -3281 ft |
| -2000 m / -6562 ft |

MARITIME SOUTHEAST ASIA

SINGAPORE

0 km 10
0 miles 10

MALAYSIA

Johore Strait

Causeway
Pulau Ubin
Pulau Tekong
Lim Chu Kang
Hougang
Bukit Panjang New Town
Changi
Choa Chu Kang
Bukit Timah 176m
1°20'
Jurong Industrial Estate
Queenstown
City
Bedok New Town
Telok Blangah
Sentosa
Selat Pandan
Pulau Sudong
103°50'
Pulau Pawai
103°40'

Strait of Singapore

Urban areas
Open areas
Nature reserves

MYANMAR (BURMA)

LAOS

VIETNAM

THAILAND

CAMBODIA

Mekong

Gulf of Tongking

Hainan Dao (to China)

PARACEL ISLANDS
(disputed by China, Taiwan and Vietnam)

South China Sea

SPRATLY ISLANDS
(disputed by China, Malaysia, Philippines, Taiwan and Vietnam)

Andaman Sea

Gulf of Thailand

Mouths of the Mekong

Nicobar Islands (to India)

Isthmus of Kra

Bandaaceh
Sigli
George Town
Kota Bharu
Kota Kinabalu
Gunung Kir
Balaba
Butterworth
Pulau Pinang
Kuala Terengganu
BANDAR SERI BEGAWAN
Meulaboh
Langsa
Taiping
Ipoh
Dungun
Cukai
BRUNEI
Miri
Medan
Klang
Kuantan
Kepulauan Natuna
Bintulu
Tebingtinggi
KUALA LUMPUR
Pematangsiantar
Seremban
MALAYSIA
Pulau Simeulue
Melaka
Keluang
Selat Serasan
Sibu
Batang Raja
Sungai Ka
Kepulauan Banyak
Muar
Johor Bahru
Sarawak
Danau Toba
Batu Pahat
SINGAPORE
Kuching
Sri Aman
Sibolga
Singkawang
Pegunungan Muller
Sungai Mahi
Pulau Nias
Pekanbaru
Sidas
Borneo
Equator
Solok
Rengat
Kepulauan Lingga
Pontianak
Sungai Kapuas
Samarind
Padang
Batang Hari
Selat Karimata
Kalimantan
Balikpapan
Pulau Siberut
Sungaipenuh
Jambi
Bangka
Sampit
Amunt
Kandar
Kepulauan Mentawai
Pangkalpinang
Palembang
Kandar
Pulau Belitung
Lahat
Banjarmasin
Bengkulu
Pulau Laut
Kotabumi
Java Sea
Sumatera (Sumatra)
Bandarlampung
Cirebon
Tegal
Serang
JAKARTA
Pekalongan
Pulau Madura
Bogor
Semarang
Selat Sunda
Sukabumi
Kudus
Surabaya
Bandung
Probolinggo
Jember Mat
Tasikmalaya
Malang
Denpa
Jawa (Java)
Cilacap
Kediri
Bali
Pulau Lombok
Magelang
Madiun
Yogyakarta
Surakarta

INDIAN OCEAN

10°

POPULATION

Over 500,000

100,000 - 500,000

50,000 - 100,000

Less than 50,000

National capital

0 km 400
0 miles 400

116

E | F | G | H

120° · *Luzon Strait* · 130° · 140°

Babuyan Island
Babuyan Channel

Philippine

Sea

109

NORTHERN
MARIANA
ISLANDS
(to US)

Tuguegarao
Ilagan

Luzon

Dagupan
Cabanatuan

GUAM
(to US)

ILA · Lucena
ngas · Naga
Legaspi

PHILIPPINES

Mindoro

Calbayog

P A C I F I C

10°

*Sibuyan
Sea* · *Samar*

Roxas City

Yap

Cadiz · Tacloban
*Panay
Island* · *Leyte*

MICRONESIA

Iloilo
Bacolod
City · Cebu

Negros · *Bohol Sea*
Butuan

Babeldaob

Iligan · Cagayan de Oro
Bislig

O C E A N

mboanga · *Mindanao*

*Moro
Gulf* · Davao

P A L A U

Basilan
kan · Lebak
General
Santos

Davao Gulf

Sulu Archipelago

*Kepulauan
Talaud*

Celebes Sea

Equator

Manado · Bitung

Pulau Morotai

*Pulau
Halmahera*

Gorontalo

Molucca Sea

Pulau Waigeo

*Pulau
Biak*

Jayapura

*Gulf of
Tomini*

*Halmahera
Sea*

Sorong

*Pulau
Yapen*

122

*Maluku
(Moluccas)*

Selat Dampier

*Jazirah
Doberai*

*Teluk
Cenderawasih*

Sungai Mamberamo

*Kepulauan
Banggai*

*Sulawesi
(Celebes)*

*Kepulauan
Sula*

Ceram Sea

*Pulau
Misool*

Teluk Berau

Pegunungan Maoke

PAPUA

*Danau
Towuti*

Waflia

Wahai

*Puncak Jaya
5030m* △

**NEW
GUINEA**

N

Tifu

Kendari

*Pulau
Buru*

Ambon

E

*Pulau
Seram*

S

I

A

Irian Jaya

New Guinea

Kolaka

*Pulau
Buton*

*Kepulauan
Kai*

*Kepulauan
Aru*

Watampone
Ujungpandang

Banda Sea

Bulukumba

*Kepulauan
Tanimbar*

Sungai Digul

Tenggara

*Pulau
Wetar*

DILI

Kepulauan Leti

Torres Strait

Flores
Kepulauan Alor

EAST TIMOR
(under UN Transitional
Authority from Feb 2000)

Arafura Sea

10°

Savu Sea

Timor

Nikiniki
Kupang

Timor Sea

126

A U S T R A L I A

120° · 130° · 140°

E | F | G | H

ELEVATION

4000 m / 13 124 ft
2000 m / 6562 ft
1000 m / 3281 ft
500 m / 1640 ft
250 m / 820 ft
100 m / 328 ft
Sea Level / Sea Level
250 m / -820 ft
-500 m / -1640 ft
-1000 m / -3281 ft
-2000 m / -6562 ft
-3000 m / -9843 ft
-4000 m / -13 124 ft

THE INDIAN OCEAN

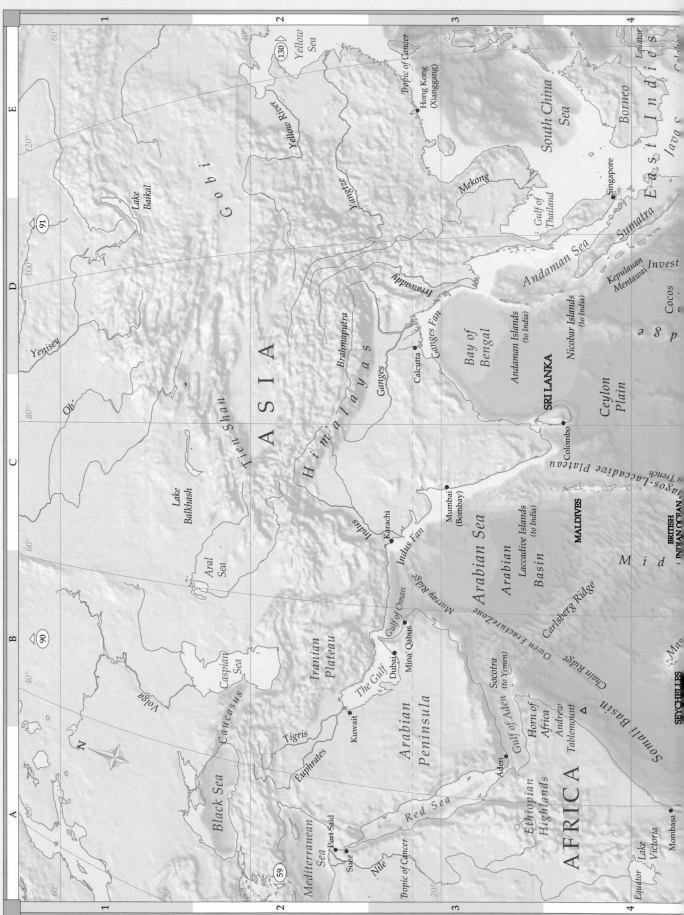

A S I A

Gobi

Lake Baikal

Yenisey

Ob'

Lake Balkhash

Tien Shan

Aral Sea

Caspian Sea

Volga

Black Sea

Caucasus

Mediterranean Sea

Tigris

Euphrates

Port Said

Suez

Nile

Iranian Plateau

The Gulf

Kuwait

Arabian Peninsula

Red Sea

Ethiopian Highlands

AFRICA

Gulf of Aden

Aden

Horn of Africa

Socotra (to Yemen)

Andrew Tablemount

Gulf of Oman

Mina Qabus

Dubai

Murray Ridge

Karachi

Indus

Indus Fan

Mumbai (Bombay)

Arabian Sea

Arabian Basin

Laccadive Islands (to India)

Owen Fracture Zone

Chain Ridge

Carlsberg Ridge

Somali Basin

SEYCHELLES

Equator

Lake Victoria

Mombasa

Himalayas

Brahmaputra

Ganges

Ganges Fan

Calcutta

Bay of Bengal

Andaman Islands (to India)

SRI LANKA

Colombo

Ceylon Plain

Chagos-Laccadive Plateau

Trench

MALDIVES

BRITISH INDIAN OCEAN

Mid

Irrawaddy

Mekong

Yellow River

Yangtze

Yellow Sea

Hong Kong (Xianggang)

Tropic of Cancer

Gulf of Thailand

South China Sea

Andaman Sea

Nicobar Islands (to India)

Singapore

Sumatra

East Indies

Borneo

Java Sea

Kepulauan Mentawai Invest

Cocos

Ridge

Equator

Tropic of Cancer

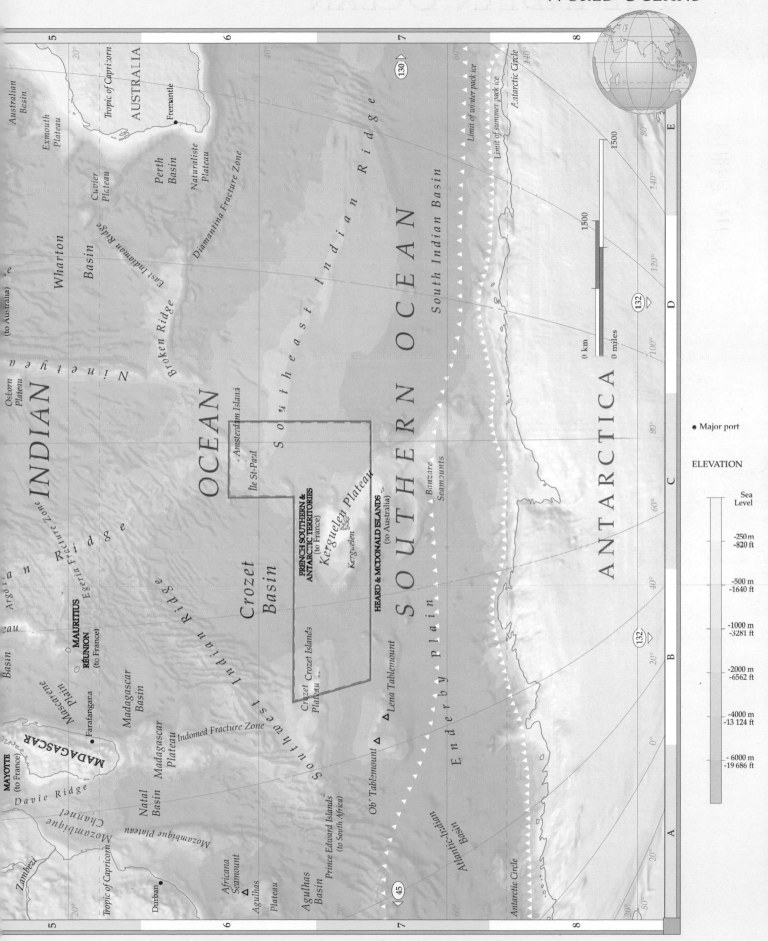

5
6
7
8

20°
40°
60°
80°
140°
120°
100°

Tropic of Capricorn

AUSTRALIA

Fremantle

Australian Basin

Exmouth Plateau

Cuvier Plateau

Perth Basin

Naturaliste Plateau

Diamantina Fracture Zone

Wharton Basin

East Indian Ridge

Broken Ridge

Ninetyeast Ridge

Southeast Indian Ridge

South Indian Basin

Limit of winter pack ice

Limit of summer pack ice

Antarctic Circle

1500

1500

0 km

0 miles

130

132

132

45

INDIAN

OCEAN

SOUTHERN OCEAN

ANTARCTICA

Osborn Plateau

Argana Ridge

Egeria Fracture Zone

Southwest Indian Ridge

Amsterdam Island

Île St-Paul

Banzare Seamounts

Kerguelen Plateau

FRENCH SOUTHERN & ANTARCTIC TERRITORIES
(to France)

Kerguelen

Kerguelen

HEARD & McDONALD ISLANDS
(to Australia)

MAURITIUS

RÉUNION
(to France)

Crozet Basin

Crozet Islands

Crozet Plateau

Lena Tablemount

Ob' Tablemount

Enderby Plain

Prince Edward Islands
(to South Africa)

Indomed Fracture Zone

MAYOTTE
(to France)

MADAGASCAR

Farafangana

Mascarene Plain

Madagascar Basin

Madagascar Plateau

Natal Basin

Davie Ridge

Mozambique Plateau

Mozambique Channel

Zambezi

Tropic of Capricorn

Durban

Africana Seamount

Agulhas Plateau

Agulhas Basin

Atlantic-Indian Basin

Antarctic Circle

20°

40°

60°

80°

0°

20°

40°

60°

80°

20°

● Major port

ELEVATION

Sea Level

-250 m
-820 ft

-500 m
-1640 ft

-1000 m
-3281 ft

-2000 m
-6562 ft

-4000 m
-13 124 ft

- 6000 m
-19 686 ft

5
6
7
8

AUSTRALASIA & OCEANIA

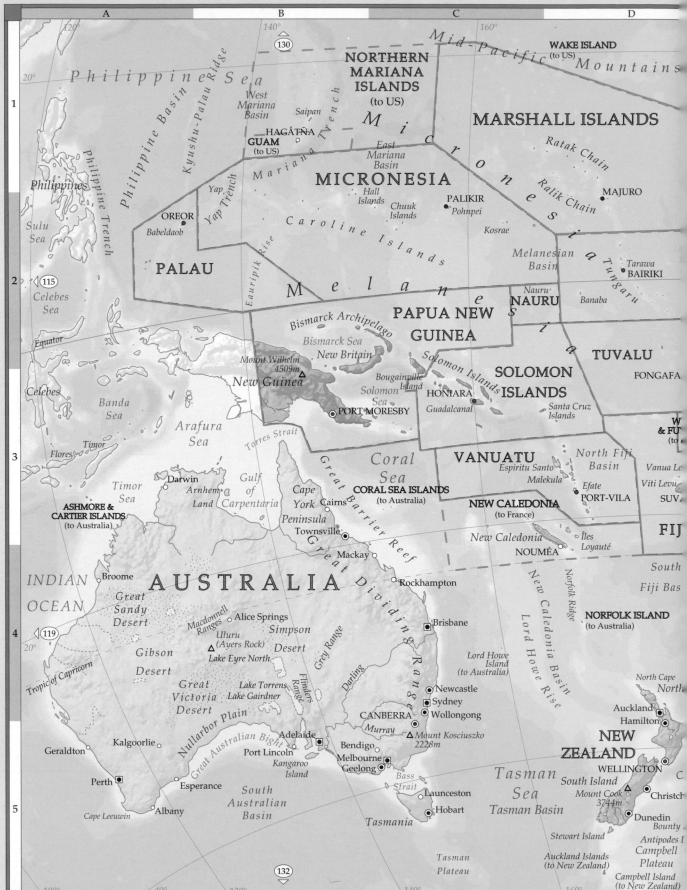

POPULATION

- ◉ Over 500,000
- ◉ 100,000 – 500,000
- ○ 50,000 – 100,000
- ○ Less than 50,000
- ● National capital

WAKE ISLAND (to US)

NORTHERN MARIANA ISLANDS (to US)

MARSHALL ISLANDS

Philippine Sea

West Mariana Basin

Saipan

HAGÅTNA
GUAM (to US)

Ratak Chain

MICRONESIA

Ralik Chain

● MAJURO

Philippine Basin

Kyushu-Palau Ridge

Mariana Trench

Mid-Pacific Mountains

East Mariana Basin

Hall Islands

Chuuk Islands

PALIKIR
● *Pohnpei*

Philippine Trench

Yap

OREOR
Babeldaob

Yap Trench

Caroline Islands

Kosrae

Melanesian Basin

Tarawa
BAIRIKI

Tungaru

Philippines

PALAU

Eauripik Rise

Nauru ●
NAURU

Banaba

Sulu Sea

Celebes Sea

Melanesia

PAPUA NEW GUINEA

TUVALU
FONGAFA

Equator

Bismarck Archipelago

Bismarck Sea
New Britain

Solomon Islands

SOLOMON ISLANDS

W & FU
(to

Celebes

Banda Sea

Mount Wilhelm 4509m △
New Guinea

Bougainville Island

HONIARA ●

Santa Cruz Islands

North Fiji Basin

Espíritu Santo
Malekula

Vanua L

Flores

Timor

Arafura Sea

Solomon Sea

Guadalcanal

VANUATU

Efate
● PORT-VILA

Viti Levu
SUV

Timor Sea

Torres Strait

PORT MORESBY ●

Coral Sea

CORAL SEA ISLANDS (to Australia)

NEW CALEDONIA (to France)

FIJ

Darwin ○

Arnhem Land

Gulf of Carpentaria

Cape York

Great Barrier Reef

New Caledonia

NOUMÉA ●

Îles Loyauté

ASHMORE & CARTIER ISLANDS (to Australia)

Peninsula

Cairns ○

Townsville ○

Great Dividing Range

Mackay ○

New Caledonia Ridge

Norfolk Ridge

South Fiji Bas

INDIAN OCEAN

Broome ○

Great Sandy Desert

AUSTRALIA

Rockhampton ○

Lord Howe Basin

Lord Howe Rise

Macdonnell Ranges
Alice Springs ○

Simpson Desert

Brisbane ■

Lord Howe Island (to Australia)

NORFOLK ISLAND (to Australia)

North Cape
North

Gibson Desert

Uluru (Ayers Rock) △
Lake Eyre North

Grey Range

Tropic of Capricorn

Great Victoria Desert

Lake Torrens
Lake Gairdner

Flinders Range

Darling

Newcastle ○
Sydney ◉
Wollongong ○

Auckland ■
Hamilton ○

Kalgoorlie ○

Nullarbor Plain

Adelaide ■

Geraldton ○

Great Australian Bight

Port Lincoln ○
Kangaroo Island

Bendigo ○
Melbourne ■
Geelong ○

CANBERRA ◉

Murray

△ Mount Kosciuszko 2228m

NEW ZEALAND

WELLINGTON ●

Perth ■

Esperance ○

South Australian Basin

Bass Strait

Launceston ○

Hobart ○

Tasman Sea

Tasman Basin

South Island

Mount Cook 3744m △

Christch

Albany ○
Cape Leeuwin

Tasmania

Tasman Plateau

Stewart Island

Auckland Islands (to New Zealand)

Dunedin ○
Bounty

Antipodes I
Campbell Plateau

Campbell Island (to New Zealand)

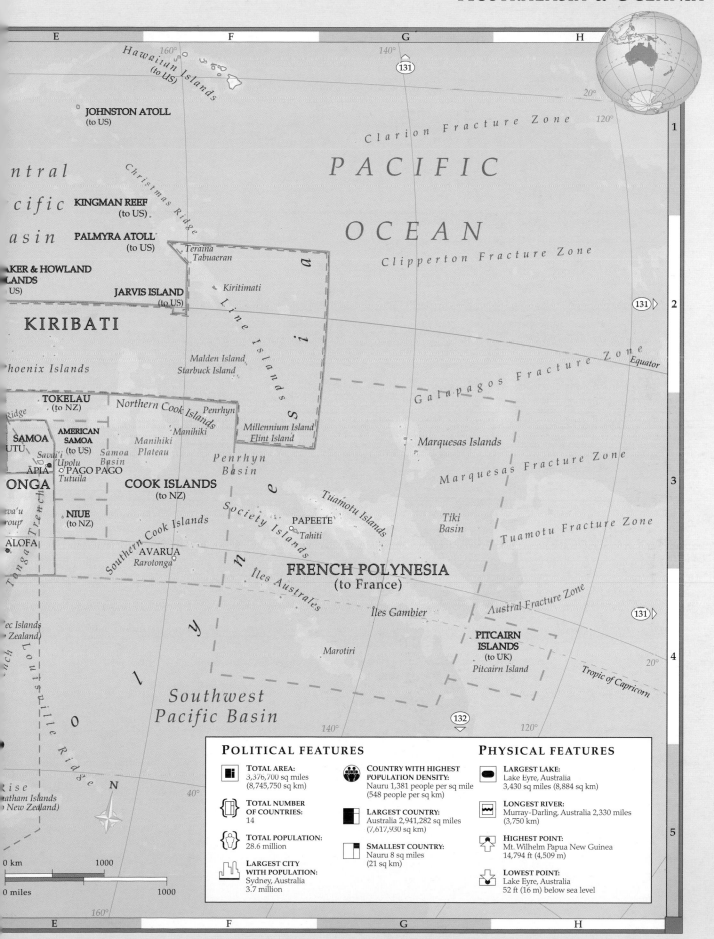

E   F   G   H

160°   140°

Hawaiian Islands
(to US)

° JOHNSTON ATOLL
(to US)

20°

120°

131

1

Clarion Fracture Zone

PACIFIC

ntral

Christmas Ridge

cific

KINGMAN REEF
(to US)

PALMYRA ATOLL
(to US)

Teraina
Tabuaeran

OCEAN

Clipperton Fracture Zone

asin

AKER & HOWLAND
LANDS
US)

Kiritimati

JARVIS ISLAND
(to US)

131

2

KIRIBATI

Line Islands

a

b

i

r

i

K

Galapagos Fracture Zone
Equator

hoenix Islands

Malden Island
Starbuck Island

TOKELAU
(to NZ)

Northern Cook Islands

Penrhyn

Marquesas Islands

Ridge

SAMOA
UTU

AMERICAN
SAMOA
(to US)

Manihiki

Manihiki
Plateau

Millennium Island
Flint Island

Suvai'i
Upolu ° PAGO PAGO
Tuitula

APIA

Samoa
Basin

Penrhyn
Basin

Marquesas Fracture Zone

Tiki
Basin

ONGA

COOK ISLANDS
(to NZ)

Society Islands

Tuamotu Islands

Tuamotu Fracture Zone

va'u
roup

NIUE
(to NZ)

Southern Cook Islands

PAPEETE
° *Tahiti*

e

ALOFA

AVARUA
Rarotonga

FRENCH POLYNESIA
(to France)

Îles Australes

n

y

Îles Gambier

Austral Fracture Zone

131

ec Islands
Zealand)

Marotiri

PITCAIRN
ISLANDS
(to UK)
Pitcairn Island

Tropic of Capricorn

20°

4

Southwest
Pacific Basin

l

o

Louisville Ridge

Rise
hatham Islands
New Zealand)

N

40°

132

140°

120°

5

0 km   1000

0 miles   1000

E   F   G   H

THE SOUTHWEST PACIFIC

POPULATION

- Over 500,000
- 100,000 – 500,000
- 50,000 – 100,000
- Less than 50,000
- National capital

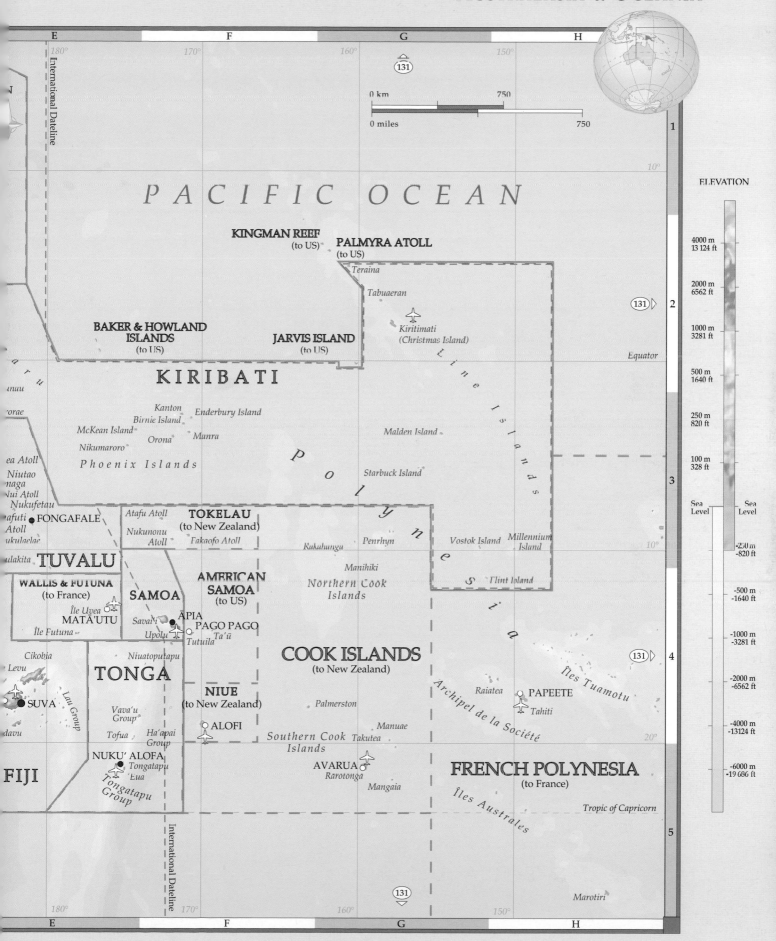

E · 180° · F · 170° · G · 160° · H · 150°

131

0 km — 750
0 miles — 750

1

10°

ELEVATION

PACIFIC OCEAN

4000 m
13 124 ft

KINGMAN REEF
(to US)

PALMYRA ATOLL
(to US)

2000 m
6562 ft

Teraina

Tabuaeran

131

2

1000 m
3281 ft

BAKER & HOWLAND ISLANDS
(to US)

JARVIS ISLAND
(to US)

Kiritimati
(Christmas Island)

500 m
1640 ft

Equator

KIRIBATI

Kanton

Enderbury Island

250 m
820 ft

Birnie Island

McKean Island

Malden Island

Orona

Munra

100 m
328 ft

Nikumaroro

Phoenix Islands

Starbuck Island

3

rae

P

Line Islands

Sea Level

Sea Level

Niutao
naga

o l

Nui Atoll
Nukufetau

y

Vostok Island

Millennium Island

-250 m
-820 ft

nafuti ● **FONGAFALE**

Atafu Atoll

TOKELAU
(to New Zealand)

n

Penrhyn

10°

ukulaelae

Nukunonu Atoll

e

Rakahanga

Atoll

Takaofo Atoll

Flint Island

-500 m
-1640 ft

ulakita

TUVALU

Manihiki

s

AMERICAN SAMOA
(to US)

Northern Cook Islands

i

WALLIS & FUTUNA
(to France)

SAMOA

-1000 m
-3281 ft

Île Uvea
MATĀ'UTU

Savai'i

ĀPIA
PAGO PAGO

a

Île Futuna

Upolu

Ta'ū
Tutuila

Cikobia

Niuatoputapu

COOK ISLANDS
(to New Zealand)

Raiatea

Îles Tuamotu

131

4

Levu

TONGA

NIUE
(to New Zealand)

PAPEETE

Tahiti

-2000 m
-6562 ft

● **SUVA**

Lau Group

Vava'u Group

Palmerston

Archipel de la Société

Tofua

○ **ALOFI**

Manuae

-4000 m
-13124 ft

davu

Ha'apai Group

Southern Cook Takutea
Islands

20°

FIJI

NUKU'ALOFA

Tongatapu
'Eua

AVARUA
Rarotonga

FRENCH POLYNESIA
(to France)

-6000 m
-19 686 ft

Tongatapu Group

Mangaia

Îles Australes

Tropic of Capricorn

5

International Dateline

131

Marotiri

E · 180° · F · 170° · G · 160° · H · 150°

WESTERN AUSTRALIA

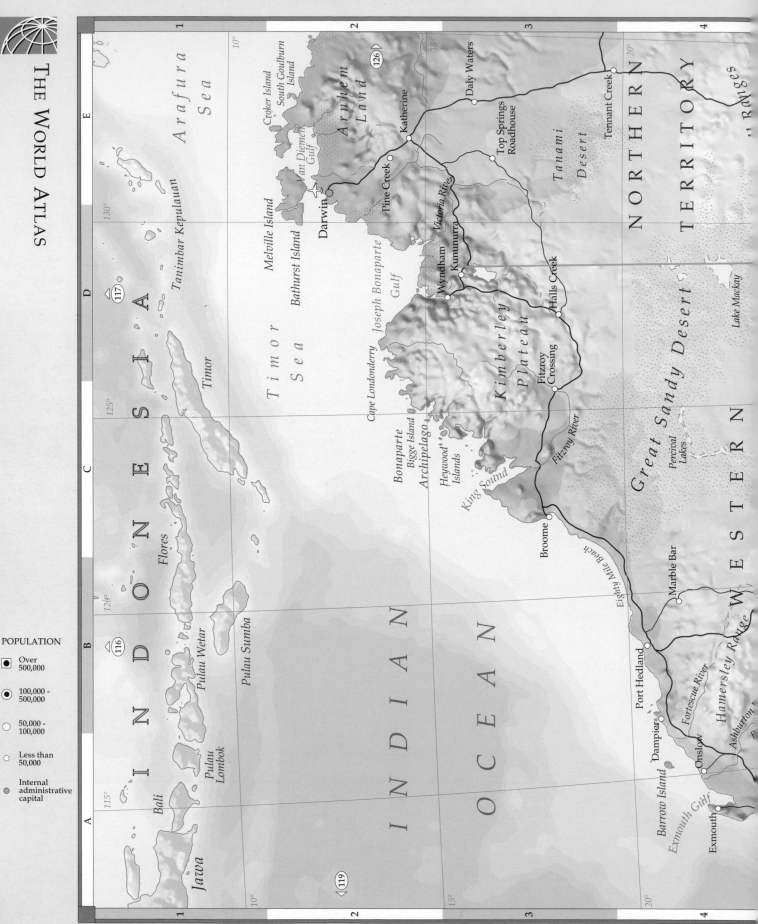

POPULATION

- Over 500,000
- 100,000 - 500,000
- 50,000 - 100,000
- Less than 50,000
- Internal administrative capital

Arafura Sea

INDONESIA

Croker Island
South Goulburn Island

Tanimbar Kepulauan

Melville Island

Bathurst Island

Van Diemen Gulf

Arnhem Land

Katherine

Daly Waters

Top Springs Roadhouse

Tennant Creek

NORTHERN TERRITORY

Tanami Desert

Timor

Timor Sea

Darwin

Pine Creek

Victoria River

Kununurra

Wyndham

Cape Londonderry

Joseph Bonaparte Gulf

Kimberley Plateau

Halls Creek

Lake Mackay

Bonaparte Archipelago
Bigge Island

Heywood Islands

Fitzroy Crossing

Fitzroy River

Great Sandy Desert

Percival Lakes

King Sound

Broome

Eighty Mile Beach

WESTERN

INDIAN OCEAN

Flores

Pulau Sumba

Pulau Wetar

Pulau Lombok

Bali

Jawa

Marble Bar

Port Hedland

Hamersley Range

Barrow Island

Dampier

Onslow

Fortescue River

Ashburton

Exmouth Gulf

Exmouth

AUSTRALIA

SOUTH AUSTRALIA

Musgrave Ranges

Uluru (Ayers Rock)
862m

Great Victoria Desert

Nullarbor Plain

Coober Pedy

Tarcoola

Lake Everard

Penong

Lake Gairdner

Ceduna

Elliston

Port Lincoln

Eucla

Reid

Great Australian Bight

AUSTRALIA

WESTERN AUSTRALIA

Lake Carnegie

Lake Wells

Robinson Range

Lake Carey

Lake Rebecca

Lake Barlee

Lake Moore

Lake Cowan

Zanthus

Balladonia

Norseman

Esperance

Kalgoorlie

Coolgardie

Southern Cross

Merredin

Meekatharra

Mount Magnet

Murchison River

Moora

Gingin

Northam

Brookton

Narrogin

Wagin

Katanning

Collie

Manjimup

Perth

Fremantle

Rockingham

Mandurah

Bunbury

Busselton

Augusta

Albany

Geraldton

Kalbarri

Denham

Shark Bay

Dorre Island

Dirk Hartog Island

INDIAN OCEAN

N

ELEVATION

4000 m
13 124 ft

2000 m
6562 ft

1000 m
3281 ft

500 m
1640 ft

250 m
820 ft

100 m
328 ft

Sea Level

Sea Level

-250 m
-820 ft

-500 m
-1640 ft

-1000 m
-3281 ft

-2000 m
-6562 ft

-3000 m
-9843 ft

-4000 m
-13 124 ft

0 km

0 miles

400

400

Eastern Australia

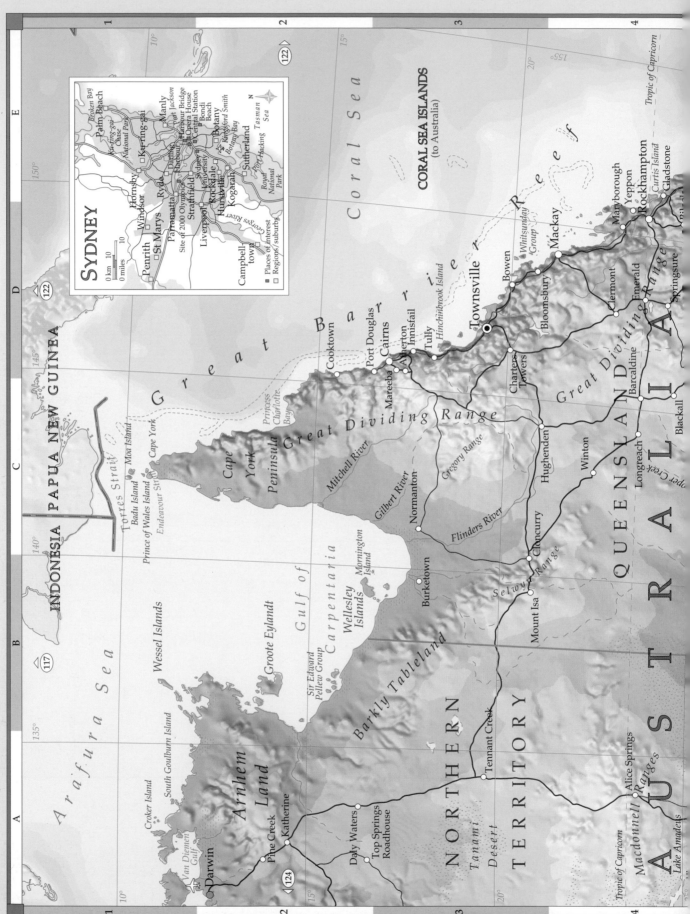

SYDNEY

Broken Bay
Palm Beach
Ku-ring-gai Chase
Ka-ring-gai
National Park
Manly
Hornsby
Windsor
Dural
Darling Harbour
Harbour Bridge
Port Jackson
Opera House
Central Station
Ryde
St Marys
Parramatta
Strathfield
Sydney
University
Rockdale
Kogarah
Penrith
Liverpool
Hurstville
Sutherland
Port Hacking
Royal National Park
Campbelltown
Georges River
Bondi Beach
Botany
Kingsford Smith
Botany Bay
Kurnell
Bare Island

N

Tasman Sea

■ Places of interest
□ Regions / suburbs

0 km 10
0 miles 10

CORAL SEA ISLANDS
(to Australia)

Coral Sea

INDONESIA PAPUA NEW GUINEA

Great Barrier Reef

Torres Strait
Moa Island
Badu Island
Prince of Wales Island
Endeavour Str.
Cape York

Cape York Peninsula

Princess Charlotte Bay

Cooktown
Port Douglas
Cairns
Mareeba
Atherton
Innisfail
Tully
Hinchinbrook Island
Townsville
Bowen
Bloomsbury
Whitsunday Group
Mackay
Marlborough
Yeppoon
Rockhampton
Curtis Island
Gladstone

Charters Towers
Clermont
Emerald
Springsure
Barcaldine
Blackall

Great Dividing Range

Mitchell River
Gregory Range
Gilbert River
Flinders River
Normanton
Hughenden
Winton
Longreach
Cooper Creek

Gulf of Carpentaria

Mornington Island
Wellesley Islands
Sir Edward Pellew Group
Groote Eylandt

Burketown
Selwyn Range
Cloncurry
Mount Isa

QUEENSLAND

AUSTRALIA

Wessel Islands
South Goulburn Island
Croker Island
Van Diemen Gulf
Darwin
Katherine
Pine Creek

Arnhem Land

Arafura Sea

Barkly Tableland

NORTHERN TERRITORY

Daly Waters
Top Springs Roadhouse
Tanami Desert
Tennant Creek
Macdonnell Ranges
Alice Springs
Tropic of Capricorn
Lake Amadeus

150°
145°
140°
135°
10°
15°
20°

POPULATION

◉ Over 500,000
◉ 100,000 - 500,000
○ 50,000 - 100,000
○ Less than 50,000
● National capital
● Internal administrative capital

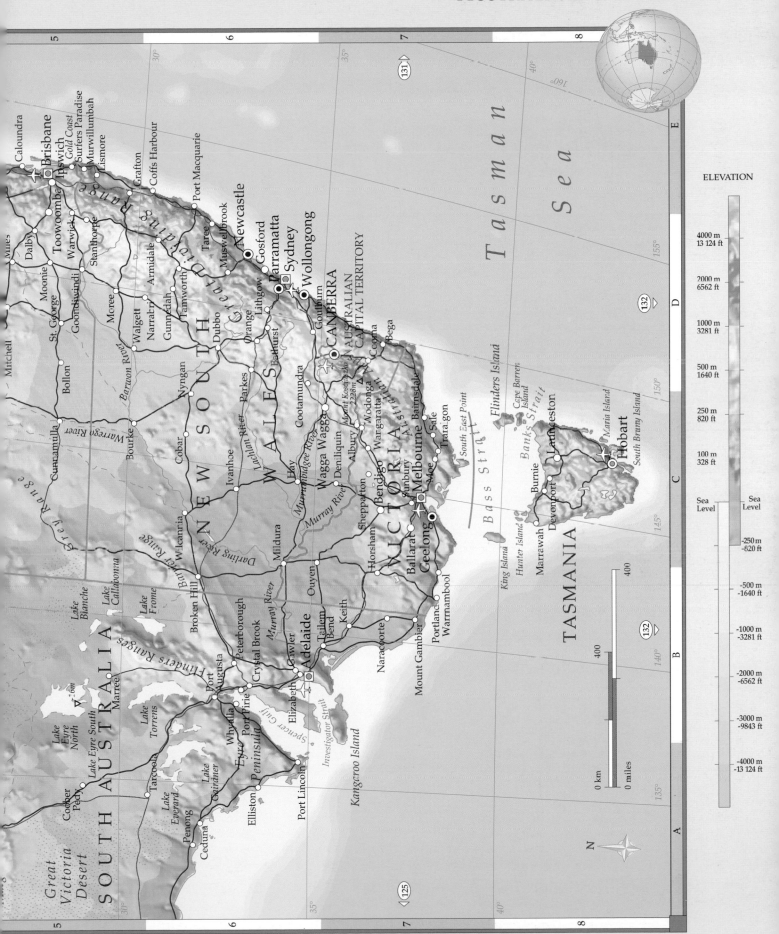

NEW ZEALAND

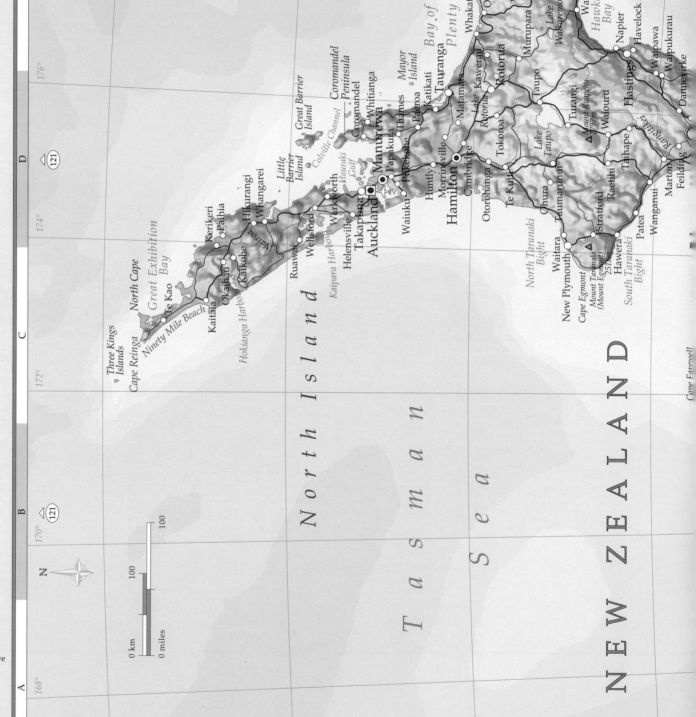

E

D

C

B

A

1   2   3   4

178° 34° 36° 38° 40°

176°

174°

172°

170°

168°

34°

36°

38°

40°

POPULATION

◪ Over
500,000

◉ 100,000 –
500,000

○ 50,000 –
100,000

○ Less than
50,000

● National
capital

◔ Internal
administrative
capital

100

100

N

0 km

0 miles

Three Kings
Islands

Cape Reinga

North Cape

Great Exhibition
Bay

Te Kao

Ninety Mile Beach

Kaitaia

Okaihau

Kaikohe

Hokianga Harbour

Kerikeri

Paihia

Hikurangi

Whangarei

Waitoa

Ruawai

Wellsford

Kaipara Harbour

Helensville

Warkworth

Takapuna

Auckland

Waiuku

Pukekohe

Manurewa

Papakura

Huntly

Morrinsville

Cambridge

Hamilton

Otorohanga

Te Kuiti

Te Awamutu

Little
Barrier
Island

Great Barrier
Island

Hauraki
Gulf

Colville Channel

Coromandel

Coromandel
Peninsula

Whitianga

Thames

Paeroa

Katikati

Tauranga

Matamata

Kawerau

Whakatane

Opotiki

Murupara

Rotorua

Lake
Rotorua

Tokoroa

Taupo

Lake
Taupo

Mayor
Island

Bay of
Plenty

East Cape

Ruatoria

Gisborne

Poverty Bay

Mahia
Peninsula

Lake
Waikaremoana

Wairoa

Hawke
Bay

Napier

Hastings

Havelock North

Waipawa

Waipukurau

Dannevirke

Raukumara Range

Turangi

Mount Ruapehu
2797m

Waiouru

Taihape

Raetihi

Ohura

Taumarunui

New Plymouth

Waitara

Cape Egmont

Mount Taranaki
(Mount Egmont)
2518m

North Taranaki
Bight

Stratford

Hawera

South Taranaki
Bight

Patea

Wanganui

Marton

Feilding

Rangitikei

North Island

T a s m a n   S e a

N E W   Z E A L A N D

Cape Farewell

124

121

121

121

128

ELEVATION

4000 m	13 124 ft
2000 m	6562 ft
1000 m	3281 ft
500 m	1640 ft
250 m	820 ft
100 m	328 ft
Sea Level	Sea Level
-250 m	-820 ft
-500 m	-1640 ft
-1000 m	-3281 ft
-2000 m	-6562 ft
-3000 m	-9843 ft
-4000 m	-13 124 ft

South Island

PACIFIC OCEAN

Lower Hutt
WELLINGTON
Cape Palliser
Cook
Seddon
Cape Campbell
Clarence
Kaikoura
Kaikoura Peninsula
Blenheim
Richmond
Mount Owen △ 1875m
Wairau
Richmond Range
Clarence
Harmer Springs
Springs Junction
Hurunui
Wapara
Pegasus
Rangiora
Kaiapoi Bay
Banks Peninsula
Christchurch
Lyttelton
Reefton
Lake Brunner
Otira
Arthur's Pass 920m
Oxford
Darfield
Waimakariri
Ashburton Ellesmere
Canterbury Bight
Seddonville
Westport
Cape Foulwind
Runanga
Greymouth
Hokitika
Ross
Waiau
Mayfield
Rakaia
Canterbury Plains
Hinds
Geraldine
Temuka
Timaru
Studholme
Oamaru
Abut Head
Whataroa
Mt Cook △ 3744m
Mount Cook
Fairlie
Waitaki
Waimate
Hampden
Fox Glacier
Lake Pukaki
Lake Hawea
Wanaka
Cromwell
Alexandra
Clutha
Taieri
Otago Peninsula
Dunedin
Mosgiel
Milton
Balclutha
Haast
Lake Wanaka
Lake Wakatipu
Queenstown
Lumsden
Mataura
Gore
Mataura
Tokanui
Jackson Head
Eyre Mts
Livingstone Mts
Te Anau
Lake Manapouri
Waiau
Winton
Riverton
Invercargill
Tokanui
Toetoes Bay
Ruapuke Island
Milford Sound
George Sound
Caswell Sound
Milford Sound
Lake Te Anau
Te Anau
Lake Hauroka
Ta Waewae Bay
Foveaux Strait
Codfish Island
Halfmoon Bay
Muttonbird Islands
Stewart Island
South West Cape
Resolution Island
West Cape
Fiordland
Puysegur

THE PACIFIC OCEAN

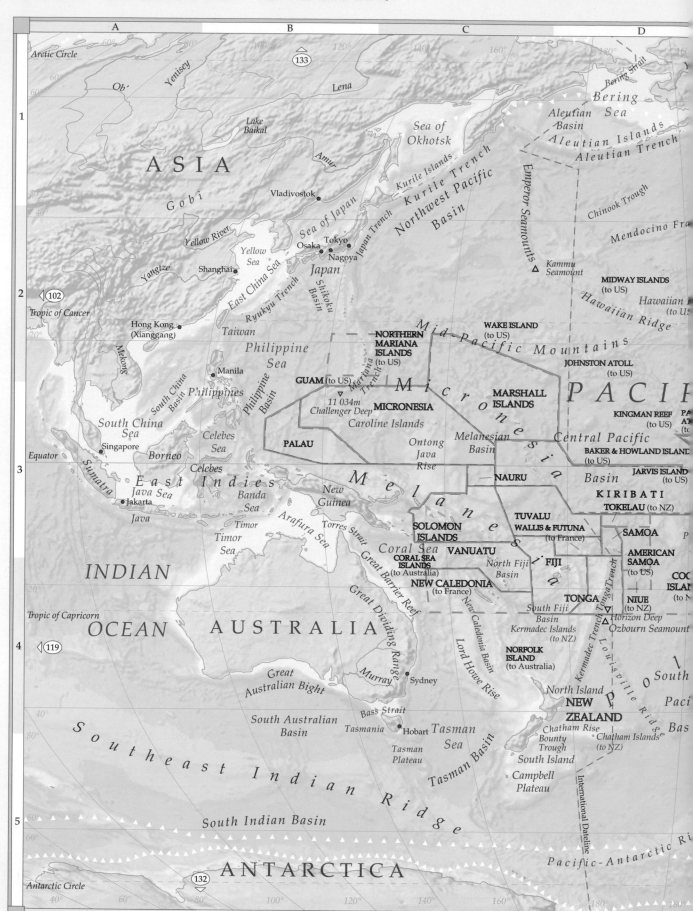

Arctic Circle

A · B · C · D

ASIA

Arctic Circle
Ob'
Yenisey
Lena
60°
Lake Baikal
Gobi
Amur
Vladivostok
Yellow River
Yellow Sea
Shanghai
Yangtze
40°
Sea of Okhotsk
Kurile Islands
Kurile Trench
Northwest Pacific Basin
Sea of Japan
Osaka Tokyo
Nagoya
Japan
Japan Trench
Shikoku Basin
East China Sea
Ryukyu Trench
Emperor Seamounts
Kammu Seamount

133

Bering Sea
Bering Strait
Aleutian Basin
Aleutian Islands
Aleutian Trench
Chinook Trough
Mendocino Fra
MIDWAY ISLANDS (to US)
Hawaiian (to US)

Tropic of Cancer
20°

102

Hong Kong (Xianggang)
Taiwan
Philippine Sea
Mekong
Manila
Philippines
Philippine Basin
South China Basin
NORTHERN MARIANA ISLANDS (to US)
Mariana Trench
GUAM (to US)
11 034m
Challenger Deep
MICRONESIA
Caroline Islands
WAKE ISLAND (to US)
Mid-Pacific Mountains
Micronesia
Melanesian Basin
JOHNSTON ATOLL (to US)
MARSHALL ISLANDS
KINGMAN REEF (to US)
Central Pacific
PA
A
(to
PACIFI

South China Sea
Singapore
Equator
Borneo
Celebes Sea
Sumatra
East Indies
Java Sea
Jakarta
Java
Celebes
Banda Sea
Timor
Timor Sea
Arafura Sea
New Guinea
PALAU
Ontong Java Rise
Melanesia
Melanesian Basin
BAKER & HOWLAND ISLAND (to US)
JARVIS ISLAND (to US)
NAURU
KIRIBATI
TOKELAU (to NZ)
TUVALU
WALLIS & FUTUNA (to France)
SAMOA
Basin

3

INDIAN

Torres Strait
Great Barrier Reef
Coral Sea
CORAL SEA ISLANDS (to Australia)
SOLOMON ISLANDS
VANUATU
NEW CALEDONIA (to France)
North Fiji Basin
FIJI
AMERICAN SAMOA (to US)
COOK ISLAN (to N
NIUE (to NZ)
TONGA

OCEAN

20°
Tropic of Capricorn

119

AUSTRALIA
Great Australian Bight
Great Dividing Range
Murray
Sydney
Lord Howe Rise
New Caledonia Basin
South Fiji Basin
Kermadec Islands (to NZ)
NORFOLK ISLAND (to Australia)
Kermadec Trench
Tonga Trench
Horizon Deep
Ozbourn Seamount
Louisville Ridge
P
South
Paci
Bas

4

40°
South Australian Basin
Bass Strait
Tasmania
Hobart
Tasman Plateau
Tasman Sea
Tasman Basin
NEW ZEALAND
North Island
Chatham Rise
Chatham Islands (to NZ)
South Island
Bounty Trough
Campbell Plateau

Southeast Indian Ridge

80°
60°
International Dateline

5
60°
South Indian Basin
Pacific-Antarctic Ri

ANTARCTICA

132

Antarctic Circle
40° · 60° · 80° · 100° · 120° · 140° · 160° · 180°

A · B · C · D

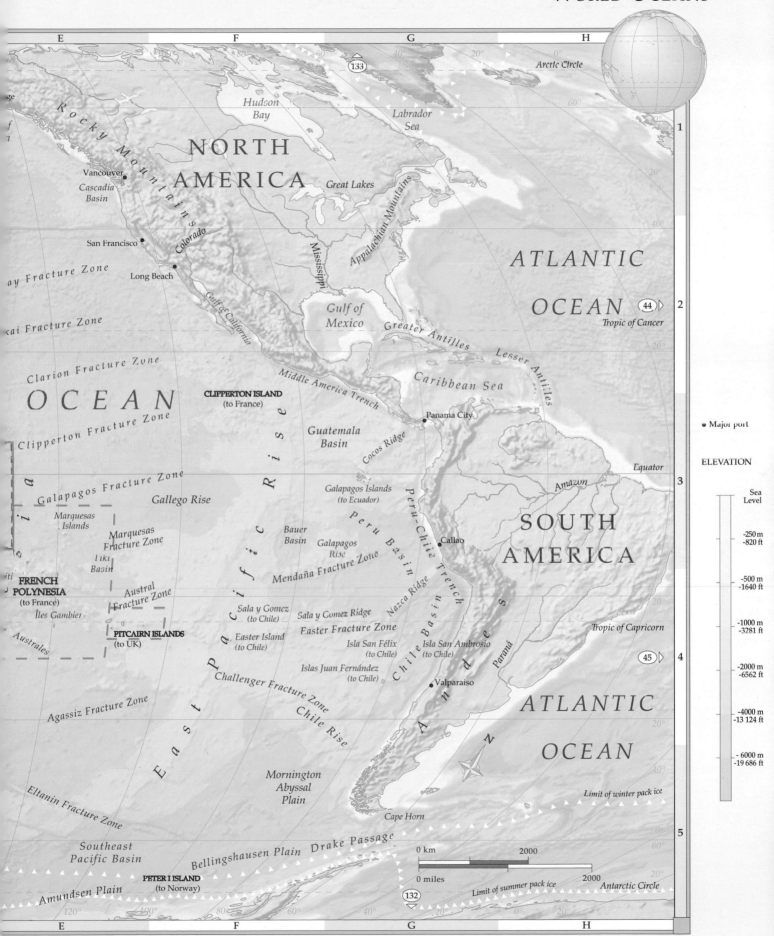

E F G H

80° 60° 40° 20°

133

Arctic Circle

60°

Hudson Bay

Labrador Sea

20°

NORTH AMERICA

1

Rocky Mountains

Vancouver

Cascadia Basin

Great Lakes

40°

San Francisco

Colorado

ATLANTIC

Long Beach

Mississippi

Appalachian Mountains

OCEAN

44

2

...ay Fracture Zone

Gulf of California

Gulf of Mexico

Greater Antilles

Tropic of Cancer

...ai Fracture Zone

20°

Clarion Fracture Zone

Middle America Trench

Caribbean Sea

Lesser Antilles

OCEAN

CLIPPERTON ISLAND
(to France)

Clipperton Fracture Zone

Panama City

Guatemala Basin

Cocos Ridge

Equator

ELEVATION

Galapagos Fracture Zone

Gallego Rise

Galapagos Islands
(to Ecuador)

3

Sea Level

Marquesas Islands

East Pacific Rise

Bauer Basin

Galapagos Rise

Peru Basin

SOUTH AMERICA

–250 m
–820 ft

Marquesas Fracture Zone

...iki Basin

Mendaña Fracture Zone

Peru–Chile Trench

Callao

Amazon

–500 m
–1640 ft

FRENCH POLYNESIA
(to France)

Austral Fracture Zone

Sala y Gomez
(to Chile)

Sala y Gomez Ridge

Nazca Ridge

Andes

–1000 m
–3281 ft

Îles Gambier

Easter Fracture Zone

Tropic of Capricorn

PITCAIRN ISLANDS
(to UK)

Easter Island
(to Chile)

Isla San Félix
(to Chile)

Isla San Ambrosio
(to Chile)

Paraná

45

4

Australes

Islas Juan Fernández
(to Chile)

Chile Basin

Valparaiso

–2000 m
–6562 ft

Challenger Fracture Zone

20°

Agassiz Fracture Zone

Chile Rise

–4000 m
–13 124 ft

Mornington Abyssal Plain

N

–6000 m
–19 686 ft

Eltanin Fracture Zone

ATLANTIC

OCEAN

Limit of winter pack ice

Cape Horn

5

Southeast Pacific Basin

Bellingshausen Plain

Drake Passage

0 km 2000

20°

0 miles 2000

PETER I ISLAND
(to Norway)

Amundsen Plain

Limit of summer pack ice

Antarctic Circle

132

120° 100° 80° 60° 40° 20° 0° 20°

E F G H

● Major port

ANTARCTICA

ELEVATION

4000 m 13 124 ft	
2000 m 6562 ft	
1000 m 3281 ft	
500 m 1640 ft	
250 m 820 ft	
100 m 328 ft	
Sea Level	Sea Level
-250 m -820 ft	
-500 m -1640 ft	
-1000 m -3281 ft	
-2000 m -6562 ft	
-3000 m -9843 ft	
-4000 m -13 124 ft	

ATLANTIC OCEAN

INDIAN OCEAN

Atlantic-Indian Basin

Limit of winter pack ice

Antarctic Circle

Lazarev Sea

Enderby Plain

SOUTH GEORGIA (to UK)

SOUTH SANDWICH ISLANDS (to UK)

Scotia Sea

South Sandwich Trench

America-Antarctica Ridge

Weddell Plain

Sanae (South Africa)

Novolazarevskaya (Russian Federation)

Georg von Neumayer (Germany)

Dronning Maud Land

Lützow Holmbukta

Molodezhnaya (Russian Federation)

Syowa (Japan)

Enderby Land

Orcadas (Argentina)

Signy (UK)

South Orkney Islands

South Shetland Islands

Drake Passage

Limit of summer pack ice

Weddell Sea

Halley (UK)

Coats Land

Mawson (Australia)

Cape Darnley

Esperanza (Argentina)

Capitán Arturo Prat (Chile)

Belgrano II (Argentina)

Berkner Island

Mackenzie Bay

Prydz Bay

Palmer (US)

Antarctic Peninsula

Graham Land

Palmer Land

Ronne Ice Shelf

Princess Elizabeth Land

Davis (Australia)

Rothera (UK)

San Martín (Argentina)

Alexander Island

ANTARCTICA

Bellingshausen Sea

Vinson Massif 4897m △

Greater

Davis Sea

PETER I ISLAND (to Norway)

Ellsworth Land

Lesser

Amundsen-Scott (US) South Pole

Antarctica

Mirny (Russian Federation)

Transantarctic Mountains

South Geomagnetic Pole

Vostok (Russian Federation)

Shackleton Ice Shelf

Antarctica

Marie Byrd Land

Mount Kirkpatrick 4528m △

Mount Markham 4351m △

Ross Ice Shelf

Wilkes Land

Casey (Australia)

Amundsen Sea

Mount Sidley 4181m △

Cape Poinsett

Mount Siple 3100m △

Roosevelt Island

Scott Base (N.Z)

McMurdo Base (US) △

Mount Erebus 3794m

Victoria Land

Terre Adélie

PACIFIC OCEAN

Amundsen Plain

Ross Sea

George V Land

Dumont d'Urville (France)

South Indian Basin

Cape Adare

Leningradskaya (Russian Federation)

Limit of summer pack ice

Scott Island

Balleny Islands

Limit of winter pack ice

Pacific-Antarctic Ridge

Macquarie Ridge

Eltanin Fracture Zone

Udintsev Fracture Zone

0 km	500
0 miles	500

○ Antarctic research station

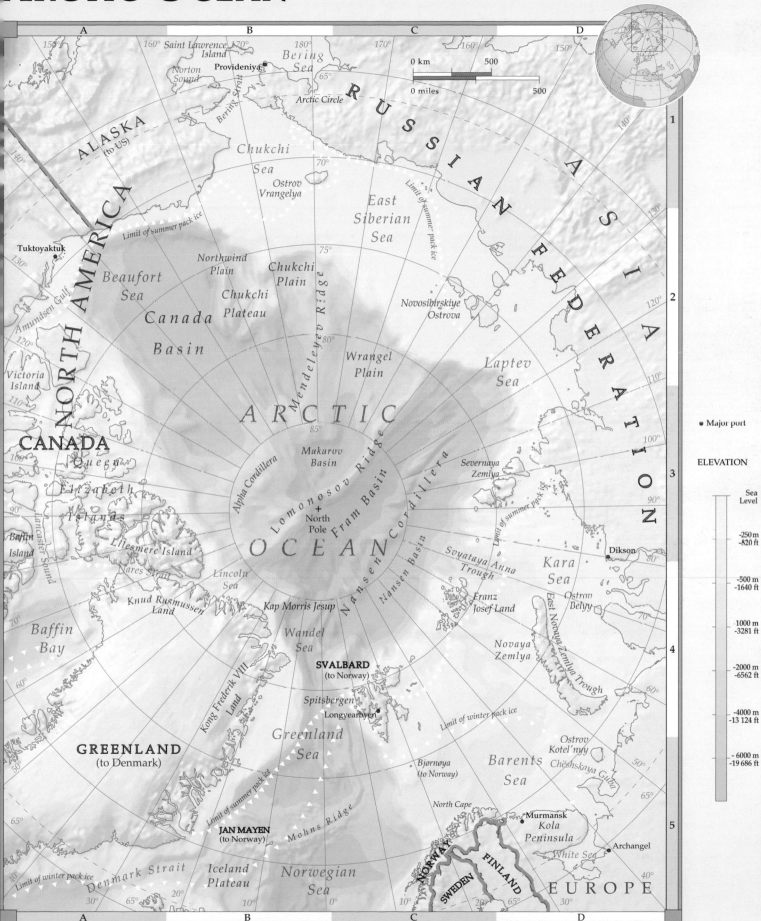

ARCTIC OCEAN — Polar Regions

Labels on map:

ALASKA (to US)
NORTH AMERICA
CANADA
RUSSIAN FEDERATION
EUROPE
GREENLAND (to Denmark)
NORWAY
SWEDEN
FINLAND

Saint Lawrence Island
Providentiya
Norton Sound
Bering Strait
Bering Sea
Arctic Circle
Chukchi Sea
Ostrov Vrangelya
East Siberian Sea
Tuktoyaktuk
Northwind Plain
Chukchi Plain
Chukchi Plateau
Beaufort Sea
Canada Basin
Amundsen Gulf
Wrangel Plain
Mendeleyev Ridge
Novosibirskiye Ostrova
Laptev Sea
Victoria Island
ARCTIC
Alpha Cordillera
Makarov Basin
Lomonosov Ridge
North Pole
Fram Basin
Nansen Cordillera
Severnaya Zemlya
Queen Elizabeth Islands
OCEAN
Nansen Basin
Svyataya Anna Trough
Kara Sea
Dikson
Baffin Island
Ellesmere Island
Nares Strait
Lincoln Sea
Kap Morris Jesup
Wandel Sea
Franz Josef Land
Ostrov Belyy
East Novaya Zemlya Trough
Lancaster Sound
Knud Rasmussen Land
Baffin Bay
Kong Frederik VIII Land
SVALBARD (to Norway)
Novaya Zemlya
Ostrov Kotel'nyy
Spitsbergen
Longyearbyen
Limit of winter pack ice
GREENLAND (to Denmark)
Greenland Sea
Bjørnøya (to Norway)
Barents Sea
Chëshskaya Guba
North Cape
Murmansk
Kola Peninsula
Archangel
White Sea
JAN MAYEN (to Norway)
Mohns Ridge
Denmark Strait
Iceland Plateau
Norwegian Sea
Limit of summer pack ice
Limit of winter pack ice

Scale:
0 km ... 500
0 miles ... 500

• Major port

ELEVATION

Sea Level	
-250 m	-820 ft
-500 m	-1640 ft
-1000 m	-3281 ft
-2000 m	-6562 ft
-4000 m	-13 124 ft
-6000 m	-19 686 ft

OVERSEAS TERRITORIES AND DEPENDENCIES

DESPITE THE RAPID PROCESS of decolonization since the end of the Second World War, around 10 million people in more than 50 territories around the world continue to live under the protection of France, Australia, the Netherlands, Denmark, Norway, New Zealand, the United Kingdom, or the USA. These remnants of former colonial empires may have persisted for economic, strategic or political reasons, and are administered in a variety of ways.

AUSTRALIA

AUSTRALIA'S OVERSEAS territories have not been an issue since Papua New Guinea became independent in 1975. Consequently there is no overriding policy toward them. Some of Norfolk Island is inhabited by descendants of the H.M.S Bounty mutineers and more recent Australian migrants.

ASHMORE & CARTIER ISLANDS
Indian Ocean
Status External territory
Claimed 1978
Capital *not applicable*
Population None
Area 5.2 sq km (2 sq miles)

 CHRISTMAS ISLAND
Indian Ocean
Status External territory
Claimed 1958
Capital Flying Fish Cove
Population 1,275
Area 134.6 sq km (52 sq miles)

COCOS ISLANDS
Indian Ocean
Status External territory
Claimed 1955
Capital No official capital
Population 670
Area 14.24 sq km (5.5 sq miles)

CORAL SEA ISLANDS
South Pacific
Status External territory
Claimed 1969
Capital None
Population 8 (meteorologists)
Area Less than 3 sq km
(1.16 sq miles)

HEARD & MCDONALD ISLANDS
Indian Ocean
Status External territory
Claimed 1947
Capital *not applicable*
Population None
Area 417 sq km
(161 sq miles)

 NORFOLK ISLAND
South Pacific
Status External territory
Claimed 1774
Capital Kingston
Population 2,181
Area 34.4 sq km
(13.3 sq miles)

DENMARK

THE FAEROE ISLANDS have been under Danish administration since Queen Margreth I of Denmark inherited Norway in 1380. The Home Rule Act of 1948 gave the Faeroese control over all their internal affairs. Greenland first came under Danish rule in 1380. Today, Denmark remains responsible for the island's foreign affairs and defense.

 FAEROE ISLANDS
North Atlantic
Status External territory
Claimed 1380
Capital Tórshavn
Population 43,382
Area 1,399 sq km
(540 sq miles)

 GREENLAND
North Atlantic
Status External territory
Claimed 1380
Capital Nuuk
Population 56,076
Area 2,175,516 sq km
(840,000 sq miles)

FRANCE

France has developed economic ties with its overseas territories, thereby stressing interdependence over independence. Overseas départements, officially part of France, have their own governments. Territorial collectivités and overseas territoires have varying degrees of autonomy.

CLIPPERTON ISLAND
East Pacific
Status Dependency
of French Polynesia
Claimed 1930
Capital *not applicable*
Population None
Area 7 sq km
(2.7 sq miles)

FRENCH GUIANA
South America
Status Overseas department
Claimed 1817
Capital Cayenne
Population 152,300
Area 90,996 sq km
(35,135 sq miles)

 FRENCH POLYNESIA
South Pacific
Status Overseas territory
Claimed 1843
Capital Papeete
Population 219,521
Area 4,165 sq km (1,608 sq miles)

GUADELOUPE
West Indies
Status Overseas department
Claimed 1635
Capital Basse-Terre
Population 419,500
Area 1,780 sq km (687 sq miles)

MARTINIQUE
West Indies
Status Overseas department
Claimed 1635
Capital Fort-de-France
Population 381,200
Area 1,100 sq km (425 sq miles)

MAYOTTE
Indian Ocean
Status Territorial collectivity
Claimed 1843
Capital Mamoudzou
Population 131,320
Area 374 sq km (144 sq miles)

NEW CALEDONIA
South Pacific
Status Overseas territory
Claimed 1853
Capital Nouméa
Population 196,836
Area 19,103 sq km (7,374 sq miles)

RÉUNION
Indian Ocean
Status Overseas department
Claimed 1638
Capital Saint-Denis
Population 697,000
Area 2,512 sq km (970 sq miles)

ST. PIERRE & MIQUELON
North America
Status Territorial collectivity
Claimed 1604
Capital Saint-Pierre
Population 6,600
Area 242 sq km (93.4 sq miles)

WALLIS & FUTUNA
South Pacific
Status Overseas territory
Claimed 1842
Capital Matā'Utu
Population 15,000
Area 274 sq km (106 sq miles)

NETHERLANDS

THE COUNTRY'S TWO remaining overseas territories were formerly part of the Dutch West Indies. Both are now self-governing, but the Netherlands remains responsible for their defense.

 ARUBA
West Indies
Status Autonomous part
of the Netherlands
Claimed 1643
Capital Oranjestad
Population 88,000
Area 194 sq km (75 sq miles)

 NETHERLANDS ANTILLES
West Indies
Status Autonomous part
of the Netherlands
Claimed 1816
Capital Willemstad
Population 207,175
Area 800 sq km (308 sq miles)

NEW ZEALAND

NEW ZEALAND'S GOVERNMENT has no desire to retain any overseas territories. However, the economic weakness of its dependent territory, Tokelau and its freely associated states, Niue and the Cook Islands, has forced New Zealand to remain responsible for their foreign policy and defense.

 COOK ISLANDS
South Pacific
Status Associated territory
Claimed 1901
Capital Avarua
Population 20,200
Area 293 sq km (113 sq miles)

 NIUE
South Pacific
Status Associated territory
Claimed 1901
Capital Alofi
Population 2,080
Area 264 sq km (102 sq miles)

TOKELAU
South Pacific
Status Dependent territory
Claimed 1926
Capital *not applicable*
Population 1,577
Area 10.4 sq km (4 sq miles)

NORWAY

IN 1920, 41 nations signed the Spitsbergen treaty recognizing Norwegian sovereignty over Svalbard. There is a NATO base on Jan Mayen. Bouvet Island is a nature reserve.

BOUVET ISLAND
South Atlantic
Status Dependency
Claimed 1928
Capital *not applicable*
Population None
Area 58 sq km (22 sq miles)

JAN MAYEN
North Atlantic
Status Dependency
Claimed 1929
Capital *not applicable*
Population None
Area 381 sq km (147 sq miles)

PETER I ISLAND
Southern Ocean
Status Dependency
Claimed 1931
Capital *not applicable*
Population None
Area 180 sq km (69 sq miles)

SVALBARD
Arctic Ocean
Status Dependency
Claimed 1920
Capital Longyearbyen
Population 3,231
Area 62,906 sq km
(24,289 sq miles)

UNITED KINGDOM

THE UK STILL has the largest number of overseas territories. Locally-governed by a mixture of elected representatives and appointed officials, they all enjoy a large measure of internal self-government, but certain powers, such as foreign affairs and defense, are reserved for Governors of the British Crown.

 ANGUILLA
West Indies
Status Dependent territory
Claimed 1650
Capital The Valley
Population 10,300
Area 96 sq km (37 sq miles)

ASCENSION ISLAND
South Atlantic
Status Dependency of St. Helena
Claimed 1673
Capital Georgetown
Population 1,099
Area 88 sq km (34 sq miles)

 BERMUDA
North Atlantic
Status Crown colony
Claimed 1612
Capital Hamilton
Population 60,144
Area 53 sq km (20.5 sq miles)

 BRITISH INDIAN OCEAN TERRITORY
Indian Ocean
Status Dependent territory
Claimed 1814
Capital Diego Garcia
Population 930
Area 60 sq km (23 sq miles)

 BRITISH VIRGIN ISLANDS
West Indies
Status Dependent territory
Claimed 1672
Capital Road Town
Population 17,896
Area 153 sq km (59 sq miles)

 CAYMAN ISLANDS
West Indies
Status Dependent territory
Claimed 1670
Capital George Town
Population 35,000
Area 259 sq km
(100 sq miles)

 FALKLAND ISLANDS
South Atlantic
Status Dependent territory
Claimed 1832
Capital Stanley
Population 2,564
Area 12,173 sq km
(4,699 sq miles)

 GIBRALTAR
Southwest Europe
Status Crown colony
Claimed 1713
Capital Gibraltar
Population 27,086
Area 6.5 sq km
(2.5 sq miles)

 GUERNSEY
Channel Islands
Status Crown dependency
Claimed 1066
Capital St Peter Port
Population 56,681
Area 65 sq km
(25 sq miles)

 ISLE OF MAN
British Isles
Status Crown dependency
Claimed 1765
Capital Douglas
Population 71,714
Area 572 sq km
(221 sq miles)

 **JERSEY**
Channel Islands
Status Crown dependency
Claimed 1066
Capital St. Helier
Population 85,150
Area 116 sq km
(45 sq miles)

 MONTSERRAT
West Indies
Status Dependent territory
Claimed 1632
Capital Plymouth
(uninhabited)
Population 2,850
Area 102 sq km
(40 sq miles)

 PITCAIRN ISLANDS
South Pacific
Status Dependent territory
Claimed 1887
Capital Adamstown
Population 55
Area 3.5 sq km
(1.35 sq miles)

 ST. HELENA
South Atlantic
Status Dependent territory
Claimed 1673
Capital Jamestown
Population 6,472
Area 122 sq km (47 sq miles)

SOUTH GEORGIA & the SOUTH SANDWICH ISLANDS
South Atlantic
Status Dependent territory
Claimed 1775
Capital *not applicable*
Population No permanent residents
Area 3,592 sq km (1,387 sq miles)

TRISTAN DA CUNHA
South Atlantic
Status Dependency of St. Helena
Claimed 1612
Capital Edinburgh
Population 297
Area 98 sq km (38 sq miles)

 TURKS & CAICOS ISLANDS
West Indies
Status Dependent territory
Claimed 1766
Capital Cockburn Town
Population 13,800
Area 430 sq km (166 sq miles)

UNITED STATES OF AMERICA

AMERICA'S OVERSEAS TERRITORIES have been seen as strategically useful, if expensive, links with its "backyards." The US has, in most cases, given the local population a say in deciding their own status. A US Commonwealth territory, such as Puerto Rico has a greater level of independence than that of a US unincorporated or external territory

 AMERICAN SAMOA
South Pacific
Status Unincorporated territory
Claimed 1900
Capital Pago Pago
Population 60,000
Area 195 sq km (75 sq miles)

BAKER & HOWLAND ISLANDS
South Pacific
Status Unincorporated territory
Claimed 1856
Capital *not applicable*
Population None
Area 1.4 sq km (0.54 sq miles)

 GUAM
West Pacific
Status Unincorporated territory
Claimed 1898
Capital Hagåtña
Population 149,249
Area 549 sq km (212 sq miles)

JARVIS ISLAND
South Pacific
Status Unincorporated territory
Claimed 1856
Capital *not applicable*
Population None
Area 4.5 sq km (1.7 sq miles)

JOHNSTON ATOLL
Central Pacific
Status Unincorporated territory
Claimed 1858
Capital *not applicable*
Population 327
Area 2.8 sq km
(1 sq mile)

KINGMAN REEF
Central Pacific
Status Administered territory
Claimed 1856
Capital *not applicable*
Population None
Area 1 sq km (0.4 sq miles)

MIDWAY ISLANDS
Central Pacific
Status Administered territory
Claimed 1867
Capital *not applicable*
Population 453
Area 5.2 sq km
(2 sq miles)

NAVASSA ISLAND
West Indies
Status Unincorporated territory
Claimed 1856
Capital *not applicable*
Population None
Area 5.2 sq km (2 sq miles)

 NORTHERN MARIANA ISLANDS
West Pacific
Status Commonwealth territory
Claimed 1947
Capital Saipan
Population 58,846
Area 457 sq km
(177 sq miles)

PALMYRA ATOLL
Central Pacific
Status Unincorporated territory
Claimed 1898
Capital *not applicable*
Population None
Area 12 sq km (5 sq miles)

 PUERTO RICO
West Indies
Status Commonwealth territory
Claimed 1898
Capital San Juan
Population 3.8 million
Area 8,959 sq km
(3,458 sq miles)

 VIRGIN ISLANDS
West Indies
Status Unincorporated territory
Claimed 1917
Capital Charlotte Amalie
Population 101,809
Area 355 sq km
(137 sq miles)

WAKE ISLAND
Central Pacific
Status Unincorporated territory
Claimed 1898
Capital *not applicable*
Population 302
Area 6.5 sq km
(2.5 sq miles)

AFGHANISTAN

Page 100 D4

Landlocked in central Asia, three-quarters of Afghanistan is inaccessible. Since 1996 most of the country has been controlled by a militant Islamic group.

Official name Islamic State of Afghanistan
Formation 1919
Capital Kabul
Population 22.7 million / 90 people per sq mile (35 people per sq km)
Total area 251,771 sq miles (652,090 sq km)
Languages Persian, Pashtu, Dari
Religions Sunni Muslim 84%, Shi'a Muslim 15%, other 1%
Ethnic mix Pashto 52%, Tajik 21%, Hazara 19%, Uzbek 5%, other 3%
Government Islamic regime
Currency Afghani = 100 puls
Literacy rate 31.5%
Calorie consumption 1,523 kilocalories

ANDORRA

Page 69 B6

A tiny landlocked principality, Andorra lies high in the eastern Pyrenees between France and Spain. It held its first full elections in 1993.

Official name Principality of Andorra
Formation 1278
Capital Andorra la Vella
Population 66,000 / 367 people per sq mile (142 people per sq km)
Total area 180 sq miles (465 sq km)
Languages Catalan, Spanish, French Portuguese
Religions Roman Catholic 94%, other 6%
Ethnic mix Catalan 61%, Spanish Castilian 30%, other 9%
Government Parliamentary democracy
Currency French franc and Spanish peseta
Literacy rate 99%
Calorie consumption 3,708 kilocalories

ARGENTINA

Page 43 B5

Most of the southern half of South America is occupied by Argentina. The country returned to civilian rule in 1983 after a series of military coups.

Official name Argentine Republic
Formation 1816
Capital Buenos Aires
Population 37 million / 35 people per sq mile (14 people per sq km)
Total area 1,056,636 sq miles (2,736,690 sq km)
Languages Spanish, Italian, Amerindian languages
Religions Roman Catholic 90%, Jewish 2%, Protestant 2%, other 6%
Ethnic mix European 85%, other 15%
Government Multiparty republic
Currency Argentine peso = 100 centavos
Literacy rate 95%
Calorie consumption 2,880 kilocalories

AUSTRIA

Page 73 D7

Bordering eight countries in the heart of Europe, Austria was created in 1920 after the collapse of the Austro-Hungarian Empire the previous year.

Official name Republic of Austria
Formation 1920
Capital Vienna
Population 8.2 million / 257 people per sq mile (99 people per sq km)
Total area 31,942 sq miles (82,730 sq km)
Languages German, Croatian, Slovene
Religions Roman Catholic 78%, non-religious 9%, Protestant 5%, Muslim 2%, other (including Jewish) 6%
Ethnic mix German 93%, Croatian, Slovene, Hungarian 6%, other 1%
Government Multiparty republic
Currency Schilling = 100 groschen
Literacy rate 99%
Calorie consumption 3,497 kilocalories

ALBANIA

Page 79 C6

Lying at the southeastern end of the Adriatic Sea, Albania held its first multiparty elections in 1991, after nearly five decades of communism.

Official name Republic of Albania
Formation 1912
Capital Tiranë
Population 3 million / 293 people per sq mile (113 people per sq km)
Total area 10,579 sq miles (27,400 sq km) sq miles
Languages Albanian, Greek
Religions Sunni Muslim 70%, Greek Orthodox 20%, Roman Catholic 10%
Ethnic mix Albanian 96%, Greek 2%, other (including Macedonian) 2%
Government Multiparty republic
Currency Lek = 100 qindars
Literacy rate 85%
Calorie consumption 2,605 kilocalories

ANGOLA

Page 56 B2

Located in southwest Africa, Angola has been in a state of civil war following its independence from Portugal, except for a brief period from 1994–98.

Official name Republic of Angola
Formation 1975
Capital Luanda
Population 13 million /27 people per sq mile (10 people per sq km)
Total area 481,351 sq miles (1,246,700 sq km)
Languages Portuguese, Umbundu, Kimbundu, Kikongo
Religions Roman Catholic/Protestant 64%, Traditional beliefs 34%, other 2%
Ethnic mix Ovimbundu 37%, Mbundu 25%, Bakongo 13%, other 25%
Government Multiparty republic
Currency Readjusted kwanza = 100 lwei
Literacy rate 45%
Calorie consumption 1,839 kilocalories

ARMENIA

Page 95 F3

Smallest of the former USSR's republics, Armenia lies in the Lesser Caucasus mountains. Territorial war with Azerbaijan ended in a 1994 ceasefire.

Official name Republic of Armenia
Formation 1991
Capital Yerevan
Population 3.5 million / 304 people per sq mile (117 people per sq km)
Total area 11,506 sq miles (29,800 sq km)
Languages Armenian, Russian
Religions The Armenian Apostolic Church 94%, other 6%
Ethnic mix Armenian 93%, Azeri 3%, Russian 2%, other 2%
Government Multiparty republic
Currency Dram = 100 louma
Literacy rate 99%
Calorie consumption not available

AZERBAIJAN

Page 95 G2

Situated on the western coast of the Caspian Sea, Azerbaijan was the first Soviet republic to declare independence from Moscow in 1991.

Official name Republic of Azerbaijan
Formation 1991
Capital Baku
Population 7.7 million / 230 people per sq mile (89 people per sq km)
Total area 33,436 sq miles (86,600 sq km)
Languages Azerbaijani, Russian
Religions Muslim 83%, Armenian Apostolic and Russian Orthodox 17%
Ethnic mix Azeri 83%, Armenian 6%, Russian 5%, Daghestani 3%, other 3%
Government Multiparty republic
Currency Manat = 100 gopik
Literacy rate 96.3%
Calorie consumption not available

ALGERIA

Page 48 C3

Algeria achieved independence from France in 1962. Today, its military-dominated government faces a severe challenge from Islamic extremists.

Official name Democratic and Popular Republic of Algeria
Formation 1962
Capital Algiers
Population 31.5 million / 34 people per sq mile (13 people per sq km)
Total area 919,590 sq miles (2,381,740 sq km)
Languages Arabic, Berber, French
Religions Sunni Muslim 99%, other 1%
Ethnic mix Arab 75%, Berber 24%, European 1%
Government Multiparty republic
Currency Algerian dinar = 100 centimes
Literacy rate 60.3%
Calorie consumption 2,897 kilocalories

ANTIGUA & BARBUDA

Page 33 H3

Lying on the Atlantic edge of the Leeward Islands, Antigua and Barbuda's area includes the uninhabited islet of Redonda.

Official name Antigua and Barbuda
Formation 1981
Capital St. John's
Population 69,000 / 404 people per sq mile (156 people per sq km)
Total area 170 sq miles (440 sq km)
Languages English, English patois
Religions Anglican 44%, other Protestant 86%, Roman Catholic 10%, Rastafarian 1%, other 3%
Ethnic mix Black 98%, other 2%
Government Parliamentary democracy
Currency Eastern Caribbean dollar = 100 cents
Literacy rate 95%
Calorie consumption 2,458 kilocalories

AUSTRALIA

Page 120 A4

An island continent located between the Indian and Pacific oceans, Australia was settled by Europeans 200 years ago, but now has many Asian immigrants.

Official name Commonwealth of Australia
Formation 1901
Capital Canberra
Population 19 million / 6 people per sq mile (2 people per sq km)
Total area 2,941,282 sq miles (7,617,930 sq km)
Languages English, Greek, Italian, Vietnamese, Aboriginal languages
Religions Christian 64%, other 34%
Ethnic mix European 95%, Asian 4%, Aboriginal and other 1%
Government Parliamentary democracy
Currency Australian dollar = 100 cents
Literacy rate 99%
Calorie consumption 3,179 kilocalories

BAHAMAS

Page 32 C1

Located in the western Atlantic, off the Florida coast, the Bahamas comprise some 700 islands and 2,400 cays, only 30 of which are inhabited.

Official name Commonwealth of the Bahamas
Formation 1973
Capital Nassau
Population 307,000 / 79 people per sq mile (31 people per sq km)
Total area 3,864 sq miles (10,010 sq km)
Languages English, English Creole, French Creole
Religions Baptist 32%, Anglican 20%, Roman Catholic 19%, Church of God 6%, Methodist 6%, other 17%
Ethnic mix Black 85%, White 15%
Government Parliamentary democracy
Currency Bahamian dollar = 100 cents
Literacy rate 95.8%
Calorie consumption 2,624 kilocalories

BAHRAIN

Page 98 C4

Bahrain is an archipelago of 33 islands between the Qatar peninsula and the Saudi Arabian mainland. Only three of these islands are inhabited.

Official name State of Bahrain
Formation 1971
Capital Manama
Population 617,000 / 2,350 people per sq mile (891 people per sq km)
Total area 263 sq miles (680 sq km)
Languages Arabic, English
Religions Muslim (mainly Shi'a) 85%, Christian 7%, other 8%
Ethnic mix Bahraini 70%, Iranian, Indian, Pakistani 24%, other Arab 6%
Government Monarchy with Consultative Council
Currency Bahrain dinar = 1,000 fils
Literacy rate 86.3%
Calorie consumption not available

BELARUS

Page 85 B6

Formerly known as White Russia, Belarus lies landlocked in eastern Europe. The country reluctantly became independent of the USSR in 1991.

Official name Republic of Belarus
Formation 1991
Capital Minsk
Population 10.2 million / 127 people per sq mile (49 people per sq km)
Total area 80,154 sq miles (207,600 sq km)
Languages Belorussian, Russian
Religions Russian Orthodox 60%, Roman Catholic 8%, other 32%
Ethnic mix Belorussian 78%, Russian 13%, Polish 4%, other 5%
Government Multiparty republic
Currency Belorussian rouble = 100 kopeks
Literacy rate 99%
Calorie consumption not available

BENIN

Page 53 F4

Stretching north from the West African coast, Benin became one of the pioneers of African democratization in 1990, ending years of military rule.

Official name Republic of Benin
Formation 1960
Capital Porto-Novo
Population 6 million / 143 people per sq mile (55 people per sq km)
Total area 42,710 sq miles (110,620 sq km)
Languages French, Fon, Bariba, Yoruba, Adja, Houeda, Somba
Religions Traditional beliefs 70%, Muslim 15%, Christian 15%
Ethnic mix Fon 39%, Yoruba 12%, Adja 10%, other tribal groups 39%
Government Multiparty republic
Currency CFA franc = 100 centimes
Literacy rate 34%
Calorie consumption 2,532 kilocalories

BOSNIA & HERZEGOVINA

Page 78 B3

At the heart of the western Balkans, Bosnia and Herzegovina was the focus of the bitter conflict surrounding the breakup of former Yugoslavia.

Official name Republic of Bosnia and Herzegovina
Formation 1992
Capital Sarajevo
Population 4 million /203 people per sq mile (78 people per sq km)
Total area 19,741 sq miles (51,130 sq km)
Languages Serbian, Croatian
Religions Muslim 40%, Serbian Orthodox 31%, other 29%
Ethnic mix Bosnian 44%, Serb 33%, Croat 17%, other 6%
Government Multiparty republic
Currency Marka = 100 pfenniga
Literacy rate 92.7%
Calorie consumption not available

BANGLADESH

Page 113 G3

Bangladesh lies at the north of the Bay of Bengal. It seceded from Pakistan in 1971 and, after much political instability, returned to democracy in 1991.

Official name People's Republic of Bangladesh
Formation 1971
Capital Dhaka
Population 129 million / 2,499 people per sq mile (965 people per sq km)
Total area 51,702 sq miles (133,910 sq km)
Languages Bengali, Urdu, Chakma, Marma (Magh), Garo, Khasi, Santhali
Religions Muslim (mainly Sunni) 87%, Hindu 12%, other 1%
Ethnic mix Bengali 98%, other 2%
Government Multiparty republic
Currency Taka = 100 paisa
Literacy rate 40%
Calorie consumption 2,019 kilocalories

BELGIUM

Page 65 B6

Located in northwestern Europe, Belgium's history has been marked by the division between its Flemish- and French-speaking communities.

Official name Kingdom of Belgium
Formation 1830
Capital Brussels
Population 10.2 million / 805 people per sq mile (311 people per sq km)
Total area 12,671 sq miles 32,820 sq km)
Languages Flemish, French, German
Religions Roman Catholic 88%, Muslim 2%, other 10%
Ethnic mix Fleming 58%, Walloon 33%, Italian 2%, Moroccan 1%, other 6%
Government Constitutional monarchy
Currency Franc = 100 centimes
Literacy rate 99%
Calorie consumption 3,681 kilocalories

BHUTAN

Page 113 G3

The landlocked Buddhist kingdom of Bhutan is perched in the eastern Himalayas between India and China. Gradual reforms protect its cultural identity.

Official name Kingdom of Bhutan
Formation 1656
Capital Thimpu
Population 2.1 million/ 116 people per sq mile (45 people per sq km)
Total area 18,147 sq miles (47,000 sq km)
Languages Dzongkha, Nepali, Assamese
Religions Mahayana Buddhist 70%, Hindu 24%, other 6%
Ethnic mix Bhote 60%, Nepalese 25%, Indigenous tribes 15%
Government Absolute monarchy
Currency Ngultrum = 100 chetrum
Literacy rate 44.2%
Calorie consumption 2,553 kilocalories

BOTSWANA

Page 56 C3

Once the British protectorate of Bechuanaland, Botswana lies landlocked in southern Africa. Diamonds provide it with a prosperous economy.

Official name Republic of Botswana
Formation 1966
Capital Gaborone
Population 1.6 million / 7 people per sq mile (3 people per sq km)
Total area 218,814 sq miles (566,730 sq km)
Languages English, Tswana, Shona, San, Khoikhoi, Ndebele
Religions Traditional beliefs 50%, Christian 50%
Ethnic mix Tswana 98% other 2%
Government Multiparty republic
Currency Pula = 100 thebe
Literacy rate 74.4%
Calorie consumption 2,266 kilocalories

BARBADOS

Page 33 H4

Barbados is the most easterly of the Caribbean Windward Islands. Under British rule for 339 years, it became fully independent in 1966.

Official name Barbados
Formation 1966
Capital Bridgetown
Population 270,000 /1,626 people per sq mile (628 people per sq km)
Total area 166 sq miles (430 sq km)
Languages English, Bajan (Barbadian English)
Religions Anglican 40%, non-religious 17%, Pentecostal 8%, Methodist 7%, Catholic 4%, other 24%
Ethnic mix Black 80%, mixed 15%, White 4%, other 1%
Government Parliamentary democracy
Currency Barbados dollar = 100 cents
Literacy rate 97.6%
Calorie consumption 3,207 kilocalories

BELIZE

Page 30 B1

The last Central American country to gain independence, this former British colony lies on the eastern shore of the Yucatan Peninsula.

Official name Belize
Formation 1981
Capital Belmopan
Population 200,000 / 23 people per sq mile (9 people per sq km)
Total area 8,803 sq miles (22,800 sq km)
Languages English, English Creole, Spanish, Maya, Garifuna (Carib)
Religions Christian 87%, other 13%
Ethnic mix Mestizo 44%, Creole 30%, Maya 11%, Garifuna 7%, Asian 4%, other 4%
Government Parliamentary democracy
Currency Belizean dollar = 100 cents
Literacy rate 75%
Calorie consumption 2,662 kilocalories

BOLIVIA

Page 39 F3

Bolivia lies landlocked high in central South America. Mineral riches once made it the region's wealthiest state. Today, it is the poorest.

Official name Republic of Bolivia
Formation 1825
Capital Sucre (official)/La Paz (administrative)
Population 8.3 million / 20 people per sq mile (8 people per sq km)
Total area 418,682 sq miles (1,084,390 sq km)
Languages Spanish, Aymara, Quechua
Religions Roman Catholic 93%, other 7%
Ethnic mix Quechua 37%, Aymara 32%, mixed 13%, European 10%, other 8%
Government Multiparty republic
Currency Boliviano = 100 centavos
Literacy rate 83.6%
Calorie consumption 2,094 kilocalories

BRAZIL

Page 40 C2

Brazil covers more than half of South America and is the site of the world's largest rain forest. The country has immense natural resources.

Official name Federative Republic of Brazil
Formation 1822
Capital Brasilia
Population 170 million / 52 people per sq mile (20 people per sq km)
Total area 3,265,058 sq miles (8,456,510 sq km)
Languages Portuguese, German, Italian, Spanish, Polish, Japanese
Religions Roman Catholic 89%, Protestant 6%, other 5%
Ethnic mix White 66%, other 34%
Government Multiparty republic
Currency Real = 100 centavos
Literacy rate 84%
Calorie consumption 2,824 kilocalories

BRUNEI

Page 116 D3

Lying on the northwestern coast of the island of Borneo, Brunei is surrounded and divided in two by the Malaysian state of Sarawak.

Official name Sultanate of Brunei
Formation 1984
Capital Bandar Seri Begawan
Population 328,000 / 161 people per sq mile (62 people per sq km)
Total area 2,034 sq miles (5,270 sq km)
Languages Malay, English, Chinese
Religions Muslim 63%, Buddhist 14%, Christian 10%, other 13%
Ethnic mix Malay 67%, Chinese 16%, Indigenous 6%, other 11%
Government Absolute monarchy
Currency Brunei dollar = 100 cents
Literacy rate 90%
Calorie consumption 2,745 kilocalories

BULGARIA

Page 82 C2

Located in southeastern Europe, Bulgaria has made slow progress toward democracy since the fall of its communist regime in 1990.

Official name Republic of Bulgaria
Formation 1908
Capital Sofia
Population 8.2 million / 194 people per sq mile (74 people per sq km)
Total area 42,683 sq miles (110,550 sq km)
Languages Bulgarian, Turkish, Macedonian, Romany, Armenian, Russian
Religions Bulgarian Orthodox 84%, Muslim 13%, other 3%
Ethnic mix Bulgarian 85%, Turkish 9%, Macedonian 3%, Romany 3%
Government Multiparty republic
Currency Lev = 100 stoninki
Literacy rate 98.2%
Calorie consumption 2,831 kilocalories

BURKINA FASO

Page 53 E4

Known as Upper Volta until 1984, the West African state of Burkina Faso has been under military rule for most of its post-independence history.

Official name Burkina Faso
Formation 1960
Capital Ouagadougou
Population 11.6 million / 113 people per sq mile (43 people per sq km)
Total area 105,714 sq miles (273,800 sq km)
Languages French, Mossi, Fulani, Tuareg, Dyula, Songhai
Religions Traditional beliefs 55%, Muslim 35%, Roman Catholic 9%, other Christian 1%
Ethnic mix Mossi 50%, other 50%
Government Multiparty republic
Currency CFA franc = 100 centimes
Literacy rate 20.7%
Calorie consumption 2,387 kilocalories

BURUNDI

Page 51 B7

Small, landlocked Burundi lies just south of the Equator, on the Nile-Congo watershed in Central Africa. Since 1993 it has been marked by violent ethnic conflict.

Official name Republic of Burundi
Formation 1962
Capital Bujumbura
Population 6.7 million / 677 people per sq mile (261 people per sq km)
Total area 9,903 sq miles (25,650 sq km)
Languages Kirundi, French, Swahili
Religions Christian 68%, Traditional beliefs 32%
Ethnic mix Hutu 85%, Tutsi 14%, Twa 1%
Government Multiparty republic
Currency Burundi franc = 100 centimes
Literacy rate 44.6%
Calorie consumption 1,941 kilocalories

CAMBODIA

Page 115 D5

Located in mainland Southeast Asia, Cambodia has emerged from two decades of civil war and invasion from Vietnam.

Official name Kingdom of Cambodia
Formation 1953
Capital Phnom Penh
Population 11.2 million / 164 people per sq mile (63 people per sq km)
Total area 68,154 sq miles (176,520 sq km)
Languages Khmer, French, Chinese, Vietnamese, Cham
Religions Theravada Buddhist 95%, other 5%
Ethnic mix Khmer 94%, Chinese 4%, Vietnamese 1%, other 1%
Government Constitutional monarchy
Currency Riel = 100 sen
Literacy rate 66%
Calorie consumption 2,021 kilocalories

CAMEROON

Page 54 A4

Situated on the central West African coast, Cameroon was effectively a one-party state for 30 years. Multiparty elections were held in 1992.

Official name Republic of Cameroon
Formation 1960
Capital Yaoundé
Population 15 million / 84 people per sq mile (32 people per sq km)
Total area 179,690 sq miles (465,400 sq km)
Languages English, French, Bamileke, Fang, Fulani
Religions Traditional beliefs 25%, Christian 53%, Muslim 22%
Ethnic mix Cameroon highlanders 31%, Bantu 19%, Kirdi 11%, other 39%
Government Multiparty republic
Currency CFA franc = 100 centimes
Literacy rate 72%
Calorie consumption 1,981 kilocalories

CANADA

Page 15 E4

Canada extends from its US border north to the Arctic Ocean. In recent years, French-speaking Quebec has sought independence from the rest of the country.

Official name Canada
Formation 1867
Capital Ottawa
Population 31 million / 9 people per sq mile (3 people per sq km)
Total area 3,560,216 sq miles (9,220,970 sq km)
Languages English, French, Chinese
Religions Roman Catholic 47%, Protestant 41%, non-religious 12%
Ethnic mix British origin 44%, French origin 25%, other European 20%. other (including indigenous Indian) 11%
Government Parliamentary democracy
Currency Canadian dollar = 100 cents
Literacy rate 99%
Calorie consumption 3,094 kilocalories

CAPE VERDE

Page 52 A2

Off the west coast of Africa, in the Atlantic Ocean, lies the group of islands that make up Cape Verde, a Portuguese colony until 1975.

Official name Republic of Cape Verde
Formation 1975
Capital Praia
Population 428,000/ 275 people per sq mile (106 people per sq km)
Total area 1,556 sq miles (4,030 sq km)
Languages Portuguese, Portuguese Creole
Religions Roman Catholic 97%, Protestant 1%, other 2%
Ethnic mix Creole 60%, African 30%, other 10%
Government Multiparty republic
Currency Cape Verde escudo = 100 centavos
Literacy rate 71%
Calorie consumption 2,805 kilocalories

CENTRAL AFRICAN REPUBLIC

Page 54 C4

This landlocked country lies between the basins of the Chad and Congo rivers. Its arid north sustains less than 2% of the population.

Official name Central African Republic
Formation 1960
Capital Bangui
Population 3.6 million / 15 people per sq mile (6 people per sq km)
Total area 240,532 sq miles (622,980 sq km)
Languages French, Sango, Banda, Gbaya
Religions Christian 50%, Traditional beliefs 24%, Muslim 15%, other 11%
Ethnic mix Baya 34%, Banda 27%, Mandjia 21%, Sara 10%, other 8%
Government Multiparty republic
Currency CFA franc = 100 centimes
Literacy rate 42.4%
Calorie consumption 1,690 kilocalories

CHAD

Page 54 C3

Landlocked in north central Africa, Chad has been torn by intermittent periods of civil war since it gained independence from France in 1960.

Official name Republic of Chad
Formation 1960
Capital N'Djamena
Population 7.7 million / 16 people per sq mile (6 people per sq km)
Total area 486,177 sq miles (1,259,200 sq km)
Languages French, Arabic, Sara, Maba
Religions Muslim 50%, Traditional beliefs 43%, Christian 7%
Ethnic mix Over 200 ethnic groups divided between the Arabic nomads (north) and black Africans (south)
Government Multiparty republic
Currency CFA franc = 100 centimes
Literacy rate 50.3%
Calorie consumption 1,989 kilocalories

CHILE

Page 42 B3

Chile extends in a ribbon down the west coast of South America. It returned to democracy in 1989 after a referendum rejected its military dictator.

Official name Republic of Chile
Formation 1818
Capital Santiago
Population 15.2 million / 53 people per sq mile (20 people per sq km)
Total area 289,111 sq miles (748,800 sq km)
Languages Spanish, Amerindian languages
Religions Roman Catholic 80%, other and non-religious 20%
Ethnic mix Mixed and European 90%, Indian 10%
Government Multiparty republic
Currency Chilean peso = 100 centavos
Literacy rate 95.2%
Calorie consumption 2,582 kilocalories

CHINA

Page 104 C4

This vast East Asian country was dominated by Mao Zedong, who founded the Communist republic, and Deng Xiaoping, his successor (1976–1997).

Official name People's Republic of China
Formation 1949
Capital Beijing
Population 1.3 billion / 355 people per sq mile (137 people per sq km)
Total area 3,600,926 sq miles (9,326,410 sq km)
Languages Mandarin, Wu, Cantonese, Hsiang, Min, Hakka, Kan
Religions Non-religious 59%, Traditional beliefs 20%, other 21%
Ethnic mix Han 93%, other 7%
Government Single-party republic
Currency Yuan = 10 jiao
Literacy rate 84%
Calorie consumption 2,727 kilocalories

COLOMBIA

Page 36 B3

Lying in northwest South America, Colombia is one of the world's most violent countries, with powerful drugs cartels and guerrilla activity.

Official name Republic of Columbia
Formation 1819
Capital Bogotá
Population 42.3 million / 105 people per sq mile (41 people per sq km) (1,038,700 sq km)
Total area 401,042 sq miles
Languages Spanish, Amerindian languages, English Creole
Religions Roman Catholic 95%, other 5%
Ethnic mix Mestizo 58%, other 42%
Government Multiparty republic
Currency Colombian peso = 100 centavos
Literacy rate 91%
Calorie consumption 2,677 kilocalories

COMOROS

Page 57 F2

In the Indian Ocean, between Mozambique and Madagascar, lie the Comoros, comprising three main islands, and a number of smaller islets.

Official name Federal Islamic Republic of the Comoros
Formation 1975
Capital Moroni
Population 694,000 / 806 people per sq mile (311 people per sq km)
Total area 861 sq miles (2,230 sq km)
Languages Arabic, French, Comoran
Religions Muslim (mainly Sunni) 98%, Roman Catholic 1%, other 1%
Ethnic mix Comorian 96%, other 4%
Government Islamic republic
Currency Comoros franc = 100 centimes
Literacy rate 55.4%
Calorie consumption 1,897 kilocalories

CONGO

Page 55 B5

Astride the Equator in west central Africa, this former French colony emerged from 26 years of Marxist-Leninist rule in 1990.

Official name Republic of the Congo
Formation 1960
Capital Brazzaville
Population 3 million / 22 people per sq mile (8 people per sq km)
Total area 131,853 sq miles (341,500 sq km)
Languages French, Kongo, Teke, Lingala
Religions Christian 50%, Traditional beliefs 48%, other 2%
Ethnic mix Bakongo 48%, Sangha 20%, Teke 17%, Mbochi 12%, other 3%
Government Multiparty republic
Currency CFA franc = 100 centimes
Literacy rate 77%
Calorie consumption 2,296 kilocalories

CONGO (ZAIRE)

Page 55 C6

Straddling the Equator in east central Africa, Congo (Zaire) is one of Africa's largest countries. It achieved independence from Belgium in 1960.

Official name Democratic Republic of the Congo
Formation 1960
Capital Kinshasa
Population 51.3 million / 59 people per sq mile (22 people per sq km)
Total area 875,520 sq miles (2,267,600 sq km)
Languages French, Kiswahili, Tshiluba
Religions Traditional beliefs 50%, Roman Catholic 37%, Protestant 13%
Ethnic mix Bantu and Hamitic 45%, other 55%
Government Single-party republic
Currency Franc = 100 centimes
Literacy rate 77%
Calorie consumption 2,060 kilocalories

COSTA RICA

Page 31 E4

Costa Rica is the most stable country in Central America. Its neutrality in foreign affairs is long-standing, but it has very strong ties with the US.

Official name Republic of Costa Rica
Formation 1838
Capital San José
Population 4 million / 203 people per sq mile (78 people per sq km)
Total area 19,714 sq miles (51,060 sq km)
Languages Spanish, English Creole, Bribri, Cabecar
Religions Roman Catholic 76%, other (including Protestant) 24%
Ethnic mix White 96%, Black 2%, other 2%
Government Multiparty republic
Currency Costa Rican colón = 100 centimes
Literacy rate 95%
Calorie consumption 2,883 kilocalories

CÔTE D'IVOIRE

Page 52 D4

One of the larger nations along the coast of West Africa, Côte d'Ivoire remains under the influence of its former colonial ruler, France.

Official name Republic of Côte d'Ivoire
Formation 1960
Capital Yamoussoukro
Population 14.8 million / 121 people per sq mile (47 people per sq km)
Total area 122,779 sq miles (318,000 sq km)
Languages French, Akan, Kru, Voltaic
Religions Traditional beliefs 63%, Muslim 25%, Christian 12%
Ethnic mix Baoule 23%, Bete 18%, Kru 17%, Malinke 15%, other 27%
Government Transitional
Currency CFA franc = 100 centimes
Literacy rate 42.6%
Calorie consumption 2,491 kilocalories

CROATIA

Page 78 B2

Post-independence fighting in this former Yugoslav republic, thwarted its plans to capitalize on its prime location along the east Adriatic coast.

Official name Republic of Croatia
Formation 1991
Capital Zagreb
Population 4.5 million / 206 people per sq mile (80 people per sq km)
Total area 21,830 sq miles (56,540 sq km)
Languages Croatian, Serbian
Religions Roman Catholic 76%, Orthodox 11%, Muslim 1%, other 12%
Ethnic mix Croat 78%, Serb 12%, Yugoslav 2%, other 8%
Government Multiparty republic
Currency Kuna = 100 lipa
Literacy rate 97.7%
Calorie consumption not available

CUBA

Page 32 C2

Cuba is the largest island in the Caribbean and the only Communist country in the Americas. It has been led by Fidel Castro since 1959.

Official name Republic of Cuba
Formation 1902
Capital Havana
Population 11.2 million / 262 people per sq mile (101 people per sq km)
Total area 42,803 sq miles (110,860 sq km)
Languages Spanish
Religions Non-religious 49%, Roman Catholic 40%, Protestant 1%, other 10%
Ethnic mix White 66%, European-African 22%, Black 12%
Government Socialist republic
Currency Cuban peso = 100 centavos
Literacy rate 96%
Calorie consumption 2,833 kilocalories

CYPRUS

Page 80 C5

Cyprus lies in the eastern Mediterranean. Since 1974, it has been partitioned between the Turkish-occupied north and the Greek south.

Official name Republic of Cyprus
Formation 1960
Capital Nicosia
Population 786,000 / 220 people per sq mile (85 people per sq km)
Total area 3,567 sq miles (9,240 sq km)
Languages Greek, Turkish, English
Religions Greek Orthodox 77%, Muslim 18%, other 5%
Ethnic mix Greek 77%, Turkish 18%, other (mainly British) 5%
Government Multiparty republic
Currency Cyprus pound / Turkish lira
Literacy rate 96%
Calorie consumption 3,779 kilocalories

CZECH REPUBLIC

Page 77 A5

Once part of Czechoslovakia in eastern Europe, it became independent in 1993, after peacefully dissolving its federal union with Slovakia.

Official name Czech Republic
Formation 1993
Capital Prague
Population 10.2 million / 335 people per sq mile (129 people per sq km)
Total area 30,449 sq miles (78,864 sq km)
Languages Czech, Slovak, Hungarian
Religions Non-religious 40%, Roman Catholic 39%, Protestant 2%, other 19%
Ethnic mix Czech 85%, Moravian 13%, other 2%
Government Multiparty republic
Currency Czech koruna = 100 halura
Literacy rate 99%
Calorie consumption 3,156 kilocalories

DENMARK

Page 63 A7

The country occupies the Jutland peninsula and over 400 islands in Scandinavia. Greenland and the Faeroe Islands are self-governing associated territories.

Official name Kingdom of Denmark
Formation AD 950
Capital Copenhagen (Koebenhavn)
Population 5.3 million / 324 people per sq mile (125 people per sq km)
Total area 16,359 sq miles (42,370 sq km)
Languages Danish
Religions Evangelical Lutheran 89%, Roman Catholic 1%, other 10%
Ethnic mix Danish 96%, Faeroe and Inuit 1%, other (including Scandinavian) 3%
Government Constitutional monarchy
Currency Danish krone = 100 ore
Literacy rate 99%
Calorie consumption 3,664 kilocalories

DJIBOUTI

Page 50 D4

A city state with a desert hinterland, Djibouti lies in northeast Africa. Once known as French Somaliland, its economy relies on its port.

Official name Republic of Djibouti
Formation 1977
Capital Djibouti
Population 638,000 / 71 people per sq mile (28 people per sq km)
Total area 8,949 sq miles (23,180 sq km)
Languages French, Arabic, Somali, Afar
Religions Christian 87%, other 13%
Ethnic mix Issa 60%, Afar 35%, other 5%
Government Multiparty republic
Currency Djibouti franc = 100 centimes
Literacy rate 48.6%
Calorie consumption 2,338 kilocalories

DOMINICA

Page 33 H4

The Caribbean island Dominica resisted European colonization until the 18th century, when it first came under the French, and then, the British.

Official name Commonwealth of Dominica
Formation 1978
Capital Roseau
Population 73,000 / 252 people per sq mile (97 people per sq km)
Total area 290 sq miles (750 sq km)
Languages English, French Creole
Religions Roman Catholic 77%, Protestant 15%, other 8%
Ethnic mix Black 98%, Amerindian 2%
Government Multiparty republic
Currency East Caribbean dollar = 100 cents
Literacy rate 94%
Calorie consumption 2,778 kilocalories

EGYPT

Page 50 B2

Egypt occupies the northeast corner of Africa. Its essentially pro-Western, military-backed regime is being challenged by Islamic fundamentalists.

Official name Arab Republic of Egypt
Formation 1936
Capital Cairo
Population 68.5 million / 178 people per sq mile (69 people per sq km)
Total area 384,343 sq miles (995,456 sq km)
Languages Arabic, French, English
Religions Muslim (mainly Sunni) 94%, Coptic Christian and other 6%
Ethnic mix Eastern Hamitic 90%, other (Nubian, Armenian, Greek) 10%
Government Multiparty republic
Currency Egyptian pound = 100 piastres
Literacy rate 52.7%
Calorie consumption 3,335 kilocalories

ERITREA

Page 50 C3

Lying on the shores of the Red Sea, Eritrea effectively seceded from Ethopia in 1993, following a 30-year war for independence.

Official name State of Eritrea
Formation 1993
Capital Asmara
Population 4 million / 86 people per sq mile (33 people per sq km)
Total area 45,405 sq miles (117,600 sq km)
Languages Tigrinya, Tigre, Afar, Arabic, Bilen, Kunama, Nara, Saho
Religions Christian 45%, Muslim 45%, other 10%
Ethnic mix Tigray (majority), Afars
Government Transitional
Currency Nafka = 100 cents
Literacy rate 25%
Calorie consumption 1,610 kilocalories

FIJI

Page 123 E5

A volcanic archipelago, Fiji comprises 882 islands in the southern Pacific Ocean. Ethnic Fijians and Indo-Fijians have been in conflict since 1987.

Official name Republic of Fiji
Formation 1970
Capital Suva
Population 817,000 / 116 people per sq mile (45 people per sq km)
Total area 7,054 sq miles (18,270 sq km)
Languages Fijian, English, Hindi, Urdu, Tamil, Telegu
Religions Hindu 38%, Methodist 37%, Roman Catholic 9%, other 16%
Ethnic mix Indian 49%, Indigenous Fijian 46%, other 5%
Government Multiparty republic
Currency Fiji dollar = 100 cents
Literacy rate 91.8%
Calorie consumption 3,089 kilocalories

DOMINICAN REPUBLIC

Page 33 E2

The republic occupies the eastern two-thirds of the island of Hispaniola in the Caribbean. Frequent coups and a strong US influence mark its recent past.

Official name Dominican Republic
Formation 1865
Capital Santo Domingo
Population 8.45 million / 455 people per sq mile (176 people per sq km)
Total area 18,679 sq miles (48,380 sq km)
Languages Spanish, French Creole
Religions Roman Catholic 92%, other and non-religious 8%
Ethnic mix European-African 73%, White 16%, Black 11%
Government Multiparty republic
Currency Dominican Republic peso = 100 centavos
Literacy rate 82.6%
Calorie consumption 2,286 kilocalories

EL SALVADOR

Page 30 B3

El Salvador is Central America's smallest state. A 12-year war between US-backed government troops and left-wing guerrillas ended in 1992.

Official name Republic of El Salvador
Formation 1856
Capital San Salvador
Population 6.3 million / 788 people per sq mile (304 people per sq km)
Total area 7,999 sq miles (20,720 sq km)
Languages Spanish
Religions Roman Catholic 80%, Evangelical 18%, other 2%
Ethnic mix Mestizo 89%, Indian 10%, White 1%
Government Multiparty republic
Currency Salvadorean colón = 100 centavos
Literacy rate 77%
Calorie consumption 2,663 kilocalories

ESTONIA

Page 84 D2

Estonia is the smallest and most developed of the three Baltic states. It has the highest standard of living of any of the former Soviet republics.

Official name Republic of Estonia
Formation 1991
Capital Tallinn
Population 1.4 million / 80 people per sq mile (31 people per sq km)
Total area 17,422 sq miles (45,125 sq km)
Languages Estonian, Russian
Religions Evangelical Lutheran 98%, Eastern Orthodox or Baptist 2%
Ethnic mix Russian 62%, Estonian 30%, other 8%
Government Multiparty republic
Currency Kroon = 100 cents
Literacy rate 99%
Calorie consumption not available

FINLAND

Page 62 D4

Finland's distinctive language and national identity have been influenced by both its Scandinavian and its Russian neighbors.

Official name Republic of Finland
Formation 1917
Capital Helsinki
Population 5.2 million / 44 people per sq mile (17 people per sq km)
Total area 117,609 sq miles (304,610 sq km)
Languages Finnish, Swedish, Lappish
Religions Evangelical Lutheran 89%, Finnish Orthodox 1%, Roman Catholic 1%, other 9%
Ethnic mix Finnish 93%, Swedish 6%, other (including Sami) 1%
Government Multiparty republic
Currency Markka = 100 pennia
Literacy rate 99%
Calorie consumption 3,018 kilocalories

ECUADOR

Page 38 A2

Ecuador sits high on South America's western coast. Once part of the Inca heartland, its territory includes the Galapagos Islands, to the west.

Official name Republic of Ecuador
Formation 1830
Capital Quito
Population 12.4 million / 118 people per sq mile (46 people per sq km)
Total area 106,887 sq miles (276,840 sq km)
Languages Spanish, Quechua, other Amerindian languages
Religions Roman Catholic 93%, Protestant, Jewish and other 7%
Ethnic mix Mestizo 55%, Indian 25%, Black 10%, White 10%
Government Multiparty republic
Currency Sucre = 100 centavos
Literacy rate 90.7%
Calorie consumption 2,583 kilocalories

EQUATORIAL GUINEA

Page 55 A5

The country comprises the Rio Muni mainland and five islands on the west coast of central Africa. Free elections were first held in 1988.

Official name Republic of Equatorial Guinea
Formation 1968
Capital Malabo
Population 453,000 / 42 people per sq mile (16 people per sq km)
Total area 10,830 sq miles (28,050 sq km)
Languages Spanish, Fang, Bubi
Religions Roman Catholic 90%, other 10%
Ethnic mix Fang 72%, Bubi 14%, Duala 3%, other 11%
Government Multiparty republic
Currency CFA franc = 100 centimes
Literacy rate 80%
Calorie consumption not available

ETHIOPIA

Page 51 C5

Located in northeast Africa, Ethiopia was a Marxist regime from 1974–91. It has suffered a series of economic, civil, and natural crises.

Official name Federal Democratic Republic of Ethiopia
Formation 1896
Capital Addis Ababa
Population 62.6 million / 179 people per sq mile (60 people per sq km)
Total area 349,490 sq miles (905,450 sq km)
Languages Amharic, Tigrinya, Galla
Religions Muslim 40%, Ethopian Orthodox 40%, other 20%
Ethnic mix Oromo 40%, Amhara 25%, Sidamo 9%, Shankella 6%, other 20%
Government Multiparty republic
Currency Ethopian birr = 100 cents
Literacy rate 35.4%
Calorie consumption 1,610 kilocalories

FRANCE

Page 68 B4

Straddling Western Europe from the English Channel to the Mediterranean Sea, France, is one of the world's leading industrial powers.

Official name French Republic
Formation AD 486
Capital Paris
Population 59 million / 278 people per sq mile (107 people per sq km)
Total area 212,393 sq miles (550,100 sq km)
Languages French, Provenial, German, Breton, Catalan, Basque
Religions Roman Catholic 88%, Muslim 8%, Protestant 2%, other 2%
Ethnic mix French 90%, North African 6%, German 2%, other 2%
Government Multiparty republic
Currency French franc = 100 centimes
Literacy rate 99%
Calorie consumption 3,633 kilocalories

GABON

Page 55 A5

A former French colony straddling the Equator on Africa's west coast, it returned to multiparty politics in 1990, after 22 years of one-party rule.

Official name Gabonese Republic
Formation 1960
Capital Libreville
Population 1.2 million / 12 people per sq mile (5 people per sq km)
Total area 99,486 sq miles (257,670 sq km)
Languages French, Fang, Punu, Sira, Nzebi, Mpongwe
Religions Christian 96%, Muslim 2%, other 2%
Ethnic mix Fang 35%, other Bantu 29%, Eshira 25%, other 11%
Government Multiparty republic
Currency CFA franc = 100 centimes
Literacy rate 66%
Calorie consumption 2,500 kilocalories

GERMANY

Page 72 B4

Europe's strongest economic power, Germany's democratic west and Communist east were re-unified in 1990, after the fall of the east's regime.

Official name Federal Republic of Germany
Formation 1871
Capital Berlin
Population 82.2 million / 609 people per sq mile (235 people per sq km)
Total area 134,949 sq miles (349,520 sq km)
Languages German
Religions Protestant 36%, Roman Catholic 35%, Muslim 2%, other 27%
Ethnic mix German 92%, other 8%
Government Multiparty republic
Currency Deutsche Mark = 100 pfennigs
Literacy rate 99%
Calorie consumption 3,344 kilocalories

GRENADA

Page 33 G5

The Windward island of Grenada became a focus of attention in 1983, when the US mounted an invasion to sever its growing links with Cuba.

Official name Grenada
Formation 1974
Capital St. George's
Population 96,000 / 731 people per sq mile (282 people per sq km)
Total area 131 sq miles (340 sq km)
Languages English, English Creole
Religions Roman Catholic 68%, Anglican 17%, other 15%
Ethnic mix Black 84%, European-African 13%, South Asian 3%
Government Parliamentary democracy
Currency East Caribbean dollar = 100 cents
Literacy rate 96%
Calorie consumption 2,402 kilocalories

GUINEA-BISSAU

Page 52 B4

Known as Portuguese Guinea during its days as a colony, Guinea-Bissau is situated on Africa's west coast, bordered by Senegal and Guinea.

Official name Republic of Guinea-Bissau
Formation 1974
Capital Bissau
Population 1.2 million / 111 people per sq mile (43 people per sq km)
Total area 10,857 sq miles (28,120 sq km)
Languages Portuguese, Creole, Balante
Religions Traditional beliefs 52%, Muslim 40%, Christian 8%
Ethnic mix Balante 30%, Fila (Fulani) 22%, Malinke 12%, other 36%
Government Multiparty republic
Currency Guinea peso = 100 centavos
Literacy rate 33.6%
Calorie consumption 2,556 kilocalories

GAMBIA

Page 52 D3

A narrow state on the west coast of Africa, The Gambia was renowned for its stability until its government was overthrown in a coup in 1994.

Official name Republic of The Gambia
Formation 1965
Capital Banjul
Population 1.3 million / 338 people per sq mile (131 people per sq km)
Total area 3,861 sq miles (10,000 sq km)
Languages English, Mandinka, Fulani, Wolof, Diola, Soninke
Religions Muslim 90%, Christian 9%, Traditional beliefs 1%
Ethnic mix Mandingo 42%, Fulani 18%, Wolof 16%, Jola 10%, Serahuli 9%, other 5%
Government Multiparty republic
Currency Dalasi = 100 butut
Literacy rate 33%
Calorie consumption 2,360 kilocalories

GHANA

Page 53 E5

Once known as the Gold Coast, Ghana in West Africa has experienced intermittent periods of military rule since independence in 1957.

Official name Republic of Ghana
Formation 1957
Capital Accra
Population 20.2 million / 227 people per sq mile (88 people per sq km)
Total area 88,810 sq miles (230,020 sq km)
Languages English, Twi, Fanti, Ewe, Ga, Adangbe, Gurma, Dagomba
Religions Christian 43%, Traditional beliefs 38%, Muslim 11%, other 8%
Ethnic mix Akan 44%, Moshi-Dagomba 16%, Ewe 13%, Ga 8%, other 19%
Government Multiparty republic
Currency Cedi = 100 pesewas
Literacy rate 66.4%
Calorie consumption 2,199 kilocalories

GUATEMALA

Page 30 A2

The largest state on the Central American isthmus, Guatemala returned to civilian rule in 1986, after 32 years of repressive military rule.

Official name Republic of Guatemala
Formation 1838
Capital Guatemala City
Population 11.4 million / 272 people per sq mile (105 people per sq km)
Total area 41,864 sq miles (108,430 sq km)
Languages Spanish, Quiché, Mam, Cakchiquel, Kekchí
Religions Christian 99%, other 1%
Ethnic mix Amerindian 60%, Mestizo 30%, other 10%
Government Multiparty republic
Currency Quetzal = 100 centavos
Literacy rate 66.6%
Calorie consumption 2,255 kilocalories

GUYANA

Page 37 F3

The only English-speaking country in South America, Guyana gained independence from Britain in 1966, and became a republic in 1970.

Official name Cooperative Republic of Guyana
Formation 1966
Capital Georgetown
Population 861,000 / 11 people per sq mile (4 people per sq km)
Total area 76,003 sq miles (196,850 sq km)
Languages English, English Creole, Hindi, Tamil, Amerindian languages
Religions Christian 57%, Hindu 33%, Muslim 9%, other 1%
Ethnic mix East Indian 52%, Black African 38%, other 10%
Government Multiparty republic
Currency Guyana dollar = 100 cents
Literacy rate 98%
Calorie consumption 2,384 kilocalories

GEORGIA

Page 95 F2

Located on the eastern shore of the Black Sea, Georgia's northern provinces have been torn by civil war since independence from the USSR in 1991.

Official name Republic of Georgia
Formation 1991
Capital Tbilisi
Population 5 million / 186 people per sq mile (72 people per sq km)
Total area 26,911 sq miles (69,700 sq km)
Languages Georgian, Russian
Religions Georgian Orthodox 70%, Russian Orthodox 10%, other 20%
Ethnic mix Georgian 70%, Armenian 8%, Russian 6%, Azeri 6%, Ossetian 3%, other 7%
Government Multiparty republic
Currency Lari = 100 tetri
Literacy rate 99%
Calorie consumption not available

GREECE

Page 83 A5

Greece is the southernmost Balkan nation. Surrounded by the Mediterranean, Aegean, and Ionian Seas, it has a strong seafaring tradition.

Official name Hellenic Republic
Formation 1829
Capital Athens
Population 10.6 million / 210 people per sq mile (81 people per sq km)
Total area 50,520 sq miles (130,850 sq km)
Languages Greek, Turkish, Macedonian, Albanian
Religions Greek Orthodox 98%, Muslim 1%, other 1%
Ethnic mix Greek 98%, other 2%
Government Multiparty republic
Currency Drachma = 100 lepta
Literacy rate 96.6%
Calorie consumption 3,815 kilocalories

GUINEA

Page 52 C4

Facing the Atlantic Ocean, on the west coast of Africa, Guinea became the first French colony in Africa to gain independence, in 1958.

Official name Republic of Guinea
Formation 1958
Capital Conakry
Population 7.4 million / 78 people per sq mile (30 people per sq km)
Total area 94,926 sq miles (245,860 sq km)
Languages French, Fulani, Malinke, Soussou
Religions Muslim 85%, Christian 8%, Traditional beliefs 7%
Ethnic mix Fila (Fulani) 30%, Malinke 30%, Soussou 15%, other 25%
Government Multiparty republic
Currency Guinea franc = 100 centimes
Literacy rate 38%
Calorie consumption 2,389 kilocalories

HAITI

Page 32 D3

Haiti shares the Caribbean island of Hispaniola with the Dominican Republic. At independence, in 1804, it became the world's first Black republic.

Official name Republic of Haiti
Formation 1804
Capital Port-au-Prince
Population 8.2 million / 761 people per sq mile (298 people per sq km)
Total area 10,640 sq miles (27,560 sq km)
Languages French, French Creole
Religions Roman Catholic 80%, Protestant 16%, non-religious 1%, other 3%
Ethnic mix Black 95%, European-African 5%
Government Multiparty republic
Currency Gourde = 100 centimes
Literacy rate 45.8%
Calorie consumption 1,706 kilocalories

HONDURAS

Page 30 C2

Honduras straddles the Central American isthmus. The country returned to full democratic civilian rule in 1984, after a succession of military regimes.

Official name Republic of Honduras
Formation 1838
Capital Tegucigalpa
Population 6.3 million / 150 people per sq mile (58 people per sq km)
Total area 43,200 sq miles (111,890 sq km)
Languages Spanish, Black Carib, English Creole
Religions Roman Catholic 97%, other (including Protestant) 3%
Ethnic mix Mestizo 90%, Black African 5%, Amerindian 4%, White 1%
Government Multiparty republic
Currency Lempira = 100 centavos
Literacy rate 70.7%
Calorie consumption 2,305 kilocalories

INDIA

Page 112 D4

Separated from the rest of Asia by the Himalayan mountain ranges, India forms a subcontinent. It is the world's second most populous country.

Official name Republic of India
Formation 1947
Capital New Delhi
Population 1 billion / 883 people per sq mile (341 people per sq km)
Total area 1,147,948 sq miles (2,973,190 sq km)
Languages Hindi, English, and 16 regional languages
Religions Hindu 83%, Muslim 11%, Christian 2%, Sikh 2%, other 2%
Ethnic mix Indo-Aryan 72%, Dravidian 25%, Mongoloid and other 3%
Government Multiparty republic
Currency Indian rupee = 100 paisa
Literacy rate 53.5%
Calorie consumption 2,395 kilocalories

IRAQ

Page 98 B3

Oil-rich Iraq is situated in the central Middle East. Since the removal of the monarchy in 1958, it has experienced considerable political turmoil.

Official name Republic of Iraq
Formation 1932
Capital Baghdad
Population 23 million / 137 people per sq mile (53 people per sq km)
Total area 168,868 sq miles (437,370 sq km)
Languages Arabic, Kurdish, Armenian, Assyrian
Religions Shi'a ithna Muslim 62%, Sunni Muslim 33%, other 5%
Ethnic mix Arab 79%, Kurdish 16%, Persian 3%, Turkoman 2%
Government Single-party republic
Currency Iraqi dinar = 1,000 fils
Literacy rate 58%
Calorie consumption 2,121 kilocalories

ITALY

Page 74 B3

Projecting into the Mediterranean Sea in Southern Europe, Italy is an ancient land, but also one of the continent's newest unified states.

Official name Italian Republic
Formation 1871
Capital Rome
Population 57.3 million / 505 people per sq mile (195 people per sq km)
Total area 113,536 sq miles (294,060 sq km)
Languages Italian, German, French, Rhaeto-Romanic, Sardinian
Religions Roman Catholic 83%, other and non-religious 17%
Ethnic mix Italian 94%, Sardinian 2%, other 4%
Government Multiparty republic
Currency Italian lira = 100 centesimi
Literacy rate 98.3%
Calorie consumption 3,561 kilocalories

HUNGARY

Page 77 C6

Hungary is bordered by seven states in Central Europe. It has changed its economic and political policies to develop closer ties with the EU.

Official name Republic of Hungary
Formation 1918
Capital Budapest
Population 10 million / 280 people per sq mile (108 people per sq km)
Total area 35,652 sq miles (92,340 sq km)
Languages Hungarian
Religions Roman Catholic 64%, Calvinist 20%, non-religious 7%, Lutheran 4%, other 5%
Ethnic mix Magyar 90%, German 2%, Romany 1%, Slovak 1%, other 6%
Government Multiparty republic
Currency Forint = 100 filler
Literacy rate 99%
Calorie consumption 3,503 kilocalories

INDONESIA

Page 116 C4

Formerly the Dutch East Indies, Indonesia, the world's largest archipelago, stretches over 5,000 km (3,100 miles), from the Indian Ocean to the Pacific Ocean.

Official name Republic of Indonesia
Formation 1949
Capital Jakarta
Population 212 million / 303 people per sq mile (117 people per sq km)
Total area 699,447 sq miles (1,811,570 sq km)
Languages Bahasa Indonesia, Javanese, Madurese, Sundanese, Dutch
Religions Muslim 87%, Protestant 6%, Roman Catholic 3%, other 4%
Ethnic mix Javanese 45%, Sundanese 14%, Coastal Malays 8%, Madurese 8%, other 25%
Government Multiparty republic
Currency Rupiah = 100 sen
Literacy rate 85%
Calorie consumption 2,752 kilocalories

IRELAND

Page 67 A6

The Republic of Ireland occupies about 85% of the island of Ireland, with the remainder (Northern Ireland) being part of the United Kingdom.

Official name Republic of Ireland
Formation 1922
Capital Dublin
Population 3.7 million / 139 people per sq mile (54 people per sq km)
Total area 26,598 sq miles (68,890 sq km)
Languages English, Irish Gaelic
Religions Roman Catholic 88%, Anglican 3%, other and non-religious 9%,
Ethnic mix Mostly Celtic with English minority
Government Multiparty republic
Currency Punt = 100 pence
Literacy rate 99%
Calorie consumption 3,847 kilocalories

JAMAICA

Page 32 C3

First colonized by the Spanish and then, from 1655, by the English, Jamaica was the first of the Caribbean island nations to achieve independence, in 1962.

Official name Jamaica
Formation 1962
Capital Kingston
Population 2.6 million / 622 people per sq mile (240 people per sq km)
Total area 4,181 sq miles (10,830 sq km)
Languages English, English Creole
Religions Christian (Church of God, Baptist, Anglican, other Protestant) 55%, other and non-religious 45%
Ethnic mix Black 75%, mixed 15%, South Asian 5%, other 5%
Government Parliamentary democracy
Currency Jamaican dollar = 100 cents
Literacy rate 85.5%
Calorie consumption 2,607 kilocalories

ICELAND

Page 61 E4

Europe's westernmost country, Iceland lies in the North Atlantic, straddling the mid-Atlantic ridge. Its spectacular, volcanic landscape is largely uninhabited.

Official name Republic of Iceland
Formation 1944
Capital Reykjavik
Population 281,000 / 7 people per sq mile (3 people per sq km)
Total area 38,706 sq miles (100,250 sq km)
Languages Icelandic
Religions Evangelical Lutheran 93%, non-religious 6%, other Christian 1%
Ethnic mix Icelandic 98%, other 2%
Government Constitutional republic
Currency Icelandic króna = 100 aurar
Literacy rate 99%
Calorie consumption 3,058 kilocalories

IRAN

Page 98 C3

Since the 1979 revolution led by Ayatollah Khomeini, which sent Iran's Shah into exile, this Middle Eastern country has become the world's largest theocracy.

Official name Islamic Republic of Iran
Formation 1906
Capital Tehran
Population 67.7 million / 107 people per sq mile (41 people per sq km)
Total area 631,659 sq miles (1,636,000 sq km)
Languages Farsi (Persian), Azerbaijani, Gilaki, Mazanderani, Kurdish, Baluchi
Religions Shi'a Muslim 95%, Sunni Muslim 4%, other 1%
Ethnic mix Persian 50%, Azeri 20%, Lur and Bakhtiari 10%, Kurd 8%, other 12%
Government Islamic republic
Currency Iranian rial = 100 dinars
Literacy rate 73.3%
Calorie consumption 2,860 kilocalories

ISRAEL

Page 97 A7

Israel was created as a new state in 1948 on the east coast of the Mediterranean. Following wars with its Arab neighbors, it has extended its boundaries.

Official name State of Israel
Formation 1948
Capital Jerusalem
Population 6.2 million / 790 people per sq mile (305 people per sq km)
Total area 7,849 sq miles (20,330 sq km)
Languages Hebrew, Arabic, Yiddish, German, Russian, Polish, Romanian
Religions Jewish 82%, Muslim (mainly Sunni) 14%, other (including Druze) 4%
Ethnic mix Jewish 82%, other (mostly Arab) 18%
Government Multiparty republic
Currency New Israeli shekel = 100 agorat
Literacy rate 95.4%
Calorie consumption 3,050 kilocalories

JAPAN

Page 108 C4

Japan comprises four principal islands and over 3,000 smaller ones. With the emperor as constitutional head, it is now the world's most powerful economy.

Official name Japan
Formation 1600
Capital Tokyo
Population 126.7 million / 872 people per sq mile (337 people per sq km)
Total area 145,374 sq miles (376,520 sq km)
Languages Japanese, Korean, Chinese
Religions Shinto and Buddhist 76%, Buddhist 16%, other (including Christian) 8%
Ethnic mix Japanese 99%, other (mainly Korean) 1%
Government Constitutional monarchy
Currency Yen = 100 sen
Literacy rate 99%
Calorie consumption 2,903 kilocalories

JORDAN

Page 97 B6

The kingdom of Jordan lies east of Israel. In 1993, King Hussein responded to calls for greater democracy by agreeing to multiparty elections.

Official name Hashemite Kingdom of Jordan
Formation 1946
Capital Amman
Population 6.7 million / 195 people per sq mile (75 people per sq km)
Total area 34,335 sq miles (88,930 sq km)
Languages Arabic
Religions Muslim (mainly Sunni) 92%, other (mostly Christian) 8%
Ethnic mix Arab 98% (Palestinian 40%), Armenian 1%, Circassian 1%
Government Constitutional monarchy
Currency Jordanian dinar = 1,000 fils
Literacy rate 87.2%
Calorie consumption 3,022 kilocalories

KIRIBATI

Page 123 F3

Part of the British colony of the Gilbert and Ellice Islands until independence in 1979, Kiribati comprises 33 islands in the mid-Pacific Ocean.

Official name Republic of Kiribati
Formation 1979
Capital Bairiki (Tarawa Atoll)
Population 84,000 / 306 people per sq mile (118 people per sq km)
Total area 274 sq miles (710 sq km)
Languages English, Micronesian dialect
Religions Roman Catholic 53%, Kiribati Protestant Church 39%, other 8%
Ethnic mix Micronesian 98%, other 2%
Government Multiparty republic
Currency Australian dollar = 100 cents
Literacy rate 98%
Calorie consumption 2,651 kilocalories

LAOS

Page 114 D4

A former French colony, independent in 1953, Laos lies landlocked in Southeast Asia. It has been under communist rule since 1975.

Official name Lao People's Democratic Republic
Formation 1953
Capital Vientiane
Population 5.4 million / 61 people per sq mile (23 people per sq km)
Total area 89,111 sq miles (230,800 sq km)
Languages Lao, Miao, Yao
Religions Buddhist 85%, other (including Animist) 15%
Ethnic mix Lao Loum 56%, Lao Theung 34%, Lao Soung 9%, other 1%
Government Single-party republic
Currency New kip = 100 cents
Literacy rate 58.6%
Calorie consumption 2,259 kilocalories

LESOTHO

Page 56 D4

The landlocked kingdom of Lesotho is entirely surrounded by South Africa, which provides all its land transportation links with the outside world.

Official name Kingdom of Lesotho
Formation 1966
Capital Maseru
Population 2.2 million / 188 people per sq mile (72 people per sq km)
Total area 11,718 sq miles (30,350 sq km)
Languages English, Sesotho, Zulu
Religions Christian 90%, Traditional beliefs 10%
Ethnic mix Basotho 97%, European and Asian 3%
Government Constitutional monarchy
Currency Loti = 100 lisente
Literacy rate 82.3%
Calorie consumption 2,201 kilocalories

KAZAKHSTAN

Page 92 B4

Second largest of the former Soviet republics, mineral-rich Kazakhstan has the potential to become the major Central Asian economic power.

Official name Republic of Kazakhstan
Formation 1991
Capital Astana
Population 16.2 million / 15 people per sq mile (6 people per sq km)
Total area 1,049,150 sq miles (2,717,300 sq km)
Languages Kazakh, Russian, German
Religions Muslim (mainly Sunni) 47%, Russian Orthodox 15%, other 38%
Ethnic mix Kazakh 44%, Russian 36%, Ukranian 5%, German 4%, Uzbek and Tartar 2%, other 9%
Government Multiparty republic
Currency Tenge = 100 tein
Literacy rate 99%
Calorie consumption not available

KUWAIT

Page 98 C4

Kuwait lies on the northwest extreme of the Persian Gulf. The state was a British protectorate from 1914 until 1961, when full independence was granted.

Official name State of Kuwait
Formation 1961
Capital Kuwait City
Population 2 million / 291 people per sq mile (112 people per sq km)
Total area 6880 sq miles (17,820 sq km)
Languages Arabic, English
Religions Muslim (mainly Sunni) 92%, Christian 6%, other 2%
Ethnic mix Kuwaiti 45%, other Arab 35%, South Asian 9%, Iranian 4%, other 7%
Government Constitutional monarchy
Currency Kuwaiti dinar = 1,000 fils
Literacy rate 80.4%
Calorie consumption 2,523 kilocalories

LATVIA

Page 84 C3

Situated on the east coast of the Baltic Sea, Latvia, like its Baltic neighbors, became independent in 1991. It retains a large Russian population.

Official name Republic of Latvia
Formation 1991
Capital Riga
Population 2.4 million / 96 people per sq mile (37 people per sq km)
Total area 24,938 sq miles (64,589 sq km)
Languages Latvian, Russian
Religions Evangelical Lutheran 85%, other Christian 15%
Ethnic mix Latvian 52%, Russian 34%, Belorussian 5%, Ukranian 4%, other 5%
Government Multiparty republic
Currency Lat = 100 santimi
Literacy rate 99%
Calorie consumption not available

LIBERIA

Page 52 C5

Liberia faces the Atlantic Ocean in equatorial West Africa. Africa's oldest republic, it was established in 1847. Today, it is torn by civil war.

Official name Republic of Liberia
Formation 1847
Capital Monrovia
Population 3.2 million / 86 people per sq mile (33 people per sq km)
Total area 37,189 sq miles (96,320 sq km)
Languages English, Kpelle, Vai, Bassa, Kru, Grebo, Kissi, Gola, Loma
Religions Christian 68%, Traditional beliefs 18%, Muslim 14%
Ethnic mix Indigenous tribes (16 main groups) 95%, Americo-Liberians 5%
Government Multiparty republic
Currency Liberian dollar = 100 cents
Literacy rate 38.3%
Calorie consumption 1,640 kilocalories

KENYA

Page 51 C6

Kenya straddles the Equator on Africa's east coast. It became a multiparty democracy in 1992 and has been led by President Moi since 1978.

Official name Republic of Kenya
Formation 1963
Capital Nairobi
Population 30 million / 138 people per sq mile (53 people per sq km)
Total area 218,907 sq miles (566,970 sq km)
Languages Swahili, English, Kikuyu, Luo, Kamba
Religions Christian 60%, Traditional beliefs 25%, Muslim 6%, other 9%
Ethnic mix Kikuyu 21%, Luhya 14%, Luo 13%, Kalenjin 11%, other 41%
Government Multiparty republic
Currency Kenya shilling = 100 cents
Literacy rate 79.3%
Calorie consumption 2,075 kilocalories

KYRGYZSTAN

Page 101 F2

A mountainous, landlocked state in Central Asia. The most rural of the ex-Soviet republics, it only gradually developed its own cultural nationalism.

Official name Kyrgyz Republic
Formation 1991
Capital Bishkek
Population 4.7 million / 61 people per sq mile (24 people per sq km)
Total area 76,640 sq miles (198,500 sq km)
Languages Kyrgyz, Russian
Religions Muslim 65%, other (mainly Russian Orthodox) 35%
Ethnic mix Kyrgyz 57%, Russian 19%, Uzbek 13%, Tartar 2%, Ukranian 2%, other 7%
Government Multiparty republic
Currency Som = 100 teen
Literacy rate 97%
Calorie consumption not available

LEBANON

Page 96 A4

Lebanon is dwarfed by its two powerful neighbors, Syria and Israel. The state started rebuilding in 1989, after 14 years of intense civil war.

Official name Republic of Lebanon
Formation 1944
Capital Beirut
Population 3.3 million / 835 people per sq mile (323 people per sq km)
Total area 3,949 sq miles (10,230 sq km)
Languages Arabic, French, Armenian
Religions Muslim (mainly Shi'a) 70%, Christian (mainly Maronite) 30%
Ethnic mix Arab 93% (Lebanese 83%, Palestinian 10%), other 7%
Government Multiparty republic
Currency Lebanese pound = 100 piastres
Literacy rate 84.4%
Calorie consumption 3,317 kilocalories

LIBYA

Page 49 F3

Situated on the Mediterranean coast of North Africa, Libya is a Muslim dictatorship, politically marginalized by the West for its terrorist links.

Official name Great Socialist People's Libyan Arab Jamahariyah
Formation 1951
Capital Tripoli/Benghazi
Population 5.6 million / 8 people per sq mile (3 people per sq km)
Total area 679,358 sq miles (1,759,540 sq km)
Languages Arabic, Tuareg
Religions Muslim (mainly Sunni) 97%, other 3%
Ethnic mix Arab and Berber 95%, other 5%
Government Single-party state
Currency Libyan dinar = 1,000 dirhams
Literacy rate 76.5%
Calorie consumption 3,308 kilocalories

LIECHTENSTEIN

Page 73 B7

Tucked in the Alps between Switzerland and Austria, Liechtenstein became an independent principality of the Holy Roman Empire in 1719.

Official name Principality of Liechtenstein
Formation 1719
Capital Vaduz
Population 32,000/ 508 people per sq mile (200 people per sq km)
Total area 62 sq miles (160 sq km)
Languages German, Alemannish dialect, Italian
Religions Roman Catholic 81%, Protestant 7%, other 12%
Ethnic mix Liectensteiner 63%, Swiss 15%, German 9%, other 13%
Government Constitutional monarchy
Currency Swiss franc = 100 centimes
Literacy rate 99%
Calorie consumption not available

MACEDONIA

Page 79 D6

Landlocked in the southern Balkans, Macedonia has been affected by sanctions imposed on its northern trading partners and by Greek antagonism.

Official name Former Yugoslav Republic of Macedonia
Formation 1991
Capital Skopje
Population 2 million / 201 people per sq mile (78 people per sq km)
Total area 9,929 sq miles (25,715 sq km)
Languages Macedonian, Serbian, Croatian
Religions Christian 80%, Muslim 20%
Ethnic mix Macedonian 67%, Albanian 23%, Turkish 4%, other 6%
Government Multiparty republic
Currency Macedonian denar = 100 deni
Literacy rate 94%
Calorie consumption not available

MALAYSIA

Page 116 B3

Malaysia's three separate territories include Malaya, Sarawak, and Sabah. A financial crisis in 1997 ended a decade of spectacular financial growth.

Official name Federation of Malaysia
Formation 1963
Capital Kuala Lumpur
Population 22.2 million / 175 people per sq mile (68 people per sq km)
Total area 126,853 sq miles (328,550 sq km)
Languages English, Bahara Malay
Religions Muslim 53%, Buddhist 19%, Chinese faiths 12%, other 16%
Ethnic mix Malay 47%, Chinese 32%, Indigenous tribes 12%, other 9%
Government Federal constitutional monarchy
Currency Ringgit = 100 cents
Literacy rate 85.7%
Calorie consumption 2,888 kilocalories

MALTA

Page 80 A5

The Maltese archipelago lies off southern Sicily, midway between Europe and North Africa. The only inhabited islands are Malta, Gozo, and Kemmuna.

Official name Republic of Malta
Formation 1964
Capital Valetta
Population 389,000 / 3,148 people per sq mile (1,216 people per sq km)
Total area 124 sq miles (320 sq km)
Languages Maltese, English
Religions Roman Catholic 98%, other and non-religious 2%
Ethnic mix Maltese (mixed Arab, Sicilian, Norman, Spanish, Italian, English) 98%, other 2%
Government Multiparty republic
Currency Maltese lira = 100 cents
Literacy rate 91%
Calorie consumption 3,486 kilocalories

LITHUANIA

Page 84 B4

The largest, most powerful and stable of the Baltic states, Lithuania was the first Baltic country to declare independence from Moscow, in 1991.

Official name Republic of Lithuania
Formation 1991
Capital Vilnius
Population 3.7 million / 147 people per sq mile (57 people per sq km)
Total area 25,174 sq miles (65,200 sq km)
Languages Lithuanian, Russian
Religions Roman Catholic 87%, Russian Orthodox 10%, other 3%
Ethnic mix Lithuanian 80%, Russian 9%, Polish 7%, other 4%
Government Multiparty republic
Currency Litas = 100 centas
Literacy rate 99%
Calorie consumption not available

MADAGASCAR

Page 57 F4

Lying in the Indian Ocean, Madagascar is the world's fourth largest island. Free elections in 1993 ended 18 years of radical socialist government.

Official name Republic of Madagascar
Formation 1960
Capital Antananarivo
Population 16 million / 71 people per sq mile (27 people per sq km)
Total area 224,532 sq miles (581,540 sq km)
Languages French, Malagasy
Religions Traditional beliefs 52%, Christian 41%, Muslim 7%
Ethnic mix Merina 26%, Betsimisaraka 15%, other 59%
Government Multiparty republic
Currency Malagasy franc = 100 centimes
Literacy rate 47%
Calorie consumption 2,135 kilocalories

MALDIVES

Page 110 A4

Only 200 of the more than 1,000 Maldivian small coral islands in the Indian Ocean, are inhabited. Government rests in the hands of a few influential families.

Official name Republic of Maldives
Formation 1965
Capital Malé
Population 286,000 / 2,469 people per sq mile (953 people per sq km)
Total area 116 sq miles (300 sq km)
Languages Dhivehi (Maldivian), Sinhala, Tamil
Religions Sunni Muslim 100%
Ethnic mix Maldivian 99%, other 1%
Government Republic
Currency Rufiyaa (Maldivian rupee) = 100 laari
Literacy rate 95.7%
Calorie consumption 2,580 kilocalories

MARSHALL ISLANDS

Page 122 D1

A group of 34 atolls, the Marshall Islands were under US rule as part of the UN Trust Territory of the Pacific Islands until 1986. The economy depends on US aid.

Official name Republic of the Marshall Islands
Formation 1986
Capital Delap district
Population 51,000 / 728 people per sq mile (281 people per sq km)
Total area 70 sq miles (181 sq km)
Languages Marshallese, English, Japanese, German
Religions Protestant 80%, Roman Catholic 15%, other 5%
Ethnic mix Micronesian 97%, other 3%
Government Republic
Currency US dollar = 100 cents
Literacy rate 91%
Calorie consumption not available

LUXEMBOURG

Page 65 D8

Making up part of the plateau of the Ardennes in Western Europe, Luxembourg is Europe's last independent duchy and one of its richest states.

Official name Grand Duchy of Luxembourg
Formation 1867
Capital Luxembourg
Population 431,000/ 432 people per sq mile (165 people per sq km)
Total area 998 sq miles (2,586 sq km)
Languages French, German, Letzeburghish
Religions Roman Catholic 97%, other 3%
Ethnic mix Luxembourger 72%, Portuguese 9%, Italian 5%, other 14%
Government Constitutional monarchy
Currency Franc = 100 centimes
Literacy rate 99%
Calorie consumption 3,681 kilocalories

MALAWI

Page 57 E1

A former British colony, Malawi lies landlocked in southeast Africa. Its name means "the land where the sun is reflected in the water like fire."

Official name Republic of Malawi
Formation 1964
Capital Lilongwe
Population 11 million / 300 people per sq mile (116 people per sq km)
Total area 36,324 sq miles (94,080 sq km)
Languages English, Chewa, Lomwe
Religions Protestant 55%, Roman Catholic 20%, Muslim 20%, other 5%
Ethnic mix Maravi 55%, Lomwe 17%, Yao 13%, other 15%
Government Multiparty republic
Currency Malawi kwacha = 100 tambala
Literacy rate 57.7%
Calorie consumption 1,825 kilocalories

MALI

Page 53 E2

Landlocked in the heart of West Africa, Mali held its first free elections in 1992, more than 30 years after it gained independence from France.

Official name Republic of Mali
Formation 1960
Capital Bamako
Population 11.2 million / 24 people per sq mile (9 people per sq km)
Total area 471,115 sq miles (1,220,190 sq km)
Languages French, Bambara, Fulani, Senufo, Soninké
Religions Muslim (mainly Sunni) 80%, Traditional beliefs 18%, other 2%
Ethnic mix Mande 50%, Peul 17%, Voltaic 12%, Songhai 6%, other 15%
Government Multiparty republic
Currency CFA franc = 100 centimes
Literacy rate 35.5%
Calorie consumption 2,278 kilocalories

MAURITANIA

Page 52 C2

Situated in northwest Africa, two-thirds of Mauritania's territory is desert. A former French colony, it achieved independence in 1960.

Official name Islamic Republic of Mauritania
Formation 1960
Capital Nouakchott
Population 2.7 million / 7 people per sq mile (3 people per sq km)
Total area 395,953 sq miles (1,025,520 sq km)
Languages Hassaniyah Arabic, French, Wolof
Religions Muslim (Maliki) 100%
Ethnic mix Maur 30%, Black 30%, mixed 40%
Government Multiparty republic
Currency Ouguiya = 5 khoums
Literacy rate 38.4%
Calorie consumption 2,685 kilocalories

MAURITIUS

Page 57 H3

Located to the east of Madagascar in the Indian Ocean, Mauritius became a republic 25 years after it gained independence. Tourism is a mainstay of its economy.

Official name Mauritius
Formation 1968
Capital Port Louis
Population 1.2 million / 1,671 people per sq mile (645 people per sq km)
Total area 718 sq miles (1,860 sq km)
Languages English, French, French Creole, Hindi, Urdu, Tamil, Chinese
Religions Hindu 52%, Roman Catholic 26%, Muslim 17%, Protestant 2%, other 3%
Ethnic mix Creole 55%, South Asian 40%, Chinese 3%, other 2%
Government Multiparty republic
Currency Mauritian rupee = 100 cents
Literacy rate 83%
Calorie consumption 2,690 kilocalories

MOLDOVA

Page 86 D3

The smallest and most densely populated of the ex-Soviet republics, Moldova has strong linguistic and cultural links with Romania to the west.

Official name Republic of Moldova
Formation 1991
Capital Chisinau
Population 4.4 million / 338 people per sq mile (131 people per sq km)
Total area 13,000 sq miles (33,700 sq km)
Languages Romanian, Moldovan
Religions Roman Orthodox 98%, Jewish 1%, other 1%
Ethnic mix Moldovan 65%, Ukranian 14%, Russian 13%, Gagauz 4%, other 4%
Government Multiparty republic
Currency Moldovan leu = 100 bani
Literacy rate 98.3%
Calorie consumption not available

MOROCCO

Page 48 C2

A former French colony in northwest Africa, independent in 1956, Morocco has occupied the disputed territory of Western Sahara since 1975.

Official name Kingdom of Morocco
Formation 1956
Capital Rabat
Population 28.4 million / 165 people per sq mile (64 people per sq km)
Total area 172,316 sq miles (446,300 sq km)
Languages Arabic, Berber (Shluh, Tamazight, Riffian), French, Spanish
Religions Muslim 98%, other 2%
Ethnic mix Arab and Berber 99%, European 1%
Government Constitutional monarchy
Currency Moroccan dirham = 100 centimes
Literacy rate 45.9%
Calorie consumption 2,984 kilocalories

NAMIBIA

Page 56 B3

Located in southwestern Africa, Namibia became free of South African control in 1990, after years of uncertainty and guerrilla activity.

Official name Republic of Namibia
Formation 1990
Capital Windhoek
Population 1.7 million / 5 people per sq mile (2 people per sq km)
Total area 317,872 sq miles (823,290 sq km)
Languages English, Ovambo, Kavango, Bergdama, German
Religions Christian 90%, other 10%
Ethnic mix Ovambo 50%,, Kavango 9%, Herero 8%, Damara 8%, other 25%
Government Multiparty republic
Currency Namibian dollar = 100 cents, South African rand = 100 cents
Literacy rate 79.8%
Calorie consumption 2,134 kilocalories

MEXICO

Page 28 D3

Located between the United States of America and the Central American states, Mexico was a Spanish colony for 300 years until 1836.

Official name United States of Mexico
Formation 1836
Capital Mexico City
Population 99 million / 134 people per sq mile (52 people per sq km)
Total area 736,945 sq miles (1,908,690 sq km)
Languages Spanish, Nahuatl, Maya, Zapotec, Mixtec, Otomi, Totonac
Religions Roman Catholic 95%, Protestant 1%, other 4%
Ethnic mix Mestizo 55%, Indigenous Indian 20%, European 16%, other 9%
Government Multiparty republic
Currency Mexican peso = 100 centavos
Literacy rate 90%
Calorie consumption 3,146 kilocalories

MONACO

Page 69 F6

A jet-set image and a thriving service sector define the modern identity of this tiny enclave on the Côte d'Azur in southeastern France.

Official name Principality of Monaco
Formation 1861
Capital Monaco
Population 32,000 / 42,503 people per sq mile (16,410 people per sq km)
Total area 0.75 sq miles (1.95 sq km)
Languages French, Italian, Monégasque, English
Religions Roman Catholic, 89%, Protestant 6%, other 5%
Ethnic mix French 47%, Monégasque 16%, Italian 16%, other 21%
Government Constitutional monarchy
Currency French franc = 100 centimes
Literacy rate 99%
Calorie consumption not available

MOZAMBIQUE

Page 57 F3

Mozambique lies on the southeast African coast. It was torn by a civil war between the Marxist government and a rebel group from 1977–1992.

Official name Republic of Mozambique
Formation 1975
Capital Maputo
Population 19.7 million / 65 people per sq mile (25 people per sq km)
Total area 302,737 sq miles (784,090 sq km)
Languages Portuguese, Makua, Tsonga, Sena, Lomwe
Religions Traditional beliefs 60%, Christian 30%, Muslim 10%
Ethnic mix Makua-Lomwe 47%, Thonga 23%, Malawi 12%, other 18%
Government Multiparty republic
Currency Metical = 100 centavos
Literacy rate 40.5%
Calorie consumption 1,680 kilocalories

NAURU

Page 122 D3

Nauru lies in the Pacific, 4,000 km (2,480 miles) northeast of Australia. Phosphate deposits have made its citizens among the richest in the world.

Official name Republic of Nauru
Formation 1968
Capital No official capital
Population 11,500 / 1,381 people per sq mile (548 people per sq km)
Total area 8.2 sq miles (21.2 sq km)
Languages Nauruan, English, Kiribati, Chinese, Tuvaluan
Religions Christian 95%, other 5%
Ethnic mix Nauruan 62%, other Pacific islanders 25%, Chinese and Vietnamese 8%, European 5%
Government Parliamentary democracy
Currency Australian dollar = 100 cents
Literacy rate 99%
Calorie consumption not available

MICRONESIA

Page 122 B1

The Federated States of Micronesia, situated in the western Pacific, comprise 607 islands and atolls grouped into four main island states.

Official name Federated States of Micronesia
Formation 1986
Capital Palikir (Pohnpei island)
Population 111,500 / 411 people per sq mile (159 people per sq km)
Total area 271 sq miles (702 sq km)
Languages English, Trukese, Pohnpeian, Mortlockese, Losrean
Religions Roman Catholic 50%, Protestant 48%, other 2%
Ethnic mix Micronesian 99%, other 1%
Government Republic
Currency US dollar = 100 cents
Literacy rate 89%
Calorie consumption not available

MONGOLIA

Page 104 D2

Lying between Russia and China, Mongolia is a vast and isolated country with a small population. Over two-thirds of the country is desert.

Official name Mongolia
Formation 1924
Capital Ulan Bator
Population 2.7 million / 4 people per sq mile (2 people per sq km)
Total area 604,247 sq miles (1,565,000 sq km)
Languages Khalka Mongol, Turkic, Chinese, Russian
Religions Predominantly Tibetan Buddhist, with a Muslim minority
Ethnic mix Mongol 90%, Kazakh 4%, Chinese 2%, Russian 2%, other 2%
Government Multiparty republic
Currency Tugrik (togrog) = 100 möngös
Literacy rate 84%
Calorie consumption 1,899 kilocalories

MYANMAR (BURMA)

Page 114 A3

Myanmar forms the eastern shores of the Bay of Bengal and the Andaman Sea in Southeast Asia. Since 1988 it has been ruled by a repressive military regime.

Official name Union of Myanmar
Formation 1948
Capital Yangon (Rangoon)
Population 45.6 million / 180 people per sq mile (69 people per sq km)
Total area 253,876 sq miles (657,540 sq km)
Languages Burmese, Karen, Shan, Chin, Kachin, Mon, Palaung, Wa
Religions Buddhist 87%, Christian 6%, Muslim 4%, Hindu 1%, other 2%
Ethnic mix Burman (Bamah) 68%, Shan 9%, Karen 6%, other 17%
Government Military regime
Currency Kyat = 100 pyas
Literacy rate 83.6%
Calorie consumption 2,598 kilocalories

NEPAL

Page 113 E3

Nepal lies between India and China, on the shoulder of the southern Himalayas. The elections of 1991 ended a period of absolute monarchy.

Official name Kingdom of Nepal
Formation 1769
Capital Kathmandu
Population 24 million / 452 people per sq mile (175 people per sq km)
Total area 52,818 sq miles (136,800 sq km)
Languages Nepali, Maithili, Bhojpuri
Religions Hindu 90%, Buddhist 4%, Muslim 3%, Christian 1%, other 2%
Ethnic mix Nepalese 58%, Bihari 19%, Tamang 6%, other 17%
Government Constitutional monarchy
Currency Nepalese rupee = 100 paisa
Literacy rate 38%
Calorie consumption 1,957 kilocalories

NETHERLANDS

Page 64 C3

Astride the delta of five major rivers in northwest Europe, the Netherlands has a long trading tradition. Rotterdam is the world's largest port.

Official name Kingdom of the Netherlands
Formation 1815
Capital Amsterdam, The Hague
Population 15.8 million / 1,206 people per sq mile (466 people per sq km)
Total area 13,096 sq miles (33,920 sq km)
Languages Dutch, Frisian
Religions Roman Catholic 36%, Protestant 27%, Muslim 3%, other 34%
Ethnic mix Dutch 96%, other 4%
Government Constitutional monarchy
Currency Netherlands guilder (guilder) or florin = 100 cents
Literacy rate 99%
Calorie consumption 3,222 kilocalories

NIGER

Page 53 F3

Niger lies landlocked in West Africa, but it is linked to the sea by the River Niger. Since 1973 it has suffered civil unrest and two major droughts.

Official name Republic of Niger
Formation 1960
Capital Niamey
Population 10.7 million / 22 people per sq mile (8 people per sq km)
Total area 489,072 sq miles (1,266,700 sq km)
Languages French, Hausa, Djerma
Religions Muslim 85%, Traditional beliefs 14%, Christian 1%
Ethnic mix Hausa 54%, Djerma and Songhai 21%, Fulani 10%, Tuareg 9%, other 6%
Government Multiparty republic
Currency CFA franc = 100 centimes
Literacy rate 14.3%
Calorie consumption 2,257 kilocalories

NORWAY

Page 63 A5

The Kingdom of Norway traces the rugged western coast of Scandinavia. Settlements are largely restricted to southern and coastal areas.

Official name Kingdom of Norway
Formation 1905
Capital Oslo
Population 4.5 million / 38 people per sq mile (15 people per sq km)
Total area 118,467 sq miles (306,830 sq km)
Languages Norwegian, Lappish
Religions Evangelical Lutheran 89%, Roman Catholic 1%, other and non-religious 10%
Ethnic mix Norwegian 95%, Lapp 1%, other 4%
Government Constitutional monarchy
Currency Norwegian krone = 100 ore
Literacy rate 99%
Calorie consumption 3,244 kilocalories

PALAU

Page 122 A2

The Palau archipelago, a group of over 200 islands, lies in the western Pacific Ocean. In 1994, it became the world's newest independent state.

Official name Republic of Palau
Formation 1994
Capital Koror
Population 18,500 million / 94 people per sq mile (36 people per sq km)
Total area 196 sq miles (508 sq km)
Languages Belauan (Palauan), English, Japanese
Religions Roman Catholic 66%, Modekngei 34%
Ethnic mix Polynesian 96%, other 4%
Government Multiparty republic
Currency US dollar = 100 cents
Literacy rate 92%
Calorie consumption not available

NEW ZEALAND

Page 128 A4

One of the Pacific Rim countries, New Zealand lies southeast of Australia, and comprises the North and South Islands, separated by the Cook Strait.

Official name Dominion of New Zealand
Formation 1947
Capital Wellington
Population 4 million /38 people per sq mile (15 people per sq km)
Total area 103,730 sq miles (268,680 sq km)
Languages English, Maori
Religions Protestant 47%, non-religious 16%, Roman Catholic 15%, other 22%
Ethnic mix European 82%, Maori 9%, Pacific Islanders 3%, other 6%
Government Parliamentary democracy
Currency New Zealand dollar = 100 cents
Literacy rate 99%
Calorie consumption 3,669 kilocalories

NIGERIA

Page 53 F4

Africa's most populous state Nigeria, in West Africa, is a federation of 30 states. It adopted civilian rule in 1999 after 33 years of military government.

Official name Federal Republic of Nigeria
Formation 1960
Capital Abuja
Population 112 million / 317 people per sq mile (122 people per sq km)
Total area 351,648 sq miles (910,770 sq km)
Languages English, Hausa, Yoruba, Ibo
Religions Muslim 50%, Christian 40%, Traditional beliefs 10%
Ethnic mix Hausa 21%, Yoruba 21%, Ibo 18%, Fulani 11%, other 29%
Government Multiparty republic
Currency Naira = 100 kobo
Literacy rate 59.5%
Calorie consumption 2,124 kilocalories

OMAN

Page 99 D6

Situated on the eastern coast of the Arabian Peninsula, Oman is the least developed of the Gulf states, despite modest oil exports.

Official name Sultanate of Oman
Formation 1951
Capital Muscat
Population 2.5 million / 30 people per sq mile (12 people per sq km)
Total area 82,030 sq miles (212,460 sq km)
Languages Arabic, Baluchi
Religions Ibadhi Muslim 75%, other Muslim and Hindu 25%
Ethnic mix Arab 75%, Baluchi 15%, other 10%
Government Monarchy with Consultative Council
Currency Omani rial = 1,000 baizas
Literacy rate 67%
Calorie consumption 3,013 kilocalories

PANAMA

Page 31 F5

Southernmost of the Central American countries. The Panama Canal (returned to Panama from US control in 2000) links the Pacific and Atlantic oceans.

Official name Republic of Panama
Formation 1903
Capital Panama City
Population 3 million / 99 people per sq mile (38 people per sq km)
Total area 29,339 sq miles (75,990 sq km)
Languages Spanish, English Creole, Amerindian languages, Chibchan
Religions Roman Catholic 93%, other 7%
Ethnic mix Mestizo 60%, White 14%, Black 12%, Amerindian 8%, Asian 4%, other 2%
Government Multiparty republic
Currency Balboa = 100 centesimos
Literacy rate 91%
Calorie consumption 2,242 kilocalories

NICARAGUA

Page 30 D3

Nicaragua lies at the heart of Central America. An 11-year war between left-wing Sandinistas and right-wing US-backed Contras ended in 1989.

Official name Republic of Nicaragua
Formation 1838
Capital Managua
Population 5 million / 111 people per sq mile (43 people per sq km)
Total area 45,849 sq miles (118,750 sq km)
Languages Spanish, English Creole, Miskito
Religions Roman Catholic 95%, other 5%
Ethnic mix Mestizo 69%, White 14%, Black 8%, other 9%
Government Multiparty republic
Currency Córdoba oro = 100 pence
Literacy rate 63.4%
Calorie consumption 2,293 kilocalories

NORTH KOREA

Page 106 E3

North Korea comprises the northern half of the Korean peninsula. A communist state since 1948, it is largely isolated from the outside world.

Official name Democratic People's Republic of Korea
Formation 1948
Capital Pyongyang
Population 24 million / 516 people per sq mile (199 people per sq km)
Total area 46,490 sq miles (120,410 sq km)
Languages Korean, Chinese
Religions Non-religious 68%, Traditional beliefs 16%, Ch'ondogyo 14%, Buddhist 2%
Ethnic mix Korean 100%
Government Single-party republic
Currency N Korean won = 100 chon
Literacy rate 95%
Calorie consumption 2,833 kilocalories

PAKISTAN

Page 112 B2

Once a part of British India, Pakistan was created in 1947 as an independent Muslim state. Today, the country is divided into four provinces.

Official name Islamic Republic of Pakistan
Formation 1947
Capital Islamabad
Population 156.5 million / 526 people per sq mile (203 people per sq km)
Total area 297,636 sq miles (770,880 sq km)
Languages Urdu, Punjabi, Sindhi
Religions Sunni Muslim 77%, Shi'a Muslim 29%, Hindu 2%, Christian 1%
Ethnic mix Punjabi 50%, Sindhi 15%, Pashto 15%, Mohajir 8%, other 12%
Government Multiparty republic
Currency Pakistani rupee = 100 paisa
Literacy rate 41%
Calorie consumption 2,315 kilocalories

PAPUA NEW GUINEA

Page 122 B3

Achieving independence from Australia in 1975, PNG occupies the eastern section of the island of New Guinea and several other island groups.

Official name Independent State of Papua New Guinea
Formation 1975
Capital Port Moresby
Population 4.8 million / 27 people per sq mile (10 people per sq km)
Total area 174,849 sq miles (452,860 sq km)
Languages English, Pidgin English, Papuan, c.750 native languages
Religions Christian 62%, Traditional beliefs 34%, other 4%
Ethnic mix Papuan 85%, other 15%
Government Parliamentary democracy
Currency Kina = 100 toea
Literacy rate 73.7%
Calorie consumption 2,613 kilocalories

PARAGUAY

Page 42 D2

Landlocked in central South America. Its post-independence history has included periods of military rule. Free elections were held in 1993.

Official name Republic of Paraguay
Formation 1811
Capital Asunción
Population 5.5 million /
36 people per sq mile (14 people per sq km)
Total area 153,397 sq miles
(397,300 sq km)
Languages Spanish, Guaraní
Religions Roman Catholic 90%, other 10%
Ethnic mix Mestizo 90%, Amerindian 2%, other 8%
Government Multiparty republic
Currency Guaraní = 100 centimos
Literacy rate 92.4%
Calorie consumption 2,670 kilocalories

POLAND

Page 76 B3

With its seven international borders and strategic location in the heart of Europe, Poland has always played an important role in European affairs.

Official name Republic of Poland
Formation 1918
Capital Warsaw
Population 38.8 million /
330 people per sq mile (127 people per sq km)
Total area 117,552 sq miles
(304,460 sq km)
Languages Polish
Religions Roman Catholic 93%, Eastern Orthodox 2%, other and non-religious 5%
Ethnic mix Polish 98%, other 2%
Government Multiparty republic
Currency Zloty = 100 groszy
Literacy rate 99%
Calorie consumption 3,301 kilocalories

ROMANIA

Page 86 B4

Romania lies on the Black Sea coast. Since the overthrow of its communist regime in 1989, it has been slowly converting to a free-market economy.

Official name Romania
Formation 1878
Capital Bucharest
Population 22.3 million / 251 people per sq mile (97 people per sq km)
Total area 88,934 sq miles
(230,340 sq km)
Languages Romanian, Hungarian, German
Religions Romanian Orthodox 87%, Roman Catholic 5%, other 8%
Ethnic mix Romanian 89%, Magyar 9%, Romany 1%, other 1%
Government Multiparty republic
Currency Leu = 100 bani
Literacy rate 97.8%
Calorie consumption 3,051 kilocalories

SAINT KITTS & NEVIS

Page 33 G3

Separated by a channel, the two islands of Saint Kitts and Nevis are part of the Leeward Islands chain in the Caribbean. Nevis is the less developed of the two.

Official name Federation of Saint Christopher and Nevis
Formation 1983
Capital Basseterre
Population 41,000 / 289 people per sq mile (111 people per sq km)
Total area 139 sq miles
(360 sq km)
Languages English, English Creole
Religions Anglican 33%, Methodist 29%, Roman Catholic 7%, other 31%
Ethnic mix Black 95%, mixed 5%
Government Parliamentary democracy
Currency Eastern Caribbean dollar = 100 cents
Literacy rate 90%
Calorie consumption 2,419 kilocalories

PERU

Page 38 C3

Once the heart of the Inca empire, before the Spanish conquest in the 16th century, Peru lies on the Pacific coast of South America.

Official name Republic of Peru
Formation 1824
Capital Lima
Population 25.7 million /
52 people per sq mile (20 people per sq km)
Total area 494,208 sq miles
(1,280,000 sq km)
Languages Spanish, Quechua, Aymará
Religions Roman Catholic 95%, other 5%
Ethnic mix Amerindian 54%, Mestizo 32%, White 12%, other 2%
Government Multiparty republic
Currency New sol = 100 centimos
Literacy rate 88.7%
Calorie consumption 1,882 kilocalories

PORTUGAL

Page 70 B3

Facing the Atlantic on the western side of the Iberian Peninsula, Portugal is the most westerly country on the European mainland.

Official name Republic of Portugal
Formation 1140
Capital Lisbon
Population 10 million /
279 people per sq mile (108 people per sq km)
Total area 35,501 sq miles
(91,950 sq km)
Languages Portuguese
Religions Roman Catholic 97%, Protestant 1%, other 2%
Ethnic mix Portuguese 99%, African 1%
Government Multiparty republic
Currency Portuguese escudo = 100 centavos
Literacy rate 90.8%
Calorie consumption 3,634 kilocalories

RUSSIAN FEDERATION

Page 92 D4

Still the world's largest state, despite the breakup of the USSR in 1991, the Russian Federation is struggling to capitalize on its diversity.

Official name Russian Federation
Formation 1991
Capital Moscow
Population 147 million /
22 people per sq mile (9 people per sq km)
Total area 6,563,700 sq miles
(17,000,000 sq km)
Languages Russian
Religions Russian Orthodox 75%, other 25%
Ethnic mix Russian 82%, Tatar 4%, Ukrainian 3%, Chuvash 1%, other 10%
Government Multiparty republic
Currency Rouble = 100 kopeks
Literacy rate 99%
Calorie consumption not available

SAINT LUCIA

Page 33 G4

Among the most beautiful of the Caribbean Windward Islands, Saint Lucia retains both French and British influences from its colonial history.

Official name Saint Lucia
Formation 1979
Capital Castries
Population 152,000 /
641 people per sq mile (248 people per sq km)
Total area 235 sq miles
(610 sq km)
Languages English, French Creole
Religions Roman Catholic 90%, other 10%
Ethnic mix Black 90%, African-European 6%, South Asian 4%
Government Parliamentary democracy
Currency Eastern Caribbean dollar = 100 cents
Literacy rate 82%
Calorie consumption 2,588 kilocalories

PHILIPPINES

Page 117 E1

An archipelago of 7,107 islands between the South China Sea and the Pacific. After 21 years of dictatorship, democracy was restored in 1986.

Official name Republic of the Philippines
Formation 1946
Capital Manila
Population 76 million / 660 people per sq mile (255 people per sq km)
Total area 115,123 sq miles
(298,170 sq km)
Languages Filipino, English, Cebuano
Religions Roman Catholic 83%, Protestant 9%, Muslim 5%, other 3%
Ethnic mix Malay 50%, Indonesian and Polynesian 30%, other 20%
Government Multiparty republic
Currency Peso = 100 centavos
Literacy rate 94.6%
Calorie consumption 2,257 kilocalories

QATAR

Page 98 C4

Projecting north from the Arabian Peninsula into the Persian Gulf, Qatar's reserves of oil and gas make it one of the region's wealthiest states.

Official name State of Qatar
Formation 1971
Capital Doha
Population 699,000 /
165 people per sq mile (64 people per sq km)
Total area 4,247 sq miles
(11,000 sq km)
Languages Arabic
Religions Sunni Muslim 86%, Hindu 10%, Christian 4%
Ethnic mix Arab 40%, Pakistani 18%, Indian 18%, Iranian 10%, other 14%
Government Absolute monarchy
Currency Qatar riyal = 100 dirhams
Literacy rate 80%
Calorie consumption not available

RWANDA

Page 51 B6

Rwanda lies just south of the Equator in east central Africa. Since independence from France in 1962, ethnic tensions have dominated politics.

Official name Republic of Rwanda
Formation 1982
Capital Kigali
Population 7.7 million / 799 people per sq mile (309 people per sq km)
Total area 9,633 sq miles
(24,950 sq km)
Languages French, Rwandan, Kiswahili, English
Religions Roman Catholic 65%, Protestant 9%, Muslim 1%, other 25%
Ethnic mix Hutu 90%, Tutsi 8%, other (including Twa) 2%
Government Multiparty republic
Currency Rwanda franc = 100 centimes
Literacy rate 63%
Calorie consumption 1,821 kilocalories

SAINT VINCENT & THE GRENADINES

Page 33 G4

Formerly ruled by Britain, these volcanic islands form part of the Caribbean Windward Islands.

Official name Saint Vincent and the Grenadines
Formation 1979
Capital Kingston
Population 111,000 / 846 people per sq mile (327 people per sq km)
Total area 131 sq miles (340 sq km)
Languages English, English Creole
Religions Anglican 42%, Methodist 20%, Roman Catholic 19%, other 19%
Ethnic mix Black 82%, mixed 14%, White 3%, South Asian 1%
Government Parliamentary democracy
Currency Eastern Caribbean dollar = 100 cents
Literacy rate 82%
Calorie consumption 2,347 kilocalories

SAMOA

Page 123 F4

The southern Pacific islands of Samoa gained independence from New Zealand in 1962. Four of the nine islands are inhabited.

Official name Independent State of Samoa
Formation 1962
Capital Apia
Population 180,000/ 165 people per sq mile (64 people per sq km)
Total area 1,092 sq miles (2,830 sq km)
Languages Samoan, English
Religions Christian 100%
Ethnic mix Polynesian 90%, Euronesian 9%, other 1%
Government Parliamentary state
Currency Tala = 100 sene
Literacy rate 98%
Calorie consumption 2,828 kilocalories

SAUDI ARABIA

Page 99 B5

Occupying most of the Arabian Peninsula, the desert kingdom of Saudi Arabia, rich in oil and gas, covers an area the size of Western Europe.

Official name Kingdom of Saudi Arabia
Formation 1932
Capital Riyadh
Population 21.6 million / 26 people per sq mile (10 people per sq km)
Total area 829,995 sq miles (2,149,690 sq km)
Languages Arabic
Religions Sunni Muslim 85%, Shi'a Muslim 15%
Ethnic mix Arab 90%, Afroasian 10%
Government Absolute monarchy
Currency Saudi riyal = 100 malalah
Literacy rate 73.4%
Calorie consumption 2,735 kilocalories

SIERRA LEONE

Page 52 C4

The West African state of Sierra Leone achieved independence from the British in 1961. Today, it is one of the world's poorest nations.

Official name Republic of Sierra Leone
Formation 1961
Capital Freetown
Population 5 million / 177 people per sq mile (68 people per sq km)
Total area 27,652 sq miles (71,620 sq km)
Languages English, Mende, Temne, Krio
Religions Traditional beliefs 52%, Muslim 40%, Christian 8%
Ethnic mix Mende 35%, Temne 32%, Limba 8%, Kuranko 4%, other 21%
Government Multiparty republic
Currency Leone = 100 cents
Literacy rate 33.3%
Calorie consumption 1,694 kilocalories

SLOVENIA

Page 73 D8

Northernmost of the former Yugoslav republics, Slovenia has the closest links with Western Europe. In 1991, it gained independence with little violence.

Official name Republic of Slovenia
Formation 1991
Capital Ljubljana
Population 2 million / 256 people per sq mile (99 people per sq km)
Total area 7820 sq miles (20,250 sq km)
Languages Slovene, Serbian, Croatian
Religions Roman Catholic 94%, Orthodox Catholic 2%, Muslim 1%, other 3%
Ethnic mix Slovene 88%, Croat 3%, Serb 2%, Bosnian 1%, other 6%
Government Multiparty republic
Currency Tolar = 100 stotins
Literacy rate 99%
Calorie consumption not available

SAN MARINO

Page 74 C3

Perched on the slopes of Monte Titano in the Italian Appennino, San Marino has maintained its independence since the 4th century AD.

Official name Republic of San Marino
Formation AD 301
Capital San Marino
Population 26,000 / 1,115 people per sq mile (431 people per sq km)
Total area 24 sq miles (61 sq km)
Languages Italian
Religions Roman Catholic 93%, other and non-religious 7%
Ethnic mix Sanmaranesi 95%, other 5%
Government Multiparty republic
Currency Lira = 100 centesimi
Literacy rate 96%
Calorie consumption 3,561 kilocalories

SENEGAL

Page 52 B3

A former French colony, Senegal achieved independence in 1960. Its capital, Dakar, stands on the westernmost cape of Africa.

Official name Republic of Senegal
Formation 1960
Capital Dakar
Population 9.5 million / 128 people per sq mile (49 people per sq km)
Total area 74,335 sq miles (192,530 sq km)
Languages French, Wolof, Fulani, Serer, Diola, Malinke, Soninke, Arabic
Religions Muslim 90%, Christian (mainly Roman Catholic) 5%, Traditional beliefs 5%
Ethnic mix Wolof 36%, Fulani 17%, Serer 17%, other 30%
Government Multiparty republic
Currency CFA franc = 100 centimes
Literacy rate 34.6%
Calorie consumption 2,262 kilocalories

SINGAPORE

Page 116 A1

A city state linked to the southernmost tip of the Malay Peninsula by a causeway, Singapore is one of Asia's most important commercial centers.

Official name Republic of Singapore
Formation 1965
Capital Singapore
Population 3.6 million / 15,285 people per sq mile (5,902 people per sq km)
Total area 236 sq miles (610 sq km)
Languages Malay, English, Mandarin Chinese, Tamil
Religions Buddhist and Daoist 53%, Muslim 16%, Hindu 4%, Christian 1%, other 26%
Ethnic mix Chinese 78%, Malay 14%, Indian 6%, other 2%
Government Multiparty republic
Currency Singapore dollar = 100 cents
Literacy rate 91.4%
Calorie consumption 3,128 kilocalories

SOLOMON ISLANDS

Page 122 C3

The Solomon archipelago comprises several hundred islands scattered in the southwestern Pacific. Independence from Britain came in 1978.

Official name Solomon Islands
Formation 1978
Capital Honiara
Population 444,000 / 41 people per sq mile (16 people per sq km)
Total area 10,806 sq miles (27,990 sq km)
Languages English, Pidgin English, Melanesian Pidgin
Religions Anglican 34%, Roman Catholic 19%, South Seas Evangelical Church 17%, Methodist 11%, other 19%
Ethnic mix Melanesian 94%, other 6%
Government Parliamentary democracy
Currency Solomon Islands dollar = 100 cents
Literacy rate 62%
Calorie consumption 2,173 kilocalories

SAO TOME & PRINCIPE

Page 55 E1

A former Portuguese colony off Africa's west coast, comprising two main islands and smaller islets. The 1991 elections ended 15 years of Marxism.

Official name Democratic Republic of São Tomé and Príncipe
Formation 1975
Capital São Tomé
Population 142,000 / 383 people per sq mile (148 people per sq km)
Total area 370 sq miles (960 sq km)
Languages Portuguese, Portuguese Creole
Religions Roman Catholic 90%, other Christian 10%
Ethnic mix Black 90%, Portuguese and Creole 10%
Government Multiparty republic
Currency Dobra = 100 centimos
Literacy rate 75%
Calorie consumption 2,129 kilocalories

SEYCHELLES

Page 57 G1

A former British colony comprising 115 islands in the Indian Ocean. Under one-party rule for 16 years, it became a multiparty democracy in 1993.

Official name Republic of the Seychelles
Formation 1976
Capital Victoria
Population 79,000/ 758 people per sq mile (293 people per sq km)
Total area 108 sq miles (280 sq km)
Languages Seselwa (French Creole), English, French
Religions Roman Catholic 90%, Anglican 8%, other 2%
Ethnic mix Seychellois (mixed Asian, African, and European) 100%
Government Multiparty republic
Currency Seychelles rupee = 100 cents
Literacy rate 84%
Calorie consumption 2,287 kilocalories

SLOVAKIA

Page 77 C6

Landlocked in Central Europe, Slovakia has been independent since 1993. It is the less developed half of the former Czechoslovakia.

Official name Slovak Republic
Formation 1993
Capital Bratislava
Population 5.4 million / 285 people per sq mile (110 people per sq km)
Total area 18,932 sq miles (49,036 sq km)
Languages Slovak, Hungarian, Czech
Religions Roman Catholic 60%, Atheist 10%, Protestant 8%, Orthodox 4%, other 18%
Ethnic mix Slovak 85%, Hungarian 9%, Czech 1%, other 5%
Government Multiparty republic
Currency Koruna = 100 halierov
Literacy rate 99%
Calorie consumption 3,156 kilocalories

SOMALIA

Page 51 E5

Italian and British Somaliland were united in 1960 to create this semiarid state occupying the horn of Africa. It has suffered years of civil war.

Official name Somali Democratic Republic
Formation 1960
Capital Mogadishu
Population 10 million / 42 people per sq mile (16 people per sq km)
Total area 242,215 sq miles (627,340 sq km)
Languages Arabic, Somali, English, Italian
Religions Sunni Muslim 98%, other 2%
Ethnic mix Somali 85%, other 15%
Government Transitional
Currency Somali shilling = 100 cents
Literacy rate 24%
Calorie consumption 1,499 kilocalories

SOUTH AFRICA

Page 56 C4

South Africa is the most southerly nation on the African continent. The multiracial elections of 1994 overturned 80 years of white minority rule.

Official name Republic of South Africa
Formation 1934
Capital Pretoria
Population 40.4 million / 86 people per sq mile (33 people per sq km)
Total area 471,443 sq miles (1,221,040 sq km)
Languages Afrikaans, English, 11 African languages
Religions Protestant 39%, Roman Catholic 8%, other 53%
Ethnic mix Zulu 23%, other Black 38%, White 16%, Mixed 10%, other 13%
Government Multiparty republic
Currency Rand = 100 cents
Literacy rate 84%
Calorie consumption 2,695 kilocalories

SRI LANKA

Page 110 D3

The island republic of Sri Lanka is separated from India by the narrow Palk Strait. Since 1983, the Sinhalese and Tamil population have been in conflict.

Official name Democratic Socialist Republic of Sri Lanka
Formation 1948
Capital Colombo
Population 18.6 million / 752 people per sq mile (290 people per sq km)
Total area 24,996 sq miles (64,740 sq km)
Languages Sinhalese, Tamil, English
Religions Buddhist 70%, Hindu 15%, Christian 8%, Muslim 7%
Ethnic mix Sinhala 74%, Tamil 18%, Moor 7%, other 1%
Government Multiparty republic
Currency Sri Lanka rupee = 100 cents
Literacy rate 90.7%
Calorie consumption 2,273 kilocalories

SWAZILAND

Page 56 D4

The tiny southern African kingdom of Swaziland gained independence from Britain in 1968. It is economically dependent on South Africa.

Official name Kingdom of Swaziland
Formation 1968
Capital Mbabane
Population 1 million / 152 people per sq mile (59 people per sq km)
Total area 6,640 sq miles (17,200 sq km)
Languages Siswati, English, Zulu
Religions Christian 60%, Traditional beliefs 40%
Ethnic mix Swazi 95%, other 5%
Government Executive monarchy
Currency Lilangeni = 100 cents
Literacy rate 77.5%
Calorie consumption 2,706 kilocalories

SYRIA

Page 96 B3

Stretching from the eastern Mediterranean to the River Tigris, Syria's borders were created on its independence from France in 1946.

Official name Syrian Arab Republic
Formation 1946
Capital Damascus
Population 16 million / 227 people per sq mile (87 people per sq km)
Total area 71,065 sq miles (184,060 sq km)
Languages Arabic, French, Kurdish
Religions Sunni Muslim 74%, other Muslim 16%, Christian 10%
Ethnic mix Arab 89%, Kurdish 6%, Armenian, Turkmen, Circassian 2%, other 3%
Government Single-party republic
Currency Syrian pound = 100 piastres
Literacy rate 71.6%
Calorie consumption 3,175 kilocalories

SOUTH KOREA

Page 106 E4

South Korea occupies the southern half of the Korean peninsula. It was separated from the communist North in 1948.

Official name Republic of Korea
Formation 1948
Capital Seoul
Population 46.8 million / 1,228 people per sq mile (474 people per sq km)
Total area 38,119 sq miles (98,730 sq km)
Languages Korean, Chinese
Religions Mahayana Buddhist 47%, Protestant 38%, Roman Catholic 11%, Confucian 3%, other 1%
Ethnic mix Korean 100%
Government Multiparty republic
Currency Korean won = 100 chon
Literacy rate 97.2%
Calorie consumption 3,285 kilocalories

SUDAN

Page 50 D4

The largest country in Africa, part of Sudan borders the Red Sea. In 1989, an army coup installed a military Islamic fundamentalist regime.

Official name Republic of Sudan
Formation 1956
Capital Khartoum
Population 29.5 million / 32 people per sq mile (12 people per sq km)
Total area 917,373 sq miles (2,376,000 sq km)
Languages Arabic, Dinka, Nuer, Nubian, Beja, Zande, Bari, Fur, Shilluk
Religions Muslim (mainly Sunni) 70%, Traditional beliefs 20%, other 10%
Ethnic mix Arab 51%, Dinka 13%, Nuba 9%, Beja 7%, other 20%
Government Military regime
Currency Sudanese pound or dinar = 100 piastres
Literacy rate 53.3%
Calorie consumption 2,202 kilocalories

SWEDEN

Page 62 B4

The largest Scandinavian country in both population and area, Sweden's strong industrial base helps to fund its extensive welfare system.

Official name Kingdom of Sweden
Formation 1809
Capital Stockholm
Population 8.9 million / 56 people per sq mile (22 people per sq km)
Total area 158,926 sq miles (411,620 sq km)
Languages Swedish, Finnish, Lappish
Religions Evangelical Lutheran 89%, Roman Catholic 2%, other 9%
Ethnic mix Swedish 91%, Finnish and Lapp 3%, other European 6%
Government Constitutional monarchy
Currency Swedish krona = 100 ore
Literacy rate 99%
Calorie consumption 2,972 kilocalories

TAIWAN

Page 107 D6

The island republic of Taiwan lies 130 km (80 miles) off the southeast coast of mainland China. China considers it to be one of its provinces.

Official name Republic of China (Taiwan)
Formation 1949
Capital Taipei
Population 22 million / 1,756 people per sq mile (678 people per sq km)
Total area 12,455 sq miles (32,260 sq km)
Languages Mandarin Chinese, Amoy Chinese, Hakka Chinese
Religions Buddhist, Confucian, Taoist 93%, Christian 5%, other 2%
Ethnic mix Indigenous Chinese 84%, Mainland Chinese 14%, Aborigine 2%
Government Multiparty republic
Currency Taiwan dollar = 100 cents
Literacy rate 94%
Calorie consumption not available

SPAIN

Page 70 D2

Lodged between mainland Europe and Africa, the Atlantic and the Mediterranean, Spain has occupied a pivotal position since it was united in 1492.

Official name Kingdom of Spain
Formation 1492
Capital Madrid
Population 39.6 million / 205 people per sq mile (79 people per sq km)
Total area 192,833 sq miles (499,440 sq km)
Languages Spanish, Catalan, Galician
Religions Roman Catholic 96%, other 4%
Ethnic mix Castilian Spanish 72%, Catalan 17%, Galician 6%, other 5%
Government Constitutional monarchy
Currency Spanish peseta = 100 centimos
Literacy rate 97.2%
Calorie consumption 3,708 kilocalories

SURINAME

Page 37 G3

Suriname is a former Dutch colony on the north coast of South America. Democracy was restored in 1991, after almost 11 years of military rule.

Official name Republic of Suriname
Formation 1975
Capital Paramaribo
Population 417,000 / 7 people per sq mile (3 people per sq km)
Total area 62,343 sq miles (161,470 sq km)
Languages Dutch, Pidgin English, Hindi, Javanese, Saramacca, Carib
Religions Christian 48%, Hindu 27%, Muslim 20%, other 5%
Ethnic mix Hindustani 34%, Creole 34%, Javanese 18%, Black 9%, other 5%
Government Multiparty republic
Currency Suriname guilder = 100 cents
Literacy rate 93.5%
Calorie consumption 2,547 kilocalories

SWITZERLAND

Page 73 A7

One of the world's most prosperous countries, with a long tradition of neutrality in foreign affairs, it lies at the center of Western Europe.

Official name Swiss Confederation
Formation 1291
Capital Berne
Population 7.4 million / 482 people per sq mile (186 people per sq km)
Total area 15,355 sq miles (39,770 sq km)
Languages German, French, Italian, Swiss German, Romansch
Religions Roman Catholic 46%, Protestant 40%, other 14%
Ethnic mix German 65%, French 18%, Italian 10%, Romansh 1%, other 6%
Government Federal republic
Currency Swiss franc = 100 centimes
Literacy rate 99%
Calorie consumption 3,379 kilocalories

TAJIKISTAN

Page 101 F3

Tajikistan lies landlocked on the western slopes of the Pamirs in Central Asia. The Tajiks' language and traditions are similar to those of Iran.

Official name Republic of Tajikistan
Formation 1991
Capital Dushanbe
Population 6.2 million / 112 people per sq mile (43 people per sq km)
Total area 55,251 sq miles (143,100 sq km)
Languages Tajik, Russian
Religions Sunni Muslim 80%, Shi'a Muslim 5%, other 15%
Ethnic mix Tajik 62%, Uzbek 24%, Russian 4%, Tatar 2%, other 8%
Government Multiparty republic
Currency Tajik rouble = 100 kopeks
Literacy rate 99%
Calorie consumption not available

TANZANIA

Page 51 B7

The East African state of Tanzania was formed in 1964 by the union of Tanganyika and Zanzibar. A third of its area is game reserve or national park.

Official name United Republic of Tanzania
Formation 1961
Capital Dodoma
Population 33.5 million / 98 people per sq mile (38 people per sq km)
Total area 342,100 sq miles (886,040 sq km)
Languages English, Swahili, Sukuma
Religions Muslim 33%, Christian 33%, Traditional beliefs 30%, other 4%
Ethnic mix 120 small ethnic Bantu groups 99%, other 1%
Government Multiparty republic
Currency Tanzanian shilling = 100 cents
Literacy rate 71.6%
Calorie consumption 2,018 kilocalories

TONGA

Page 123 E4

Northeast of New Zealand, in the South Pacific, Tonga is an archipelago of 170 islands, 45 of which are inhabited. Politics is effectively controlled by the king.

Official name Kingdom of Tonga
Formation 1970
Capital Nuku'alofa
Population 98,000 / 353 people per sq mile (136 people per sq km)
Total area 278 sq miles (720 sq km)
Languages Tongan, English
Religions Free Wesleyan 64%, Roman Catholic 15%, Other 21%
Ethnic mix Polynesian 99%, other Pacific groups and European 1%
Government Constitutional monarchy
Currency Pa'anga (Tongan dollar) = 100 seniti
Literacy rate 99%
Calorie consumption 2,946 kilocalories

TURKEY

Page 94 B3

Lying partly in Europe, but mostly in Asia, Turkey's position gives it significant influence in the Mediterranean, Black Sea, and Middle East.

Official name Republic of Turkey
Formation 1923
Capital Ankara
Population 66.6 million / 224 people per sq mile (87 people per sq km)
Total area 297,154 sq miles (769,630 sq km)
Languages Turkish, Kurdish, Arabic, Circassian, Armenian, Greek, Georgian
Religions Muslim (mainly Sunni) 99%, other 1%
Ethnic mix Turkish 70%, Kurdish 20%, Arab 2%, other 8%
Government Multiparty republic
Currency Turkish lira = 100 krural
Literacy rate 83.2%
Calorie consumption 3,429 kilocalories

UGANDA

Page 51 B6

Uganda lies landlocked in East Africa. It was ruled by one of Africa's more eccentric leaders, the dictator Idi Amin Dada, from 1971–1980.

Official name Republic of Uganda
Formation 1962
Capital Kampala
Population 21.8 million / 283 people per sq mile (109 people per sq km)
Total area 77,046 sq miles (199,550 sq km)
Languages English, Swahili, Luganda
Religions Roman Catholic 38%, Protestant 33%, Traditional beliefs 13%, Muslim (mainly Sunni) 5%, other 11%
Ethnic mix African 99%, other 1%
Government Multiparty republic
Currency New Uganda shilling = 100 cents
Literacy rate 64%
Calorie consumption 2,159 kilocalories

THAILAND

Page 115 C5

Thailand lies at the heart of mainland Southeast Asia. Continuing rapid industrialization has resulted in massive congestion in the capital.

Official name Kingdom of Thailand
Formation 1782
Capital Bangkok
Population 61.4 million / 311 people per sq mile (120 people per sq km)
Total area 197,254 sq miles (510,890 sq km)
Languages Thai, Chinese, Malay, Khmer, Mon, Karen, Miao
Religions Theravada Buddhist 95%, Muslim 3%, other 2%
Ethnic mix Thai 80%, Chinese 12%, Malay 4%, Khmer and other 4%
Government Constitutional monarchy
Currency Baht = 100 stangs
Literacy rate 94.7%
Calorie consumption 2,432 kilocalories

TRINIDAD & TOBAGO

Page 33 H5

The former British colony of Trinidad and Tobago is the most southerly of the West Indies, lying just 15 km (9 miles) off the coast of Venezuela.

Official name Republic of Trinidad and Tobago
Formation 1962
Capital Port-of-Spain
Population 1.3 million / 656 people per sq mile (253 people per sq km)
Total area 1981 sq miles (5,130 sq km)
Languages English, English Creole
Religions Christian 58%, Hindu 30%, Muslim 8%, other 4%
Ethnic mix Asian 40%, Black 40%, Mixed 19%, White and Chinese 1%
Government Multiparty republic
Currency Trinidad and Tobago dollar = 100 cents
Literacy rate 97.8%
Calorie consumption 2,585 kilocalories

TURKMENISTAN

Page 100 B2

Stretching from the Caspian Sea into the deserts of Central Asia, the ex-Soviet state of Turkmenistan has adjusted better than most to independence.

Official name Turkmenistan
Formation 1991
Capital Ashgabat
Population 4.5 million / 24 people per sq mile (9 people per sq km)
Total area 188,455 sq miles (488,100 sq km)
Languages Turkmen, Uzbek, Russian
Religions Sunni Muslim 87%, Eastern Orthodox 11%, other 2%
Ethnic mix Turkmen 72%, Russian 9%, Uzbek 9%, other 10%
Government Multiparty republic
Currency Manat = 100 tenge
Literacy rate 98%
Calorie consumption not available

UKRAINE

Page 86 C2

Bordered by seven states, the former "breadbasket of the Soviet Union" balances assertive nationalism with concerns over its relations with Russia.

Official name Ukraine
Formation 1991
Capital Kiev
Population 50.7 million / 218 people per sq mile (84 people per sq km)
Total area 223,090 sq miles (603,700 sq km)
Languages Ukrainian, Russian, Tartar
Religions Ukrainian Autonomous and Autocephalous Orthodox, with Roman Catholic (Uniate), Protestant and Jewish minorities
Ethnic mix Ukrainian 73%, Russian 22%, other 4%, Jewish 1%
Government Multiparty republic
Currency Hryvnia = 100 kopiykas
Literacy rate 99%
Calorie consumption not available

TOGO

Page 53 F4

Togo lies sandwiched between Ghana and Benin in West Africa. The 1993–94 presidential elections were the first since its independence in 1960.

Official name Togolese Republic
Formation 1960
Capital Lomé
Population 4.6 million / 219 people per sq mile (85 people per sq km)
Total area 20,999 sq miles (54,390 sq km)
Languages French, Ewe, Kabye, Gurma
Religions Traditional beliefs 50%, Christian 35%, Muslim 15%
Ethnic mix Ewe 43%, Kabye 26%, Gurma 16%, other 15%
Government Multiparty republic
Currency CFA franc = 100 centimes
Literacy rate 53.2%
Calorie consumption 2,242 kilocalories

TUNISIA

Page 49 E2

Tunisia, in North Africa, has traditionally been one of the more liberal Arab states, but is now facing a challenge from Islamic fundamentalists.

Official name Republic of Tunisia
Formation 1956
Capital Tunis
Population 9.6 million / 160 people per sq mile (62 people per sq km)
Total area 59,984 sq miles (155,360 sq km)
Languages Arabic, French
Religions Muslim 98%, Christian 1%, Jewish 1%
Ethnic mix Arab and Berber 98%, European 1%, other 1%
Government Multiparty republic
Currency Tunisian dinar = 1,000 millimes
Literacy rate 67%
Calorie consumption 3,330 kilocalories

TUVALU

Page 123 E3

The former Ellice Islands, linked to the Gilbert Islands as a British colony until 1978, Tuvalu is an isolated chain of nine atolls in the Central Pacific.

Official name Tuvalu
Formation 1978
Capital Fongafale, on Funafuti Atoll
Population 11,100 / 1,106 people per sq mile (427 people per sq km)
Total area 10 sq miles (26 sq km)
Languages English, Tuvaluan, Kiribati
Religions Church of Tuvalu 97%, Seventh Day Adventist 1%, Baha'i 1%, other 1%
Ethnic mix Polynesian 95%, other 5%
Government Constitutional monarchy
Currency Australian dollar and Tuvaluan dollar = 100 cents
Literacy rate 95%
Calorie consumption not available

UNITED ARAB EMIRATES

Page 99 D5

Bordering the Persian Gulf on the northern coast of the Arabian Peninsula, is the United Arab Emirates, a working federation of seven states.

Official name United Arab Emirates
Formation 1971
Capital Abu Dhabi
Population 2.4 million / 74 people per sq mile (29 people per sq km)
Total area 32,278 sq miles (83,600 sq km)
Languages Arabic, Persian, English, Indian and Pakistani languages
Religions Muslim 96%, other 4%
Ethnic mix Asian 50%, Emirian 19%, other Arab 23%, other 8%
Government Federation of monarchs
Currency UAE dirham = 100 fils
Literacy rate 74.8%
Calorie consumption 3,384 kilocalories

UNITED KINGDOM

Page 67 B5

Separated from continental Europe by the North Sea and the English Channel, the UK comprises England, Wales, Scotland, and Northern Ireland.

Official name United Kingdom of Great Britain and Northern Ireland
Formation 1707
Capital London
Population 58.8 million / 630 people per sq mile (243 people per sq km)
Total area 93,281 sq miles (241,600 sq km)
Languages English, Welsh, Scottish
Religions Protestant 52%, Roman Catholic 9%, Muslim 3%, other 36%
Ethnic mix English 80%, Scottish 10%, Northern Irish 4%, Welsh 2%, other 4%
Government Constitutional monarchy
Currency Pound sterling = 100 pence
Literacy rate 99%
Calorie consumption 3,317 kilocalories

UZBEKISTAN

Page 100 D2

Sharing the Aral Sea coastline with its northern neighbor, Kazakhstan, Uzbekistan lies on the ancient Silk Road between Asia and Europe.

Official name Republic of Uzbekistan
Formation 1991
Capital Tashkent
Population 24.3 million / 141 people per sq mile (54 people per sq km)
Total area 172,741 sq miles (447,400 sq km)
Languages Uzbek, Russian
Religions Sunni Muslim 88%, Eastern Orthodox 9%, other 3%
Ethnic mix Uzbek 71%, Russian 8%, Tajik 5%, Kazakh 4%, other 12%
Government Multiparty republic
Currency Som = 100 teen
Literacy rate 99%
Calorie consumption not available

VENEZUELA

Page 36 D2

Located on the north coast of South America, Venezuela has the continent's most urbanized society. Most people live in the northern cities.

Official name Bolivarian Republic of Venezuela
Formation 1821
Capital Caracas
Population 24.2 million / 71 people per sq mile (27 people per sq km)
Total area 340,559 sq miles (882,050 sq km)
Languages Spanish, Amerindian languages
Religions Roman Catholic 89%, Protestant and other 11%
Ethnic mix Mestizo 69%, other 31%
Government Multiparty republic
Currency Bolivar = 100 centimos
Literacy rate 92%
Calorie consumption 2,618 kilocalories

YUGOSLAVIA (SERBIA & MONTENEGRO)

Page 78 D4

The Federal Republic of Yugoslavia is the successor state to the former Yugoslavia.

Official name Federal Republic of Yugoslavia
Formation 1992
Capital Belgrade
Population 10.6 million / 269 people per sq mile (104 people per sq km)
Total area 39,449 sq miles (102,173 sq km)
Languages Serbian, Croatian, Albanian
Religions Eastern Orthodox 65%, Muslim 19%, other 16%
Ethnic mix Serb 62%, Albanian 17%, Montenegrin 5%, other 16%
Government Multiparty republic
Currency Yugoslav dinar = 100 para
Literacy rate 93.3%
Calorie consumption not available

UNITED STATES OF AMERICA

Page 13 B5

Stretching across the most temperate part of North America, and with many natural resources, the USA is the sole truly global superpower.

Official name United States of America
Formation 1787
Capital Washington DC
Population 278.4 million / 79 people per sq mile (30 people per sq km)
Total area 3,539,224 sq miles (9,166,600 sq km)
Languages English, Spanish, Italian, German, French, Polish, Chinese, Greek
Religions Protestant 61%, Roman Catholic 25%, Jewish 2%, other 12%
Ethnic mix White (including Hispanic) 84%, Black 12%, Chinese 1%, Amerindian 1%, other 2%
Government Multiparty republic
Currency US dollar = 100 cents
Literacy rate 99%
Calorie consumption 3,732 kilocalories

VANUATU

Page 122 D4

An archipelago of 82 islands and islets in the Pacific Ocean, it was ruled jointly by Britain and France from 1906 until independence in 1980.

Official name Republic of Vanuatu
Formation 1980
Capital Port-Vila
Population 200,000 / 42 people per sq mile (16 people per sq km)
Total area 4,706 sq miles (12,190 sq km)
Languages Bislama, English, French
Religions Presbyterian 37%, other Protestant 21%, Roman Catholic 15%, Traditional beliefs 8%, other 19%
Ethnic mix Melanesian 94%, French 4%, other 2%
Government Multiparty republic
Currency Vatu = 100 centimes
Literacy rate 64%
Calorie consumption 2,739 kilocalories

VIETNAM

Page 114 D4

Situated in the far east of mainland Southeast Asia, the country is still rebuilding after the devastating 1962–1975 Vietnam War.

Official name Socialist Republic of Vietnam
Formation 1976
Capital Hanoi
Population 79.8 million / 635 people per sq mile (245 people per sq km)
Total area 125,621 sq miles (325,360 sq km)
Languages Vietnamese, Chinese, Thai, Khmer, Muong, Nung, Miao, Yao
Religions Buddhist 55%, Christian 7%, other 38%
Ethnic mix Vietnamese 88%, Chinese 4%, Thai 2%, other 6%
Government Single-party republic
Currency Dông = 10 hao = 100 xu
Literacy rate 92%
Calorie consumption 2,250 kilocalories

ZAMBIA

Page 56 C2

Zambia lies landlocked at the heart of southern Africa. In 1991, it made a peaceful transition from single-party rule to multiparty democracy.

Official name Republic of Zambia
Formation 1964
Capital Lusaka
Population 9.2 million / 32 people per sq mile (12 people per sq km)
Total area 285,992 sq miles (740,720 sq km)
Languages English, Bemba, Nyanja, Tonga, Koonde, Lunda, Luvale, Lozi
Religions Christian 63%, Traditional beliefs 36%, other 1%
Ethnic mix Bemba 36%, Maravi 18%, Tonga 15%, other 31%
Government Multiparty republic
Currency Zambian kwacha = 100 ngwee
Literacy rate 75%
Calorie consumption 1,931 kilocalories

URUGUAY

Page 42 D4

Uruguay is situated in southeastern South America. It returned to civilian government in 1985, after 12 years of military dictatorship.

Official name Eastern Republic of Uruguay
Formation 1828
Capital Montevideo
Population 3.3 million / 49 people per sq mile (19 people per sq km)
Total area 67,494 sq miles (174,810 sq km)
Languages Spanish
Religions Roman Catholic 66%, non-religious 30%, other 4%
Ethnic mix White 90%, other 10%
Government Multiparty republic
Currency Uruguayan peso = 100 centimes
Literacy rate 97.5%
Calorie consumption 2,750 kilocalories

VATICAN CITY

Page 75 A8

The Vatican City, seat of the Roman Catholic Church, is a walled enclave in the city of Rome. It is the world's smallest fully independent state.

Official name State of the Vatican City
Formation 1929
Capital Vatican City
Population 1,000 / 5,886 people per sq mile (2,273 people per sq km)
Total area 0.17 sq miles (0.44 sq km)
Languages Italian, Latin
Religions Roman Catholic 100%
Ethnic mix Italian 90%, Swiss 10% (including the Swiss Guard which is responsible for papal security)
Government Papal Commission
Currency Lira and Italian lira = 100 centesimi
Literacy rate 99%
Calorie consumption 3,561 kilocalories

YEMEN

Page 99 C7

Located in southern Arabia, Yemen was formerly two countries – a socialist regime in the south, and a republic in the north. Both united in 1990.

Official name Republic of Yemen
Formation 1990
Capital Sana'a
Population 18 million / 89 people per sq mile (34 people per sq km)
Total area 203,849 sq miles (527,970 sq km)
Languages Arabic
Religions Shi'a Muslim 55%, Sunni Muslim 42%, Christian, Hindu and Jewish 3%
Ethnic mix Arab 95%, Afro-Arab 3%, Indian, Somali and European 2%
Government Multiparty republic
Currency Rial and Dinar
Literacy rate 42.5%
Calorie consumption 2,203 kilocalories

ZIMBABWE

Page 56 D3

The former British colony of Southern Rhodesia became fully independent as Zimbabwe in 1980, after 15 years of troubled white minority rule.

Official name Republic of Zimbabwe
Formation 1980
Capital Harare
Population 11.7 million / 78 people per sq mile (30 people per sq km)
Total area 149,293 sq miles (386,670 sq km)
Languages English, Shona, Ndebele
Religions Syncretic (Christian and traditional beliefs) 50%, Christian 25%, Traditional beliefs 24%, other 1%
Ethnic mix Shona 71%, Ndebele 16%, other African 11%, Asian 1%, White 1%
Government Multiparty republic
Currency Zimbabwe dollar = 100 cents
Literacy rate 91%
Calorie consumption 1,985 kilocalories

GEOGRAPHICAL COMPARISONS

LARGEST COUNTRIES

Russ. Fed.	6,592,812 sq miles	(17,075,400 sq km)
China	3,600,926 sq miles	(9,326,410 sq km)
Canada	3,560,216 sq miles	(9,220,970 sq km)
USA	3,539,224 sq miles	(9,166,600 sq km)
Brazil	3,265,058 sq miles	(8,456,510 sq km)
Australia	2,941,282 sq miles	(7,617,930 sq km)
India	1,147,948 sq miles	(2,973,190 sq km)
Argentina	1,056,636 sq miles	(2,736,690 sq km)
Kazakhstan	1,049,150 sq miles	(2,717,300 sq km)
Sudan	917,373 sq miles	(2,376,000 sq km)

SMALLEST COUNTRIES

Vatican City	0.17 sq miles	(0.44 sq km)
Monaco	0.75 sq miles	(1.95 sq km)
Nauru	8 sq miles	(21 sq km)
Tuvalu	10 sq miles	(26 sq km)
San Marino	24 sq miles	(61 sq km)
Liechtenstein	62 sq miles	(160 sq km)
Marshall Islands	70 sq miles	(181 sq km)
Seychelles	108 sq miles	(280 sq km)
Maldives	116 sq miles	(300 sq km)
Malta	124 sq miles	(320 sq km)

LARGEST ISLANDS

(TO THE NEAREST 1,000 - OR 100,000 FOR THE LARGEST)

Greenland	849,400 sq miles	(2,200,000 sq km)
New Guinea	312,000 sq miles	(808,000 sq km)
Borneo	292,222 sq miles	(757,050 sq km)
Madagascar	229,300 sq miles	(594,000 sq km)
Sumatra	202,300 sq miles	(524,000 sq km)
Baffin Island	183,800 sq miles	(476,000 sq km)
Honshu	88,800 sq miles	(230,000 sq km)
Britain	88,700 sq miles	(229,800 sq km)

RICHEST COUNTRIES

(GNP PER CAPITA, IN US$)

Liechtenstein	52,200
Luxembourg	45,360
Switzerland	39,980
Japan	38,160
Norway	36,100
Denmark	34,890
Singapore	32,810
USA	29,080
Germany	28,280
Austria	27,920

POOREST COUNTRIES

(GNP PER CAPITA, IN US$)

Somalia	100
Ethiopia	110
Congo, Dem. Rep. (Zaire)	110
Mozambique	140
Burundi	140
Sierra Leone	160
Niger	200
Tanzania	210
Malawi	210
Rwanda	210

MOST POPULOUS COUNTRIES

China	1,300,000,000
India	1,000,000,000
USA	278,400,000
Indonesia	212,000,000
Brazil	170,000,000
Pakistan	156,500,000
Russian Federation	147,000,000

MOST POPULOUS COUNTRIES continued

Bangladesh	129,000,000
Japan	126,700,000
Nigeria	112,000,000

LEAST POPULOUS COUNTRIES

Vatican City	1,000
Tuvalu	11,100
Nauru	11,500
Palau	18,500
San Marino	26,000
Liechtenstein	32,000
Monaco	32,000
St. Kitts & Nevis	41,000
Marshall Islands	51,000
Andorra	66,000

MOST DENSELY POPULATED COUNTRIES

Monaco	42,503 people per sq mile	(16,410 per sq km)
Singapore	15,285 people per sq mile	(5,902 per sq km)
Vatican City	5,886 people per sq mile	(2,273 per sq km)
Malta	3,148 people per sq mile	(1,216 per sq km)
Bangladesh	2,499 people per sq mile	(965 per sq km)
Maldives	2,469 people per sq mile	(953 per sq km)
Bahrain	2,350 people per sq mile	(891 per sq km)
Taiwan	1,756 people per sq mile	(678 per sq km)
Mauritius	1,671 people per sq mile	(645 per sq km)
Barbados	1,626 people per sq mile	(628 per sq km)

MOST SPARSELY POPULATED COUNTRIES

Mongolia	4 people per sq mile	(2 per sq km)
Namibia	5 people per sq mile	(2 per sq km)
Australia	6 people per sq mile	(2 per sq km)
Mauritania	6 people per sq mile	(2 per sq km)
Suriname	7 people per sq mile	(3 per sq km)
Botswana	7 people per sq mile	(3 per sq km)
Iceland	7 people per sq mile	(3 per sq km)
Canada	8 people per sq mile	(3 per sq km)
Libya	9 people per sq mile	(3 per sq km)
Guyana	11 people per sq mile	(4 per sq km)

MOST WIDELY SPOKEN LANGUAGES

1. Chinese (Mandarin)	6. Arabic
2. English	7. Bengali
3. Hindi	8. Portuguese
4. Spanish	9. Malay-Indonesian
5. Russian	10. French

COUNTRIES WITH THE MOST LAND BORDERS

14: China (Afghanistan, Bhutan, Myanmar, India, Kazakhstan, Kyrgyzstan, Laos, Mongolia, Nepal, North Korea, Pakistan, Russian Federation, Tajikistan, Vietnam)

14: Russ. Fed. (Azerbaijan, Belarus, China, Estonia, Finland, Georgia, Kazakhstan, Latvia, Lithuania, Mongolia, North Korea, Norway, Poland, Ukraine)

10: Brazil (Argentina, Bolivia, Colombia, French Guiana, Guyana, Paraguay, Peru, Suriname, Uruguay, Venezuela)

9: Congo, Dem. Rep. (Zaire) (Angola, Burundi, Central African Republic, Congo, Rwanda, Sudan, Tanzania, Uganda, Zambia)

9: Germany (Austria, Belgium, Czech Republic, Denmark, France, Luxembourg, Netherlands, Poland, Switzerland)

9: Sudan (Central African Republic, Chad, Congo, Dem. Rep. (Zaire), Egypt, Eritrea, Ethiopia, Kenya, Libya, Uganda)

8: Austria (Czech Republic, Germany, Hungary, Italy, Liechtenstein, Slovakia, Slovenia, Switzerland)

8: France (Andorra, Belgium, Germany, Italy, Luxembourg, Monaco, Spain, Switzerland)

8: Tanzania (Burundi, Congo, Dem. Rep. (Zaire), Kenya, Malawi, Mozambique, Rwanda, Uganda, Zambia)

8: Turkey (Armenia, Azerbaijan, Bulgaria, Georgia, Greece, Iran, Iraq, Syria)

LONGEST RIVERS

River	Length (miles)	Length (km)
Nile (NE Africa)	4,160 miles	(6,695 km)
Amazon (South America)	4,049 miles	(6,516 km)
Yangtze (China)	3,915 miles	(6,299 km)
Mississippi/Missouri (US)	3,710 miles	(5,969 km)
Ob'-Irtysh (Russ. Fed.)	3,461 miles	(5,570 km)
Yellow River (China)	3,395 miles	(5,464 km)
Congo (Central Africa)	2,900 miles	(4,667 km)
Mekong (Southeast Asia)	2,749 miles	(4,425 km)
Lena (Russian Federation)	2,734 miles	(4,400 km)
Mackenzie (Canada)	2,640 miles	(4,250 km)

HIGHEST MOUNTAINS

(HEIGHT ABOVE SEA LEVEL)

Mountain	Height (ft)	Height (m)
Everest	29,030 ft	(8,848 m)
K2	28,253 ft	(8,611 m)
Kanchenjunga I	28,210 ft	(8,598 m)
Makalu I	27,767 ft	(8,463 m)
Cho Oyu	26,907 ft	(8,201 m)
Dhaulagiri I	26,796 ft	(8,167 m)
Manaslu I	26,783 ft	(8,163 m)
Nanga Parbat I	26,661 ft	(8,126 m)
Annapurna I	26,547 ft	(8,091 m)
Gasherbrum I	26,471 ft	(8,068 m)

LARGEST BODIES OF INLAND WATER

(WITH AREA AND DEPTH)

Caspian Sea	143,243 sq miles (371,000 sq km)	3,215 ft (980 m)
Lake Superior	32,150 sq miles (83,270 sq km)	1,289 ft (393 m)
Lake Victoria	26,828 sq miles (69,484 sq km)	328 ft (100 m)
Lake Huron	23,436 sq miles (60,700 sq km)	751 ft (229 m)
Lake Michigan	22,402 sq miles (58,020 sq km)	922 ft (281 m)
Lake Tanganyika	12,703 sq miles (32,900 sq km)	4,700 ft (1,435 m)
Great Bear Lake	12,274 sq miles (31,790 sq km)	1,047 ft (319 m)
Lake Baikal	11,776 sq miles (30,500 sq km)	5,712 ft (1,741 m)
Great Slave Lake	10,981 sq miles (28,440 sq km)	459 ft (140 m)
Lake Erie	9,915 sq miles (25,680 sq km)	197 ft (60 m)

DEEPEST OCEAN FEATURES

Feature	Depth (ft)	Depth (m)
Challenger Deep, Marianas Trench (Pacific)	36,201 ft	(11,034 m)
Vityaz III Depth, Tonga Trench (Pacific)	35,704 ft	(10,882 m)
Vityaz Depth, Kurile-Kamchatka Trench (Pacific)	34,588 ft	(10,542 m)
Cape Johnson Deep, Philippine Trench (Pacific)	34,441 ft	(10,497 m)
Kermadec Trench (Pacific)	32,964 ft	(10,047 m)
Ramapo Deep, Japan Trench (Pacific)	32,758 ft	(9,984 m)
Milwaukee Deep, Puerto Rico Trench (Atlantic)	30,185 ft	(9,200 m)
Argo Deep, Torres Trench (Pacific)	30,070 ft	(9,165 m)
Meteor Depth, South Sandwich Trench (Atlantic)	30,000 ft	(9,144 m)
Planet Deep, New Britain Trench (Pacific)	29,988 ft	(9,140 m)

GREATEST WATERFALLS

(MEAN FLOW OF WATER)

Waterfall	Flow (cu. ft/sec)	Flow (cu. m/sec)
Boyoma (Congo (Zaire))	600,400 cu. ft/sec	(17,000 cu.m/sec)
Khône (Laos/Cambodia)	410,000 cu. ft/sec	(11,600 cu.m/sec)
Niagara (USA/Canada)	195,000 cu. ft/sec	(5,500 cu.m/sec)
Grande (Uruguay)	160,000 cu. ft/sec	(4,500 cu.m/sec)
Paulo Afonso (Brazil)	100,000 cu. ft/sec	(2,800 cu.m/sec)
Urubupunga (Brazil)	97,000 cu. ft/sec	(2,750 cu.m/sec)
Iguaçu (Argentina/Brazil)	62,000 cu. ft/sec	(1,700 cu.m/sec)
Maribondo (Brazil)	53,000 cu. ft/sec	(1,500 cu.m/sec)
Victoria (Zimbabwe)	39,000 cu. ft/sec	(1,100 cu.m/sec)
Kabalega (Uganda)	42,000 cu. ft/sec	(1,200 cu.m/sec)

HIGHEST WATERFALLS

Waterfall	Height (ft)	Height (m)
Angel (Venezuela)	3,212 ft	(979 m)
Tugela (South Africa)	3,110 ft	(948 m)
Utigard (Norway)	2,625 ft	(800 m)
Mongefossen (Norway)	2,539 ft	(774 m)
Mtarazi (Zimbabwe)	2,500 ft	(762 m)
Yosemite (USA)	2,425 ft	(739 m)
Ostre Mardola Foss (Norway)	2,156 ft	(657 m)
Tyssestrengane (Norway)	2,119 ft	(646 m)
*Cuquenan (Venezuela)	2,001 ft	(610 m)
Sutherland (New Zealand)	1,903 ft	(580 m)

* indicates that the total height is a single leap

LARGEST DESERTS

Desert	Area (sq miles)	Area (sq km)
Sahara	3,450,000 sq miles	(9,065,000 sq km)
Gobi	500,000 sq miles	(1,295,000 sq km)
Ar Rub al Khali	289,600 sq miles	(750,000 sq km)
Great Victorian	249,800 sq miles	(647,000 sq km)
Sonoran	120,000 sq miles	(311,000 sq km)
Kalahari	120,000 sq miles	(310,800 sq km)
Kara Kum	115,800 sq miles	(300,000 sq km)
Takla Makan	100,400 sq miles	(260,000 sq km)
Namib	52,100 sq miles	(135,000 sq km)
Thar	33,670 sq miles	(130,000 sq km)

NB – Most of Antarctica is a polar desert, with only
50 mm of precipitation annually

HOTTEST INHABITED PLACES

Place	Temp (°F)	Temp (°C)
Djiboutl (Djibouti)	86° F	(30 °C)
Timbouctou (Mali)	84.7° F	(29.3 °C)
Tirunelveli (India)		
Tuticorin (India)		
Nellore (India)	84.5° F	(29.2 °C)
Santa Marta (Colombia)		
Aden (Yemen)	84° F	(28.9 °C)
Madurai (India)		
Niamey (Niger)		
Hodeida (Yemen)	83.8° F	(28.8 °C)

DRIEST INHABITED PLACES

Place	Rainfall (in)	Rainfall (mm)
Aswân (Egypt)	0.02 in	(0.5 mm)
Luxor (Egypt)	0.03 in	(0.7 mm)
Arica (Chile)	0.04 in	(1.1 mm)
Ica (Peru)	0.1 in	(2.3 mm)
Antofagasta (Chile)	0.2 in	(4.9 mm)
El Minya (Egypt)	0.2 in	(5.1 mm)
Asyût (Egypt)	0.2 in	(5.2 mm)
Callao (Peru)	0.5 in	(12.0 mm)
Trujillo (Peru)	0.55 in	(14.0 mm)
El Faiyûm (Egypt)	0.8 in	(19.0 mm)

WETTEST INHABITED PLACES

Place	Rainfall (in)	Rainfall (mm)
Buenaventura (Colombia)	265 in	(6,743 mm)
Monrovia (Liberia)	202 in	(5,131 mm)
Pago Pago (American Samoa)	196 in	(4,990 mm)
Moulmein (Myanmar)	191 in	(4,852 mm)
Lae (Papua New Guinea)	183 in	(4,645 mm)
Baguio (Luzon Island, Philippines)	180 in	(4,573 mm)
Sylhet (Bangladesh)	176 in	(4,457 mm)
Padang (Sumatra, Indonesia)	166 in	(4,225 mm)
Bogor (Java, Indonesia)	166 in	(4,225 mm)
Conakry (Guinea)	171 in	(4,341 mm)

Aachen – Alexándria

GLOSSARY OF ABBREVIATIONS
This Glossary provides a comprehensive guide to the abbreviations used in this Atlas, and in the Index.

A **abbrev.** abbreviated
Afr. Afrikaans
Alb. Albanian
Amh. Amharic
anc. ancient
Ar. Arabic
Arm. Armenian
Az. Azerbaijani
B **Basq.** Basque
Bel. Belorussian
Ben. Bengali
Bibl. Biblical
Bret. Breton
Bul. Bulgarian
Bur. Burmese
C **Cam.** Cambodian
Cant. Cantonese
Cast. Castilian
Cat. Catalan
Chin. Chinese
Cro. Croat
Cz. Czech
D **Dan.** Danish
Dut. Dutch
E **Eng.** English
Est. Estonian
est. estimated
F **Faer.** Faeroese
Fij. Fijian
Fin. Finnish
Flem. Flemish
Fr. French
Fris. Frisian
G **Geor.** Georgian
Ger. German
Gk. Greek
Guj. Gujarati
H **Haw.** Hawaiian
Heb. Hebrew
Hind. Hindi
hist. historical
Hung. Hungarian
I **Icel.** Icelandic
Ind. Indonesian
Ir. Irish
It. Italian
J **Jap.** Japanese
K **Kaz.** Kazakh
Kir. Kirghiz
Kor. Korean
Kurd. Kurdish
L **Lao.** Laotian
Lapp. Lappish
Lat. Latin
Latv. Latvian
Lith. Lithanian
Lus. Lusatian
M **Mac.** Macedonian
Mal. Malay
Malg. Malagasy
Malt. Maltese
Mong. Mongolian
N **Nepali.** Nepali
Nor. Norwegian
O **off.** officially
P **Pash.** Pashtu
Per. Persian
Pol. Polish
Port. Portuguese
prev. previously
R **Rmsch.** Romansch
Roman. Romanian
Rus. Russian
S **SCr.** Serbo–Croatian
Serb. Serbian
Slvk. Slovak
Slvn. Slovene
Som. Somali
Sp. Spanish
Swa. Swahili
Swe. Swedish
T **Taj.** Tajik
Th. Thai
Tib. Tibetan
Turk. Turkish
Turkm. Turkmenistan
U **Uigh.** Uighur
Ukr. Ukrainian
Uzb. Uzbek
V **var.** variant
Vtn. Vietnamese
W **Wel.** Welsh
X **Xh.** Xhosa
Y **Yugo.** Yugoslavia

INDEX

INDEX

A

Aachen 72 A4 Dut. Aken, Fr.Aix-la-Chapelle; anc. Aquae Grani, Aquisgranum. Nordrhein-Westfalen, W Germany
Aaiún see Laâyoune
Aalborg see Ålborg
Aalen 73 B6 Baden-Württemberg, S Germany
Aalsmeer 64 C3 Noord-Holland, C Netherlands
Aalst 65 B6 Fr. Alost. Oost-Vlaanderen, C Belgium
Aalten 64 E4 Gelderland, E Netherlands
Aalter 65 B5 Oost-Vlaanderen, NW Belgium
Äänekoski 63 D5 Länsi-Suomi, W Finland
Aar see Aare
Aare 73 A7 var. Aar. River W Switzerland
Aarhus see Århus
Aat see Ath
Aba 53 G5 Abia, S Nigeria
Aba 55 E5 Orientale, NE Dem. Rep. Congo (Zaire)
Abā as Su'ūd see Najrān
Abaco Island see Great Abaco
Ābādān 98 C4 Khūzestān, SW Iran
Abai see Blue Nile
Abakan 92 D4 Respublika Khakasiya, S Russian Federation
Abancay 38 D4 Apurímac, SE Peru
Abariringa see Kanton
Abashiri 108 D2 var. Abasiri. Hokkaidō, NE Japan
Abasiri see Abashiri
Ābaya Hāyk' 51 C5 Eng. Lake Margherita, It. Abbaia. Lake SW Ethiopia
Ābay Wenz see Blue Nile
Abbeville 68 C2 anc. Abbatis Villa. Somme, N France
'Abd al 'Azīz, Jabal 96 D2 mountain range NE Syria
Abéché 54 C3 var. Abécher, Abeshr. Ouaddaï, SE Chad
Abécher see Abéché
Abela see Ávila
Abemama 122 D2 var. Apamama; prev. Roger Simpson Island. Atoll Tungaru, W Kiribati
Abengourou 53 E5 E Côte d'Ivoire
Aberdeen 66 D3 anc. Devana. NE Scotland, UK
Aberdeen 23 E2 South Dakota, N USA
Aberdeen 24 B2 Washington, NW USA
Abergwaun see Fishguard
Abertawe see Swansea
Aberystwyth 67 C6 W Wales, UK
Abeshr see Abéché
Abhā 99 B6 'Asīr, SW Saudi Arabia
Abidavichy 85 D7 Rus. Obidovichi. Mahilyowskaya Voblasts', E Belarus
Abidjan 53 E5 S Côte d'Ivoire
Abilene 27 F3 Texas, SW USA
Abingdon see Pinta, Isla
Abkhazia 95 E1 autonomous republic NW Georgia
Åbo 63 D6 Länsi-Suomi, W Finland
Aboisso 53 E5 SE Côte d'Ivoire
Abo, Massif d' 54 B1 mountain range NW Chad
Abomey 53 F5 S Benin
Abou-Déïa 54 C3 Salamat, SE Chad
Abrantes 70 B3 var. Abrántes. Santarém, C Portugal
Abrolhos Bank 34 E4 undersea feature W Atlantic Ocean
Abrova 85 B6 Rus. Obrovo. Brestskaya Voblasts', SW Belarus
Abrud 86 B4 Ger. Gross-Schlatten, Hung. Abrudbánya. Alba, SW Romania
Abruzzese, Appennino 74 C4 mountain range C Italy
Absaroka Range 22 B2 mountain range Montana/Wyoming, NW USA
Abū aḍ Ḍuhūr 96 B3 Fr. Aboudouhour. Idlib, NW Syria
Abu Dhabi see Abū Ẓaby
Abu Hamed 50 C3 River Nile, N Sudan
Abū Ḥardān 96 E3 var. Hajîne. Dayr az Zawr, E Syria
Abuja 53 G4 country capital (Nigeria) Federal Capital District, C Nigeria
Abū Kamāl 96 E3 Fr. Abou Kémal. Dayr az Zawr, E Syria
Abula see Ávila
Abunã, Rio 40 C2 var. Río Abuná. River Bolivia/Brazil
Abut Head 129 B6 headland South Island, NZ
Ābuyē Mēda 50 D4 mountain C Ethiopia
Abū Ẓabī see Abū Ẓaby
Abū Ẓaby 99 C5 var. Abū Ẓabī, Eng. Abu Dhabi. Country capital (UAE) Abū Ẓaby, C UAE
Abyla see Ávila
Acalayong 55 A5 SW Equatorial Guinea
Acaponeta 28 D4 Nayarit, C Mexico
Acapulco 29 E5 var. Acapulco de Juárez. Guerrero, S Mexico
Acapulco de Juárez see Acapulco
Acarai Mountains 37 F4 Sp. Serra Acaraí. Mountain range Brazil/Guyana
Acarigua 36 D2 Portuguesa, N Venezuela
Accra 53 E5 country capital (Ghana) SE Ghana
Achacachi 39 E4 La Paz, W Bolivia
Acklins Island 32 C2 island SE Bahamas
Aconcagua, Cerro 42 B4 mountain W Argentina
Açores see Azores
A Coruña 70 B1 Cast. La Coruña, Eng. Corunna; anc. Caronium. Galicia, NW Spain
Acre 40 C2 off. Estado do Acre. State W Brazil
Açu 41 G2 var. Assu. Rio Grande do Norte, E Brazil
Ada 27 G2 Oklahoma, C USA
Ada 78 D3 Serbia, N Yugoslavia
Adalia, Gulf of see Antalya Körfezi
Adama see Nazrēt
Adamawa Highlands 54 B4 plateau NW Cameroon
'Adan 99 B7 Eng. Aden. SW Yemen
Adana 94 D4 var. Seyhan. Adana, S Turkey
Adapazarı 94 B2 prev. Ada Bazar. Sakarya, NW Turkey
Adare, Cape 132 B4 headland Antarctica
Ad Dahnā' 98 C4 desert E Saudi Arabia
Ad Dakhla 48 A4 var. Dakhla. SW Western Sahara
Ad Dalanj see Dilling
Ad Damar see Ed Damer
Ad Damazīn see Ed Damazin
Ad Dāmir see Ed Damer
Ad Dammān 98 C4 var. Dammām. Ash Sharqīyah, NE Saudi Arabia
Ad Dāmūr see Damoûr
Ad Dawḥah 98 C4 Eng. Doha. Country capital (Qatar) C Qatar
Aḍ Ḍiffah see Libyan Plateau
Addis Ababa see Ādīs Ābeba
Addu Atoll 110 A5 atoll S Maldives
Adelaide 127 B6 state capital South Australia
Aden see 'Adan
Aden, Gulf of 99 C7 gulf SW Arabian Sea
Adige 74 C2 Ger. Etsch. River N Italy
Adirondack Mountains 19 F2 mountain range New York, NE USA
Ādīs Ābeba 51 C5 Eng. Addis Ababa. Country capital (Ethiopia) C Ethiopia
Adıyaman 95 E4 Adıyaman, SE Turkey
Adjud 86 C4 Vrancea, E Romania
Admiralty Islands 122 B3 island group N PNG
Adra 71 E5 Andalucía, S Spain
Adrar 48 D3 C Algeria
Adrar des Iforas see Ifôghas, Adrar des
Adrian 18 C3 Michigan, N USA
Adriatic Sea 81 E2 Alb. Deti Adriatik, It. Mare Adriatico, SCr. Jadransko More, Slvn. Jadransko Morje. Sea N Mediterranean Sea
Adycha 93 F2 river NE Russian Federation
Aegean Sea 83 C5 Gk. Aigaíon Pélagos, Aigaío Pélagos, Turk. Ege Denizi. Sea NE Mediterranean Sea
Aegviidu 84 D2 Ger. Charlottenhof. Harjumaa, NW Estonia
Aelana see Al 'Aqabah
Aelok see Ailuk Atoll
Aelōnlaplap see Ailinglaplap Atoll
Aeolian Islands see Eolie, Isole
Afar Depression see Danakil Desert
Afghanistan 100 C4 off. Islamic State of Afghanistan, Per. Dowlat-e Eslāmī-ye Afghānestān; prev. Republic of Afghanistan. Country C Asia
Afmadow 51 D6 Jubbada Hoose, S Somalia
Africa 46 continent
Africa, Horn of 46 E4 physical region Ethiopia/Somalia
Africana Seamount 119 A6 undersea feature SW Indian Ocean
'Afrīn 96 B2 Ḥalab, N Syria
Afyon 94 B3 prev. Afyonkarahisar. Afyon, W Turkey
Agadez 53 G3 prev. Agadès. Agadez, C Niger
Agadir 48 B3 SW Morocco
Agana/Agaña see Hagåtña
Āgaro 51 C5 C Ethiopia
Agassiz Fracture Zone 121 G5 tectonic feature S Pacific Ocean
Agathónisi 83 D6 island Dodekánisos, Greece, Aegean Sea
Agde 69 C6 anc. Agatha. Hérault, S France
Agedabia see Ajdābiyā
Agen 69 B5 anc. Aginnum. Lot-et-Garonne, SW France
Aghri Dagh see Büyükağrı Dağı
Agiá 82 B4 var. Ayiá. Thessalía, C Greece
Agialoúsa 80 D4 var. Yenierenköy. NE Cyprus
Agía Marína 83 E6 Léros, Dodekánisos, Greece, Aegean Sea
Ágios Nikólaos 83 D8 var. Áyios Nikólaos. Kríti, Greece, E Mediterranean Sea
Āgra 112 D3 Uttar Pradesh, N India
Agram see Zagreb
Ağrı 95 F3 var. Karaköse; prev. Karakılısse. Ağrı, NE Turkey
Agri Dagi see Büyükağrı Dağı
Agrigento 75 C7 Gk. Akragas; prev. Girgenti. Sicilia, Italy, C Mediterranean Sea
Agriovótano 83 C5 Évvoia, C Greece
Agropoli 75 D5 Campania, S Italy
Aguachica 36 B2 Cesar, N Colombia
Aguadulce 31 F5 Coclé, S Panama
Agua Prieta 28 B1 Sonora, NW Mexico
Aguascalientes 28 D4 Aguascalientes, C Mexico
Aguaytía 38 C3 Ucayali, C Peru
Aguilas 71 E4 Murcia, SE Spain
Aguililla 28 D4 Michoacán de Ocampo, SW Mexico
Agulhas Basin 47 D8 undersea feature SW Indian Ocean
Agulhas Plateau 45 D6 undersea feature SW Indian Ocean
Ahaggar 53 F2 high plateau region SE Algeria
Ahlen 72 B4 Nordrhein-Westfalen, W Germany
Ahmadābād 112 C4 var. Ahmedabad. Gujarāt, W India
Ahmadnagar 112 C5 var. Ahmednagar. Mahārāshtra, W India
Ahmedabad see Ahmadābād
Ahmednagar see Ahmadnagar
Ahuachapán 30 B3 Ahuachapán, W El Salvador
Ahvāz 98 C3 var. Ahwāz; prev. Nāsiri. Khūzestān, SW Iran
Ahvenanmaa see Åland
Ahwāz see Ahvāz
Aïdin see Aydın
Aígina 83 C6 var. Aíyina, Egina. Aígina, C Greece
Aígio 83 B5 var. Egio; prev. Aíyion. Dytikí Ellás, S Greece
Aiken 21 E2 South Carolina, SE USA
Ailigandí 31 G4 San Blas, NE Panama
Ailinglaplap Atoll 122 D2 var. Aelōnlaplap. Atoll Ralik Chain, S Marshall Islands
Ailuk Atoll 122 D1 var. Aelok. Atoll Ratak Chain, NE Marshall Islands
Ainaži 84 D3 Est. Heinaste, Ger. Hainasch. Limbaži, N Latvia
'Aïn Ben Tili 52 D1 Tiris Zemmour, N Mauritania
Aintab see Gaziantep
Aïoun el Atrous see 'Ayoûn el 'Atroûs
Aïoun el Atroûss see 'Ayoûn el 'Atroûs
Aiquile 39 F4 Cochabamba, C Bolivia
Aïr see Aïr, Massif de l'
Air du Azbine see Aïr, Massif de l'
Aïr, Massif de l' 53 G2 var. Aïr, Air du Azbine, Asben. Mountain range NC Niger
Aiud 86 B4 Ger. Strassburg, Hung. Nagyenyed; prev. Engeten. Alba, SW Romania
Aix see Aix-en-Provence
Aix-en-Provence 69 D6 var. Aix; anc. Aquae Sextiae. Bouches-du-Rhône, SE France
Aíyina see Aígina
Aíyion see Aígio
Aizkraukle 84 C4 Aizkraukle, S Latvia
Ajaccio 69 E7 Corse, France, C Mediterranean Sea
Ajaria 95 F2 autonomous republic SW Georgia
Aj Bogd Uul 104 D2 mountain SW Mongolia
Ajdābiyā 49 G2 var. Agedabia, Ajdābiyah. NE Libya
Ajdābiyah see Ajdābiyā
Ajjinena see El Geneina
Ajmer 112 D3 var. Ajmere. Rājasthān, N India
Ajmere see Ajmer
Ajo 26 A3 Arizona, SW USA
Akaba see Al 'Aqabah
Akamagaseki see Shimonoseki
Akasha 50 B3 Northern, N Sudan
Akchâr 52 C2 desert W Mauritania
Akhalts'ikhe 95 F2 SW Georgia
Akhisar 94 A3 Manisa, W Turkey
Akhmīm 50 B2 anc. Panopolis. C Egypt
Akhtubinsk 89 C7 Astrakhanskaya Oblast', SW Russian Federation
Akimiski Island 16 C3 island Northwest Territories, C Canada
Akinovka 87 F4 Zaporiz'ka Oblast', S Ukraine
Akita 108 D4 Akita, Honshū, C Japan
Akjoujt 52 C2 prev. Fort-Repoux. Inchiri, W Mauritania
Akkeshi 108 E2 Hokkaidō, NE Japan
Aklavik 14 D3 Northwest Territories, NW Canada
Akmola see Astana
Akpatok Island 17 E1 island Northwest Territories, E Canada
Akra Dhrepanon see Drépano, Akrotírio
Akra Kanestron see Palioúri, Akrotírio
Akron 18 D4 Ohio, N USA
Akrotiri see Akrotírion
Akrotírion 80 C5 var. Akrotiri. UK air base S Cyprus
Aksai Chin 102 B2 Chin. Aksayqin. Disputed region China/India
Aksaray 94 C4 Aksaray, C Turkey
Akşehir 94 B4 Konya, W Turkey
Aktau 92 A4 Kaz. Aqtaū; prev. Shevchenko. Mangistau, W Kazakhstan
Aktsyabrski 85 C7 Rus. Oktyabr'skiy; prev. Karpilovka. Homyel'skaya Voblasts', SE Belarus
Aktyubinsk 92 B4 Kaz. Aqtöbe. Aktyubinsk, NW Kazakhstan
Akula 55 C5 Equateur, NW Dem. Rep. Congo (Zaire)
Akureyri 61 E4 Nordhurland Eystra, N Iceland
Akyab see Sittwe
Alabama 29 G1 off. State of Alabama; also known as Camellia State, Heart of Dixie, The Cotton State, Yellowhammer State. State S USA
Alabama River 20 C3 river Alabama, S USA
Alaca 94 C3 Çorum, N Turkey
Alagoas 41 G2 off. Estado de Alagoas. State E Brazil
Alajuela 31 E4 Alajuela, C Costa Rica
Alakanuk 14 C2 Alaska, USA
Al 'Alamayn see El 'Alamein
Al 'Amārah 98 C3 var. Amara. E Iraq
Alamo 25 D6 Nevada, W USA
Alamogordo 26 D3 New Mexico, SW USA
Alamosa 22 C5 Colorado, C USA
Åland 63 C6 var. Aland Islands, Fin. Ahvenanmaa. Island group SW Finland
Aland Islands see Åland
Aland Sea see Ålands Hav
Ålands Hav 63 C6 var. Aland Sea. Strait Baltic Sea/Gulf of Bothnia
Alanya 94 C4 Antalya, S Turkey
Alappuzha see Alleppey
Al 'Aqabah 97 B8 var. Akaba, Aqaba, 'Aqaba; anc. Aelana, Elath. Ma'ān, SW Jordan
Alasca, Golfo de see Alaska, Gulf of
Alaşehir 94 A4 Manisa, W Turkey
Al 'Ashārah 96 E3 var. Ashara. Dayr az Zawr, E Syria
Alaska 14 C3 off. State of Alaska; also known as Land of the Midnight Sun, The Last Frontier, Seward's Folly; prev. Russian America. State NW USA
Alaska, Gulf of 14 C4 var. Golfo de Alasca. Gulf Canada/USA
Alaska Peninsula 14 C3 peninsula Alaska, USA
Alaska Range 12 B2 mountain range Alaska, USA
Al-Asnam see Chlef
Al Awaynāt see Al 'Uwaynāt
Al 'Aynā 97 B7 Al Karak, W Jordan
Alazeya 93 G2 river NE Russian Federation
Al Bāb 96 B2 Ḥalab, N Syria
Albacete 71 E3 Castilla-La Mancha, C Spain
Al Baghdādī 98 B3 var. Khān al Baghdādī. SW Iraq
Al Bāha see Al Bāḥah
Al Bāḥah 99 B5 var. Al Bāha. Al Bāḥah, SW Saudi Arabia
Al Baḥr al Mayyit see Dead Sea
Alba Iulia 86 B4 Ger. Weissenburg, Hung. Gyulafehérvár; prev. Bălgrad, Karlsburg, Károly-Fehérvár. Alba, W Romania
Albania 79 C7 off. Republic of Albania, Alb. Republika e Shqipërisë, Shqipëria; prev. People's Socialist Republic of Albania. Country SE Europe
Albany 16 C3 river Ontario, S Canada
Albany 19 F3 state capital New York, NE USA
Albany 20 D3 Georgia, SE USA
Albany 24 B3 Oregon, NW USA
Albany 125 B7 Western Australia
Al Bāridah 96 C4 var. Bāridah. Ḥimş, C Syria
Al Başrah 98 C3 Eng. Basra; hist. Busra, Bussora. SE Iraq
Al Batrūn see Batroûn
Al Bayḍā' 49 G2 var. Beida. NE Libya
Albemarle Island see Isabela, Isla
Albemarle Sound 21 G1 inlet W Atlantic Ocean
Albergaria-a-Velha 70 B2 Aveiro, N Portugal
Albert 68 C3 Somme, N France
Alberta 15 E4 province SW Canada
Albert Edward Nyanza see Edward, Lake
Albert, Lake 51 B6 var. Albert Nyanza, Lac Mobutu Sese Seko. Lake Uganda/Dem. Rep. Congo (Zaire)
Albert Lea 23 F3 Minnesota, N USA
Albert Nyanza see Albert, Lake
Albi 69 C6 anc. Albiga. Tarn, S France
Ålborg 58 D3 var. Aalborg, Ålborg-Nørresundby; anc. Alburgum. Nordjylland, N Denmark
Ålborg-Nørresundby see Ålborg
Alborz, Reshteh-ye Kūhhā-ye 98 C2 Eng. Elburz Mountains. Mountain range N Iran
Albuquerque 26 D2 New Mexico, SW USA
Al Burayqah see Marsá al Burayqah
Alburgum see Ålborg
Albury 127 C7 New South Wales, SE Australia
Alcácer do Sal 70 B4 Setúbal, W Portugal
Alcalá de Henares 71 E3 Ar. Alkal'a; anc. Complutum. Madrid, C Spain
Alcamo 75 C7 Sicilia, Italy, C Mediterranean Sea
Alcañiz 71 F2 Aragón, NE Spain
Alcántara, Embalse de 70 C3 reservoir W Spain
Alcaudete 70 D4 Andalucía, S Spain
Alcázar see Ksar-el-Kebir
Alcoi see Alcoy
Alcoy 71 F4 var. Alcoi. País Valenciano, E Spain
Aldabra Group 57 G2 island group SW Seychelles
Aldan 93 F3 river NE Russian Federation
al Dar al Baida see Rabat
Alderney 68 A2 island Channel Islands
Aleg 52 C3 Brakna, SW Mauritania
Aleksandropol' see Gyumri
Aleksin 89 B5 Tul'skaya Oblast', W Russian Federation
Aleksinac 78 E4 Serbia, SE Yugoslavia
Alençon 68 B3 Orne, N France
Alenquer 41 E2 Pará, NE Brazil
Aleppo see Ḥalab
Alert 15 F1 Ellesmere Island, Nunavut, N Canada
Alès 69 C6 prev. Alais. Gard, S France
Aleşd 86 B3 Hung. Élesd. Bihor, SW Romania
Alessandria 74 B2 Fr. Alexandrie. Piemonte, N Italy
Ålesund 63 A5 Møre og Romsdal, S Norway
Aleutian Basin 91 G3 undersea feature Bering Sea
Aleutian Islands 14 A3 island group Alaska, USA
Aleutian Range 12 A2 mountain range Alaska, USA
Aleutian Trench 91 H3 undersea feature S Bering Sea
Alexander Archipelago 14 D4 island group Alaska, USA
Alexander City 20 D2 Alabama, S USA
Alexander Island 132 A3 island Antarctica
Alexandra 129 B7 Otago, South Island, NZ
Alexándreia 82 B4 var. Alexándria. Kentrikí Makedonía, N Greece
Alexandria 50 B1 Ar. Al Iskandarīyah. N Egypt
Alexándria see Alexándreia

Alexandria – Aquitaine

Alexandria 20 B3 Louisiana, S USA
Alexandria 23 F2 Minnesota, N USA
Alexandria 86 C5 Teleorman, S Romania
Alexandroúpoli 82 D3 var. Alexandroúpolis, Turk. Dedeagaç, Dedeagach. Anatolikí Makedonía kai Thráki, NE Greece
Alexandroúpolis see Alexandroúpoli
Al Fāshir see El Fasher
Alfatar 82 E1 Silistra, NE Bulgaria
Alfeiós 83 B6 prev. Alfiós, anc. Alpheius, Alpheus. River S Greece
Alföld see Great Hungarian Plain
Alga 92 B4 Kaz. Algha. Aktyubinsk, NW Kazakhstan
Algarve 70 B4 cultural region S Portugal
Algeciras 70 C5 Andalucía, SW Spain
Algemesí 71 F3 País Valenciano, E Spain
Al-Genain see El Geneina
Alger 49 E1 var. Algiers, El Djazaïr, Al Jazair. Country capital (Algeria) N Algeria
Algeria 48 C3 off. Democratic and Popular Republic of Algeria. Country N Africa
Algerian Basin 58 C5 var. Balearic Plain undersea feature W Mediterranean Sea
Al Ghābah 99 E5 var. Ghaba. C Oman
Alghero 75 A5 Sardegna, Italy, C Mediterranean Sea
Al Ghurdaqah see Hurghada
Algiers see Alger
Al Golea see El Goléa
Algona 23 F3 Iowa, C USA
Al Ḩajār al Gharbī 99 D5 mountain range N Oman
Al Ḩasakah 96 D2 var. Al Hasijah, El Haseke, Fr. Hassetché. Al Ḩasakah, NE Syria
Al Hasijah see Al Ḩasakah
Al Ḩillah 98 B3 var. Hilla. C Iraq
Al Ḩisā 97 B7 Aṭ Ṭafīlah, W Jordan
Al Ḩudaydah 99 B6 Eng. Hodeida. W Yemen
Al Hufūf 98 C4 var. Hofuf. Ash Sharqīyah, NE Saudi Arabia
Aliákmonas 82 B4 prev. Aliákmon, anc. Haliacmon. N Greece
Alíartos 83 C5 Stereá Ellás, C Greece
Alicante 71 F4 Cat. Alacant; País Valenciano, SE Spain
Alice 27 G5 Texas, SW USA
Alice Springs 126 A4 Northern Territory, C Australia
Aliki see Alykí
Alima 55 B6 river C Congo
Alindao 54 C4 Basse-Kotto, S Central African Republic
Aliquippa 18 D4 Pennsylvania, NE USA
Alistráti 82 C3 Kentrikí Makedonía, NE Greece
Alivéri 83 C5 var. Alivérion. Évvoia, C Greece
Alivérion see Alivéri
Al Jabal al Akhḑar 49 G2 mountain range NE Libya
Al Jabal ash Sharqī see Anti-Lebanon
Al Jafr 97 B7 Ma'ān, S Jordan
Al Jaghbūb 49 H3 NE Libya
Al Jahrā' 98 C4 var. Al Jahrah, Jahra. C Kuwait
Al Jahrah see Al Jahrā'
Al Jawf 98 B4 var. Jauf. Al Jawf, NW Saudi Arabia
Al Jazair see Alger
Al Jazīrah 96 E2 physical region Iraq/Syria
Al Jīzah see El Giza
Al Junaynah see El Geneina
Al Karak 97 B7 var. El Kerak, Karak, Kerak, anc. Kir Moab, Kir of Moab. Al Karak, W Jordan
Al-Kasr al-Kebir see Ksar-el-Kebir
Al Khalīl see Hebron
Al Khārijah see El Khârga
Al Khufrah 49 H4 SE Libya
Al Khums 49 F2 var. Homs, Khoms, Khums. NW Libya
Alkmaar 64 C2 Noord-Holland, NW Netherlands
Al Kūt 98 C3 var. Kūt al 'Amārah, Kut al Imara. E Iraq
Al-Kuwait see Al Kuwayt
Al Kuwayt 98 C4 var. Al-Kuwait, Eng. Kuwait, Kuwait City; prev. Qurein. Country capital (Kuwait) E Kuwait
Al Lādhiqīyah 96 A3 Eng. Latakia, Fr. Lattaquié; anc. Laodicea, Laodicea ad Mare. Al Lādhiqīyah, W Syria
Allahābād 113 E3 Uttar Pradesh, N India
Allanmyo 114 B4 Magwe, C Myanmar
Allegheny Plateau 19 E3 mountain range New York/Pennsylvania, NE USA
Allentown 19 F4 Pennsylvania, NE USA
Alleppey 110 C3 var. Alappuzha; prev. Alleppi. Kerala, SW India
Alleppi see Alleppey
Alliance 22 D3 Nebraska, C USA
Al Līth 99 B5 Makkah, SW Saudi Arabia
Alma-Ata see Almaty
Almada 70 B4 Setúbal, W Portugal
Al Madīnah 99 A5 Eng. Medina. Al Madīnah, W Saudi Arabia
Al Mafraq 97 B6 var. Mafraq. Al Mafraq, N Jordan
Al Mahdīyah see Mahdia
Al Mahrah 99 C6 mountain range E Yemen
Al Majma'ah 98 B4 Ar Riyāḑ, C Saudi Arabia
Al Mālikīyah 96 E1 Al Ḩasakah, NE Syria
Al Manāmah 98 C4 Eng. Manama. Country capital (Bahrain) N Bahrain
Al Manāşif 96 E3 mountain range E Syria
Almansa 71 F4 Castilla-La Mancha, C Spain
Al Marj 49 G2 var. Barka, It. Barce. NE Libya
Almaty 92 C5 var. Alma-Ata. Almaty, SE Kazakhstan
Al Mawşil 98 B2 Eng. Mosul. N Iraq
Al Mayādīn 96 D3 var. Mayadin, Fr. Meyadine. Dayr az Zawr, E Syria
Al Mazra' see Al Mazra'ah
Al Mazra'ah 97 B6 var. Al Mazra', Mazra'a. Al Karak, W Jordan
Almelo 64 E3 Overijssel, E Netherlands
Almendra, Embalse de 70 C2 reservoir Castilla-León, NW Spain
Almendralejo 70 C4 Extremadura, W Spain
Almere 64 C3 var. Almere-stad. Flevoland, C Netherlands
Almere-stad see Almere
Almería 71 E5 Ar. Al-Mariyya; anc. Unci, Lat. Portus Magnus. Andalucía, S Spain
Al'met'yevsk 89 D5 Respublika Tatarstan, W Russian Federation
Al Mīnā' see El Mina
Al Minyā see El Minya
Almirante 31 E4 Bocas del Toro, NW Panama
Al Mudawwarah 97 B8 Ma'ān, SW Jordan
Al Mukallā 99 C6 var. Mukalla. SE Yemen
Al Obayyid see El Obeid
Alofi 123 F4 dependent territory capital (Niue) W Niue
Aloja 84 D3 Limbaži, N Latvia
Alónnisos 83 C5 island Vóreioi Sporádes, Greece, Aegean Sea
Álora 70 D5 Andalucía, S Spain
Alor, Kepulauan 117 E5 island group E Indonesia
Al Oued see El Oued
Alpen see Alps
Alpena 18 D2 Michigan, N USA
Alpes see Alps
Alpha Cordillera 133 B3 var. Alpha Ridge. Undersea feature Arctic Ocean
Alpha Ridge see Alpha Cordillera
Alphen see Alphen aan den Rijn
Alphen aan den Rijn 64 C3 var. Alphen. Zuid-Holland, C Netherlands
Alpi see Alps
Alpine 27 E4 Texas, SW USA
Alpi Transilvaniei see Carpaţii Meridionali
Alps 80 C1 Fr. Alpes, Ger. Alpen, It. Alpi. Mountain range C Europe
Al Qaḑārif see Gedaref
Al Qāmishlī 96 E1 var. Kamishli, Qamishly. Al Ḩasakah, NE Syria
Al Qaşrayn see Kasserine
Al Qayrawān see Kairouan
Al-Qsar see Ksar-el-Kebir
Al Qubayyāt see Qoubaïyât
Al Qunayţirah 97 B5 var. El Kuneitra, El Quneitra, Kuneitra, Qunaytra. Al Qunayţirah, SW Syria
Al Quşayr 96 B4 var. El Quseir, Quşayr, Fr. Kousseir. Ḩimş, W Syria
Al Quwayrah 97 B8 var. El Quweira. Ma'ān, SW Jordan
Alsace 68 E3 cultural region NE France
Alsdorf 72 A4 Nordrhein-Westfalen, W Germany
Alt see Olt
Alta 62 D2 Fin. Alattio. Finnmark, N Norway
Altai see Altai Mountains
Altai Mountains 104 C2 var. Altai, Chin. Altay Shan, Rus. Altay. Mountain range Asia/Europe
Altamaha River 21 E3 river Georgia, SE USA
Altamira 41 E2 Pará, NE Brazil
Altamura 75 E5 anc. Lupatia. Puglia, SE Italy
Altar, Desierto de 28 A1 var. Sonoran Desert. Desert Mexico/USA see also Sonoran Desert
Altay 104 C2 Chin. A-le-t'ai, Mong. Sharasume; prev. Ch'eng-hua, Chenghwa. Xinjiang Uygur Zizhiqu, NW China
Altay see Altai Mountains
Altay 104 D2 Govĭ-Altay, W Mongolia
Altay Shan see Altai Mountains
Altin Köprü 98 B3 var. Altun Kupri. N Iraq
Altiplano 39 F4 physical region W South America
Alton 18 B5 Illinois, N USA
Alton 18 B4 Missouri, C USA
Altoona 19 E4 Pennsylvania, NE USA
Alto Paraná see Paraná
Altun Kupri see Altin Köprü
Altun Shan 104 C3 var. Altyn Tagh. Mountain range NW China
Altus 27 F2 Oklahoma, C USA
Altyn Tagh see Altun Shan
Al Ubayyiḑ see El Obeid
Alūksne 84 D3 Ger. Marienburg. Alūksne, NE Latvia
Al 'Ulā 98 A4 Al Madīnah, NW Saudi Arabia
Al 'Umarī 97 C6 'Ammān, E Jordan
Alupka 87 F5 Respublika Krym, S Ukraine
Alushta 87 F5 Respublika Krym, S Ukraine
Al 'Uwaynāt 49 F4 var. Al Awaynāt. SW Libya
Alva 27 F1 Oklahoma, C USA
Alvarado 29 F4 Veracruz-Llave, E Mexico
Alvin 27 H4 Texas, SW USA
Al Wajh 98 A4 Tabūk, NW Saudi Arabia
Alwar 112 D3 Rājasthān, N India
Al Wari'ah 98 C4 Ash Sharqīyah, N Saudi Arabia
Alykí 82 C4 var. Aliki. Thásos, N Greece
Alytus 85 B5 Pol. Olita. Alytus, S Lithuania
Alzette 65 D8 river S Luxembourg
Amadeus, Lake 125 D5 seasonal lake Northern Territory, C Australia
Amadi 51 B5 Western Equatoria, SW Sudan
Amadjuak Lake 15 G3 lake Baffin Island, Nunavut, N Canada
Amakusa-nada 109 A7 gulf Kyūshū, SW Japan
Åmål 63 B6 Västra Götaland, S Sweden
Amami-guntō 108 A3 island group SW Japan
Amami-Ō-shima 108 A3 island S Japan
Amantea 75 D6 Calabria, SW Italy
Amapá 41 E1 Amapá, NE Brazil
Amara see Al 'Amārah
Amarapura 114 B3 Mandalay, C Myanmar
Amarillo 27 E2 Texas, SW USA
Amay 65 C6 Liège, E Belgium
Amazon 41 E1 Sp. Amazonas. River Brazil/Peru
Amazon Basin 40 D2 basin N South America
Amazon, Mouths of the 41 F1 delta NE Brazil
Ambam 55 B5 Sud, S Cameroon
Ambanja 57 G2 Antsirañana, N Madagascar
Ambarchik 93 G2 Respublika Sakha (Yakutiya), NE Russian Federation
Ambato 38 B1 Tungurahua, C Ecuador
Ambérieu-en-Bugey 69 D5 Ain, E France
Amboasary 57 F4 Toliara, S Madagascar
Ambon 117 F4 prev. Amboina, Amboyna. Pulau Ambon, E Indonesia
Ambositra 57 G3 Fianarantsoa, SE Madagascar
Ambrim see Ambrym
Ambriz 56 A1 Bengo, NW Angola
Ambrym 122 D4 var. Ambrim. Island C Vanuatu
Amchitka Island 14 A2 island Aleutian Islands, Alaska, USA
Amdo 104 C5 Xizang Zizhiqu, W China
Ameland 64 D1 Fris. It Amelân. Island Waddeneilanden, N Netherlands
America-Antarctica Ridge 45 C7 undersea feature S Atlantic Ocean
American Falls Reservoir 24 E4 reservoir Idaho, NW USA
American Samoa 123 E4 US unincorporated territory W Polynesia
Amersfoort 64 D3 Utrecht, C Netherlands
Ames 23 F3 Iowa, C USA
Amfilochía 83 A5 var. Amfilokhía. Dytikí Ellás, C Greece
Amfilokhía see Amfilochía
Amga 93 F3 river NE Russian Federation
Amherst 17 F4 Nova Scotia, SE Canada
Amida see Diyarbakır
Amiens 68 C3 anc. Ambianum, Samarobriva. Somme, N France
Amíndaion see Amýntaio
Amindeo see Amýntaio
Amīndīvi Islands 110 A2 island group Lakshadweep, India, N Indian Ocean
Amirante Islands 57 G1 var. Amirantes Group. Island group C Seychelles
Amirantes Group see Amirante Islands
Amistad Reservoir 27 F4 var. Presa de la Amistad. Reservoir Mexico/USA
'Ammān 97 B6 var. Amman; anc. Philadelphia, Bibl. Rabbah Ammon, Rabbath Ammon. Country capital (Jordan) 'Ammān, NW Jordan
Amman see 'Ammān
Ammassalik 60 D4 var. Angmagssalik. S Greenland
Ammóchostos 80 D5 var. Famagusta, Gazimağusa. E Cyprus
Āmol 98 D2 var. Amul. Mazandarān, N Iran
Amorgós 83 D6 island Kykládes, Greece, Aegean Sea
Amorgós 83 D6 Amorgós, Kykládes, Greece, Aegean Sea
Amos 16 D4 Québec, SE Canada
Amourj 52 D3 Hodh ech Chargui, SE Mauritania
Amoy see Xiamen
Ampato, Nevado 39 E4 mountain S Peru
Amposta 71 F2 Cataluña, NE Spain
Amrāvati 112 D4 prev. Amraoti. Mahārāshtra, C India
Amritsar 112 D2 Punjab, N India
Amstelveen 64 C3 Noord-Holland, C Netherlands
Amsterdam 64 C3 country capital (Netherlands) Noord-Holland, C Netherlands
Amsterdam Island 119 C6 island NE French Southern and Antarctic Territories
Am Timan 54 C3 Salamat, SE Chad
Amu Darya 100 D2 Rus. Amudar'ya, Taj. Dar"yoi Amu, Turkm. Amyderya, Uzb. Amudaryo; anc. Oxus. River C Asia
Amu-Dar'ya 101 E3 Lebapskiy Velayat, NE Turkmenistan
Amul see Āmol
Amund Ringnes Island 15 F2 island Nunavut, N Canada
Amundsen Basin see Fram Basin
Amundsen Gulf 15 E2 gulf Northwest Territories, N Canada
Amundsen Plain 132 A4 undersea feature S Pacific Ocean
Amundsen-Scott 132 B3 US research station Antarctica
Amundsen Sea 132 A4 sea S Pacific Ocean
Amuntai 116 D4 prev. Amoentai. Borneo, C Indonesia
Amur 93 G4 Chin. Heilong Jiang. River China/Russian Federation
Amvrosiyivka 87 H3 Rus. Amvrosiyevka. Donets'ka Oblast', SE Ukraine
Amýntaio 82 B4 var. Amindeo; prev. Amíndaion. Dytikí Makedonía, N Greece
Anabar 93 E2 river NE Russian Federation
An Abhainn Mhór see Blackwater
Anaco 37 E2 Anzoátegui, NE Venezuela
Anaconda 22 B2 Montana, NW USA
Anacortes 24 B1 Washington, NW USA
Anadolu Dağları see Doğu Karadeniz Dağları
Anadyr' 93 G1 river NE Russian Federation
Anadyr' 93 H1 Chukotskiy Avtonomnyy Okrug, NE Russian Federation
Anadyr, Gulf of see Anadyrskiy Zaliv
Anadyrskiy Zaliv 93 H1 Eng. Gulf of Anadyr. Gulf NE Russian Federation
Anáfi 83 D7 anc. Anaphe. Island Kykládes, Greece, Aegean Sea
'Ānah see 'Annah
Anaheim 24 E2 California, W USA
Anaiza see 'Unayzah
Analalava 57 G2 Mahajanga, NW Madagascar
Anamur 94 C5 İçel, S Turkey
Anantapur 110 C2 Andhra Pradesh, S India
Anápolis 41 F3 Goiás, C Brazil
Anār 98 D3 Kermān, C Iran
Anatolia 94 C4 plateau C Turkey
Anatom see Aneityum
Añatuya 42 C3 Santiago del Estero, N Argentina
An Bhearú see Barrow
Anchorage 14 C3 Alaska, USA
Ancona 74 C3 Marche, C Italy
Ancud 43 B6 prev. San Carlos de Ancud. Los Lagos, S Chile
Åndalsnes 63 A5 Møre og Romsdal, S Norway
Andalucía 70 D4 cultural region S Spain
Andalusia 20 C3 Alabama, S USA
Andaman Islands 102 B4 island group India, NE Indian Ocean
Andaman Sea 102 C4 sea NE Indian Ocean
Andenne 65 C6 Namur, SE Belgium
Anderlues 65 B7 Hainaut, S Belgium
Anderson 18 C4 Indiana, N USA
Andes 42 B3 mountain range W South America
Andhra Pradesh 113 E5 state E India
Andijon 101 F2 Rus. Andizhan. Andijon Wiloyati, E Uzbekistan
Andikíthira see Antikýthira
Andipaxi see Antípaxoi
Andípsara see Antípsara
Ándissa see Ántissa
Andkhvoy 100 D3 Fāryāb, N Afghanistan
Andorra 69 A7 off. Principality of Andorra, Cat. Valls d'Andorra, Fr. Vallée d'Andorre. Country SW Europe
Andorra see Andorra la Vella
Andorra la Vella 69 A8 var. Andorra, Fr. Andorre la Vielle, Sp. Andorra la Vieja. Country capital (Andorra) C Andorra
Andorra la Vieja see Andorra la Vella
Andorre la Vielle see Andorra la Vella
Andover 67 D7 S England, UK
Andøya 62 C2 island C Norway
Andreanof Islands 14 A3 island group Aleutian Islands, Alaska, USA
Andrews 27 E3 Texas, SW USA
Andrew Tablemount 118 A4 var. Gora Andryu. Undersea feature W Indian Ocean
Andria 75 D5 Puglia, SE Italy
An Droichead Nua see Newbridge
Ándros 83 C6 island Kykládes, Greece, Aegean Sea
Ándros 83 D6 Ándros, Kykládes, Greece, Aegean Sea
Andros Island 32 B2 island NW Bahamas
Andros Town 32 C1 Andros Island, NW Bahamas
Aneityum 122 D5 var. Anatom; prev. Kéamu. Island S Vanuatu
Ānewetak see Enewetak Atoll
Angara 93 E4 river C Russian Federation
Angarsk 93 E4 Irkutskaya Oblast', S Russian Federation
Ånge 63 C5 Västernorrland, C Sweden
Ángel de la Guarda, Isla 28 B2 island NW Mexico
Angeles 117 E1 off. Angeles City. Luzon, N Philippines
Angel Falls see Ángel, Salto
Ángel, Salto 37 E3 Eng. Angel Falls. Waterfall E Venezuela
Ångermanälven 62 C4 river N Sweden
Angermünde 72 D3 Brandenburg, NE Germany
Angers 68 B4 anc. Juliomagus. Maine-et-Loire, NW France
Anglesey 67 C5 island NW Wales, UK
Anglet 69 A6 Pyrénées-Atlantiques, SW France
Angleton 27 H4 Texas, SW USA
Angmagssalik see Ammassalik
Ang Nam Ngum 114 C4 lake C Laos
Angola 56 B2 off. Republic of Angola; prev. People's Republic of Angola, Portuguese West Africa. Country SW Africa
Angola Basin 47 B5 undersea feature E Atlantic Ocean
Angostura, Presa de la 29 G5 reservoir SE Mexico
Angoulême 69 B5 anc. Iculisma. Charente, W France
Angoumois 69 B5 cultural region W France
Angren 101 F2 Toshkent Wiloyati, E Uzbekistan
Anguilla 33 G3 UK dependent territory E West Indies
Anguilla Cays 32 B2 islets SW Bahamas
Anhui 106 C5 var. Anhui Sheng, Anhwei, Wan. Admin. region province E China
Anhui Sheng see Anhui
Anhwei see Anhui
Anina 86 A4 Ger. Steierdorf, Hung. Stájerlakanina; prev. Ştaierdorf-Anina, Steierdorf-Anina, Steyerlak-Anina. Caraş-Severin, SW Romania
Anjou 68 B4 cultural region NW France
Anjouan 57 F2 var. Nzwani, Johanna Island. Island SE Comoros
Ankara 94 C3 prev. Angora, anc. Ancyra. Country capital (Turkey) Ankara, C Turkey
Ankeny 23 F3 Iowa, C USA
Anklam 72 D2 Mecklenburg-Vorpommern, NE Germany
Anykščiai 84 C4 Anykščiai, E Lithuania
An Longfort see Longford
An Mhuir Cheilteach see Celtic Sea
Annaba 49 E1 prev. Bône. NE Algeria
An Nafūd 98 B4 desert NW Saudi Arabia
'Annah 98 B3 var. 'Ānah. NW Iraq
An Najaf 98 B3 var. Najaf. S Iraq
Annamitique, Chaîne 114 D4 mountain range C Laos
Annapolis 19 F4 state capital Maryland, NE USA
Annapurna 113 E3 mountain C Nepal
An Nāqūrah see En Nâqoûra
Ann Arbor 18 C3 Michigan, N USA
An Nāşirīyah 98 C3 var. Nasiriya. SE Iraq
Annecy 69 D5 anc. Anneciacum. Haute-Savoie, E France
An Nīl al Azraq see Blue Nile
Anniston 20 D2 Alabama, S USA
Annotto Bay 32 B4 C Jamaica
An Ómaigh see Omagh
Anqing 106 D5 Anhui, E China
Anse La Raye 33 F1 NW Saint Lucia
Anshun 106 B6 Guizhou, S China
Ansongo 53 E3 Gao, E Mali
An Srath Bán see Strabane
Antakya 94 D4 anc. Antioch, Antiochia. Hatay, S Turkey
Antalaha 57 G2 Antsirañana, NE Madagascar
Antalya 94 B4 prev. Adalia, anc. Attaleia, Bibl. Attalia. Antalya, SW Turkey
Antalya, Gulf of see Antalya Körfezi
Antalya Körfezi 94 B4 var. Gulf of Adalia, Eng. Gulf of Antalya. Gulf SW Turkey
Antananarivo 57 G3 prev. Tananarive. Country capital (Madagascar) Antananarivo, C Madagascar
Antarctica 132 B3 continent
Antarctic Peninsula 132 A2 peninsula Antarctica
Antep see Gaziantep
Antequera 70 D5 anc. Anticaria, Antiquaria. Andalucía, S Spain
Antequera see Oaxaca
Antibes 69 D6 anc. Antipolis. Alpes-Maritimes, SE France
Anticosti, Île d' 17 F3 Eng. Anticosti Island. Island Québec, E Canada
Antigua 33 G3 island S Antigua and Barbuda, Leeward Islands
Antigua and Barbuda 33 G3 country E West Indies
Antikýthira 83 B7 var. Andikíthira. Island S Greece
Anti-Lebanon 96 B4 var. Jebel esh Sharqi, Ar. Al Jabal ash Sharqī, Fr. Anti-Liban. Mountain range Lebanon/Syria
Anti-Liban see Anti-Lebanon
Antípaxoi 83 A5 var. Andipaxi. Island Iónioi Nísoi, Greece, C Mediterranean Sea
Antipodes Islands 120 D5 island group S NZ
Antípsara 83 D5 var. Andípsara. Island E Greece
Ántissa 83 D5 var. Ándissa. Lésvos, E Greece
An tIúr see Newry
Antofagasta 42 B2 Antofagasta, N Chile
Antony 68 E2 Hauts-de-Seine, N France
Antserana see Antsirañana
An tSionainn see Shannon
Antsirañana 57 G2 var. Antserana; prev. Antsirane, Diégo-Suarez. Antsirañana, N Madagascar
Antsirane see Antsirañana
Antsohihy 57 G2 Mahajanga, NW Madagascar
An-tung see Dandong
Antwerp see Antwerpen
Antwerpen 65 C5 Eng. Antwerp, Fr. Anvers. Antwerpen, N Belgium
Anuradhapura 110 D3 North Central Province, C Sri Lanka
Anyang 106 C4 Henan, C China
A'nyêmaqên Shan 104 D4 mountain range C China
Anzio 75 C5 Lazio, C Italy
Aomen see Macao
Aomori 108 D3 Aomori, Honshū, C Japan
Aóos see Vjosës, Lumi i
Aosta 74 A1 anc. Augusta Praetoria. Valle d'Aosta, NW Italy
Ao Thai see Thailand, Gulf of
Aoukâr 52 D3 var. Aouker. Plateau C Mauritania
Aouk, Bahr 54 C4 river Central African Republic/Chad
Aouker see Aoukâr
Aozou 54 C1 Borkou-Ennedi-Tibesti, N Chad
Apalachee Bay 20 D3 bay Florida, SE USA
Apalachicola River 20 D3 river Florida, SE USA
Apamama see Abemama
Apaporis, Río 36 C4 river Brazil/Colombia
Apatity 88 C2 Murmanskaya Oblast', NW Russian Federation
Ape 84 D3 Alūksne, NE Latvia
Apeldoorn 64 D3 Gelderland, E Netherlands
Apennines see Appennino
Āpia 123 F4 country capital (Samoa) Upolu, SE Samoa
Apoera 37 G3 Sipaliwini, NW Suriname
Apostle Islands 18 B1 island group Wisconsin, N USA
Appalachian Mountains 13 D5 mountain range E USA
Appennino 74 E2 Eng. Apennines. Mountain range Italy/San Marino
Appingedam 64 E1 Groningen, NE Netherlands
Appleton 18 B2 Wisconsin, N USA
Apure, Río 36 C2 river W Venezuela
Apurímac, Río 38 D3 river S Peru
Apuseni, Munţii 86 A4 mountain range W Romania
'Aqaba see Al 'Aqabah
'Aqaba, Gulf of 98 A4 var. Gulf of Elat, Ar. Khalīj al 'Aqabah; anc. Sinus Aelaniticus. Gulf NE Red Sea
Āqchah 101 E3 var. Āqcheh. Jowzjān, N Afghanistan
Āqcheh see Āqchah
Aquae Augustae see Dax
Aquae Sextiae see Aix-en-Provence
Aquae Tarbelicae see Dax
Aquidauana 41 E4 Mato Grosso do Sul, S Brazil
Aquila see L'Aquila
Aquila degli Abruzzo see L'Aquila
Aquitaine 69 B6 cultural region SW France

Bahama Islands – Bemmel

Bahama Islands see Bahamas
Bahamas 32 C2 off. Commonwealth of the Bahamas. Country N West Indies
Bahamas 13 D6 var. Bahama Islands. Island group N West Indies
Bahāwalpur 112 C2 Punjab, E Pakistan
Bahia 41 F3 off. Estado da Bahia. State E Brazil
Bahía Blanca 43 C5 Buenos Aires, E Argentina
Bahía, Islas de la 30 C1 Eng. Bay Islands. Island group N Honduras
Bahir Dar 50 C4 var. Bahr Dar, Bahrdar Giyorgis. NW Ethiopia
Bahraich 113 E3 Uttar Pradesh, N India
Bahrain 98 C4 off. State of Bahrain, Dawlat al Bahrayn, Ar. Al Baḩrayn; prev. Bahrein, anc. Tylos or Tyros. Country SW Asia
Baḩr al Milḩ see Razāzah, Buḩayrat ar
Baḩrat Lūṭ see Dead Sea
Baḩrat Ṭabariya see Tiberias, Lake
Bahr Dar see Bahir Dar
Bahrdar Giyorgis see Bahir Dar
Bahr el Azraq see Blue Nile
Bahr el Jebel see White Nile
Bahret Lut see Dead Sea
Bahr Tabariya, Sea of see Tiberias, Lake
Bahushewsk 85 E6 Rus. Bogushëvsk. Vitsyebskaya Voblasts', NE Belarus
Baia Mare 86 B3 Ger. Frauenbach, Hung. Nagybánya; prev. Neustadt. Maramureş, NW Romania
Baia Sprie 86 B3 Ger. Mittelstadt, Hung. Felsőbánya. Maramureş, NW Romania
Baïbokoum 54 B4 Logone-Oriental, SW Chad
Baidoa see Baydhabo
Baie-Comeau 17 E3 Québec, SE Canada
Baikal, Lake see Baykal, Ozero
Baile Átha Luain see Athlone
Bailén 70 D4 Andalucía, S Spain
Baile na Mainistreach see Newtownabbey
Băileşti 86 B5 Dolj, SW Romania
Ba Illi 54 B3 Chari-Baguirmi, SW Chad
Bainbridge 20 D3 Georgia, SE USA
Bā'ir see Bāyir
Baireuth see Bayreuth
Bairiki 122 D2 country capital (Kiribati) Tarawa, NW Kiribati
Bairnsdale 127 C7 Victoria, SE Australia
Baishan 107 E3 prev. Hunjiang. Jilin, NE China
Baiyin 106 B4 Gansu, C China
Baja 77 C7 Bács-Kiskun, S Hungary
Baja California 26 A4 Eng. Lower California. Peninsula NW Mexico
Baja California 28 B2 state NW Mexico
Bajo Boquete see Boquete
Bajram Curri 79 D5 Kukës, N Albania
Bakala 54 C4 Ouaka, C Central African Republic
Bakan see Shimonoseki
Baker 24 C3 Oregon, NW USA
Baker and Howland Islands 123 E2 US unincorporated territory W Polynesia
Baker Lake 15 F3 Nunavut, N Canada
Bakersfield 25 C7 California, W USA
Bakharden 100 C3 Turkm. Bäherden; prev. Bakherden. Akhalskiy Velayat, C Turkmenistan
Bakhchysaray 87 F5 Rus. Bakhchisaray. Respublika Krym, S Ukraine
Bakhmach 87 F1 Chernihivs'ka Oblast', N Ukraine
Bākhtarān 98 C3 prev. Kermānshāh, Qahremānshahr. Kermānshāh, W Iran
Bakı 95 H2 Eng. Baku. Country capital (Azerbaijan) E Azerbaijan
Bakony 77 C7 Eng. Bakony Mountains, Ger. Bakonywald. Mountain range W Hungary
Baku see Bakı
Balabac Island 107 C8 island W Philippines
Balabac Strait 116 D2 var. Selat Balabac. Strait Malaysia/Philippines
Ba'labakk see Baalbek
Balaguer 71 F2 Cataluña, NE Spain
Balakovo 89 C6 Saratovskaya Oblast', W Russian Federation
Bālā Morghāb 100 D4 Laghmān, NW Afghanistan
Balashov 89 B6 Saratovskaya Oblast', W Russian Federation
Balaton C7 var. Lake Balaton, Ger. Plattensee. Lake W Hungary
Balaton, Lake see Balaton
Balbina, Represa 40 D1 reservoir NW Brazil
Balboa 31 G4 Panamá, C Panama
Balcarce 43 D5 Buenos Aires, E Argentina
Balclutha 129 B7 Otago, South Island, NZ
Baldy Mountain 22 C1 mountain Montana, NW USA
Bâle see Basel
Baleares, Islas 71 G3 Eng. Balearic Islands. Island group Spain, W Mediterranean Sea
Balearic Islands see Baleares, Islas
Balearic Plain see Algerian Basin
Baleine, Rivière à la 17 E2 river Québec, E Canada
Balen 65 C5 Antwerpen, N Belgium
Bāleshwar 113 F4 prev. Balasore. Orissa, E India
Bali 116 D5 island C Indonesia
Balıkesir 94 A3 Balıkesir, W Turkey
Balīkh, Nahr 96 C2 river N Syria
Balikpapan 116 D4 Borneo, C Indonesia
Balkan Mountains 82 C2 Bul./SCr. Stara Planina. Mountain range Bulgaria/Yugoslavia
Balkh 101 E3 anc. Bactra. Balkh, N Afghanistan
Balkhash 92 C5 Kaz. Balqash. Karaganda, SE Kazakhstan
Balkhash, Lake see Balkhash, Ozero
Balkhash, Ozero 92 C5 Eng. Lake Balkhash, Kaz. Balqash. Lake SE Kazakhstan
Balladonia 125 C6 Western Australia
Ballarat 127 C7 Victoria, SE Australia
Balleny Islands 132 B5 island group Antarctica
Ballinger 27 F3 Texas, SW USA
Balochistān see Baluchistān
Balş 86 B5 Olt, S Romania
Balsas 41 F2 Maranhão, E Brazil
Balsas, Río 29 E5 var. Río Mexcala. River S Mexico
Bal'shavik 85 D7 Rus. Bol'shevik. Homyel'skaya Voblasts', SE Belarus
Balta 86 D3 Odes'ka Oblast', SW Ukraine
Bălţi 86 D3 Rus. Bel'tsy. N Moldova
Baltic Sea 63 C7 Ger. Ostee, Rus. Baltiskoye More. Sea N Europe
Baltimore 19 F4 Maryland, NE USA
Baltkrievija see Belarus
Baluchistān 112 B3 var. Balochistān, Beluchistan. Admin. region province SW Pakistan
Balvi 84 D4 Balvi, NE Latvia
Balykchy 101 G2 Kir. Ysyk-Köl; prev. Issyk-Kul', Rybach'ye. Issyk-Kul'skaya Oblast', NE Kyrgyzstan
Balzers 72 E2 S Liechtenstein
Bam 98 E4 Kermān, SE Iran
Bamako 52 D4 country capital (Mali) Capital District, SW Mali
Bambari 54 C4 Ouaka, C Central African Republic
Bamberg 73 C5 Bayern, SE Germany
Bamenda 54 A4 Nord-Ouest, W Cameroon
Banaba 122 D2 var. Ocean Island. Island Tungaru, W Kiribati
Bandaaceh 116 A3 var. Banda Atjeh; prev. Koetaradja, Kutaradja, Kutaraja. Sumatera, W Indonesia
Banda Atjeh see Bandaaceh
Bandama 52 D5 var. Bandama Fleuve. River S Côte d'Ivoire
Bandama Fleuve see Bandama
Bandar 'Abbās see Bandar-e 'Abbās
Bandarbeyla 51 E5 var. Bender Beila, Bender Beyla. Bari, NE Somalia
Bandar-e 'Abbās 98 D4 var. Bandar 'Abbās; prev. Gombroon. Hormozgān, S Iran
Bandar-e Būshehr 98 C4 var. Būshehr, Eng. Bushire. Būshehr, S Iran
Bandar-e Khamīr 98 D4 Hormozgān, S Iran
Bandar-e Langeh 98 D4 var. Bandar-e Lengeh, Lingeh. Hormozgān, S Iran
Bandar-e Lengeh see Bandar-e Langeh
Bandar Kassim see Boosaaso
Bandarlampung 116 C4 prev. Tanjungkarang, Teloekbetoeng, Telukbetung. Sumatera, W Indonesia
Bandar Maharani see Muar
Bandar Masulipatnam see Machilīpatnam
Bandar Seri Begawan 116 D3 prev. Brunei Town. Country capital (Brunei) N Brunei
Bandar Sri Aman see Sri Aman
Banda Sea 117 F5 var. Laut Banda. Sea E Indonesia
Bandiagara 53 E3 Mopti, C Mali
Bandırma 94 A3 var. Penderma. Balıkesir, NW Turkey
Bandundu 55 C6 prev. Banningville. Bandundu, W Dem. Rep. Congo (Zaire)
Bandung 116 C5 prev. Bandoeng. Jawa, C Indonesia
Bangalore 110 C2 Karnātaka, S India
Bangassou 54 D4 Mbomou, SE Central African Republic
Banggai, Kepulauan 117 E4 island group C Indonesia
Banghāzī 49 G2 Eng. Bengazi, Benghazi, It. Bengasi. NE Libya
Bangka, Pulau 116 C4 island W Indonesia
Bangkok see Krung Thep
Bangkok, Bight of see Krung Thep, Ao
Bangladesh 113 G3 off. People's Republic of Bangladesh; prev. East Pakistan. Country S Asia
Bangor 67 B5 Ir. Beannchar. E Northern Ireland, UK
Bangor 19 G2 Maine, NE USA
Bangor 67 C6 NW Wales, UK
Bangui 55 B5 country capital (Central African Republic) Ombella-Mpoko, SW Central African Republic
Bangweulu, Lake 51 B8 var. Lake Bengweulu. Lake N Zambia
Ban Hat Yai see Hat Yai
Ban Hin Heup 114 C4 Viangchan, C Laos
Ban Houayxay see Houayxay
Ban Houei Sai see Houayxay
Ban Hua Hin 115 C6 var. Hua Hin. Prachuap Khiri Khan, SW Thailand
Bani 52 D3 river S Mali
Banias see Bāniyās
Banī Suwayf see Beni Suef
Bāniyās 96 B3 var. Banias, Baniyas, Paneas. Ṭarṭūs, W Syria
Baniyas see Bāniyās
Banja Luka 78 B3 Republika Srpska, NW Bosnia and Herzegovina
Banjarmasin 116 D4 prev. Bandjarmasin. Borneo, C Indonesia
Banjul 52 B3 prev. Bathurst. Country capital (Gambia) W Gambia
Banks Island 15 E2 island Banks Island, Northwest Territories, NW Canada
Banks Islands 122 D4 Fr. Îles Banks. Island group N Vanuatu
Banks Lake 24 B1 reservoir Washington, NW USA
Banks Peninsula 129 C6 peninsula South Island, NZ
Banks Strait 127 C8 strait SW Tasman Sea
Bānkura 113 F4 West Bengal, NE India
Ban Mak Khaeng see Udon Thani
Banmo see Bhamo
Bañolas see Banyoles
Ban Pak Phanang see Pak Phanang
Ban Sichon see Sichon
Banská Bystrica 77 C6 Ger. Neusohl, Hung. Besztercebánya. Banskobystrický Kraj, C Slovakia
Bantry Bay 67 A7 Ir. Bá Bheanntraí. Bay SW Ireland
Banya 82 E2 Burgas, E Bulgaria
Banyak, Kepulauan 116 A3 prev. Kepulauan Banjak. Island group NW Indonesia
Banyo 54 B4 Adamaoua, NW Cameroon
Banyoles 71 G2 var. Bañolas. Cataluña, NE Spain
Banzare Seamounts 119 C7 undersea feature S Indian Ocean
Baoji 106 B4 var. Pao-chi, Paoki. Shaanxi, C China
Baoro 54 B4 Nana-Mambéré, W Central African Republic
Baoshan 106 A6 var. Pao-shan. Yunnan, SW China
Baotou 105 F3 var. Pao-t'ou, Paotow. Nei Mongol Zizhiqu, N China
Ba'qūbah 98 B3 var. Qubba. C Iraq
Baquerizo Moreno see Puerto Baquerizo Moreno
Bar 79 C5 It. Antivari. Montenegro, SW Yugoslavia
Baraawe 51 D6 It. Brava. Shabeellaha Hoose, S Somalia
Baraji, Hirfanli 94 C3 lake C Turkey
Bārāmati 112 C5 Mahārāshtra, W India
Baranavichy 85 B6 Pol. Baranowicze, Rus. Baranovichi. Brestskaya Voblasts', SW Belarus
Barbados 33 G1 country SE West Indies
Barbastro 71 F2 Aragón, NE Spain
Barbate de Franco 70 C5 Andalucía, S Spain
Barbuda 33 G3 island N Antigua and Barbuda
Barcaldine 126 C4 Queensland, E Australia
Barce see Al Marj
Barcelona 71 G2 anc. Barcino, Barcinona. Cataluña, E Spain
Barcelona 37 E2 Anzoátegui, NE Venezuela
Barcoo see Cooper Creek
Barcs 77 C7 Somogy, SW Hungary
Bardaï 54 C1 Borkou-Ennedi-Tibesti, N Chad
Bardejov 77 D5 Ger. Bartfeld, Hung. Bártfa. Prešovský Kraj, E Slovakia
Bardera see Baardheere
Bardere see Baardheere
Bareilly 113 E3 var. Bareli. Uttar Pradesh, N India
Bareli see Bareilly
Barendrecht 64 C4 Zuid-Holland, SW Netherlands
Barentin 68 C3 Seine-Maritime, N France
Barentsburg 61 G2 Spitsbergen, W Svalbard
Barentsøya 61 G2 island E Svalbard
Barents Sea 88 C2 Nor. Barents Havet, Rus. Barentsevo More. Sea Arctic Ocean
Barents Trough 59 E1 undersea feature SW Barents Sea
Bar Harbor 19 H2 Mount Desert Island, Maine, NE USA
Bari 75 E5 var. Bari delle Puglie; anc. Barium. Puglia, SE Italy
Bāridah see Al Bāridah
Bari delle Puglie see Bari
Barikot see Barīkowṭ
Barīkowṭ 101 F4 var. Barikot. Kunar, NE Afghanistan
Barillas 30 A2 var. Santa Cruz Barillas. Huehuetenango, NW Guatemala
Barinas 36 C2 Barinas, W Venezuela
Barisal 113 G4 Khulna, S Bangladesh
Barisan, Pegunungan 116 B4 mountain range Sumatera, W Indonesia
Barito, Sungai 116 D4 river Borneo, C Indonesia
Barium see Bari
Barka see Al Marj
Barkly Tableland 126 B3 plateau Northern Territory/Queensland, N Australia
Bârlad 86 D4 prev. Bîrlad. Vaslui, E Romania
Barlavento, Ilhas de 52 A2 var. Windward Islands. Island group N Cape Verde
Bar-le-Duc 68 D3 var. Bar-sur-Ornain. Meuse, NE France
Barlee, Lake 125 B6 lake Western Australia
Barlee Range 124 A4 mountain range Western Australia
Barletta 75 D5 anc. Barduli. Puglia, SE Italy
Barlinek 76 B3 Ger. Berlinchen. Zachodniopomorskie, NW Poland
Barmouth 67 C6 NW Wales, UK
Barnaul 92 D4 Altayskiy Kray, C Russian Federation
Barnet 67 A7 SE England, UK
Barnstaple 67 C7 SW England, UK
Baroghil Pass 101 F3 var. Kowtal-e Barowghīl. Pass Afghanistan/Pakistan
Baron'ki 85 E7 Rus. Boron'ki. Mahilyowskaya Voblasts', E Belarus
Barquisimeto 36 C2 Lara, NW Venezuela
Barra 66 B3 island NW Scotland, UK
Barra de Río Grande 31 E3 Región Autónoma Atlántico Sur, E Nicaragua
Barragem de Sobradinho see Sobradinho, Represa de
Barranca 38 C3 Lima, W Peru
Barrancabermeja 36 B2 Santander, N Colombia
Barranquilla 36 B1 Atlántico, N Colombia
Barreiro 70 B4 Setúbal, W Portugal
Barrier Range 127 C6 hill range New South Wales, SE Australia
Barrow 67 B6 Ir. An Bhearú. River SE Ireland
Barrow 14 D2 Alaska, USA
Barrow-in-Furness 67 C5 NW England, UK
Barrow Island 124 A4 island Western Australia
Barstow 25 C7 California, W USA
Bar-sur-Ornain see Bar-le-Duc
Bartang 101 F3 river SE Tajikistan
Bartica 37 F3 N Guyana
Bartın 94 C2 Bartın NW Turkey
Bartlesville 27 G1 Oklahoma, C USA
Bartoszyce 76 D2 Ger. Bartenstein. Warmińsko-Mazurskie, NE Poland
Baruun-Urt 105 F2 Sühbaatar, E Mongolia
Barú, Volcán 31 E5 var. Volcán de Chiriquí. Volcano W Panama
Barwon River 127 D5 river New South Wales, SE Australia
Barysaw 85 D6 Rus. Borisov. Minskaya Voblasts', NE Belarus
Basarabeasca 86 D4 Rus. Bessarabka. SE Moldova
Basel 73 A7 Eng. Basle, Fr. Bâle. Basel-Stadt, NW Switzerland
Basilan 117 E3 island SW Philippines
Basle see Basel
Basra see Al Başrah
Bassano del Grappa 74 C2 Veneto, NE Italy
Bassein 114 A4 var. Pathein. Irrawaddy, SW Myanmar
Basse-Terre 33 G4 dependent territory capital (Guadeloupe) Basse Terre, SW Guadeloupe
Basse Terre 33 G4 island W Guadeloupe
Basseterre 33 G3 country capital (Saint Kitts and Nevis) Saint Kitts, Saint Kitts and Nevis
Bassikounou 52 D3 Hodh ech Chargui, SE Mauritania
Bass Strait 127 C7 strait SE Australia
Bassum 72 B3 Niedersachsen, NW Germany
Bastia 69 E7 Corse, France, C Mediterranean Sea
Bastogne 65 D7 Luxembourg, SE Belgium
Bastrop 20 B2 Louisiana, S USA
Bastyn' 85 B7 Rus. Bostyn'. Brestskaya Voblasts', SW Belarus
Basuo see Dongfang
Bata 55 A5 NW Equatorial Guinea
Batabanó, Golfo de 32 A2 gulf W Cuba
Batajnica 78 D3 Serbia, N Yugoslavia
Batangas 117 E2 off. Batangas City. Luzon, N Philippines
Bătdâmbâng 115 C5 prev. Battambang. Bătdâmbâng, NW Cambodia
Batéké, Plateaux 55 B6 plateau S Congo
Bath 67 D7 hist. Akermanceaster, anc. Aquae Calidae, Aquae Solis. SW England, UK
Bathinda 112 D2 Punjab, NW India
Bathsheba 33 G1 E Barbados
Bathurst 17 F4 New Brunswick, SE Canada
Bathurst 127 D6 New South Wales, SE Australia
Bathurst Island 124 D2 island Northern Territory, N Australia
Bathurst Island 15 F2 island Parry Islands, Nunavut, N Canada
Bāṭin, Wādī al 136 C4 dry watercourse SW Asia
Batman 95 E4 var. Iluh. Batman, SE Turkey
Batna 49 E2 NE Algeria
Baton Rouge 20 B3 state capital Louisiana, S USA
Batroûn 96 A4 var. Al Batrūn. N Lebanon
Batticaloa 110 D3 Eastern Province, E Sri Lanka
Battipaglia 75 D5 Campania, S Italy
Bat'umi 95 F2 W Georgia
Batu Pahat 116 B3 prev. Bandar Penggaram. Johor, Peninsular Malaysia
Bauchi 53 G4 Bauchi, NE Nigeria
Bauer Basin 131 F3 undersea feature E Pacific Ocean
Bauska 84 C3 Ger. Bauske. Bauska, S Latvia
Bautzen 72 D4 Lus. Budyšin. Sachsen, E Germany
Bavarian Alps 73 C7 Ger. Bayrische Alpen. Mountain range Austria/Germany
Bavispe, Río 28 C2 river NW Mexico
Bawīṭī 50 B2 N Egypt
Bawku 53 E4 N Ghana
Bayamo 32 C3 Granma, E Cuba
Bayan Har Shan 104 D4 var. Bayan Khar. Mountain range C China
Bayanhongor 104 D2 Bayanhongor, C Mongolia
Bayan Khar see Bayan Har Shan
Bayano, Lago 31 G4 lake E Panama
Bay City 18 C3 Michigan, N USA
Bay City 27 G4 Texas, SW USA
Baydhabo 51 D6 var. Baydhowa, Isha Baydhabo, It. Baidoa. Bay, SW Somalia
Baydhowa see Baydhabo
Bayern 73 C6 cultural region SE Germany
Bayeux 68 B3 anc. Augustodurum. Calvados, N France
Bāyir 97 C7 var. Bā'ir. Ma'ān, S Jordan
Baykal, Ozero 93 E4 Eng. Lake Baikal. Lake S Russian Federation
Baymak 89 D6 Respublika Bashkortostan, W Russian Federation
Bayonne 69 A6 anc. Lapurdum. Pyrénées-Atlantiques, SW France
Bayramaly 100 D3 prev. Bayram-Ali. Maryyskiy Velayat, S Turkmenistan
Bayreuth 73 C5 var. Baireuth. Bayern, SE Germany
Bayrūt see Beyrouth
Baytown 27 H4 Texas, SW USA
Baza 71 E4 Andalucía, S Spain
Beagle Channel 43 C8 channel Argentina/Chile
Béal Feirste see Belfast
Beannchar see Bangor
Bear Lake 24 E4 lake Idaho/Utah, NW USA
Beas de Segura 71 E4 Andalucía, S Spain
Beata, Isla 33 E3 island SW Dominican Republic
Beatrice 23 F4 Nebraska, C USA
Beaufort Sea 14 D2 sea Arctic Ocean
Beaufort West 56 C5 Afr. Beaufort-Wes. Western Cape, SW South Africa
Beaumont 27 H3 Texas, SW USA
Beaune 68 D4 Côte d'Or, C France
Beauvais 68 C3 anc. Bellovacum, Caesaromagus. Oise, N France
Beaver Island 18 C2 island Michigan, N USA
Beaver Lake 27 H1 reservoir Arkansas, C USA
Beaver River 27 F1 river Oklahoma, C USA
Beāwar 112 C3 Rājasthān, N India
Bečej 78 D3 Ger. Altbetsche, Hung. Óbecse, Rácz-Becse; prev. Magyar-Becse, Stari Bečej. Serbia, N Yugoslavia
Béchar 48 D2 prev. Colomb-Béchar. W Algeria
Beckley 18 D5 West Virginia, NE USA
Bedford 67 D6 E England, UK
Bedum 64 E1 Groningen, NE Netherlands
Be'ér Menuḩa 97 B7 var Be'er Menukha. Southern, S Israel
Be'er Menukha see Be'ér Menuḩa
Beernem 65 A5 West-Vlaanderen, NW Belgium
Beersheba see Be'ér Sheva'
Be'ér Sheva' 97 A7 var. Beersheba, Ar. Bir es Saba. Southern, S Israel
Beesel 65 D5 Limburg, SE Netherlands
Beeville 27 G4 Texas, SW USA
Bega 127 D7 New South Wales, SE Australia
Beida see Al Bayḑā'
Beihai 106 B6 Guangxi Zhuangzu Zizhiqu, S China
Beijing 106 C3 var. Pei-ching, Eng. Peking; prev. Pei-p'ing. Country/municipality capital (China) Beijing Shi, E China
Beilen 64 E2 Drenthe, NE Netherlands
Beira 57 E3 Sofala, C Mozambique
Beirut see Beyrouth
Beit Leḩm see Bethlehem
Beiuş 86 B3 Hung. Belényes. Bihor, NW Romania
Beja 70 B4 anc. Pax Julia. Beja, SE Portugal
Béjar 70 C3 Castilla-León, N Spain
Bejraburi see Phetchaburi
Békéscsaba 77 D7 Rom. Bichiş-Ciaba. Békés, SE Hungary
Bekobod 101 E2 Rus. Bekabad; prev. Begovat. Toshkent Wiloyati, E Uzbekistan
Bela Crkva 78 E3 Ger. Weisskirchen, Hung. Fehértemplom. Serbia, W Yugoslavia
Belarus 85 B6 off. Republic of Belarus, var. Belorussia, Latv. Baltkrievija; prev. Belorussian SSR, Rus. Belorusskaya SSR. Country E Europe
Belau see Palau
Belchatow see Bełchatów
Bełchatów 76 C4 var. Belchatow. Łódzkie, C Poland
Belcher Islands 16 C2 Fr. Îles Belcher. Island group Northwest Territories, SE Canada
Beledweyne 51 D5 var. Belet Huen, It. Belet Uen. Hiiraan, C Somalia
Belém 41 F1 var. Pará. State capital Pará, N Brazil
Belen 26 D2 New Mexico, SW USA
Belén 30 D4 Rivas, SW Nicaragua
Belet Huen see Beledweyne
Belet Uen see Beledweyne
Belfast 67 B5 Ir. Béal Feirste. Admin capital E Northern Ireland, UK
Belfield 22 D2 North Dakota, N USA
Belfort 68 E4 Territoire-de-Belfort, E France
Belgaum 110 B1 Karnātaka, W India
Belgium 65 B6 off. Kingdom of Belgium, Dut. België, Fr. Belgique. Country NW Europe
Belgorod 89 A6 Belgorodskaya Oblast', W Russian Federation
Belgrade see Beograd
Belgrano II 132 B2 Argentinian research station Antarctica
Belice see Belize City
Beligrad see Berat
Beli Manastir 78 C3 Hung. Pélmonostor; prev. Monostor. Osijek-Baranja, NE Croatia
Bélinga 55 B5 Ogooué-Ivindo, NE Gabon
Belitung, Pulau 116 C4 island W Indonesia
Belize 30 B1 Sp. Belice; prev. British Honduras, Colony of Belize. Country Central America
Belize 30 B1 river Belize/Guatemala
Belize see Belize City
Belize City 30 C1 var. Belize, Sp. Belice. Belize, NE Belize
Belkofski 14 B3 Alaska, USA
Belle Île 68 A4 island NW France
Belle Isle, Strait of 17 G3 strait Newfoundland and Labrador, E Canada
Belleville 18 B4 Illinois, N USA
Bellevue 23 F4 Iowa, C USA
Bellevue 24 B2 Washington, NW USA
Bellingham 24 B1 Washington, NW USA
Belling Hausen Mulde see Southeast Pacific Basin
Bellingshausen Abyssal Plain see Bellingshausen Plain
Bellingshausen Plain 131 F5 var. Bellingshausen Abyssal Plain. Undersea feature SE Pacific Ocean
Bellingshausen Sea 132 A3 sea Antarctica
Bellinzona 73 B8 Ger. Bellenz. Ticino, S Switzerland
Bello 36 B2 Antioquia, W Colombia
Bellville 56 B5 Western Cape, SW South Africa
Belmopan 30 C1 country capital (Belize) Cayo, C Belize
Belogradchik 82 B1 Vidin, NW Bulgaria
Belo Horizonte 41 F4 prev. Bello Horizonte. State capital Minas Gerais, SE Brazil
Belomorsk 88 B3 Respublika Kareliya, NW Russian Federation
Beloretsk 89 D6 Respublika Bashkortostan, W Russian Federation
Belorussia/Belorussian SSR see Belarus
Belorusskaya SSR see Belarus
Beloye More 88 C3 Eng. White Sea. Sea NW Russian Federation
Belozersk 88 B4 Vologodskaya Oblast', NW Russian Federation
Belton 27 G3 Texas, SW USA
Beluchistan see Baluchistān
Belukha, Gora 92 D5 mountain Kazakhstan/Russian Federation
Belyy, Ostrov 92 D2 island N Russian Federation
Bemaraha 57 F3 var. Plateau du Bemaraha. Mountain range W Madagascar
Bemidji 23 F1 Minnesota, N USA
Bemmel 64 D4 Gelderland, SE Netherlands

Benaco – Bouar

INDEX

Benaco see Garda, Lago di
Benavente 70 D2 Castilla-León, N Spain
Bend 24 B3 Oregon, NW USA
Bender Beila see Bandarbeyla
Bender Beyla see Bandarbeyla
Bender Cassim see Boosaaso
Bendern 72 E1 NW Liechtenstein
Bender Qaasim see Boosaaso
Bendigo 127 C7 Victoria, SE Australia
Benešov 77 B5 Ger. Beneschau. Středočesky Kraj, W Czech Republic
Benevento 75 D5 anc. Beneventum, Malventum. Campania, S Italy
Bengal, Bay of 102 C4 bay N Indian Ocean
Bengbu 106 D5 var. Peng-pu. Anhui, E China
Benghazi see Banghāzī
Bengkulu 116 B4 prev. Bengkoeloe, Benkoelen, Benkulen. Sumatera, W Indonesia
Benguela 56 A2 var. Benguella. Benguela, W Angola
Benguella see Benguela
Bengweulu, Lake see Bangweulu, Lake
Ben Hope 66 B2 mountain N Scotland, UK
Beni 34 B4 var. El Beni. Admin. region department N Bolivia
Beni 55 E5 Nord Kivu, NE Dem. Rep. Congo (Zaire)
Benidorm 71 F4 País Valenciano, SE Spain
Beni-Mellal 48 C2 C Morocco
Benin 53 F4 off. Republic of Benin; prev. Dahomey. Country W Africa
Benin, Bight of 53 F5 gulf W Africa
Benin City 53 F5 Edo, SW Nigeria
Beni, Río 39 E3 river N Bolivia
Beni Suef 50 B2 var. Banī Suwayf. N Egypt
Ben Nevis 66 C3 mountain N Scotland, UK
Benson 26 B3 Arizona, SW USA
Bent Jbaïl 97 A5 var. Bint Jubayl. S Lebanon
Benton 20 B1 Arkansas, C USA
Benue 54 B4 Fr. Bénoué. River Cameroon/Nigeria
Benue 53 G4 state SE Nigeria
Beograd 78 D3 Eng. Belgrade, Ger. Belgrad; anc. Singidunum. Country capital (Yugoslavia) Serbia, N Yugoslavia
Berane 79 D5 prev. Ivangrad. Montenegro, SW Yugoslavia
Berat 79 C6 var. Berati, SCr. Beligrad. Berat, C Albania
Berati see Berat
Berau, Teluk 117 G4 var. MacCluer Gulf. Bay Irian Jaya, E Indonesia
Berbera 50 D4 Woqooyi Galbeed, NW Somalia
Berbérati 55 B5 Mambéré-Kadéï, SW Central African Republic
Berck-Plage 68 C2 Pas-de-Calais, N France
Berdyans'k 87 G4 Rus. Berdyansk; prev. Osipenko. Zaporiz'ka Oblast', SE Ukraine
Berdychiv 86 D2 Rus. Berdichev. Zhytomyrs'ka Oblast', N Ukraine
Berehove 86 B3 Cz. Berehovo, Hung. Beregszász, Rus. Beregovo. Zakarpats'ka Oblast', W Ukraine
Berettyó 77 D7 Rom. Barcău; prev. Berătău, Beretău. River Hungary/Romania
Berettyóújfalu 77 D6 Hajdú-Bihar, E Hungary
Berezhany 86 C2 Pol. Brzeżany. Ternopil's'ka Oblast', W Ukraine
Berezniki 89 D5 Permskaya Oblast', NW Russian Federation
Berga 71 G2 Cataluña, NE Spain
Bergamo 74 B2 anc. Bergomum. Lombardia, N Italy
Bergara 71 E1 País Vasco, N Spain
Bergen 63 A5 Hordaland, S Norway
Bergen 72 D2 Mecklenburg-Vorpommern, NE Germany
Bergen 64 C2 Noord-Holland, NW Netherlands
Bergerac 69 B5 Dordogne, SW France
Bergeyk 65 C5 Noord-Brabant, S Netherlands
Bergse Maas 64 D4 river S Netherlands
Beringen 65 C5 Limburg, NE Belgium
Bering Sea 14 A2 sea N Pacific Ocean
Bering Strait 14 C2 Rus. Beringov Proliv. Strait Bering Sea/Chukchi Sea
Berja 71 E5 Andalucía, S Spain
Berkeley 25 B6 California, W USA
Berkner Island 132 A2 island Antarctica
Berkovitsa 82 C2 Montana, NW Bulgaria
Berlin 72 D3 country capital (Germany) Berlin, NE Germany
Berlin 19 G2 New Hampshire, NE USA
Bermejo, Río 42 C2 river N Argentina
Bermeo 71 E1 País Vasco, N Spain
Bermuda 13 D6 var. Bermuda Islands, Bermudas; prev. Somers Islands. UK crown colony NW Atlantic Ocean
Bermuda Islands see Bermuda
Bermuda Rise 13 E6 undersea feature C Sargasso Sea
Bermudas see Bermuda
Bern 73 A7 Fr. Berne. Country capital (Switzerland) Bern, W Switzerland
Bernau 72 D3 Brandenburg, NE Germany
Bernburg 72 C4 Sachsen-Anhalt, C Germany
Berne see Bern
Berner Alpen 73 A7 var. Berner Oberland, Eng. Bernese Oberland. Mountain range SW Switzerland
Berner Oberland see Berner Alpen
Bernese Oberland see Berner Alpen
Bernier Island 125 A5 island Western Australia
Berry 68 C4 cultural region C France
Berry Islands 32 C1 island group N Bahamas
Bertoua 55 B5 Est, E Cameroon
Beru 123 E2 var. Peru. Atoll Tungaru, W Kiribati
Berwick-upon-Tweed 66 D4 N England, UK
Berytus see Beyrouth
Besançon 68 D4 anc. Besontium, Vesontio. Doubs, E France
Beskra see Biskra
Betafo 57 G3 Antananarivo, C Madagascar
Betanzos 70 B1 Galicia, NW Spain
Bethlehem 97 B6 Ar. Beit Laḥm, Heb. Bet Lehem. C West Bank
Bethlehem 56 D4 Free State, C South Africa
Béticos, Sistemas 70 D4 var. Sistema Penibético, Eng. Baetic Cordillera, Baetic Mountains. Mountain range S Spain
Bet Lehem see Bethlehem
Bétou 55 C5 La Likouala, N Congo
Bette, Picco see Bette, Pic
Bette, Pic 49 G4 var. Bikkū Bīttī, It. Picco Bette. Mountain S Libya
Bette, Picco see Bette, Pic
Beulah 18 C2 Michigan, N USA
Beuthen see Bytom
Beveren 65 B5 Oost-Vlaanderen, N Belgium
Beverley 67 D5 E England, UK
Bexley 67 B8 SE England, UK
Beyla 52 D4 Guinée-Forestière, SE Guinea
Beyrouth 96 A4 var. Bayrūt, Eng. Beirut; anc. Berytus. Country capital (Lebanon) W Lebanon
Beyşehir 94 B4 Konya, SW Turkey
Beyşehir Gölü 94 B4 lake C Turkey
Béziers 69 C6 anc. Baeterrae, Baeterrae Septimanorum, Julia Beterrae. Hérault, S France
Bhadrāvati 110 C2 Karnātaka, SW India
Bhāgalpur 113 F3 Bihār, NE India
Bhaktapur 113 F3 Central, C Nepal
Bhamo 114 B2 var. Banmo. Kachin State, N Myanmar
Bharūch 112 C4 Gujarāt, W India
Bhāvnagar 112 C4 prev. Bhaunagar. Gujarāt, W India
Bhopāl 112 D4 Madhya Pradesh, C India
Bhubaneshwar 113 F5 prev. Bhubaneswar, Bhuvaneshwar. Orissa, E India
Bhuket see Phuket
Bhusāwal 112 D4 prev. Bhusaval. Mahārāshtra, C India
Bhutan 113 G3 off. Kingdom of Bhutan, var. Druk-yul. Country S Asia
Biak, Pulau 117 G4 island E Indonesia
Biała Podlaska 76 E3 Lubelskie, E Poland
Białogard 76 B2 Ger. Belgard. Zachodniopomorskie, NW Poland
Białystok 76 E3 Rus. Belostok, Bielostok. Podlaskie, NE Poland
Biarritz 69 A6 Pyrénées-Atlantiques, SW France
Bicaz 86 C3 Hung. Békás. Neamț, NE Romania
Biddeford 19 G2 Maine, NE USA
Bideford 67 C7 SW England, UK
Biel 73 A7 Fr. Bienne. Bern, W Switzerland
Bielefeld 72 B4 Nordrhein-Westfalen, NW Germany
Bielsko-Biała 77 C5 Ger. Bielitz, Bielitz-Biala. Śląskie, S Poland
Bielsk Podlaski 76 E3 Podlaskie, NE Poland
Bien Bien see Điên Biên
Biên Hoa 115 E6 Đông Nai, S Vietnam
Bienville, Lac 16 D2 lake Québec, C Canada
Bié, Planalto do 56 B2 var. Bié Plateau. Plateau C Angola
Bié Plateau see Bié, Planalto do
Big Cypress Swamp 21 E5 wetland Florida, SE USA
Bigge Island 124 C2 island Western Australia
Bighorn Mountains 22 C2 mountain range Wyoming, C USA
Bighorn River 22 C2 river Montana/Wyoming, NW USA
Bignona 52 B3 SW Senegal
Big Sioux River 23 E2 river Iowa/South Dakota, N USA
Big Spring 27 E3 Texas, SW USA
Bihać 78 B3 Federacija Bosna I Hercegovina, NW Bosnia and Herzegovina
Bihār 113 F4 prev. Behar. Admin. region state N India
Biharamulo 51 B7 Kagera, NW Tanzania
Bihosava 85 D5 Rus. Bigosovo. Vitsyebskaya Voblasts', NW Belarus
Bijeljina 78 C3 Republika Srpska, NE Bosnia and Herzegovina
Bijelo Polje 79 D5 Montenegro, SW Yugoslavia
Bīkāner 112 C3 Rājasthān, NW India
Bikin 93 G4 Khabarovskiy Kray, SE Russian Federation
Bikini Atoll 122 C1 var. Pikinni. Atoll Ralik Chain, NW Marshall Islands
Bīkkū Bīttī see Bette, Pic
Bilāspur 113 E4 Madhya Pradesh, C India
Biläsuvar 95 H3 Rus. Bilyasuvar; prev. Pushkino. SE Azerbaijan
Bila Tserkva 87 E2 Rus. Belaya Tserkov'. Kyyivs'ka Oblast', N Ukraine
Bilauktaung Range 115 C6 var. Thanintari Taungdan. Mountain range Myanmar/Thailand
Bilbao 71 E1 Basq. Bilbo. País Vasco, N Spain
Bilecik 94 B3 Bilecik, NW Turkey
Billings 22 C2 Montana, NW USA
Bilma, Grand Erg de 53 H3 desert NE Niger
Biloela 126 D4 Queensland, E Australia
Biloxi 20 C3 Mississippi, S USA
Biltine 54 C3 Biltine, E Chad
Bilwi see Puerto Cabezas
Bilzen 65 D6 Limburg, NE Belgium
Bimini Islands 32 C1 island group W Bahamas
Binche 65 B7 Hainaut, S Belgium
Bindloe Island see Marchena, Isla
Binghamton 19 F3 New York, NE USA
Bingöl 95 E3 Bingöl, E Turkey
Bint Jubayl see Bent Jbaïl
Bintulu 116 D3 Sarawak, East Malaysia
Binzhou 106 D4 Shandong, E China
Bío Bío, Río 43 B5 river C Chile
Bioco, Isla de 55 A5 var. Bioko, Eng. Fernando Po, Sp. Fernando Póo; prev. Macías Nguema Biyogo. Island NW Equatorial Guinea
Bioko see Bioco, Isla de
Birāk 49 F3 var. Brak. C Libya
Birao 54 D3 Vakaga, NE Central African Republic
Biratnagar 113 F3 Eastern, SE Nepal
Bir es Saba see Be'ér Sheva'
Birhār Sharīf 113 F3 Bihar, N India
Bīrjand 98 E3 Khorāsān, E Iran
Birkenfeld 73 A5 Rheinland-Pfalz, SW Germany
Birkenhead 67 C5 NW England, UK
Birmingham 20 C2 Alabama, S USA
Birmingham 67 C6 C England, UK
Bir Moghrein see Bîr Mogreïn
Bîr Mogreïn 52 C1 var. Bir Moghrein; prev. Fort-Trinquet. Tiris Zemmour, N Mauritania
Birnie Island 123 E3 atoll Phoenix Islands, C Kiribati
Birni-Nkonni see Birnin Konni
Birnin Konni 53 F3 var. Birni-Nkonni. Tahoua, SW Niger
Birobidzhan 93 G4 Yevreyskaya Avtonomnaya Oblast', SE Russian Federation
Birsk 89 D5 Respublika Bashkortostan, W Russian Federation
Biržai 84 C4 Ger. Birsen. Biržai, NE Lithuania
Birżebbuġa 80 B5 SE Malta
Bisbee 26 B3 Arizona, SW USA
Biscay, Bay of 58 B4 Sp. Golfo de Vizcaya, Port. Baía de Biscaia. Bay France/Spain
Biscay Plain 58 B3 undersea feature SE Bay of Biscay
Bīshah, Wādī 99 B5 dry watercourse C Saudi Arabia
Bishkek 101 G2 var. Pishpek; prev. Frunze. Country capital (Kyrgyzstan) Chuyskaya Oblast', N Kyrgyzstan
Bishop's Lynn see King's Lynn
Bishrī, Jabal 96 D3 mountain range E Syria
Biskara see Biskra
Biskra 49 E2 var. Beskra, Biskara. NE Algeria
Biskupiec 76 D2 Ger. Bischofsburg. Warmińsko-Mazurskie, NE Poland
Bislig 117 F2 Mindanao, S Philippines
Bismarck 23 E2 state capital North Dakota, N USA
Bismarck Archipelago 122 B3 island group NE PNG
Bismarck Sea 122 B3 sea W Pacific Ocean
Bisnulok see Phitsanulok
Bissau 52 B4 country capital (Guinea-Bissau) W Guinea-Bissau
Bistrița 86 B3 Ger. Bistritz, Hung. Beszterce; prev. Nösen. Bistrița-Năsăud, N Romania
Bitam 55 B5 Woleu-Ntem, N Gabon
Bitburg 73 A5 Rheinland-Pfalz, SW Germany
Bitlis 95 F3 Bitlis, SE Turkey
Bitola 79 D6 Turk. Monastir; prev. Bitolj. S FYR Macedonia
Bitonto 75 D5 anc. Butuntum. Puglia, SE Italy
Bitterroot Range 24 D2 mountain range Idaho/Montana, NW USA
Bitung 117 F3 prev. Bitoeng. Sulawesi, C Indonesia
Biu 53 H4 Borno, E Nigeria
Biwa-ko 109 C6 lake Honshū, SW Japan
Bizerte 49 E1 Ar. Banzart, Eng. Bizerta. N Tunisia
Bjelovar 78 B2 Hung. Belovár. Bjelovar-Bilogora, N Croatia
Bjørnøya 61 F3 Eng. Bear Island. Island N Norway
Blackall 126 C4 Queensland, E Australia
Black Drin 79 D6 Alb. Lumi i Drinit të Zi, SCr. Crni Drim. River Albania/FYR Macedonia
Blackfoot 24 E4 Idaho, NW USA
Black Forest see Schwarzwald
Black Hills 22 D3 mountain range South Dakota/Wyoming, N USA
Blackpool 67 C5 NW England, UK
Black Range 26 C2 mountain range New Mexico, SW USA
Black River 114 C3 Chin. Babian Jiang, Lixian Jiang, Fr. Rivière Noire, Vtn. Sông Đa. River China/Vietnam
Black River 32 A5 W Jamaica
Black Rock Desert 25 C5 desert Nevada, W USA
Black Sand Desert see Garagumy
Black Sea 94 B1 var. Euxine Sea, Bul. Cherno More, Rom. Marea Neagră, Rus. Chernoye More, Turk. Karadeniz, Ukr. Chorne More. Sea Asia/Europe
Black Sea Lowland 87 E4 Ukr. Prychornomors'ka Nyzovyna. Depression SE Europe
Black Volta 53 E4 var. Borongo, Mouhoun, Moun Hou, Fr. Volta Noire. River W Africa
Blackwater 67 A6 Ir. An Abhainn Mhór. River S Ireland
Blagoevgrad 82 C3 prev. Gorna Dzhumaya. Blagoevgrad, SW Bulgaria
Blagoveshchensk 93 G4 Amurskaya Oblast', SE Russian Federation
Blake Plateau 13 D6 var. Blake Terrace. Undersea feature W Atlantic Ocean
Blake Terrace see Blake Plateau
Blanca, Bahía 43 C5 bay E Argentina
Blanca, Costa 71 F4 physical region SE Spain
Blanche, Lake 127 B5 lake South Australia
Blanc, Mont 69 D5 It. Monte Bianco. Mountain France/Italy
Blanco, Cape 24 A4 headland Oregon, NW USA
Blanes 71 G2 Cataluña, NE Spain
Blankenberge 65 A5 West-Vlaanderen, NW Belgium
Blankenheim 73 A5 Nordrhein-Westfalen, W Germany
Blanquilla, Isla 37 E1 var. La Blanquilla. Island N Venezuela
Blantyre 57 E2 var. Blantyre-Limbe. Southern, S Malawi
Blantyre-Limbe see Blantyre
Blaricum 64 C3 Noord-Holland, C Netherlands
Blenheim 129 C5 Marlborough, South Island, NZ
Blida 48 D2 var. El Boulaida, El Boulaïda. N Algeria
Bloemfontein 56 C4 var. Mangaung. Country capital (South Africa-judicial capital) Free State, C South Africa
Blois 68 C4 anc. Blesae. Loir-et-Cher, C France
Bloomfield 26 C1 New Mexico, SW USA
Bloomington 18 B4 Illinois, N USA
Bloomington 18 C4 Indiana, N USA
Bloomington 23 F2 Minnesota, N USA
Bloomsbury 126 D3 Queensland, NE Australia
Bluefield 18 D5 West Virginia, NE USA
Bluefields 31 E3 Región Autónoma Atlántico Sur, SE Nicaragua
Blue Mountain Peak 32 B5 mountain E Jamaica
Blue Mountains 24 C3 mountain range Oregon/Washington, NW USA
Blue Nile 46 D4 var. Abai, Bahr el Azraq, Amh. Äbay Wenz, Ar. An Nīl al Azraq. River Ethiopia/Sudan
Blue Nile 50 C4 state E Sudan
Blumenau 41 E5 Santa Catarina, S Brazil
Blythe 25 D8 California, W USA
Blytheville 20 C1 Arkansas, C USA
Bo 52 C4 S Sierra Leone
Boaco 30 D3 Boaco, S Nicaragua
Boa Vista 52 A3 island Ilhas de Barlavento, E Cape Verde
Boa Vista 40 D1 state capital Roraima, NW Brazil
Bobaomby, Tanjona 57 G2 Fr. Cap d'Ambre. Headland N Madagascar
Bobigny 68 E1 Seine-St-Denis, N France
Bobo-Dioulasso 52 D4 SW Burkina faso
Bobrynets' 87 E3 Rus. Bobrinets. Kirovohrads'ka Oblast', C Ukraine
Boca Raton 21 F5 Florida, SE USA
Bocay 30 D2 Jinotega, N Nicaragua
Bocche del Po see Po, Foci del
Bocholt 72 A4 Nordrhein-Westfalen, W Germany
Bochum 72 A4 Nordrhein-Westfalen, W Germany
Bocșa 86 A4 Ger. Bokschen, Hung. Boksánbánya. Caraș-Severin, SW Romania
Bodaybo 93 F4 Irkutskaya Oblast', E Russian Federation
Boden 62 D4 Norrbotten, N Sweden
Bodmin 67 C7 SW England, UK
Bodø 62 C3 Nordland, C Norway
Bodrum 94 A4 Muğla, SW Turkey
Boende 55 C5 Equateur, C Dem. Rep. Congo (Zaire)
Boetoeng see Buton, Pulau
Bogale 114 B4 Irrawaddy, SW Myanmar
Bogalusa 20 B3 Louisiana, S USA
Bogatynia 76 B4 Ger. Reichenau. Dolnośląskie, SW Poland
Boğazlıyan 94 D3 Yozgat, C Turkey
Bogor 116 C5 Dut. Buitenzorg. Jawa, C Indonesia
Bogotá 36 B3 prev. Santa Fe, Santa Fe de Bogotá. Country capital (Colombia) Cundinamarca, C Colombia
Bo Hai 106 D4 var. Gulf of Chihli. Gulf NE China
Bohemia 77 A5 Cz. Čechy, Ger. Böhmen. Cultural and historical region W Czech Republic
Bohemian Forest 73 C5 Cz. Ceský Les, Šumava, Ger. Böhmerwald. Mountain range C Europe
Böhmisch-Krumau see Český Krumlov
Bohol Sea 117 E2 var. Mindanao Sea. Sea S Philippines
Bohoro Shan 104 B2 mountain range NW China
Bohuslav 87 E2 Rus. Boguslav. Kyyivs'ka Oblast', N Ukraine
Boise 24 D3 var. Boise City. State capital Idaho, NW USA
Boise City see Boise
Boise City 27 E1 Oklahoma, C USA
Boizenburg 72 C3 Mecklenburg-Vorpommern, N Germany
Bojador see Boujdour
Bojnūrd 98 D2 var. Bujnurd. Khorāsān, N Iran
Bokāro 113 F4 Bihār, N India
Boké 52 C4 Guinée-Maritime, W Guinea
Bokhara see Bukhoro
Boknafjorden 63 A6 fjord S Norway
Bol 54 B3 Lac, W Chad
Bolgatanga 53 E4 N Ghana
Bolhrad 86 D4 Rus. Bolgrad. Odes'ka Oblast', SW Ukraine
Bolívar, Pico 36 C2 mountain W Venezuela
Bolivia 39 F3 off. Republic of Bolivia. Country W South America
Bollène 69 D6 Vaucluse, SE France
Bollnäs 63 C5 Gävleborg, C Sweden
Bollon 127 D5 Queensland, C Australia
Bologna 74 C3 Emilia-Romagna, N Italy
Bol'shevik, Ostrov 93 E2 island Severnaya Zemlya, N Russian Federation
Bol'shezemel'skaya Tundra 88 E3 physical region NW Russian Federation
Bol'shoy Lyakhovskiy, Ostrov 93 F2 island NE Russian Federation
Bolton 67 D5 prev. Bolton-le-Moors. NW England, UK
Bolu 94 B3 Bolu, NW Turkey
Bolungarvík 61 E4 Vestfirdhir, NW Iceland
Bolyarovo 82 D3 prev. Pashkeni. Yambol, E Bulgaria
Bolzano 74 C1 Ger. Bozen; anc. Bauzanum. Trentino-Alto Adige, N Italy
Boma 55 B6 Bas-Zaïre, W Dem. Rep. Dem. Rep. Congo (Zaire)
Bombay see Mumbai
Bomu 54 D4 var. Mbomou, Mbomu, M'Bomu. River Central African Republic/Dem. Rep. Congo (Zaire)
Bonaire 33 F5 island E Netherlands Antilles
Bonanza 30 D2 Región Autónoma Atlántico Norte, NE Nicaragua
Bonaparte Archipelago 124 C2 island group Western Australia
Bon, Cap 80 D3 headland N Tunisia
Bonda 55 B6 Ogooué-Lolo, C Gabon
Bondoukou 53 E4 E Côte d'Ivoire
Bone see Watampone
Bone, Teluk 117 E4 bay Sulawesi, C Indonesia
Bongaigaon 113 G3 Assam, NE India
Bongo, Massif des 54 D4 var. Chaîne des Mongos. Mountain range NE Central African Republic
Bongor 54 B3 Mayo-Kébbi, SW Chad
Bonifacio 69 E7 Corse, France, C Mediterranean Sea
Bonifacio, Strait of 74 A4 Fr. Bouches de Bonifacio, It. Bocche de Bonifacio. Strait C Mediterranean Sea
Bonn 73 A5 Nordrhein-Westfalen, W Germany
Bononia see Boulogne-sur-Mer
Boosaaso 50 E4 var. Bandar Kassim, Bender Qaasim, Bosaso, It. Bender Cassim. Bari, N Somalia
Boothia, Gulf of 15 F2 gulf Nunavut, NE Canada
Boothia Peninsula 15 F2 prev. Boothia Felix. Peninsula Nunavut, NE Canada
Boppard 73 A5 Rheinland-Pfalz, W Germany
Boquete 31 E5 var. Bajo Boquete. Chiriquí, W Panama
Boquillas 28 D2 var. Boquillas del Carmen. Coahuila de Zaragoza, NE Mexico
Boquillas del Carmen see Boquillas
Bor 51 B5 Jonglei, S Sudan
Bor 78 E4 Serbia, E Yugoslavia
Borås 63 B7 Västra Götaland, S Sweden
Borborema, Planalto da 34 E3 plateau NE Brazil
Bordeaux 69 B5 anc. Burdigala. Gironde, SW France
Bordj Omar Driss 49 E3 E Algeria
Børgefjellet 62 C4 mountain range C Norway
Borger 64 E2 Drenthe, NE Netherlands
Borger 27 E1 Texas, SW USA
Borgholm 63 C7 Kalmar, S Sweden
Borgo Maggiore 74 E1 NW San Marino
Borisoglebsk 89 B6 Voronezhskaya Oblast', W Russian Federation
Borlänge 63 C6 Kopparberg, C Sweden
Borne 64 E3 Overijssel, E Netherlands
Borneo 116 C4 island Brunei/Indonesia/Malaysia
Bornholm 63 B8 island E Denmark
Borohoro Shan 101 H1 mountain range NW China
Borongo see Black Volta
Borovan 82 C2 Vratsa, NW Bulgaria
Borovichi 88 B4 Novgorodskaya Oblast', W Russian Federation
Borovo 78 C3 Vukovar-Srijem, NE Croatia
Borşa 86 C3 Hung. Borsa. Maramureș, N Romania
Boryslav 86 B2 Pol. Borysław, Rus. Borislav. L'vivs'ka Oblast', NW Ukraine
Bosanska Dubica 78 B3 var. Kozarska Dubica. Republika Srpska, NW Bosnia and Herzegovina
Bosanska Gradiška 78 B3 var. Gradiška. Republika Srpska, N Bosnia and Herzegovina
Bosanski Novi 78 B3 var. Novi Grad. Republika Srpska, NW Bosnia and Herzegovina
Bosanski Šamac 78 C3 var. Šamac, Republika Srpska, N Bosnia and Herzegovina
Bosaso see Boosaaso
Boskovice 77 B5 Ger. Boskowitz. Brněnský Kraj, SE Czech Republic
Bosna 78 C4 river N Bosnia and Herzegovina
Bosna I Hercegovina, Federacija Admin. region republic Bosnia and Herzegovina
Bosnia and Herzegovina 78 B3 off. Republic of Bosnia and Herzegovina. Country SE Europe
Bōsō-hantō 109 D6 peninsula Honshū, S Japan
Bosphorus see İstanbul Boğazı
Bosporus see İstanbul Boğazı
Bosporus Cimmerius see Kerch Strait
Bosporus Thracius see İstanbul Boğazı
Bossangoa 54 C4 Ouham, C Central African Republic
Bossembélé 54 C4 Ombella-Mpoko, C Central African Republic
Bossier City 20 A2 Louisiana, S USA
Bosten Hu 104 C3 var. Bagrax Hu. Lake NW China
Boston 67 E6 prev. St.Botolph's Town. E England, UK
Boston 19 G3 state capital Massachusetts, NE USA
Boston Mountains 20 B1 mountain range Arkansas, C USA
Botany 126 E2 New South Wales, SE Australia
Botany Bay 126 E2 inlet New South Wales, SE Australia
Boteti 56 C3 var. Botletle. River N Botswana
Bothnia, Gulf of 63 D5 Fin. Pohjanlahti, Swe. Bottniska Viken. Gulf N Baltic Sea
Botletle see Boteti
Botoșani 86 C3 Hung. Botosány. Botoșani, NE Romania
Botou 106 C4 prev. Bozhen. Hebei, E China
Botrange 65 D6 mountain E Belgium
Botswana 56 C3 off. Republic of Botswana. Country S Africa
Bouar 54 B4 Nana-Mambéré, W Central African Republic

Bou Craa – Cantaura

Bou Craa 48 B3 var. Bu Craa. NW Western Sahara
Bougainville Island 120 B3 island NE PNG
Bougaroun, Cap 80 C3 headland NE Algeria
Bougouni 52 D4 Sikasso, SW Mali
Boujdour 48 A3 var. Bojador. W Western Sahara
Boulder 22 C4 Colorado, C USA
Boulder 22 B2 Montana, NW USA
Boulogne see Boulogne-sur-Mer
Boulogne-Billancourt 68 D1 prev. Boulogne-sur-Seine. Hauts-de-Seine, N France
Boulogne-sur-Mer 68 C2 var. Boulogne; anc. Bononia, Gesoriacum, Gessoriacum. Pas-de-Calais, N France
Boûmdeïd 52 C3 var. Boumdeït. Assaba, S Mauritania
Boumdeït see Boûmdeïd
Boundiali 52 D4 N Côte d'Ivoire
Bountiful 22 B4 Utah, W USA
Bounty Basin see Bounty Trough
Bounty Islands 120 D5 island group S NZ
Bounty Trough 130 C5 var. Bounty Basin. Undersea feature S Pacific Ocean
Bourbonnais 68 C4 Illinois, N USA
Bourg see Bourg-en-Bresse
Bourgas see Burgas
Bourge-en-Bresse see Bourg-en-Bresse
Bourg-en-Bresse 69 D5 var. Bourg, Bourge-en-Bresse. Ain, E France
Bourges 68 C4 anc. Avaricum. Cher, C France
Bourgogne 68 C4 Eng. Burgundy. Cultural region E France
Bourke 127 C5 New South Wales, SE Australia
Bournemouth 67 D7 S England, UK
Boutilimit 52 C3 Trarza, SW Mauritania
Bouvet Island 45 D7 Norwegian dependency S Atlantic Ocean
Bowen 126 D3 Queensland, NE Australia
Bowling Green 18 B5 Kentucky, S USA
Bowling Green 18 C3 Ohio, N USA
Boxmeer 64 D4 Noord-Brabant, SE Netherlands
Boyarka 87 E2 Kyyivs'ka Oblast', N Ukraine
Boysun 101 E3 Rus. Baysun. Surkhondaryo Wiloyati, S Uzbekistan
Bozeman 22 B2 Montana, NW USA
Bozüyük 94 B3 Bilecik, NW Turkey
Brač 78 B4 var. Brach, It. Brazza; anc. Brattia. Island S Croatia
Brach see Brač
Bradford 67 D5 N England, UK
Brady 27 F3 Texas, SW USA
Braga 70 B2 anc. Bracara Augusta. Braga, NW Portugal
Bragança 70 C2 Eng. Braganza; anc. Julio Briga. Bragança, NE Portugal
Brahmanbaria 113 G4 Chittagong, E Bangladesh
Brahmapur 113 F5 Orissa, E India
Brahmaputra 113 H3 var. Padma, Tsangpo, Ben. Jamuna, Chin. Yarlung Zangbo Jiang, Ind. Bramaputra, Dihang, Siang. River S Asia
Brăila 86 D4 Brăila, E Romania
Braine-le-Comte 65 B6 Hainaut, SW Belgium
Brainerd 23 F2 Minnesota, N USA
Brak see Birāk
Bramaputra see Brahmaputra
Brampton 16 D5 Ontario, S Canada
Branco, Rio 34 C3 river N Brazil
Brandberg 56 A3 mountain NW Namibia
Brandenburg 72 C3 var. Brandenburg an der Havel. Brandenburg, NE Germany
Brandenburg an der Havel see Brandenburg
Brandon 15 F5 Manitoba, S Canada
Braniewo 76 D2 Ger. Braunsberg. Warmińsko-Mazurskie, NE Poland
Brasília 41 F3 country capital (Brazil) Distrito Federal, C Brazil
Brașov 86 C4 Ger. Kronstadt, Hung. Brassó; prev. Orașul Stalin. Brașov, C Romania
Bratislava 77 C6 Ger. Pressburg, Hung. Pozsony. Country capital (Slovakia) Bratislavský Kraj, SW Slovakia
Bratsk 93 E4 Irkutskaya Oblast', C Russian Federation
Brattia see Brač
Braunschweig 72 C4 Eng./Fr. Brunswick. Niedersachsen, N Germany
Brava, Costa 71 H2 coastal region NE Spain
Bravo del Norte see Grande, Rio
Bravo del Norte, Río see Bravo, Río
Bravo del Norte, Río see Bravo, Río
Bravo del Norte, Río see Grande, Rio
Bravo, Río 28 C1 var. Río Bravo del Norte, Rio Grande. River Mexico/USA
Bravo, Río see Grande, Rio
Brawley 25 D8 California, W USA
Brazil 40 C2 off. Federative Republic of Brazil, Port. República Federativa do Brasil, Sp. Brasil; prev. United States of Brazil. Country South America
Brazil Basin 45 C5 var. Brazilian Basin, Brazil'skaya Kotlovina. Undersea feature W Atlantic Ocean
Brazilian Basin see Brazil Basin
Brazilian Highlands see Central, Planalto
Brazil'skaya Kotlovina see Brazil Basin
Brazos River 27 G3 river Texas, SW USA
Brazza see Brač
Brazzaville 55 B6 country capital (Congo) Capital District, S Congo
Brčko 78 C3 Republika Srpska, NE Bosnia and Herzegovina
Brecht 65 C5 Antwerpen, N Belgium
Brecon Beacons 67 C6 mountain range S Wales, UK
Breda 64 C4 Noord-Brabant, S Netherlands
Bree 65 D5 Limburg, NE Belgium
Bregalnica 79 E6 river E FYR Macedonia
Bregenze 35 B7 anc. Brigantium. Vorarlberg, W Austria
Bregovo 82 B1 Vidin, NW Bulgaria
Bremen 72 B3 Fr. Brême. Bremen, NW Germany
Bremerhaven 72 B3 Bremen, NW Germany
Bremerton 24 B2 Washington, NW USA
Brenham 27 G3 Texas, SW USA
Brenner Pass 74 C1 var. Brenner Sattel, Fr. Col du Brenner, Ger. Brennerpass, It. Passo del Brennero. Pass Austria/Italy
Brennerpass see Brenner Pass
Brenner Sattel see Brenner Pass
Brescia 74 B2 anc. Brixia. Lombardia, N Italy
Bressanone 74 C1 Ger. Brixen. Trentino-Alto Adige, N Italy
Brest 85 A6 Pol. Brześć nad Bugiem, Rus. Brest-Litovsk; prev. Brześć Litewski. Brestskaya Voblasts', SW Belarus
Brest 68 A3 Finistère, NW France
Bretagne 68 A3 Eng. Brittany; Lat. Britannia Minor. Cultural region NW France
Brewton 20 C3 Alabama, S USA
Brezovo 82 D2 prev. Abrashlare. Plovdiv, C Bulgaria
Bria 54 D4 Haute-Kotto, C Central African Republic
Briançon 69 D5 anc. Brigantio. Hautes-Alpes, SE France
Bridgeport 19 F3 Connecticut, NE USA
Bridgetown 33 G2 country capital (Barbados) SW Barbados
Bridlington 67 D5 E England, UK
Bridport 67 D7 S England, UK
Brig 73 A7 Fr. Brigue, It. Briga. Valais, SW Switzerland
Brigham City 22 B3 Utah, W USA
Brighton 22 D4 Colorado, C USA
Brighton 67 E7 SE England, UK
Brindisi 75 E5 anc. Brundisium, Brundusium. Puglia, SE Italy
Brisbane 127 E5 state capital Queensland, E Australia
Bristol 67 D7 anc. Bricgstow. SW England, UK
Bristol 19 F3 Connecticut, NE USA
Bristol 18 D5 Virginia, NE USA
Bristol Bay 14 B3 bay Alaska, USA
Bristol Channel 67 C7 inlet England/Wales, UK
Britain 58 C3 var. Great Britain. Island UK
British Columbia 14 D4 Fr. Colombie-Britannique. Province SW Canada
British Indian Ocean Territory 119 B5 UK dependent territory C Indian Ocean
British Isles 67 island group NW Europe
British Virgin Islands 33 F3 var. Virgin Islands. UK dependent territory E West Indies
Brive-la-Gaillarde 69 C5 prev. Brive, anc. Briva Curretia. Corrèze, C France
Brno 77 B5 Ger. Brünn. Brněnský Kraj, SE Czech Republic
Brocēni 84 B3 Saldus, SW Latvia
Brodeur Peninsula 15 F2 peninsula Baffin Island, Nunavut, NE Canada
Brodnica 76 C3 Ger. Buddenbrock. Kujawski-pomorskie, C Poland
Broek-in-Waterland 64 C3 Noord-Holland, C Netherlands
Broken Arrow 27 G1 Oklahoma, C USA
Broken Bay 126 E1 bay New South Wales, SE Australia
Broken Hill 127 B6 New South Wales, SE Australia
Broken Ridge 119 D6 undersea feature S Indian Ocean
Bromley 67 B8 SE England, UK
Brookhaven 20 B3 Mississippi, S USA
Brookings 23 F3 South Dakota, N USA
Brooks Range 14 D2 mountain range Alaska, USA
Brookton 125 B6 Western Australia
Broome 124 B3 Western Australia
Broomfield 22 D4 Colorado, C USA
Broucsella see Brussel
Brovary 87 E2 Kyyivs'ka Oblast', N Ukraine
Brownfield 27 E2 Texas, SW USA
Brownville 27 G5 Texas, SW USA
Brownwood 27 F3 Texas, SW USA
Brozha 85 D7 Mahilyowskaya Voblasts', E Belarus
Brugge 65 A5 Fr. Bruges. West Vlaanderen, NW Belgium
Brummen 64 D3 Gelderland, E Netherlands
Brunei 116 D3 off. Sultanate of Brunei, Mal. Negara Brunei Darussalam. Country SE Asia
Brunner, Lake 129 C5 lake South Island, NZ
Brunswick 21 E3 Georgia, SE USA
Brusa see Bursa
Brus Laguna 30 D2 Gracias a Dios, E Honduras
Brussa see Bursa
Brussel var. Brussels, Fr. Bruxelles, Ger. Brüssel; anc. Broucsella. Country capital (Belgium) Brussels, C Belgium see also Bruxelles
Brüssel see Brussel
Brussels see Brussel
Bruxelles see Brussels
Bryan 27 G3 Texas, SW USA
Bryansk 89 A5 Bryanskaya Oblast', W Russian Federation
Brzeg 76 C4 Ger. Brieg; anc. Civitas Altae Ripae. Opolskie, S Poland
Bucaramanga 36 B2 Santander, N Colombia
Buchanan 52 C5 prev. Grand Bassa. SW Liberia
Buchanan, Lake 27 F3 reservoir Texas, SW USA
Bucharest see București
Bu Craa see Bou Craa
București 86 C5 Eng. Bucharest, Ger. Bukarest; prev. Altenburg, anc. Cetatea Damboviței. Country capital (Romania) București, S Romania
Buda-Kashalyova 85 D7 Rus. Buda-Koshelëvo. Homyel'skaya Voblasts', SE Belarus
Budapest 77 C6 off. Budapest Főváros, SCr. Budimpešta. Country capital (Hungary) Pest, N Hungary
Budaun 112 D3 Uttar Pradesh, N India
Buena Park 24 E2 California, W USA
Buenaventura 36 A3 Valle del Cauca, W Colombia
Buena Vista 71 H5 S Gibraltar
Buena Vista 39 G4 Santa Cruz, C Bolivia
Buenos Aires 42 D4 hist. Santa Maria del Buen Aire. Country capital (Argentina) Buenos Aires, E Argentina
Buenos Aires 31 E5 Puntarenas, SE Costa Rica
Buenos Aires, Lago 43 B6 var. Lago General Carrera. Lake Argentina/Chile
Buffalo 19 E3 New York, NE USA
Buffalo Narrows 15 F4 Saskatchewan, C Canada
Buff Bay 32 B5 E Jamaica
Buftea 86 C5 București, S Romania
Bug 59 E3 Bel. Zakhodni Buh, Eng. Western Bug, Rus. Zapadnyy Bug, Ukr. Zakhidnyy Buh. River E Europe
Buga 36 B3 Valle del Cauca, W Colombia
Bughotu see Santa Isabel
Buguruslan 89 D6 Orenburgskaya Oblast', W Russian Federation
Buḩayrat Nāşir see Nasser, Lake
Buheiret Nâşir see Nasser, Lake
Bujalance 70 D4 Andalucía, S Spain
Bujanovac 79 E5 Serbia, SE Yugoslavia
Bujnurd see Bojnūrd
Bujumbura 51 B7 prev. Usumbura. Country capital (Burundi) W Burundi
Bukavu 55 E6 prev. Costermansville. Sud Kivu, E Dem. Rep. Congo (Zaire)
Bukhara see Bukhoro
Bukhoro 100 D2 var. Bokhara, Rus. Bukhara. Bukhoro Wiloyati, C Uzbekistan
Bukoba 51 B6 Kagera, NW Tanzania
Bülach 73 B7 Zürich, NW Switzerland
Bulawayo 56 D3 var. Buluwayo. Matabeleland North, SW Zimbabwe
Buldur see Burdur
Bulgan 105 E2 Bulgan, N Mongolia
Bulgaria 82 C2 off. Republic of Bulgaria, Bul. Bŭlgariya; prev. People's Republic of Bulgaria. Country SE Europe
Bull Shoals Lake 20 B1 reservoir Arkansas/Missouri, C USA
Bulukumba 117 E4 prev. Boeloekoemba. Sulawesi, C Indonesia
Buluwayo see Bulawayo
Bumba 55 D5 Equateur, N Dem. Rep. Congo (Zaire)
Bunbury 125 A7 Western Australia
Bundaberg 126 E4 Queensland, E Australia
Bungo-suidō 109 B7 strait SW Japan
Bunia 55 E5 Orientale, NE Dem. Rep. Congo (Zaire)
Bünyan 94 D3 Kayseri, C Turkey
Buraida see Buraydah
Buraydah 98 B4 var. Buraida. Al Qaşīm, N Saudi Arabia
Burdur 94 B4 var. Buldur. Burdur, SW Turkey
Burdur Gölü 94 B4 salt lake SW Turkey
Burē 50 C4 C Ethiopia
Burgas 82 E2 var. Bourgas. Burgas, E Bulgaria
Burgaski Zaliv 82 E2 gulf E Bulgaria
Burgos 70 D2 Castilla-León, N Spain
Burhan Budai Shan 104 D4 mountain range C China
Buri Ram see Buriram
Buriram 115 D5 var. Buri Ram, Puriramya. Buri Ram, E Thailand
Burjassot 71 F3 País Valenciano, E Spain
Burkburnett 27 F2 Texas, SW USA
Burketown 126 B3 Queensland, NE Australia
Burkina see Burkina Faso
Burkina Faso 53 E4 off. Burkina Faso, var. Burkina; prev. Upper Volta. Country W Africa
Burley 24 D4 Idaho, NW USA
Burlington 23 G4 Iowa, C USA
Burlington 19 F2 Vermont, NE USA
Burma see Myanmar
Burnie 127 C8 Tasmania, SE Australia
Burns 24 C3 Oregon, NW USA
Burnside 15 F3 river Nunavut, NW Canada
Burnsville 23 F2 Minnesota, N USA
Burrel 79 D6 var. Burreli. Dibër, C Albania
Burreli see Burrel
Burriana 71 F3 País Valenciano, E Spain
Bursa 94 B3 var. Brussa; prev. Brusa, anc. Prusa. Bursa, NW Turkey
Burtnieks see Burtnieku Ezers
Burtnieku Ezers 84 C3 var. Burtnieks. Lake N Latvia
Burundi 51 B7 off. Republic of Burundi; prev. Kingdom of Burundi, Urundi. Country C Africa
Buru, Pulau 117 F4 prev. Boeroe. Island E Indonesia
Buşayrah 96 D3 Dayr az Zawr, E Syria
Büshehr see Bandar-e Büshehr
Bushire see Bandar-e Büshehr
Busselton 125 A7 Western Australia
Buta 55 D5 Orientale, N Dem. Rep. Congo (Zaire)
Butembo 55 E5 Nord Kivu, NE Dem. Rep. Congo (Zaire)
Butler 19 E4 Pennsylvania, NE USA
Buton, Pulau 117 E4 var. Pulau Butung; prev. Boetoeng. Island C Indonesia
Butte 22 B2 Montana, NW USA
Butterworth 116 B3 Pinang, Peninsular Malaysia
Button Islands 17 E1 island group Northwest Territories, NE Canada
Butuan 117 F2 off. Butuan City. Mindanao, S Philippines
Buulobarde 51 D5 var. Buulo Berde. Hiiraan, C Somalia Africa
Buulo Berde see Buulobarde
Buur Gaabo 51 D6 Jubbada Hoose, S Somalia
Buynaksk 89 B8 Respublika Dagestan, SW Russian Federation
Büyükağrı Dağı 95 F3 var. Aghri Dagh, Agri Dagi, Koh I Noh, Masis, Eng. Great Ararat, Mount Ararat. Mountain E Turkey
Büyükmenderes Nehri 94 A4 river SW Turkey
Buzău 86 C4 Buzău, SE Romania
Buzuluk 89 D6 Akmola, C Kazakhstan
Byahoml' 85 D5 Rus. Begoml'. Vitsyebskaya Voblasts', N Belarus
Byalynichy 85 D6 Rus. Belynichi. Mahilyowskaya Voblasts', E Belarus
Bydgoszcz 76 C3 Ger. Bromberg. Kujawski-pomorskie, C Poland
Byelaruskaya Hrada 85 B6 Rus. Belorusskaya Gryada. Ridge N Belarus
Byerezino 85 D6 Rus. Berezina. River C Belarus
Byron Island see Nikunau
Bytom 77 C5 Ger. Beuthen. Śląskie, S Poland
Bytča 77 C5 Žilinský Kraj, N Slovakia
Bytów 76 C2 Ger. Bütow. Pomorskie, N Poland
Byuzmeyin 100 C3 Turkm. Büzmeyin; prev. Bezmein. Akhalskiy Velayat, C Turkmenistan
Byval'ki 85 D8 Homyel'skaya Voblasts', SE Belarus
Byzantium see İstanbul

C

Caála 56 B2 var. Kaala, Robert Williams, Port. Vila Robert Williams. Huambo, C Angola
Caazapá 42 D3 Caazapá, S Paraguay
Caballo Reservoir 26 C3 reservoir New Mexico, SW USA
Cabañaquinta 70 D1 Asturias, N Spain
Cabanatuan 117 E1 off. Cabanatuan City. Luzon, N Philippines
Cabimas 36 C1 Zulia, NW Venezuela
Cabinda 56 A1 var. Kabinda. Cabinda, NW Angola
Cabinda 56 A1 var. Kabinda. Admin. region province NW Angola
Cabora Bassa, Lake see Cahora Bassa, Albufeira de
Caborca 28 B1 Sonora, NW Mexico
Cabot Strait 17 G4 strait E Canada
Cabras, Ilha das 54 E2 island S Sao Tome and Principe
Cabrera 71 G3 anc. Capraria. Island Islas Baleares, Spain, W Mediterranean Sea
Cáceres 70 C3 Ar. Qazris. Extremadura, W Spain
Cachimbo, Serra do 41 E2 mountain range C Brazil
Caconda 56 B2 Huíla, C Angola
Čadca 77 C5 Hung. Csaca. Žilinský Kraj, N Slovakia
Cadillac 18 C2 Michigan, N USA
Cadiz 117 E2 off. Cadiz City. Negros, C Philippines
Cádiz 70 C5 anc. Gades, Gadier, Gadir, Gadire. Andalucía, SW Spain
Cádiz, Golfo de 70 B5 Eng. Gulf of Cadiz. Gulf Portugal/Spain
Cadiz, Gulf of see Cádiz, Golfo de
Caen 68 B3 Calvados, N France
Caene see Qena
Caenepolis see Qena
Caerdydd see Cardiff
Caer Gybi see Holyhead
Caesarea Mazaca see Kayseri
Cafayate 42 C2 Salta, N Argentina
Cagayan de Oro 117 E2 off. Cagayan de Oro City. Mindanao, S Philippines
Cagliari 75 A6 anc. Caralis. Sardegna, Italy, C Mediterranean Sea
Caguas 33 F3 E Puerto Rico
Cahora Bassa, Albufeira de 56 D2 var. Lake Cabora Bassa. Reservoir NW Mozambique
Cahors 69 C5 anc. Cadurcum. Lot, S France
Cahul 86 D4 Rus. Kagul. S Moldova
Caicos Passage 32 D2 strait Bahamas/Turks and Caicos Islands
Caiffa see Hefa
Cailungo 74 E1 N San Marino
Caiphas see Hefa
Cairns 126 D3 Queensland, NE Australia
Cairo 50 B2 Ar. Al Qāhirah, var. El Qâhira. Country capital (Egypt) N Egypt
Caisleán an Bharraigh see Castlebar
Cajamarca 38 B3 prev. Caxamarca. Cajamarca, NW Peru
Čakovec 78 B2 Ger. Csakathurn, Hung. Csáktornya; prev. Ger. Tschakathurn. Međimurje, N Croatia
Calabar 53 G5 Cross River, S Nigeria
Calabozo 36 D2 Guárico, C Venezuela
Calafat 86 B5 Dolj, SW Romania
Calafate see El Calafate
Calahorra 71 E2 La Rioja, N Spain
Calais 19 H2 Maine, NE USA
Calais 68 C2 Pas-de-Calais, N France
Calama 42 B2 Antofagasta, N Chile
Calamianes see Calamian Group
Calamian Group 107 C7 var. Calamianes. Island group W Philippines
Călăras see Călărași
Călărași 86 D3 var. Călăras, Rus. Kalarash. C Moldova
Călărași 86 C5 Călărași, SE Romania
Calatayud 71 E2 Aragón, NE Spain
Calbayog 117 E2 off. Calbayog City. Samar, C Philippines
Calcutta 113 G4 West Bengal, NE India
Caldas da Rainha 70 B3 Leiria, W Portugal
Caldera 42 B3 Atacama, N Chile
Caldwell 24 C3 Idaho, NW USA
Caledonia 30 C1 Corozal, N Belize
Caleta see Catalan Bay
Caleta Olivia 43 B6 Santa Cruz, SE Argentina
Calgary 15 E5 Alberta, SW Canada
Cali 36 B3 Valle del Cauca, W Colombia
Calicut 110 C2 var. Kozhikode. Kerala, SW India
California 25 B7 off. State of California; also known as El Dorado, The Golden State. State W USA
California, Golfo de 28 B2 Eng. Gulf of California; prev. Sea of Cortez. Gulf W Mexico
California, Gulf of see California, Golfo de
Călimănești 86 B4 Vâlcea, SW Romania
Callabonna, Lake 127 B5 lake South Australia
Callao 38 C4 Callao, W Peru
Callosa de Segura 71 F4 País Valenciano, E Spain
Calmar see Kalmar
Caloundra 127 E5 Queensland, E Australia
Caltanissetta 75 C7 Sicilia, Italy, C Mediterranean Sea
Caluula 50 E4 Bari, NE Somalia
Camabatela 56 B1 Cuanza Norte, NW Angola
Camacupa 56 B2 var. General Machado, Port. Vila General Machado. Bié, C Angola
Camagüey 32 C2 prev. Puerto Príncipe. Camagüey, C Cuba
Camagüey, Archipiélago de 32 C2 island group C Cuba
Camaná 39 E4 Arequipa, SW Peru
Camargue 69 D6 physical region SE France
Ca Mau 115 D6 prev. Quan Long. Minh Hai, S Vietnam
Cambodia 115 D5 off. Kingdom of Cambodia, var. Democratic Kampuchea, Roat Kampuchea, Cam. Kampuchea; prev. People's Democratic Republic of Kampuchea. Country SE Asia
Cambrai 68 C2 Flem. Kambryk; prev. Cambray, anc. Cameracum. Nord, N France
Cambrian Mountains 67 C6 mountain range C Wales, UK
Cambridge 67 E6 Lat. Cantabrigia. E England, UK
Cambridge 19 F4 Maryland, NE USA
Cambridge 18 D4 Ohio, NE USA
Cambridge 32 A4 W Jamaica
Cambridge 128 D3 Waikato, North Island, NZ
Cambridge Bay 15 F3 district capital Victoria Island, Nunavut, NW Canada
Camden 20 B2 Arkansas, C USA
Cameroon 54 A4 off. Republic of Cameroon, Fr. Cameroun. Country W Africa
Camocim 41 F2 Ceará, E Brazil
Camopi 37 H3 E French Guiana
Campamento 30 C2 Olancho, C Honduras
Campania 75 D5 cultural region SE Italy
Campbell, Cape 129 D5 headland South Island, NZ
Campbell Island 120 D5 island S NZ
Campbell Plateau 120 D5 undersea feature SW Pacific Ocean
Campbell River 14 D5 Vancouver Island, British Columbia, SW Canada
Campeche 29 G4 Campeche, SE Mexico
Campeche, Bahía de 29 F4 Eng. Bay of Campeche. Bay E Mexico
Câm Pha 114 E3 Quang Ninh, N Vietnam
Câmpina 86 C4 prev. Cîmpina. Prahova, SE Romania
Campina Grande 41 G2 Paraíba, E Brazil
Campinas 41 F4 São Paulo, S Brazil
Campobasso 75 D5 Molise, C Italy
Campo Criptana see Campo de Criptana
Campo de Criptana 71 E3 var. Campo Criptana. Castilla-La Mancha, C Spain
Campo dos Goitacazes see Campos
Campo Grande 41 E4 state capital Mato Grosso do Sul, SW Brazil
Campos 41 F4 var. Campo dos Goitacazes. Rio de Janeiro, SE Brazil
Câmpulung 86 B4 prev. Câmpulung-Mușcel, Cîmpulung. Argeș, S Romania
Campus Stellae see Santiago
Cam Ranh 115 E6 Khanh Hoa, S Vietnam
Canada 12 B4 country N North America
Canada Basin 12 C2 undersea feature Arctic Ocean
Canadian River 27 E2 river SW USA
Çanakkale 94 A3 var. Dardanelli; prev. Chanak, Kale Sultanie. Çanakkale, W Turkey
Çanakkale Boğazı 94 A2 Eng. Dardanelles. Strait NW Turkey
Cananea 28 B1 Sonora, NW Mexico
Canarias, Islas 48 A2 Eng. Canary Islands. Island group Spain, NE Atlantic Ocean
Canarreos, Archipiélago de los 32 B2 island group W Cuba
Canary Islands see Canarias, Islas
Cañas 30 D4 Guanacaste, NW Costa Rica
Canaveral, Cape 21 E4 headland Florida, SE USA
Canavieiras 41 G3 Bahia, E Brazil
Canberra 120 C4 country capital (Australia) Australian Capital Territory, SE Australia
Cancún 29 H3 Quintana Roo, SE Mexico
Candia see Irákleio
Canea see Chaniá
Cangzhou 106 D4 Hebei, E China
Caniapiscau 17 E2 river Québec, E Canada
Caniapiscau, Réservoir de 16 D3 reservoir Québec, C Canada
Canik Dağları 94 D2 mountain range N Turkey
Canillo 69 A7 C Andorra
Çankiri 94 C3 var. Chankiri; anc. Gangra, Germanicopolis. Çankırı, N Turkey
Cannanore 110 B2 var. Kananur, Kannur. Kerala, SW India
Cannes 69 D6 Alpes-Maritimes, SE France
Canoas 41 E5 Rio Grande do Sul, S Brazil
Canon City 22 C5 Colorado, C USA
Cantabria 70 D1 cultural region N Spain
Cantábrica, Cordillera 70 C1 mountain range N Spain
Cantaura 37 E2 Anzoátegui, NE Venezuela

Chiapa – Corsicana

iapa see Chiapa de Corzo
iapa de Corzo 29 G5 var. Chiapa. Chiapas, SE Mexico
iayi see Chiai
iba 108 B1 var. Tiba. Chiba, Honshū, Japan
ibougamau 16 D3 Québec, SE Canada
icago 18 B3 Illinois, N USA
'i-ch'i-ha-erh see Qiqihar
ickasha 27 G2 Oklahoma, C USA
iclayo 38 B3 Lambayeque, NW Peru
ico 25 B5 California, W USA
ico, Río 43 B6 river S Argentina
ico, Río 43 B7 river SE Argentina
icoutimi 17 E4 Québec, SE Canada
iengmai see Chiang Mai
ienrai see Chiang Rai
iesanuova 74 D2 SW San Marino
ieti 74 D4 var. Teate. Abruzzo, C Italy
ifeng 105 G2 var. Ulanhad. Nei Mongol Zizhiqu, N China
ih-fu see Yantai
ihli see Hebei
ihli, Gulf of see Bo Hai
ihuahua 28 C2 Chihuahua, NW Mexico
ildress 27 F2 Texas, SW USA
ile 42 B3 off. Republic of Chile. Country SW South America
ile Basin 35 A5 undersea feature E Pacific Ocean
ile Chico 43 B6 Aisén, W Chile
ile Rise 35 A7 undersea feature SE Pacific Ocean
ililabombwe 56 D2 Copperbelt, C Zambia
i-lin see Jilin
illán 43 B5 Bío Bío, C Chile
illicothe 18 D4 Ohio, N USA
iloé, Isla de 43 A6 var. Isla Grande de Chiloé. Island W Chile
ilpancingo 29 E5 var. Chilpancingo de los Bravos. Guerrero, S Mexico
ilpancingo de los Bravos see Chilpancingo
ilung 106 D6 var. Keelung, Jap. Kirun, Kirun'; prev. Sp. Santissima Trinidad. N Taiwan
imán 31 G5 Panamá, E Panama
imborazo 38 A1 volcano C Ecuador
imbote 38 C3 Ancash, W Peru
imboy 100 D1 Rus. Chimbay. Qoraqalpoghiston Respublikasi, NW Uzbekistan
imoio 57 E3 Manica, C Mozambique
ina 102 C2 off. People's Republic of China, Chin. Chung-hua Jen-min Kung-ho-kuo, Zhonghua Renmin Gongheguo; prev. Chinese Empire. Country E Asia
i-nan see Jinan
inandega 30 C3 Chinandega, NW Nicaragua
incha Alta 38 D4 Ica, SW Peru
in-chiang see Quanzhou
in-chou see Jinzhou
inchow see Jinzhou
indwin 114 B2 river N Myanmar
'ing Hai see Qinghai Hu
ingola 56 D2 Copperbelt, C Zambia
ing-Tao see Qingdao
inguetti 52 C2 var. Chinguetti. Adrar, Mauritania
in Hills 114 A3 mountain range W Myanmar
inhsien see Jinzhou
innereth see Tiberias, Lake
inook Trough 91 H4 undersea feature N Pacific Ocean
ioggia 74 C2 anc. Fossa Claudia. Veneto, NE Italy
íos 83 D5 var. Hios, Khíos, It. Scio, Turk. Sakiz-Adasi. Chíos, E Greece
íos 83 D5 var. Khíos. Island E Greece
ipata 56 D2 prev. Fort Jameson. Eastern, Zambia
iquián 38 C3 Ancash, W Peru
iquimula 30 B2 Chiquimula, SE Guatemala
irāla 110 D1 Andhra Pradesh, E India
irchiq 101 E2 Rus. Chirchik. Toshkent Wiloyati, E Uzbekistan
iriquí, Golfo de 31 E5 Eng. Chiriqui Gulf. Gulf SW Panama
iriquí, Laguna de 31 E5 lagoon NW Panama
irripó Grande, Cerro 30 D4 var. Cerro Chirripó. Mountain SE Costa Rica
isec 30 B2 Alta Verapaz, C Guatemala
isholm 23 F1 Minnesota, N USA
hisimaio see Kismaayo
hisimayu see Kismaayo
hişinău 86 D4 Rus. Kishinev. Country capital (Moldova) C Moldova
hita 93 F4 Chitinskaya Oblast', S Russian Federation
hitato 56 C1 Lunda Norte, NE Angola
hitina 14 D3 Alaska, USA
hitose 108 D2 var. Titose. Hokkaidō, NE Japan
hitré 31 F5 Herrera, S Panama
hittagong 113 G4 Ben. Chāttagām. Chittagong, SE Bangladesh
hitungwiza 56 D3 prev. Chitungwiza. Mashonaland East, NE Zimbabwe
hlef 48 D2 var. Ech Cheliff, Ech Chleff; prev. Al-Asnam, El Asnam, Orléansville. NW Algeria
hocolate Mountains 25 D8 mountain range California, W USA
hodzież 76 C3 Wielkopolskie, C Poland
hoele Choel 43 C5 Río Negro, C Argentina
hoiseul 122 C3 var. Lauru. Island NW Solomon Islands
hojnice 76 C2 Ger. Knoitz. Pomorskie, N Poland
h'ok'ē 50 C4 var. Choke Mountains. Mountain range NW Ethiopia
hoke Mountains see Ch'ok'ē
holet 68 B4 Maine-et-Loire, NW France
Choluteca 30 C3 Choluteca, S Honduras
Choluteca, Río 30 C3 river SW Honduras
Choma 56 D2 Southern, S Zambia
Chomutov 76 A4 Ger. Komotau. Ústecký Kraj, NW Czech Republic
Chona 91 E2 river C Russian Federation
Chon Buri 115 C5 prev. Bang Pla Soi. Chon Buri, S Thailand
Chone 38 A1 Manabí, W Ecuador
Ch'ŏngjin 107 E3 NE North Korea
Chongqing 106 B5 var. Ch'ung-ching, Ch'ung-ch'ing, Chungking, Pahsien, Tchongking, Yuzhou. Chongqing, C China
Chongqing 106 B5 Admin. region province C China
Chonos, Archipiélago de los 43 A6 island group S Chile
Chorne More see Black Sea
Chornomors'ke 87 E4 Rus. Chernomorskoye. Respublika Krym, S Ukraine
Chortkiv 86 C2 Rus. Chortkov. Ternopil's'ka Oblast', W Ukraine
Chorum see Çorum
Chorzów 77 C5 Ger. Königshütte; prev. Królewska Huta. Śląskie, S Poland
Chōshi 109 D5 var. Tyôsi. Chiba, Honshū, S Japan
Choszczno 76 B3 Ger. Arnswalde. Zachodniopomorskie, NW Poland
Chota Nāgpur 113 E4 plateau N India
Chott el-Hodna see Hodna, Chott El
Chott Melrhir see Melghir, Chott
Choûm 52 C2 Adrar, C Mauritania
Choybalsan 105 F2 Dornod, E Mongolia
Christchurch 129 C6 Canterbury, South Island, NZ
Christiana 32 B5 C Jamaica
Christiansand see Kristiansand
Christianshåb see Qasigiannguit
Christiansund see Kristiansund
Christmas Island 119 D5 Australian external territory E Indian Ocean
Christmas Ridge 121 E1 undersea feature C Pacific Ocean
Chuan see Sichuan
Ch'uan-chou see Quanzhou
Chubut 35 B7 off. Provincia de Chubut. Admin. region province S Argentina
Chubut, Río 43 B6 river SE Argentina
Ch'u-chiang see Shaoguan
Chūgoku-sanchi 109 B6 mountain range Honshū, SW Japan
Chuí see Chuy
Chukai see Cukai
Chukchi Plain 133 B2 undersea feature Arctic Ocean
Chukchi Plateau 12 C2 undersea feature Arctic Ocean
Chukchi Sea 12 B2 Rus. Chukotskoye More. Sea Arctic Ocean
Chula Vista 25 C8 California, W USA
Chulucanas 38 B2 Piura, NW Peru
Chulym 92 D4 river C Russian Federation
Chumphon 115 C6 var. Jumporn. Chumphon, SW Thailand
Ch'unch'ŏn 107 E4 Jap. Shunsen. N South Korea
Ch'ung-ching see Chongqing
Chungking see Chongqing
Chunya 93 E3 river C Russian Federation
Chuquicamata 42 B2 Antofagasta, N Chile
Chur 73 B7 Fr. Coire, It. Coira, Rmsch. Cuera, Quera, anc. Curia Rhaetorum. Graubünden, E Switzerland
Churchill 16 B2 river Manitoba/Saskatchewan, C Canada
Churchill 17 F2 river Newfoundland and Labrador, E Canada
Churchill 15 G4 Manitoba, C Canada
Chuska Mountains 26 C1 mountain range Arizona/New Mexico, SW USA
Chusovoy 89 D5 Permskaya Oblast', NW Russian Federation
Chuuk Islands 122 B2 var. Hogoley Islands; prev. Truk Islands. Island group Caroline Islands, C Micronesia
Chuy 42 F4 var. Chuí. Rocha, E Uruguay
Chyhyryn 87 E2 Rus. Chigirin. Cherkas'ka Oblast', N Ukraine
Ciadîr-Lunga 86 D4 var. Ceadâr-Lunga, Rus. Chadyr-Lunga. S Moldova
Cide 94 C2 Kastamonu, N Turkey
Ciechanów 76 D3 prev. Zichenau. Mazowieckie, C Poland
Ciego de Ávila 32 C2 Ciego de Ávila, C Cuba
Ciénaga 36 B1 Magdalena, N Colombia
Cienfuegos 32 B2 Cienfuegos, C Cuba
Cieza 71 E4 Murcia, SE Spain
Cihanbeyli 94 C3 Konya, C Turkey
Cikobia 123 E4 prev. Thikombia. Island N Fiji
Cilacap 116 C5 prev. Tjilatjap. Jawa, C Indonesia
Cill Airne see Killarney
Cill Chainnigh see Kilkenny
Cill Mhantáin see Wicklow
Cincinnati 18 C4 Ohio, N USA
Ciney 65 C7 Namur, SE Belgium
Cinto, Monte 69 E7 mountain Corse, France, C Mediterranean Sea
Cipolletti 43 B5 Río Negro, C Argentina
Cirebon 116 C4 prev. Tjirebon. Jawa, S Indonesia
Ciro Marino 75 E6 Calabria, S Italy
Cisnădie 86 B4 Ger. Heltau, Hung. Nagydisznód. Sibiu, SW Romania
Citlaltépetl see Orizaba, Volcán Pico de
Citrus Heights 25 B5 California, W USA
Ciudad Bolívar 37 E2 prev. Angostura. Bolívar, E Venezuela
Ciudad Acuña see Villa Acuña
Cuidad Camargo 28 D2 Chihuahua, N Mexico
Ciudad Cortés see Cortés
Ciudad Darío 30 D3 var. Dario. Matagalpa, W Nicaragua
Ciudad de Dolores Hidalgo see Dolores Hidalgo
Ciudad de Guatemala 30 B2 var. Gautemala City Eng. Guatemala City; prev. Santiago de los Caballeros. Country capital (Guatemala) Guatemala, C Guatemala
Ciudad del Carmen see Carmen
Ciudad del Este 42 E2 prev. Cuidad Presidente Stroessner, Presidente Stroessner, Puerto Presidente Stroessner. Alto Paraná, SE Paraguay
Ciudad Delicias see Delicias
Ciudad de México see México
Ciudad de Panamá see Panamá
Ciudad Guayana 37 E2 prev. San Tomé de Guayana, Santo Tomé de Guayana. Bolívar, NE Venezuela
Ciudad Guzmán 28 D4 Jalisco, SW Mexico
Ciudad Hidalgo 29 G5 Chiapas, SE Mexico
Ciudad Juárez 28 C1 Chihuahua, N Mexico
Ciudad Lerdo 28 D3 Durango, C Mexico
Ciudad Madero 29 E3 var. Villa Cecilia. Tamaulipas, C Mexico
Ciudad Mante 29 E3 Tamaulipas, C Mexico
Ciudad Miguel Alemán 29 E2 Tamaulipas, C Mexico
Ciudad Obregón 28 B2 Sonora, NW Mexico
Ciudad Ojeda 36 C1 Zulia, NW Venezuela
Ciudad Porfirio Díaz see Piedras Negras
Ciudad Quesada see Quesada
Ciudad Real 70 D3 Castilla-La Mancha, C Spain
Ciudad-Rodrigo 70 C3 Castilla-León, N Spain
Ciudad Valles 29 E3 San Luis Potosí, C Mexico
Ciudad Victoria 29 E3 Tamaulipas, C Mexico
Ciutadella see Ciutadella de Menorca
Ciutadella de Menorca 71 H3 var. Ciutadella. Menorca, Spain, W Mediterranean Sea
Civitanova Marche 74 D3 Marche, C Italy
Civitavecchia 74 C4 anc. Centum Cellae, Trajani Portus. Lazio, C Italy
Claremore 27 G1 Oklahoma, C USA
Clarence 129 C5 river South Island, NZ
Clarence 129 C5 Canterbury, South Island, NZ
Clarence Town 32 D2 Long Island, C Bahamas
Clarinda 23 F4 Iowa, C USA
Clarion Fracture Zone 131 E2 tectonic feature NE Pacific Ocean
Clarión, Isla 28 A5 island W Mexico
Clark Fork 22 A1 river Idaho/Montana, NW USA
Clark Hill Lake 21 E2 var. J.Storm Thurmond Reservoir. Reservoir Georgia/South Carolina, SE USA
Clarksburg 18 D4 West Virginia, NE USA
Clarksdale 20 B2 Mississippi, S USA
Clarksville 20 C1 Tennessee, S USA
Clayton 27 E1 New Mexico, SW USA
Clearwater 21 E4 Florida, SE USA
Clearwater Mountains 24 D2 mountain range Idaho, NW USA
Cleburne 27 G3 Texas, SW USA
Clermont 126 D4 Queensland, E Australia
Clermont-Ferrand 69 C5 Puy-de-Dôme, C France
Cleveland 18 D3 Ohio, N USA
Cleveland 20 D1 Tennessee, S USA
Clifton 26 C2 Arizona, SW USA
Clinton 20 B2 Mississippi, S USA
Clinton 27 F1 Oklahoma, C USA
Clipperton Fracture Zone 131 E3 tectonic feature E Pacific Ocean
Clipperton Island 13 A7 French dependency of French Polynesia E Pacific Ocean
Cloncurry 126 B3 Queensland, C Australia
Clonmel 67 B6 Ir. Cluain Meala. S Ireland
Cloppenburg 72 B3 Niedersachsen, NW Germany
Cloquet 23 G2 Minnesota, N USA
Cloud Peak 22 C3 mountain Wyoming, C USA
Clovis 27 E2 New Mexico, SW USA
Cluain Meala see Clonmel
Cluj-Napoca 86 B3 Ger. Klausenburg, Hung. Kolozsvár; prev. Cluj. Cluj, NW Romania
Clutha 129 B7 river South Island, NZ
Clyde 66 C4 river W Scotland, UK
Coari 40 D2 Amazonas, N Brazil
Coast Mountains 14 D4 Fr. Chaîne Côtière. Mountain range Canada/USA
Coast Ranges 24 A4 mountain range W USA
Coats Island 15 G3 island Nunavut, NE Canada
Coats Land 132 B2 physical region Antarctica
Coatzacoalcos 29 G4 var. Quetzalcoalco; prev. Puerto México. Veracruz-Llave, E Mexico
Cobán 30 B2 Alta Verapaz, C Guatemala
Cobar 127 C6 New South Wales, SE Australia
Cobija 39 E3 Pando, NW Bolivia
Coburg 73 C5 Bayern, SE Germany
Coca see Puerto Francisco de Orellana
Cochabamba 39 F4 hist. Oropeza. Cochabamba, C Bolivia
Cochin 110 C3 var. Kochi. Kerala, SW India
Cochinos, Bahía de 32 B2 Eng. Bay of Pigs. Bay SE Cuba
Cochrane 43 B7 Aisén, S Chile
Cochrane 16 C4 Ontario, S Canada
Cocibolca see Nicaragua, Lago de
Cockburn Town 33 E2 var. Grand Turk. dependent territory capital (Turks and Caicos Islands) Grand Turk Island, SE Turks and Caicos Islands
Cockpit Country, The 32 A4 physical region W Jamaica
Cocobeach 55 A5 Estuaire, NW Gabon
Coconino Plateau 26 B1 plain Arizona, SW USA
Coco, Río 31 E2 var. Río Wanki, Segoviao Wangkí. River Honduras/Nicaragua
Cocos Basin 102 C5 undersea feature E Indian Ocean
Cocos Island Ridge see Cocos Ridge
Cocos Islands 119 D5 island group E Indian Ocean
Cocos Ridge 13 C8 var. Cocos Island Ridge. Undersea feature E Pacific Ocean
Cod, Cape 19 G3 headland Massachusetts, NE USA
Codfish Island 129 A8 island SW NZ
Codlea 86 C4 Ger. Zeiden, Hung. Feketehalom. Braşov, C Romania
Cody 22 C2 Wyoming, C USA
Coeur d'Alene 24 C2 Idaho, NW USA
Coevorden 64 E2 Drenthe, NE Netherlands
Coffs Harbour 127 E6 New South Wales, SE Australia
Cognac 69 B5 anc. Compniacum. Charente, W France
Coiba, Isla de 31 E5 island SW Panama
Coihaique 43 B6 var. Coyhaique. Aisén, S Chile
Coimbatore 110 C3 Tamil Nādu, S India
Coimbra 70 B3 anc. Conimbria, Conimbriga. Coimbra, W Portugal
Coín 70 D5 Andalucía, S Spain
Coirib, Loch see Corrib, Lough
Colby 23 E4 Kansas, C USA
Colchester 67 E6 hist. Colneceaste, anc. Camulodunum. E England, UK
Col du Brenner see Brenner Pass
Coleman 27 F3 Texas, SW USA
Coleraine 66 B4 Ir. Cúil Raithin. N Northern Ireland, UK
Colesberg 56 C5 Northern Cape, C South Africa
Colima 28 D4 Colima, S Mexico
Coll 66 B3 island W Scotland, UK
College Station 27 G3 Texas, SW USA
Collie 125 A7 Western Australia
Colmar 68 E4 Ger. Kolmar. Haut-Rhin, NE France
Cöln see Köln
Cologne see Köln
Colombia 36 B3 off. Republic of Colombia. Country N South America
Colombian Basin 34 A1 undersea feature SW Caribbean Sea
Colombo 110 C4 country capital (Sri Lanka) Western Province, W Sri Lanka
Colón 31 G4 prev. Aspinwall. Colón, C Panama
Colonia Agrippina see Köln
Colón Ridge 13 B8 undersea feature E Pacific Ocean
Colorado 22 C4 off. State of Colorado; also known as Centennial State, Silver State. State C USA
Colorado City 27 F3 Texas, SW USA
Colorado Plateau 26 B1 plateau W USA
Colorado, Río 43 C5 river E Argentina
Colorado, Río see Colorado River
Colorado River 13 B5 var. Río Colorado. River Mexico/USA
Colorado River 27 G4 river Texas, SW USA
Colorado Springs 22 D5 Colorado, C USA
Columbia 24 B3 river Canada/USA
Columbia 21 E2 state capital South Carolina, SE USA
Columbia 19 E4 Maryland, NE USA
Columbia 23 G4 Missouri, C USA
Columbia 20 C1 Tennessee, S USA
Columbia Plateau 24 C3 plateau Idaho/Oregon, NW USA
Columbus 18 D4 state capital Ohio, N USA
Columbus 20 D2 Georgia, SE USA
Columbus 18 C4 Indiana, N USA
Columbus 20 C2 Mississippi, S USA
Columbus 23 F4 Nebraska, C USA
Colville Channel 128 D2 channel North Island, NZ
Colville River 14 D2 river Alaska, USA
Comacchio 74 C3 var. Commachio; anc. Comactium. Emilia-Romagna, N Italy
Comactium see Comacchio
Comalcalco 29 G4 Tabasco, SE Mexico
Coma Pedrosa, Pic de 69 A7 mountain NW Andorra
Comarapa 39 F4 Santa Cruz, C Bolivia
Comayagua 30 C2 Comayagua, W Honduras
Comer See see Como, Lago di
Comilla 113 G4 Ben. Kumillā. Chittagong, E Bangladesh
Comino 80 A5 Malt. Kemmuna. Island C Malta
Comitán 29 G5 var. Comitán de Domínguez. Chiapas, SE Mexico
Comitán de Domínguez see Comitán
Commachio see Comacchio
Commissioner's Point 20 A5 headland W Bermuda
Communism Peak see Kommunizm, Qullai
Como 74 B2 anc. Comum. Lombardia, N Italy
Comodoro Rivadavia 43 B6 Chubut, SE Argentina
Como, Lago di 74 B2 var. Lario, Eng. Lake Como, Ger. Comer See. Lake N Italy
Como, Lake see Como, Lago di
Comoros 57 F2 off. Federal Islamic Republic of the Comoros, Fr. République Fédérale Islamique des Comores. Country W Indian Ocean
Compiègne 68 C3 Oise, N France
Compostella see Santiago
Comrat 86 D4 Rus. Komrat. S Moldova
Conakry 52 C4 country capital (Guinea) Conakry, SW Guinea
Concarneau 68 A3 Finistère, NW France
Concepción 42 D2 var. Villa Concepción. Concepción, C Paraguay
Concepción see La Concepción
Concepción 43 B5 Bío Bío, C Chile
Concepción 39 G3 Santa Cruz, E Bolivia
Concepción de la Vega see La Vega
Conchos, Río 28 D2 river C Mexico
Conchos, Río 26 D4 river NW Mexico
Concord 19 G3 state capital New Hampshire, NE USA
Concordia 42 D4 Entre Ríos, E Argentina
Concordia 23 E4 Kansas, C USA
Côn Đao 115 E7 var. Con Son. Island S Vietnam
Condate see Cosne-Cours-sur-Loire
Condega 30 D3 Estelí, NW Nicaragua
Congo 55 B5 off. Republic of the Congo, Fr. Moyen-Congo; prev. Middle Congo. Country C Africa
Congo 55 C6 off. Democratic Republic of Congo; prev. Zaire, Belgian Congo, Congo (Kinshasa). Country C Africa
Congo 55 C6 var. Kongo, Fr. Zaire. River C Africa
Congo Basin 55 C6 drainage basin W Dem. Rep. Congo (Zaire)
Connacht see Connaught
Connaught 67 A5 var. Connacht, Ir. Chonnacht, Cúige. Cultural region W Ireland
Connecticut 19 F3 off. State of Connecticut; also known as Blue Law State, Constitution State, Land of Steady Habits, Nutmeg State. State NE USA
Connecticut 19 G3 river Canada/USA
Conroe 27 G3 Texas, SW USA
Consolación del Sur 32 A2 Pinar del Río, W Cuba
Con Son see Côn Đao
Constance see Konstanz
Constance, Lake B7 Ger. Bodensee. Lake C Europe
Constanţa 86 D5 var. Küstendje, Eng. Constanza, Ger. Konstanza, Turk. Küstence. Constanţa, SE Romania
Constantia see Konstanz
Constantine 49 E2 var. Qacentina, Ar. Qoussantîna. NE Algeria
Constantinople see İstanbul
Constanz see Konstanz
Constanza see Constanţa
Coober Pedy 127 A5 South Australia
Cookeville 20 D1 Tennessee, S USA
Cook Islands 123 F4 territory in free association with NZ S Pacific Ocean
Cook, Mount 129 B6 prev. Aoraki, Aorangi. Mountain South Island, NZ
Cook Strait 129 D5 var. Raukawa. Strait NZ
Cooktown 126 D2 Queensland, NE Australia
Coolgardie 125 B6 Western Australia
Cooma 127 D7 New South Wales, SE Australia
Coon Rapids 23 F2 Minnesota, N USA
Cooper Creek 126 C4 var. Barcoo, Cooper's Creek. Seasonal river Queensland/South Australia
Cooper's Creek see Cooper Creek
Coos Bay 24 A3 Oregon, NW USA
Cootamundra 127 D6 New South Wales, SE Australia
Copacabana 39 E4 La Paz, W Bolivia
Copenhagen see København
Copiapó 42 B3 Atacama, N Chile
Copperas Cove 27 G3 Texas, SW USA
Coppermine see Kugluktuk
Coquimbo 42 B3 Coquimbo, N Chile
Corabia 86 B5 Olt, S Romania
Coral Harbour 15 G3 Southampton Island, Nunavut, NE Canada
Coral Sea 120 B3 sea SW Pacific Ocean
Coral Sea Islands 122 B4 Australian external territory SW Pacific Ocean
Corantijn Rivier see Courantyne River
Corcaigh see Cork
Corcovado, Golfo 43 B6 gulf S Chile
Cordele 20 D3 Georgia, SE USA
Cordillera Ibérica see Ibérico, Sistema
Cordoba see Córdoba
Córdoba 70 D4 var. Cordoba, Eng. Cordova, anc. Corduba. Andalucía, SW Spain
Córdoba 42 C3 Córdoba, C Argentina
Córdoba 29 F4 Veracruz-Llave, E Mexico
Cordova see Córdoba
Cordova 14 C3 Alaska, USA
Corduba see Córdoba
Corentyne River see Courantyne River
Corfu see Kérkyra
Coria 70 C3 Extremadura, W Spain
Corinth see Kórinthos
Corinth 20 C1 Mississippi, S USA
Corinth, Gulf of see Korinthiakós Kólpos
Corinthiacus Sinus see Korinthiakós Kólpos
Corinto 30 C3 Chinandega, NW Nicaragua
Cork 67 A6 Ir. Corcaigh. S Ireland
Çorlu 94 A2 Tekirdağ, NW Turkey
Corner Brook 17 G3 Newfoundland, Newfoundland and Labrador, E Canada
Corn Islands see Maíz, Islas del
Cornwallis Island 15 F2 island Nunavut, N Canada
Coro 36 C1 prev. Santa Ana de Coro. Falcón, NW Venezuela
Corocoro 39 F4 La Paz, W Bolivia
Coromandel 128 D2 Waikato, North Island, NZ
Coromandel Coast 110 D2 coast E India
Coromandel Peninsula 128 D2 peninsula North Island, NZ
Coronado, Bahía de 30 D5 bay S Costa Rica
Coronel Dorrego 43 C5 Buenos Aires, E Argentina
Coronel Oviedo 42 D2 Caaguazú, SE Paraguay
Corozal 30 C1 Corozal, N Belize
Corpus Christi 27 G4 Texas, SW USA
Corrales 26 D2 New Mexico, SW USA
Corrib, Lough 67 A5 Ir. Loch Coirib. Lake W Ireland
Corrientes 42 D3 Corrientes, NE Argentina
Corriza see Korçë
Corse 69 E7 Eng. Corsica. Island France, C Mediterranean Sea
Corsica see Corse
Corsicana 27 G3 Texas, SW USA

Dimashq – El Ḩank

mashq *97 B5 var.* Ash Shām, Esh Sham, *Eng.* Damascus, *Fr.* Damas, *It.* Damasco. *Country capital* (Syria) Dimashq, SW Syria
mitrovgrad *82 D3* Khaskovo, S Bulgaria
mitrovgrad *89 C6* Ul'yanovskaya Oblast', W Russian Federation
movo *82 B1* Vidin, NW Bulgaria
najpur *113 F3* Rajshahi, NW Bangladesh
nan *68 B3* Côtes d'Armor, NW France
nant *65 C7* Namur, S Belgium
nar *94 B4* Afyon, SW Turkey
nara *see* Dinaric Alps
naric Alps *78 C4 var.* Dinara. *Mountain range* Bosnia and Herzegovina/Croatia
ndigul *110 C3* Tamil Nādu, SE India
ngle Bay *67 A6 Ir.* Bá an Daingin. *Bay* SW Ireland
nguiraye *52 C4* Haute-Guinée, N Guinea
ourbel *52 B3* W Senegal
rē Dawa *51 D5* E Ethiopia
rk Hartog Island *125 A5 island* Western Australia
sappointment, Lake *124 C4 salt lake* Western Australia
spur *113 G3* Assam, NE India
vinópolis *41 F4* Minas Gerais, SE Brazil
vo *52 D5* S Côte d'Ivoire
yarbakır *95 E4 var.* Diarbekr; *anc.* Amida. Diyarbakır, SE Turkey
zful *see* Dezfūl
ajapura *see* Jayapura
akovica *see* Đakovica
akovo *see* Đakovo
ambala *55 B6* Plateaux, C Congo
ambi *see* Jambi
anet *49 E4 prev.* Fort Charlet. SE Algeria
éblé *see* Jablah
elfa *48 D2 var.* El Djelfa. N Algeria
éma *54 D4* Haut-Mbomou, E Central African Republic
érablous *see* Jarābulus
erba *see* Jerba, Île de
jérem *54 B4 river* C Cameroon
evdjelija *see* Gevgelija
jibouti *50 D4 off.* Republicof Djibouti, *var.* Jibuti; *prev.* French Somaliland, French Territory of the Afars and Issas, *Fr.* Côte Française des Somalis, Territoire Français des Afars et des Issas. *Country* E Africa
jibouti *50 D4 var.* Jibuti. *Country capital* (Djibouti) E Djibouti
ourab, Erg du *54 C2 dunes* N Chad
júpivogur *61 E5* Austurland, SE Iceland
nieper *59 F4 Bel.* Dnyapro, *Rus.* Dnepr, *Ukr.* Dnipro. *River* E Europe
nieper Lowland *87 E2 Bel.* Prydnyaprowskaya Nizina, *Ukr.* Prydniprovs'ka Nyzovyna. *Lowlands* Belarus/Ukraine
niester *59 E4 Rom.* Nistru, *Rus.* Dnestr, *Ukr.* Dnister; *anc.* Tyras. *River* Moldova/Ukraine
nipro *see* Dnieper
niprodzerzhyns'k *87 F3 Rus.* Dneprodzerzhinsk; *prev.* Kamenskoye. Dnipropetrovs'ka Oblast', E Ukraine
niprodzerzhyns'ke Vodoskhovyshche *87 F3 Rus.* Dneprodzerzhinskoye Vodokhranilishche. *Reservoir* C Ukraine
nipropetrovs'k *87 F3 Rus.* Dnepropetrovsk; *prev.* Yekaterinoslav. Dnipropetrovs'ka Oblast', E Ukraine
niprorudne *87 F3 Rus.* Dneprorudnoye. Zaporiz'ka Oblast', SE Ukraine
oba *54 C4* Logone-Oriental, S Chad
öbeln *72 D4* Sachsen, E Germany
oberai, Jazirah *117 G4 Dut.* Vogelkop. *Peninsula* Irian Jaya, E Indonesia
oboj *78 C3* Republika Srpska, N Bosnia and Herzegovina
obre Miasto *76 D2 Ger.* Guttstadt. Warmińsko-Mazurskie, NE Poland
obrich *82 E1 Rom.* Bazargic; *prev.* Tolbukhin. Dobrich, NE Bulgaria
obrush *85 D7* Homyel'skaya Voblasts', SE Belarus
odecánese *see* Dodekánisos
odekánisos *83 D6 var.* Nóties Sporádes, *Eng.* Dodecanese; *prev.* Dhodhekánisos. *Island group* SE Greece
odge City *23 E5* Kansas, C USA
odoma *47 D5 country capital* (Tanzania) Dodoma, C Tanzania
odoma *51 C7 region* C Tanzania
ogana *74 E1* NE San Marino
ōgo *109 B6 island* Oki-shotō, SW Japan
ogondoutchi *53 F3* Dosso, SW Niger
oğubayazıt *95 F3* Ağrı, E Turkey
oğu Karadeniz Dağları *95 E3 var.* Anadolu Dağları. *Mountain range* NE Turkey
oha *see* Ad Dawḩah
oire *see* Londonderry
okkum *64 D1* Friesland, N Netherlands
okuchayevs'k *87 G3 var.* Dokuchayevsk. Donets'ka Oblast', SE Ukraine
okuchayevsk *see* Dokuchayevs'k
oldrums Fracture Zone *44 C4 tectonic feature* W Atlantic Ocean
ôle *68 D4* Jura, E France
olisie *55 B6 prev.* Loubomo. Le Niari, S Congo
olomites *see* Dolomitiche, Alpi
olomiti *see* Dolomitiche, Alpi
olomitiche, Alpi *74 C1 var.* Dolomiti, *Eng.* Dolomites. *Mountain range* NE Italy
olores *42 D4* Buenos Aires, E Argentina
olores *30 B1* Petén, N Guatemala
olores *42 D4* Soriano, SW Uruguay
olores Hidalgo *29 E4 var.* Ciudad de Dolores Hidalgo. Guanajuato, C Mexico
olyna *86 B2 Rus.* Dolina. Ivano-Frankivs'ka Oblast', W Ukraine
olyns'ka *87 F3 Rus.* Dolinskaya. Kirovohrads'ka Oblast', S Ukraine
omachëvo *see* Damachava
omaczewo *see* Damachava
ombås *63 B5* Oppland, S Norway
Domel Island *see* Letsôk-aw Kyun
Domeyko *42 B3* Atacama, N Chile
Dominica *33 H4 off.* Commonwealth of Dominica. *Country* E West Indies
Dominica Channel *see* Martinique Passage
Dominican Republic *33 E2 country* C West Indies
Domokós *83 B5 var.* Dhomokós. Stereá Ellás, C Greece
Don *89 B6 var.* Duna, Tanais. *River* SW Russian Federation
Donau *see* Danube
Donauwörth *73 C6* Bayern, S Germany
Don Benito *70 C3* Extremadura, W Spain
Doncaster *67 D5 anc.* Danum. N England, UK
Dondo *56 B1* Cuanza Norte, NW Angola
Donegal *67 B5 Ir.* Dún na nGall. NW Ireland
Donegal Bay *67 A5 Ir.* Bá Dhún na nGall. *Bay* NW Ireland
Donets *87 G2 var. Sivers'kyy Donets', Rus.* Severskiy Donets. Serra Acaraí. *river* Russian Federation/Ukraine
Donets'k *87 G3 Rus.* Donetsk; *prev.* Stalino. Donets'ka Oblast', E Ukraine
Dongfang *106 B7 var.* Basuo. Hainan, S China
Dongguan *106 C6* Guangdong, S China
Đông Ha *114 E4* Quang Tri, C Vietnam
Đông Hơi *114 D4* Quang Binh, C Vietnam
Dongliao *see* Liaoyuan
Dongola *50 B3 var.* Donqola, Dunqulah. Northern, N Sudan
Dongou *55 C5* La Likouala, NE Congo
Dongting Hu *106 C5 var.* Tung-t'ing Hu. *Lake* S China
Donji Vakuf *var.* Srbobran, Federacija Bosna I Hercegovina, N Yugoslavia
Donostia-San Sebastián *71 E1* País Vasco, N Spain
Donqola *see* Dongola
Doolow *51 D5* E Ethiopia
Doornik *see* Tournai
Door Peninsula *18 C2 peninsula* Wisconsin, N USA
Dooxo Nugaaleed *51 E5 var.* Nogal Valley. *Valley* E Somalia
Dordogne *69 B5 cultural region* SW France
Dordogne *69 B5 river* W France
Dordrecht *64 C4 var.* Dordt, Dort. Zuid-Holland, SW Netherlands
Dordt *see* Dordrecht
Dorohoi *86 C3* Botoşani, NE Romania
Dorotea *62 C4* Västerbotten, N Sweden
Dorre Island *125 A5 island* Western Australia
Dort *see* Dordrecht
Dortmund *72 A4* Nordrhein-Westfalen, W Germany
Dos Hermanas *70 C4* Andalucía, S Spain
Dospad Dagh *see* Rhodope Mountains
Dospat *82 C3* Smolyan, S Bulgaria
Dothan *20 D3* Alabama, S USA
Dotnuva *84 B4* Kėdainiai, C Lithuania
Douai *68 C2 prev.* Douay, *anc.* Duacum. Nord, N France
Douala *55 A5 var.* Duala. Littoral, W Cameroon
Douglas *67 C5 dependent territory capital* (Isle of Man) E Isle of Man
Douglas *26 C3* Arizona, SW USA
Douglas *22 D3* Wyoming, C USA
Douro *70 B2 Sp.* Duero. *River* Portugal/Spain *see also* Duero
Dover *67 E7 Fr.* Douvres; *Lat.* Dubris Portus. SE England, UK
Dover *19 F4 state capital* Delaware, NE USA
Dover, Strait of *68 C2 var.* Straits of Dover, *Fr.* Pas de Calais. *Strait* England, UK/France
Dover, Straits of *see* Dover, Strait of
Dovrefjell *63 B5 plateau* S Norway
Downpatrick *67 B5 Ir.* Dún Pádraig. SE Northern Ireland, UK
Dōzen *109 B6 island* Oki-shotō, SW Japan
Drač *see* Durrës
Drachten *64 D2* Friesland, N Netherlands
Drăgăşani *86 B5* Vâlcea, SW Romania
Dragoman *82 B2* Sofiya, W Bulgaria
Dra, Hamada du *48 C3 var.* Hammada du Drâa, Haut Plateau du Dra. *Plateau* W Algeria
Drahichyn *85 B6 Pol.* Drohiczyn Poleski, *Rus.* Drogichin. Brestskaya Voblasts', SW Belarus
Drakensberg *56 D5 mountain range* Lesotho/South Africa
Drake Passage *35 B8 passage* Atlantic Ocean/Pacific Ocean
Dralfa *82 D2* Tŭrgovishte, N Bulgaria
Dráma *82 C3 var.* Dhráma. Anatolikí Makedonía kai Thráki, NE Greece
Drammen *63 B6* Buskerud, S Norway
Drau *see* Drava
Drava *78 C3 var.* Drau, *Eng.* Drave, *Hung.* Dráva. *River* C Europe *see also* Drau
Dráva *see* Drava
Drave *see* Drava
Drawsko Pomorskie *76 B3 Ger.* Dramburg. Zachodniopomorskie, NW Poland
Drépano, Akrotírio *82 C4 var.* Akra Dhrepanon. *Headland* N Greece
Dresden *72 D4* Sachsen, E Germany
Drin *see* Drinit, Lumi i
Drina *78 C3 river* Bosnia and Herzegovina/Yugoslavia
Drinit, Lumi i *79 D5 var.* Drin. *River* NW Albania
Drobeta-Turnu Severin *86 B5 prev.* Turnu Severin. Mehedinţi, SW Romania
Drogheda *67 B5 Ir.* Droichead Átha. NE Ireland
Drohobych *86 B2 Pol.* Drohobycz, *Rus.* Drogobych. L'vivs'ka Oblast', NW Ukraine
Droichead Átha *see* Drogheda
Drôme *69 D5 cultural region* SE France
Dronning Maud Land *132 B2 physical region* Antarctica
Drummondville *17 E4* Québec, SE Canada
Druskininkai *85 B5 Pol.* Druskienniki. Druskininkai, S Lithuania
Dryden *16 B3* Ontario, C Canada
Drysa *85 D5 Rus.* Drissa. *River* N Belarus
Duala *see* Douala
Dubai *see* Dubayy
Dubăsari *86 D3 Rus.* Dubossary. NE Moldova
Dubawnt *15 F4 river* Northwest Territories/Nunavut, NW Canada
Dubayy *98 D4 Eng.* Dubai. Dubayy, NE UAE
Dubbo *127 D6* New South Wales, SE Australia
Dublin *67 B5 Ir.* Baile Átha Cliath; *anc.* Eblana. *Country capital* (Ireland), E Ireland
Dublin *21 E2* Georgia, SE USA
Dubno *86 C2* Rivnens'ka Oblast', NW Ukraine
Dubrovnik *79 B5 It.* Ragusa. Dubrovnik-Neretva, SE Croatia
Dubuque *23 G3* Iowa, C USA
Dudelange *65 D8 var.* Forge du Sud, *Ger.* Dudelingen. Luxembourg, S Luxembourg
Dudelingen *see* Dudelange
Duero *70 D2 Port.* Douro. *River* Portugal/Spain *see also* Douro
Duesseldorf *see* Düsseldorf
Duffel *65 C5* Antwerpen, C Belgium
Dugi Otok *78 A4 var.* Isola Grossa, *It.* Isola Lunga. *Island* W Croatia
Duisburg *72 A4 prev.* Duisburg-Hamborn. Nordrhein-Westfalen, W Germany
Duiven *64 D4* Gelderland, E Netherlands
Duk Faiwil *51 B5* Jonglei, SE Sudan
Dulan *104 D4 var.* Qagan Us. Qinghai, C China
Dulce, Golfo *31 E5 gulf* S Costa Rica
Dülmen *72 A4* Nordrhein-Westfalen, W Germany
Dulovo *82 E1* Silistra, NE Bulgaria
Duluth *23 G2* Minnesota, N USA
Dūmā *97 B5 Fr.* Douma. Dimashq, SW Syria
Dumas *27 E1* Texas, SW USA
Dumfries *66 C4* S Scotland, UK
Dumont d'Urville *132 C4 French research station* Antarctica
Dumyât *50 B1 Eng.* Damietta. N Egypt
Duna *see* Danube
Duna *see* Don
Dunaj *see* Danube
Dunaújváros *77 C7 prev.* Dunapentele, Sztálinváros. Fejér, C Hungary
Dunav *see* Danube
Dunavska Ravnina *82 C2 Eng.* Danubian Plain. *Plain* N Bulgaria
Duncan *27 G2* Oklahoma, C USA
Dundalk *67 B5 Ir.* Dún Dealgan. NE Ireland
Dún Dealgan *see* Dundalk
Dundee *66 C4* E Scotland, UK
Dundee *56 D4* KwaZulu/Natal, E South Africa
Dunedin *129 B7* Otago, South Island, NZ
Dunfermline *66 C4* C Scotland, UK
Dungu *55 E5* Orientale, NE Dem. Rep. Congo (Zaire)
Dungun *116 B3 var.* Kuala Dungun. Terengganu, Peninsular Malaysia
Dunkerque *68 C2 Eng.* Dunkirk, *Flem.* Duinekerke; *prev.* Dunquerque. Nord, N France
Dún Laoghaire *67 B6 Eng.* Dunleary; *prev.* Kingstown. E Ireland
Dún na nGall *see* Donegal
Dún Pádraig *see* Downpatrick
Dunqulah *see* Dongola
Dunărea *see* Danube
Dupnitsa *82 C2 prev.* Marek, Stanke Dimitrov. Kyustendil, W Bulgaria
Duqm *99 E5 var.* Daqm. E Oman
Durance *69 D6 river* SE France
Durango *28 D3 var.* Victoria de Durango. Durango, W Mexico
Durango *22 C5* Colorado, C USA
Durankulak *82 E1 Rom.* Răcari; *prev.* Blatnitsa, Duranulac. Dobrich, NE Bulgaria
Durant *27 G2* Oklahoma, C USA
Durazzo *see* Durrës
Durban *56 D4 var.* Port Natal. KwaZulu/Natal, E South Africa
Durbe *84 B3 Ger.* Durben. Liepāja, W Latvia
Durg *113 E4 prev.* Drug. Madhya Pradesh, C India
Durham *67 D5 hist.* Dunholme. N England, UK
Durham *21 F1* North Carolina, SE USA
Durostorum *see* Silistra
Durrës *79 C6 var.* Durrësi, Dursi, *It.* Durazzo, *SCr.* Drač, *Turk.* Draç. Durrës, W Albania
Durrësi *see* Durrës
Dursi *see* Durrës
Durūz, Jabal ad *97 C5 mountain* SW Syria
D'Urville Island *128 C4 island* C NZ
Dusa Mareb *see* Dhuusa Marreeb
Dusa Marreb *see* Dhuusa Marreeb
Dushanbe *101 E3 var.* Dyushambe; *prev.* Stalinabad, *Taj.* Stalinobod. *Country capital* (Tajikistan) W Tajikistan
Düsseldorf *72 A4 var.* Duesseldorf. Nordrhein-Westfalen, W Germany
Düstí *101 E3 Rus.* Dusti. SW Tajikistan
Dutch Harbor *14 B3* Unalaska Island, Alaska, USA
Dutch New Guinea *see* Irian Jaya
Duzdab *see* Zāhedān
Dvina *see* Severnaya Dvina
Dvina Bay *see* Chëshskaya Guba
Dyanev *see* Deynau
Dyersburg *20 C1* Tennessee, S USA
Dyushambe *see* Dushanbe
Dza Chu *see* Mekong
Dzerzhinsk *89 C5* Nizhegorodskaya Oblast', W Russian Federation
Dzhalal-Abad *101 F2 Kir.* Jalal-Abad. Dzhalal-Abadskaya Oblast', W Kyrgyzstan
Dzhambul *see* Taraz
Dzhankoy *87 F4* Respublika Krym, S Ukraine
Dzhelandy *101 F3* SE Tajikistan
Dzhergalan *101 G2 Kir.* Jyrgalan. Issyk-Kul'skaya Oblast', NE Kyrgyzstan
Dzhugdzhur, Khrebet *93 G3 mountain range* E Russian Federation
Dzhusaly *92 B4 Kaz.* Zholsaly. Kyzylorda, SW Kazakhstan
Działdowo *76 D3* Warmińsko-Mazurskie, NE Poland
Dzuunmod *105 E2* Töv, C Mongolia

E

Eagle Pass *27 F4* Texas, SW USA
East Açores Fracture Zone *see* East Azores Fracture Zone
East Antarctica *see* Greater Antarctica
East Australian Basin *see* Tasman Basin
East Azores Fracture Zone *44 C3 var.* East Açores Fracture Zone. *Tectonic feature* E Atlantic Ocean
Eastbourne *67 E7* SE England, UK
East Cape *128 E3 headland* North Island, NZ
East China Sea *103 E2 Chin.* Dong Hai. *Sea* W Pacific Ocean
Easter Fracture Zone *131 G4 tectonic feature* E Pacific Ocean
Easter Island *131 F4 var.* Rapa Nui, *island* E Pacific Ocean
Eastern Desert *46 D3 var.* Aş Şaḩrā' ash Sharqīyah, *Eng.* Arabian Desert, Eastern Desert. *Desert* E Egypt
Eastern Ghats *102 B3 mountain range* SE India
Eastern Sayans *93 E4 Mong.* Dzüün Soyonï Nuruu, *Rus.* Vostochnyy Sayan. *Mountain range* Mongolia/Russian Federation
East Falkland *43 D8 var.* Isla Soledad. *Island* E Falkland Islands
East Grand Forks *23 E1* Minnesota, N USA
East Indiaman Ridge *119 D6 undersea feature* E Indian Ocean
East Indies *130 A3 island group* SE Asia
East Kilbride *66 C4* S Scotland, UK
East Korea Bay *107 E3 bay* E North Korea
Eastleigh *67 D7* S England, UK
East London *56 D5 Afr.* Oos-Londen; *prev.* Emonti, Port Rex. Eastern Cape, S South Africa
Eastmain *16 D3 river* Québec, C Canada
East Mariana Basin *120 B1 undersea feature* W Pacific Ocean
East Novaya Zemlya Trench *90 C1 var.* Novaya Zemlya Trench. *Undersea feature* W Kara Sea
East Pacific Rise *131 F4 undersea feature* E Pacific Ocean
East Saint Louis *18 B4* Illinois, N USA
East Scotia Basin *45 C7 undersea feature* SE Scotia Sea
East Sea *see* Japan, Sea of
East Siberian Sea *see* Vostochno-Sibirskoye More
East Timor *117 F5 var.* Loro Sae *prev.* Portuguese Timor, Timor Timur. Dependent territory, *disputed territory,* SE Asia
Eau Claire *18 A2* Wisconsin, N USA
Eauripik Rise *120 B2 undersea feature* W Pacific Ocean
Ebensee *73 D6* Oberösterreich, N Austria
Eberswalde-Finow *72 D3* Brandenburg, E Germany
Ebetsu *108 D2 var.* Ebetu. Hokkaidō, NE Japan
Ebetu *see* Ebetsu
Ebolowa *55 A5* Sud, S Cameroon
Ebon Atoll *122 D2 var.* Epoon. *Atoll* Ralik Chain, S Marshall Islands
Ebro *71 E2 river* NE Spain
Ebusus *see* Eivissa
Ech Cheliff *see* Chlef
Ech Chleff *see* Chlef
Echo Bay *15 E3* Northwest Territories, NW Canada
Echt *65 D5* Limburg, SE Netherlands
Ecija *70 D4 anc.* Astigi. Andalucía, SW Spain
Ecuador *38 B1 off.* Republic of Ecuador. *Country* NW South America
Ed Da'ein *50 A4* Southern Darfur, W Sudan
Ed Damazin *50 C4 var.* Ad Damazīn. Blue Nile, E Sudan
Ed Damer *50 C3 var.* Ad Damar, Ad Dāmir. River Nile, NE Sudan
Ed Debba *50 B3* Northern, N Sudan
Ede *64 D4* Gelderland, C Netherlands
Ede *53 F5* Osun, SW Nigeria
Edéa *55 A5* Littoral, SW Cameroon
Edeyin Murzuq *see* Murzuq, Idhān
Edfu *see* Idfu
Edgeøya *61 G2 island* S Svalbard
Edgware *67 A7* SE England, UK
Edinburg *27 G5* Texas, SW USA
Edinburgh *66 C4 admin capital* S Scotland, UK
Edirne *94 A2 Eng.* Adrianople; *anc.* Adrianopolis, Hadrianopolis. Edirne, NW Turkey
Edmonds *24 B2* Washington, NW USA
Edmonton *15 E5* Alberta, SW Canada
Edmundston *17 E4* New Brunswick, SE Canada
Edna *27 G4* Texas, SW USA
Edolo *74 B1* Lombardia, N Italy
Edremit *94 A3* Balıkesir, NW Turkey
Edward, Lake *55 E5 var.* Albert Edward Nyanza, Edward Nyanza, Lac Idi Amin, Lake Rutanzige. *Lake* Uganda/Zaire
Edward Nyanza *see* Edward, Lake
Edwards Plateau *27 F3 plain* Texas, SW USA
Eeklo *65 B5 var.* Eekloo. Oost-Vlaanderen, NW Belgium
Edzo *53 E4 prev.* Rae-Edzo. Northwest Territories, NW Canada
Eekloo *see* Eeklo
Eersel *65 C5* Noord-Brabant, S Netherlands
Efate *122 D4 var.* Éfaté *Fr.* Vaté; *prev.* Sandwich Island. *Island* C Vanuatu
Effingham *18 B4* Illinois, N USA
Eforie Sud *86 D5* Constanţa, E Romania
Efstrátios, Ágios *82 D4 var.* Ayios Evstratios. *Island* E Greece
Egadi, Isole *75 B7 island group* S Italy
Eger *77 D6 Ger.* Erlau. Heves, NE Hungary
Egeria Fracture Zone *119 C5 tectonic feature* W Indian Ocean
Éghezée *65 C6* Namur, C Belgium
Egina *see* Aígina
Egio *see* Aígio
Egmont, Mount *see* Taranaki, Mount
Egmont, Cape *128 C4 headland* North Island, NZ
Egoli *see* Johannesburg
Egypt *50 B2 off.* Arab Republic of Egypt, *Ar.* Jumhūrīyah Mişr al 'Arabīyah; *prev.* United Arab Republic, *anc.* Aegyptus. *Country* NE Africa
Eibar *71 E1* País Vasco, N Spain
Eibergen *64 E3* Gelderland, E Netherlands
Eidfjord *63 A5* Hordaland, S Norway
Eier-Berg *see* Suur Munamägi
Eifel *73 A5 plateau* W Germany
Eiger *73 B7 mountain* C Switzerland
Eigg *66 B3 island* W Scotland, UK
Eight Degree Channel *110 B3 channel* India/Maldives
Eighty Mile Beach *124 B4 beach* Western Australia
Eijsden *65 D6* Limburg, SE Netherlands
Eilat *see* Elat
Eindhoven *65 D5* Noord-Brabant, S Netherlands
Eipel *see* Ipel'
Eipel *see* Ipoly
Eisenhüttenstadt *72 D4* Brandenburg, E Germany
Eisenstadt *73 E6* Burgenland, E Austria
Eisleben *72 C4* Sachsen-Anhalt, C Germany
Eivissa *71 G3 var.* Iviza, *Cast.* Ibiza; *anc.* Ebusus. *Island Islas Baleares,* Spain, W Mediterranean Sea
Eivissa *71 G3 var.* Iviza, *Cast.* Ibiza; *anc.* Ebusus. Eivissa, Spain, W Mediterranean Sea
Ejea de los Caballeros *71 E2* Aragón, NE Spain
Ejin Qi *104 D3 var.* Dalain Hob. Nei Mongol Zizhiqu, N China
Ekapa *see* Cape Town
Ekiatapskiy Khrebet *93 G1 mountain range* NE Russian Federation
El 'Alamein *50 B1 var.* Al 'Alamayn. N Egypt
El Asnam *see* Chlef
Elat *97 B8 var.* Eilat, Elath. Southern, S Israel
Elat, Gulf of *see* Aqaba, Gulf of
Elath *see* Al 'Aqabah
Elath *see* Elat
El'Atrun *50 B3* Northern Darfur, NW Sudan
Elâzığ *95 E3 var.* Elâziz. Elâzığ, E Turkey
Elâziz *see* Elâzığ
Elba, Isola d' *74 B4 island* Archipelago Toscano, C Italy
Elbasan *79 D6 var.* Elbasani. Elbasan, C Albania
Elbasani *see* Elbasan
Elbe *58 D3 Cz.* Labe. *River* Czech Republic/Germany
El Beni *see* Beni
Elbert, Mount *22 C4 mountain* Colorado, C USA
Elbing *see* Elbląg
Elbląg *76 C2 var.* Elblag, *Ger.* Elbing. Warmińsko-Mazurskie, NE Poland
El Boulaida *see* Blida
El'brus *89 A8 var.* Gora El'brus. *Mountain* SW Russian Federation
El Burgo de Osma *71 E2* Castilla-León, C Spain
El Cajon *25 C8* California, W USA
El Calafate *43 B7 var.* Calafate. Santa Cruz, S Argentina
El Callao *37 E2* Bolívar, E Venezuela
El Campo *27 G4* Texas, SW USA
El Carmen de Bolívar *36 B2* Bolívar, NW Colombia
El Centro *25 D8* California, W USA
Elche *71 F4 var.* Elx-Elche; *anc.* Ilici, *Lat.* Illicis. País Valenciano, E Spain
Elda *71 F4* País Valenciano, E Spain
El Djazaïr *see* Alger
El Djelfa *see* Djelfa
El Dorado *20 B2* Arkansas, C USA
El Dorado *37 F2* Bolívar, E Venezuela
El Dorado *23 F5* Kansas, C USA
El Dorado *28 C3* Sinaloa, C Mexico
Eldorado *42 E3* Misiones, NE Argentina
Eldoret *51 C6* Rift Valley, W Kenya
Elektrostal' *89 B5* Moskovskaya Oblast', W Russian Federation
Elemi Triangle *51 B5 disputed region* Kenya/Sudan
Elephant Butte Reservoir *26 C2 reservoir* New Mexico, SW USA
Eleuthera Island *32 C1 island* N Bahamas
El Fasher *50 A4 var.* Al Fāshir. Northern Darfur, W Sudan
El Ferrol *see* Ferrol
El Ferrol del Caudillo *see* Ferrol
El Gedaref *see* Gedaref
El Geneina *50 A4 var.* Ajjinena, Al-Genain, Al Junaynah. Western Darfur, W Sudan
Elgin *18 B3* Illinois, N USA
Elgin *66 C3* NE Scotland, UK
El Gîza *50 B1 var.* Al Jīzah, Gîza, Gizeh. N Egypt
El Goléa *48 D3 var.* Al Golea. C Algeria
El Ḩank *52 D1 cliff* N Mauritania

Forel, Mont – Glendale

orel, Mont *60 D4 mountain* SE Greenland
orfar *66 C3* E Scotland, UK
orge du Sud *see* Dudelange
orlì *74 C3 anc.* Forum Livii. Emilia-Romagna, N Italy
ormentera *71 G4 anc.* Ophiusa, *Lat.* Frumentum. *Island* Islas Baleares, Spain, W Mediterranean Sea
ormosa *42 D2* Formosa, NE Argentina
ormosa, Serra *41 F3 mountain range* C Brazil
ormosa Strait *see* Taiwan Strait
orrest City *20 B1* Arkansas, C USA
ort Albany *16 C3* Ontario, C Canada
ortaleza *41 G2 prev.* Ceará. *State capital* Ceará, NE Brazil
ortaleza *39 F2* Pando, N Bolivia
ort-Bayard *see* Zhanjiang
ort-Cappolani *see* Tidjikja
ort Collins *22 D4* Colorado, C USA
ort Davis *27 E3* Texas, SW USA
ort-de-France *33 H4 prev.* Fort-Royal. *Dependent territory capital* (Martinique) W Martinique
ort Dodge *23 F3* Iowa, C USA
ortescue River *124 A4 river* Western Australia
ort Frances *16 B4* Ontario, S Canada
ort Good Hope *15 E3 var.* Good Hope. Northwest Territories, NW Canada
ort Gouraud *see* Fdérik
orth *66 C4 river* C Scotland, UK
orth, Firth of *66 C4 estuary* E Scotland, UK
ort-Lamy *see* Ndjamena
ort Lauderdale *21 F5* Florida, SE USA
ort Liard *15 E4 var.* Liard. Northwest Territories, W Canada
ort Madison *23 G4* Iowa, C USA
ort McMurray *15 E4* Alberta, C Canada
ort McPherson *14 D3 var.* McPherson. Northwest Territories, NW Canada
ort Morgan *22 D4* Colorado, C USA
ort Myers *21 E5* Florida, SE USA
ort Nelson *15 E4* British Columbia, W Canada
ort Peck Lake *22 C1 reservoir* Montana, NW USA
ort Pierce *21 F4* Florida, SE USA
ort Providence *15 E4 var.* Providence. Northwest Territories, W Canada
ort St.John *15 E4* British Columbia, W Canada
ort Scott *23 F5* Kansas, C USA
ort Severn *16 C2* Ontario, C Canada
ort-Shevchenko *92 A4* Mangistau, W Kazakhstan
ort Simpson *15 E4 var.* Simpson. Northwest Territories, W Canada
ort Smith *15 E4 district capital* Northwest Territories, W Canada
ort Smith *20 B1* Arkansas, C USA
ort Stockton *27 E3* Texas, SW USA
ort-Trinquet *see* Bîr Mogreïn
ort Vermilion *15 E4* Alberta, W Canada
ort Walton Beach *20 C3* Florida, SE USA
ort Wayne *18 C4* Indiana, N USA
ort William *66 C3* N Scotland, UK
ort Worth *27 G2* Texas, SW USA
ort Yukon *14 D3* Alaska, USA
ougamou *55 A6* Ngounié, C Gabon
ougères *68 B3* Ille-et-Vilaine, NW France
ou-hsin *see* Fuxin
oulwind, Cape *129 B5 headland* South Island, NZ
oumban *54 A4* Ouest, NW Cameroon
ou-shan *see* Fushun
oveaux Strait *129 A8 strait* S NZ
oxe Basin *15 G3 sea* Nunavut, N Canada
ox Glacier *129 B6* West Coast, South Island, NZ
ox Mine *15 F4* Manitoba, C Canada
raga *71 F2* Aragón, NE Spain
ram Basin *133 C3 var.* Amundsen Basin. *Undersea feature* Arctic Ocean
rance *68 B4 off.* French Republic, *It./Sp.* Francia; *prev.* Gaul, Gaule, *Lat.* Gallia. *Country* W Europe
ranceville *55 B6 var.* Massoukou, Masuku. Haut-Ogooué, E Gabon
rancfort prev *see* Frankfurt am Main
ranche-Comté *68 D4 cultural region* E France
rancis Case, Lake *23 E3 reservoir* South Dakota, N USA
rancisco Escárcega *29 G4* Campeche, SE Mexico
rancistown *56 D3* North East, NE Botswana
ranconian Jura *see* Fränkische Alb
rankenalb *see* Fränkische Alb
rankenstein *see* Ząbkowice Śląskie
rankenstein in Schlesien *see* Ząbkowice Śląskie
rankfort *18 C5 state capital* Kentucky, S USA
rankfort on the Main *see* Frankfurt am Main
rankfurt *see* Frankfurt am Main
rankfurt am Main *73 B5 var.* Frankfurt, *Fr.* Francfort; prev. *Eng.* Frankfort on the Main. Hessen, SW Germany
Frankfurt an der Oder *72 D3* Brandenburg, E Germany
Fränkische Alb *73 C6 var.* Frankenalb, *Eng.* Franconian Jura. *Mountain range* S Germany
Franklin *20 C1* Tennessee, S USA
Franklin D.Roosevelt Lake *24 C1 reservoir* Washington, NW USA
Frantsa-Iosifa, Zemlya *92 D1 Eng.* Franz Josef Land. *Island group* N Russian Federation
Franz Josef Land *see* Frantsa-Iosifa, Zemlya
Fraserburgh *66 D3* NE Scotland, UK
Fraser Island *126 E4 var.* Great Sandy Island. *Island* Queensland, E Australia
Fredericksburg *19 E5* Virginia, NE USA
Fredericton *17 F4* New Brunswick, SE Canada
Frederikshåb *see* Paamiut
Fredrikstad *63 B6* Østfold, S Norway
Freeport *32 C1* Grand Bahama Island, N Bahamas
Freeport *27 H4* Texas, SW USA
Freetown *52 C4 country capital* (Sierra Leone) W Sierra Leone
Freiburg *see* Freiburg im Breisgau
Freiburg im Breisgau *73 A6 var.* Freiburg, *Fr.* Fribourg-en-Brisgau. Baden-Württemberg, SW Germany
Fremantle *125 A6* Western Australia
Fremont *23 F4* Nebraska, C USA
French Guiana *37 H3 var.* Guiana, Guyane. *French overseas department* N South America
French Polynesia *121 F4 French overseas territory* C Polynesia
French Southern and Antarctic Territories *119 B7 Fr.* Terres Australes et Antarctiques Françaises. *French overseas territory* S Indian Ocean
Fresnillo *28 D3 var.* Fresnillo de González Echeverría. Zacatecas, C Mexico
Fresnillo de González Echeverría *see* Fresnillo
Fresno *25 C6* California, W USA
Frías *42 C3* Catamarca, N Argentina
Fribourg-en-Brisgau *see* Freiburg im Breisgau
Friedrichshafen *73 B7* Baden-Württemberg, S Germany
Frobisher Bay *60 B3 inlet* Baffin Island, Northwest Territories, NE Canada
Frohavet *62 B4 sound* C Norway
Frome, Lake *127 B6 salt lake* South Australia
Frontera *29 G4* Tabasco, SE Mexico
Frontignan *69 C6* Hérault, S France
Frostviken *see* Kvarnbergsvattnet
Frøya *62 A4 island* W Norway
Frunze *see* Bishkek
Frýdek-Místek *77 C5 Ger.* Friedek-Mistek. Ostravský Kraj, E Czech Republic
Fu-chien *see* Fujian
Fu-chou *see* Fuzhou
Fuengirola *70 D5* Andalucía, S Spain
Fuerte Olimpo *12 D2 var.* Olimpo. Alto Paraguay, NE Paraguay
Fuerte, Río *26 C5 river* C Mexico
Fuerteventura *48 B3 island* Islas Canarias, Spain, NE Atlantic Ocean
Fuhkien *see* Fujian
Fu-hsin *see* Fuxin
Fuji *109 D6 var.* Huzi. Shizuoka, Honshū, S Japan
Fujian *106 D6 var.* Fu-chien, Fuhkien, Fujian Sheng, Fukien, Min. Admin. region *province* SE China
Fujian Sheng *see* Fujian
Fuji-san *109 C6 var.* Fujiyama, *Eng.* Mount Fuji. *Mountain* Honshū, SE Japan
Fujiyama *see* Fuji-san
Fukang *104 C2* Xinjiang Uygur Zizhiqu, W China
Fukien *see* Fujian
Fukui *109 C6 var.* Hukui. Fukui, Honshū, SW Japan
Fukuoka *109 A7 var.* Hukuoka; *hist.* Najima. Fukuoka, Kyūshū, SW Japan
Fukushima *108 D4 var.* Hukusima. Fukushima, Honshū, C Japan
Fulda *73 B5* Hessen, C Germany
Funafuti *see* Fongafale
Funafuti Atoll *123 E3 atoll* C Tuvalu
Funchal *48 A2* Madeira, Portugal, NE Atlantic Ocean
Fundy, Bay of *17 F3 bay* Canada/USA
Furnes *see* Veurne
Fürth *73 C5* Bayern, S Germany
Furukawa *108 D4 var.* Hurukawa. Miyagi, Honshū, C Japan
Fushun *106 D3 var.* Fou-shan, Fu-shun. Liaoning, NE China
Fu-shun *see* Fushun
Fusin *see* Fuxin
Füssen *73 C7* Bayern, S Germany
Futog *78 D3* Serbia, NW Yugoslavia
Futuna, Île *123 E4 island* S Wallis and Futuna
Fuxin *106 D3 var.* Fou-hsin, Fu-hsin, Fusin. Liaoning, NE China
Fuzhou *106 D6 var.* Foochow, Fu-chou. Fujian, SE China
Fuzhou *see* Linchuan
Fyn *63 B8 Ger.* Fünen. *Island* C Denmark
Fyzabad *see* Feyẕābād

G

Gaafu Alifu Atoll *see* North Huvadhu Atoll
Gaafu Dhaalu Atoll *see* South Huvadhu Atoll
Gaalkacyo *51 E5 var.* Galka'yo, *It.* Galcaio. Mudug, C Somalia
Gabela *56 B2* Cuanza Sul, W Angola
Gabès *49 E2 var.* Qābis. E Tunisia
Gabès, Golfe de *49 F2 Ar.* Khalīj Qābis. *Gulf* E Tunisia
Gabon *55 B6 off.* Gabonese Republic. *Country* C Africa
Gaborone *56 C4 prev.* Gaberones. *Country capital* (Botswana) South East, SE Botswana
Gabrovo *82 D2* Gabrovo, N Bulgaria
Gadag *110 C1* Karnātaka, W India
Gadsden *20 D2* Alabama, S USA
Gaeta *75 C5* Lazio, C Italy
Gaeta, Golfo di *75 C5 var.* Gulf of Gaeta. *Gulf* C Italy
Gaeta, Gulf of *see* Gaeta, Golfo di
Gäfle *see* Gävle
Gafsa *49 E2 var.* Qafṣah. W Tunisia
Gagnoa *52 D5* C Côte d'Ivoire
Gagra *95 E1* NW Georgia
Gaillac *69 C6 var.* Gaillac-sur-Tarn. Tarn, S France
Gaillac-sur-Tarn *see* Gaillac
Gaillimh *see* Galway
Gainesville *21 E3* Florida, SE USA
Gainesville *20 D2* Georgia, SE USA
Gainesville *27 G2* Texas, SW USA
Gairdner, Lake *127 A6 salt lake* South Australia
Gaizin *see* Gaizina Kalns
Gaizina Kalns *84 C3 var.* Gaiziņ. *Mountain* E Latvia
Galán, Cerro *42 B3 mountain* NW Argentina
Galanta *77 C6 Hung.* Galánta. Trnavský Kraj, W Slovakia
Galapagos Fracture Zone *131 E3 tectonic feature* E Pacific Ocean
Galapagos Islands *131 F3 var.* Islas de los Galápagos,*Tortoise Islands. Island group* Ecuador, E Pacific Ocean
Galapagos Rise *131 F3 undersea feature* E Pacific Ocean
Galashiels *66 C4* SE Scotland, UK
Galaṭi *86 D4 Ger.* Galatz. Galaṭi, E Romania
Galcaio *see* Gaalkacyo
Galesburg *18 B3* Illinois, N USA
Galicia *70 B1 cultural region* NW Spain
Galicia Bank *58 B4 undersea feature* E Atlantic Ocean
Galilee, Sea of *see* Tiberias, Lake
Galka'yo *see* Gaalkacyo
Galle *110 D4 prev.* Point de Galle. Southern Province, SW Sri Lanka
Gallego Rise *131 F3 undersea feature* E Pacific Ocean
Gallegos *see* Río Gallegos
Gallipoli *75 E6* Puglia, SE Italy
Gällivare *62 C3* Norrbotten, N Sweden
Gallup *26 C1* New Mexico, SW USA
Galtat-Zemmour *48 B3* C Western Sahara
Galveston *27 H4* Texas, SW USA
Galway *67 A5 Ir.* Gaillimh. W Ireland
Galway Bay *67 A6 Ir.* Cuan na Gaillimhe. *Bay* W Ireland
Gambell *14 C2* Saint Lawrence Island, Alaska, USA
Gambia *52 C3 Fr.* Gambie. *River* W Africa
Gambia *52 B3 off.* Republic of The Gambia, The Gambia. *Country* W Africa
Gambier, Îles *121 G4 island group* E French Polynesia
Gamboma *55 B6* Plateaux, E Congo
Gan *see* Gansu
Gan *see* Jiangxi
Gan *110 B5* Addu Atoll, C Maldives
Gäncä *95 G2 Rus.* Gyandzha; *prev.* Kirovabad, Yelisavetpol. W Azerbaijan
Gandajika *55 D7* Kasai Oriental, S Dem. Rep. Congo (Zaire)
Gander *17 G3* Newfoundland, Newfoundland and Labrador, SE Canada
Gāndhīdhām *112 C4* Gujarāt, W India
Gandía *71 F3* País Valenciano, E Spain
Ganges *113 F3 Ben.* Padma. *River* Bangladesh/India *see also* Padma
Ganges Cone *see* Ganges Fan
Ganges Fan *118 D3 var.* Ganges Cone. *Undersea feature* N Bay of Bengal
Ganges, Mouths of the *113 G4 delta* Bangladesh/India
Gangra *see* Çankırı
Gangtok *113 F3* Sikkim, N India
Gansu *106 B4 var.* Gan, Gansu Sheng, Kansu. Admin. region *province* N China
Gansu Sheng *see* Gansu
Ganzhou *106 D6* Jiangxi, S China
Gao *53 E3* Gao, E Mali
Gaoual *52 C4* Moyenne-Guinée, N Guinea
Gaoxiong *see* Kaohsiung
Gap *69 D5 anc.* Vapincum. Hautes-Alpes, SE France
Gar *104 A4 var.* Gar Xincun. Xizang Zizhiqu, W China
Garachiné *31 G5* Darién, SE Panama
Garagum *see* Garagumy
Garagum Kanaly *see* Garagumskiy Kanal
Garagumskiy Kanal *100 D3 var.* Kara Kum Canal, Karakumskiy Kanal, *Turkm.* Garagum Kanaly. *Canal* C Turkmenistan
Garagumy *100 C3 var.* Qara Qum, *Eng.* Black Sand Desert, Kara Kum, *Turkm.* Garagum; *prev.* Peski Karakumy. *Desert* C Turkmenistan
Gara Khitrino *82 D2* Shumen, NE Bulgaria
Garda, Lago di *C2 var.* Benaco, *Eng.* Lake Garda, *Ger.* Gardasee. *Lake* NE Italy
Garda, Lake *see* Garda, Lago di
Gardasee *see* Garda, Lago di
Garden City *23 E5* Kansas, C USA
Gardeyz *see* Gardēz
Gardēz *101 E4 var.* Gardeyz, Gordiaz. Paktīā, E Afghanistan
Gargždai *84 B3* Gargždai, W Lithuania
Garissa *51 D6* Coast, E Kenya
Garland *27 G2* Texas, SW USA
Garman, Loch *see* Wexford
Garoe *see* Garoowe
Garonne *69 B5 anc.* Garumna. *River* S France
Garoowe *51 E5 var.* Garoe. Nugaal, N Somalia
Garoua *54 B4 var.* Garua. Nord, N Cameroon
Garrygala *see* Kara-Kala
Garry Lake *15 F3 lake* Nunavut, N Canada
Garsen *51 D6* Coast, S Kenya
Garua *see* Garoua
Garwolin *76 D4* Mazowieckie, C Poland
Gar Xincun *see* Gar
Gary *18 B3* Indiana, N USA
Garzón *36 B4* Huila, S Colombia
Gascogne *69 B6 Eng.* Gascony. *Cultural region* S France
Gascoyne River *125 A5 river* Western Australia
Gaspé *17 F3* Québec, SE Canada
Gaspé, Péninsule de *17 E4 var.* Péninsule de la Gaspésie. *Peninsula* Québec, SE Canada
Gastonia *21 E1* North Carolina, SE USA
Gastoúni *83 B6* Dytikí Ellás, S Greece
Gatchina *88 B4* Leningradskaya Oblast', NW Russian Federation
Gatineau *16 D4* Québec, SE Canada
Gatún, Lago *31 F4 reservoir* C Panama
Gauja *84 D3 Ger.* Aa. *River* Estonia/Latvia
Gauteng *see* Johannesburg
Gāvbandī *98 D4* Hormozgān, S Iran
Gávdos *83 C8 island* SE Greece
Gavere *65 B6* Oost-Vlaanderen, NW Belgium
Gävle *63 C6 var.* Gäfle; *prev.* Gefle. Gävleborg, C Sweden
Gawler *127 B6* South Australia
Gaya *113 F3* Bihār, N India
Gayndah *127 E5* Queensland, E Australia
Gaza *97 A6 Ar.* Ghazzah, *Heb.* 'Azza. NE Gaza Strip
Gaz-Achak *100 D2 Turkm.* Gazojak. Lebapskiy Velayat, NE Turkmenistan
Gazandzhyk *100 B2 Turkm.* Gazanjyk; *prev.* Kazandzhik. Balkanskiy Velayat, W Turkmenistan
Gaza Strip *97 A7 Ar.* Qiṭā' Ghazzah. *Disputed region* SW Asia
Gazi Antep *see* Gaziantep
Gaziantep *94 D4 var.* Gazi Antep; *prev.* Aintab, Antep. Gaziantep, S Turkey
Gazimağusa *see* Ammóchostos
Gazimağusa Körfezi *see* Kólpos Ammóchostos
Gazli *100 D2* Bukhoro Wiloyati, C Uzbekistan
Gbanga *52 D5 var.* Gbarnga. N Liberia
Gbarnga *see* Gbanga
Gdańsk *76 C2 Fr.* Dantzig, *Ger.* Danzig. Pomorskie, N Poland
Gdan'skaya Bukhta *see* Danzig, Gulf of
Pomorskie, Gulf of *see* Danzig, Gulf of
Gdynia *76 C2 Ger.* Gdingen. Pomorskie, N Poland
Gedaref *50 C4 var.* Al Qaḍārif, El Gedaref. Gedaref, E Sudan
Gediz *94 B3* Kütahya, W Turkey
Gediz Nehri *94 A3 river* W Turkey
Geel *65 C5 var.* Gheel. Antwerpen, N Belgium
Geelong *127 C7* Victoria, SE Australia
Ge'e'mu *see* Golmud
Gefle *see* Gävle
Geilo *63 A5* Buskerud, S Norway
Gejiu *106 B6 var.* Kochiu. Yunnan, S China
Gökdepe *see* Geok-Tepe
Gela *75 C7 prev.* Terranova di Sicilia. Sicilia, Italy, C Mediterranean Sea
Geldermalsen *64 C4* Gelderland, C Netherlands
Geleen *65 D6* Limburg, SE Netherlands
Gelinsoor *see* Gellinsoor
Gellinsoor *51 E5 var.* Gelinsoor. Mudug, NE Somalia
Gembloux *65 C6* Namur, Belgium
Gemena *55 C5* Equateur, NW Dem. Rep. Congo (Zaire)
Gemona del Friuli *74 D2* Friuli-Venezia Giulia, NE Italy
Genck *see* Genk
General Alvear *42 B4* Mendoza, W Argentina
General Eugenio A.Garay *42 C1* Guairá, S Paraguay
General Machado *see* Camacupa
General Santos *117 F3 off.* General Santos City. Mindanao, S Philippines
Genova *see* Genova
Geneva, Lake *A7 Fr.* Lac de Genève, Lac Léman, le Léman, *Ger.* Genfer See. *Lake* France/Switzerland
Genève *73 A7 Eng.* Geneva, *Ger.* Genf, *It.* Ginevra. Genève, SW Switzerland
Genf *see* Genève
Genk *65 D6 var.* Genck. Limburg, NE Belgium
Gennep *64 D4* Limburg, SE Netherlands
Genoa *see* Genova
Genova *80 D1 Eng.* Genoa, *Fr.* Gênes; *anc.* Genua. Liguria, NW Italy
Genova, Golfo di *74 A3 Eng.* Gulf of Genoa. *Gulf* NW Italy
Genovesa, Isla *38 B5 var.* Tower Island. *Island* Galapagos Islands, Ecuador, E Pacific Ocean
Gent *65 B5 Eng.* Ghent, *Fr.* Gand. Oost-Vlaanderen, NW Belgium
Geok-Tepe *100 C3 var.* Gëkdepe, *Turkm.* Gökdepe. Akhalskiy Velayat, C Turkmenistan
George *60 A4 river* Newfoundland and Labrador/Québec, E Canada
George *56 C5* Western Cape, S South Africa
George, Lake *21 E3 lake* Florida, SE USA
Georges Bank *13 D5 undersea feature* W Atlantic Ocean
George Sound *129 A7 sound* South Island, NZ
Georges River *126 D2 river* New South Wales, SE Australia
George Town *32 B3 var.* Georgetown. *Dependent territory capital* (Cayman Islands) Grand Cayman, SW Cayman Islands
George Town *116 B3 var.* Penang, Pinang. Pinang, Peninsular Malaysia
George Town *32 C2* Great Exuma Island, C Bahamas
Georgetown *37 F2 country capital* (Guyana) N Guyana
Georgetown *21 F2* South Carolina, SE USA
George V Land *132 C4 physical region* Antarctica
Georgia *95 F2 off.* Republic of Georgia, *Geor.* Sak'art'velo, *Rus.* Gruzinskaya SSR, Gruziya; *prev.* Georgian SSR. *Country* SW Asia
Georgia *20 D2 off.* State of Georgia; also known as Empire State of the South, Peach State. *State* SE USA
Georgian Bay *18 D2 lake bay* Ontario, S Canada
Georgia, Strait of *24 A1 strait* British Columbia, W Canada
Georg von Neumayer *132 A2 German research station* Antarctica
Gera *72 C4* Thüringen, E Germany
Geráki *83 B6* Pelopónnisos, S Greece
Geraldine *129 B6* Canterbury, South Island, NZ
Geraldton *125 A6* Western Australia
Geral, Serra *35 D5 mountain range* S Brazil
Gerede *94 C2* Bolu, N Turkey
Gereshk *100 D5* Helmand, SW Afghanistan
Gering *22 D3* Nebraska, C USA
Germanicopolis *see* Çankırı
Germany *72 B4 off.* Federal Republic of Germany, *Ger.* Bundesrepublik Deutschland, Deutschland. *Country* N Europe
Geroliménas *83 B7* Pelopónnisos, S Greece
Gerona *see* Girona
Gerpinnes *65 C7* Hainaut, S Belgium
Gerunda *see* Girona
Gerze *94 D2* Sinop, N Turkey
Gesoriacum *see* Boulogne-sur-Mer
Gessoriacum *see* Boulogne-sur-Mer
Getafe *70 D3* Madrid, C Spain
Gevaş *95 F3* Van, SE Turkey
Gevgeli *see* Gevgelija
Gevgelija *79 E6 var.* Đevđelija, Djevdjelija, *Turk.* Gevgeli. SE FYR Macedonia
Ghaba *see* Al Ghābah
Ghana *53 E5 off.* Republic of Ghana. *Country* W Africa
Ghanzi *56 C3 var.* Khanzi. Ghanzi, W Botswana
Gharandal *97 B7* Ma'ān, SW Jordan
Ghardaïa *18 D2* N Algeria
Gharvān *see* Gharyān
Gharyān *49 F2 var.* Gharvān. NW Libya
Ghaznī *101 E4 var.* Ghazni. Ghaznī, E Afghanistan
Ghazni *see* Ghaznī
Gheel *see* Geel
Gheorgheni *86 C4 prev.* Gheorghieni, Sînt Miclăuş, *Ger.* Niklasmarkt, *Hung.* Gyergyószentmiklós. Harghita, C Romania
Ghijduwon *100 D2 Rus.* Gizhduvan. Bukhoro Wiloyati, C Uzbekistan
Ghŭdara *101 F3 var.* Gudara, *Rus.* Kudara. SE Tajikistan
Ghurdaqah *see* Hurghada
Ghūriān *100 D4* Herāt, W Afghanistan
Giannitsá *82 B4 var.* Yiannitsá. Kentrikí Makedonía, N Greece
Gibraltar *71 G4 UK dependent territory* SW Europe
Gibraltar, Bay of *71 G5 bay* Gibraltar/Spain
Gibraltar, Strait of *70 C5 Fr.* Détroit de Gibraltar, *Sp.* Estrecho de Gibraltar. *Strait* Atlantic Ocean/Mediterranean Sea
Gibson Desert *125 B5 desert* Western Australia
Giedraičiai *85 C5* Molėtai, E Lithuania
Giessen *73 B5* Hessen, W Germany
Gifu *109 C6 var.* Gihu. Gifu, Honshū, SW Japan
Giganta, Sierra de la *28 B3 mountain range* W Mexico
Gihu *see* Gifu
Gijón *70 D1 var.* Xixón. Asturias, NW Spain
Gilani *see* Gnjilane
Gila River *26 A2 river* Arizona, SW USA
Gilbert River *126 C3 river* Queensland, NE Australia
Gilf Kebir Plateau *50 A2 Ar.* Haḍabat al Jilf al Kabīr. *Plateau* SW Egypt
Gillette *22 D3* Wyoming, C USA
Gilroy *25 B6* California, W USA
Gimie, Mount *33 F1 mountain* C Saint Lucia
Gimma *see* Jīma
Ginevra *see* Genève
Gingin *125 A6* Western Australia
Giohar *see* Jawhar
Girardot *36 B3* Cundinamarca, C Colombia
Giresun *95 E2 var.* Kerasunt; *anc.* Cerasus, Pharnacia. Giresun, NE Turkey
Girin *see* Jilin
Girne *see* Kerýneia
Girona *71 G2 var.* Gerona; *anc.* Gerunda. Cataluña, NE Spain
Gisborne *128 E3* Gisborne, North Island, NZ
Gissar Range *101 E3 Rus.* Gissarskiy Khrebet. *Mountain range* Tajikistan/Uzbekistan
Githio *see* Gýtheio
Giulianova *74 D4* Abruzzo, C Italy
Giumri *see* Gyumri
Giurgiu *86 C5* Giurgiu, S Romania
Gîza *see* El Gîza
Gizeh *see* El Gîza
Giżycko *76 D2* Warmińsko-Mazurskie, NE Poland
Gjakovë *see* Đakovica
Gjilan *see* Gnjilane
Gjinokastër *see* Gjirokastër
Gjirokastër *79 C7 var.* Gjirokastra; *prev.* Gjinokastër, *Gk.* Argyrokastron, *It.* Argirocastro. Gjirokastër, S Albania
Gjirokastra *see* Gjirokastër
Gjoa Haven *15 F3* King William Island, Nunavut, NW Canada
Gjøvik *63 B5* Oppland, S Norway
Glace Bay *17 G4* Cape Breton Island, Nova Scotia, SE Canada
Gladstone *126 E4* Queensland, E Australia
Glåma *63 B5 river* SE Norway
Glasgow *66 C4* S Scotland, UK
Glavn'a Morava *see* Velika Morava
Glazov *89 D5* Udmurtskaya Respublika, NW Russian Federation
Glendale *26 B2* Arizona, SW USA

Hai-la-erh – Huainan

ai-la-erh see Hailar
ailar 105 F1 var. Hai-la-erh; prev. Hulun. Nei Mongol Zizhiqu, N China
ailuoto 62 D4 Swe. Karlö. Island W Finland
ainan 106 B7 var. Hainan Sheng, Qiong. Admin. region province S China
ainan Dao 106 C7 island S China
ainan Sheng see Hainan
aines 14 D4 Alaska, USA
ainichen 72 D4 Sachsen, E Germany
ai Phong 114 D3 var. Haifong, Haiphong. N Vietnam
aiphong see Hai Phong
aiti 32 D3 off. Republic of Haiti. Country C West Indies
aiya 50 C3 Red Sea, NE Sudan
ajdúhadház 77 D6 Hajdú-Bihar, E Hungary
ajîne see Abū Ḩardān
ajnówka 76 E3 Ger. Hermhausen. Podlaskie, NE Poland
akodate 108 D3 Hokkaidō, NE Japan
alab 96 B2 Eng. Aleppo, Fr. Alep; anc. Beroea. Ḩalab, NW Syria
alāniyāt, Juzur al 137 D6 var. Jazā'ir Bin Ghalfān, Eng. Kuria Muria Islands. Island group S Oman
alberstadt 72 C4 Sachsen-Anhalt, C Germany
alden 63 B6 prev. Fredrikshald. Østfold, S Norway
alfmoon Bay 129 A8 var. Oban. Stewart Island, Southland, NZ
alifax 17 F4 Nova Scotia, SE Canada
alkida see Chalkída
alle 65 B6 Fr. Hal. Vlaams Brabant, C Belgium
alle 72 C4 var. Halle an der Saale. Sachsen-Anhalt, C Germany
alle an der Saale see Halle
alle-Neustadt 72 C4 Sachsen-Anhalt, C Germany
alley 132 B2 UK research station Antarctica
all Islands 120 B2 island group C Micronesia
alls Creek 124 C3 Western Australia
almahera, Pulau 117 F3 prev. Djailolo, Gilolo, Jailolo. Island E Indonesia
almahera Sea 117 F4 Ind. Laut Halmahera. Sea E Indonesia
almstad 63 B7 Halland, S Sweden
ama see Ḩamāh
amada 109 B6 Shimane, Honshū, SW Japan
amadān 98 C3 anc. Ecbatana. Hamadān, W Iran
amāh 96 B3 var. Hama; anc. Epiphania, Bibl. Hamath. Ḩamāh, W Syria
amamatsu 109 D6 var. Hamamatu. Shizuoka, Honshū, S Japan
amamatu see Hamamatsu
amar 63 B5 prev. Storhammer. Hedmark, S Norway
amath see Ḩamāh
amburg 72 B3 Hamburg, N Germany
amd, Wādī al 136 A4 dry watercourse W Saudi Arabia
ämeenlinna 63 D5 Swe. Tavastehus. Etelä-Suomi, S Finland
amersley Range 124 A4 mountain range Western Australia
amhŭng 107 E3 C North Korea
ami 104 C3 var. Ha-mi, Uigh. Kumul, Qomul. Xinjiang Uygur Zizhiqu, NW China
ami see Hami
amilton 20 C2 Alabama, S USA
amilton 16 D5 Ontario, S Canada
amilton 66 C4 S Scotland, UK
amilton 128 D3 Waikato, North Island, NZ
amīm, Wādī al 87 G2 river NE Libya
amīs Musait see Khamīs Mushayt
amiton 20 A5 dependent territory capital (Bermuda) C Bermuda
amm 72 B4 var. Hamm in Westfalen. Nordrhein-Westfalen, W Germany
ammada du Drâa see Dra, Hamada du
ammamet, Golfe de 80 D3 Ar. Khalīj al Ḩammāmāt. Gulf NE Tunisia
ammār, Hawr al 136 C3 lake SE Iraq
amm in Westfalen see Hamm
ampden 129 B7 Otago, South Island, NZ
ampstead 67 A7 SE England, UK
amrun 80 B5 C Malta
ancești see Hîncești
andan 106 C4 var. Han-tan. Hebei, E China
aneda 108 A2 international airport (Tōkyō) Tōkyō, Honshū, S Japan
aNegev 97 A7 Eng. Negev. Desert S Israel
anford 25 C6 California, W USA
angayn Nuruu 104 D2 mountain range C Mongolia
ang-chou see Hangzhou
angchow see Hangzhou
angö see Hanko
angzhou 106 D5 var. Hang-chou, Hangchow. Zhejiang, SE China
ania see Chaniá
anka, Lake see Khanka, Lake
anko 63 D6 Swe. Hangö. Etelä-Suomi, SW Finland
an k'ou see Wuhan
ankow see Wuhan
anmer Springs 129 C5 Canterbury, South Island, NZ
annibal 23 G4 Missouri, C USA
annover 72 B3 Eng. Hanover. Niedersachsen, NW Germany
anöbukten 63 B7 bay S Sweden
a Nôi 114 D3 Eng. Hanoi, Fr. Ha noï. Country capital (Vietnam) N Vietnam
anoi see Ha Nôi
an Shui 105 E4 river C China
an-tan see Handan
antsavichy 85 B6 Pol. Hancewicze, Rus. Gantsevichi. Brestskaya Voblasts', SW Belarus
anyang see Wuhan
Hanzhong 106 B5 Shaanxi, C China
Hāora 113 F4 prev. Howrah. West Bengal, NE India
Haparanda 62 D4 Norrbotten, N Sweden
Haradok 85 E5 Rus. Gorodok. Vitsyebskaya Voblasts', N Belarus
Haradzyets 85 B6 Rus. Gorodets. Brestskaya Voblasts', SW Belarus
Haramachi 108 D4 Fukushima, Honshū, E Japan
Harany 85 D5 Rus. Gorany. Vitsyebskaya Voblasts', N Belarus
Harare 56 D3 prev. Salisbury. Country capital (Zimbabwe) Mashonaland East, NE Zimbabwe
Harbavichy 85 E6 Rus. Gorbovichi. Mahilyowskaya Voblasts', E Belarus
Harbel 52 C5 W Liberia
Harbin 107 E2 var. Haerbin, Ha-erh-pin, Kharbin; prev. Haerhpin, Pingkiang, Pinkiang. Heilongjiang, NE China
Hardangerfjorden 63 A6 fjord S Norway
Hardangervidda 63 A6 plateau S Norway
Hardenberg 64 E3 Overijssel, E Netherlands
Harelbeke 65 A6 var. Harlebeke. West-Vlaanderen, W Belgium
Harem see Ḩārim
Haren 64 E2 Groningen, NE Netherlands
Hārer 51 D5 E Ethiopia
Hargeisa see Hargeysa
Hargeysa 51 D5 var. Hargeisa. Woqooyi Galbeed, NW Somalia
Hariana see Haryāna
Hari, Batang 116 B4 prev. Djambi. River Sumatera, W Indonesia
Ḩārim 96 B2 var. Harem. Idlib, W Syria
Harima-nada 109 B6 sea S Japan
Harīrūd var. Tedzhen, Turkm. Tejen. River Afghanistan/Iran see also Tedzhen
Harlan 23 F3 Iowa, C USA
Harlebeke see Harelbeke
Harlingen 64 D2 Fris. Harns. Friesland, N Netherlands
Harlingen 27 G5 Texas, SW USA
Harlow 67 E6 E England, UK
Harney Basin 24 B4 basin Oregon, NW USA
Härnösand 63 C5 var. Hernösand. Vasternorrland, C Sweden
Har Nuur 104 C2 lake NW Mongolia
Harper 52 D5 var. Cape Palmas. NE Liberia
Harricana 16 D3 river Québec, SE Canada
Harris 66 B3 physical region NW Scotland, UK
Harrisburg 19 E4 state capital Pennsylvania, NE USA
Harrisonburg 19 E4 Virginia, NE USA
Harrison, Cape 17 F2 headland Newfoundland and Labrador, E Canada
Harris Ridge see Lomonosov Ridge
Harrogate 67 D5 N England, UK
Hârșova 86 D5 prev. Hîrșova. Constanța, SE Romania
Harstad 62 C2 Troms, N Norway
Hartford 19 G3 state capital Connecticut, NE USA
Hartlepool 67 D5 N England, UK
Harunabad see Eslāmābād
Harwich 67 E6 E England, UK
Haryāna 112 D2 var. Hariana. Admin. region state N India
Hasselt 65 C6 Limburg, NE Belgium
Hassetché see Al Ḩasakah
Hastings 128 E4 Hawke's Bay, North Island, NZ
Hastings 23 E4 Nebraska, C USA
Hastings 67 E7 SE England, UK
Hațeg 86 B4 Ger. Wallenthal, Hung. Hátszeg; prev. Hatzeg, Hötzing. Hunedoara, SW Romania
Hatizyô Zima see Hachijō-jima
Hattem 64 D3 Gelderland, E Netherlands
Hatteras, Cape 21 G1 headland North Carolina, SE USA
Hatteras Plain 13 D6 undersea feature W Atlantic Ocean
Hattiesburg 20 C3 Mississippi, S USA
Hatton Bank see Hatton Ridge
Hatton Ridge 58 B2 var. Hatton Bank. Undersea feature N Atlantic Ocean
Hat Yai 115 C7 var. Ban Hat Yai. Songkhla, SW Thailand
Haugesund 63 A6 Rogaland, S Norway
Haukeligrend 63 A6 Telemark, S Norway
Haukivesi 63 E5 lake SE Finland
Hauraki Gulf 128 D2 gulf North Island, NZ
Hauroko, Lake 129 A7 lake South Island, NZ
Haut Atlas 48 B3 Eng. High Atlas. Mountain range C Morocco
Hautes Fagnes 65 D6 Ger. Hohes Venn. Mountain range E Belgium
Haut Plateau du Dra see Dra, Hamada du
Hauts Plateaux 48 D2 plateau Algeria/Morocco
Hauzenberg 73 D6 Bayern, SE Germany
Havana see La Habana
Havana 13 D6 Illinois, N USA
Havant 67 D7 S England, UK
Havelock 21 F1 North Carolina, SE USA
Havelock North 128 E4 Hawke's Bay, North Island, NZ
Haverfordwest 67 C6 SW Wales, UK
Havířov 77 C5 Ostravský Kraj, E Czech Republic
Havre 22 C1 Montana, NW USA
Havre-St-Pierre 17 F3 Québec, E Canada
Hawaii 25 B8 Haw. Hawai'i. Island Hawaiian Islands, USA, C Pacific Ocean
Hawaii 25 A8 off. State of Hawaii; also known as Aloha State, Paradise of the Pacific. State USA, C Pacific Ocean
Hawaiian Islands 130 D2 prev. Sandwich Islands. Island group Hawaii, USA, C Pacific Ocean
Hawaiian Ridge 91 H4 undersea feature N Pacific Ocean
Hawash see Āwash
Hawea, Lake 129 B6 lake South Island, NZ
Hawera 128 D4 Taranaki, North Island, NZ
Hawick 66 C4 SE Scotland, UK
Hawke Bay 128 E4 bay North Island, NZ
Hawlēr see Arbīl
Hawthorne 25 C6 Nevada, W USA
Hay 127 C6 New South Wales, SE Australia
Hayes 16 B2 river Manitoba, C Canada
Hay River 15 E4 Northwest Territories, W Canada
Hays 23 E5 Kansas, C USA
Haysyn 86 D3 Rus. Gaysin. Vinnyts'ka Oblast', C Ukraine
Heard and McDonald Islands 119 B7 Australian external territory S Indian Ocean
Hearst 16 C4 Ontario, S Canada
Heathrow 67 A8 international airport (London)SE England, UK
Hebei 106 C4 var. Hebei Sheng, Hopeh, Hopei, Ji; prev. Chihli. Admin. region province E China
Hebei Sheng see Hebei
Hebron 97 A6 var. Al Khalīl, El Khalil, Heb. Ḥevron; anc. Kiriath-Arba. S West Bank
Hebrus see Maritsa
Heemskerk 64 C3 Noord-Holland, W Netherlands
Heerde 64 D3 Gelderland, E Netherlands
Heerenveen 64 D2 Fris. It Hearrenfean. Friesland, N Netherlands
Heerhugowaard 64 C2 Noord-Holland, NW Netherlands
Heerlen 65 D6 Limburg, SE Netherlands
Heerwegen see Polkowice
Ḥefa 97 A5 var. Haifa; hist. Caiffa, Caiphas, anc. Sycaminum. Haifa, N Israel
Ḥefa, Mifraz 97 A5 Eng. Bay of Haifa. Bay N Israel
Hefei 106 D5 var. Hofei; hist. Luchow. Anhui, E China
Hegang 107 E2 Heilongjiang, NE China
Hei see Heilongjiang
Heide 72 B2 Schleswig-Holstein, N Germany
Heidelberg 73 B5 Baden-Württemberg, SW Germany
Heidenheim see Heidenheim an der Brenz
Heidenheim an der Brenz 73 B6 var. Heidenheim. Baden-Württemberg, S Germany
Heilbronn 73 B6 Baden-Württemberg, SW Germany
Heilongjiang 106 D2 var. Hei, Heilongjiang Sheng, Hei-lung-chiang, Heilungkiang. Admin. region province NE China
Heilongjiang Sheng see Heilongjiang
Heiloo 64 C3 Noord-Holland, NW Netherlands
Hei-lung-chiang see Heilongjiang
Heilungkiang see Heilongjiang
Heimdal 63 B5 Sør-Trøndelag, S Norway
Hekimhan 94 D3 Malatya, C Turkey
Helena 22 B2 state capital Montana, NW USA
Helensville 128 D2 Auckland, North Island, NZ
Helgoland Bay see Helgoländer Bucht
Helgoländer Bucht 72 A2 var. Helgoland Bay, Heligoland Bight. Bay NW Germany
Heligoland Bight see Helgoländer Bucht
Heliopolis see Baalbek
Hellevoetsluis 64 B4 Zuid-Holland, SW Netherlands
Hellín 71 E4 Castilla-La Mancha, C Spain
Helmand, Daryā-ye var. Rūd-e Hīrmand. River Afghanistan/Iran see also Hīrmand, Rūd-e
Helmond 65 D5 Noord-Brabant, S Netherlands
Helsingborg 63 B7 prev. Hälsingborg. Skåne, S Sweden
Helsinki 63 D6 Swe. Helsingfors. Country capital (Finland) Etelä-Suomi, S Finland
Henan 106 C5 var. Henan Sheng, Honan, Yu. Admin. region province C China
Henan Sheng see Henan
Henderson 18 B5 Kentucky, S USA
Henderson 25 D7 Nevada, W USA
Henderson 27 H3 Texas, SW USA
Hengchow see Hengyang
Hengduan Shan 106 A5 mountain range SW China
Hengelo 64 E3 Overijssel, E Netherlands
Hengnan see Hengyang
Hengyang 106 C6 var. Hengnan, Heng-yang; prev. Hengchow. Hunan, S China
Heng-yang see Hengyang
Heniches'k 87 F4 Rus. Genichesk. Khersons'ka Oblast', S Ukraine
Hennebont 68 A3 Morbihan, NW France
Henzada 114 B4 Irrawaddy, SW Myanmar
Herakleion see Irákleio
Herāt 100 D4 var. Herat; anc. Aria. Herāt, W Afghanistan
Herat see Herāt
Heredia 31 E4 Heredia, C Costa Rica
Hereford 27 E2 Texas, SW USA
Herford 72 B4 Nordrhein-Westfalen, NW Germany
Herk-de-Stad 65 C6 Limburg, NE Belgium
Hermansverk 63 A5 Sogn Og Fjordane, S Norway
Hermhausen see Hajnówka
Hermiston 24 C2 Oregon, NW USA
Hermon, Mount 97 B5 Ar. Jabal ash Shaykh. Mountain S Syria
Hermosillo 28 B2 Sonora, NW Mexico
Hermoupolis see Ermoúpoli
Hernösand see Härnösand
Herrera del Duque 70 D3 Extremadura, W Spain
Herselt 65 C5 Antwerpen, C Belgium
Herstal 65 D6 Fr. Héristal. Liège, E Belgium
Hessen 73 B5 cultural region C Germany
Ḥevron see Hebron
Heydebrech see Kędzierzyn-Kole
Heywood Islands 124 C3 island group Western Australia
Hibbing 23 F1 Minnesota, N USA
Hidalgo del Parral 28 C2 var. Parral. Chihuahua, N Mexico
Hida-sanmyaku 109 C5 mountain range Honshū, S Japan
Hierro 48 A3 var. Ferro. Island Islas Canarias, Spain, NE Atlantic Ocean
High Plains see Great Plains
High Point 21 E1 North Carolina, SE USA
High Veld see Great Karoo
Hiiumaa 84 C2 Ger. Dagden, Swe. Dagö. Island W Estonia
Hikurangi 128 D2 Northland, North Island, NZ
Hildesheim 72 B4 Niedersachsen, N Germany
Hilla see Al Ḩillah
Hillaby, Mount 33 G1 mountain N Barbados
Hill Bank 30 C1 Orange Walk, N Belize
Hillegom 64 C3 Zuid-Holland, W Netherlands
Hilo 25 B8 Hawaii, USA, C Pacific Ocean
Hilton Head Island 21 E2 South Carolina, SE USA
Hilversum 64 C3 Noord-Holland, C Netherlands
Himalaya see Himalayas
Himalayas 113 E2 var. Himalaya, Chin. Himalaya Shan. Mountain range S Asia
Himalaya Shan see Himalayas
Himeji 109 C6 var. Himezi. Hyōgo, Honshū, SW Japan
Himezi see Himeji
Ḩimş 96 B4 var. Homs; anc. Emesa. Ḩimş, C Syria
Hîncești 86 D4 var. Hâncești; prev. Kotovsk. C Moldova
Hinchinbrook Island 126 D3 island Queensland, NE Australia
Hinds 129 C6 Canterbury, South Island, NZ
Hindu Kush 101 F4 Per. Hendū Kosh. Mountain range Afghanistan/Pakistan
Hinesville 21 E3 Georgia, SE USA
Hinnøya 62 C3 island C Norway
Hinson Bay 20 A5 bay W Bermuda
Hios see Chíos
Hirosaki 108 D3 Aomori, Honshū, C Japan
Hiroshima 109 B6 var. Hirosima. Hiroshima, Honshū, SW Japan
Hirosima see Hiroshima
Hirson 68 D3 Aisne, N France
Hispaniola 34 B1 island Dominion Republic/Haiti
Hitachi 109 D5 var. Hitati. Ibaraki, Honshū, S Japan
Hitati see Hitachi
Hitra 62 A4 prev. Hitteren. Island S Norway
Hjälmaren 63 C6 Eng. Lake Hjalmar. Lake C Sweden
Hjørring 63 B7 Nordjylland, N Denmark
Hkakabo Razi 114 B1 mountain Myanmar/China
Hlobyne 87 F2 Rus. Globino. Poltavs'ka Oblast', NE Ukraine
Hlukhiv 87 F1 Rus. Glukhov. Sums'ka Oblast', NE Ukraine
Hlybokaye 85 D5 Rus. Glubokoye. Vitsyebskaya Voblasts', N Belarus
Hoa Binh 114 D3 Hoa Binh, N Vietnam
Hoang Liên Sơn 114 D3 mountain range N Vietnam
Hobart 127 C8 prev. Hobarton, Hobart Town. State capital Tasmania, SE Australia
Hobbs 27 E3 New Mexico, SW USA
Hobro 63 A7 Nordjylland, N Denmark
Hô Chi Minh 115 E6 var. Ho Chi Minh City, prev. Saigon. S Vietnam
Ho Chi Minh City see Hô Chi Minh
Hódmezővásárhely 77 D7 Csongrád, SE Hungary
Hodna, Chott El 118 C4 var. Chott el-Hodna, Ar. Shatt al-Hodna. Salt lake N Algeria
Hodonín 77 C5 Ger. Göding. Brněnský Kraj, SE Czech Republic
Hoë Karoo see Great Karoo
Hof 73 C5 Bayern, SE Germany
Hofei see Hefei
Hōfu 109 B7 Yamaguchi, Honshū, SW Japan
Hofuf see Al Hufūf
Hogoley Islands see Chuuk Islands
Hohe Tauern 73 C7 mountain range W Austria
Hohhot 105 F3 var. Huhehot, Huhuohaote, Mong. Kukukhoto; prev. Kweisui, Kwesui. Nei Mongol Zizhiqu, N China
Hôi An 115 E5 prev. Faifo. Quang Nam-Đa Năng, C Vietnam
Hoï-Hao see Haikou
Hoihow see Haikou
Hokianga Harbour 128 C2 inlet SE Tasman Sea
Hokitika 129 B5 West Coast, South Island, NZ
Hokkaidō 108 C2 prev. Ezo, Yeso, Yezo. Island NE Japan
Hola Prystan' 87 E4 Rus. Golaya Pristan. Khersons'ka Oblast', S Ukraine
Holbrook 26 B2 Arizona, SW USA
Holetown 33 G1 prev. Jamestown. W Barbados
Holguín 32 C2 Holguín, SE Cuba
Hollabrunn 73 E6 Niederösterreich, NE Austria
Hollandia see Jayapura
Holly Springs 20 C1 Mississippi, S USA
Holman 15 E3 Victoria Island, Northwest Territories, N Canada
Holmsund 62 D4 Västerbotten, N Sweden
Ḥolon 97 A6 var. Kholon. Tel Aviv, C Israel
Holovanivs'k 87 E3 Rus. Golovanevsk. Kirovohrads'ka Oblast', C Ukraine
Holstebro 63 A7 Ringkøbing, W Denmark
Holsteinborg see Sisimiut
Holsteinsborg see Sisimiut
Holstenborg see Sisimiut
Holstensborg see Sisimiut
Holyhead 67 C5 Wel. Caer Gybi. NW Wales, UK
Hombori 53 E3 Mopti, S Mali
Homs see Al Khums
Homs see Ḩimş
Homyel' 85 D7 Rus. Gomel'. Homyel'skaya Voblasts', SE Belarus
Honan see Henan
Honan see Luoyang
Hondo see Honshū
Hondo 27 F4 Texas, SW USA
Honduras 30 C2 off. Republic of Honduras. Country Central America
Honduras, Gulf of 30 C2 Sp. Golfo de Honduras. Gulf W Caribbean Sea
Hønefoss 63 B6 Buskerud, S Norway
Honey Lake 25 B5 lake California, W USA
Hon Gai see Hông Gai
Hongay see Hông Gai
Hông Gai 114 E3 var. Hon Gai, Hongay. Quang Ninh, N Vietnam
Hong Kong 106 A1 Chin. Xianggang. S China
Hong Kong Island 106 B2 Chin. Xianggang. Island S China
Honiara 122 C3 country capital (Solomon Islands) Guadalcanal, C Solomon Islands
Honjō 108 D4 var. Honzyô. Akita, Honshū, C Japan
Honolulu 25 A8 admin capital Oahu, Hawaii, USA, C Pacific Ocean
Honshū 109 E5 var. Hondo, Honsyû. Island SW Japan
Honsyû see Honshū
Honzyô see Honjō
Hoogeveen 64 E2 Drenthe, NE Netherlands
Hoogezand-Sappemeer 64 E2 Groningen, NE Netherlands
Hoorn 64 C2 Noord-Holland, NW Netherlands
Hopa 95 E2 Artvin, NE Turkey
Hope 14 C3 British Columbia, SW Canada
Hopedale 17 F2 Newfoundland and Labrador, NE Canada
Hopeh see Hebei
Hopei see Hebei
Hopkinsville 18 B5 Kentucky, S USA
Horasan 95 F3 Erzurum, NE Turkey
Horizon Deep 130 D4 undersea feature W Pacific Ocean
Horki 85 E6 Rus. Gorki. Mahilyowskaya Voblasts', E Belarus
Horlivka 87 G3 Rom. Adâncata, Rus. Gorlovka. Donets'ka Oblast', E Ukraine
Hormuz, Strait of 98 D4 var. Strait of Ormuz, Per. Tangeh-ye Hormoz. Strait Iran/Oman
Hornos, Cabo de 43 C8 Eng. Cape Horn. Headland S Chile
Hornsby 126 E1 New South Wales, SE Australia
Horodnya 87 E1 Rus. Gorodnya. Chernihivs'ka Oblast', NE Ukraine
Horodyshche 87 E2 Rus. Gorodishche. Cherkas'ka Oblast', C Ukraine
Horokok 86 B2 Pol. Gródek Jagielloński, Rus. Gorodok, Gorodok Yagellonski. L'vivs'ka Oblast', NW Ukraine
Horoshiri-dake 108 D2 var. Horosiri Dake. Mountain Hokkaidō, N Japan
Horosiri Dake see Horoshiri-dake
Horsburgh Atoll 110 A4 atoll N Maldives
Horseshoe Bay 20 A5 bay W Bermuda
Horseshoe Seamounts 58 A4 undersea feature E Atlantic Ocean
Horsham 127 B7 Victoria, SE Australia
Horst 65 D5 Limburg, SE Netherlands
Horten 63 B6 Vestfold, S Norway
Horyn' 85 B7 Rus. Goryn. River NW Ukraine
Hosingen 65 D7 Diekirch, NE Luxembourg
Hospitalet see L'Hospitalet de Llobregat
Hotan 104 B4 var. Khotan, Chin. Ho-t'ien. Xinjiang Uygur Zizhiqu, NW China
Ho-t'ien see Hotan
Hoting 62 C4 Jämtland, C Sweden
Hot Springs 20 B1 Arkansas, C USA
Houayxay 114 C3 var. Ban Houayxay, Ban Houei Sai. Bokèo, N Laos
Houghton 18 B1 Michigan, N USA
Houilles 69 B5 Yvelines, N France
Houlton 19 H1 Maine, NE USA
Houma 20 B3 Louisiana, S USA
Houston 27 H4 Texas, SW USA
Hovd 104 C2 var. Khovd. Hovd, W Mongolia
Hove 67 E7 SE England, UK
Hoverla, Hora 86 C3 Rus. Gora Goverla. Mountain W Ukraine
Hovsgol, Lake see Hövsgöl Nuur
Hövsgöl Nuur 104 D1 var. Lake Hovsgol. Lake N Mongolia
Howar, Wādi 50 A3 var. Ouadi Howa. River Chad/Sudan see also Howa, Ouadi
Hoy 66 C2 island N Scotland, UK
Hoyerswerda 72 D4 Sachsen, E Germany
Hradec Králové 77 B5 Ger. Königgrätz. Hradecký Kraj, N Czech Republic
Hrandzichy 85 B5 Rus. Grandichi. Hrodzyenskaya Voblasts', W Belarus
Hranice 77 C5 Ger. Mährisch-Weisskirchen. Olomoucký Kraj, E Czech Republic
Hrebinka 87 E2 Rus. Grebenka. Poltavs'ka Oblast', NE Ukraine
Hrodna 85 B5 Pol. Grodno. Hrodzyenskaya Voblasts', W Belarus
Hsia-men see Xiamen
Hsiang-t'an see Xiangtan
Hsi Chiang see Xi Jiang
Hsing-k'ai Hu see Khanka, Lake
Hsining see Xining
Hsinking see Changchun
Hsin-yang see Xinyang
Hsu-chou see Xuzhou
Huacho 38 C4 Lima, W Peru
Hua Hin see Ban Hua Hin
Huaihua 106 C5 Hunan, S China
Huailai 106 C3 prev. Shacheng. Hebei, E China
Huainan 106 D5 var. Huai-nan, Hwainan. Anhui, E China

Jajce – Karakolka

Jajce 78 B3 Federacija Bosna I Hercegovina, W Bosnia and Herzegovina
Jakarta 116 C5 *prev.* Djakarta, *Dut.* Batavia. *Country capital* (Indonesia) Jawa, C Indonesia
Jakobstad 62 D4 *Fin.* Pietarsaari. Länsi-Suomi, W Finland
Jalālābād 101 F4 *var.* Jalalabad, Jelalabad. Nangarhār, E Afghanistan
Jalandhar 112 D2 *prev.* Jullundur. Punjab, N India
Jalapa *see* Xalapa
Jalapa 30 D3 Nueva Segovia, NW Nicaragua
Jalapa Enríquez *see* Xalapa
Jalpa 28 D4 Zacatecas, C Mexico
Jālū 49 G3 *var.* Jūlā. NE Libya
Jaluit Atoll 122 D2 *var.* Jālwōj. *Atoll* Ralik Chain, S Marshall Islands
Jālwōj *see* Jaluit Atoll
Jamaame 51 D6 *It.* Giamame; *prev.* Margherita. Jubbada Hoose, S Somalia
Jamaica 32 A4 *country* W West Indies
Jamaica 34 A1 *island* W West Indies
Jamaica Channel 32 D3 *channel* Haiti/Jamaica
Jamālpur 113 F3 Bihār, NE India
Jambi 116 B4 *var.* Telanaipura; *prev.* Djambi. Sumatera, W Indonesia
James Bay 16 C3 *bay* Ontario/Québec, E Canada
James River 23 E2 *river* North Dakota/South Dakota, N USA
James River 19 E5 *river* Virginia, NE USA
Jamestown 19 E3 New York, NE USA
Jamestown 23 E2 North Dakota, N USA
Jammu 112 D2 *prev.* Jummoo. Jammu and Kashmir, NW India
Jammu and Kashmīr 112 D1 *disputed region* India/Pakistan
Jāmnagar 112 C4 *prev.* Navanagar. Gujarāt, W India
Jamshedpur 113 F4 Bihār, NE India
Jamuna *see* Brahmaputra
Janaúba 41 F3 Minas Gerais, SE Brazil
Janesville 18 B3 Wisconsin, N USA
Janīn *see* Jenīn
Janina *see* Ioánnina
Jan Mayen 61 F4 *Norwegian dependency* N Atlantic Ocean
Jánoshalma 77 C7 *SCr.* Jankovac. Bács-Kiskun, S Hungary
Japan 108 C4 *var.* Nippon, *Jap.* Nihon. *Country* E Asia
Japan, Sea of 108 A4 *var.* East Sea, *Rus.* Yapanskoye More. *Sea* NW Pacific Ocean
Japan Trench 103 F1 *undersea feature* NW Pacific Ocean
Japim 40 C2 *var.* Máncio Lima. Acre, W Brazil
Japurá, Rio 40 C2 *var.* Río Caquetá, Yapura. *River* Brazil/Colombia *see also* Caquetá, Río
Jaqué 31 G5 Darién, SE Panama
Jaquemel *see* Jacmel
Jarablos *see* Jarābulus
Jarābulus 96 C2 *var.* Jarablos, Jerablus, *Fr.* Djérablous. Ḩalab, N Syria
Jardines de la Reina, Archipiélago de los 32 B2 *island group* C Cuba
Jarocin 76 C4 Wielkopolskie, C Poland
Jarosław 77 E5 *Ger.* Jaroslau, *Rus.* Yaroslav. Podkarpackie, SE Poland
Jarqŭrghon 101 E3 *Rus.* Dzharkurgan. Surkhondaryo Wiloyati, S Uzbekistan
Jarvis Island 123 G2 *US unincorporated territory* C Pacific Ocean
Jasło 77 D5 Podkarpackie, SE Poland
Jastrzębie-Zdrój 77 C5 Śląskie, S Poland
Jataí 41 E3 Goiás, C Brazil
Játiva *see* Xátiva
Jauf *see* Al Jawf
Jaunpiebalga 84 D3 Gulbene, NE Latvia
Jaunpur 113 E3 Uttar Pradesh, N India
Java 130 A3 *prev.* Djawa. *Island* C Indonesia
Javalambre 71 E3 *mountain* E Spain
Javari, Rio 40 C2 *var.* Yavarí. *River* Brazil/Peru
Java Sea 116 D4 *Ind.* Laut Jawa. *Sea* W Indonesia
Java Trench 102 D5 *var.* Sunda Trench. *Undersea feature* E Indian Ocean
Jawhar 51 D6 *var.* Jowhar, *It.* Giohar. Shabeellaha Dhexe, S Somalia
Jaya, Puncak 117 G4 *prev.* Puntjak Carstensz, Puntjak Sukarno. *Mountain* Irian Jaya, E Indonesia
Jayapura 117 H4 *var.* Djajapura, *Dut.* Hollandia; *prev.* Kotabaru, Sukarnapura. Irian Jaya, E Indonesia
Jazā'ir Bin Ghalfān *see* Ḩalāniyāt, Juzur al
Jazīrat Jarbah *see* Jerba, Île de
Jazīreh-ye Qeshm *see* Qeshm
Jaz Mūrīān, Hāmūn-e 98 E4 *lake* SE Iran
Jebba 53 F4 Kwara, W Nigeria
Jebel esh Sharqi *see* Anti-Lebanon
Jebel Uweinat *see* 'Uwaynāt, Jabal al
Jeble *see* Jablah
Jędrzejów 76 D4 *Ger.* Endersdorf. Świętokrzyskie, C Poland
Jefferson City 23 G5 *state capital* Missouri, C USA
Jega 53 F4 Kebbi, NW Nigeria
Jehol *see* Chengde
Jēkabpils 84 D4 *Ger.* Jakobstadt. Jēkabpils, S Latvia
Jelalabad *see* Jalālābād
Jelenia Góra 76 B4 *Ger.* Hirschberg, Hirschberg im Riesengebirge, Hirschberg in Riesengebirge, Hirschberg in Schlesien. Dolnośląskie, SW Poland
Jelgava 84 C3 *Ger.* Mitau. Jelgava, C Latvia
Jemappes 65 B6 Hainaut, S Belgium
Jember 116 D5 *prev.* Djember. Jawa, C Indonesia
Jena 72 C4 Thüringen, C Germany
Jenīn 97 A6 *var.* Janīn, Jinīn; *anc.* Engannim. N West Bank
Jerablus *see* Jarābulus
Jerada 48 D2 NE Morocco
Jerba, Île de 49 F2 *var.* Djerba, Jazīrat Jarbah. *Island* E Tunisia
Jérémie 32 D3 SW Haiti
Jerez *see* Jeréz de la Frontera
Jeréz de la Frontera 70 C5 *var.* Jerez; *prev.* Xeres. Andalucía, SW Spain
Jeréz de los Caballeros 70 C4 Extremadura, W Spain
Jericho 97 B6 *Ar.* Arīḩā, *Heb.* Yeriḥo. E West Bank
Jerid, Chott el 87 E2 *var.* Shaṭṭ al Jarīd. *Salt lake* SW Tunisia
Jersey 67 D8 *UK dependent territory* NW Europe
Jerusalem 97 H4 *Ar.* El Quds, *Heb.* Yerushalayim; *anc.* Hierosolyma. *Country capital* (Israel) Jerusalem, NE Israel
Jerusalem 90 A4 Admin. region *district* E Israel
Jesenice 73 D7 *Ger.* Assling. NW Slovenia
Jessore 113 G4 Khulna, W Bangladesh
Jesús María 42 C3 Córdoba, C Argentina
Jhānsi 112 D3 Uttar Pradesh, N India
Jhelum 112 C2 Punjab, NE Pakistan
Ji *see* Hebei
Ji *see* Jilin
Jiangmen 106 C6 Guangdong, S China
Jiangsu 106 D4 *var.* Chiang-su, Jiangsu Sheng, Kiangsu, Su. Admin. region *province* E China
Jiangsu Sheng *see* Jiangsu
Jiangxi 106 C6 *var.* Chiang-hsi, Gan, Jiangxi Sheng, Kiangsi. Admin. region *province* S China
Jiangxi Sheng *see* Jiangxi
Jiaxing 106 D5 Zhejiang, SE China
Jiayi *see* Chiai
Jibuti *see* Djibouti
Jiddah 99 A5 *Eng.* Jedda. Makkah, W Saudi Arabia
Jih-k'a-tse *see* Xigazê
Jihlava 77 B5 *Ger.* Iglau, *Pol.* Igława. Jihlavský Kraj, C Czech Republic
Jilib 51 D6 *It.* Gelib. Jubbada Dhexe, S Somalia
Jilin 106 D3 *var.* Chi-lin, Girin, Ji, Jilin Sheng, Kirin. Admin. region *province* NE China
Jilin 107 E3 *var.* Chi-lin, Girin, Kirin; *prev.* Yungki, Yunki. Jilin, NE China
Jilin Sheng *see* Jilin
Jīma 51 C5 *var.* Jimma, *It.* Gimma. C Ethiopia
Jimbolia 86 A4 *Ger.* Hatzfeld, *Hung.* Zsombolya. Timiş, W Romania
Jiménez 28 D2 Chihuahua, N Mexico
Jimma *see* Jīma
Jimsar 104 C3 Xinjiang Uygur Zizhiqu, NW China
Jin *see* Shanxi
Jin *see* Tianjin Shi
Jinan 106 C4 *var.* Chinan, Chi-nan, Tsinan. Shandong, E China
Jingdezhen 106 C5 Jiangxi, S China
Jinghong 106 A6 *var.* Yunjinghong. Yunnan, SW China
Jinhua 106 D5 Zhejiang, SE China
Jinīn *see* Jenīn
Jining 105 F3 Shandong, E China
Jinja 51 C6 S Uganda
Jinotega 30 D3 Jinotega, NW Nicaragua
Jinotepe 30 D3 Carazo, SW Nicaragua
Jinsha Jiang 106 A5 *river* SW China
Jinzhou 106 D3 *var.* Chin-chou, Chinchow; *prev.* Chinhsien. Liaoning, NE China
Jisr ash Shadadi *see* Ash Shadādah
Jiu 86 B5 *Ger.* Schil, Schyl, *Hung.* Zsil, Zsily. *River* S Romania
Jiujiang 106 C5 Jiangxi, S China
Jixi 107 E2 Heilongjiang, NE China
Jīzān 99 B6 *var.* Qīzān. Jīzān, SW Saudi Arabia
Jizzakh 101 E2 *Rus.* Dzhizak. Jizzakh Wiloyati, C Uzbekistan
João Pessoa 41 G2 *prev.* Paraíba. *State capital* Paraíba, E Brazil
Jo'burg *see* Johannesburg
Jo-ch'iang *see* Ruoqiang
Jodhpur 112 C3 Rājasthān, NW India
Joensuu 63 E5 Itä-Suomi, E Finland
Jōetsu 109 C5 *var.* Zyôetu. Niigata, Honshū, C Japan
Johanna Island *see* Anjouan
Johannesburg 56 D4 *var.* Egoli, Erautini, Gauteng, *abbrev.* Jo'burg. Gauteng, NE South Africa
John Day River 24 C3 *river* Oregon, NW USA
John o'Groats 66 C2 N Scotland, UK
Johnston Atoll 121 E1 *US unincorporated territory* C Pacific Ocean
Johor Baharu *see* Johor Bahru
Johor Bahru 116 B3 *var.* Johor Baharu, Johore Bahru. Johor, Peninsular Malaysia
Johore Bahru *see* Johor Bahru
Johore Strait 116 A1 *Mal.* Selat Johor. *Strait* Malaysia/Singapore
Joinvile *see* Joinville
Joinville 41 E4 *var.* Joinvile. Santa Catarina, S Brazil
Jokkmokk 62 C3 Norrbotten, N Sweden
Joliet 18 B3 Illinois, N USA
Jonava 84 B4 *Ger.* Janow, *Pol.* Janów. Jonava, C Lithuania
Jonesboro 20 B1 Arkansas, C USA
Joniškis 84 C3 *Ger.* Janischken. Joniškis, N Lithuania
Jönköping 63 B7 Jönköping, S Sweden
Jonquière 17 E4 Québec, SE Canada
Joplin 23 F5 Missouri, C USA
Jordan 97 B5 *Ar.* Urdunn, *Heb.* HaYarden. *River* SW Asia
Jordan 97 B6 *off.* Hashemite Kingdom of Jordan, *Ar.* Al Mamlakah al Urdunīyah al Hāshimīyah, Al Urdunn; *prev.* Transjordan. *Country* SW Asia
Jorhāt 113 H3 Assam, NE India
Jos 53 G4 Plateau, C Nigeria
Joseph Bonaparte Gulf 124 D2 *gulf* N Australia
Jos Plateau 53 G4 *plateau* C Nigeria
Jotunheimen 63 A5 *mountain range* S Norway
Joûnié 96 A4 *var.* Junīyah. W Lebanon
Joure 64 D2 *Fris.* De Jouwer. Friesland, N Netherlands
Joutseno 63 E5 Etelä-Suomi, S Finland
Jowhar *see* Jawhar
JStorm Thurmond Reservoir *see* Clark Hill Lake
Juan Aldama 28 D3 Zacatecas, C Mexico
Juan de Fuca, Strait of 24 A1 *strait* Canada/USA
Juan Fernández, Islas 35 A6 *Eng.* Juan Fernandez Islands. *Island group* W Chile
Juazeiro 41 G2 *prev.* Joazeiro. Bahia, E Brazil
Juazeiro do Norte 41 G2 Ceará, E Brazil
Juba 51 D6 *Amh.* Genalē Wenz, *It.* Guiba, *Som.* Ganaane, Webi Jubba. *River* Ethiopia/Somalia
Juba 51 B5 *var.* Jūbā. Bahr el Gabel, S Sudan
Júcar 71 E3 *var.* Jucar. *River* C Spain
Juchitán 29 F5 *var.* Juchitán de Zaragosa. Oaxaca, SE Mexico
Juchitán de Zaragosa *see* Juchitán
Judayyidat Hāmir 98 B3 S Iraq
Judenburg 73 D7 Steiermark, C Austria
Juigalpa 30 D3 Chontales, S Nicaragua
Juiz de Fora 41 F4 Minas Gerais, SE Brazil
Jujuy *see* San Salvador de Jujuy
Jūlā *see* Jālū
Juliaca 39 E4 Puno, SE Peru
Juliana Top 37 G3 *mountain* C Suriname
Jumilla 71 E4 Murcia, SE Spain
Jumporn *see* Chumphon
Junction City 23 F4 Kansas, C USA
Juneau 14 D4 *state capital* Alaska, USA
Junín 42 C4 Buenos Aires, E Argentina
Junīyah *see* Joûnié
Junkseylon *see* Phuket
Jur 51 B5 *river* C Sudan
Jura 66 B4 *island* SW Scotland, UK
Jura 73 A7 *canton* NW Switzerland
Jura 68 D4 *department* E France
Jurbarkas 84 B4 *Ger.* Georgenburg, Jurburg. Jurbarkas, W Lithuania
Jūrmala 84 C3 Rīga, C Latvia
Juruá, Rio 40 C2 *var.* Río Yuruá. *River* Brazil/Peru
Juruena, Rio 40 D3 *river* W Brazil
Jutiapa 30 B2 Jutiapa, S Guatemala
Juticalpa 30 D2 Olancho, C Honduras
Juventud, Isla de la 32 A2 *var.* Isla de Pinos, *Eng.* Isle of Youth; *prev.* The Isle of the Pines. *Island* W Cuba
Južna Morava 79 E5 *Ger.* Südliche Morava. *River* SE Yugoslavia
Juzur Qarqannah *see* Kerkenah, Îles de
Jwaneng 56 C4 Southern, SE Botswana
Jylland 63 A7 *Eng.* Jutland. *Peninsula* W Denmark
Jyväskylä 63 D5 Länsi-Suomi, W Finland

K

K2 104 A4 *Chin.* Qogir Feng, *Eng.* Mount Godwin Austen. *Mountain* China/Pakistan
Kaafu Atoll *see* Male' Atoll
Kaaimanston 37 G3 Sipaliwini, N Suriname
Kaakhka 100 C3 *var.* Kaka. Akhalskiy Velayat, S Turkmenistan
Kaala *see* Caála
Kaamanen 62 D2 *Lapp.* Gámas. Lappi, N Finland
Kaapstad *see* Cape Town
Kaaresuvanto 62 C3 *Lapp.* Gárassavon. Lappi, N Finland
Kabale 51 B6 SW Uganda
Kabinda *see* Cabinda
Kabinda 55 D7 Kasai Oriental, SE Dem. Rep. Congo (Zaire)
Kābol *see* Kābul
Kabompo 56 C2 *river* W Zambia
Kābul 101 F4 *var.* Kabul, *Per.* Kābol. *Country capital* (Afghanistan) Kābul, E Afghanistan
Kabul *see* Kābul
Kabwe 56 D2 Central, C Zambia
Kachchh, Gulf of 112 B4 *var.* Gulf of Cutch, Gulf of Kutch. *Gulf* W India
Kachchh, Rann of 112 B4 *var.* Rann of Kachh, Rann of Kutch. *Salt marsh* India/Pakistan
Kachh, Rann of *see* Kachchh, Rann of
Kadan Kyun 115 B5 *prev.* King Island. *Island* Mergui Archipelago, S Myanmar
Kadavu 123 E4 *prev.* Kandavu. *Island* S Fiji
Kadoma 56 D3 *prev.* Gatooma. Mashonaland West, C Zimbabwe
Kadugli 50 B4 Southern Kordofan, S Sudan
Kaduna 53 G4 Kaduna, C Nigeria
Kadzhi-Say 101 G2 *Kir.* Kajisay. Issyk-Kul'skaya Oblast', NE Kyrgyzstan
Kaédi 52 C3 Gorgol, S Mauritania
Kaffa *see* Feodosiya
Kafue 56 C2 *river* C Zambia
Kafue 56 D2 Lusaka, SE Zambia
Kaga Bandoro 54 C4 *prev.* Fort-Crampel. Nana-Grébizi, C Central African Republic
Kāghet 52 D1 *var.* Karet. *Physical region* N Mauritania
Kagi *see* Chiai
Kagoshima 109 B8 *var.* Kagosima. Kagoshima, Kyūshū, SW Japan
Kagoshima-wan 109 A8 *bay* SW Japan
Kagosima *see* Kagoshima
Kahmard, Daryā-ye 101 E4 *prev.* Darya-i-Surkhab. *River* NE Afghanistan
Kahraman Maraş *see* Kahramanmaraş
Kahramanmaraş 94 D4 *var.* Kahraman Maraş, Maraş, Marash. Kahramanmaraş, S Turkey
Kaiapoi 129 C6 Canterbury, South Island, NZ
Kaifeng 106 C4 Henan, C China
Kai, Kepulauan 117 F4 *prev.* Kei Islands. *Island group* Maluku, SE Indonesia
Kaikohe 128 C2 Northland, North Island, NZ
Kaikoura 129 C5 Canterbury, South Island, NZ
Kaikoura Peninsula 129 C5 *peninsula* South Island, NZ
Kainji Lake *see* Kainji Reservoir
Kainji Reservoir 53 F4 *var.* Kainji Lake. *Reservoir* W Nigeria
Kaipara Harbour 128 C2 *harbour* North Island, NZ
Kairouan 49 E2 *var.* Al Qayrawān. E Tunisia
Kaisaria *see* Kayseri
Kaiserslautern 73 A5 Rheinland-Pfalz, SW Germany
Kaišiadorys 85 B5 Kaišiadorys, S Lithuania
Kaitaia 128 C2 Northland, North Island, NZ
Kajaani 62 E4 *Swe.* Kajana. Oulu, C Finland
Kaka *see* Kaakhka
Kake 14 D4 Kupreanof Island, Alaska, USA
Kakhovka 87 F4 Khersons'ka Oblast', S Ukraine
Kakhovs'ka Vodoskhovyshche 87 F4 *Rus.* Kakhovskoye Vodokhranilishche. *Reservoir* SE Ukraine
Kākināda 110 D1 *prev.* Cocanada. Andhra Pradesh, E India
Kaktovik 14 D2 Alaska, USA
Kalahari Desert 56 B4 *desert* Southern Africa
Kalamariá 82 B4 Kentrikí Makedonía, N Greece
Kalámata 83 B6 *prev.* Kalámai. Pelopónnisos, S Greece
Kalamazoo 18 C3 Michigan, N USA
Kalambaka *see* Kalampáka
Kálamos 83 C5 Attikí, C Greece
Kalampáka 82 B4 *var.* Kalambaka. Thessalía, C Greece
Kalanchak 87 F4 Khersons'ka Oblast', S Ukraine
Kalarash *see* Călăraşi
Kalasin 114 D4 *var.* Muang Kalasin. Kalasin, E Thailand
Kalāt 101 E5 *Per.* Qalāt. Zābul, S Afghanistan
Kālat 112 B2 *var.* Kelat, Khelat. Baluchistān, SW Pakistan
Kalbarri 125 A5 Western Australia
Kalecik 94 C3 Ankara, N Turkey
Kalemie 55 E6 *prev.* Albertville. Shaba, SE Dem. Rep. Congo (Zaire)
Kale Sultanie *see* Çanakkale
Kalgan *see* Zhangjiakou
Kalgoorlie 125 B6 Western Australia
Kalima 55 D6 Maniema, E Dem. Rep. Congo (Zaire)
Kalimantan 116 D4 *Eng.* Indonesian Borneo. *Geopolitical region* Borneo, C Indonesia
Kálimnos *see* Kálymnos
Kaliningrad *see* Kaliningradskaya Oblast'
Kaliningrad 84 A4 Kaliningradskaya Oblast', W Russian Federation
Kaliningradskaya Oblast' 84 B4 *var.* Kaliningrad. Admin. region *province and enclave* W Russian Federation
Kalinkavichy 85 C7 *Rus.* Kalinkovichi. Homyel'skaya Voblasts', SE Belarus
Kalispell 22 B1 Montana, NW USA
Kalisz 76 C4 *Ger.* Kalisch, *Rus.* Kalish; *anc.* Calisia. Wielkopolskie, C Poland
Kalix 62 D4 Norrbotten, N Sweden
Kalixälven 62 D3 *river* N Sweden
Kallaste 84 E3 *Ger.* Krasnogor. Tartumaa, SE Estonia
Kallavesi 63 E5 *lake* SE Finland
Kalloní 83 D5 Lésvos, E Greece
Kalmar 63 C7 *var.* Calmar. Kalmar, S Sweden
Kalmthout 65 C5 Antwerpen, N Belgium
Kalpáki 82 A4 Ípeiros, W Greece
Kalpeni Island 110 B3 *island* Lakshadweep, India, N Indian Ocean
Kaluga 89 B5 Kaluzhskaya Oblast', W Russian Federation
Kalush 86 C2 *Pol.* Kałusz. Ivano-Frankivs'ka Oblast', W Ukraine
Kalutara 110 D4 Western Province, SW Sri Lanka
Kalvarija 85 B5 *Pol.* Kalwaria. Marijampolė, S Lithuania
Kalyān 112 C5 Mahārāshtra, W India
Kálymnos 83 D6 *var.* Kálimnos. *Island* Dodekánisos, Greece, Aegean Sea
Kama 88 D4 *river* NW Russian Federation
Kamarang 37 F3 W Guyana
Kamchatka *see* Kamchatka, Poluostrov
Kamchatka, Poluostrov 93 G3 *Eng.* Kamchatka. *Peninsula* E Russian Federation
Kamensk-Shakhtinskiy 89 B6 Rostovskaya Oblast', SW Russian Federation
Kamina 55 D7 Shaba, S Dem. Rep. Congo (Zaire)
Kamishli *see* Al Qāmishlī
Kamloops 15 E5 British Columbia, SW Canada
Kammu Seamount 130 C2 *undersea feature* N Pacific Ocean
Kampala 51 B6 *country capital* (Uganda) S Uganda
Kâmpóng Cham 115 D6 *prev.* Kompong Cham. Kâmpóng Cham, C Cambodia
Kâmpóng Chhnăng 115 D6 *prev.* Kompong. Kâmpóng Chhnăng, C Cambodia
Kâmpóng Saôm 115 D6 *prev.* Kompong Som, Sihanoukville. Kâmpóng Saôm, SW Cambodia
Kâmpóng Spoe 115 D6 *prev.* Kompong Speu. Kâmpóng Spœ, S Cambodia
Kâmpôt 115 D6 Kâmpôt, SW Cambodia
Kam"yanets'-Podil's'kyy 86 C3 *Rus.* Kamenets-Podol'skiy. Khmel'nyts'ka Oblast', W Ukraine
Kam"yanka-Dniprovs'ka 87 F3 *Rus.* Kamenka Dneprovskaya. Zaporiz'ka Oblast', SE Ukraine
Kamyshin 89 B6 Volgogradskaya Oblast', SW Russian Federation
Kanaky *see* New Caledonia
Kananga 55 D6 *prev.* Luluabourg. Kasai Occidental, S Dem. Rep. Congo (Zaire)
Kananur *see* Cannanore
Kanara *see* Karnātaka
Kanash 89 C5 Chuvashskaya Respublika, W Russian Federation
Kanazawa 109 C5 Ishikawa, Honshu, SW Japan
Kanbe 114 B4 Yangon, SW Myanmar
Kānchīpuram 110 C2 *prev.* Conjeeveram. Tamil Nādu, SE India
Kandahār 101 E5 *Per.* Qandahār. Kandahār, S Afghanistan
Kandalakša *see* Kandalaksha
Kandalaksha 88 B2 *var.* Kandalakša, *Fin.* Kantalahti. Murmanskaya Oblast', NW Russian Federation
Kandangan 116 D4 Borneo, C Indonesia
Kandava 84 C3 *Ger.* Kandau. Tukums, W Latvia
Kandi 53 F4 N Benin
Kandy 110 D3 Central Province, C Sri Lanka
Kane Fracture Zone 44 B4 *tectonic feature* NW Atlantic Ocean
Kaneohe 25 A8 *Haw.* Kāne'ohe. Oahu, Hawaii, USA, C Pacific Ocean
Kangān 98 D4 Būshehr, S Iran
Kangaroo Island 127 A7 *island* South Australia
Kangertittivaq 61 E4 *Dan.* Scoresby Sund. *Fjord* E Greenland
Kangikajik 61 E4 *var.* Kap Brewster. *Headland* E Greenland
Kaniv 87 E2 *Rus.* Kanëv. Cherkas'ka Oblast', C Ukraine
Kanivs'ke Vodoskhovyshche 87 E2 *Rus.* Kanevskoye Vodokhranilishche. *Reservoir* C Ukraine
Kanjiža 78 D2 *Ger.* Altkanischa, *Hung.* Magyarkanizsa, Ókanizsa; *prev.* Stara Kanjiža. Serbia, N Yugoslavia
Kankaanpää 63 D5 Länsi-Suomi, W Finland
Kankakee 18 B3 Illinois, N USA
Kankan 52 D4 Haute-Guinée, E Guinea
Kannur *see* Cannanore
Kano 53 G4 Kano, N Nigeria
Kānpur 113 E3 *Eng.* Cawnpore. Uttar Pradesh, N India
Kansas 27 F1 *off.* State of Kansas; *also known as* Jayhawker State, Sunflower State. *State* C USA
Kansas 23 F5 Kansas, C USA
Kansas City 23 F4 Kansas, C USA
Kansas City 23 F4 Missouri, C USA
Kansas River 23 F5 *river* Kansas, C USA
Kansk 93 E4 Krasnoyarskiy Kray, S Russian Federation
Kansu *see* Gansu
Kantalahti *see* Kandalaksha
Kántanos 83 C7 Kríti, Greece, E Mediterranean Sea
Kantemirovka 89 B6 Voronezhskaya Oblast', W Russian Federation
Kanton 123 F3 *var.* Abariringa, Canton Island; *prev.* Mary Island. *Atoll* Phoenix Islands, C Kiribati
Kanye 56 C4 Southern, SE Botswana
Kaohsiung 106 D6 *var.* Gaoxiong, *Jap.* Takao, Takow. S Taiwan
Kaolack 52 B3 *var.* Kaolak. W Senegal
Kaolak *see* Kaolack
Kaolan *see* Lanzhou
Kaoma 56 C2 Western, W Zambia
Kap Brewster *see* Kangikajik
Kapelle 65 B5 Zeeland, SW Netherlands
Kapellen 65 C5 Antwerpen, N Belgium
Kap Farvel *see* Uummannarsuaq
Kapka, Massif du 54 C2 *mountain range* E Chad
Kaplangky, Plato 100 C2 *ridge* Turkmenistan/Uzbekistan
Kapoeta 51 C5 Eastern Equatoria, SE Sudan
Kaposvár 77 C7 Somogy, SW Hungary
Kappeln 72 B2 Schleswig-Holstein, N Germany
Kapstad *see* Cape Town
Kaptsevichy 85 C7 *Rus.* Koptsevichi. Homyel'skaya Voblasts', SE Belarus
Kapuas, Sungai 116 C4 *prev.* Kapoeas. *River* Borneo, C Indonesia
Kapuskasing 16 C4 Ontario, S Canada
Kapyl' 85 C6 *Rus.* Kopyl'. Minskaya Voblasts', C Belarus
Kap York *see* Innaanganeq
Kara-Balta 101 F2 Chuyskaya Oblast', N Kyrgyzstan
Karabil', Vozvyshennost' 100 D3 *mountain range* S Turkmenistan
Karabük 94 C2 Karabük NW Turkey
Karāchi 112 B3 Sind, SE Pakistan
Karadeniz *see* Black Sea
Karadeniz Boğazı *see* İstanbul Boğazı
Karaferiye *see* Véroia
Karaganda 92 C4 *Kaz.* Qaraghandy. Karaganda, C Kazakhstan
Karaginskiy, Ostrov 93 H2 *island* E Russian Federation
Karak *see* Al Karak
Kara-Kala 100 C3 *var.* Garrygala. Balkanskiy Velayat, W Turkmenistan
Karakax *see* Moyu
Karakılısse *see* Ağrı
Karakol 101 G2 *prev.* Przheval'sk. Issyk-Kul'skaya Oblast', NE Kyrgyzstan
Karakol 101 G2 *var.* Karakolka. Issyk-Kul'skaya Oblast', NE Kyrgyzstan
Karakolka *see* Karakol

Kitwe – Kuruktag

Kitwe *56 D2 var.* Kitwe-Nkana. Copperbelt, C Zambia
Kitwe-Nkana *see* Kitwe
Kitzbühler Alpen *73 C7 mountain range* W Austria
Kivalina *14 C2* Alaska, USA
Kivalo *62 D3 ridge* C Finland
Kivertsi *86 C1 Pol.* Kiwerce, *Rus.* Kivertsy. Volyns'ka Oblast', NW Ukraine
Kivu, Lake *55 E6 Fr.* Lac Kivu. *Lake* Rwanda/Dem. Rep. Congo (Zaire)
Kızıl Irmak *94 C3 river* C Turkey
Kizil Kum *see* Kyzyl Kum
Kladno *77 A5* Středočesky Kraj, NW Czech Republic
Klagenfurt *73 D7 Slvn.* Celovec. Kärnten, S Austria
Klaipėda *84 B3 Ger.* Memel. Klaipėda, NW Lithuania
Klamath Falls *24 B4* Oregon, NW USA
Klamath Mountains *24 A4 mountain range* California/Oregon, W USA
Klang *116 B3 var.* Kelang; *prev.* Port Swettenham. Selangor, Peninsular Malaysia
Klarälven *63 B6 river* Norway/Sweden
Klatovy *77 A5 Ger.* Klattau. Plzeňský Kraj, W Czech Republic
Klazienaveen *64 E2* Drenthe, NE Netherlands
Klein Karas *56 B4* Karas, S Namibia
Kleisoúra *83 A5* Ípeiros, W Greece
Klerksdorp *56 D4* North-West, N South Africa
Klimavichy *85 E7 Rus.* Klimovichi. Mahilyowskaya Voblasts', E Belarus
Klintsy *89 A5* Bryanskaya Oblast', W Russian Federation
Klisura *82 C2* Plovdiv, C Bulgaria
Ključ *78 B3* Federacija Bosna I Hercegovina, NW Bosnia and Herzegovina
Kłobuck *76 C4* Śląskie, S Poland
Klosters *73 B7* Graubünden, SE Switzerland
Kluang *see* Keluang
Kluczbork *76 C4 Ger.* Kreuzburg, Kreuzburg in Oberschlesien. Opolskie, S Poland
Klyuchevskaya Sopka, Vulkan *93 H3 volcano* E Russian Federation
Knin *78 B4* Šibenik Knin, S Croatia
Knjaževac *78 E4* Serbia, E Yugoslavia
Knokke-Heist *65 A5* West-Vlaanderen, NW Belgium
Knoxville *20 D1* Tennessee, S USA
Knud Rasmussen Land *60 D1 physical region* N Greenland
Kōbe *109 C6* Hyōgo, Honshū, SW Japan
København *63 B7 Eng.* Copenhagen; *anc.* Hafnia. *Country capital* (Denmark) Sjælland, København, E Denmark
Kobenni *52 D3* Hodh el Gharbi, S Mauritania
Koblenz *73 A5 prev.* Coblenz, *Fr.* Coblence, *anc.* Confluentes. Rheinland-Pfalz, W Germany
Kobryn *85 A6 Pol.* Kobryn, *Rus.* Kobrin. Brestskaya Voblasts', SW Belarus
K'obulet'i *95 F2* W Georgia
Kočani *79 E6* NE FYR Macedonia
Kočevje *73 D8 Ger.* Gottschee. S Slovenia
Koch Bihār *113 G3* West Bengal, NE India
Kōchi *109 B7 var.* Kôti. Kōchi, Shikoku, SW Japan
Kochi *see* Cochin
Kochiu *see* Gejiu
Kodiak *14 C3* Kodiak Island, Alaska, USA
Kodiak Island *14 C3 island* Alaska, USA
Koeln *see* Köln
Ko-erh-mu *see* Golmud
Koetai *see* Mahakam, Sungai
Koetaradja *see* Bandaaceh
Kōfu *109 D5 var.* Kôhu. Yamanashi, Honshū, S Japan
Kogarah *126 E2* New South Wales, SE Australia
Kogon *100 D2 Rus.* Kagan. Bukhoro Wiloyati, C Uzbekistan
Kohīma *113 H3* Nāgāland, E India
Koh I Noh *see* Büyükağrı Dağı
Kohtla-Järve *84 E2* Ida-Virumaa, NE Estonia
Kôhu *see* Kōfu
Kokand *see* Qŭqon
Kokkola *62 D4 Swe.* Karleby; *prev. Swe.* Gamlakarleby. Länsi-Suomi, W Finland
Koko *see* Qinghai Hu
Koko *53 F4* Kebbi, W Nigeria
Kokomo *18 C4* Indiana, N USA
Koko Nor *see* Qinghai
Kokrines *14 C2* Alaska, USA
Kokshaal-Tau *101 G2 Rus.* Khrebet Kakshaal-Too. *Mountain range* China/Kyrgyzstan
Kokshetau *92 C4 Kaz.* Kökshetaū; *prev.* Kokchetav. Severnyy Kazakhstan, N Kazakhstan
Koksijde *65 A5* West-Vlaanderen, W Belgium
Koksoak *16 D2 river* Québec, E Canada
Kokstad *56 D5* KwaZulu/Natal, E South Africa
Kola *see* Kol'skiy Poluostrov
Kolaka *117 E4* Sulawesi, C Indonesia
Kolam *see* Quilon
K'o-la-ma-i *see* Karamay
Kola Peninsula *see* Kol'skiy Poluostrov
Kolari *62 D3* Lappi, NW Finland
Kolárovo *77 C6 Ger.* Gutta; *prev.* Guta, *Hung.* Gúta. Nitriansky Kraj, SW Slovakia
Kolda *52 C3* S Senegal
Kolding *63 A7* Vejle, C Denmark
Kölen *59 E1 Nor.* Kjølen. *Mountain range* Norway/Sweden
Kolguyev, Ostrov *88 C2 island* NW Russian Federation
Kolhāpur *110 B1* Mahārāshtra, SW India
Kolhumadulu Atoll *110 A5 var.* Kolumadulu Atoll, Thaa Atoll. *Atoll* S Maldives
Kolín *77 B5 Ger.* Kolin. Středočesky Kraj, C Czech Republic
Kolka *84 C2* Talsi, NW Latvia
Kolkasrags *84 C2 prev. Eng.* Cape Domesnes. *Headland* NW Latvia
Kollam *see* Quilon
Köln *72 A4 var.* Koeln, *Eng./Fr.* Cologne; *prev.* Cöln, *anc.* Colonia Agrippina, Oppidum Ubiorum. Nordrhein-Westfalen, W Germany
Koło *76 C3* Wielkopolskie, C Poland
Kołobrzeg *76 B2 Ger.* Kolberg. Zachodniopomorskie, NW Poland
Kolokani *52 D3* Koulikoro, W Mali
Kolomna *89 B5* Moskovskaya Oblast', W Russian Federation
Kolomyya *86 C3 Ger.* Kolomea. Ivano-Frankivs'ka Oblast', W Ukraine
Kolpa *78 A2 Ger.* Kulpa, *SCr.* Kupa. *River* Croatia/Slovenia
Kolpino *88 B4* Leningradskaya Oblast', NW Russian Federation
Kólpos Ammóchostos *80 C5 var.* Famagusta Bay, *bay* E Cyprus
Kol'skiy Poluostrov *88 C2 Eng.* Kola Peninsula. *Peninsula* NW Russian Federation
Kolumadulu Atoll *see* Kolhumadulu Atoll
Kolwezi *55 D7* Shaba, S Dem. Rep. Congo (Zaire)
Kolyma *93 G2 river* NE Russian Federation
Kolyma Range *91 G2 var.* Khrebet Kolymskiy, *Eng.* Kolyma Range. *Mountain range* E Russian Federation
Komatsu *109 C5 var.* Komatu. Ishikawa, Honshū, SW Japan
Komatu *see* Komatsu
Kommunizma Pik *see* Kommunizm, Qullai
Kommunizm, Qullai *101 F3 var.* Qullai Garmo, *Eng.* Communism Peak, *Rus.* Kommunizma Pik; *prev.* Stalin Peak. *Mountain* E Tajikistan
Komoé *53 E4 var.* Komoé Fleuve. *River* E Côte d'Ivoire
Komoé Fleuve *see* Komoé
Komotiní *82 D3 var.* Gümüljina, *Turk.* Gümülcine. Anatolikí Makedonía kai Thráki, NE Greece
Komsomolets, Ostrov *93 E1 island* Severnaya Zemlya, N Russian Federation
Komsomol'sk-na-Amure *93 G4* Khabarovskiy Kray, SE Russian Federation
Kondolovo *82 E3* Burgas, E Bulgaria
Kondopoga *88 B3* Respublika Kareliya, NW Russian Federation
Kondoz *see* Kunduz
Kondūz *see* Kunduz
Kong Christian IX Land *60 D4 Eng.* King Christian IX Land. *Physical region* SE Greenland
Kong Frederik IX Land *60 C3 Eng.* King Frederik IX Land. *Physical region* SW Greenland
Kong Frederik VIII Land *61 E2 Eng.* King Frederik VIII Land. *Physical region* NE Greenland
Kong Frederik VI Kyst *60 C4 Eng.* King Frederik VI Coast. *Physical region* SE Greenland
Kong Karls Land *61 G2 Eng.* King Charles Islands. *Island group* SE Svalbard
Kongo *see* Congo
Kongolo *55 D6* Shaba, E Dem. Rep. Congo (Zaire)
Kongor *51 B5* Jonglei, SE Sudan
Kong Oscar Fjord *61 E3 fjord* E Greenland
Kongsberg *63 B6* Buskerud, S Norway
Kông, Tônle *115 E5 Lao.* Xê Kong. *River* Cambodia/Laos
Konia *see* Konya
Konieh *see* Konya
Konin *76 C3 Ger.* Kuhnau. Wielkopolskie, C Poland
Konispol *79 C7 var.* Konispoli. Vlorë, S Albania
Konispoli *see* Konispol
Kónitsa *82 A4* Ípeiros, W Greece
Konitz *see* Chojnice
Konjic *78 C4* Federacija Bosna I Hercegovina, S Bosnia and Herzegovina
Konosha *88 C4* Arkhangel'skaya Oblast', NW Russian Federation
Konotop *87 F1* Sums'ka Oblast', NE Ukraine
Konstanz *73 B7 var.* Constanz, *Eng.* Constance; *hist.* Kostnitz, *anc.* Constantia. Baden-Württemberg, S Germany
Konstanza *see* Constanța
Konya *94 C4 var.* Konieh; *prev.* Konia, *anc.* Iconium. Konya, C Turkey
Kopaonik *79 D5 mountain range* S Yugoslavia
Koper *73 D8 It.* Capodistria; *prev.* Kopar. SW Slovenia
Kopetdag Gershi *100 C3 mountain range* Iran/Turkmenistan
Koppeh Dāgh *98 D2 var.* Khrebet Kopetdag. *Mountain range* Iran/Turkmenistan
Koprivnica *78 B2 Ger.* Kopreinitz, *Hung.* Kaproncza. Koprivnica-Križevci, N Croatia
Korat *see* Nakhon Ratchasima
Korat Plateau *114 D4 plateau* E Thailand
Korba *113 E4* Madhya Pradesh, C India
Korça *see* Korçë
Korçë *79 D6 var.* Korça, *Gk.* Korytsa, *It.* Corriza; *prev.* Koritsa. Korçë, SE Albania
Korčula *78 B4 It.* Curzola; *anc.* Corcyra Nigra. *Island* S Croatia
Korea Bay *105 G3 bay* China/North Korea
Korea Strait *109 A7 Jap.* Chōsen-kaikyō, *Kor.* Taehan-haehyŏp. *Channel* Japan/South Korea
Korhogo *52 D4* N Côte d'Ivoire
Korinthiakós Kólpos *83 B5 Eng.* Gulf of Corinth; *anc.* Corinthiacus Sinus. *Gulf* C Greece
Kórinthos *83 B6 Eng.* Corinth; *anc.* Corinthus. Pelopónnisos, S Greece
Koritsa *see* Korçë
Kōriyama *109 D5* Fukushima, Honshū, C Japan
Korla *104 C3 Chin.* K'u-erh-lo. Xinjiang Uygur Zizhiqu, NW China
Körmend *77 B7* Vas, W Hungary
Koróni *83 B6* Pelopónnisos, S Greece
Koror *see* Oreor
Korosten' *86 D1* Zhytomyrs'ka Oblast', NW Ukraine
Koro Toro *54 C2* Borkou-Ennedi-Tibesti, N Chad
Kortrijk *65 A6 Fr.* Courtrai. West-Vlaanderen, W Belgium
Koryak Range *see* Koryakskoye Nagor'ye
Koryakskiy Khrebet *see* Koryakskoye Nagor'ye
Koryakskoye Nagor'ye *93 H2 var.* Koryakskiy Khrebet, *Eng.* Koryak Range. *Mountain range* NE Russian Federation
Koryazhma *88 C4* Arkhangel'skaya Oblast', NW Russian Federation
Korytsa *see* Korçë
Kos *83 E6 It.* Coo; *anc.* Cos. *Island* Dodekánisos, Greece, Aegean Sea
Kos *83 E6* Kos, Dodekánisos, Greece, Aegean Sea
Kō-saki *109 A7 headland* Nagasaki, Tsushima, SW Japan
Kościan *76 B4 Ger.* Kosten. Wielkopolskie, C Poland
Koscian *see* Lubań
Kościerzyna *76 C2* Pomorskie, NW Poland
Kosciusko, Mount *see* Kosciuszko, Mount
Kosciuszko, Mount *127 C7 prev.* Mount Kosciusko. *Mountain* New South Wales, SE Australia
Koshikijima-rettō *109 A8 var.* Kosikizima Rettô. *Island group* SW Japan
Košice *77 D6 Ger.* Kaschau, *Hung.* Kassa. Košický Kraj, E Slovakia
Kosikizima Rettô *see* Koshikijima-rettō
Koson *101 E3 Rus.* Kasan. Qashqadaryo Wiloyati, S Uzbekistan
Kosovo *79 D5 prev.* Autonomous Province of Kosovo and Metohija. *Region* S Yugoslavia
Kosovo Polje *79 D5* Serbia, S Yugoslavia
Kosovska Mitrovica *79 D5 Alb.* Mitrovicë; *prev.* Mitrovica, Titova Mitrovica. Serbia, S Yugoslavia
Kosrae *122 C2 prev.* Kusaie. *Island* Caroline Islands, E Micronesia
Kossou, Lac de *52 D5 lake* C Côte d'Ivoire
Kostanay *130 C1 var.* Kustanay, *Kaz.* Qostanay. Kostanay, N Kazakhstan
Kosten *see* Lubań
Kostenets *82 C2 prev.* Georgi Dimitrov. Sofiya, W Bulgaria
Kostnitz *see* Konstanz
Kostroma *88 B4* Kostromskaya Oblast', NW Russian Federation
Kostyantynivka *87 G3 Rus.* Konstantinovka. Donets'ka Oblast', SE Ukraine
Koszalin *76 B2 Ger.* Köslin. Zachodniopomorskie, NW Poland
Kota *112 D3 prev.* Kotah. Rājasthān, N India
Kota Baharu *see* Kota Bharu
Kota Bahru *see* Kota Bharu
Kotabaru *see* Jayapura
Kota Bharu *116 B3 var.* Kota Baharu, Kota Bahru. Kelantan, Peninsular Malaysia
Kotabumi *116 B4 prev.* Kotaboemi. Sumatera, W Indonesia
Kota Kinabalu *116 D3 prev.* Jesselton. Sabah, East Malaysia
Kotel'nyy, Ostrov *93 E2 island* Novosibirskiye Ostrova, N Russian Federation
Kôti *see* Kōchi
Kotka *63 E5* Kymi, S Finland
Kotlas *88 C4* Arkhangel'skaya Oblast', NW Russian Federation
Kotonu *see* Cotonou
Kotor *79 C5 It.* Cattaro. Montenegro, SW Yugoslavia
Kotovs'k *86 D3 Rus.* Kotovsk. Odes'ka Oblast', SW Ukraine
Kotovsk *see* Hîncești
Kotte *see* Sri Jayawardanapura
Kotto *54 D4 river* Central African Republic/Dem. Rep. Congo (Zaire)
Kotuy *93 E2 river* N Russian Federation
Koudougou *53 E4* C Burkina faso
Koulamoutou *55 B6* Ogooué-Lolo, C Gabon
Koulikoro *52 D3* Koulikoro, SW Mali
Koumra *54 C4* Moyen-Chari, S Chad
Kourou *37 H3* N French Guiana
Kousseir *see* Al Quşayr
Kousséri *54 B3 prev.* Fort-Foureau. Extrême-Nord, NE Cameroon
Koutiala *52 D4* Sikasso, S Mali
Kouvola *63 E5* Kymi, S Finland
Kovel' *86 C1 Pol.* Kowel. Volyns'ka Oblast', NW Ukraine
Kowloon *106 A2 Chin.* Jiulong. Hong Kong, S China
Kowtal-e Barowghīl *see* Baroghil Pass
Kowtal-e Khaybar *see* Khyber Pass
Kozáni *82 B4* Dytikí Makedonía, N Greece
Kozara *78 B3 mountain range* NW Bosnia and Herzegovina
Kozarska Dubica *see* Bosanska Dubica
Kozhikode *see* Calicut
Kōzu-shima *109 D6 island* E Japan
Kozyatyn *86 D2 Rus.* Kazatin. Vinnyts'ka Oblast', C Ukraine
Kpalimé *53 E5 var.* Palimé. SW Togo
Krâchéh *115 D6 prev.* Kratie. Krâchéh, E Cambodia
Kragujevac *78 D4* Serbia, C Yugoslavia
Kra, Isthmus of *115 B6 isthmus* Malaysia/Thailand
Kraków *77 D5 Eng.* Cracow, *Ger.* Krakau; *anc.* Cracovia. Małopolskie, S Poland
Krâlănh *115 D5* Siĕmréab, NW Cambodia
Kraljevo *78 D4 prev.* Rankovićevo. Serbia, C Yugoslavia
Kramators'k *87 G3 Rus.* Kramatorsk. Donets'ka Oblast', SE Ukraine
Kramfors *63 C5* Västernorrland, C Sweden
Kranéa *82 B4* Dytikí Makedonía, N Greece
Kranj *73 D7 Ger.* Krainburg. NW Slovenia
Krāslava *84 D4* Krāslava, SE Latvia
Krasnaye *85 C5 Rus.* Krasnoye. Minskaya Voblasts', C Belarus
Krasnoarmeysk *89 C6* Saratovskaya Oblast', W Russian Federation
Krasnodar *89 A7 prev.* Ekaterinodar, Yekaterinodar. Krasnodarskiy Kray, SW Russian Federation
Krasnodon *87 H3* Luhans'ka Oblast', E Ukraine
Krasnohvardiys'ke *87 F4 Rus.* Krasnogvardeyskoye. Respublika Krym, S Ukraine
Krasnokamensk *93 F4* Chitinskaya Oblast', S Russian Federation
Krasnokamsk *89 D5* Permskaya Oblast', W Russian Federation
Krasnoperekops'k *87 F4 Rus.* Krasnoperekopsk. Respublika Krym, S Ukraine
Krasnovodskiy Zaliv *100 A2 Turkm.* Krasnowodsk Aylagy. *Lake gulf* W Turkmenistan
Krasnoyarsk *92 D4* Krasnoyarskiy Kray, S Russian Federation
Krasnystaw *76 E4 Rus.* Krasnostav. Lubelskie, E Poland
Krasnyy Kut *89 C6* Saratovskaya Oblast', W Russian Federation
Krasnyy Luch *87 H3 prev.* Krindachevka. Luhans'ka Oblast', E Ukraine
Krâvanh, Chuŏr Phnum *115 C6 Eng.* Cardamom Mountains, *Fr.* Chaîne des Cardamomes. *Mountain range* W Cambodia
Krefeld *72 A4* Nordrhein-Westfalen, W Germany
Kremenchuk *87 F2 Rus.* Kremenchug. Poltavs'ka Oblast', NE Ukraine
Kremenchuts'ke Vodoskhovyshche *87 F2 Eng.* Kremenchuk Reservoir, *Rus.* Kremenchugskoye Vodokhranilishche. *Reservoir* C Ukraine
Kremenets' *86 C2 Pol.* Krzemieniec, *Rus.* Kremenets. Ternopil's'ka Oblast', W Ukraine
Kreminna *87 G2 Rus.* Kremennaya. Luhans'ka Oblast', E Ukraine
Kresena *see* Kresna
Kresna *82 C3 var.* Kresena. Blagoevgrad, SW Bulgaria
Kretikon Delagos *see* Kritikó Pélagos
Kretinga *84 B3 Ger.* Krottingen. Kretinga, NW Lithuania
Krishna *110 C1 prev.* Kistna. *River* C India
Krishnagiri *110 C2* Tamil Nādu, SE India
Kristiansand *63 A6 var.* Christiansand. Vest-Agder, S Norway
Kristianstad *63 B7* Skåne, S Sweden
Kristiansund *62 A4 var.* Christiansund. Møre og Romsdal, S Norway
Kríti *83 C7 Eng.* Crete. *Island* Greece, Aegean Sea
Kritikó Pélagos *83 D7 var.* Kretikon Delagos, *Eng.* Sea of Crete; *anc.* Mare Creticum. *Sea* Greece, Aegean Sea
Križevci *78 B2 Ger.* Kreuz, *Hung.* Kőrös. Varaždin, NE Croatia
Krk *78 A3 It.* Veglia; *anc.* Curieta. *Island* NW Croatia
Krolevets' *87 F1 Rus.* Krolevets. Sums'ka Oblast', NE Ukraine
Kronach *73 C5* Bayern, E Germany
Kroonstad *56 D4* Free State, C South Africa
Kropotkin *89 A7* Krasnodarskiy Kray, SW Russian Federation
Krosno *77 D5 Ger.* Krossen. Podkarpackie, SE Poland
Krosno Odrzańskie *76 B3 Ger.* Crossen, Kreisstadt. Lubuskie, W Poland
Krško *73 E8 Ger.* Gurkfeld; *prev.* Videm-Krško. E Slovenia
Kruhlaye *85 D6 Rus.* Krugloye. Mahilyowskaya Voblasts', E Belarus
Kruja *see* Krujë
Krujë *79 C6 var.* Kruja, *It.* Croia. Durrës, C Albania
Krummau *see* Český Krumlov
Krung Thep *115 C5 var.* Krung Thep Mahanakhon, *Eng.* Bangkok. *Country capital* (Thailand) Bangkok, C Thailand
Krung Thep, Ao *115 C5 var.* Bight of Bangkok. *Bay* S Thailand
Krung Thep Mahanakhon *see* Krung Thep
Krupki *85 D6 Rus.* Krupki. Minskaya Voblasts', C Belarus
Krychaw *85 E7 Rus.* Krichëv. Mahilyowskaya Voblasts', E Belarus
Krym *see* Crimea
Krymskaya Oblast' *see* Crimea
Kryms'ki Hory *87 F5 mountain range* S Ukraine
Kryms'kyy Pivostriv *87 F5 peninsula* S Ukraine
Krynica *77 D5 Ger.* Tannenhof. Małopolskie, S Poland
Kryve Ozero *87 E3* Odes'ka Oblast', SW Ukraine
Kryvyy Rih *87 F3 Rus.* Krivoy Rog. Dnipropetrovs'ka Oblast', SE Ukraine
Ksar al Kabir *see* Ksar-el-Kebir
Ksar al Soule *see* Er-Rachidia
Ksar-el-Kebir *48 C2 var.* Alcázar, Ksar al Kabir, Ksar-el-Kébir, *Ar.* Al-Kasr al-Kebir, Al-Qsar al-Kbir, *Sp.* Alcazarquivir. NW Morocco
Ksar-el-Kébir *see* Ksar-el-Kebir
Kuala Dungun *see* Dungun
Kuala Lumpur *116 B3 country capital* (Malaysia) Kuala Lumpur, Peninsular Malaysia
Kuala Terengganu *116 B3 var.* Kuala Trengganu. Terengganu, Peninsular Malaysia
Kuala Trengganu *see* Kuala Terengganu
Kualatungkal *116 B4* Sumatera, W Indonesia
Kuang-chou *see* Guangzhou
Kuang-hsi *see* Guangxi Zhuangzu Zizhiqu
Kuang-tung *see* Guangdong
Kuang-yuan *see* Guangyuan
Kuantan *116 B3* Pahang, Peninsular Malaysia
Kuban' *87 G5 var.* Hypanis. *River* SW Russian Federation
Kubango *see* Cubango
Kuching *116 C3 prev.* Sarawak. Sarawak, East Malaysia
Kuchnay Darweyshan *100 D5* Helmand, S Afghanistan
Kuçova *see* Kuçovë
Kuçovë *79 C6 var.* Kuçova; *prev.* Qyteti Stalin. Berat, C Albania
Kudara *see* Ghŭdara
Kudus *116 C5 prev.* Koedoes. Jawa, C Indonesia
Kuei-chou *see* Guizhou
Kuei-lin *see* Guilin
Kuei-Yang *see* Guiyang
Kueyang *see* Guiyang
Kugluktuk 53 E3 *var.* Qurlurtuuq *prev.* Coppermine. Nunavut, NW Canada
Kuhmo *62 E4* Oulu, E Finland
Kühnö *see* Kihnu
Kuibyshev *see* Kuybyshevskoye Vodokhranilishche
Kuito *56 B2 Port.* Silva Porto. Bié, C Angola
Kuji *108 D3 var.* Kuzi. Iwate, Honshū, C Japan
Kukës *79 D5 var.* Kukësi. Kukës, NE Albania
Kukësi *see* Kukës
Kukong *see* Shaoguan
Kukukhoto *see* Hohhot
Kula Kangri *113 G3 var.* Kulhakangri. *Mountain* Bhutan/China
Kuldīga *84 B3 Ger.* Goldingen. Kuldīga, W Latvia
Kuldja *see* Yining
Kulhakangri *see* Kula Kangri
Kullorsuaq *60 D2 var.* Kuvdlorssuak. C Greenland
Kulmsee *see* Chełmża
Külob *101 F3 Rus.* Kulyab. SW Tajikistan
Kulu *94 C3* Konya, W Turkey
Kulunda Steppe *92 C4 Kaz.* Qulyndy Zhazyghy, *Rus.* Kulundinskaya Ravnina. *Grassland* Kazakhstan/Russian Federation
Kum *see* Qom
Kuma *89 B7 river* SW Russian Federation
Kumamoto *109 A7* Kumamoto, Kyūshū, SW Japan
Kumanovo *79 E5 Turk.* Kumanova. N FYR Macedonia
Kumasi *53 E5 prev.* Coomassie. C Ghana
Kumayri *see* Gyumri
Kumba *55 A5* Sud-Ouest, W Cameroon
Kumertau *89 D6* Respublika Bashkortostan, W Russian Federation
Kumo *53 G4* Gombe, E Nigeria
Kumon Range *114 B2 mountain range* N Myanmar
Kumul *see* Hami
Kunashiri *see* Kunashir, Ostrov
Kunashir, Ostrov *108 E1 var.* Kunashiri. *Island* Kuril'skiye Ostrova, SE Russian Federation
Kunda *84 E2* Lääne-Virumaa, NE Estonia
Kunduz *101 E3 var.* Kondoz, Kundūz, Qondūz, *Per.* Kondūz. Kunduz, NE Afghanistan
Kuneitra *see* Al Qunayṭirah
Kunene *see* Cunene
Kungsbacka *63 B7* Halland, S Sweden
Kungur *89 D5* Permskaya Oblast', NW Russian Federation
Kunlun Mountains *see* Kunlun Shan
Kunlun Shan *104 B4 Eng.* Kunlun Mountains. *Mountain range* NW China
Kunming *106 B6 var.* K'un-ming; *prev.* Yunnan. Yunnan, SW China
K'un-ming *see* Kunming
Kununurra *124 D3* Western Australia
Kuopio *63 E5* Itä-Suomi, C Finland
Kupang *117 E5 prev.* Koepang. Timor, C Indonesia
Kup"yans'k *87 G2 Rus.* Kupyansk. Kharkivs'ka Oblast', E Ukraine
Kura *95 H3 Az.* Kür, *Geor.* Mtkvari, *Turk.* Kura Nehri. *River* SW Asia
Kurashiki *109 B6 var.* Kurasiki. Okayama, Honshū, SW Japan
Kurasiki *see* Kurashiki
Kurdistan *95 F4 cultural region* SW Asia
Kŭrdzhali *82 D3 var.* Kirdzhali. Kŭrdzhali, S Bulgaria
Kure *109 B7* Hiroshima, Honshū, SW Japan
Küre Dağları *94 C2 mountain range* N Turkey
Kuressaare *84 C2 Ger.* Arensburg; *prev.* Kingissepp. Saaremaa, W Estonia
Kureyka *90 D2 river* N Russian Federation
Kuria Muria Islands *see* Ḩalāniyāt, Juzur al
Kurile Islands *see* Kuril'skiye Ostrova
Kurile-Kamchatka Depression *see* Kurile Trench
Kurile Trench *91 F3 var.* Kurile-Kamchatka Depression. *Undersea feature* NW Pacific Ocean
Kuril'sk *108 E1* Kuril'skiye Ostrova, Sakhalinskaya Oblats', SE Russian Federation
Kuril'skiye Ostrova *93 H4 Eng.* Kurile Islands. *Island group* SE Russian Federation
Ku-ring-gai *126 E1* New South Wales, SE Australia
Kurnool *110 C1 var.* Karnul. Andhra Pradesh, S India
Kursk *89 A6* Kurskaya Oblast', W Russian Federation
Kuršumlija *79 D5* Serbia, S Yugoslavia
Kuruktag *104 C3 mountain range* NW China

L'Hospitalet de Llobregat – Maceió

L'Hospitalet de Llobregat 71 G2 var. Hospitalet. Cataluña, NE Spain
Liancourt Rocks 109 A5 Jap. Take-shima, Kor. Tok-Do. Island group Japan/South Korea
Lianyungang 106 D4 var. Xinpu. Jiangsu, E China
Liao see Liaoning
Liaodong Wan 105 G3 Eng. Gulf of Lantung, Gulf of Liaotung. Gulf NE China
Liao He 103 E1 river NE China
Liaoning 106 D3 var. Liao, Liaoning Sheng, Shengking; hist. Fengtien, Shenking. Admin. region province NE China
Liaoyuan 107 E3 var. Dongliao, Shuang-liao, Jap. Chengchiatun. Jilin, NE China
Liard see Fort Liard
Liban, Jebel 96 B4 Ar. Jabal al Gharbt, Jabal Lubnān, Eng. Mount Lebanon. Mountain range C Lebanon
Libby 22 A1 Montana, NW USA
Liberal 23 E5 Kansas, C USA
Liberec 76 B4 Ger. Reichenberg. Liberecký Kraj, N Czech Republic
Liberia 52 C5 off. Republic of Liberia. Country W Africa
Liberia 30 D4 Guanacaste, NW Costa Rica
Libian Desert see Libyan Desert
Libourne 69 B5 Gironde, SW France
Libreville 55 A5 country capital (Gabon) Estuaire, NW Gabon
Libya 49 F3 off. Socialist People's Libyan Arab Jamahiriya, Ar. Al Jamāhīrīyah al 'Arabīyah al Lībīyah ash Sha'bīyah al Ishtirākīyah; prev. Libyan Arab Republic. Country N Africa
Libyan Desert 49 H4 var. Libian Desert, Ar. Aş Şahrā' al Lībīyah. Desert N Africa
Libyan Plateau 81 F4 var. Aḍ Ḍiffah. Plateau Egypt/Libya
Lichtenfels 73 C5 Bayern, SE Germany
Lichtenvoorde 64 E4 Gelderland, E Netherlands
Lichuan 106 C5 Hubei, C China
Lida 85 B5 Rus. Lida. Hrodzyenskaya Voblasts', W Belarus
Lidköping 63 B6 Västra Götaland, S Sweden
Lidorïki 83 B5 prev. Lidhorikíon, Lidokhorikion. Stereá Ellás, C Greece
Lidzbark Warmiński 76 D2 Ger. Heilsberg. Warmińsko-Mazurskie, NE Poland
Liechtenstein 72 D1 off. Principality of Liechtenstein. Country C Europe
Liège 65 D6 Dut. Luik, Ger. Lüttich. Liège, E Belgium
Lienz 73 D7 Tirol, W Austria
Liepāja 84 B3 Ger. Libau. Liepaja, W Latvia
Liezen 73 D7 Steiermark, C Austria
Liffey 67 B6 river E Ireland
Lifou 122 D5 island Îles Loyauté, E New Caledonia
Liger see Loire
Ligure, Appennino 74 A2 Eng. Ligurian Mountains. Mountain range NW Italy
Ligurian Sea 74 A3 Fr. Mer Ligurienne, It. Mar Ligure. Sea N Mediterranean Sea
Lihue 25 A7 Haw. Līhu'e. Kauai, Hawaii, USA, C Pacific Ocean
Lihula 84 D2 Ger. Leal. Läänemaa, W Estonia
Likasi 55 D7 prev. Jadotville. Shaba, SE Dem. Rep. Congo (Zaire)
Liknes 63 A6 Vest-Agder, S Norway
Lille 68 C2 var. l'Isle, Dut. Rijssel, Flem. Ryssel, prev. Lisle, anc. Insula. Nord, N France
Lillehammer 63 B5 Oppland, S Norway
Lillestrøm 63 B6 Akershus, S Norway
Lilongwe 57 E2 country capital (Malawi) Central, W Malawi
Lima 38 C4 country capital (Peru) Lima, W Peru
Limanowa 77 D5 Małopolskie, S Poland
Limassol see Lemesós
Limerick 67 A6 Ir. Luimneach. SW Ireland
Límnos 81 F3 anc. Lemnos. Island E Greece
Limoges 69 C5 anc. Augustoritum Lemovicensium, Lemovices. Haute-Vienne, C France
Limón 31 E4 var. Puerto Limón. Limón, E Costa Rica
Limón 30 D2 Colón, NE Honduras
Limousin 69 C5 cultural region C France
Limoux 69 C6 Aude, S France
Limpopo 56 D3 var. Crocodile. River S Africa
Linares 70 D4 Andalucía, S Spain
Linares 42 B4 Maule, C Chile
Linares 29 E3 Nuevo León, NE Mexico
Linchuan 106 D5 var. Fuzhou. Jiangxi, S China
Lincoln 67 D5 anc. Lindum, Lindum Colonia. E England, UK
Lincoln 23 F4 state capital Nebraska, C USA
Lincoln 19 H2 Maine, NE USA
Lincoln Sea 12 D2 sea Arctic Ocean
Linden 37 F3 E Guyana
Líndhos see Líndos
Lindi 51 D8 Lindi, SE Tanzania
Líndos 83 E7 var. Líndhos. Ródos, Dodekánisos, Greece, Aegean Sea
Line Islands 123 G3 island group E Kiribati
Lingeh see Bandar-e Langeh
Lingen 72 A3 var. Lingen an der Ems. Niedersachsen, NW Germany
Lingen an der Ems see Lingen
Lingga, Kepulauan 116 B4 island group W Indonesia
Linköping 63 C6 Östergötland, S Sweden
Linz 73 D6 anc. Lentia. Oberösterreich, N Austria
Lion, Golfe du 69 C7 Eng. Gulf of Lion, Gulf of Lions; anc. Sinus Gallicus. Gulf S France
Lipari Islands see Eolie, Isole
Lipari, Isola 75 D6 island Isole Eolie, S Italy
Lipetsk 89 B5 Lipetskaya Oblast', W Russian Federation
Lipno 76 C3 Kujawsko-pomorskie, C Poland
Lipova 86 A4 Hung. Lippa. Arad, W Romania
Liqeni i Ohrit see Ohrid, Lake
Lira 51 B6 N Uganda
Lisala 55 C5 Equateur, N Dem. Rep. Congo (Zaire)
Lisboa 70 B4 Eng. Lisbon; anc. Felicitas Julia, Olisipo. Country capital (Portugal) Lisboa, W Portugal
Lisbon see Lisboa
Lisieux 68 B3 anc. Noviomagus. Calvados, N France
Liski 89 B6 prev. Georgiu-Dezh. Voronezhskaya Oblast', W Russian Federation
Lisle see Lille
l'Isle see Lille
Lismore 127 E5 Victoria, SE Australia
Lisse 64 C3 Zuid-Holland, W Netherlands
Litang 106 A5 Sichuan, C China
Līṭāni, Nahr el 135 B5 var. Nahr al Litant. River C Lebanon
Lithgow 127 D6 New South Wales, SE Australia
Lithuania 84 B4 off. Republic of Lithuania, Ger. Litauen, Lith. Lietuva, Pol. Litwa, Rus. Litva; prev. Lithuanian SSR, Rus. Litovskaya SSR. Country NE Europe
Litóchoro 82 B4 var. Litohoro, Litókhoron. Kentrikí Makedonía, N Greece
Litohoro see Litóchoro
Litókhoron see Litóchoro
Little Alföld 77 C6 Ger. Kleines Ungarisches Tiefland, Hung. Kisalföld, Slvk. Podunajská Rovina. Plain Hungary/Slovakia
Little Andaman 111 F2 island Andaman Islands, India, NE Indian Ocean
Little Barrier Island 128 D2 island N NZ
Little Bay 71 H5 bay S Gibraltar
Little Cayman 32 B3 island E Cayman Islands
Little Falls 23 F2 Minnesota, N USA
Littlefield 27 E2 Texas, SW USA
Little Inagua 32 D2 var. Inagua Islands. Island S Bahamas
Little Minch, The 66 B3 strait NW Scotland, UK
Little Missouri River 22 D2 river NW USA
Little Nicobar 111 G3 island Nicobar Islands, India, NE Indian Ocean
Little Rock 20 B1 state capital Arkansas, C USA
Little Saint Bernard Pass 69 D5 Fr. Col du Petit St-Bernard, It. Colle di Piccolo San Bernardo. Pass France/Italy
Little Sound 20 A5 bay Bermuda, NW Atlantic Ocean
Littleton 22 D4 Colorado, C USA
Liu-chou see Liuzhou
Liuchow see Liuzhou
Liuzhou 106 C6 var. Liu-chou, Liuchow. Guangxi Zhuangzu Zizhiqu, S China
Livanátes 83 B5 prev. Livanátai. Stereá Ellás, C Greece
Līvāni 84 D4 Ger. Lievenhof. Preiļi, SE Latvia
Liverpool 126 D2 New South Wales, SE Australia
Liverpool 17 F5 Nova Scotia, SE Canada
Liverpool 67 C5 NW England, UK
Livingston 22 B2 Montana, NW USA
Livingstone 56 C3 var. Maramba. Southern, S Zambia
Livingstone 27 H3 Texas, SW USA
Livingstone Mountains 129 A7 mountain range South Island, NZ
Livno 78 B4 Federacija Bosna I Hercegovina, SW Bosnia and Herzegovina
Livojoki 62 D4 river C Finland
Livonia 18 D3 Michigan, N USA
Livorno 74 B3 Eng. Leghorn. Toscana, C Italy
Lixoúri 83 A5 prev. Lixoúrion. Kefallinía, Iónioi Nísoi, Greece, C Mediterranean Sea
Ljubljana 73 D7 Ger. Laibach, It. Lubiana; anc. Aemona, Emona. Country capital (Slovenia) C Slovenia
Ljungby 63 B7 Kronoberg, S Sweden
Ljusdal 63 C5 Gävleborg, C Sweden
Ljusnan 63 C5 river C Sweden
Llanelli 67 C6 prev. Llanelly. SW Wales, UK
Llanes 70 D1 Asturias, N Spain
Llanos 36 D2 physical region Colombia/Venezuela
Lleida 71 F2 Cast. Lérida; anc. Ilerda. Cataluña, NE Spain
Lluchmayor see Llucmajor
Llucmajor 71 G3 var. Lluchmayor. Mallorca, Spain, W Mediterranean Sea
Loaita Island 106 C8 island W Spratly Islands
Loanda see Luanda
Lobatse 56 C4 var. Lobatsi. Kgatleng, SE Botswana
Lobatsi see Lobatse
Löbau 72 D4 Sachsen, E Germany
Lobito 56 B2 Benguela, W Angola
Lob Nor see Lop Nur
Loburi see Lop Buri
Locarno 73 B8 Ger. Luggarus. Ticino, S Switzerland
Lochem 64 E3 Gelderland, E Netherlands
Lockport 19 E3 New York, NE USA
Lodja 55 D6 Kasai Oriental, C Dem. Rep. Congo (Zaire)
Lodwar 51 C6 Rift Valley, NW Kenya
Łódź 76 D4 Rus. Lodz. Łódzkie, C Poland
Loei 114 C4 var. Loey, Muang Loei. Loei, C Thailand
Loey see Loei
Lofoten 62 B3 var. Lofoten Islands. Island group C Norway
Lofoten Islands see Lofoten
Logan 22 B3 Utah, W USA
Logan, Mount 14 D3 mountain Yukon Territory, W Canada
Logroño 71 E1 anc. Vareia, Lat. Juliobriga. La Rioja, N Spain
Loibl Pass 73 D7 Ger. Loiblpass, Slvn. Ljubelj. Pass Austria/Slovenia
Loi-Kaw 114 B4 Kayah State, C Myanmar
Loire 68 B4 var. Liger. River C France
Loja 38 B2 Loja, S Ecuador
Lokitaung 51 C5 Rift Valley, NW Kenya
Lokoja 53 G4 Kogi, C Nigeria
Loksa 84 E2 Ger. Loxa. Harjumaa, NW Estonia
Lolland 63 B8 prev. Laaland. Island S Denmark
Lom 82 C1 prev. Lom-Palanka. Montana, NW Bulgaria
Lomami 55 D6 river C Dem. Rep. Congo (Zaire)
Lomas 38 D4 Arequipa, SW Peru
Lomas de Zamora 42 D4 Buenos Aires, E Argentina
Lombardia 74 B2 cultural region N Italy
Lombok, Pulau 116 D5 island Nusa Tenggara, C Indonesia
Lomé 53 F5 country capital (Togo) S Togo
Lomela 55 D6 Kasai Oriental, C Dem. Rep. Congo (Zaire)
Lommel 65 C5 Limburg, N Belgium
Lomond, Loch 66 B4 lake C Scotland, UK
Lomonosov Ridge 133 B3 var. Harris Ridge, Rus. Khrebet Lomonsova. Undersea feature Arctic Ocean
Lompoc 25 B7 California, W USA
Lom Sak 114 C4 var. Muang Lom Sak. Phetchabun, C Thailand
Łomża 76 D3 off. Województwo Łomżyńskie, Rus. Lomzha. Podlaskie, NE Poland
Loncoche 43 B5 Araucanía, C Chile
London 67 A7 anc. Augusta, Lat. Londinium. Country capital (UK) SE England, UK
London 18 C5 Kentucky, S USA
London 16 C5 Ontario, S Canada
Londonderry 66 B4 var. Derry, Ir. Doire. NW Northern Ireland, UK
Londonderry, Cape 124 C2 headland Western Australia
Londrina 41 E4 Paraná, S Brazil
Longa, Proliv 93 G1 Eng. Long Strait. Strait NE Russian Federation
Long Bay 21 F2 bay North Carolina/South Carolina, E USA
Long Beach 25 C7 California, W USA
Longford 67 B5 Ir. An Longfort. C Ireland
Long Island 32 D2 island C Bahamas
Long Island 19 G4 island New York, NE USA
Long Island see Bermuda
Longlac 16 C3 Ontario, S Canada
Longmont 22 D4 Colorado, C USA
Longreach 126 C4 Queensland, E Australia
Long Strait see Longa, Proliv
Longview 27 H3 Texas, SW USA
Longview 24 B2 Washington, NW USA
Long Xuyên 115 D6 var. Longxuyen. An Giang, S Vietnam
Longxuyen see Long Xuyên
Longyan 106 D6 Fujian, SE China
Longyearbyen 61 G2 dependent territory capital (Svalbard) Spitsbergen, W Svalbard
Lons-le-Saunier 68 D4 anc. Ledo Salinarius. Jura, E France
Lop Buri 115 C5 var. Loburi. Lop Buri, C Thailand
Lop Nor see Lop Nur
Lop Nur 104 C3 var. Lob Nor, Lop Nor, Lo-pu Po. Seasonal lake NW China
Loppersum 64 E1 Groningen, NE Netherlands
Lo-pu Po see Lop Nur
Lorca 71 E4 Ar. Lurka; anc. Eliocroca, Lat. Illur co. Murcia, S Spain
Lord Howe Island 120 C4 island E Australia
Lord Howe Rise 120 C4 undersea feature SW Pacific Ocean
Loreto 28 B3 Baja California Sur, W Mexico
Lorient 68 A3 prev. l'Orient. Morbihan, NW France
Lorn, Firth of 66 B4 inlet W Scotland, UK
Loro Sae see East Timor
Lörrach 73 A7 Baden-Württemberg, S Germany
Lorraine 68 D3 cultural region NE France
Los Alamos 26 C1 New Mexico, SW USA
Los Amates 30 B2 Izabal, E Guatemala
Los Angeles 25 C7 California, W USA
Los Ángeles 43 B5 Bío Bío, C Chile
Lošinj 78 A3 Ger. Lussin, It. Lussino. Island W Croatia
Los Mochis 28 C3 Sinaloa, C Mexico
Los Roques, Islas 36 D1 island group N Venezuela
Los Testigos, Isla 33 G5 island NE Venezuela
Lost River Range 24 D3 mountain range Idaho, C USA
Lot 69 B5 cultural region C France
Lot 69 B5 river S France
Lotagipi Swamp 51 C5 wetland Kenya/Sudan
Louangnamtha 114 C3 var. Luong Nam Tha. Louang Namtha, N Laos
Louangphabang 102 D3 var. Louangphrabang, Luang Prabang. Louangphabang, N Laos
Louangphrabang see Louangphabang
Loudéac 68 A3 Côtes d'Armor, NW France
Loudi 106 C5 Hunan, S China
Louga 52 B3 NW Senegal
Louisiade Archipelago 122 B4 island group SE PNG
Louisiana 20 A2 off. State of Louisiana; also known as Creole State, Pelican State. State S USA
Louisville 18 C5 Kentucky, S USA
Louisville Ridge 121 E4 undersea feature S Pacific Ocean
Loup River 23 E4 river Nebraska, C USA
Lourdes 69 B6 Hautes-Pyrénées, S France
Louth 67 E5 E England, UK
Loutrá 82 C4 Kentrikí Makedonía, N Greece
Lóuva 56 C1 Lunda Norte, NE Angola
Louvain-la Neuve 65 C6 Wallon Brabant, C Belgium
Louviers 68 C3 Eure, N France
Lovech 82 C2 Lovech, N Bulgaria
Loveland 22 D4 Colorado, C USA
Lovosice 76 A4 Ger. Lobositz. Ústecký Kraj, NW Czech Republic
Lowell 19 G3 Massachusetts, NE USA
Lower California see Baja California
Lower Hutt 129 D5 Wellington, North Island, NZ
Lower Lough Erne 67 A5 lake SW Northern Ireland, UK
Lower Red Lake 23 F1 lake Minnesota, N USA
Lower Tunguska see Nizhnyaya Tunguska
Lowestoft 67 E6 E England, UK
Lo-yang see Luoyang
Loyauté, Îles 122 D5 island group S New Caledonia
Loyew 85 D8 Rus. Loyev. Homyel'skaya Voblasts', SE Belarus
Loznica 78 C3 Serbia, W Yugoslavia
Lu see Shandong
Lualaba 55 D6 Fr. Loualaba. River SE Dem. Rep. Congo (Zaire)
Luanda 56 A1 var. Loanda, Port. São Paulo de Loanda. Country capital (Angola) Luanda, NW Angola
Luang Prabang see Louangphabang
Luang, Thale 115 C7 lagoon S Thailand
Luangua, Rio see Luangwa
Luangwa 51 B8 var. Aruângua, Rio Luangua. River Mozambique/Zambia
Luanshya 56 D2 Copperbelt, C Zambia
Luarca 70 C1 Asturias, N Spain
Lubaczów 77 E5 var. Lúbaczów. Podkarpackie, SE Poland
Lubań 76 B4 var. Koscian, Ger. Kosten. Dolnośląskie, SW Poland
Lubānas Ezers see Lubāns
Lubango 56 B2 Port. Sá da Bandeira. Huíla, SW Angola
Lubāns 84 D4 var. Lubānas Ezers. Lake E Latvia
Lubao 55 D6 Kasai Oriental, C Dem. Rep. Congo (Zaire)
Lübben 72 D4 Brandenburg, E Germany
Lübbenau 72 D4 Brandenburg, E Germany
Lubbock 27 E2 Texas, SW USA
Lübeck 72 C2 Schleswig-Holstein, N Germany
Lubelska, Wyżyna 76 E4 plateau SE Poland
Lubin 76 B4 Ger. Lüben. Dolnośląskie, W Poland
Lublin 76 E4 Rus. Lyublin. Lubelskie, E Poland
Lubliniec 76 C4 Śląskie, S Poland
Lubny 87 F2 Poltavs'ka Oblast', NE Ukraine
Lubsko 76 B4 Ger. Sommerfeld. Lubuskie, W Poland
Lubumbashi 55 E8 prev. Élisabethville. Shaba, SE Dem. Rep. Congo (Zaire)
Lubutu 55 D6 Maniema, E Dem. Rep. Congo (Zaire)
Lucan 67 B5 Ir. Leamhcán. E Ireland
Lucano, Appennino 75 D5 Eng. Lucanian Mountains. Mountain range S Italy
Lucapa 56 C1 var. Lukapa. Lunda Norte, NE Angola
Lucca 74 B3 anc. Luca. Toscana, C Italy
Lucea 32 A4 W Jamaica
Lucena 117 E1 off. Lucena City. Luzon, N Philippines
Lucena 70 D4 Andalucía, S Spain
Lučenec 77 D6 Ger. Losontz, Hung. Losonc. Banskobystrický Kraj, C Slovakia
Luchow see Hefei
Lucknow 113 E3 var. Lakhnau. Uttar Pradesh, N India
Lüda see Dalian
Luda Kamchiya 82 D2 river E Bulgaria
Lüderitz 56 B4 prev. Angra Pequena. Karas, SW Namibia
Ludhiāna 112 D2 Punjab, N India
Ludington 18 C2 Michigan, N USA
Luduş 86 B4 Ger. Ludasch, Hung. Marosludas. Mureş, C Romania
Ludvika 63 C6 Kopparberg, C Sweden
Ludwiglust 72 C3 Mecklenburg-Vorpommern, N Germany
Ludwigsburg 73 B6 Baden-Württemberg, SW Germany
Ludwigsfelde 72 D3 Brandenburg, NE Germany
Ludwigshafen 73 B5 var. Ludwigshafen am Rhein. Rheinland-Pfalz, W Germany
Ludwigshafen am Rhein see Ludwigshafen
Ludza 84 D4 Ger. Ludsan. Ludza, E Latvia
Luebo 55 C6 Kasai Occidental, SW Dem. Rep. Congo (Zaire)
Luena 56 C2 var. Lwena, Port. Luso. Moxico, E Angola
Lufira 55 E7 river SE Dem. Rep. Congo (Zaire)
Lufkin 27 H3 Texas, SW USA
Luga 88 A4 Leningradskaya Oblast', NW Russian Federation
Lugano 73 B8 Ger. Lauis. Ticino, S Switzerland
Lugenda, Rio 57 E2 river N Mozambique
Lugo 70 C1 anc. Lugus Augusti. Galicia, NW Spain
Lugoj 86 A4 Ger. Lugosch, Hung. Lugos. Timiş, W Romania
Luhans'k 87 H3 Rus. Lugansk; prev. Voroshilovgrad. Luhans'ka Oblast', E Ukraine
Luimneach see Limerick
Lukapa see Lucapa
Lukenie 55 C6 river C Dem. Rep. Congo (Zaire)
Lukovit 82 C2 Lovech, NW Bulgaria
Łuków 76 E4 Ger. Bogendorf. Lubelskie, E Poland
Lukuga 55 D7 river SE Dem. Rep. Congo (Zaire)
Luleå 62 D4 Norrbotten, N Sweden
Luleälven 62 C3 river N Sweden
Lulonga 55 C5 river NW Dem. Rep. Congo (Zaire)
Lulua 55 D7 river S Dem. Rep. Congo (Zaire)
Lumbo 57 F2 Nampula, NE Mozambique
Lumsden 129 A7 Southland, South Island, NZ
Lund 63 B7 Skåne, S Sweden
Lüneburg 72 C3 Niedersachsen, N Germany
Lungkiang see Qiqihar
Lungué-Bungo 56 C2 var. Lungwebungu. River Angola/Zambia see also Lungwebungu
Lungwebungu see Lungué-Bungo
Luninyets 85 B7 Pol. Łuniniec, Rus. Luninets. Brestskaya Voblasts', SW Belarus
Lunteren 64 D4 Gelderland, C Netherlands
Luong Nam Tha see Louangnamtha
Luoyang 106 C4 var. Honan, Lo-yang. Henan, C China
Lúrio 57 F2 Nampula, NE Mozambique
Lúrio, Rio 57 E2 river NE Mozambique
Lusaka 56 D2 country capital (Zambia) Lusaka, SE Zambia
Lushnja see Lushnjë
Lushnjë 79 C6 var. Lushnja. Fier, C Albania
Luso see Luena
Lūt, Dasht-e 98 D3 var. Kavīr-e Lūt. Desert E Iran
Luton 67 D6 SE England, UK
Łutselk'e 15 F4 prev. Snowdrift. Northwest Territories, W Canada
Luts'k 86 C1 Pol. Łuck, Rus. Lutsk. Volyns'ka Oblast', NW Ukraine
Lutzow-Holm Bay see Lützow Holmbukta
Lützow Holmbukta 132 C2 var. Lutzow-Holm Bay. Bay Antarctica
Luuq 51 D6 It. Lugh Ganana. Gedo, SW Somalia
Luvua 55 D7 river SE Dem. Rep. Congo (Zaire)
Luwego 51 C8 river S Tanzania
Luxembourg 65 D8 off. Grand Duchy of Luxembourg, var. Lëtzebuerg, Luxemburg. Country NW Europe
Luxembourg 65 D8 country capital (Luxembourg) Luxembourg, S Luxembourg
Luxor 50 B2 Ar. Al Uqşur. E Egypt
Luza 88 C4 Kirovskaya Oblast', NW Russian Federation
Luz, Costa de la 70 C5 coastal region SW Spain
Luzern 73 B7 Fr. Lucerne, It. Lucerna. Luzern, C Switzerland
Luzon 117 E1 island N Philippines
Luzon Strait 103 E3 strait Philippines/Taiwan
L'viv 86 B2 Ger. Lemberg, Pol. Lwów, Rus. L'vov. L'vivs'ka Oblast', W Ukraine
Lwena see Luena
Lyakhavichy 85 B6 Rus. Lyakhovichi. Brestskaya Voblasts', SW Belarus
Lycksele 62 C4 Västerbotten, N Sweden
Lycopolis see Asyūt
Lyel'chytsy 85 C7 Rus. Lel'chitsy. Homyel'skaya Voblasts', SE Belarus
Lyepyel' 85 D5 Rus. Lepel'. Vitsyebskaya Voblasts', N Belarus
Lyme Bay 67 C7 bay S England, UK
Lynchburg 19 E5 Virginia, NE USA
Lynn Regis see King's Lynn
Lyon 69 D5 Eng. Lyons; anc. Lugdunum. Rhône, E France
Lyozna 85 E6 Rus. Liozno. Vitsyebskaya Voblasts', NE Belarus
Lypovets' 86 D2 Rus. Lipovets. Vinnyts'ka Oblast', C Ukraine
Lysychans'k 87 H3 Rus. Lisichansk. Luhans'ka Oblast', E Ukraine
Lyttelton 129 C6 Canterbury, South Island, NZ
Lyubotyn 87 G2 Rus. Lyubotin. Kharkivs'ka Oblast', E Ukraine
Lyulyakovo 82 E2 prev. Keremitlik. Burgas, E Bulgaria
Lyusina 85 B6 Rus. Lyusino. Brestskaya Voblasts', SW Belarus

M

Ma'ān 97 B7 Ma'ān, SW Jordan
Maardu 84 D2 Ger. Maart. Harjumaa, NW Estonia
Ma'aret-en-Nu'man see Ma'arrat an Nu'mān
Ma'arrat an Nu'mān 96 B3 var. Ma'aret-en-Nu'man, Fr. Maarret enn Naamâne. Idlib, NW Syria
Maarret enn Naamâne see Ma'arrat an Nu'mān
Maaseik 65 D5 prev. Maeseyck. Limburg, NE Belgium
Maastricht 65 D6 var. Maestricht; anc. Traietum ad Mosam, Traiectum Tungorum. Limburg, SE Netherlands
Macao 107 C6 Chin. Aomen, Port. Macao. S China
Macapá 41 E1 state capital Amapá, N Brazil
Macassar see Ujungpandang
MacCluer Gulf see Berau, Teluk
Macdonnell Ranges 124 D4 mountain range Northern Territory, C Australia
Macedonia, FYR 79 D6 off. the Former Yugoslav Republic of Macedonia, var. Macedonia, Mac. Makedonija, abbrev. FYR Macedonia, FYROM. Country SE Europe
Maceió 41 G3 state capital Alagoas, E Brazil

Masai Steppe – Mi Tho

Masai Steppe 51 C7 grassland NW Tanzania
Masaka 51 B6 SW Uganda
Masallı 95 H3 Rus. Masally. S Azerbaijan
Masasi 51 C8 Mtwara, SE Tanzania
Masawa see Massawa
Masaya 30 D3 Masaya, W Nicaragua
Mascarene Basin 119 B5 undersea feature W Indian Ocean
Mascarene Islands 57 H4 island group W Indian Ocean
Mascarene Plain 119 B5 undersea feature W Indian Ocean
Mascarene Plateau 119 B5 undersea feature W Indian Ocean
Maseru 56 D4 country capital (Lesotho) W Lesotho
Mas-ha 59 D7 W Bank
Mashhad 98 E2 var. Meshed. Khorāsān, NE Iran
Masindi 51 B6 W Uganda
Masīra see Maşīrah, Jazīrat
Masira, Gulf of see Maşīrah, Khalīj
Maşīrah, Jazīrat 99 E5 var. Masīra. Island E Oman
Maşīrah, Khalīj 99 E5 var. Gulf of Masira. Bay E Oman
Masis see Büyükağrı Dağı
Maskat see Masqaţ
Mason City 23 F3 Iowa, C USA
Masqaţ 99 E5 var. Maskat, Eng. Muscat. Country capital (Oman) NE Oman
Massa 74 B3 Toscana, C Italy
Massachusetts 19 G3 off. Commonwealth of Massachusetts; also known as Bay State, Old Bay State, Old Colony State. State NE USA
Massawa 50 C4 var. Masawa, Amh. Mits'iwa. E Eritrea
Massenya 54 B3 Chari-Baguirmi, SW Chad
Massif Central 69 C5 plateau C France
Massif du Makay see Makay
Massoukou see Franceville
Masterton 129 D5 Wellington, North Island, NZ
Masty 85 B5 Rus. Mosty. Hrodzyenskaya Voblasts', W Belarus
Masuda 109 B6 Shimane, Honshū, SW Japan
Masuku see Franceville
Masvingo 56 D3 prev. Fort Victoria, Nyanda, Victoria. Masvingo, SE Zimbabwe
Maşyāf 96 B3 Fr. Misiaf. Ḩamāh, C Syria
Matadi 55 B6 Bas-Zaïre, W Dem. Rep. Congo (Zaire)
Matagalpa 30 D3 Matagalpa, C Nicaragua
Matale 110 D3 Central Province, C Sri Lanka
Matam 52 C3 NE Senegal
Matamata 128 D3 Waikato, North Island, NZ
Matamoros 28 D3 Coahuila de Zaragoza, NE Mexico
Matamoros 29 E2 Tamaulipas, C Mexico
Matane 17 E4 Québec, SE Canada
Matanzas 32 B2 Matanzas, NW Cuba
Matara 110 D4 Southern Province, S Sri Lanka
Mataram 116 D5 Pulau Lombok, C Indonesia
Mataró 71 G2 anc. Illuro. Cataluña, E Spain
Mataura 129 B7 river South Island, NZ
Mataura 129 B7 Southland, South Island, NZ
Mata Uta see Matā'utu
Matā'utu 123 E4 var. Mata Uta. Dependent territory capital (Wallis and Futuna) Île Uvea, Wallis and Futuna
Matera 75 E5 Basilicata, S Italy
Matías Romero 29 F5 Oaxaca, SE Mexico
Mato Grosso 41 E4 prev. Vila Bela da Santissima Trindade. Mato Grosso, W Brazil
Mato Grosso do Sul 41 E4 off. Estado de Mato Grosso do Sul. State S Brazil
Mato Grosso, Planalto de 34 C4 plateau C Brazil
Matosinhos 70 B2 prev. Matozinhos. Porto, NW Portugal
Matsue 109 B6 var. Matsuye, Matue. Shimane, Honshū, SW Japan
Matsumoto 109 C5 var. Matumoto. Nagano, Honshū, S Japan
Matsuyama 109 B7 var. Matuyama. Ehime, Shikoku, SW Japan
Matsuye see Matsue
Matterhorn 73 A8 It. Monte Cervino. Mountain Italy/Switzerland see also Cervino, Monte
Matthews Ridge 37 F2 N Guyana
Matthew Town 32 D2 Great Inagua, S Bahamas
Matucana 38 C4 Lima, W Peru
Matue see Matsue
Matumoto see Matsumoto
Maturín 37 E2 Monagas, NE Venezuela
Matuyama see Matsuyama
Mau 113 E3 var. Maunāth Bhanjan. Uttar Pradesh, N India
Maui 25 B8 island Hawaii, USA, C Pacific Ocean
Maulmain see Moulmein
Maun 56 C3 Ngamiland, C Botswana
Maunāth Bhanjan see Mau
Mauren 72 E1 NE Liechtenstein
Mauritania 52 C2 off. Islamic Republic of Mauritania, Ar. Mūrītānīyah. Country W Africa
Mauritius 57 H3 off. Republic of Mauritius, Fr. Maurice. Country W Indian Ocean
Mauritius 119 B5 island W Indian Ocean
Mawlamyine see Moulmein
Mawson 132 D2 Australian research station Antarctica
Maya 30 B1 river E Russian Federation
Mayadin see Al Mayādīn
Mayaguana 32 D2 island SE Bahamas
Mayaguana Passage 32 D2 passage SE Bahamas
Mayagüez 33 F3 W Puerto Rico
Mayamey 98 D2 Semnān, N Iran
Maya Mountains 30 B2 Sp. Montañas Mayas. Mountain range Belize/Guatemala
Maych'ew 50 C4 var. Mai Chio, It. Mai Ceu. N Ethiopia
Maydān Shahr 101 E4 Wardag, E Afghanistan
Mayebashi see Maebashi
Mayfield 129 B6 Canterbury, South Island, NZ
Maykop 89 A7 Respublika Adygeya, SW Russian Federation
Maymana see Meymaneh
Maymyo 114 B3 Mandalay, C Myanmar
Mayo see Maio
Mayor Island 128 D3 island NE NZ
Mayor Pablo Lagerenza see Capitán Pablo Lagerenza
Mayotte 57 F2 French territorial collectivity E Africa
May Pen 32 B5 C Jamaica
Mazabuka 56 D2 Southern, S Zambia
Mazaca see Kayseri
Mazār-e Sharīf 101 E3 var. Mazār-i Sharif. Balkh, N Afghanistan
Mazār-i Sharif see Mazār-e Sharīf
Mazatlán 28 C3 Sinaloa, C Mexico
Mažeikiai 84 B3 Mažeikiai, NW Lithuania
Mazirbe 84 C2 Talsi, NW Latvia
Mazra'a see Al Mazra'ah
Mazury 76 D3 physical region NE Poland
Mazyr 85 C7 Rus. Mozyr'. Homyel'skaya Voblasts', SE Belarus
Mbabane 56 D4 country capital (Swaziland) NW Swaziland
Mbacké see Mbaké
M'Baiki see Mbaïki
Mbaïki 55 C5 var. M'Baiki. Lobaye, SW Central African Republic
Mbaké 52 B3 var. Mbacké. W Senegal
Mbala 56 D1 prev. Abercorn. Northern, NE Zambia
Mbale 51 C6 E Uganda
Mbandaka 55 C5 prev. Coquilhatville. Equateur, NW Dem. Rep. Congo (Zaire)
M'Banza Congo 56 B1 var. Mbanza Congo; prev. São Salvador, São Salvador do Congo. Zaire, NW Angola
Mbanza-Ngungu 55 B6 Bas-Zaïre, W Dem. Rep. Congo (Zaire)
Mbarara 51 B6 SW Uganda
Mbé 54 B4 Nord, N Cameroon
Mbeya 51 C7 Mbeya, SW Tanzania
Mbomou see Bomu
M'Bomu see Bomu
Mbour 52 B3 W Senegal
Mbuji-Mayi 55 D7 prev. Bakwanga. Kasai Oriental, S Dem. Rep. Congo (Zaire)
McAlester 27 G2 Oklahoma, C USA
McAllen 27 G5 Texas, SW USA
McCamey 27 E3 Texas, SW USA
McClintock Channel 15 F2 channel Nunavut, N Canada
McComb 20 B3 Mississippi, S USA
McCook 23 E4 Nebraska, C USA
McKean Island 123 E3 island Phoenix Islands, C Kiribati
McKinley, Mount 14 C3 var. Denali. Mountain Alaska, USA
McKinley Park 14 C3 Alaska, USA
McMinnville 24 B3 Oregon, NW USA
McMurdo Base 132 B4 US research station Antarctica
McPherson see Fort McPherson
McPherson 23 E5 Kansas, C USA
Mdantsane 56 D5 Eastern Cape, SE South Africa
Mead, Lake 25 D6 reservoir Arizona/Nevada, W USA
Mecca see Makkah
Mechelen 65 C5 Eng. Mechlin, Fr. Malines. Antwerpen, C Belgium
Mecklenburger Bucht 72 C2 bay N Germany
Mecsek 77 C7 mountain range SW Hungary
Medan 116 B3 Sumatera, E Indonesia
Medeba see Ma'dabā
Medellín 36 B3 Antioquia, NW Colombia
Médenine 49 F2 var. Madanīyīn. SE Tunisia
Medford 24 B4 Oregon, NW USA
Medgidia 86 D5 Constanţa, SE Romania
Mediaş 86 B4 Ger. Mediasch, Hung. Medgyes. Sibiu, C Romania
Medicine Hat 15 F5 Alberta, SW Canada
Medinaceli 71 E2 Castilla-León, N Spain
Medina del Campo 70 D2 Castilla-León, N Spain
Mediterranean Sea 80 D3 Fr. Mer Méditerranée. Sea Africa/Asia/Europe
Médoc 69 B5 cultural region SW France
Medvezh'yegorsk 88 B3 Respublika Kareliya, NW Russian Federation
Meekatharra 125 B5 Western Australia
Meemu Atoll see Mulaku Atoll
Meerssen 65 D6 var. Mersen. Limburg, SE Netherlands
Meerut 112 D2 Uttar Pradesh, N India
Mehdia see Mahdia
Meheso see Mī'ēso
Me Hka see Nmai Hka
Mehrīz 98 D3 Yazd, C Iran
Mehtar Lām see Mehtarlām
Mehtarlām 101 F4 var. Mehtar Lām, Meterlam, Methariam, Metharlam. Laghmān, E Afghanistan
Meiktila 114 B3 Mandalay, C Myanmar
Mejillones 42 B2 Antofagasta, N Chile
Mek'elē 50 C4 var. Makale. N Ethiopia
Mékhé 52 B3 NW Senegal
Mekong 102 D3 var. Lan-ts'ang Chiang, Cam. Mékôngk, Chin. Lancang Jiang, Lao. Mènam Khong, Th. Mae Nam Khong, Tib. Dza Chu, Vtn. Sông Tiên Giang. River SE Asia
Mékôngk see Mekong
Mekong, Mouths of the 115 E6 delta S Vietnam
Melaka 116 B3 var. Malacca. Melaka, Peninsular Malaysia
Melanesia 122 D3 island group W Pacific Ocean
Melanesian Basin 120 C2 undersea feature W Pacific Ocean
Melbourne 127 C7 state capital Victoria, SE Australia
Melbourne 21 E4 Florida, SE USA
Melghir, Chott 49 E2 var. Chott Melrhir. Salt lake E Algeria
Melilla 58 B5 anc. Rusaddir, Russadir. Melilla, Spain, N Africa
Melilla 48 D2 enclave Spain, N Africa
Melita 15 F5 Manitoba, S Canada
Melitopol' 87 F4 Zaporiz'ka Oblast', SE Ukraine
Melle 65 B5 Oost-Vlaanderen, NW Belgium
Mellerud 63 B6 Västra Götaland, S Sweden
Mellieha 80 B5 E Malta
Mellizo Sur, Cerro 43 A7 mountain S Chile
Melo 42 E4 Cerro Largo, NE Uruguay
Melsungen 72 B4 Hessen, C Germany
Melun 68 C3 anc. Melodunum. Seine-et-Marne, N France
Melville Island 124 D2 island Northern Territory, N Australia
Melville Island 15 E2 island Parry Islands, Northwest Territories/Nunavut, NW Canada
Melville, Lake 17 F2 lake Newfoundland and Labrador, E Canada
Melville Peninsula 15 G3 peninsula Northwest Territories, NE Canada
Membidj see Manbij
Memmingen 73 B6 Bayern, S Germany
Memphis 20 C1 Tennessee, S USA
Ménaka 53 F3 Goa, E Mali
Menaldum 64 D1 Fris. Menaam. Friesland, N Netherlands
Mènam Khong see Mekong
Mendaña Fracture Zone 131 F4 tectonic feature E Pacific Ocean
Mende 69 C5 anc. Mimatum. Lozère, S France
Mendeleyev Ridge 133 B2 undersea feature Arctic Ocean
Mendocino Fracture Zone 130 D2 tectonic feature NE Pacific Ocean
Mendoza 42 B4 Mendoza, W Argentina
Menemen 94 A3 İzmir, W Turkey
Menengiyn Tal 105 F2 plain E Mongolia
Menongue 56 B2 var. Vila Serpa Pinto, Port. Serpa Pinto. Cuando Cubango, C Angola
Menorca 71 H3 Eng. Minorca; anc. Balearis Minor. Island Islas Baleares, Spain, W Mediterranean Sea
Mentawai, Kepulauan 116 A4 island group W Indonesia
Meppel 64 D2 Drenthe, NE Netherlands
Merano 74 C1 Ger. Meran. Trentino-Alto Adige, N Italy
Merca see Marka
Mercedes see Villa Mercedes
Mercedes 42 D3 Corrientes, NE Argentina
Mercedes 42 D4 Soriano, SW Uruguay
Meredith, Lake 27 E1 reservoir Texas, SW USA
Merefa 87 G2 Kharkivs'ka Oblast', E Ukraine
Mergui 115 B6 Tenasserim, S Myanmar
Mergui Archipelago 115 B6 island group S Myanmar
Meriç see Maritsa
Mérida 70 C4 anc. Augusta Emerita. Extremadura, W Spain
Mérida 36 C2 Mérida, W Venezuela
Mérida 29 H3 Yucatán, SW Mexico
Meridian 20 C2 Mississippi, S USA
Mérignac 69 B5 Gironde, SW France
Merkinė 85 B5 Varėna, S Lithuania
Merowe 50 B3 desert W Sudan
Merredin 125 B6 Western Australia
Mersen see Meerssen
Mersey 67 D5 river NW England, UK
Mersin 94 C4 İçel, S Turkey
Mērsrags 84 C3 Talsi, NW Latvia
Meru 51 C6 Eastern, C Kenya
Merzifon 94 D2 Amasya, N Turkey
Merzig 73 A5 Saarland, SW Germany
Mesa 26 B2 Arizona, SW USA
Meshed see Mashhad
Mesopotamia 35 C5 var. Mesopotamia Argentina. Physical region NE Argentina
Mesopotamia Argentina see Mesopotamia
Messalo, Rio 57 E2 var. Mualo. River NE Mozambique
Messana see Messina
Messene see Messina
Messina 75 D7 var. Messana, Messene; anc. Zancle. Sicilia, Italy, C Mediterranean Sea
Messina 56 D3 Northern, NE South Africa
Messina, Stretto di 75 D7 Eng. Strait of Messina. Strait SW Italy
Messíni 83 B6 Pelopónnisos, S Greece
Mestghanem see Mostaganem
Mestia 95 F1 var. Mestiya. N Georgia
Mestiya see Mestia
Mestre 74 C2 Veneto, NE Italy
Meta 34 B2 off. Departamento del Meta. Province C Colombia
Metairie 20 B3 Louisiana, S USA
Metán 42 C2 Salta, N Argentina
Metapán 30 B2 Santa Ana, NW El Salvador
Meta, Río 36 D3 river Colombia/Venezuela
Meterlam see Mehtarlām
Methariam see Mehtarlām
Metharlam see Mehtarlām
Metković 78 B4 Dubrovnik-Neretva, SE Croatia
Métsovo 82 B4 prev. Métsovon. Ípeiros, C Greece
Metz 68 D3 anc. Divodurum Mediomatricum, Mediomatrica, Metis. Moselle, NE France
Meulaboh 116 A3 Sumatera, W Indonesia
Meuse 65 C6 Dut. Maas. River W Europe see also Maas
Meuse 68 D3 department NE France
Mexcala, Río see Balsas, Río
Mexicali 28 A1 Baja California, NW Mexico
Mexico 28 C3 off. United Mexican States, var. Méjico, México, Sp. Estados Unidos Mexicanos. Country N Central America
Mexico 23 G4 Missouri, C USA
México 29 E4 var. Ciudad de México, Eng. Mexico City. Country capital (Mexico) México, C Mexico
Mexico City see México
Mexico, Gulf of 29 F2 Sp. Golfo de México. Gulf W Atlantic Ocean
Meyadine see Al Mayādīn
Meymaneh 100 D3 var. Maimāna, Maymana. Fāryāb, NW Afghanistan
Mezen' 88 D3 river NW Russian Federation
Mezőtúr 77 D7 Jász-Nagykun-Szolnok, E Hungary
Mġarr 80 A5 Gozo, N Malta
Miahuatlán 29 F5 var. Miahuatlán de Porfirio Díaz. Oaxaca, SE Mexico
Miahuatlán de Porfirio Díaz see Miahuatlán
Miami 21 F5 Florida, SE USA
Miami 27 G1 Oklahoma, C USA
Miami Beach 21 F5 Florida, SE USA
Mīāneh 98 C2 var. Miyāneh. Āzarbāyjān-e Khāvarī, NW Iran
Mianyang 106 B5 Sichuan, C China
Miastko 76 C2 Ger. Rummelsburg in Pommern. Pomorskie, N Poland
Mi Chai see Nong Khai
Michalovce 77 E5 Ger. Grossmichel, Hung. Nagymihály. Košický Kraj, E Slovakia
Michigan 18 C1 off. State of Michigan; also known as Great Lakes State, Lake State, Wolverine State. State N USA
Michigan, Lake 18 C2 lake N USA
Michurinsk 89 B5 Tambovskaya Oblast', W Russian Federation
Micoud 33 F2 SE Saint Lucia
Micronesia 122 B1 off. Federated States of Micronesia. Country W Pacific Ocean
Micronesia 122 C1 island group W Pacific Ocean
Mid-Atlantic Cordillera see Mid-Atlantic Ridge
Mid-Atlantic Ridge 44 C3 var. Mid Atlantic Cordillera, Mid-Atlantic Rise, Mid-Atlantic Swell. Undersea feature Atlantic Ocean
Mid-Atlantic Rise see Mid-Atlantic Ridge
Mid-Atlantic Swell see Mid-Atlantic Ridge
Middelburg 65 B5 Zeeland, SW Netherlands
Middelharnis 64 B4 Zuid-Holland, SW Netherlands
Middelkerke 65 A5 West-Vlaanderen, W Belgium
Middle America Trench 13 B7 undersea feature E Pacific Ocean
Middle Andaman 111 F2 island Andaman Islands, India, NE Indian Ocean
Middlesboro 18 C5 Kentucky, S USA
Middlesbrough 67 D5 N England, UK
Middletown 19 F4 New Jersey, NE USA
Middletown 19 F3 New York, NE USA
Mid-Indian Basin 119 C5 undersea feature N Indian Ocean
Mid-Indian Ridge 119 C5 var. Central Indian Ridge. Undersea feature C Indian Ocean
Midland 18 C3 Michigan, N USA
Midland 16 D5 Ontario, S Canada
Midland 27 E3 Texas, SW USA
Mid-Pacific Mountains 130 C2 var. Mid-Pacific Seamounts. Undersea feature NW Pacific Ocean
Mid-Pacific Seamounts see Mid-Pacific Mountains
Midway Islands 130 D2 US territory C Pacific Ocean
Miechów 77 D5 Małopolskie, S Poland
Międzyrzec Podlaski 76 E3 Lubelskie, E Poland
Międzyrzecz 76 B3 Ger. Meseritz. Lubuskie, W Poland
Mielec 77 D5 Podkarpackie, SE Poland
Miercurea-Ciuc 86 C4 Ger. Szeklerburg, Hung. Csíkszereda. Harghita, C Romania
Mieres del Camín see Mieres del Camino
Mieres del Camino 108 D1 var. Mieres del Camín. Asturias, NW Spain
Mieresch see Mureş
Mī'ēso 51 D5 var. Meheso, Miesso. C Ethiopia
Miesso see Mī'ēso
Miguel Asua 28 D3 var. Miguel Auza. Zacatecas, C Mexico
Miguel Auza see Miguel Asua
Mijdrecht 64 C3 Utrecht, C Netherlands
Mikashevichy 85 C7 Pol. Mikaszewicze, Rus. Mikashevichi. Brestskaya Voblasts', SW Belarus
Mikhaylovka 89 B6 Volgogradskaya Oblast', SW Russian Federation
Míkonos see Mýkonos
Mikre 82 C2 Lovech, N Bulgaria
Mikun' 88 D4 Respublika Komi, NW Russian Federation
Mikuni-sanmyaku 109 D5 mountain range Honshū, N Japan
Mikura-jima 109 D6 island E Japan
Milagro 38 B2 Guayas, SW Ecuador
Milan see Milano
Milange 57 E2 Zambézia, NE Mozambique
Milano 74 B2 Eng. Milan, Ger. Mailand; anc. Mediolanum. Lombardia, N Italy
Milas 94 A4 Muğla, SW Turkey
Milashavichy 85 C7 Rus. Milashevichi. Homyel'skaya Voblasts', SE Belarus
Mildura 127 C6 Victoria, SE Australia
Mile see Mili Atoll
Miles 127 D5 Queensland, E Australia
Miles City 22 C2 Montana, NW USA
Milford Haven 67 C6 prev. Milford. SW Wales, UK
Milford Sound 129 A6 inlet South Island, NZ
Milford Sound 129 A6 Southland, South Island, NZ
Mili Atoll 122 D2 var. Mile. Atoll Ratak Chain, SE Marshall Islands
Mil'kovo 93 H3 Kamchatskaya Oblast', E Russian Federation
Milk River 22 C1 river Montana, NW USA
Milk River 15 E5 Alberta, SW Canada
Milk, Wadi el 88 B4 var. Wadi al Malik. River C Sudan
Milledgeville 21 E2 Georgia, SE USA
Mille Lacs Lake 23 F2 lake Minnesota, N USA
Millennium Island 160 C8 prev. Caroline Island, Thornton Island. Atoll Line Islands, E Kiribati
Millerovo 89 B6 Rostovskaya Oblast', SW Russian Federation
Mílos 83 C7 island Kykládes, Greece, Aegean Sea
Mílos 83 C6 Mílos, Kykládes, Greece, Aegean Sea
Milton 129 B7 Otago, South Island, NZ
Milton Keynes 67 D6 SE England, UK
Milwaukee 18 B3 Wisconsin, N USA
Min see Fujian
Mīnā' Qābūs 118 B3 NE Oman
Minas Gerais 41 F3 off. Estado de Minas Gerais. State E Brazil
Minatitlán 29 F4 Veracruz-Llave, E Mexico
Minbu 114 A3 Magwe, W Myanmar
Minch, The 66 B3 var. North Minch. Strait NW Scotland, UK
Mindanao 117 F2 island S Philippines
Mindanao Sea see Bohol Sea
Mindelheim 73 C6 Bayern, S Germany
Mindello see Mindelo
Mindelo 52 A2 var. Mindello; prev. Porto Grande. São Vicente, N Cape Verde
Minden 72 B4 anc. Minthun. Nordrhein-Westfalen, NW Germany
Mindoro 117 E2 island N Philippines
Mindoro Strait 117 E2 strait W Philippines
Mineral Wells 27 F2 Texas, SW USA
Mingäçevir 95 G2 Rus. Mingechaur, Mingechevir. C Azerbaijan
Mingāora 112 C1 var. Mingora, Mongora. North-West Frontier Province, N Pakistan
Mingora see Mingāora
Minho 70 B2 former province N Portugal
Minho, Rio 70 B2 Sp. Miño. river Portugal/Spain see also Mino
Minicoy Island 110 B3 island SW India
Minius see Miño
Minna 53 G4 Niger, C Nigeria
Minneapolis 23 F2 Minnesota, N USA
Minnesota 23 F2 off. State of Minnesota; also known as Gopher State, New England of the West, North Star State. State N USA
Miño 70 B2 var. Mino, Minius, Port. Rio Minho. River Portugal/Spain see also Minho, Rio
Mino see Miño
Minot 23 E1 North Dakota, N USA
Minsk 85 C6 country capital (Belarus) Minskaya Voblasts', C Belarus
Minskaya Wzvyshsha 85 C6 mountain range C Belarus
Mińsk Mazowiecki 76 D3 var. Nowo Minsk. Mazowieckie, C Poland
Minto, Lac 16 D2 lake Québec, C Canada
Minya see El Minya
Miraflores 28 C3 Baja California Sur, W Mexico
Miranda de Ebro 71 E1 La Rioja, N Spain
Miri 116 D3 Sarawak, East Malaysia
Mirim Lagoon 41 E5 var. Lake Mirim, Sp. Laguna Merín. Lagoon Brazil/Uruguay
Mirim, Lake see Mirim Lagoon
Mírina see Mýrina
Mīrjāveh 98 E4 Sīstān va Balūchestān, SE Iran
Mirny 132 C3 Russian research station Antarctica
Mirnyy 93 F3 Respublika Sakha (Yakutiya), NE Russian Federation
Mīrpur Khās 112 B3 Sind, SE Pakistan
Mirtóo Pélagos 83 C6 Eng. Mirtoan Sea; anc. Myrtoum Mare. Sea S Greece
Miskito Coast see Mosquito Coast
Miskitos, Cayos 31 E2 island group NE Nicaragua
Miskolc 77 D6 Borsod-Abaúj-Zemplén, NE Hungary
Misool, Pulau 117 F4 island Maluku, E Indonesia
Mişrātah 49 F2 var. Misurata. NW Libya
Mission 27 G5 Texas, SW USA
Mississippi 20 B2 off. State of Mississippi; also known as Bayou State, Magnolia State. State SE USA
Mississippi Delta 20 B4 delta Louisiana, S USA
Mississippi River 13 C6 river C USA
Missoula 22 B1 Montana, NW USA
Missouri 23 F5 off. State of Missouri; also known as Bullion State, Show Me State. State C USA
Missouri River 23 E3 river C USA
Mistassini, Lac 16 D3 lake Québec, SE Canada
Mistelbach an der Zaya 73 E6 Niederösterreich, NE Austria
Misti, Volcán 39 E4 mountain S Peru
Misurata see Mişrātah
Mitchell 127 D5 Queensland, E Australia
Mitchell 23 E3 South Dakota, N USA
Mitchell, Mount 21 E1 mountain North Carolina, SE USA
Mitchell River 126 C2 river Queensland, NE Australia
Mi Tho see My Tho

Nadur – Niuatoputapu

Nadur 80 A5 Gozo, N Malta
Nadvirna 86 C3 Pol. Nadwórna, Rus. Nadvornaya. Ivano-Frankivs'ka Oblast', W Ukraine
Nadvoitsy 88 B3 Respublika Kareliya, NW Russian Federation
Nadym 92 C3 Yamalo-Nenetskiy Avtonomnyy Okrug, N Russian Federation
Náfpaktos 83 B5 var. Návpaktos. Dytikí Ellás, C Greece
Náfplio 83 B6 prev. Návplion. Pelopónnisos, S Greece
Naga 117 E2 off. Naga City; prev. Nueva Caceres. Luzon, N Philippines
Nagano 109 C5 Nagano, Honshū, S Japan
Nagaoka 109 D5 Niigata, Honshū, C Japan
Nagara Pathom see Nakhon Pathom
Nagara Sridharmaraj see Nakhon Si Thammarat
Nagara Svarga see Nakhon Sawan
Nagasaki 109 A7 Nagasaki, Kyūshū, SW Japan
Nagato 109 A7 Yamaguchi, Honshū, SW Japan
Nāgercoil 110 C3 Tamil Nādu, SE India
Nagorno-Karabakhskaya Avtonomnaya Oblast see Nagornyy Karabakh
Nagornyy Karabakh 95 G3 var. Nagorno-Karabakhskaya Avtonomnaya Oblast, Arm. Lernayin Gharabakh, Az. Dağliq Qarabağ. Former autonomous region SW Azerbaijan
Nagoya 109 C6 Aichi, Honshū, SW Japan
Nāgpur 112 D4 Mahārāshtra, C India
Nagqu 104 C5 Chin. Na-ch'ii; prev. Hei-ho. Xizang Zizhiqu, W China
Nagykálló 77 E6 Szabolcs-Szatmár-Bereg, E Hungary
Nagykanizsa 77 C7 Ger. Grosskanizsa. Zala, SW Hungary
Nagykőrös 77 D7 Pest, C Hungary
Nagyszentmiklós see Sânnicolau Mare
Naha 108 A3 Okinawa, Okinawa, SW Japan
Nahariya see Nahariyya
Nahariyya 97 A5 var. Nahariya. Northern, N Israel
Nahr al 'Āṣī see Orantes
Nahr al Litant see Lītani, Nahr el
Nahr an Nīl see Nile
Nahr el Aassi see Orantes
Nahuel Huapi, Lago 43 B5 lake W Argentina
Nā'īn 98 D3 Eşfahān, C Iran
Nain 17 F2 Newfoundland and Labrador, NE Canada
Nairobi 47 E5 country capital (Kenya) Nairobi Area, S Kenya
Nairobi 51 C6 international airport Nairobi Area, S Kenya
Najaf see An Najaf
Najima see Fukuoka
Najin 107 E3 NE North Korea
Najrān 99 B6 var. Abā as Su'ūd. Najrān, S Saudi Arabia
Nakambé see White Volta
Nakamura 109 B7 Kōchi, Shikoku, SW Japan
Nakatsugawa 109 C6 var. Nakatugawa. Gifu, Honshū, SW Japan
Nakatugawa see Nakatsugawa
Nakhodka 93 G5 Primorskiy Kray, SE Russian Federation
Nakhon Pathom 115 C5 var. Nagara Pathom, Nakorn Pathom. Nakhon Pathom, W Thailand
Nakhon Ratchasima 115 C5 var. Khorat, Korat. Nakhon Ratchasima, E Thailand
Nakhon Sawan 115 C5 var. Muang Nakhon Sawan, Nagara Svarga. Nakhon Sawan, W Thailand
Nakhon Si Thammarat 115 C7 var. Nagara Sridharmaraj, Nakhon Sithamnaraj. Nakhon Si Thammarat, SW Thailand
Nakhon Sithamnaraj see Nakhon Si Thammarat
Nakorn Pathom see Nakhon Pathom
Nakuru 51 C6 Rift Valley, SW Kenya
Nal'chik 89 B8 Kabardino-Balkarskaya Respublika, SW Russian Federation
Nālūt 49 F2 NW Libya
Namakan Lake 18 A1 lake Canada/USA
Namangan 101 F2 Namangan Wiloyati, E Uzbekistan
Nambala 56 D2 Central, C Zambia
Nam Co 104 C5 lake W China
Nam Định 114 D3 Nam Ha, N Vietnam
Namib Desert 56 B3 desert W Namibia
Namibe 56 A2 Port. Moçâmedes, Mossâmedes. Namibe, SW Angola
Namibia 56 B3 off. Republic of Namibia, var. South West Africa, Afr. Suidwes-Afrika, Ger. Deutsch-Südwestafrika; prev. German Southwest Africa, South-West Africa. Country S Africa
Namo see Namu Atoll
Nam Ou 114 C3 river N Laos
Nampa 24 D3 Idaho, NW USA
Nampula 57 E2 Nampula, NE Mozambique
Namsos 62 B4 Nord-Trøndelag, C Norway
Nam Tha 114 C4 river N Laos
Namu Atoll 122 D2 var. Namo. Atoll Ralik Chain, C Marshall Islands
Namur 65 C6 Dut. Namen. Namur, SE Belgium
Namyit Island 106 C8 island S Spratly Islands
Nan 114 C4 var. Muang Nan. Nan, NW Thailand
Nanaimo 14 D5 Vancouver Island, British Columbia, SW Canada
Nanchang 106 C5 var. Nan-ch'ang, Nanch'ang-hsien. Jiangxi, S China
Nanch'ang-hsien see Nanchang
Nan-ching see Nanjing
Nancy 68 D3 Meurthe-et-Moselle, NE France
Nandaime 30 D3 Granada, SW Nicaragua
Nānded 112 D5 Mahārāshtra, C India
Nandyāl 110 C1 Andhra Pradesh, E India
Nanjing 106 D5 var. Nan-ching, Nanking; prev. Chianning, Chian-ning, Kiang-ning. Jiangsu, E China
Nanking see Nanjing
Nanning 106 B6 var. Nan-ning; prev. Yung-ning. Guangxi Zhuangzu Zizhiqu, S China
Nan-ning see Nanning
Nanortalik 60 C5 S Greenland
Nanpan Jiang 114 D2 river S China
Nanping 106 D6 var. Nan-p'ing; prev. Yenping. Fujian, SE China
Nansei-shotō 108 A2 var. Ryukyu Islands. Island group SW Japan
Nansei Syotō Trench see Ryukyu Trench
Nansen Basin 133 C4 undersea feature Arctic Ocean
Nansen Cordillera 133 B3 var. Arctic-Mid Oceanic Ridge, Nansen Ridge. Undersea feature Arctic Ocean
Nansen Ridge see Nansen Cordillera
Nanterre 68 D1 Hauts-de-Seine, N France
Nantes 68 B4 Bret. Naoned; anc. Condivincum, Namnetes. Loire-Atlantique, NW France
Nantucket Island 19 G3 island Massachusetts, NE USA
Nanumaga 123 E3 var. Nanumanga. Atoll NW Tuvalu
Nanumanga see Nanumaga
Nanumea Atoll 123 E3 atoll NW Tuvalu
Nanyang 106 C5 var. Nan-yang. Henan, C China
Napa 25 B6 California, W USA
Napier 128 E4 Hawke's Bay, North Island, NZ
Naples 58 D5 anc. Neapolis. Campania, S Italy
Naples 21 E5 Florida, SE USA
Napo 34 A3 province NE Ecuador
Napo, Río 38 C1 river Ecuador/Peru
Naracoorte 127 B7 South Australia
Naradhivas see Narathiwat
Narathiwat 115 C7 var. Naradhivas. Narathiwat, SW Thailand
Narbada see Narmada
Narbonne 69 C6 anc. Narbo Martius. Aude, S France
Narborough Island see Fernandina, Isla
Nares Abyssal Plain see Nares Plain
Nares Plain 13 E6 var. Nares Abyssal Plain. Undersea feature NW Atlantic Ocean
Nares Strait 60 D1 Dan. Nares Stræde. Strait Canada/Greenland
Narew 76 E3 river E Poland
Narmada 102 B3 var. Narbada. River C India
Narowlya 85 C8 Rus. Narovlya. Homyel'skaya Voblasts', SE Belarus
Närpes 63 D5 Fin. Närpiö. Länsi-Suomi, W Finland
Narrabri 127 D6 New South Wales, SE Australia
Narrogin 125 B6 Western Australia
Narva 84 E2 prev. Narova. River Estonia/Russian Federation
Narva 84 E2 Ida-Virumaa, NE Estonia
Narva Bay 84 E2 Est. Narva Laht, Ger. Narwa-Bucht, Rus. Narvskiy Zaliv. Bay Estonia/Russian Federation
Narva Reservoir 84 E2 Est. Narva Veehoidla, Rus. Narvskoye Vodokhranilishche. Reservoir Estonia/Russian Federation
Narvik 62 C3 Nordland, C Norway
Nar'yan-Mar 88 D3 prev. Beloshchel'ye, Dzerzhinskiy. Nenetskiy Avtonomnyy Okrug, NW Russian Federation
Naryn 101 G2 Narynskaya Oblast', C Kyrgyzstan
Năsăud 86 B3 Ger. Nussdorf, Hung. Naszód. Bistriţa-Năsăud, N Romania
Nase see Naze
Nāshik 112 C5 prev. Nāsik. Mahārāshtra, W India
Nashua 19 G3 New Hampshire, NE USA
Nashville 20 C1 state capital Tennessee, S USA
Näsijärvi 63 D5 lake SW Finland
Nāsiri see Ahvāz
Nasiriya see An Nāṣirīyah
Nassau 32 C1 country capital (Bahamas) New Providence, N Bahamas
Nasser, Lake 50 B3 var. Buhayrat Nasir, Buḥayrat Nāşir, Buḥeiret Nâşir. Lake Egypt/Sudan
Nata 56 C3 Central, NE Botswana
Natal 41 G2 Rio Grande do Norte, E Brazil
Natal Basin 119 A6 var. Mozambique Basin. Undersea feature W Indian Ocean
Natanya see Netanya
Natchez 20 B3 Mississippi, S USA
Natchitoches 20 A2 Louisiana, S USA
Nathanya see Netanya
Natitingou 53 F4 NW Benin
Natsrat see Nazerat
Natuna Islands 102 D4 island group W Indonesia
Naturaliste Plateau 119 E6 undersea feature E Indian Ocean
Naugard see Nowogard
Naujamiestis 84 C4 Panevėžys, C Lithuania
Nauru 122 D2 off. Republic of Nauru; prev. Pleasant Island. Country W Pacific Ocean
Nauta 38 C2 Loreto, N Peru
Navahrudak 85 C6 Pol. Nowogródek, Rus. Novogrudok. Hrodzyenskaya Voblasts', W Belarus
Navapolatsk 85 D5 Rus. Novopolotsk. Vitsyebskaya Voblasts', N Belarus
Navarra 71 E2 cultural region N Spain
Navassa Island 32 C3 US unincorporated territory C West Indies
Navojoa 28 C2 Sonora, NW Mexico
Navolat see Navolato
Navolato 66 C3 var. Navolat. Sinaloa, C Mexico
Návpaktos see Náfpaktos
Nawabashah see Nawābshāh
Nawābshāh 112 B3 var. Nawabashah. Sind, S Pakistan
Nawoiy 101 E2 Rus. Navoi. Nawoiy Wiloyati, C Uzbekistan
Naxçıvan 95 G3 Rus. Nakhichevan'. SW Azerbaijan
Náxos 83 D6 var. Naxos. Náxos, Kykládes, Greece, Aegean Sea
Náxos 83 D6 island Kykládes, Greece, Aegean Sea
Nayoro 108 D2 Hokkaidō, NE Japan
Nazca 38 D4 Ica, S Peru
Nazca Ridge 35 A5 undersea feature E Pacific Ocean
Naze 108 B3 var. Nase. Kagoshima, Amami-ōshima, SW Japan
Nazerat 97 A5 var. Natsrat, Ar. En Nazira, Eng. Nazareth. Northern, N Israel
Nazilli 94 A4 Aydın, SW Turkey
Nazrēt 51 C5 var. Adama, Hadama. C Ethiopia
N'Dalatando 56 B1 Port. Salazar, Vila Salazar. Cuanza Norte, NW Angola
Ndélé 54 C4 Bamingui-Bangoran, N Central African Republic
Ndendé 55 B6 Ngounié, S Gabon
Ndindi 55 A6 Nyanga, S Gabon
Ndjamena 54 B3 var. N'Djamena; prev. Fort-Lamy. Country capital (Chad) Chari-Baguirmi, W Chad
Ndjolé 55 A5 Moyen-Ogooué, W Gabon
Ndola 56 D2 Copperbelt, C Zambia
Neagh, Lough 67 B5 lake E Northern Ireland, UK
Néa Moudanía 82 C4 var. Néa Moudhaniá. Kentrikí Makedonía, N Greece
Néa Moudhaniá see Néa Moudanía
Neápoli 82 B4 prev. Neápolis. Dytikí Makedonía, N Greece
Neápoli 83 D8 Kríti, Greece, E Mediterranean Sea
Neápoli 83 C7 Pelopónnisos, S Greece
Neapolis see Nablus
Near Islands 14 A2 island group Aleutian Islands, Alaska, USA
Néa Zíchni 82 C3 var. Néa Zíkhni; prev. Néa Zíkhna. Kentrikí Makedonía, NE Greece
Néa Zíkhna see Néa Zíchni
Néa Zíkhni see Néa Zíchni
Nebaj 30 B2 Quiché, W Guatemala
Nebitdag 100 B2 Balkanskiy Velayat, W Turkmenistan
Neblina, Pico da 40 C1 mountain NW Brazil
Nebraska 22 D4 off. State of Nebraska; also known as Blackwater State, Cornhusker State, Tree Planters State. State C USA
Nebraska City 23 F4 Nebraska, C USA
Neches River 27 H3 river Texas, SW USA
Neckar 73 B6 river SW Germany
Necochea 43 D5 Buenos Aires, E Argentina
Neder Rijn 64 D4 Eng. Lower Rhine. River C Netherlands
Nederweert 65 D5 Limburg, SE Netherlands
Neede 64 E3 Gelderland, E Netherlands
Neerpelt 65 D5 Limburg, NE Belgium
Neftekamsk 89 D5 Respublika Bashkortostan, W Russian Federation
Negēlē 51 D5 var. Negelli, It. Neghelli. C Ethiopia
Negelli see Negēlē
Neghelli see Negēlē
Negomane 57 E2 var. Negomano. Cabo Delgado, N Mozambique
Negomano see Negomane
Negombo 110 C3 Western Province, SW Sri Lanka
Negotin 78 E4 Serbia, E Yugoslavia
Negra, Punta 38 A3 headland NW Peru
Negreşti-Oaş 86 B3 Hung. Avasfelsőfalu; prev. Negreşti. Satu Mare, NE Romania
Negro, Río 43 C5 river E Argentina
Negro, Rio 40 D1 river N South America
Negro, Río 42 D4 river Brazil/Uruguay
Negros 117 E2 island C Philippines
Nehbandān 98 E3 Khorāsān, E Iran
Neijiang 106 B5 Sichuan, C China
Nei Monggol Zizhiqu see Inner Mongolia
Nei Mongol see Inner Mongolia
Neiva 36 B3 Huila, S Colombia
Nellore 110 D2 Andhra Pradesh, E India
Nelson 15 G4 river Manitoba, C Canada
Nelson 129 C5 Nelson, South Island, NZ
Néma 52 D3 Hodh ech Chargui, SE Mauritania
Neman 84 A4 Bel. Nyoman, Ger. Memel, Lith. Nemunas, Pol. Niemen, Rus. Neman. River NE Europe
Neman 84 B4 Ger. Ragnit. Kaliningradskaya Oblast', W Russian Federation
Neméa 83 B6 Pelopónnisos, S Greece
Nemours 68 C3 Seine-et-Marne, N France
Nemuro 108 E2 Hokkaidō, NE Japan
Neochóri 83 B5 Dytikí Ellás, C Greece
Nepal 113 E3 off. Kingdom of Nepal. Country S Asia
Nereta 84 C4 Aizkraukle, S Latvia
Neretva 78 C4 river Bosnia and Herzegovina/Croatia
Neringa 84 A3 Ger. Nidden; prev. Nida. Neringa, SW Lithuania
Neris 85 C5 Bel. Viliya, Pol. Wilia; prev. Pol. Wilja. River Belarus/Lithuania
Nerva 70 C4 Andalucía, S Spain
Neryungri 93 F4 Respublika Sakha (Yakutiya), NE Russian Federation
Neskaupstadhur 61 E5 Austurland, E Iceland
Ness, Loch 66 C3 lake N Scotland, UK
Néstos 82 C3 Bul. Mesta, Turk. Kara Su. River Bulgaria/Greece see also Mesta
Netanya 97 A6 var. Natanya, Nathanya. Central, C Israel
Netherlands 64 C3 off. Kingdom of the Netherlands, var. Holland, Dut. Koninkrijk der Nederlanden, Nederland. Country NW Europe
Netherlands Antilles 33 E5 prev. Dutch West Indies. Dutch autonomous region S Caribbean Sea
Netherlands New Guinea see Irian Jaya
Nettilling Lake 15 G3 lake Baffin Island, Nunavut, N Canada
Neubrandenburg 72 D3 Mecklenburg-Vorpommern, NE Germany
Neuchâtel 73 A7 Ger. Neuenburg. Neuchâtel, W Switzerland
Neuchâtel, Lac de 73 A7 Ger. Neuenburger See. Lake W Switzerland
Neufchâteau 65 D8 Luxembourg, SE Belgium
Neumünster 72 B2 Schleswig-Holstein, N Germany
Neunkirchen 73 A5 Saarland, SW Germany
Neuquén 43 B5 Neuquén, SE Argentina
Neuruppin 72 C3 Brandenburg, NE Germany
Neusalz an der Oder see Nowa Sól
Neusiedler See 73 E6 Hung. Fertő. Lake Austria/Hungary
Neustadt an der Weinstrasse 73 B5 prev. Neustadt an der Haardt, hist. Niewenstat, anc. Nova Civitas. Rheinland-Pfalz, SW Germany
Neustrelitz 72 D3 Mecklenburg-Vorpommern, NE Germany
Neu-Ulm 73 B6 Bayern, S Germany
Neuwied 73 A5 Rheinland-Pfalz, W Germany
Neuzen see Terneuzen
Nevada 25 C5 off. State of Nevada; also known as Battle Born State, Sagebrush State, Silver State. State W USA
Nevada, Sierra 70 D5 mountain range S Spain
Nevers 68 C4 anc. Noviodunum. Nièvre, C France
Neves 54 E2 São Tomé, S Sao Tome and Principe
Nevinnomyssk 89 B7 Stavropol'skiy Kray, SW Russian Federation
Nevşehir 94 C3 var. Nevshehr. Nevşehir, C Turkey
Nevshehr see Nevşehir
Newala 51 C8 Mtwara, SE Tanzania
New Albany 18 C5 Indiana, N USA
New Amsterdam 37 G3 E Guyana
Newark 19 F4 New Jersey, NE USA
New Bedford 19 G3 Massachusetts, NE USA
Newberg 24 B3 Oregon, NW USA
New Bern 21 F1 North Carolina, SE USA
New Braunfels 27 G4 Texas, SW USA
Newbridge 67 B6 Ir. An Droichead Nua. C Ireland
New Britain 122 B3 island E PNG
New Brunswick 17 E4 Fr. Nouveau-Brunswick. Province SE Canada
New Caledonia 122 D4 var. Kanaky, Fr. Nouvelle-Calédonie. French overseas territory SW Pacific Ocean
New Caledonia 122 C5 island SW Pacific Ocean
New Caledonia Basin 120 C4 undersea feature W Pacific Ocean
Newcastle see Newcastle upon Tyne
Newcastle 127 D6 New South Wales, SE Australia
Newcastle upon Tyne 66 D4 var. Newcastle; hist. Monkchester, Lat. Pons Aelii. NE England, UK
New Delhi 112 D3 country capital (India) Delhi, N India
Newfoundland 17 G3 Fr. Terre-Neuve Island Newfoundland, SE Canada
Newfoundland 17 F2 Fr. Terre Neuve. Province SE Canada
Newfoundland Basin 44 B3 undersea feature NW Atlantic Ocean
New Georgia Islands 122 C3 island group NW Solomon Islands
New Glasgow 17 F4 Nova Scotia, SE Canada
New Goa see Panaji
New Guinea 122 A3 Dut. Nieuw Guinea, Ind. Irian. Island Indonesia/PNG
New Hampshire 19 F2 off. State of New Hampshire; also known as The Granite State. State NE USA
New Haven 19 G3 Connecticut, NE USA
New Iberia 20 B3 Louisiana, S USA
New Ireland 122 C3 island NE PNG
New Jersey 19 F4 off. State of New Jersey; also known as The Garden State. State NE USA
Newman 124 B4 Western Australia
Newmarket 67 E6 E England, UK
New Mexico 26 C2 off. State of New Mexico; also known as Land of Enchantment, Sunshine State. State SW USA
New Orleans 20 B3 Louisiana, S USA
New Plymouth 128 C4 Taranaki, North Island, NZ
Newport 18 C4 Kentucky, S USA
Newport 67 D7 S England, UK
Newport 67 C7 SE Wales, UK
Newport 19 G2 Vermont, NE USA
Newport News 19 F5 Virginia, NE USA
New Providence 32 C1 island N Bahamas
Newquay 67 C7 SW England, UK
Newry 67 B5 Ir. An tIúr. SE Northern Ireland, UK
New Sarum see Salisbury
New Siberian Islands see Novosibirskiye Ostrova
New South Wales 127 C6 state SE Australia
Newton 23 G3 Iowa, C USA
Newtownabbey 67 B5 Ir. Baile na Mainistreach. E Northern Ireland, UK
New Ulm 23 F2 Minnesota, N USA
New York 19 F4 New York, NE USA
New York 19 F3 state NE USA
New Zealand 128 A4 abbrev. NZ. Country SW Pacific Ocean
Neyveli 110 C2 Tamil Nādu, SE India
Ngangzê Co 104 B5 lake W China
Ngaoundéré 54 B4 var. N'Gaoundéré. Adamaoua, N Cameroon
N'Giva 56 B3 var. Ondjiva, Port. Vila Pereira de Eça. Cunene, S Angola
Ngo 55 B6 Plateaux, SE Congo
Ngoko 55 B5 river Cameroon/Congo
Ngourti 53 H3 Diffa, E Niger
Nguigmi 53 H3 var. N'Guigmi. Diffa, SE Niger
Nguru 53 G3 Yobe, NE Nigeria
Nha Trang 115 E6 Khanh Hoa, S Vietnam
Niagara Falls 18 D3 waterfall Canada/USA
Niagara Falls 19 E3 New York, NE USA
Niagara Falls 16 D5 Ontario, S Canada
Niamey 53 F3 country capital (Niger) Niamey, SW Niger
Niangay, Lac 53 E3 lake E Mali
Nia-Nia 55 E5 Orientale, NE Dem. Rep. Congo (Zaire)
Nias, Pulau 116 A3 island W Indonesia
Nicaragua 30 D3 off. Republic of Nicaragua. Country Central America
Nicaragua, Lago de 30 D4 var. Cocibolca, Gran Lago, Eng. Lake Nicaragua. Lake S Nicaragua
Nicaragua, Lake see Nicaragua, Lago de
Nicaria see Ikaría
Nice 69 D6 It. Nizza; anc. Nicaea. Alpes-Maritimes, SE France
Nicephorium see Ar Raqqah
Nicholas II Land see Severnaya Zemlya
Nicholls Town 32 C1 Andros Island, NW Bahamas
Nicobar Islands 102 B4 island group India, E Indian Ocean
Nicosia 80 C5 Gk. Lefkosía, Turk. Lefkoşa. Country capital (Cyprus) C Cyprus
Nicoya 30 D4 Guanacaste, W Costa Rica
Nicoya, Golfo de 30 D5 gulf W Costa Rica
Nicoya, Península de 30 D4 peninsula NW Costa Rica
Nidzica 76 D3 Ger. Niedenburg. Warmińsko-Mazurskie, NE Poland
Niedere Tauern 77 A6 mountain range C Austria
Nieuw Amsterdam 37 G3 Commewijne, NE Suriname
Nieuw-Bergen 64 D4 Limburg, SE Netherlands
Nieuwegein 64 C4 Utrecht, C Netherlands
Nieuw Nickerie 37 G3 Nickerie, NW Suriname
Niğde 94 C4 Niğde, C Turkey
Niger 53 F3 off. Republic of Niger. Country W Africa
Niger 53 F4 river W Africa
Nigeria 53 F4 off. Federal Republic of Nigeria. Country W Africa
Niger, Mouths of the 53 F5 delta S Nigeria
Nihon see Japan
Niigata 109 D5 Niigata, Honshū, C Japan
Niihama 109 B7 Ehime, Shikoku, SW Japan
Niihau 25 A7 island Hawaii, USA, C Pacific Ocean
Nii-jima 109 D6 island E Japan
Nijkerk 64 D3 Gelderland, C Netherlands
Nijlen 65 C5 Antwerpen, N Belgium
Nijmegen 64 D4 Ger. Nimwegen; anc. Noviomagus. Gelderland, SE Netherlands
Nikaria see Ikaría
Nikel' 88 C2 Murmanskaya Oblast', NW Russian Federation
Nikiniki 117 E5 Timor, S Indonesia
Nikopol' 87 F3 Pleven, N Bulgaria
Nikšić 79 C5 Montenegro, SW Yugoslavia
Nikumaroro 123 E3 prev. Gardner Island, Kemins Island. Atoll Phoenix Islands, C Kiribati
Nikunau 123 E3 var. Nukunau; prev. Byron Island. Atoll Tungaru, W Kiribati
Nile 46 D3 Ar. Nahr an Nīl. River N Africa
Nile 50 B2 former province NW Uganda
Nile Delta 50 B1 delta N Egypt
Nîmes 69 C6 anc. Nemausus, Nismes. Gard, S France
Nine Degree Channel 110 B3 channel India/Maldives
Ninetyeast Ridge 119 D5 undersea feature E Indian Ocean
Ninety Mile Beach 128 C1 beach North Island, NZ
Ningbo 106 D5 var. Ning-po, Yin-hsien; prev. Ninghsien. Zhejiang, SE China
Ninghsien see Ningbo
Ning-po see Ningbo
Ningxia 106 B4 off. Ningxia Huizu Zizhiqu, var. Ning-hsia, Ningsia, Eng. Ningsia Hui, Ningsia Hui Autonomous Region. Admin. region autonomous region N China
Ningxia Huizu Zizhiqu see Ningxia
Nio see Íos
Niobrara River 23 E3 river Nebraska/Wyoming, C USA
Nioro 52 D3 var. Nioro du Sahel. Kayes, W Mali
Nioro du Sahel see Nioro
Niort 68 B4 Deux-Sèvres, W France
Nipigon 16 B4 Ontario, S Canada
Nipigon, Lake 16 B3 lake Ontario, S Canada
Nippon see Japan
Niš 79 E5 Eng. Nish, Ger. Nisch; anc. Naissus. Serbia, SE Yugoslavia
Nişab 98 B4 Al Ḥudūd ash Shamālīyah, N Saudi Arabia
Nisibin see Nusaybin
Nisiros see Nísyros
Nisko 76 E4 Podkarpackie, SE Poland
Nísyros 83 E7 var. Nisiros. Island Dodekánisos, Greece, Aegean Sea
Nitra 77 C6 Ger. Neutra, Hung. Nyitra. River W Slovakia
Nitra 77 C6 Ger. Neutra, Hung. Nyitra. Nitriansky Kraj, SW Slovakia
Niuatobutabu see Niuatoputapu
Niuatoputapu 123 E4 var. Niuatobutabu; prev. Keppel Island. Island N Tonga

Opelika – Pátmos

Opelika 20 D2 Alabama, S USA
Opelousas 20 B3 Louisiana, S USA
Opmeer 64 C2 Noord-Holland, NW Netherlands
Opochka 88 A4 Pskovskaya Oblast', W Russian Federation
Opole 76 C4 *Ger.* Oppeln. Opolskie, S Poland
Opotiki 128 E3 Bay of Plenty, North Island, NZ
Oppidum Ubiorum *see* Köln
Oqtosh 101 E2 *Rus.* Aktash. Samarqand Wiloyati, C Uzbekistan
Oradea 86 B3 *prev.* Oradea Mare, *Ger.* Grosswardein, *Hung.* Nagyvárad. Bihor, NW Romania
Orahovac 79 D5 *Alb.* Rahovec. Serbia, S Yugoslavia
Oran 48 D2 *var.* Ouahran, Wahran. NW Algeria
Orange 69 D6 *anc.* Arausio. Vaucluse, SE France
Orange 127 D6 New South Wales, SE Australia
Orangeburg 21 E2 South Carolina, SE USA
Orange Cone *see* Orange Fan
Orange Fan 47 C7 *var.* Orange Cone. *Undersea feature* SW Indian Ocean
Orange Mouth *see* Oranjemund
Orangemund *see* Oranjemund
Orange River 56 B4 *Afr.* Oranjerivier. *River* S Africa
Orange Walk 30 C1 Orange Walk, N Belize
Oranienburg 72 D3 Brandenburg, NE Germany
Oranjemund 56 B4 *var.* Orangemund; *prev.* Orange Mouth. Karas, SW Namibia
Oranjestad 33 E5 *dependent territory capital* (Aruba) W Aruba
Orantes 96 B3 *var.* Ononte, *Ar.* Nahr el Aassi, Nahr al 'Aṣī. *River* SW Asia
Oraviţa 86 A4 *Ger.* Orawitza, *Hung.* Oravicabánya. Caraş-Severin, SW Romania
Orbetello 74 B4 Toscana, C Italy
Orcadas 132 A1 *Argentinian research station* South Orkney Islands, Antarctica
Orchard Homes 22 B1 Montana, NW USA
Ordino 69 A8 NW Andorra
Ordos Desert *see* Mu Us Shamo
Ordu 94 D2 *anc.* Cotyora. Ordu, N Turkey
Ordzhonikidze 87 F3 Dnipropetrovs'ka Oblast', E Ukraine
Orealla 37 G3 E Guyana
Örebro 63 C6 Örebro, C Sweden
Oregon 24 B3 *off.* State of Oregon; also known as Beaver State, Sunset State, Valentine State, Webfoot State. *State* NW USA
Oregon City 24 B3 Oregon, NW USA
Orël 89 B5 Orlovskaya Oblast', W Russian Federation
Orem 22 B4 Utah, W USA
Orenburg 89 D6 *prev.* Chkalov. Orenburgskaya Oblast', W Russian Federation
Orense *see* Ourense
Oreor 122 A2 *var.* Koror. *Country capital* (Palau) Oreor, N Palau
Orestiáda 82 D3 *prev.* Orestiás. Anatolikí Makedonía kai Thráki, NE Greece
Organ Peak 26 D3 *mountain* New Mexico, SW USA
Orgeyev *see* Orhei
Orhei 86 D3 *var.* Orheiu, *Rus.* Orgeyev. N Moldova
Orheiu *see* Orhei
Oriental, Cordillera 38 D3 *mountain range* Bolivia/Peru
Oriental, Cordillera 39 F4 *mountain range* C Bolivia
Oriental, Cordillera 36 B3 *mountain range* C Colombia
Orihuela 71 F4 País Valenciano, E Spain
Orikhiv 87 G3 *Rus.* Orekhov. Zaporiz'ka Oblast', SE Ukraine
Orinoco, Río 37 E2 *river* Colombia/Venezuela
Orissa 113 F4 *state* NE India
Orissaare 84 C2 *Ger.* Orissaar. Saaremaa, W Estonia
Oristano 75 A5 Sardegna, Italy, C Mediterranean Sea
Orito 36 A4 Putumayo, SW Colombia
Orizaba, Volcán Pico de 13 C7 *var.* Citlaltépetl. *Mountain* S Mexico
Orkney *see* Orkney Islands
Orkney Islands 66 C2 *var.* Orkney, Orkneys. *Island group* N Scotland, UK
Orkneys *see* Orkney Islands
Orlando 21 E4 Florida, SE USA
Orléanais 68 C4 *cultural region* C France
Orléans 68 C4 *anc.* Aurelianum. Loiret, C France
Orléansville *see* Chlef
Orly 68 E2 *international airport* (Paris) Essonne, N France
Orlya 85 B6 *Rus.* Orlya. Hrodzyenskaya Voblasts', W Belarus
Ormuz, Strait of *see* Hormuz, Strait of
Örnsköldsvik 63 C5 Västernorrland, C Sweden
Oromocto 17 F4 New Brunswick, SE Canada
Orona 123 F3 *prev.* Hull Island. *Atoll* Phoenix Islands, C Kiribati
Orosirá Rodhópis *see* Rhodope Mountains
Orpington 67 B8 SE England, UK
Orsha 85 E6 *Rus.* Orsha. Vitsyebskaya Voblasts', NE Belarus
Orsk 92 B4 Orenburgskaya Oblast', W Russian Federation
Orşova 86 A4 *Ger.* Orschowa, *Hung.* Orsova. Mehedinţi, SW Romania
Orthez 69 B6 Pyrénées-Atlantiques, SW France
Ortona 74 D4 Abruzzo, C Italy
Oruba *see* Aruba
Oruro 39 F4 Oruro, W Bolivia
Ōsaka 109 C6 *hist.* Naniwa. Ōsaka, Honshū, SW Japan
Osa, Península de 31 E5 *peninsula* S Costa Rica
Osborn Plateau 119 D5 *undersea feature* E Indian Ocean
Osh 101 F2 Oshskaya Oblast', SW Kyrgyzstan
Oshawa 16 D5 Ontario, SE Canada
Oshikango 56 B3 Ohangwena, N Namibia
Ō-shima 109 D6 *island* S Japan
Oshkosh 18 B2 Wisconsin, N USA
Osijek 78 C3 *prev.* Osiek, Osjek, *Ger.* Esseg, *Hung.* Eszék. Osijek-Baranja, E Croatia
Oskaloosa 23 G4 Iowa, C USA
Oskarshamn 63 C7 Kalmar, S Sweden
Oskil 87 G2 *Rus.* Oskol. *River* Russian Federation/Ukraine
Oslo 63 B6 *prev.* Christiania, Kristiania. *Country capital* (Norway) Oslo, S Norway
Osmaniye 94 D4 Osmaniye, admin. region *province* S Turkey
Osnabrück 72 A3 Niedersachsen, NW Germany
Osogov Mountains 120 B3 *var.* Osogovske Planine, Osogovski Planina, *Mac.* Osogovski Planini. *mountain range* Bulgaria/FYR, Macedonia
Osogovske Planine/Osogovski Planina/Osogovski Planini *see* Osogov Mountains
Osorno 43 B5 Los Lagos, C Chile
Oss 64 D4 Noord-Brabant, S Netherlands
Ossa, Serra d' 70 C4 *mountain range* SE Portugal
Ossora 93 H2 Koryakskiy Avtonomnyy Okrug, E Russian Federation
Ostend *see* Oostende
Ostende *see* Oostende
Oster 87 E1 Chernihivs'ka Oblast', N Ukraine
Östersund 63 C5 Jämtland, C Sweden
Ostfriesische Inseln 72 A3 *Eng.* East Frisian Islands. *Island group* NW Germany
Ostiglia 74 C2 Lombardia, N Italy
Ostrava 77 C5 Ostravský Kraj, E Czech Republic
Ostróda 76 D3 *Ger.* Osterode, Osterode in Ostpreussen. Warmińsko-Mazurskie, NE Poland
Ostrołęka 76 D3 *Ger.* Wiesenhof, *Rus.* Ostrolenka. Mazowieckie, C Poland
Ostrov 88 A4 *Latv.* Austrava. Karlovarský Kraj, W Czech Republic
Ostrovets *see* Ostrowiec Świętokrzyski
Ostrów *see* Ostrów Wielkopolski
Ostrowiec *see* Ostrowiec Świętokrzyski
Ostrowiec Świętokrzyski 76 D4 *var.* Ostrowiec, *Rus.* Ostrovets. Świętokrzyskie, C Poland
Ostrów Mazowiecka 76 D3 *var.* Ostrów Mazowiecki. Mazowieckie, C Poland
Ostrów Mazowiecki *see* Ostrów Mazowiecka
Ostrowo *see* Ostrów Wielkopolski
Ostrów Wielkopolski 76 C4 *var.* Ostrów, *Ger.* Ostrowo. Wielkopolskie, C Poland
Osum *see* Osumit, Lumi i
Ōsumi-shotō 109 A8 *island group* SW Japan
Osumit, Lumi i 79 D7 *var.* Osum. *River* SE Albania
Osuna 70 D4 Andalucía, S Spain
Oswego 19 F2 New York, NE USA
Otago Peninsula 129 B7 *peninsula* South Island, NZ
Otaki 128 D4 Wellington, North Island, NZ
Otaru 108 C2 Hokkaidō, NE Japan
Otavalo 38 B1 Imbabura, N Ecuador
Otavi 56 B3 Otjozondjupa, N Namibia
Oţelu Roşu 86 B4 *Ger.* Ferdinandsberg, *Hung.* Nándorhgy. Caraş-Severin, SW Romania
Otepää 84 D3 *Ger.* Odenpäh. Valgamaa, SE Estonia
Oti 53 E4 *river* W Africa
Otira 129 C6 West Coast, South Island, NZ
Otjiwarongo 56 B3 Otjozondjupa, N Namibia
Otorohanga 128 D3 Waikato, North Island, NZ
Otranto, Strait of 79 C6 *It.* Canale d'Otranto. *Strait* Albania/Italy
Otrokovice 77 C5 *Ger.* Otrokowitz. Zlínský Kraj, E Czech Republic
Ōtsu 109 C6 *var.* Ôtu. Shiga, Honshū, SW Japan
Ottawa 19 E2 *Fr.* Outaouais. Admin. region *river* Ontario/Québec, SE Canada
Ottawa 16 D5 *country capital* (Canada) Ontario, SE Canada
Ottawa 18 B3 Illinois, N USA
Ottawa 23 F5 Kansas, C USA
Ottawa Islands 16 C1 *island group* Northwest Territories, C Canada
Ottignies 65 C6 Wallon Brabant, C Belgium
Ottumwa 23 G4 Iowa, C USA
Ôtu *see* Ōtsu
Ouachita Mountains 20 A1 *mountain range* Arkansas/Oklahoma, C USA
Ouachita River 20 B2 *river* Arkansas/Louisiana, C USA
Ouadi Howa *see* Howar, Wādi
Ouagadougou 53 E4 *var.* Wagadugu. *Country capital* (Burkina Faso) C Burkina Faso
Ouahigouya 53 E3 NW Burkina faso
Ouahran *see* Oran
Oualata *see* Oualâta
Oualâta 52 D3 *var.* Oualata. Hodh ech Chargui, SE Mauritania
Ouanary 37 H3 E French Guiana
Ouanda Djallé 54 D4 Vakaga, NE Central African Republic
Ouarâne 52 D2 *desert* C Mauritania
Ouargla 49 E2 *var.* Wargla. NE Algeria
Ouarzazate 48 C3 S Morocco
Oubangui *see* Ubangi
Oubangui-Chari *see* Central African Republic
Ouessant, Île d' 68 A3 *Eng.* Ushant. *Island* NW France
Ouésso 55 B5 La Sangha, NW Congo
Oujda 48 D2 *Ar.* Oudjda, Ujda. NE Morocco
Oujeft 52 C2 Adrar, C Mauritania
Oulu 62 D4 *Swe.* Uleåborg. Oulu, C Finland
Oulujärvi 62 D4 *Swe.* Uleträsk. *Lake* C Finland
Oulujoki 62 D4 *Swe.* Uleälv. *River* C Finland
Ounasjoki 62 D3 *river* N Finland
Ounianga Kébir 54 C2 Borkou Ennedi-Tibesti, N Chad
Oup *see* Auob
Oupeye 65 D6 Liège, E Belgium
Our 65 D6 *river* NW Europe
Ourense 70 C1 *var. Cast.* Orense; *Lat.* Aurium. Galicia, NW Spain
Ourique 70 B4 Beja, S Portugal
Ourthe 65 D7 *river* E Belgium
Ouse 67 D5 *river* N England, UK
Outer Hebrides 66 B3 *var.* Western Isles. *Island group* NW Scotland, UK
Outer Islands 57 G1 *island group* SW Seychelles
Outes 70 B1 Galicia, NW Spain
Ouvéa 122 D5 *island* Îles Loyauté, NE New Caledonia
Ouyen 127 C6 Victoria, SE Australia
Ovalle 42 B3 Coquimbo, N Chile
Ovar 70 B2 Aveiro, N Portugal
Overflakkee 64 B4 *island* SW Netherlands
Overijse 65 C6 Vlaams Brabant, C Belgium
Oviedo 70 C1 *anc.* Asturias. Asturias, NW Spain
Ovruch 86 D1 Zhytomyrs'ka Oblast', N Ukraine
Owando 55 B5 *prev.* Fort-Rousset. Cuvette, C Congo
Owase 109 C6 Mie, Honshū, SW Japan
Owatonna 23 F3 Minnesota, N USA
Owen Fracture Zone 118 B4 *tectonic feature* W Arabian Sea
Owen, Mount 129 C5 *mountain* South Island, NZ
Owensboro 18 B5 Kentucky, S USA
Owen Stanley Range 122 B3 *mountain range* S PNG
Owerri 53 G5 Imo, S Nigeria
Owo 53 F5 Ondo, SW Nigeria
Owyhee River 24 C4 *river* Idaho/Oregon, NW USA
Oxford 67 D6 *Lat.* Oxonia. S England, UK
Oxford 129 C6 Canterbury, South Island, NZ
Oxkutzcab 29 H4 Yucatán, SE Mexico
Oxnard 25 B7 California, W USA
Oyama 109 D5 Tochigi, Honshū, S Japan
Oyem 55 B5 Woleu-Ntem, N Gabon
Oyo 55 B6 Cuvette, C Congo
Oyo 53 F4 Oyo, W Nigeria
Ozark 20 D3 Alabama, S USA
Ozark Plateau 23 G5 *plain* Arkansas/Missouri, C USA
Ozarks, Lake of the 23 F5 *reservoir* Missouri, C USA
Ozbourn Seamount 130 D4 *undersea feature* W Pacific Ocean
Ózd 77 D6 Borsod-Abaúj-Zemplén, NE Hungary
Ozero Khanka *see* Khanka, Lake
Ozero Ubsu-Nur *see* Uvs Nuur
Ozieri 75 A5 Sardegna, Italy, C Mediterranean Sea

P

Paamiut 60 B4 *var.* Pâmiut, *Dan.* Frederikshåb. S Greenland
Pa-an 114 B4 Karen State, S Myanmar
Pabianice 76 C4 Łodz, C Poland
Pabna 113 G4 Rajshahi, W Bangladesh
Pachuca 29 E4 *var.* Pachuca de Soto. Hidalgo, C Mexico
Pachuca de Soto *see* Pachuca
Pacific-Antarctic Ridge 132 B5 *undersea feature* S Pacific Ocean
Pacific Ocean 130 D3 *ocean*
Padalung *see* Phatthalung
Padang 116 B4 Sumatera, W Indonesia
Paderborn 72 B4 Nordrhein-Westfalen, NW Germany
Padma *see* Brahmaputra
Padova 74 C2 *Eng.* Padua; *anc.* Patavium. Veneto, NE Italy
Padre Island 27 G5 *island* Texas, SW USA
Padua *see* Padova
Paducah 18 B5 Kentucky, S USA
Paeroa 128 D3 Waikato, North Island, NZ
Páfos 80 C5 *var.* Paphos. W Cyprus
Pag 78 A3 *It.* Pago. *Island* Zadar SW Croatia
Page 26 B1 Arizona, SW USA
Pago Pago 123 F4 *dependent territory capital* (American Samoa) Tutuila, W American Samoa
Pahiatua 128 D4 Manawatu-Wanganui, North Island, NZ
Pahsien *see* Chongqing
Paide 84 D2 *Ger.* Weissenstein. Järvamaa, N Estonia
Paihia 128 D2 Northland, North Island, NZ
Päijänne 63 D5 *lake* S Finland
Paine, Cerro 43 A7 *mountain* S Chile
Painted Desert 26 B1 *desert* Arizona, SW USA
Paisley 66 C4 W Scotland, UK
País Valenciano 71 F3 *cultural region* NE Spain
País Vasco 71 E1 *cultural region* N Spain
Paita 38 B3 Piura, NW Peru
Pakanbaru *see* Pekanbaru
Pakaraima Mountains 37 E3 *var.* Serra Pacaraim, Sierra Pacaraima. *Mountain range* N South America
Pakistan 112 A2 *off.* Islamic Republic of Pakistan, *var.* Islami Jamhuriya e Pakistan. *Country* S Asia
Paknam *see* Samut Prakan
Pakokku 114 A3 Magwe, C Myanmar
Pak Phanang 115 C7 *var.* Ban Pak Phanang. Nakhon Si Thammarat, SW Thailand
Pakruojis 84 C4 Pakruojis, N Lithuania
Paks 77 C7 Tolna, S Hungary
Paksé *see* Pakxé
Pakxé 115 D5 *var.* Paksé. Champasak, S Laos
Palafrugell 71 G2 Cataluña, NE Spain
Palagruža 79 B5 *It.* Pelagosa. *Island* SW Croatia
Palaiá Epídavros 83 C6 Pelopónnisos, S Greece
Palaiseau 68 D2 Essonne, N France
Palamós 71 G2 Cataluña, NE Spain
Palamuse 84 E2 *Ger.* Sankt-Bartholomäi. Jõgevamaa, E Estonia
Pālanpur 112 C4 Gujarāt, W India
Palapye 56 D3 Central, SE Botswana
Palau 122 A2 *var.* Belau. *Country* W Pacific Ocean
Palawan 117 E2 *island* W Philippines
Palawan Passage 116 D2 *passage* W Philippines
Paldiski 84 D2 *prev.* Baltiski, *Eng.* Baltic Port, *Ger.* Baltischport. Harjumaa, NW Estonia
Palembang 116 B4 Sumatera, W Indonesia
Palencia 70 D2 *anc.* Palantia, Pallantia. Castilla-León, NW Spain
Palermo 75 C7 *Fr.* Palerme; *anc.* Panhormus, Panormus. Sicilia, Italy, C Mediterranean Sea
Pāli 112 C3 Rājasthān, N India
Palikir 122 C2 *country capital* (Micronesia) Pohnpei, E Micronesia
Palimé *see* Kpalimé
Palioúri, Akrotírio 82 C4 *var.* Akra Kanestron. *Headland* N Greece
Palk Strait 110 C3 *strait* India/Sri Lanka
Palliser, Cape 129 D5 *headland* North Island, NZ
Palma 71 G3 *var.* Palma de Mallorca. Mallorca, Spain, W Mediterranean Sea
Palma del Río 70 D4 Andalucía, S Spain
Palma de Mallorca *see* Palma
Palmar Sur 31 E5 Puntarenas, SE Costa Rica
Palma Soriano 32 C3 Santiago de Cuba, E Cuba
Palm Beach 126 E1 New South Wales, SE Australia
Palmer 132 A2 *US research station* Antarctica
Palmer Land 132 A3 *physical region* Antarctica
Palmerston 123 F4 *island* S Cook Islands
Palmerston North 128 D4 Manawatu-Wanganui, North Island, NZ
Palmi 75 D7 Calabria, SW Italy
Palmira 36 B3 Valle del Cauca, W Colombia
Palm Springs 25 D7 California, W USA
Palmyra *see* Tudmur
Palmyra Atoll 123 G2 *US privately owned unincorporated territory* C Pacific Ocean
Palo Alto 25 B6 California, W USA
Palu 117 E4 *prev.* Paloe. Sulawesi, C Indonesia
Pamiers 69 B6 Ariège, S France
Pamir *var.* Daryā-ye Pāmīr, *Taj.* Dar"yoi Pomir. *River* Afghanistan/Tajikistan *see also* Pāmīr, Daryā-ye
Pamirs 101 F3 *Pash.* Daryā-ye Pāmīr, *Rus.* Pamir. *Mountain range* C Asia
Pâmiut *see* Paamiut
Pamlico Sound 21 G1 *sound* North Carolina, SE USA
Pampa 27 E1 Texas, SW USA
Pampas 42 C4 *plain* C Argentina
Pamplona 71 E1 *Basq.* Iruña; *prev.* Pampeluna, *anc.* Pompaelo. Navarra, N Spain
Pamplona 36 C2 Norte de Santander, N Colombia
Panaji 110 B1 *var.* Pangim, Panjim, New Goa. Goa, W India
Panama 31 G5 *off.* Republic of Panama. *Country* Central America
Panamá 31 G4 *var.* Ciudad de Panamá, *Eng.* Panama City. *Country capital* (Panama) Panamá, C Panama
Panama Basin 13 C8 *undersea feature* E Pacific Ocean
Panama Canal 31 F4 *canal* E Panama
Panama City *see* Panamá
Panama City 20 D3 Florida, SE USA
Panamá, Golfo de 31 G5 *var.* Gulf of Panama. *Gulf* S Panama
Panama, Gulf of *see* Panamá, Golfo de
Panamá, Isthmus of *see* Panamá, Istmo de
Panamá, Istmo de 31 G4 *Eng.* Isthmus of Panama; *prev.* Isthmus of Darien. *Isthmus* E Panama
Panay Island 117 E2 *island* C Philippines
Pančevo 78 D3 *Ger.* Pantschowa, *Hung.* Pancsova. Serbia, N Yugoslavia
Paneas *see* Bāniyās
Panevėžys 84 C4 Panevėžys, C Lithuania
Pangim *see* Panaji
Pangkalpinang 116 C4 Pulau Bangka, W Indonesia
Pang-Nga *see* Phang-Nga
Panjim *see* Panaji
Pánormos 83 C7 Kríti, Greece, E Mediterranean Sea
Pantanal 41 E3 *var.* Pantanalmato-Grossense. *Swamp* SW Brazil
Pantanalmato-Grossense *see* Pantanal
Pantelleria, Isola di 75 B7 *island* SW Italy
Pánuco 29 E3 Veracruz-Llave, E Mexico
Pao-chi *see* Baoji
Paoki *see* Baoji
Paola 80 B5 E Malta
Pao-shan *see* Baoshan
Pao-t'ou *see* Baotou
Paotow *see* Baotou
Papagayo, Golfo de 30 C4 *gulf* NW Costa Rica
Papakura 128 D3 Auckland, North Island, NZ
Papantla 29 F4 *var.* Papantla de Olarte. Veracruz-Llave, E Mexico
Papantla de Olarte *see* Papantla
Papeete 123 H4 *dependent territory capital* (French Polynesia) Tahiti, W French Polynesia
Paphos *see* Páfos
Papilė 84 B3 Akmenė, NW Lithuania
Papillion 23 F4 Nebraska, C USA
Papua, Gulf of 122 B3 *gulf* S PNG
Papua New Guinea 122 B3 *off.* Independent State of Papua New Guinea; *prev.* Territory of Papua and New Guinea, *abbrev.* PNG. *Country* NW Melanesia
Papuk 78 C3 *mountain range* NE Croatia
Pará 41 E2 *off.* Estado do Pará. *State* NE Brazil
Pará *see* Belém
Paracel Islands 103 E3 *disputed territory* SE Asia
Paraćin 78 D4 Serbia, C Yugoslavia
Paragua, Río 37 E3 *river* SE Venezuela
Paraguay 42 D2 *var.* Río Paraguay. *River* C South America
Paraguay 42 C2 *country* C South America
Paraguay, Río *see* Paraguay
Paraíba 41 G2 *off.* Estado da Paraíba; *prev.* Parahiba, Parahyba. *State* E Brazil
Parakou 53 F4 C Benin
Paramaribo 37 G3 *country capital* (Suriname) Paramaribo, N Suriname
Paramushir, Ostrov 93 H3 *island* SE Russian Federation
Paraná 41 E5 *off.* Estado do Paraná. *State* S Brazil
Paraná 35 C5 *var.* Alto Paraná. *River* C South America
Paraná 41 E4 Entre Ríos, E Argentina
Paranéstio 82 C3 Anatolikí Makedonía kai Thráki, NE Greece
Paraparaumu 129 D5 Wellington, North Island, NZ
Parchim 72 C3 Mecklenburg-Vorpommern, N Germany
Parczew 76 E4 Lubelskie, E Poland
Pardubice 77 B5 *Ger.* Pardubitz. Pardubický Kraj, C Czech Republic
Parechcha 85 B5 *Rus.* Porech'ye. Hrodzyenskaya Voblasts', NE Belarus
Parecis, Chapada dos 40 D3 *var.* Serra dos Parecis. *Mountain range* W Brazil
Parepare 117 E4 Sulawesi, C Indonesia
Párga 83 A5 Ípeiros, W Greece
Paria, Golfo de *see* Paria, Gulf of
Paria, Gulf of 37 E1 *var.* Golfo de Paria. *Gulf* Trinidad and Tobago/Venezuela
Parika 37 F2 NE Guyana
Paris 68 D1 *anc.* Lutetia, Lutetia Parisiorum, Parisii. *Country capital* (France) Paris, N France
Paris 27 G2 Texas, SW USA
Parkersburg 18 D4 West Virginia, NE USA
Parkes 127 D6 New South Wales, SE Australia
Parma 74 B2 Emilia-Romagna, N Italy
Parnahyba *see* Parnaíba
Parnaíba 41 F2 *var.* Parnahyba. Piauí, E Brazil
Pärnu 84 D2 *Ger.* Pernau, *Latv.* Pērnava; *prev. Rus.* Pernov. Pärnumaa, SW Estonia
Pärnu 84 D2 *var.* Parnu Jõgi, *Ger.* Pernau. *River* SW Estonia
Pärnu-Jaagupi 84 D2 *Ger.* Sankt Jakobi. Pärnumaa, SW Estonia
Parnu Jõgi *see* Pärnu
Pärnu Laht 84 D2 *Ger.* Pernauer Bucht. *Bay* SW Estonia
Páros 83 C6 *island* Kykládes, Greece, Aegean Sea
Páros 83 D6 Páros, Kykládes, Greece, Aegean Sea
Parral *see* Hidalgo del Parral
Parral 42 B4 Maule, C Chile
Parramatta 126 D1 New South Wales, SE Australia
Parras 28 D3 *var.* Parras de la Fuente. Coahuila de Zaragoza, NE Mexico
Parras de la Fuente *see* Parras
Parsons 23 F5 Kansas, C USA
Pasadena 25 C7 California, W USA
Pasadena 27 H4 Texas, SW USA
Paşcani 86 C3 *Hung.* Páskán. Iaşi, NE Romania
Pasco 24 C2 Washington, NW USA
Pas de Calais *see* Dover, Strait of
Pasewalk 72 D3 Mecklenburg-Vorpommern, NE Germany
Pasinler 95 F3 Erzurum, NE Turkey
Pasłęk 76 D2 *Ger.* Preußisch Holland. Warmińsko-Mazurskie, NE Poland
Pasni 112 A3 Baluchistān, SW Pakistan
Paso de Indios 43 B6 Chubut, S Argentina
Passau 73 D6 Bayern, SE Germany
Passo del Brennero *see* Brenner Pass
Passo Fundo 41 E5 Rio Grande do Sul, S Brazil
Pastavy 85 C5 *Pol.* Postawy, *Rus.* Postavy. Vitsyebskaya Voblasts', NW Belarus
Pastaza, Río 38 B2 *river* Ecuador/Peru
Pasto 36 A4 Nariño, SW Colombia
Pasvalys 84 C4 Pasvalys, N Lithuania
Patagonia 35 B7 *physical region* Argentina/Chile
Patalung *see* Phatthalung
Patani *see* Pattani
Patavium *see* Padova
Patea 128 D4 Taranaki, North Island, NZ
Paterson 19 F3 New Jersey, NE USA
Pathein *see* Bassein
Pátmos 83 D6 *island* Dodekánisos, Greece, Aegean Sea

Port Jackson – Raga

Port Jackson *126 E1 harbour* New South Wales, SE Australia
Port Láirge *see* Waterford
Portland *19 G2* Maine, NE USA
Portland *24 B3* Oregon, NW USA
Portland *27 G4* Texas, SW USA
Portland *127 B7* Victoria, SE Australia
Portland Bight *32 B5 bay* S Jamaica
Portlaoighise *see* Portlaoise
Portlaoise *67 B6 Ir.* Portlaoighise, *prev.* Maryborough. C Ireland
Port Lavaca *27 G4* Texas, SW USA
Port Lincoln *127 A6* South Australia
Port Louis *57 H3 country capital* (Mauritius) NW Mauritius
Port Macquarie *127 E6* New South Wales, SE Australia
Portmore *32 B5* C Jamaica
Port Moresby *122 B3 country capital* (PNG) Central/National Capital District, SW PNG
Port Musgrave *127 B9 bay* Queensland, N Australia
Port Natal *see* Durban
Porto *70 B2 Eng.* Oporto; *anc.* Portus Cale. Porto, NW Portugal
Porto Alegre *41 E5 var.* Pôrto Alegre. *State capital* Rio Grande do Sul, S Brazil
Porto Alegre *54 E2* São Tomé, S Sao Tome and Principe
Porto Bello *see* Portobelo
Portobelo *31 G4 var.* Porto Bello, Puerto Bello. Colón, N Panama
Port O'Connor *27 G4* Texas, SW USA
Porto Edda *see* Sarandë
Portoferraio *74 B4* Toscana, C Italy
Port-of-Spain *33 H5 country capital* (Trinidad and Tobago) Trinidad, Trinidad and Tobago
Porto Grande *see* Mindelo
Portogruaro *74 C2* Veneto, NE Italy
Porto-Novo *53 F5 country capital* (Benin) S Benin
Porto Santo *48 A2 var.* Ilha do Porto Santo. *Island* Madeira, Portugal, NE Atlantic Ocean
Porto Torres *75 A5* Sardegna, Italy, C Mediterranean Sea
Porto Velho *40 D2 var.* Velho. *State capital* Rondônia, W Brazil
Portoviejo *38 A2 var.* Puertoviejo. Manabí, W Ecuador
Port Pirie *127 B6* South Australia
Port Said *50 B1 Ar.* Būr Sa'īd. N Egypt
Portsmouth *19 G3* New Hampshire, NE USA
Portsmouth *18 D4* Ohio, N USA
Portsmouth *67 D7* S England, UK
Portsmouth *19 F5* Virginia, NE USA
Port Stanley *see* Stanley
Port Sudan *50 C3* Red Sea, NE Sudan
Port Swettenham *see* Klang
Port Talbot *67 C7* S Wales, UK
Portugal *70 B3 off.* Republic of Portugal. *Country* SW Europe
Portuguese Timor *see* East Timor
Port-Vila *122 D4 var.* Vila. *Country capital* (Vanuatu) Éfaté, C Vanuatu
Porvenir *43 B8* Magallanes, S Chile
Porvenir *39 E3* Pando, NW Bolivia
Porvoo *63 E6 Swe.* Borgå. Etelä-Suomi, S Finland
Posadas *42 D3* Misiones, NE Argentina
Poschega *see* Požega
Postelholt *65 D5* Limburg, SE Netherlands
Postojna *73 D8 Ger.* Adelsberg, *It.* Postumia. SW Slovenia
Potamós *83 C7* Antikýthira, S Greece
Potenza *75 D5 anc.* Potentia. Basilicata, S Italy
P'ot'i *95 F2* W Georgia
Potiskum *53 G4* Yobe, NE Nigeria
Potomac River *19 E5 river* NE USA
Potosí *39 F4* Potosí, S Bolivia
Potsdam *72 D3* Brandenburg, NE Germany
Potwar Plateau *112 C2 plateau* NE Pakistan
Poŭthĭsăt *115 D6 prev.* Pursat. Poŭthĭsăt, W Cambodia
Po Valley *74 C2 It.* Valle del Po. *Valley* N Italy
Považská Bystrica *77 C5 Ger.* Waagbistritz, *Hung.* Vágbeszterce. Trenčiansky Kraj, W Slovakia
Poverty Bay *128 E4 inlet* North Island, NZ
Póvoa de Varzim *70 B2* Porto, NW Portugal
Powder River *22 D2 river* Montana/Wyoming, NW USA
Powell *22 C2* Wyoming, C USA
Powell, Lake *22 B5 lake* Utah, W USA
Požarevac *78 D4 Ger.* Passarowitz. Serbia, NE Yugoslavia
Poza Rica *29 F4 var.* Poza Rica de Hidalgo. Veracruz-Llave, E Mexico
Poza Rica de Hidalgo *see* Poza Rica
Požega *78 D4 prev.* Slavonska Požega. *Ger.* Poschega, *Hung.* Pozsega. Požega-Slavonija, NE Croatia
Pozsega *see* Požega
Poznań *76 C3 Ger.* Posen, Posnania. Wielkopolskie, C Poland
Pozoblanco *70 D4* Andalucía, S Spain
Pozzallo *75 C8* Sicilia, Italy, C Mediterranean Sea
Prachatice *77 A5 Ger.* Prachatitz. Budějovický Kraj, S Czech Republic
Prado del Ganso *see* Goose Green
Prae *see* Phrae
Prague *58 D3* Oklahoma, C USA
Praha *77 A5 Eng.* Prague, *Ger.* Prag, *Pol.* Praga. *Country capital* (Czech Republic) Středočeský Kraj, NW Czech Republic
Praia *52 A3 country capital* (Cape Verde) Santiago, S Cape Verde
Prato *74 B3* Toscana, C Italy
Pratt *23 E5* Kansas, C USA
Prattville *20 D2* Alabama, S USA
Pravda *82 D1 prev.* Dogrular. Silistra, NE Bulgaria
Pravia *70 C1* Asturias, N Spain
Prenzlau *72 D3* Brandenburg, NE Germany
Přerov *77 C5 Ger.* Prerau. Olomoucký Kraj, E Czech Republic
Presa de la Amistad *see* Amistad Reservoir
Preschau *see* Prešov
Prescott *26 B2* Arizona, SW USA
Preševo *79 D5* Serbia, SE Yugoslavia
Presidente Epitácio *41 E4* São Paulo, S Brazil
Prešov *77 D5 var.* Preschau, *Ger.* Eperies, *Hung.* Eperjes. Prešouský Kraj, E Slovakia
Prespa, Lake *79 D6 Alb.* Liqen i Prespës, *Gk.* Límni Megáli Préspa, Limni Prespa, *Mac.* Prespansko Ezero, *Serb.* Prespansko Jezero. *Lake* SE Europe
Presque Isle *19 H1* Maine, NE USA
Preston *67 D5* NW England, UK
Prestwick *66 C4* W Scotland, UK
Pretoria *56 D4 var.* Epitoli, Tshwane. *Country capital* (South Africa-administrative capital) Gauteng, NE South Africa
Préveza *83 A5* Ípeiros, W Greece
Pribilof Islands *14 A3 island group* Alaska, USA
Priboj *78 C4* Serbia, W Yugoslavia
Price *22 B4* Utah, W USA
Prichard *20 C3* Alabama, S USA
Priekulė *84 B3 Ger.* Prökuls. Gargždai, W Lithuania
Prienai *85 B5 Pol.* Preny. Prienai, S Lithuania
Prieska *56 C4* Northern Cape, C South Africa
Prijedor *78 B3* Republika Srpska, NW Bosnia and Herzegovina
Prijepolje *78 D4* Serbia, W Yugoslavia
Prilep *79 D6 Turk.* Perlepe. S FYR Macedonia
Primorsk *84 A4 Ger.* Fischhausen. Kaliningradskaya Oblast', W Russian Federation
Primorsko *82 E2 prev.* Keupriya. Burgas, E Bulgaria
Prince Albert *15 F5* Saskatchewan, S Canada
Prince Edward Island *17 F4 Fr.* Île-du Prince-Édouard. *Province* SE Canada
Prince Edward Islands *47 E8 island group* S South Africa
Prince George *15 E5* British Columbia, SW Canada
Prince of Wales Island *15 F2 island* Queen Elizabeth Islands, Nunavut, NW Canada
Prince of Wales Island *126 B1 island* Queensland, E Australia
Prince Patrick Island *15 E2 island* Parry Islands, Northwest Territories, NW Canada
Prince Rupert *14 D4* British Columbia, SW Canada
Prince's Island *see* Príncipe
Princess Charlotte Bay *126 C2 bay* Queensland, NE Australia
Princess Elizabeth Land *132 C3 physical region* Antarctica
Príncipe *55 A5 var.* Príncipe Island, *Eng.* Prince's Island. *Island* N Sao Tome and Principe
Príncipe Island *see* Príncipe
Prinzapolka *31 E3* Región Autónoma Atlántico Norte, NE Nicaragua
Pripet *85 C7 Bel.* Prypyats', *Ukr.* Pryp"yat'. *River* Belarus/Ukraine
Pripet Marshes *85 B7 wetland* Belarus/Ukraine
Priština *79 D5 Alb.* Prishtinë. Serbia, S Yugoslavia
Privas *69 D5* Ardèche, E France
Prizren *79 D5 Alb.* Prizreni. Serbia, S Yugoslavia
Probolinggo *116 D5* Jawa, C Indonesia
Progreso *29 H3* Yucatán, SE Mexico
Prokhladnyy *89 B8* Kabardino-Balkarskaya Respublika, SW Russian Federation
Prokuplje *79 D5* Serbia, SE Yugoslavia
Prome *114 B4 var.* Pyè. Pegu, C Myanmar
Promyshlennyy *88 E3* Respublika Komi, NW Russian Federation
Prostějov *77 C5 Ger.* Prossnitz, *Pol.* Prościejów. Olomoucký Kraj, E Czech Republic
Provence *69 D6 cultural region* SE France
Providence *see* Fort Providence
Providence *19 G3 state capital* Rhode Island, NE USA
Providencia, Isla de *31 F3 island* NW Colombia
Provideniya *172 B1* Chukotskiy Avtonomnyy Okrug, NE Russian Federation
Provo *22 B4* Utah, W USA
Prudhoe Bay *14 D2* Alaska, USA
Prusa *see* Bursa
Pruszków *76 D3 Ger.* Kaltdorf. Mazowieckie, C Poland
Prut *86 D4 Ger.* Pruth. *River* E Europe
Pruzhany *85 B6 Pol.* Prużana. Brestskaya Voblasts', SW Belarus
Prydz Bay *132 D3 bay* Antarctica
Pryluky *87 E2 Rus.* Priluki. Chernihivs'ka Oblast', NE Ukraine
Prymors'k *87 G4 Rus.* Primorsk; *prev.* Primorskoye. Zaporiz'ka Oblast', SE Ukraine
Przemysl *77 E5 Rus.* Peremyshl. Podkarpackie, SE Poland
Psará *83 D5 island* E Greece
Psël *87 F2 river* Russian Federation/Ukraine
Pskov *92 B2 Ger.* Pleskau, *Latv.* Pleskava. Pskovskaya Oblast', W Russian Federation
Pskov, Lake *E3 Est.* Pihkva Järv, *Ger.* Pleskauer See, *Rus.* Pskovskoye Ozero. *Lake* Estonia/Russian Federation
Ptsich *85 C7 Rus.* Ptich'. *River* SE Belarus
Ptsich *85 C7 Rus.* Ptich'. Homyel'skaya Voblasts', SE Belarus
Ptuj *73 E7 Ger.* Pettau; *anc.* Poetovio. NE Slovenia
Pucallpa *38 C3* Ucayali, C Peru
Puck *76 C2* Pomorskie, N Poland
Pudasjärvi *62 D4* Oulu, C Finland
Puduchcheri *see* Pondicherry
Puebla *29 F4 var.* Puebla de Zaragoza. Puebla, S Mexico
Puebla de Zaragoza *see* Puebla
Pueblo *22 D5* Colorado, C USA
Puerto Acosta *39 E4* La Paz, W Bolivia
Puerto Aisén *43 B6* Aisén, S Chile
Puerto Ángel *29 F5* Oaxaca, SE Mexico
Puerto Argentino *see* Stanley
Puerto Ayacucho *36 D3* Amazonas, SW Venezuela
Puerto Baquerizo Moreno *38 B5 var.* Baquerizo Moreno. Galapagos Islands, Ecuador, E Pacific Ocean
Puerto Barrios *30 C2* Izabal, E Guatemala
Puerto Bello *see* Portobelo
Puerto Berrío *36 B2* Antioquia, C Colombia
Puerto Cabello *36 D1* Carabobo, N Venezuela
Puerto Cabezas *31 E2 var.* Bilwi. Región Autónoma Atlántico Norte, NE Nicaragua
Puerto Carreño *36 D3* Vichada, E Colombia
Puerto Cortés *30 C2* Cortés, NW Honduras
Puerto Cumarebo *36 C1* Falcón, N Venezuela
Puerto Deseado *43 C7* Santa Cruz, SE Argentina
Puerto Escondido *29 F5* Oaxaca, SE Mexico
Puerto Francisco de Orellana *38 B1 var.* Coca. Napo, N Ecuador
Puerto Gallegos *see* Río Gallegos
Puerto Inírida *36 D3 var.* Obando. Guainía, E Colombia
Puerto La Cruz *37 E1* Anzoátegui, NE Venezuela
Puerto Lempira *31 E2* Gracias a Dios, E Honduras
Puerto Limón *see* Limón
Puertollano *70 D4* Castilla-La Mancha, C Spain
Puerto López *36 C1* La Guajira, N Colombia
Puerto Maldonado *39 E3* Madre de Dios, E Peru
Puerto México *see* Coatzacoalcos
Puerto Montt *43 B5* Los Lagos, C Chile
Puerto Natales *43 B7* Magallanes, S Chile
Puerto Obaldía *31 H5* San Blas, NE Panama
Puerto Plata *33 E3 var.* San Felipe de Puerto Plata. N Dominican Republic
Puerto Princesa *117 E2 off.* Puerto Princesa City. Palawan, W Philippines
Puerto Rico *33 F3 off.* Commonwealth of Puerto Rico; *prev.* Porto Rico. *US commonwealth territory* C West Indies
Puerto Rico *34 B1 island* C West Indies
Puerto Rico Trench *34 B1 undersea feature* NE Caribbean Sea
Puerto San José *see* San José
Puerto San Julián *43 B7 var.* San Julián. Santa Cruz, SE Argentina
Puerto Suárez *39 H4* Santa Cruz, E Bolivia
Puerto Vallarta *28 D4* Jalisco, SW Mexico
Puerto Varas *43 B5* Los Lagos, C Chile
Puerto Viejo *31 E4* Heredia, NE Costa Rica
Puertoviejo *see* Portoviejo
Puget Sound *24 B1 sound* Washington, NW USA
Puglia *75 E5 Eng.* Apulia. *Cultural region* SE Italy
Pukaki, Lake *129 B6 lake* South Island, NZ
Pukekohe *128 D3* Auckland, North Island, NZ
Puket *see* Phuket
Pukhavichy *85 C6 Rus.* Pukhovichi. Minskaya Voblasts', C Belarus
Pula *78 A3 It.* Pola; *prev.* Pulj. Istra, NW Croatia
Pulaski *18 D5* Virginia, NE USA
Pulau Butung *see* Buton, Pulau
Puławy *76 D4 Ger.* Neu Amerika. Lublin, E Poland
Pul-i-Khumri *see* Pol-e Khomrī
Pullman *24 C2* Washington, NW USA
Pułtusk *76 D3* Mazowieckie, C Poland
Puná, Isla *38 A2 island* SW Ecuador
Pune *112 C5 prev.* Poona. Mahārāshtra, W India
Punjab *112 C2 prev.* West Punjab, Western Punjab. *Province* E Pakistan
Puno *39 E4* Puno, SE Peru
Punta Alta *43 C5* Buenos Aires, E Argentina
Punta Arenas *43 B8 prev.* Magallanes. Magallanes, S Chile
Punta Gorda *31 E4* Región Autónoma Atlántico Sur, SE Nicaragua
Punta Gorda *30 C2* Toledo, SE Belize
Puntarenas *30 D4* Puntarenas, W Costa Rica
Punto Fijo *36 C1* Falcón, N Venezuela
Pupuya, Nevado *39 E4 mountain* W Bolivia
Puri *113 F5 var.* Jagannath. Orissa, E India
Puriramya *see* Buriram
Purmerend *64 C3* Noord-Holland, C Netherlands
Purus, Rio *40 C2 Sp.* Río Purús. *River* Brazil/Peru
Pusan *107 E4 off.* Pusan-gwangyŏksi, *var.* Busan, *Jap.* Fusan. SE South Korea
Püspökladány *77 D6* Hajdú-Bihar, E Hungary
Putorana Mountains *see* Putorana, Plato
Putorana, Plato *92 D3 var.* Gory Putorana, *Eng.* Putorana Mountains. *Mountain range* N Russian Federation
Puttalam *110 C3* North Western Province, W Sri Lanka
Puttgarden *72 C2* Schleswig-Holstein, N Germany
Putumayo, Río *36 B5 var.* Rio Içá. *River* NW South America *see also* Içá, Rio
Putumayo, Río *see* Içá, Rio
Puurmani *84 D2 Ger.* Talkhof. Jõgevamaa, E Estonia
Pyatigorsk *89 B7* Stavropol'skiy Kray, SW Russian Federation
P"yatykhatky *87 F3 Rus.* Pyatikhatki. Dnipropetrovs'ka Oblast', E Ukraine
Pyè *see* Prome
Pyetrykaw *85 C7 Rus.* Petrikov. Homyel'skaya Voblasts', SE Belarus
Pyinmana *114 B4* Mandalay, C Myanmar
Pýlos *83 B6 var.* Pilos. Pelopónnisos, S Greece
P'yŏngyang *107 E3 var.* P'yŏngyang-si, *Eng.* Pyongyang. *Country capital* (North Korea) SW North Korea
P'yŏngyang-si *see* P'yŏngyang
Pyramid Lake *25 C5 lake* Nevada, W USA
Pyrenees *80 B2 Fr.* Pyrénées, *Sp.* Pirineos; *anc.* Pyrenaei Montes. *Mountain range* SW Europe
Pýrgos *83 B6 var.* Pírgos. Dytikí Ellás, S Greece
Pyryatyn *87 E2 Rus.* Piryatin. Poltavs'ka Oblast', NE Ukraine
Pyrzyce *76 B3 Ger.* Pyritz. Zachodniopomorskie, NW Poland
Pyu *114 B4* Pegu, C Myanmar
Pyuntaza *114 B4* Pegu, SW Myanmar

Q

Qā' al Jafr *97 C7 lake* S Jordan
Qaanaaq *60 D1 var.* Qânâq, *Dan.* Thule. N Greenland
Qābis *see* Gabès
Qacentina *see* Constantine
Qafṣah *see* Gafsa
Qagan Us *see* Dulan
Qahremānshahr *see* Bākhtarān
Qaidam Pendi *104 C4 basin* C China
Qal'aikhum *101 F3 Rus.* Kalaikhum. S Tajikistan
Qal'at Bīshah *99 B5* 'Asīr, SW Saudi Arabia
Qamdo *104 D5* Xizang Zizhiqu, W China
Qamishly *see* Al Qāmishlī
Qânâq *see* Qaanaaq
Qaqortoq *60 C4 Dan.* Julianehåb. S Greenland
Qara Qum *see* Garagumy
Qarkilik *see* Ruoqiang
Qarokŭl *101 F3 Rus.* Karakul'. E Tajikistan
Qars *see* Kars
Qarshi *101 E3 Rus.* Karshi; *prev.* Bek-Budi. Qashqadaryo Wiloyati, S Uzbekistan
Qasigianguit *see* Qasigiannguit
Qasigiannguit *60 C3 var.* Qasigianguit, *Dan.* Christianshåb. C Greenland
Qasr Farâfra *50 B2* W Egypt
Qaṭanā *97 B5 var.* Katana. Dimashq, S Syria
Qatar *98 C4 off.* State of Qatar, *Ar.* Dawlat Qaṭar. *Country* SW Asia
Qattara Depression *see* Qaṭṭâra, Monkhafad el
Qaṭṭâra, Monkhafad el *88 A1 var.* Munkhafaḍ al Qaṭṭārah, *Eng.* Qattara Depression. *Desert* NW Egypt
Qazimämmäd *95 H3 Rus.* Kazi Magomed. SE Azerbaijan
Qazvīn *98 C2 var.* Kazvin. Qazvin, N Iran
Qena *50 B2 var.* Qinā; *anc.* Caene, Caenepolis. E Egypt
Qeqertarssuaq *see* Qeqertarsuaq
Qeqertarsuaq *60 C3 var.* Qeqertarssuaq, *Dan.* Godhavn. S Greenland
Qeqertarsuaq *60 C3 island* W Greenland
Qeqertarsuup Tunua *60 C3 Dan.* Disko Bugt. *Inlet* W Greenland
Qerveh *see* Qorveh
Qeshm *98 D4 var.* Jazīreh-ye Qeshm, Qeshm Island. *Island* S Iran
Qeshm Island *see* Qeshm
Qian *see* Guizhou
Qilian Shan *104 D3 var.* Kilien Mountains. *Mountain range* N China
Qimusseriarsuaq *60 C2 Dan.* Melville Bugt, *Eng.* Melville Bay. *Bay* NW Greenland
Qinā *see* Qena
Qing *see* Qinghai
Qingdao *106 D4 var.* Ching-Tao, Ch'ing-tao, Tsingtao, Tsintao, *Ger.* Tsingtau. Shandong, E China
Qinghai *104 C4 var.* Chinghai, Koko Nor, Qing, Qinghai Sheng, Tsinghai. *Admin. region province* C China
Qinghai Hu *104 D4 var.* Ch'ing Hai, Tsing Hai, *Mong.* Koko Nor. *lake* C China
Qinghai Sheng *see* Qinghai
Qingzang Gaoyuan *104 B4 var.* Xizang Gaoyuan, *Eng.* Plateau of Tibet. *Plateau* W China
Qinhuangdao *106 D3* Hebei, E China
Qinzhou *106 B6* Guangxi Zhuangzu Zizhiqu, S China
Qiong *see* Hainan
Qiqihar *106 D2 var.* Ch'i-ch'i-ha-erh, Tsitsihar; *prev.* Lungkiang. Heilongjiang, NE China
Qira *104 B4* Xinjiang Uygur Zizhiqu, NW China
Qitai *104 C3* Xinjiang Uygur Zizhiqu, NW China
Qīzān *see* Jīzān
Qizil Orda *see* Kyzylorda
Qizil Qum *see* Kyzyl Kum
Qizilrabot *101 G3 Rus.* Kyzylrabot. SE Tajikistan
Qom *98 C3 var.* Kum, Qum. Qom, N Iran
Qomul *see* Hami
Qondūz *see* Kunduz
Qorveh *98 C3 var.* Qerveh, Qurveh. Kordestān, W Iran
Qostanay *see* Kostanay
Qoubaïyât *96 B4 var.* Al Qubayyāt. N Lebanon
Qoussantîna *see* Constantine
Quang Ngai *115 E5 var.* Quangngai, Quang Nghia. Quang Ngai, C Vietnam
Quangngai *see* Quang Ngai
Quang Nghia *see* Quang Ngai
Quanzhou *106 D6 var.* Ch'uan-chou, Tsinkiang; *prev.* Chin-chiang. Fujian, SE China
Quanzhou *106 C6* Guangxi Zhuangzu Zizhiqu, S China
Qu'Appelle *15 F5 river* Saskatchewan, S Canada
Quarles, Pegunungan *117 E4 mountain range* Sulawesi, C Indonesia
Quarnero *see* Kvarner
Quartu Sant' Elena *75 A6* Sardegna, Italy, C Mediterranean Sea
Quba *95 H2 Rus.* Kuba. N Azerbaijan
Qubba *see* Ba'qūbah
Québec *17 E4 var.* Quebec. Québec, SE Canada
Quebec *16 D3 var.* Québec. *Admin. region province* SE Canada
Queen Charlotte Islands *14 C5 Fr.* Îles de la Reine-Charlotte. *Island group* British Columbia, SW Canada
Queen Charlotte Sound *14 C5 sea area* British Columbia, W Canada
Queen Elizabeth Islands *15 F2 Fr.* Îles de la Reine-Élisabeth. *Island group* Northwest Territories/Nunavut, N Canada
Queensland *126 B4 state* N Australia
Queenstown *56 D5* Eastern Cape, S South Africa
Queenstown *129 B7* Otago, South Island, NZ
Quelimane *57 E3 var.* Kilimane, Kilmain, Quilimane. Zambézia, NE Mozambique
Quepos *31 E4* Puntarenas, S Costa Rica
Querétaro *29 E4* Querétaro de Arteaga, C Mexico
Quesada *31 E4 var.* Ciudad Quesada, San Carlos. Alajuela, N Costa Rica
Quetta *112 B2* Baluchistān, SW Pakistan
Quetzalcoalco *see* Coatzacoalcos
Quetzaltenango *see* Quezaltenango
Quezaltenango *30 A2 var.* Quetzaltenango. Quezaltenango, W Guatemala
Quibdó *36 A3* Chocó, W Colombia
Quilimane *see* Quelimane
Quillabamba *38 D3* Cusco, C Peru
Quilon *110 C3 var.* Kolam, Kollam. Kerala, SW India
Quimper *68 A3 anc.* Quimper Corentin. Finistère, NW France
Quimperlé *68 A3* Finistère, NW France
Quincy *18 A4* Illinois, N USA
Qui Nhon *see* Quy Nhơn
Quissico *57 E4* Inhambane, S Mozambique
Quito *38 B1 country capital* (Ecuador) Pichincha, N Ecuador
Qullai Garmo *see* Kommunizm, Qullai
Qum *see* Qom
Qunaytra *see* Al Qunayṭirah
Qŭqon *101 F2 var.* Khokand, *Rus.* Kokand. Farghona Wiloyati, E Uzbekistan
Qurein *see* Al Kuwayt
Qŭrghonteppa *101 E3 Rus.* Kurgan-Tyube. SW Tajikistan
Qurlurtuuq *see* Kugluktuk
Qurveh *see* Qorveh
Quṣayr *see* Al Quṣayr
Quy Nhơn *115 E5 var.* Quinhon, Qui Nhon. Bình Định, C Vietnam
Qyteti Stalin *see* Kuçovë
Qyzylorda *see* Kyzylorda

R

Raab *78 B1 Hung.* Rába. *River* Austria/Hungary *see also* Rába
Raahe *62 D4 Swe.* Brahestad. Oulu, W Finland
Raalte *64 D3* Overijssel, E Netherlands
Raamsdonksveer *64 C4* Noord-Brabant, S Netherlands
Raasiku *84 D2 Ger.* Rasik. Harjumaa, NW Estonia
Rába *77 B7 Ger.* Raab. *River* Austria/Hungary *see also* Raab
Rabat *48 C2 var.* al Dar al Baida. *Country capital* (Morocco) NW Morocco
Rabat *see* Victoria
Rabat *80 B5* W Malta
Rabbah Ammon *see* 'Ammān
Rabbath Ammon *see* 'Ammān
Rabinal *30 B2* Baja Verapaz, C Guatemala
Rabka *77 D5* Małopolskie, S Poland
Râbniţa *see* Rîbniţa
Rabyanāh, Ramlat *49 G4 var.* Rebiana Sand Sea, Ṣaḥrā' Rabyanāh. *Desert* SE Libya
Race, Cape *17 H3 headland* Newfoundland, Newfoundland and Labrador, E Canada
Rach Gia *115 D6* Kiên Giang, S Vietnam
Rach Gia, Vinh *115 D6 bay* S Vietnam
Racine *18 B3* Wisconsin, N USA
Rădăuţi *86 C3 Ger.* Radautz, *Hung.* Rádóc. Suceava, N Romania
Radom *76 D4* Mazowieckie, C Poland
Radomsko *76 D4 Rus.* Novoradomsk. Łódzkie, C Poland
Radomyshl' *86 D2* Zhytomyrs'ka Oblast', N Ukraine
Radoviš *79 E6 prev.* Radovište. E FYR Macedonia
Radviliškis *84 B4* Radviliškis, N Lithuania
Radzyń Podlaski *76 E4* Lubelskie, E Poland
Rae-Edzo *see* Edzo
Raetihi *128 D4* Manawatu-Wanganui, North Island, NZ
Rafa *see* Rafah
Rafaela *42 C3* Santa Fe, E Argentina
Rafah *97 A7 var.* Rafa, Rafaḥ, *Heb.* Rafiaḥ, Raphiah. SW Gaza Strip
Rafaḥ *see* Rafah
Rafḥah *98 B4* Al Ḥudūd ash Shamālīyah, N Saudi Arabia
Rafiaḥ *see* Rafah
Raga *51 A5* Western Bahr el Ghazal, SW Sudan

Shari – Sông Tiên Giang

Shari see Chari
Shari 108 D2 Hokkaidō, NE Japan
Shark Bay 125 A5 bay Western Australia
Shashe 56 D3 var. Shashi. River Botswana/Zimbabwe
Shashi see Shashe
Shatskiy Rise 103 G1 undersea feature N Pacific Ocean
Shatt al-Hodna see Hodna, Chott El
Shaṭṭ al Jarīd see Jerīd, Chott el
Shawnee 27 G1 Oklahoma, C USA
Shchadryn 85 D7 Rus. Shchedrin. Homyel'skaya Voblasts', SE Belarus
Shchëkino 89 B5 Tul'skaya Oblast', W Russian Federation
Shchors 87 E1 Chernihivs'ka Oblast', N Ukraine
Shchuchinsk 92 C4 prev. Shchuchye. Severnyy kazakhstan, N Kazakhstan
Shchuchyn 85 B5 Pol. Szczuczyn Nowogródzki, Rus. Shchuchin. Hrodzyenskaya Voblasts', W Belarus
Shebekino 89 A6 Belgorodskaya Oblast', W Russian Federation
Shebeli 51 D5 Amh. Wabē Shebelē Wenz, It. Scebeli, Som. Webi Shabeelle. River Ethiopia/Somalia
Sheberghān 101 E3 var. Shibarghān, Shiberghan, Shiberghān. Jowzjān, N Afghanistan
Sheboygan 18 B2 Wisconsin, N USA
Shebshi Mountains 54 A4 var. Schebschi Mountains. Mountain range E Nigeria
Shechem see Nablus
Shedadi see Ash Shadādah
Sheffield 67 D5 N England, UK
Shekhem see Nablus
Shelby 22 B1 Montana, NW USA
Sheldon 23 F3 Iowa, C USA
Shelekhov Gulf see Shelikhova, Zaliv
Shelikhova, Zaliv 93 G2 Eng. Shelekhov Gulf. Gulf E Russian Federation
Shendi 50 C4 var. Shandī. River Nile, NE Sudan
Shengking see Liaoning
Shenking see Liaoning
Shenshi see Shaanxi
Shensi see Shaanxi
Shenyang 106 D3 Chin. Shen-yang, Eng. Moukden, Mukden; prev. Fengtien. Liaoning, NE China
Shepetivka 86 D2 Rus. Shepetovka. Khmel'nyts'ka Oblast', NW Ukraine
Shepparton 127 C7 Victoria, SE Australia
Sherbrooke 17 E4 Québec, SE Canada
Shereik 50 C3 River Nile, N Sudan
Sheridan 22 C2 Wyoming, C USA
Sherman 27 G2 Texas, SW USA
's-Hertogenbosch 64 C4 Fr. Bois-le-Duc, Ger. Herzogenbusch. Noord-Brabant, S Netherlands
Shetland Islands 66 D1 island group NE Scotland, UK
Shibarghān see Sheberghān
Shiberghān see Sheberghān
Shibetsu 108 D2 var. Sibetu. Hokkaidō, NE Japan
Shibh Jazīrat Sīnā' see Sinai
Shibushi-wan 109 B8 bay SW Japan
Shigatse see Xigazê
Shih-chia-chuang see Shijiazhuang
Shihezi 104 C2 Xinjiang Uygur Zizhiqu, NW China
Shihmen see Shijiazhuang
Shijiazhuang 106 C4 var. Shih-chia-chuang; prev. Shihmen. Hebei, E China
Shikārpur 112 B3 Sind, S Pakistan
Shikoku 109 C7 var. Sikoku. Island SW Japan
Shikoku Basin 103 F2 var. Sikoku Basin. Undersea feature N Philippine Sea
Shikotan, Ostrov 108 E2 Jap. Shikotan-tō. Island NE Russian Federation
Shilabo 51 D5 E Ethiopia
Shiliguri 113 F3 prev. Siliguri. West Bengal, NE India
Shilka 93 F4 river S Russian Federation
Shimbir Berris see Shimbiris
Shimbiris 50 E4 var. Shimbir Berris. Mountain N Somalia
Shimoga 110 C2 Karnātaka, W India
Shimonoseki 109 A7 var. Simonoseki; hist. Akamagaseki, Bakan. Yamaguchi, Honshū, SW Japan
Shinano-gawa 109 C5 var. Sinano Gawa. River Honshū, C Japan
Shīndand 100 D4 Farāh, W Afghanistan
Shingū 109 C6 var. Singû. Wakayama, Honshū, SW Japan
Shinjō 108 D4 var. Sinzyô. Yamagata, Honshū, C Japan
Shinyanga 51 C7 Shinyanga, NW Tanzania
Shiprock 26 C1 New Mexico, SW USA
Shirāz 98 D4 var. Shīrāz. Fārs, S Iran
Shivpuri 112 D3 Madhya Pradesh, C India
Shizugawa 108 D4 Miyagi, Honshū, NE Japan
Shizuoka 109 D6 var. Sizuoka. Shizuoka, Honshū, S Japan
Shklow 85 D6 Rus. Shklov. Mahilyowskaya Voblasts', E Belarus
Shkodër 79 C5 var. Shkodra, It. Scutari, SCr. Skadar. Shkodër, NW Albania
Shkodra see Shkodër
Shkubinit, Lumi i 79 C6 var. Shkumbî, Shkumbin. River C Albania
Shkumbî see Shkubinit, Lumi i
Shkumbin see Shkubinit, Lumi i
Sholāpur see Solāpur
Shostka 87 F1 Sums'ka Oblast', NE Ukraine
Show Low 26 B2 Arizona, SW USA
Shpola 87 E3 Cherkas'ka Oblast', N Ukraine
Shreveport 20 A2 Louisiana, S USA
Shrewsbury 67 D6 hist. Scrobesbyrig'. W England, UK
Shu 92 C5 Kaz. Shū. Zhambyl, SE Kazakhstan
Shuang-liao see Liaoyuan
Shumagin Islands 14 B3 island group Alaska, USA
Shumen 82 D2 Shumen, NE Bulgaria
Shumilina 85 E5 Rus. Shumilino. Vitsyebskaya Voblasts', NE Belarus
Shuqrah 99 B7 var. Shaqrā. SW Yemen
Shwebo 114 B3 Sagaing, C Myanmar
Shyichy 85 C7 Rus. Shiichi. Homyel'skaya Voblasts', SE Belarus
Shymkent 92 B5 prev. Chimkent. Yuzhnyy Kazakhstan, S Kazakhstan
Shyshchytsy 85 C6 Rus. Shishchitsy. Minskaya Voblasts', C Belarus
Si see Syr Darya
Siam, Gulf of see Thailand, Gulf of
Sian see Xi'an
Siang see Brahmaputra
Siangtan see Xiangtan
Šiauliai 84 B4 Ger. Schaulen. Šiauliai, N Lithuania
Sibay 89 D6 Respublika Bashkortostan, W Russian Federation
Šibenik 116 B4 It. Sebenico. Šibenik-Knin, S Croatia
Siberia see Sibir'
Siberut, Pulau 116 A4 prev. Siberoet. Island Kepulauan Mentawai, W Indonesia
Sibetu see Shibetsu
Sibi 112 B2 Baluchistān, SW Pakistan
Sibir' 93 E3 var. Siberia. Physical region NE Russian Federation
Sibiti 55 B6 La Lékoumou, S Congo
Sibiu 86 B4 Ger. Hermannstadt, Hung. Nagyszeben. Sibiu, C Romania
Sibolga 116 B3 Sumatera, W Indonesia
Sibu 116 D3 Sarawak, East Malaysia
Sibut 54 C4 prev. Fort-Sibut. Kémo, S Central African Republic
Sibuyan Sea 117 E2 sea C Philippines
Sichon 115 C6 var. Ban Sichon, Si Chon. Nakhon Si Thammarat, SW Thailand
Sichuan 106 B5 var. Chuan, Sichuan Sheng, Ssu-ch'uan, Szechuan, Szechwan. Admin. region province C China
Sichuan Pendi 106 B5 depression C China
Sichuan Sheng see Sichuan
Sicilia 75 C7 Eng. Sicily; anc. Trinacria. Island Italy, C Mediterranean Sea
Sicilian Channel see Sicily, Strait of
Sicily see Sicilia
Sicily, Strait of 75 B7 var. Sicilian Channel. Strait C Mediterranean Sea
Sicuani 39 E4 Cusco, S Peru
Sidári 82 A4 Kérkyra, Iónioi Nísoi, Greece, C Mediterranean Sea
Sidas 116 C4 Borneo, C Indonesia
Siderno 75 D7 Calabria, SW Italy
Sîdi Barrâni 50 A1 NW Egypt
Sidi Bel Abbès 48 D2 var. Sidi bel Abbès, Sidi-Bel-Abbès. NW Algeria
Sidirókastro 82 C3 prev. Sidhirókastron. Kentrikí Makedonía, NE Greece
Sidley, Mount 132 B4 mountain Antarctica
Sidney 22 D1 Montana, NW USA
Sidney 22 D4 Nebraska, C USA
Sidney 18 C4 Ohio, N USA
Sidon see Saïda
Sidra see Surt
Siedlce 76 E3 Ger. Sedlez, Rus. Sesdlets. Mazowieckie, C Poland
Siegen 72 B4 Nordrhein-Westfalen, W Germany
Siemiatycze 76 E3 Podlaskie
Siena 74 B3 Fr. Sienne, anc. Saena Julia. Toscana, C Italy
Sieradz 76 C4 Łódzkie, C Poland
Sierpc 76 D3 Mazowieckie, C Poland
Sierra de Soconusco see Sierra Madre
Sierra Leone 52 C4 off. Republic of Sierra Leone. Country W Africa
Sierra Leone Basin 44 C4 undersea feature E Atlantic Ocean
Sierra Leone Ridge see Sierra Leone Rise
Sierra Leone Rise 44 C4 var. Sierra Leone Ridge, Sierra Leone Schwelle. Undersea feature E Atlantic Ocean
Sierra Leone Schwelle see Sierra Leone Rise
Sierra Madre 30 B2 var. Sierra de Soconusco. Mountain range Guatemala/Mexico
Sierra Madre see Madre Occidental, Sierra
Sierra Nevada 25 C6 mountain range W USA
Sierra Pacaraima see Pakaraima Mountains
Sierra Vieja 26 D3 mountain range Texas, SW USA
Sierra Vista 26 B3 Arizona, SW USA
Sífnos 83 C6 anc. Siphnos. Island Kykládes, Greece, Aegean Sea
Sigli 116 A3 Sumatera, W Indonesia
Siglufjördhur 61 E4 Nordhurland Vestra, N Iceland
Signal Peak 26 A2 mountain Arizona, SW USA
Signan see Xi'an
Signy 132 A2 UK research station South Orkney Islands, Antarctica
Siguatepeque 30 C2 Comayagua, W Honduras
Siguiri 52 D4 Haute-Guinée, NE Guinea
Siilinjärvi 62 E4 Itä-Suomi, C Finland
Siirt 95 F4 var. Sert; anc. Tigranocerta. Siirt, SE Turkey
Sikandarabad see Secunderābād
Sikasso 52 D4 Sikasso, S Mali
Sikeston 23 H5 Missouri, C USA
Sikhote-Alin', Khrebet 93 G4 mountain range SE Russian Federation
Siking see Xi'an
Siklós 77 C7 Baranya, SW Hungary
Sikoku see Shikoku
Sikoku Basin see Shikoku Basin
Šilalė 84 B4 Šilalė, W Lithuania
Silchar 113 G3 Assam, NE India
Silesia 76 B4 physical region SW Poland
Silifke 94 C4 anc. Seleucia. İçel, S Turkey
Siling Co 104 C5 lake W China
Silinhot see Xilinhot
Silistra 82 E1 var. Silistria; anc. Durostorum. Silistra, NE Bulgaria
Silistria see Silistra
Sillamäe 84 E2 Ger. Sillamäggi. Ida-Virumaa, NE Estonia
Šilutė 84 B4 Ger. Heydekrug. Šilutė, W Lithuania
Silvan 95 E4 Diyarbakır, SE Turkey
Silverek 95 E4 Şanlıurfa, SE Turkey
Simanggang see Sri Aman
Simanichy 85 C7 Rus. Simonichi. Homyel'skaya Voblasts', SE Belarus
Simav 94 B3 Kütahya, W Turkey
Simav Çayı 94 A3 river NW Turkey
Simeto 75 C7 river Sicilia, Italy, C Mediterranean Sea
Simeulue, Pulau 116 A3 island NW Indonesia
Simferopol' 87 F5 Respublika Krym, S Ukraine
Simitli 82 C3 Blagoevgrad, SW Bulgaria
Şimleu Silvaniei 86 B3 Hung. Szilágsomlyó; prev. Şimlăul Silvaniei, Şimleul Silvaniei. Sălaj, NW Romania
Simonoseki see Shimonoseki
Simpelveld 65 D6 Limburg, SE Netherlands
Simplon Pass 73 B8 pass S Switzerland
Simpson see Fort Simpson
Simpson Desert 126 B4 desert Northern Territory/South Australia
Sīnā' see Sinai
Sinai 50 C2 var. Sinai Peninsula, Ar. Shibh Jazīrat Sīnā', Sīnā'. Physical region NE Egypt
Sinaia 86 C4 Prahova, SE Romania
Sinai Peninsula see Sinai
Sinano Gawa see Shinano-gawa
Sincelejo 36 B2 Sucre, NW Colombia
Sind 112 B3 var. Sindh. Admin. region province SE Pakistan
Sindelfingen 73 B6 Baden-Württemberg, SW Germany
Sindh see Sind
Sindi 84 D2 Ger. Zintenhof. Pärnumaa, SW Estonia
Sines 70 B4 Setúbal, S Portugal
Singan see Xi'an
Singapore 116 A1 off. Republic of Singapore. Country SE Asia
Singapore 116 B3 country capital (Singapore) S Singapore
Singen 73 B6 Baden-Württemberg, S Germany
Singida 51 C7 Singida, C Tanzania
Singkang 117 E4 Sulawesi, C Indonesia
Singkawang 116 C3 Borneo, C Indonesia
Singora see Songkhla
Singû see Shingū
Sining see Xining
Siniscola 75 A5 Sardegna, Italy, C Mediterranean Sea
Sinj 78 B4 Split-Dalmacija, SE Croatia
Sinkiang see Xinjiang Uygur Zizhiqu
Sinkiang Uighur Autonomous Region see Xinjiang Uygur Zizhiqu
Sinnamarie see Sinnamary
Sinnamary 37 H3 var. Sinnamarie. N French Guiana
Sînnicolau Mare see Sânnicolau Mare
Sinoie, Lacul 86 D5 prev. Lacul Sinoe. Lagoon SE Romania
Sinop 94 D2 anc. Sinope. Sinop, N Turkey
Sinsheim 73 B6 Baden-Württemberg, SW Germany
Sint Maarten 33 G3 Eng. Saint Martin. Island N Netherlands Antilles
Sint-Michielsgestel 64 C4 Noord-Brabant, S Netherlands
Sint-Niklaas 65 B5 Fr. Saint-Nicolas. Oost-Vlaanderen, N Belgium
Sint-Pieters-Leeuw 65 B6 Vlaams Brabant, C Belgium
Sintra 70 B3 prev. Cintra. Lisboa, W Portugal
Sinujiif 51 E5 Nugaal, NE Somalia
Sinus Aelaniticus see Aqaba, Gulf of
Sinyang see Xinyang
Sinzyô see Shinjō
Sion 73 A7 Ger. Sitten; anc. Sedunum. Valais, SW Switzerland
Sioux City 23 F3 Iowa, C USA
Sioux Falls 23 F3 South Dakota, N USA
Siping 106 D3 var. Ssu-p'ing, Szeping; prev. Ssu-p'ing-chieh. Jilin, NE China
Siple, Mount 132 A4 mountain Siple Island, Antarctica
Siquirres 31 E4 Limón, E Costa Rica
Siracusa 75 D7 Eng. Syracuse. Sicilia, Italy, C Mediterranean Sea
Sir Darya see Syr Darya
Sir Edward Pellew Group 126 B2 island group Northern Territory, NE Australia
Siret 86 C3 var. Siretul, Ger. Sereth, Rus. Seret, Ukr. Siret. River Romania/Ukraine
Siret see Siret
Siretul see Siret
Sirikit Reservoir 114 C4 lake N Thailand
Sīrjān 98 D4 prev. Sa'īdābād. Kermān, S Iran
Sirna see Sýrna
Şırnak 95 F4 Şırnak, SE Turkey
Síros see Sýros
Sirte see Surt
Sirte, Gulf of see Surt, Khalīj
Sisak 78 B3 var. Siscia, Ger. Sissek, Hung. Sziszek; anc. Segestica. Sisak-Moslavina, C Croatia
Siscia see Sisak
Sisimiut 60 C3 var. Holsteinborg, Holsteinsborg, Holstenborg, Holstensborg. S Greenland
Sissek see Sisak
Sistema Penibético see Béticos, Sistemas
Siteía 83 D8 var. Sitía. Kríti, Greece, E Mediterranean Sea
Sitges 71 G2 Cataluña, NE Spain
Sitía see Siteía
Sittang 114 B4 var. Sittoung. River S Myanmar
Sittard 65 D5 Limburg, SE Netherlands
Sittoung see Sittang
Sittwe 114 A3 var. Akyab. Arakan State, W Myanmar
Siuna 30 D3 Región Autónoma Atlántico Norte, NE Nicaragua
Siut see Asyût
Sivas 94 D3 anc. Sebastia, Sebaste. Sivas, C Turkey
Sivers'kyy Donets' see Donets
Siwa 50 A2 var. Sīwah. NW Egypt
Sīwah see Siwa
Six-Fours-les-Plages 69 D6 Var, SE France
Siyäzän 95 H2 Rus. Siazan'. NE Azerbaijan
Sizuoka see Shizuoka
Sjar see Sääre
Sjælland B8 Eng. Zealand, Ger. Seeland. Island E Denmark
Sjenica 79 D5 Turk. Seniça. Serbia, SW Yugoslavia
Skadar see Shkodër
Skagerak see Skagerrak
Skagerrak 63 A6 var. Skagerak. Channel N Europe
Skagit River 24 B1 river Washington, NW USA
Skalka 62 C3 lake N Sweden
Skarżysko-Kamienna 76 D4 Świętokrzyskie, C Poland
Skaudvilė 84 B4 Tauragė, SW Lithuania
Skegness 67 E6 E England, UK
Skellefteå 62 D4 Västerbotten, N Sweden
Skellefteälven 62 C4 river N Sweden
Ski 63 B6 Akershus, S Norway
Skíathos 83 C5 Skíathos, Vóreioi Sporádes, Greece, Aegean Sea
Skidal' 85 B5 Rus. Skidel'. Hrodzyenskaya Voblasts', W Belarus
Skierniewice 76 D3 Łódzkie, C Poland
Skiftet 84 C1 Fin. Kihti. Strait Gulf of Bothnia/Gulf of Finland
Skíros see Skýros
Skópelos 83 C5 Skópelos, Vóreioi Sporádes, Greece, Aegean Sea
Skopje 79 D6 var. Üsküb, Turk. Üsküp; prev. Skoplje, anc. Scupi. Country capital (FYR Macedonia) N FYR Macedonia
Skoplje see Skopje
Skovorodino 93 F4 Amurskaya Oblast', SE Russian Federation
Skuodas 84 B3 Ger. Schoden, Pol. Szkudy. Skuodas, NW Lithuania
Skye, Isle of 66 B3 island NW Scotland, UK
Skýros 83 C5 var. Skíros. Skýros, Vóreioi Sporádes, Greece, Aegean Sea
Skýros 83 C5 var. Skíros; anc. Scyros. Island Vóreioi Sporádes, Greece, Aegean Sea
Slagelse 63 B7 Vestsjælland, E Denmark
Slatina 86 B5 Olt, S Romania
Slatina 78 C3 Hung. Szlatina, prev. Podravska Slatina. Virovitica-Podravina, NE Croatia
Slavonska Požega see Požega
Slavonski Brod 78 C3 Ger. Brod, Hung. Bród; prev. Brod, Brod na Savi. Brod-Posavina, NE Croatia
Slavuta 86 C2 Khmel'nyts'ka Oblast', NW Ukraine
Slawharad 85 E7 Rus. Slavgorod. Mahilyowskaya Voblasts', E Belarus
Sławno 76 C2 Zachodniopomorskie, NW Poland
Sléibhte Chill Mhantáin see Wicklow Mountains
Slēmānī see As Sulaymānīyah
Sliema 80 B5 N Malta
Sligeach see Sligo
Sligo 67 A5 Ir. Sligeach. NW Ireland
Sliven 82 D2 var. Slivno. Sliven, C Bulgaria
Slivnitsa 82 B2 Sofiya, W Bulgaria
Slivno see Sliven
Slobozia 86 C5 Ialomiţa, SE Romania
Slonim 85 B6 Pol. Słonim, Rus. Slonim. Hrodzyenskaya Voblasts', W Belarus
Slovakia 77 C6 off. Slovenská Republika, Ger. Slowakei, Hung. Szlovákia, Slvk. Slovensko. Country C Europe
Slovak Ore Mountains see Slovenské rudohorie
Slovenia 73 D8 off. Republic of Slovenia, Ger. Slowenien, Slvn. Slovenija. Country SE Europe
Slovenské rudohorie 77 D6 Eng. Slovak Ore Mountains, Ger. Slowakisches Erzgebirge, Ungarisches Erzgebirge. Mountain range C Slovakia
Slov"yans'k 87 G3 Rus. Slavyansk. Donets'ka Oblast', E Ukraine
Slowakisches Erzgebirge see Slovenské rudohorie
Słubice 76 B3 Ger. Frankfurt. Lubuskie, W Poland
Sluch 86 D1 river NW Ukraine
Słupsk 76 C2 Ger. Stolp. Pomorskie, N Poland
Slutsk 85 C6 Rus. Slutsk. Minskaya Voblasts', S Belarus
Smallwood Reservoir 17 F2 lake Newfoundland and Labrador, S Canada
Smara 48 B3 var. Es Semara. N Western Sahara
Smarhon' 85 C5 Pol. Smorgonie, Rus. Smorgon'. Hrodzyenskaya Voblasts', W Belarus
Smederevo 78 D4 Ger. Semendria. Serbia, N Yugoslavia
Smederevska Palanka 78 D4 Serbia, C Yugoslavia
Smila 87 E2 Rus. Smela. Cherkas'ka Oblast', C Ukraine
Smiltene 84 D3 Ger. Smilten. Valka, N Latvia
Smøla 62 A4 island W Norway
Smolensk 89 A5 Smolenskaya Oblast', W Russian Federation
Snake 12 B4 river Yukon Territory, NW Canada
Snake River 24 C3 river NW USA
Snake River Plain 24 D4 plain Idaho, NW USA
Sneek 64 D2 Friesland, N Netherlands
Sněžka 76 B4 Ger. Schneekoppe. Mountain N Czech Republic
Śniardwy, Jezioro 114 D2 Ger. Spirdingsee. Lake NE Poland
Snina 77 E5 Hung. Szinna. Prešovský Kraj, E Slovakia
Snowdonia 67 C6 mountain range NW Wales, UK
Snyder 27 F3 Texas, SW USA
Sobradinho, Represa de 41 F2 var. Barragem de Sobradinho. Reservoir E Brazil
Sochi 89 A7 Krasnodarskiy Kray, SW Russian Federation
Société, Archipel de la 123 G4 var. Archipel de Tahiti, Îles de la Société, Eng. Society Islands. Island group W French Polynesia
Society Islands see Société, Archipel de la
Socorro 26 D2 New Mexico, SW USA
Socorro, Isla 28 B5 island W Mexico
Socotra see Suquṭrā
Soc Trăng 115 D6 var. Khanh. Soc Trăng, S Vietnam
Socuéllamos 71 E3 Castilla-La Mancha, C Spain
Sodankylä 62 D3 Lappi, N Finland
Sodari see Sodiri
Söderhamn 63 C5 Gävleborg, C Sweden
Södertälje 63 C6 Stockholm, C Sweden
Sodiri 50 B4 var. Sawdirī, Sodari. Northern Kordofan, C Sudan
Sofia see Sofiya
Sofiya 82 C2 var. Sophia, Eng. Sofia; Lat. Serdica. Country capital (Bulgaria) Sofiya-Grad, W Bulgaria
Sogamoso 36 B3 Boyacá, C Colombia
Sognefjorden 63 A5 fjord NE North Sea
Sohâg 50 B2 var. Sawhāj, Suliag. C Egypt
Sohar see Ṣuḥār
Sohm Plain 44 B3 undersea feature NW Atlantic Ocean
Sohrau see Żory
Sokal' 86 C2 Rus. Sokal. L'vivs'ka Oblast', NW Ukraine
Söke 94 A4 Aydın, SW Turkey
Sokhumi 95 E1 Rus. Sukhumi. NW Georgia
Sokodé 53 F4 C Togo
Sokol 88 C4 Vologodskaya Oblast', NW Russian Federation
Sokółka 76 E3 Białystok, NE Poland
Sokolov 77 A5 Ger. Falkenau an der Eger; prev. Falknov nad Ohří. Karlovarský Kraj, W Czech Republic
Sokone 52 B3 W Senegal
Sokoto 53 F4 river NW Nigeria
Sokoto 53 F3 Sokoto, NW Nigeria
Sokotra see Suquṭrā
Solāpur 102 B3 var. Sholāpur. Mahārāshtra, W India
Solca 86 C3 Ger. Solka. Suceava, N Romania
Sol, Costa del 70 D5 coastal region S Spain
Soldeu 69 B7 NE Andorra
Solec Kujawski 76 C3 Kujawsko-pomorskie, C Poland
Soledad, Isla see East Falkland
Soledad 36 B1 Anzoátegui, NE Venezuela
Solikamsk 92 C3 Permskaya Oblast', NW Russian Federation
Sol'-Iletsk 89 D6 Orenburgskaya Oblast', W Russian Federation
Solingen 72 A4 Nordrhein-Westfalen, W Germany
Sollentuna 63 C6 Stockholm, C Sweden
Solok 116 B4 Sumatera, W Indonesia
Solomon Islands 122 C3 prev. British Solomon Islands Protectorate. Country W Pacific Ocean
Solomon Islands 122 C3 island group PNG/Solomon Islands
Solomon Sea 122 B3 sea W Pacific Ocean
Soltau 72 B3 Niedersachsen, NW Germany
Sol'tsy 88 A4 Novgorodskaya Oblast', W Russian Federation
Solwezi 56 D2 North Western, NW Zambia
Sōma 108 D4 Fukushima, Honshū, C Japan
Somalia 51 D5 off. Somali Democratic Republic, Som. Jamuuriyada Demuqraadiga Soomaaliyeed, Soomaaliya; prev. Italian Somaliland, Somaliland Protectorate. Country E Africa
Somali Basin 47 E5 undersea feature W Indian Ocean
Sombor 78 C3 Hung. Zombor. Serbia, NW Yugoslavia
Someren 65 D5 Noord-Brabant, SE Netherlands
Somerset 20 A5 var. Somerset Village. W Bermuda
Somerset 18 C5 Kentucky, S USA
Somerset Island 15 F2 island Queen Elizabeth Islands, Nunavut, NW Canada
Somerset Island 20 A5 island W Bermuda
Somerset Village see Somerset
Somers Islands see Bermuda
Somerton 26 A2 Arizona, SW USA
Someş 86 B3 var. Somesch, Someşul, Szamos, Ger. Samosch. River Hungary/Romania
Somesch see Someş
Someşul see Someş
Somme 68 C2 river N France
Somotillo 30 C3 Chinandega, NW Nicaragua
Somoto 30 D3 Madriz, NW Nicaragua
Songea 51 C8 Ruvuma, S Tanzania
Sông Hông Hà see Red River
Songkhla 115 C7 var. Songkla, Mal. Singora. Songkhla, SW Thailand
Songkla see Songkhla
Sông Srepok see Srêpôk, Tônle
Sông Tiên Giang see Mekong

INDEX

Szeping – Tiberias, Lake

Szeping see Siping
Sziszek see Sisak
Szlatina see Slatina
Szolnok 77 D6 Jász-Nagykun-Szolnok, C Hungary
Szombathely 77 B6 Ger. Steinamanger; anc. Sabaria, Savaria. Vas, W Hungary
Szprotawa 76 B4 Ger. Sprottau. Lubuskie, W Poland

T

Table Rock Lake 27 G1 reservoir Arkansas/Missouri, C USA
Tábor 77 B5 Budějovický Kraj, S Czech Republic
Tabora 51 B7 Tabora, W Tanzania
Tabrīz 98 C2 var. Tebriz; anc. Tauris. Āžarbāyjān-e Khāvarī, NW Iran
Tabuaeran 123 G2 prev. Fanning Island. Atoll Line Islands, E Kiribati
Tabūk 98 A4 Tabūk, NW Saudi Arabia
Täby 63 C6 Stockholm, C Sweden
Tachov 77 A5 Ger. Tachau. Plzeňský Kraj, W Czech Republic
Tacloban 117 F2 off. Tacloban City. Leyte, C Philippines
Tacna 39 E4 Tacna, SE Peru
Tacoma 24 B2 Washington, NW USA
Tacuarembó 42 D4 prev. San Fructuoso. Tacuarembó, C Uruguay
Tademaït, Plateau du 48 D3 plateau C Algeria
Tadmor see Tudmur
Tadmur see Tudmur
Tādpatri 110 C2 Andhra Pradesh, E India
Taegu 107 E4 off. Taegu-gwangyŏksi, var. Daegu, Jap. Taikyū. SE South Korea
Taejŏn 107 E4 off. Taejŏn-gwangyŏksi, Jap. Taiden. C South Korea
Tafassâsset, Ténéré du 53 G2 desert N Niger
Tafila see Aṭ Ṭafīlah
Taganrog 89 A7 Rostovskaya Oblast', SW Russian Federation
Taganrog, Gulf of 87 G4 Rus. Taganrogskiy Zaliv, Ukr. Tahanroz'ka Zatoka. Gulf Russian Federation/Ukraine
Taguatinga 41 F3 Tocantins, C Brazil
Tagus 70 C3 Port. Rio Tejo, Sp. Río Tajo. River Portugal/Spain
Tagus Plain 58 A4 undersea feature E Atlantic Ocean
Tahat 49 E4 mountain SE Algeria
Tahiti 123 H4 island Îles du Vent, W French Polynesia
Tahlequah 27 G1 Oklahoma, C USA
Tahoe, Lake 25 B5 lake California/Nevada, W USA
Tahoua 53 F3 Tahoua, W Niger
T'aichung 106 D6 Jap. Taichū; prev. Taiwan. C Taiwan
Taieri 129 B7 river South Island, NZ
Taihape 128 D4 Manawatu-Wanganui, North Island, NZ
Tailem Bend 127 B7 South Australia
T'ainan 106 D6 Jap. Tainan; prev. Dainan. S Taiwan
T'aipei 106 D6 Jap. Taihoku; prev. Daihoku. Country capital (Taiwan) N Taiwan
Taiping 116 B3 Perak, Peninsular Malaysia
Taiwan 106 D6 off. Republic of China, var. Formosa, Formo'sa. Country E Asia
T'aiwan Haihsia see Taiwan Strait
Taiwan Haixia see Taiwan Strait
Taiwan Strait 106 D6 var. Formosa Strait, Chin. T'aiwan Haihsia, Taiwan Haixia. Strait China/Taiwan
Taiyuan 106 C4 prev. T'ai-yuan, T'ai-yüan, Yangku. Shanxi, C China
Ta'izz 99 B7 SW Yemen
Tajikistan 101 E3 off. Republic of Tajikistan, Rus. Tadzhikistan, Taj. Jumhurii Tojikiston; prev. Tajik S.S.R. Country C Asia
Tak 114 C4 var. Rahaeng. Tak, W Thailand
Takao see Kaohsiung
Takaoka 109 C5 Toyama, Honshū, SW Japan
Takapuna 128 D2 Auckland, North Island, NZ
Takhiatosh 100 C2 Rus. Takhiatash. Qoraqalpoghiston Respublikasi, W Uzbekistan
Takhtakŭpir 100 D1 Rus. Takhtakupyr. Qoraqalpoghiston Respublikasi, NW Uzbekistan
Takikawa 108 D2 Hokkaidō, NE Japan
Takla Makan Desert see Taklimakan Shamo
Taklimakan Shamo 104 B3 Eng. Takla Makan Desert. Desert NW China
Takow see Kaohsiung
Takutea 123 G4 island S Cook Islands
Talachyn 85 D6 Rus. Tolochin. Vitsyebskaya Voblasts', NE Belarus
Talamanca, Cordillera de 31 E5 mountain range S Costa Rica
Talara 38 B2 Piura, NW Peru
Talas 101 F2 Talasskaya Oblast', NW Kyrgyzstan
Talaud, Kepulauan 117 F3 island group E Indonesia
Talavera de la Reina 70 D3 anc. Caesarobriga, Talabriga. Castilla-La Mancha, C Spain
Talca 42 B4 Maule, C Chile
Talcahuano 43 B5 Bío Bío, C Chile
Taldykorgan 92 C5 Kaz. Taldyqorghan; prev. Taldy-Kurgan. Almaty, SE Kazakhstan
Taldy-Kurgan/Taldyqorghan see Taldykorgan
Ta-lien see Dalian
Taliq-an see Tāloqān
Tal'ka 85 C6 Rus. Tal'ka. Minskaya Voblasts', C Belarus
Tallahassee 20 D3 prev. Muskogean. State capital Florida, SE USA
Tall al Abyaḍ see At Tall al Abyaḍ
Tallinn 84 D2 Ger. Reval, Rus. Tallin; prev. Revel. Country capital (Estonia) Harjumaa, NW Estonia
Tall Kalakh 96 B4 var. Tell Kalakh. Ḥimṣ, C Syria
Tallulah 20 B2 Louisiana, S USA
Talnakh 92 D3 Taymyrskiy (Dolgano-Nenetskiy) Avtonomnyy Okrug, N Russian Federation
Tal'ne 87 E3 Rus. Tal'noye. Cherkas'ka Oblast', C Ukraine
Taloga 27 F1 Oklahoma, C USA
Tāloqān 101 E3 var. Taliq an. Takhār, NE Afghanistan
Talsi 84 C3 Ger. Talsen. Talsi, NW Latvia
Taltal 42 B2 Antofagasta, N Chile
Talvik 62 D2 Finnmark, N Norway
Tamabo, Banjaran 116 D3 mountain range East Malaysia
Tamale 53 E4 C Ghana
Tamana 123 E3 prev. Rotcher Island. Atoll Tungaru, W Kiribati
Tamanrasset 49 E4 var. Tamenghest. S Algeria
Tamar 67 C7 river SW England, UK
Tamar see Tudmur
Tamatave see Toamasina
Tamazunchale 29 E4 San Luis Potosí, C Mexico
Tambacounda 52 C3 SE Senegal
Tambov 89 B6 Tambovskaya Oblast', W Russian Federation
Tambura 51 B5 Western Equatoria, SW Sudan
Tamchaket see Tâmchekket
Tâmchekket 52 C3 var. Tamchaket. Hodh el Gharbi, S Mauritania
Tamenghest see Tamanrasset
Tamiahua, Laguna de 29 F4 lagoon E Mexico
Tamil Nādu 110 C3 prev. Madras. State SE India
Tam Ky 115 E5 Quang Nam Đa Năng, C Vietnam
Tampa 21 E4 Florida, SE USA
Tampa Bay 21 E4 bay Florida, SE USA
Tampere 63 D5 Swe. Tammerfors. Länsi-Suomi, W Finland
Tampico 29 E3 Tamaulipas, C Mexico
Tamworth 127 D6 New South Wales, SE Australia
Tana 62 D2 var. Tenojoki, Fin. Teno, Lapp. Deatnu. River Finland/Norway see also Teno
Tana 62 D2 Finnmark, N Norway
Tanabe 109 C7 Wakayama, Honshū, SW Japan
T'ana Hāyk' 50 C4 Eng. Lake Tana. Lake NW Ethiopia
Tanais see Don
Tanami Desert 124 D3 desert Northern Territory, N Australia
Țăndărei 86 D5 Ialomița, SE Romania
Tandil 43 D5 Buenos Aires, E Argentina
Tanega-shima 109 B8 island Nansei-shotō, SW Japan
Tane Range 114 B4 Bur. Tanen Taunggyi. Mountain range W Thailand
Tanezrouft 48 D4 desert Algeria/Mali
Ţanf, Jabal aţ 96 D4 mountain SE Syria
Tanga 47 E5 Tanga, E Tanzania
Tanga 51 C7 region E Tanzania
Tanganyika, Lake 51 B7 lake E Africa
Tangeh-ye Hormoz see Hormuz, Strait of
Tanger 48 C2 var. Tangiers, Tangier, Fr./Ger. Tangerk, Sp. Tánger; anc. Tingis. NW Morocco
Tangerk see Tanger
Tanggula Shan 104 C4 var. Dangla, Tangla Range. Mountain range W China
Tangier see Tanger
Tangiers see Tanger
Tangla Range see Tanggula Shan
Tangra Yumco 104 B5 var. Tangro Tso. Lake W China
Tangro Tso see Tangra Yumco
Tangshan 106 D3 var. T'ang-shan. Hebei, E China
T'ang-shan see Tangshan
Tanimbar, Kepulauan 117 F5 island group Maluku, E Indonesia
Tanna 122 D4 island S Vanuatu
Tannenhof see Krynica
Tan-Tan 48 B3 SW Morocco
Tan-tung see Dandong
Tanzania 51 C7 off. United Republic of Tanzania, Swa. Jamhuri ya Muungano wa Tanzania; prev. German East Africa, Tanganyika and Zanzibar. Country E Africa
Taoudenit see Taoudenni
Taoudenni 53 E2 var. Taoudenit. Tombouctou, N Mali
Tapa 84 E2 Ger. Taps. Lääne-Virumaa, NE Estonia
Tapachula 29 G5 Chiapas, SE Mexico
Tapajós, Rio 41 E2 var. Tapajóz. River NW Brazil
Tapajóz see Tapajós, Rio
Ţarābulus 49 F2 var. Ţarābulus al Gharb, Eng. Tripoli. Country capital (Libya) NW Libya
Ţarābulus see Tripoli
Ţarābulus al Gharb see Ţarābulus
Ţarābulus ash Sham see Tripoli
Taraclia 86 D4 Rus. Tarakilya. S Moldova
Taranaki, Mount 128 C4 var. Egmont, Mount. Mountain North Island, NZ
Tarancón 71 E3 Castilla-La Mancha, C Spain
Taranto 75 E5 var. Tarentum. Puglia, SE Italy
Taranto, Golfo di 75 E6 Eng. Gulf of Taranto. Gulf S Italy
Tarapoto 38 C2 San Martín, N Peru
Tarare 69 D5 Rhône, E France
Tarascon 69 D6 Bouches-du-Rhône, SE France
Tarawa 122 D2 atoll Tungaru, W Kiribati
Taraz 92 C5 prev. Aulie Ata, Auliye-Ata, Dzhambul, Zhambyl. Zhambyl, S Kazakhstan
Tarazona 71 E2 Aragón, NE Spain
Tarbes 69 B6 anc. Bigorra. Hautes-Pyrénées, S France
Tarcoola 127 A6 South Australia
Taree 127 D6 New South Wales, SE Australia
Tarentum see Taranto
Târgovişte 86 C5 prev. Tîrgovişte. Dâmboviţa, S Romania
Târgu Jiu 86 B4 prev. Tîrgu Jiu. Gorj, W Romania
Târgul-Neamţ see Târgu-Neamţ
Târgu Mureş 86 B4 prev. Oşorhei, Tîrgu Mures, Ger. Neumarkt, Hung. Marosvásárhely. Mureş, C Romania
Târgu-Neamţ 86 C3 var. Târgul-Neamţ; prev. Tîrgu-Neamţ. Neamţ, NE Romania
Târgu Ocna 86 C4 Hung. Aknavásár; prev. Tîrgu Ocna. Bacău, E Romania
Târgu Secuiesc 86 C4 Ger. Neumarkt, Szekler Neumarkt, Hung. Kezdivásárhely; prev. Chezdi-Oşorheiu, Târgul-Săcuiesc, Tîrgu Secuiesc. Covasna, E Romania
Tarija 39 G5 Tarija, S Bolivia
Tarīm 99 C6 C Yemen
Tarim Basin 102 C2 basin NW China
Tarim He 104 B3 river NW China
Tarma 38 C3 Junín, C Peru
Tarn 69 C6 cultural region S France
Tarn 69 C6 river S France
Tarnobrzeg 76 D4 Podkarpackie, SE Poland
Tarnów 77 D5 Małopolskie, S Poland
Tarragona 71 G2 anc. Tarraco. Cataluña, E Spain
Tàrrega 71 F2 var. Tarrega. Cataluña, NE Spain
Tarsus 94 C4 İçel, S Turkey
Tartu 84 D3 Ger. Dorpat; prev. Rus. Yurev, Yur'yev. Tartumaa, SE Estonia
Ţarţūs 96 A3 Fr. Tartouss; anc. Tortosa. Ţarţūs, W Syria
Ta Ru Tao, Ko 115 B7 island S Thailand
Tarvisio 74 D2 Friuli-Venezia Giulia, NE Italy
Tashi Chho Dzong see Thimphu
Tashkent see Toshkent
Tash-Kumyr 101 F2 Kir. Tash-Kömür. Dzhalal-Abadskaya Oblast', W Kyrgyzstan
Tashqurghan see Kholm
Tasikmalaya 116 C5 prev. Tasikmalaja. Jawa, C Indonesia
Tasman Basin 120 C5 var. East Australian Basin. Undersea feature S Tasman Sea
Tasman Bay 129 C5 inlet South Island, NZ
Tasmania 127 B8 prev. Van Diemen's Land. State SE Australia
Tasmania 130 B4 island SE Australia
Tasman Plateau 120 C5 var. South Tasmania Plateau. Undersea feature SW Tasman Sea
Tasman Sea 120 C5 sea SW Pacific Ocean
Tassili-n-Ajjer 49 E4 plateau E Algeria
Tatabánya 77 C6 Komárom-Esztergom, NW Hungary
Tathlīth 99 B5 'Asīr, S Saudi Arabia
Tatra Mountains 77 D5 Ger. Tatra, Hung. Tátra, Pol./Slvk. Tatry. Mountain range Poland/Slovakia
Ta-t'ung see Datong
Tatvan 95 F3 Bitlis, SE Turkey
Ta'ū 123 F4 var. Tau. Island Manua Islands, E American Samoa
Tau see Ta'ū
Taukum, Peski 101 G1 desert SE Kazakhstan
Taumarunui 128 D4 Manawatu-Wanganui, North Island, NZ
Taungdwingyi 114 B3 Magwe, C Myanmar
Taunggyi 114 B3 Shan State, C Myanmar
Taunton 67 C7 SW England, UK
Taupo 128 D3 Waikato, North Island, NZ
Taupo, Lake 128 D3 lake North Island, NZ
Tauragė 84 B4 Ger. Tauroggen. Tauragė, SW Lithuania
Tauranga 128 D3 Bay of Plenty, North Island, NZ
Tauris see Tabrīz
Tavas 94 B4 Denizli, SW Turkey
Tavira 70 C5 Faro, S Portugal
Tavoy 115 B5 var. Dawei. Tenasserim, S Myanmar
Tavoy Island see Mali Kyun
Tawakoni, Lake 27 G2 reservoir Texas, SW USA
Tawau 116 D3 Sabah, East Malaysia
Ţawkar see Tokar
Tawzar see Tozeur
Taxco 29 E4 var. Taxco de Alarcón. Guerrero, S Mexico
Taxco de Alarcón see Taxco
Tay 66 C3 river C Scotland, UK
Taylor 27 G3 Texas, SW USA
Taymā' 98 A4 Tabūk, NW Saudi Arabia
Taymyr, Ozero 93 E2 lake N Russian Federation
Taymyr, Poluostrov 93 E2 peninsula N Russian Federation
Taz 92 D3 river N Russian Federation
T'bilisi 95 G2 Eng. Tiflis. Country capital (Georgia) SE Georgia
T'bilisi 90 B4 international airport S Georgia
Tchien see Zwedru
Tchongking see Chongqing
Tczew 76 C2 Ger. Dirschau. Pomorskie, N Poland
Te Anau 129 A7 Southland, South Island, NZ
Te Anau, Lake 129 A7 lake South Island, NZ
Teapa 29 G4 Tabasco, SE Mexico
Teate see Chieti
Tebingtinggi 116 B3 Sumatera, N Indonesia
Tebriz see Tabrīz
Techirghiol 86 D5 Constanţa, SE Romania
Tecomán 28 D4 Colima, SW Mexico
Tecpan 29 E5 var. Tecpan de Galeana. Guerrero, S Mexico
Tecpan de Galeana see Tecpan
Tecuci 86 C4 Galaţi, E Romania
Tedzhen 100 C3 Turkm. Tejen. Akhalskiy Velayat, S Turkmenistan
Tedzhen see Harīrūd
Tees 67 D5 river N England, UK
Tefé 40 D2 Amazonas, N Brazil
Tegal 116 C4 Jawa, C Indonesia
Tegelen 65 D5 Limburg, SE Netherlands
Tegucigalpa 30 C3 country capital (Honduras) Francisco Morazán, SW Honduras
Teheran see Tehrān
Tehrān 98 C3 var. Teheran. Country capital (Iran) Tehrān, N Iran
Tehuacán 29 F4 Puebla, S Mexico
Tehuantepec 29 F5 var. Santo Domingo Tehuantepec. Oaxaca, SE Mexico
Tehuantepec, Golfo de 29 F5 var. Gulf of Tehuantepec. Gulf S Mexico
Tehuantepec, Gulf of see Tehuantepec, Golfo de
Tehuantepec, Isthmus of see Tehuantepec, Istmo de
Tehuantepec, Istmo de 29 F5 var. Isthmus of Tehuantepec. Isthmus SE Mexico
Tejen see Harīrūd
Te Kao 128 C1 Northland, North Island, NZ
Tekax 29 H4 var. Tekax de Álvaro Obregón. Yucatán, SE Mexico
Tekax de Álvaro Obregón see Tekax
Tekeli 92 C5 Almaty, SE Kazakhstan
Tekirdağ 94 A2 It. Rodosto; anc. Bisanthe, Raidestos, Rhaedestus. Tekirdağ, NW Turkey
Te Kuiti 128 D3 Waikato, North Island, NZ
Tela 30 C2 Atlántida, NW Honduras
Telanaipura see Jambi
Tel Aviv-Jaffa see Tel Aviv-Yafo
Tel Aviv-Yafo 97 A6 var. Tel Aviv-Jaffa. Tel Aviv, C Israel
Teles Pirés see São Manuel, Rio
Telish 82 C2 prev. Azizie. Pleven, NW Bulgaria
Tell Abiad see At Tall al Abyaḍ
Tell Abyad see At Tall al Abyaḍ
Tell Kalakh see Tall Kalakh
Tell Shedadi see Ash Shadādah
Telšiai 84 B3 Ger. Telschen. Telšiai, NW Lithuania
Teluk Irian see Cenderawasih, Teluk
Teluk Serera see Cenderawasih, Teluk
Temerin 78 D3 Serbia, N Yugoslavia
Temirtau 92 C4 prev. Samarkandski, Samarkandskoye. Karaganda, C Kazakhstan
Tempio Pausania 75 A5 Sardegna, Italy, C Mediterranean Sea
Temple 27 G3 Texas, SW USA
Temuco 43 B5 Araucanía, C Chile
Temuka 129 B6 Canterbury, South Island, NZ
Tenasserim 115 B6 Tenasserim, S Myanmar
Ténenkou 52 D3 Mopti, C Mali
Ténéré 53 G3 physical region C Niger
Tenerife 48 A3 island Islas Canarias, Spain, NE Atlantic Ocean
Tengger Shamo 105 E3 desert N China
Tengréla 52 D4 var. Tingréla. N Côte d'Ivoire
Tenkodogo 53 E4 S Burkina faso
Tennant Creek 126 A3 Northern Territory, C Australia
Tennessee 20 C1 off. State of Tennessee; also known as The Volunteer State. State SE USA
Tennessee River 20 C1 river S USA
Teno see Tana
Tenojoki see Tana
Tepelena see Tepelenë
Tepelenë 79 C7 var. Tepelena, It. Tepeleni. Gjirokastër, S Albania
Tepeleni see Tepelenë
Tepic 28 D4 Nayarit, C Mexico
Teplice 76 A4 Ger. Teplitz; prev. Teplice-Šanov, Teplitz-Schönau. Ústecký Kraj, NW Czech Republic
Tequila 28 D4 Jalisco, SW Mexico
Teraina 123 G2 prev. Washington Island. Atoll Line Islands, E Kiribati
Teramo 74 C4 anc. Interamna. Abruzzo, C Italy
Tercan 95 E3 Erzincan, NE Turkey
Terceira 70 A5 var. Ilha Terceira. Island Azores, Portugal, NE Atlantic Ocean
Teresina 41 F2 var. Therezina. State capital Piauí, NE Brazil
Termia see Kýthnos
Términos, Laguna de 29 G4 lagoon SE Mexico
Termiz 101 E3 Rus. Termez. Surkhondaryo Wiloyati, S Uzbekistan
Termoli 74 D4 Molise, C Italy
Terneuzen 65 B5 var. Neuzen. Zeeland, SW Netherlands
Terni 74 C4 anc. Interamna Nahars. Umbria, C Italy
Ternopil' 86 C2 Pol. Tarnopol, Rus. Ternopol'. Ternopil's'ka Oblast', W Ukraine
Terracina 75 C5 Lazio, C Italy
Terrassa 71 G2 Cast. Tarrasa. Cataluña, E Spain
Terre Adélie 132 C4 disputed region SE Antarctica
Terre Haute 18 B4 Indiana, N USA
Territoire du Yukon see Yukon Territory
Terschelling 64 C1 Fris. Skylge. Island Waddeneilanden, N Netherlands
Teruel 71 F3 anc. Turba. Aragón, E Spain
Tervel 82 E1 prev. Kurtbunar, Rom. Curtbunar. Dobrich, NE Bulgaria
Tervueren see Tervuren
Tervuren 65 C6 var. Tervueren. Vlaams Brabant, C Belgium
Teseney 50 C4 var. Tessenei. W Eritrea
Tessalit 53 E2 Kidal, NE Mali
Tessaoua 53 G3 Maradi, S Niger
Tessenderlo 65 C5 Limburg, NE Belgium
Tessenei see Teseney
Testigos, Islas los 37 E1 island group N Venezuela
Tete 57 E2 Tete, NW Mozambique
Teterow 72 C3 Mecklenburg-Vorpommern, NE Germany
Tétouan 48 C2 var. Tetouan, Tetuán. N Morocco
Tetovo 79 D5 Alb. Tetova, Tetovë, Turk. Kalkandelen. Razgrad, N Bulgaria
Tetuán see Tétouan
Tevere 74 C4 Eng. Tiber. River C Italy
Teverya 97 B5 var. Tiberias, Tverya. Northern, N Israel
Te Waewae Bay 129 A7 bay South Island, NZ
Texarkana 20 A2 Arkansas, C USA
Texarkana 27 H2 Texas, SW USA
Texas 27 F3 off. State of Texas; also known as The Lone Star State. State S USA
Texas City 27 H4 Texas, SW USA
Texel 64 C2 island Waddeneilanden, NW Netherlands
Texoma, Lake 27 G2 reservoir Oklahoma/Texas, C USA
Teziutlán 29 F4 Puebla, S Mexico
Thaa Atoll see Kolhumadulu Atoll
Thai Binh 114 D3 Thai Binh, N Vietnam
Thailand 115 C5 off. Kingdom of Thailand, Th. Prathet Thai; prev. Siam. Country SE Asia
Thailand, Gulf of 115 C6 var. Gulf of Siam, Th. Ao Thai, Vtn. Vinh Thai Lan. Gulf SE Asia
Thai Nguyên 114 D3 Băc Thai, N Vietnam
Thakhèk 114 D4 prev. Muang Khammouan. Khammouan, C Laos
Thamarīd see Thamarīt
Thamarīt 99 D6 var. Thamarīd, Thumrayt. SW Oman
Thames 67 B8 river S England, UK
Thames 128 D3 Waikato, North Island, NZ
Thanh Hoa 114 D3 Vinh Phu, N Vietnam
Thanintari Taungdan see Bilauktaung Range
Thar Desert 112 C3 var. Great Indian Desert, Indian Desert. Desert India/Pakistan
Tharthār, Buḥayrat ath 98 B3 lake C Iraq
Thásos 82 C4 island E Greece
Thásos 82 C4 Thásos, E Greece
Thaton 114 B4 Mon State, S Myanmar
Thayetmyo 114 A4 Magwe, C Myanmar
The Crane 33 H2 var. Crane. S Barbados
The Dalles 24 B3 Oregon, NW USA
The Flatts Village see Flatts Village
The Hague see 's-Gravenhage
Theodosia see Feodosiya
The Pas 15 F5 Manitoba, C Canada
Thera see Santorini
Thérma 83 D6 Ikaría, Dodekánisos, Greece, Aegean Sea
Thermaïkós Kólpos 82 B4 Eng. Thermaic Gulf; anc. Thermaicus Sinus. Gulf N Greece
Thermiá see Kýthnos
Thérmo 83 B5 Dytikí Ellás, C Greece
The Rock 71 H4 E Gibraltar
The Six Counties see Northern Ireland
Thessaloníki 82 C3 Eng. Salonica, Salonika, SCr. Solun, Turk. Selânik. Kentrikí Makedonía, N Greece
The Valley 33 G3 dependent territory capital (Anguilla) E Anguilla
The Village 27 G1 Oklahoma, C USA
Thiamis see Thýamis
Thibet see Xizang Zizhiqu
Thief River Falls 23 F1 Minnesota, N USA
Thienen see Tienen
Thiers 69 C5 Puy-de-Dôme, C France
Thiès 52 B3 W Senegal
Thimbu see Thimphu
Thimphu 113 G3 var. Thimbu; prev. Tashi Chho Dzong. Country capital (Bhutan) W Bhutan
Thionville 68 D3 Ger. Diedenhofen. Moselle, NE France
Thíra 83 D7 prev. Santorin, Santoríni, anc. Thera. Island Kykládes, Greece, Aegean Sea
Thíra 83 D7 Thíra, Kykládes, Greece, Aegean Sea
Thiruvanathapuram see Trivandrum
Thitu Island 106 C8 island NW Spratly Islands
Tholen 64 B4 island SW Netherlands
Thomasville 20 D3 Georgia, SE USA
Thompson 15 F4 Manitoba, C Canada
Thonon-les-Bains 69 D5 Haute-Savoie, E France
Thorlákshöfn 61 E5 Sudhurland, SW Iceland
Thornton Island see Millennium Island
Thouars 68 B4 Deux-Sèvres, W France
Thracian Sea 82 D4 Gk. Thrakikó Pélagos; anc. Thracium Mare. Sea Greece/Turkey
Three Kings Islands 128 C1 island group N NZ
Thrissur see Trichūr
Thuin 65 B7 Hainaut, S Belgium
Thule see Qaanaaq
Thumrayt see Thamarīt
Thun 73 A7 Fr. Thoune. Bern, W Switzerland
Thunder Bay 16 B4 Ontario, S Canada
Thuner See 73 A7 lake C Switzerland
Thung Song 115 C7 var. Cha Mai. Nakhon Si Thammarat, SW Thailand
Thurso 66 C2 N Scotland, UK
Thýamis 82 A4 var. Thiamis. River W Greece
Tianjin 106 D4 var. Tientsin. Tianjin Shi, E China
Tianjin see Tianjin Shi
Tianjin Shi 106 D4 var. Jin, Tianjin, T'ien-ching, Tientsin. Admin. region municipality E China
Tianshui 106 B4 Gansu, C China
Tiba see Chiba
Tiberias see Teverya
Tiberias, Lake 97 B5 var. Chinnereth, Sea of Bahr Tabariya, Sea of Galilee, Ar. Bahrat Tabariya, Heb. Yam Kinneret. Lake N Israel

Turkmenistan – Victoria Island

Turkmenistan *100 B2 off.* Turkmenistan; *prev.* Turkmenskaya Soviet Socialist Republic. *Country* C Asia
Turkmenskiy Zaliv *100 B2 Turkm.* Türkmen Aylagy. *Lake gulf* W Turkmenistan
Turks and Caicos Islands *33 E2 UK dependent territory* N West Indies
Turlock *25 B6* California, W USA
Turnagain, Cape *128 D4 headland* North Island, NZ
Turnhout *65 C5* Antwerpen, N Belgium
Turnov *76 B4 Ger.* Turnau. Liberecký Kraj, N Czech Republic
Turnu Măgurele *86 B5 var.* Turnu-Măgurele. Teleorman, S Romania
Turon Pasttekisligi *see* Turan Lowland
Turpan *104 C3 var.* Turfan. Xinjiang Uygur Zizhiqu, NW China
Turpan Pendi *104 C3 Eng.* Turpan Depression. *Depression* NW China
Türtkül *100 D2 Rus.* Turtkul'; *prev.* Petroaleksandrovsk. Qoraqalpoghiston Respublikasi, W Uzbekistan
Turuga *see* Tsuruga
Turuoka *see* Tsuruoka
Tuscaloosa *20 C2* Alabama, S USA
Tusima *see* Tsushima
Tuticorin *110 C3* Tamil Nādu, SE India
Tutrakan *82 D1* Silistra, NE Bulgaria
Tutuila *123 F4 island* W American Samoa
Tuvalu *123 E3 prev.* Ellice Islands. *Country* SW Pacific Ocean
Tuwayq, Jabal *99 C5 mountain range* C Saudi Arabia
Tuxpán *29 F4 var.* Tuxpán de Rodríguez Cano. Veracruz-Llave, E Mexico
Tuxpan *28 D4* Jalisco, C Mexico
Tuxpan *28 D4* Nayarit, C Mexico
Tuxpán de Rodríguez Cano *see* Tuxpán
Tuxtepec *29 F4 var.* San Juan Bautista Tuxtepec. Oaxaca, S Mexico
Tuxtla *29 G5 var.* Tuxtla Gutiérrez. Chiapas, SE Mexico
Tuxtla *see* San Andrés Tuxtla
Tuxtla Gutiérrez *see* Tuxtla
Tuy Hoa *115 E5* Phu Yên, S Vietnam
Tuz Gölü *94 C3 lake* C Turkey
Tuzla *78 C3* Federacija Bosna I Hercegovina, NE Bosnia and Herzegovina
Tver' *88 B4 prev.* Kalinin. Tverskaya Oblast', W Russian Federation
Tverya *see* Teverya
Twin Falls *24 D4* Idaho, NW USA
Tychy *77 D5 Ger.* Tichau. Śląskie, S Poland
Tyler *27 G3* Texas, SW USA
Tympáki *83 C8 var.* Timbaki; *prev.* Timbákion. Kríti, Greece, E Mediterranean Sea
Tynda *93 F4* Amurskaya Oblast', SE Russian Federation
Tyne *66 D4 river* N England, UK
Tyôsi *see* Chōshi
Tyre *see* Soûr
Týrnavos *82 B4 var.* Tírnavos. Thessalía, C Greece
Tyrrhenian Sea *75 B6 It.* Mare Tirreno. *Sea* N Mediterranean Sea
Tyumen' *92 C3* Tyumenskaya Oblast', C Russian Federation
Tyup *101 G2 Kir.* Tüp. Issyk-Kul'skaya Oblast', NE Kyrgyzstan
Tywyn *67 C6* W Wales, UK
Tzekung *see* Zigong
T,ong D,ong *114 D4 var.* Tuong Buong. Nghê An, N Vietnam

U

Uanle Uen *see* Wanlaweyn
Uaupés, Rio *see* Vaupés, Río
Ubangi *55 C5 Fr.* Oubangui. *River* C Africa
Ubangi-Shari *see* Central African Republic
Ube *109 B7* Yamaguchi, Honshū, SW Japan
Ubeda *71 E4* Andalucía, S Spain
Uberaba *41 F4* Minas Gerais, SE Brazil
Uberlândia *41 F4* Minas Gerais, SE Brazil
Ubol Rajadhani *see* Ubon Ratchathani
Ubol Ratchathani *see* Ubon Ratchathani
Ubon Ratchathani *115 D5 var.* Muang Ubon, Ubol Rajadhani, Ubol Ratchathani, Udon Ratchathani. Ubon Ratchathani, E Thailand
Ubrique *70 D5* Andalucía, S Spain
Ucayali, Río *38 D3 river* C Peru
Uchiura-wan *108 D3 bay* NW Pacific Ocean
Uchquduq *100 D2 Rus.* Uchkuduk. Nawoiy Wiloyati, N Uzbekistan
Uchtagan, Peski *100 C2 Turkm.* Uchtagan Gumy. *Desert* NW Turkmenistan
Udaipur *112 C3 prev.* Oodeypore. Rājasthān, N India
Uddevalla *63 B6* Västra Götaland, S Sweden
Udine *74 D2 anc.* Utina. Friuli-Venezia Giulia, NE Italy
Udintsev Fracture Zone *132 A5 tectonic feature* S Pacific Ocean
Udipi *see* Udupi
Udon Ratchathani *see* Ubon Ratchathani
Udon Thani *114 C4 var.* Ban Mak Khaeng, Udorndhani. Udon Thani, N Thailand
Udorndhani *see* Udon Thani
Udupi *110 B2 var.* Udipi. Karnātaka, SW India
Uele *55 D5 var.* Welle. *River* NE Dem. Rep. Congo (Zaire)
Uelzen *72 C3* Niedersachsen, N Germany
Ufa *89 D6* Respublika Bashkortostan, W Russian Federation
Ugāle *84 C2* Ventspils, NW Latvia
Uganda *51 B6 off.* Republic of Uganda. *Country* E Africa
Uglovka *88 B4 var.* Okulovka. Novgorodskaya Oblast', W Russian Federation
Uhuru Peak *see* Kilimanjaro
Uíge *56 B1 Port.* Carmona, Vila Marechal Carmona. Uíge, NW Angola
Uinta Mountains *22 B4 mountain range* Utah, W USA
Uitenhage *56 C5* Eastern Cape, S South Africa
Uithoorn *64 C3* Noord-Holland, C Netherlands
Ujelang Atoll *122 C1 var.* Wujlān. *Atoll* Ralik Chain, W Marshall Islands
Ujungpandang *117 E4 var.* Macassar, Makassar; *prev.* Makasar. Sulawesi, C Indonesia
Ujung Salang *see* Phuket
Ukhta *92 C3* Respublika Komi, NW Russian Federation
Ukiah *25 B5* California, W USA
Ukmergė *84 C4 Pol.* Wiłkomierz. Ukmergė, C Lithuania
Ukraine *86 C2 off.* Ukraine, *Rus.* Ukraina, *Ukr.* Ukrayina; *prev.* Ukrainian Soviet Socialist Republic, Ukrainskaya S.S.R. *Country* SE Europe
Ulaanbaatar *105 E2 Eng.* Ulan Bator. *Country capital* (Mongolia) Töv, C Mongolia
Ulaangom *104 C2* Uvs, NW Mongolia
Ulan Bator *see* Ulaanbaatar
Ulanhad *see* Chifeng
Ulan-Ude *93 E4 prev.* Verkhneudinsk. Respublika Buryatiya, S Russian Federation
Ulft *64 E4* Gelderland, E Netherlands
Ullapool *66 C3* N Scotland, UK
Ulm *73 B6* Baden-Württemberg, S Germany
Ulsan *107 E4 Jap.* Urusan. SE South Korea
Ulster *67 B5 cultural region* N Ireland
Ulungur Hu *104 B2 lake* NW China
Uluru *125 D5 var.* Ayers Rock. *Rocky outcrop* Northern Territory, C Australia
Ulyanivka *87 E3 Rus.* Ul'yanovka. Kirovohrads'ka Oblast', C Ukraine
Ul'yanovsk *89 C5 prev.* Simbirsk. Ul'yanovskaya Oblast', W Russian Federation
Uman' *87 E3 Rus.* Uman. Cherkas'ka Oblast', C Ukraine
Umán *29 H3* Yucatán, SE Mexico
Umanak *see* Uummannaq
Umanaq *see* Uummannaq
Umbro-Marchigiano, Appennino *74 C3 Eng.* Umbrian-Machigian Mountains. *Mountain range* C Italy
Umeå *62 C4* Västerbotten, N Sweden
Umeälven *62 C4 river* N Sweden
Umiat *14 D2* Alaska, USA
Umm Buru *50 A4* Western Darfur, W Sudan
Umm Durmān *see* Omdurman
Umm Ruwaba *50 C4 var.* Umm Ruwābah, Um Ruwāba. Northern Kordofan, C Sudan
Umm Ruwābah *see* Umm Ruwaba
Umnak Island *14 A3 island* Aleutian Islands, Alaska, USA
Um Ruwaba *see* Umm Ruwaba
Umtali *see* Mutare
Umtata *56 D5* Eastern Cape, SE South Africa
Una *78 B3 river* Bosnia and Herzegovina/Croatia
Unac *78 B3 river* W Bosnia and Herzegovina
Unalaska Island *14 A3 island* Aleutian Islands, Alaska, USA
'Unayzah *98 B4 var.* Anaiza. Al Qaşīm, C Saudi Arabia
Uncía *39 F4* Potosí, C Bolivia
Uncompahgre Peak *22 B5 mountain* Colorado, C USA
Ungarisches Erzgebirge *see* Slovenské rudohorie
Ungava Bay *17 E1 bay* Québec, E Canada
Ungava, Péninsule d' *16 D1 peninsula* Québec, SE Canada
Ungheni *86 D3 Rus.* Ungeny. W Moldova
Unimak Island *14 B3 island* Aleutian Islands, Alaska, USA
Union *21 E1* South Carolina, SE USA
Union City Tennessee, S USA
United Arab Emirates *99 C5 Ar.* Al Imārāt al 'Arabīyah al Muttaḩidah, *abbrev.* UAE; *prev.* Trucial States. *Country* SW Asia
United Kingdom *67 B5 off.* UK of Great Britain and Northern Ireland, *abbrev.* UK. *Country* NW Europe
United States of America *13 B5 off.* United States of America, *var.* America, The States, *abbrev.* U.S., USA. *Country* North America
Unst *66 D1 island* NE Scotland, UK
Ünye *94 D2* Ordu, W Turkey
Upala *30 D4* Alajuela, NW Costa Rica
Upata *37 E2* Bolívar, E Venezuela
Upemba, Lac *55 D7 lake* SE Dem. Rep. Congo (Zaire)
Upernavik *60 C2 var.* Upernivik. C Greenland
Upernivik *see* Upernavik
Upington *56 C4* Northern Cape, W South Africa
Upolu *123 F4 island* SE Samoa
Upper Klamath Lake *24 A4 lake* Oregon, NW USA
Upper Lough Erne *67 A5 lake* SW Northern Ireland, UK
Upper Red Lake *23 F1 lake* Minnesota, N USA
Uppsala *63 C6* Uppsala, C Sweden
Ural *90 B3 Kaz.* Zayyq. *River* Kazakhstan/Russian Federation
Ural Mountains *see* Ural'skiye Gory
Ural'sk *92 B3 Kaz.* Oral. Zapadnyy Kazakhstan, NW Kazakhstan
Ural'skiye Gory *92 C3 var.* Ural'skiy Khrebet, *Eng.* Ural Mountains. *Mountain range* Kazakhstan/Russian Federation
Ural'skiy Khrebet *see* Ural'skiye Gory
Uraricoera *40 D1* Roraima, N Brazil
Urbandale *23 F3* Iowa, C USA
Uren' *89 C5* Nizhegorodskaya Oblast', W Russian Federation
Urganch *100 D2 Rus.* Urgench; *prev.* Novo-Urgench. Khorazm Wiloyati, W Uzbekistan
Urgut *101 E3* Samarqand Wiloyati, C Uzbekistan
Uroševac *79 D5 Alb.* Ferizaj. Serbia, S Yugoslavia
Ŭroteppa *101 E2 Rus.* Ura-Tyube. NW Tajikistan
Uruapan *29 E4 var.* Uruapan del Progreso. Michoacán de Ocampo, SW Mexico
Uruapan del Progreso *see* Uruapan
Uruguai, Rio *see* Uruguay
Uruguay *42 D4 off.* Oriental Republic of Uruguay; *prev.* La Banda Oriental. *Country* E South America
Uruguay *42 D3 var.* Rio Uruguai, Río Uruguay. *River* E South America
Uruguay, Río *see* Uruguay
Urumchi *see* Ürümqi
Urumqi *see* Ürümqi
Ürümqi *104 C3 var.* Tihwa, Urumchi, Urumqi, Urumtsi, Wu-lu-k'o-mu-shi, Wu-lu-mu-ch'i; *prev.* Ti-hua. *Autonomous region capital* Xinjiang Uygur Zizhiqu, NW China
Urumtsi *see* Ürümqi
Urup, Ostrov *93 H4 island* Kuril'skiye Ostrova, SE Russian Federation
Urziceni *86 C5* Ialomiţa, SE Romania
Usa *88 E3 river* NW Russian Federation
Uşak *94 B3 prev.* Ushak. Uşak, W Turkey
Ushuaia *43 B8* Tierra del Fuego, S Argentina
Usinsk *88 E3* Respublika Komi, NW Russian Federation
Üsküb *see* Skopje
Üsküp *see* Skopje
Usmas Ezers *84 B3 lake* NW Latvia
Usol'ye-Sibirskoye *93 E4* Irkutskaya Oblast', C Russian Federation
Ussel *69 C5* Corrèze, C France
Ussuriysk *93 G5 prev.* Nikol'sk, Nikol'sk-Ussuriyskiy, Voroshilov. Primorskiy Kray, SE
Ustica, Isola d' *75 B6 island* S Italy
Ust'-Ilimsk *93 E4* Irkutskaya Oblast', C Russian Federation
Ústí nad Labem *76 A4 Ger.* Aussig. Ústecký Kraj, NW Czech Republic
Ustka *76 C2 Ger.* Stolpmünde. Pomorskie, N Poland
Ust'-Kamchatsk *93 H2* Kamchatskaya Oblast', E Russian Federation
Ust'-Kamenogorsk *92 D5 Kaz.* Öskemen. Vostochnyy Kazakhstan, E Kazakhstan
Ust'-Kut *93 E4* Irkutskaya Oblast', C Russian Federation
Ust'-Olenëk *93 E3* Respublika Sakha (Yakutiya), NE Russian Federation
Ustrzyki Dolne *77 E5* Podkarpackie, SE Poland
Ust Urt *see* Ustyurt Plateau
Ustyurt Plateau *100 B1 var.* Ust Urt, *Uzb.* Ustyurt Platosi. *Plateau* Kazakhstan/Uzbekistan
Ustyurt Platosi *see* Ustyurt Plateau
Usulután *30 C3* Usulután, SE El Salvador
Usumacinta, Río *30 B1 river* Guatemala/Mexico
Utah *26 A1 off.* State of Utah; also known as Beehive State, Mormon State. *State* W USA
Utah Lake *22 B4 lake* Utah, W USA
Utena *84 C4* Utena, E Lithuania
Utica *19 F3* New York, NE USA
Utrecht *64 C4 Lat.* Trajectum ad Rhenum. Utrecht, C Netherlands
Utsunomiya *109 D5 var.* Utunomiya. Tochigi, Honshū, S Japan
Uttar Pradesh *113 E3 prev.* United Provinces, United Provinces of Agra and Oudh. *State* N India
Utunomiya *see* Utsunomiya
Uulu *84 D2* Pärnumaa, SW Estonia
Uummannaq *60 C3 var.* Umanak, Umanaq. C Greenland
Uummannarsuaq *see* Nunap Isua
Uvalde *27 F4* Texas, SW USA
Uvaravichy *85 D7 Rus.* Uvarovichi. Homyel'skaya Voblasts', SE Belarus
Uvea, Île *123 E4 island* N Wallis and Futuna
Uvs Nuur *104 C1 var.* Ozero Ubsu-Nur. *Lake* Mongolia/Russian Federation
'Uwaynāt, Jabal al *88 A3 var.* Jebel Uweinat. *Mountain* Libya/Sudan
Uyo *53 G5* Akwa Ibom, S Nigeria
Uyuni *39 F5* Potosí, W Bolivia
Uzbekistan *100 D2 off.* Republic of Uzbekistan. *Country* C Asia
Uzhhorod *86 B2 Rus.* Uzhgorod; *prev.* Ungvár. Zakarpats'ka Oblast', W Ukraine
Užice *78 D4 prev.* Titovo Užice. Serbia, W Yugoslavia

V

Vaal *56 D4 river* C South Africa
Vaals *65 D6* Limburg, SE Netherlands
Vaasa *63 D5 Swe.* Vasa; *prev.* Nikolainkaupunki. Länsi Suomi, W Finland
Vaassen *64 D3* Gelderland, E Netherlands
Vác *77 C6 Ger.* Waitzen. Pest, N Hungary
Vadodara *112 C4 prev.* Baroda. Gujarāt, W India
Vaduz *72 E2 country capital* (Liechtenstein) W Liechtenstein
Váh *77 C5 Ger.* Waag, *Hung.* Vág. *River* W Slovakia
Väinameri *84 C2 prev.* Muhu Väin, *Ger.* Moon-Sund. *Sea* E Baltic Sea
Valachia *see* Wallachia
Valday *88 B4* Novgorodskaya Oblast', W Russian Federation
Valdecañas, Embalse de *70 D3 reservoir* W Spain
Valdepeñas *71 E4* Castilla-La Mancha, C Spain
Valdés, Península *43 C6 peninsula* SE Argentina
Valdez *14 C3* Alaska, USA
Valdia *see* Weldiya
Valdivia *43 B5* Los Lagos, C Chile
Val-d'Or *16 D4* Québec, SE Canada
Valdosta *21 E3* Georgia, SE USA
Valence *69 D5 anc.* Valentia, Valentia Julia, Ventia. Drôme, E France
Valencia *24 D1* California, W USA
Valencia *36 D1* Carabobo, N Venezuela
Valencia *71 F3* País Valenciano, E Spain
Valencia, Golfo de *71 F3 var.* Gulf of Valencia. *Gulf* E Spain
Valencia, Gulf of *see* Valencia, Golfo de
Valenciennes *68 D2* Nord, N France
Valera *36 C2* Trujillo, NW Venezuela
Valga *84 D3 Ger.* Walk, *Latv.* Valka. Valgamaa, S Estonia
Valira *69 A8 river* Andorra/Spain
Valjevo *78 C4* Serbia, W Yugoslavia
Valjok *see* Válljohka
Valka *84 D3 Ger.* Walk. Valka, N Latvia
Valkenswaard *65 D5* Noord-Brabant, S Netherlands
Valladolid *70 D2* Castilla-León, NW Spain
Valladolid *29 H3* Yucatán, SE Mexico
Vall d'Uxó *71 F3* País Valenciano, E Spain
Valle de La Pascua *36 D2* Guárico, N Venezuela
Valledupar *36 B1* Cesar, N Colombia
Vallejo *25 B6* California, W USA
Vallenar *42 B3* Atacama, N Chile
Valletta *75 C8 prev.* Valetta. *Country capital* (Malta) E Malta
Valley City *23 E2* North Dakota, N USA
Válljohka *62 D2 var.* Valjok. Finnmark, N Norway
Valls *71 G2* Cataluña, NE Spain
Valmiera *84 D3 Est.* Volmari, *Ger.* Wolmar. Valmiera, N Latvia
Valozhyn *85 C5 Pol.* Wołożyn, *Rus.* Volozhin. Minskaya Voblasts', C Belarus
Valparaiso *18 C3* Indiana, N USA
Valparaíso *42 B4* Valparaíso, C Chile
Valverde del Camino *70 C4* Andalucía, S Spain
Van *95 F3* Van, E Turkey
Vanadzor *95 F2 prev.* Kirovakan. N Armenia
Vancouver *14 D5* British Columbia, SW Canada
Vancouver *24 B3* Washington, NW USA
Vancouver Island *14 D5 island* British Columbia, SW Canada
Van Diemen Gulf *124 D2 gulf* Northern Territory, N Australia
Vänern *63 B6 Eng.* Lake Vaner; *prev.* Lake Vener. *Lake* S Sweden
Vangaindrano *57 G4* Fianarantsoa, SE Madagascar
Van Gölü *95 F3 Eng.* Lake Van; *anc.* Thospitis. *Salt lake* E Turkey
Van Horn *26 D3* Texas, SW USA
Van, Lake *see* Van Gölü
Vannes *68 A3 anc.* Dariorigum. Morbihan, NW France
Vantaa *63 D6 Swe.* Vanda. Etelä-Suomi, S Finland
Vanua Levu *123 E4 island* N Fiji
Vanuatu *122 C4 off.* Republic of Vanuatu; *prev.* New Hebrides. *Country* SW Pacific Ocean
Van Wert *18 C4* Ohio, N USA
Varakļani *84 D4* Madona, C Latvia
Vārānasi *113 E3 prev.* Banaras, Benares, *hist.* Kasi. Uttar Pradesh, N India
Varangerfjorden *62 E2 fjord* N Norway
Varangerhalvøya *62 D2 peninsula* N Norway
Varannó *see* Vranov nad Topl'ou
Varaždin *78 B2 Ger.* Warasdin, *Hung.* Varasd. Varaždin, N Croatia
Varberg *63 B7* Halland, S Sweden
Vardar *79 E6 Gk.* Axiós. *River* FYR Macedonia/Greece *see also* Axiós
Varde *63 A7* Ribe, W Denmark
Varėna *85 B5 Pol.* Orany. Varėna, S Lithuania
Varese *74 B2* Lombardia, N Italy
Vârful Moldoveanu *86 B4 var.* Moldoveanul; *prev.* Vîrful Moldoveanu. *Mountain* C Romania
Varkaus *63 E5* Itä-Suomi, C Finland
Varna *82 E2 prev.* Stalin, *anc.* Odessus. Varna, E Bulgaria
Varnenski Zaliv *82 E2 prev.* Stalinski Zaliv. *Bay* E Bulgaria
Vasilikí *83 A5* Lefkáda, Iónioi Nísoi, Greece, C Mediterranean Sea
Vasilishki *85 B5 Pol.* Wasiliszki, *Rus.* Vasilishki. Hrodzyenskaya Voblasts', W Belarus
Vaslui *86 D4* Vaslui, C Romania
Västerås *63 C6* Västmanland, C Sweden
Vasyl'kiv *87 E2 Rus.* Vasil'kov. Kyyivs'ka Oblast', N Ukraine
Vaté *see* Efate
Vatican City *75 A7 off.* Vatican City State. *Country* S Europe
Vatnajökull *61 E5 glacier* SE Iceland
Vättern *63 B6 Eng.* Lake Vatter; *prev.* Lake Vetter. *Lake* S Sweden
Vaughn *26 D2* New Mexico, SW USA
Vaupés, Río *36 C4 var.* Rio Uaupés. *River* Brazil/Colombia *see also* Uaupés, Rio
Vava'u Group *123 E4 island group* N Tonga
Vavuniya *110 D3* Northern Province, N Sri Lanka
Vawkavysk *85 B6 Pol.* Wołkowysk, *Rus.* Volkovysk. Hrodzyenskaya Voblasts', W Belarus
Växjö *63 C7 var.* Vexiö. Kronoberg, S Sweden
Vaygach, Ostrov *88 E2 island* NW Russian Federation
Veendam *64 E2* Groningen, NE Netherlands
Veenendaal *64 D4* Utrecht, C Netherlands
Vega *62 B4 island* C Norway
Veisiejai *85 B5* Lazdijai, S Lithuania
Vejer de la Frontera *70 C5* Andalucía, S Spain
Veldhoven *65 D5* Noord-Brabant, S Netherlands
Velebit *78 A3 mountain range* C Croatia
Velenje *73 E7 Ger.* Wöllan. N Slovenia
Veles *79 E6 Turk.* Köprülü. C FYR Macedonia
Velho *see* Porto Velho
Velika Morava *78 D4 var.* Glavn'a Morava, Morava, *Ger.* Grosse Morava. *River* C Yugoslavia
Velikaya *91 G2 river* NE Russian Federation
Velikiye Luki *88 A4* Pskovskaya Oblast', W Russian Federation
Veliko Tŭrnovo *82 D2 prev.* Tirnovo, Trnovo, Tŭrnovo. Veliko Tŭrnovo, N Bulgaria
Velingrad *82 C3* Pazardzhik, C Bulgaria
Vel'ký Krtíš *77 D6* Banskobystrický Kraj, C Slovakia
Vellore *110 C2* Tamil Nādu, SE India
Velobriga *see* Viana do Castelo
Velsen *see* Velsen-Noord
Velsen-Noord *64 C3 var.* Velsen. Noord-Holland, W Netherlands
Vel'sk *88 C4 var.* Velsk. Arkhangel'skaya Oblast', NW Russian Federation
Velsk *see* Vel'sk
Velvendos *see* Velvendós
Velvendós *82 B4 var.* Velvendos. Dytikí Makedonía, N Greece
Velykyy Tokmak *see* Tokmak
Vendôme *68 C4* Loir-et-Cher, C France
Venezia *74 C2 Eng.* Venice, *Fr.* Venise, *Ger.* Venedig; *anc.*Venetia. Veneto, NE Italy
Venezuela *36 D2 off.* Republic of Venezuela; *prev.* Estados Unidos de Venezuela, United States of Venezuela. *Country* N South America
Venezuela, Golfo de *36 C1 Eng.* Gulf of Maracaibo, Gulf of Venezuela. *Gulf* NW Venezuela
Venezuelan Basin *34 B1 undersea feature* E Caribbean Sea
Venice *see* Venezia
Venice *20 C4* Louisiana, S USA
Venice, Gulf of *74 C2 It.* Golfo di Venezia, *Slvn.* Beneški Zaliv. *Gulf* N Adriatic Sea
Venlo *65 D5 prev.* Venloo. Limburg, SE Netherlands
Venta *84 B3 Ger.* Windau. *River* Latvia/Lithuania
Ventimiglia *74 A3* Liguria, NW Italy
Ventspils *84 B2 Ger.* Windau. Ventspils, NW Latvia
Vera *42 D3* Santa Fe, C Argentina
Veracruz *29 F4 var.* Veracruz Llave. Veracruz-Llave, E Mexico
Veracruz Llave *see* Veracruz
Vercelli *74 A2 anc.* Vercellae. Piemonte, NW Italy
Verdalsøra *62 B4* Nord-Trøndelag, C Norway
Verde, Costa *70 D1 coastal region* N Spain
Verden *72 B3* Niedersachsen, NW Germany
Veria *see* Véroia
Verkhoyanskiy Khrebet *93 F3 mountain range* NE Russian Federation
Vermillion *23 F3* South Dakota, N USA
Vermont *19 F2 off.* State of Vermont; also known as The Green Mountain State. *State* NE USA
Vernal *22 B4* Utah, W USA
Vernon *27 F2* Texas, SW USA
Véroia *82 B4 var.* Veria, Vérroia, *Turk.* Karaferiye. Kentrikí Makedonía, N Greece
Verona *74 C2* Veneto, NE Italy
Vérroia *see* Véroia
Versailles *68 D1* Yvelines, N France
Verviers *65 D6* Liège, E Belgium
Vesdre *65 D6 river* E Belgium
Veselinovo *82 D2* Shumen, NE Bulgaria
Vesoul *68 D4 anc.* Vesulium, Vesulum. Haute-Saône, E France
Vesterålen *62 B2 island group* N Norway
Vestfjorden *62 C3 fjord* C Norway
Vestmannaeyjar *61 E5* Sudhurland, S Iceland
Vesuvio *75 D5 Eng.* Vesuvius. *Volcano* S Italy
Veszprém *77 C7 Ger.* Veszprim. Veszprém, W Hungary
Vetrino *82 E2* Varna, E Bulgaria
Veurne *65 A5 var.* Furnes. West-Vlaanderen, W Belgium
Vexiö *see* Växjö
Viacha *39 F4* La Paz, W Bolivia
Viana de Castelo *see* Viana do Castelo
Viana do Castelo *70 B2 var.* Viana de Castelo; *anc.* Velobriga. Viana do Castelo, NW Portugal
Vianen *64 C4* Zuid-Holland, C Netherlands
Viangchan *114 C4 Eng./Fr.* Vientiane. *Country capital* (Laos) C Laos
Viangphoukha *114 C3 var.* Vieng Pou Kha. Louang Namtha, N Laos
Viareggio *74 B3* Toscana, C Italy
Viborg *63 A7* Viborg, NW Denmark
Vic *71 G2 var.* Vich; *anc.* Ausa, Vicus Ausonensis. Cataluña, NE Spain
Vicenza *74 C2 anc.* Vicentia. Veneto, NE Italy
Vich *see* Vic
Vichy *69 C5* Allier, C France
Vicksburg *20 B2* Mississippi, S USA
Victoria *80 A5 var.* Rabat. Gozo, NW Malta
Victoria *57 H1 country capital* (Seychelles) Mahé, SW Seychelles
Victoria *27 G4* Texas, SW USA
Victoria *14 D5* Vancouver Island, British Columbia, SW Canada
Victoria *127 C7 state* SE Australia
Victoria Bank *see* Vitória Seamount
Victoria de Durango *see* Durango
Victoria de las Tunas *see* Las Tunas
Victoria Falls *56 C2 waterfall* Zambia/Zimbabwe
Victoria Falls *56 C3* Matabeleland North, W Zimbabwe
Victoria Island *15 F3 island* Northwest Territories/Nunavut, NW Canada

Victoria, Lake – Wicklow Mountains

INDEX

Victoria, Lake 51 B6 *var.* Victoria Nyanza. *Lake* E Africa
Victoria Land 132 C4 *physical region* Antarctica
Victoria Nyanza *see* Victoria, Lake
Victoria River 124 D3 *river* Northern Territory, N Australia
Victorville 25 C7 California, W USA
Vicus Ausonensis *see* Vic
Vidalia 21 E2 Georgia, SE USA
Vidin 82 B1 *anc.* Bononia. Vidin, NW Bulgaria
Vidzy 85 C5 *Rus.* Vidzy. Vitsyebskaya Voblasts', NW Belarus
Viedma 43 C5 Río Negro, E Argentina
Vieng Pou Kha *see* Viangphoukha
Vienna *see* Wien
Vienne 69 D5 *anc.* Vienna. Isère, E France
Vienne 68 B4 *river* W France
Vientiane *see* Viangchan
Vierzon 68 C4 Cher, C France
Viesīte 84 C4 *Ger.* Eckengraf. Jēkabpils, S Latvia
Vietnam 114 D4 *off.* Socialist Republic of Vietnam, *Vtn.* Công Hoa Xa Hôi Chu Nghia Viêt Nam. *Country* SE Asia
Vietri *see* Viêt Tri
Viêt Tri 114 D3 *var.* Vietri. Vinh Phu, N Vietnam
Vieux Fort 33 F2 S Saint Lucia
Vigo 70 B2 Galicia, NW Spain
Vijayawāda 110 D1 *prev.* Bezwada. Andhra Pradesh, SE India
Vijosa *see* Vjosës, Lumi i
Vijosë *see* Vjosës, Lumi i
Vila *see* Port-Vila
Vila Artur de Paiva *see* Cubango
Vila da Ponte *see* Cubango
Vila de Mocímboa da Praia *see* Mocímboa da Praia
Vila do Conde 70 B2 Porto, NW Portugal
Vila do Zumbo 56 D2 *prev.* Vila do Zumbu, Zumbo. Tete, NW Mozambique
Vilafranca del Penedès 71 G2 *var.* Villafranca del Panadés. Cataluña, NE Spain
Vila General Machado *see* Camacupa
Viļaka 84 D4 *Ger.* Marienhausen. Balvi, NE Latvia
Vilalba 70 C1 Galicia, NW Spain
Vila Nova de Gaia 70 B2 Porto, NW Portugal
Vila Nova de Portimão *see* Portimão
Vila Pereira de Eça *see* N'Giva
Vila Real 70 C2 *var.* Vila Rial. Vila Real, N Portugal
Vila Rial *see* Vila Real
Vila Robert Williams *see* Caála
Vila Serpa Pinto *see* Menongue
Vilhelmina 62 C4 Västerbotten, N Sweden
Vilhena 40 D3 Rondônia, W Brazil
Vília 83 C5 Attikí, C Greece
Viliya 85 C5 *Lith.* Neris, *Rus.* Viliya. *River* W Belarus
Viljandi 84 D2 *Ger.* Fellin. Viljandimaa, S Estonia
Vilkaviškis 84 B4 *Pol.* Wyłkowyszki. Vilkaviškis, SW Lithuania
Villa Acuña 28 D2 *var.* Cuidad Acuña. Coahuila de Zaragoza, NE Mexico
Villa Bella 39 F2 Beni, N Bolivia
Villacarrillo 71 E4 Andalucía, S Spain
Villa Cecilia *see* Ciudad Madero
Villach 73 D7 *Slvn.* Beljak. Kärnten, S Austria
Villacidro 75 A5 Sardegna, Italy, C Mediterranean Sea
Villa Concepción *see* Concepción
Villa del Pilar *see* Pilar
Villafranca de los Barros 70 C4 Extremadura, W Spain
Villafranca del Panadés *see* Vilafranca del Penedès
Villahermosa 29 G4 *prev.* San Juan Bautista. Tabasco, SE Mexico
Villajoyosa 71 F4 *var.* La Vila Jojosa. País Valenciano, E Spain
Villa María 42 C4 Córdoba, C Argentina
Villa Martín 39 F5 Potosí, SW Bolivia
Villa Mercedes 42 C4 *prev.* Mercedes. San Luis, C Argentina
Villanueva 28 D3 Zacatecas, C Mexico
Villanueva de la Serena 70 C3 Extremadura, W Spain
Villanueva de los Infantes 71 E4 Castilla-La Mancha, C Spain
Villarrica 42 D2 Guairá, SE Paraguay
Villavicencio 36 B3 Meta, C Colombia
Villaviciosa 70 D1 Asturias, N Spain
Villazón 39 G5 Potosí, S Bolivia
Villena 71 F4 País Valenciano, E Spain
Villeurbanne 69 D5 Rhône, E France
Villingen-Schwenningen 73 B6 Baden-Württemberg, S Germany
Vilnius 85 C5 *Pol.* Wilno, *Ger.* Wilna; *prev. Rus.* Vilna. *Country capital* (Lithuania) Vilnius, SE Lithuania
Vil'shanka 87 E3 *Rus.* Olshanka. Kirovohrads'ka Oblast', C Ukraine
Vilvoorde 65 C6 *Fr.* Vilvorde. Vlaams Brabant, C Belgium
Vilyeyka 85 C5 *Pol.* Wilejka, *Rus.* Vileyka. Minskaya Voblasts', NW Belarus
Vilyuy 93 F3 *river* NE Russian Federation
Viña del Mar 42 B4 Valparaíso, C Chile
Vinaròs 71 F3 País Valenciano, E Spain
Vincennes 18 B4 Indiana, N USA
Vindhya Mountains *see* Vindhya Range
Vindhya Range 112 D4 *var.* Vindhya Mountains. *Mountain range* N India
Vineland 19 F4 New Jersey, NE USA
Vinh 114 D4 Nghê An, N Vietnam
Vinh Loi *see* Bac Liêu
Vinh Thai Lan *see* Thailand, Gulf of
Vinishte 82 C2 Montana, NW Bulgaria
Vinita 27 G1 Oklahoma, C USA
Vinkovci 78 C3 *Ger.* Winkowitz, *Hung.* Vinkovcze. Vukovar-Srijem, E Croatia
Vinnytsya 86 D2 *Rus.* Vinnitsa. Vinnyts'ka Oblast', C Ukraine
Vinson Massif 132 A3 *mountain* Antarctica
Viranşehir 95 E4 Şanlıurfa, SE Turkey
Vîrful Moldoveanu *see* Vârful Moldoveanu
Virginia 19 E5 *off.* Commonwealth of Virginia; also known as Mother of Presidents, Mother of States, Old Dominion. *State* NE USA
Virginia 23 G1 Minnesota, N USA
Virginia Beach 19 F5 Virginia, NE USA
Virgin Islands *see* British Virgin Islands
Virgin Islands (US) 33 F3 *var.* Virgin Islands of the United States; *prev.* Danish West Indies. *US unincorporated territory* E West Indies
Virgin Islands of the United States *see* Virgin Islands (US)
Virôchey 115 E5 Rôtânôkiri, NE Cambodia
Virovitica 78 C2 *Ger.* Virovititz, *Hung.* Verőcze; *prev. Ger.* Werowitz. Virovitica-Podravina, NE Croatia
Virton 65 D8 Luxembourg, SE Belgium
Virtsu 84 D2 *Ger.* Werder. Läänemaa, W Estonia
Vis 78 B4 *It.* Lissa; *anc.* Issa. *Island* S Croatia
Vis *see* Fish
Visaginas 84 C4 *prev.* Sniečkus. Ignalina, E Lithuania
Visākhapatnam 113 E5 Andhra Pradesh, SE India
Visalia 25 C6 California, W USA
Visby 63 C7 *Ger.* Wisby. Gotland, SE Sweden
Viscount Melville Sound 15 F2 *prev.* Melville Sound. *Sound* Northwest Territories/Nunavut, N Canada
Visé 65 D6 Liège, E Belgium
Viseu 70 C2 *prev.* Vizeu. Viseu, N Portugal
Visoko 78 C4 Federacija Bosna I Hercegovina, C Bosnia and Herzegovina
Vistula *see* Wisła
Vistula Lagoon 76 C2 *Ger.* Frisches Haff, *Pol.* Zalew Wiślany, *Rus.* Vislinskiy Zaliv. *Lagoon* Poland/Russian Federation
Viterbo 74 C4 *anc.* Vicus Elbii. Lazio, C Italy
Viti Levu 123 E4 *island* W Fiji
Vitim 93 F4 *river* C Russian Federation
Vitoria *see* Vitoria-Gasteiz
Vitória 41 F4 Espírito Santo, SE Brazil
Vitoria Bank *see* Vitória Seamount
Vitória da Conquista 41 F3 Bahia, E Brazil
Vitoria-Gasteiz 71 E1 *var.* Vitoria, *Eng.* Vittoria. País Vasco, N Spain
Vitória Seamount 45 B5 *var.* Victoria Bank, Vitoria Bank. *Undersea feature* C Atlantic Ocean
Vitré 68 B3 Ille-et-Vilaine, NW France
Vitsyebsk 85 E5 *Rus.* Vitebsk. Vitsyebskaya Voblasts', NE Belarus
Vittoria *see* Vitoria-Gasteiz
Vittoria 75 C7 Sicilia, Italy, C Mediterranean Sea
Vizianagaram 113 E5 *var.* Vizianagram. Andhra Pradesh, E India
Vizianagram *see* Vizianagaram
Vjosës, Lumi i 79 C7 *var.* Vijosa, Vijosë, *Gk.* Aóos. *River* Albania/Greece *see also* Aóos
Vlaardingen 64 B4 Zuid-Holland, SW Netherlands
Vladikavkaz 89 B8 *prev.* Dzaudzhikau, Ordzhonikidze. Severnaya Osetiya-Alaniya, SW Russian Federation
Vladimir 89 B5 Vladimirskaya Oblast', W Russian Federation
Vladivostok 93 G5 Primorskiy Kray, SE Russian Federation
Vlagtwedde 64 E2 Groningen, NE Netherlands
Vlasotince 79 E5 Serbia, SE Yugoslavia
Vlieland 64 C1 *Fris.* Flylân. *Island* Waddeneilanden, N Netherlands
Vlijmen 64 C4 Noord-Brabant, S Netherlands
Vlissingen 65 B5 *Eng.* Flushing, *Fr.* Flessingue. Zeeland, SW Netherlands
Vlorë 79 C7 *prev.* Vlonë, *It.* Valona, Vlora. Vlorë, SW Albania
Vöcklabruck 73 D6 Oberösterreich, NW Austria
Vohimena, Tanjona 57 F4 *Fr.* Cap Sainte Marie. *Headland* S Madagascar
Voiron 69 D5 Isère, E France
Vojvodina 78 D3 *Ger.* Wojwodina. *Region* N Yugoslavia
Volcán de Chiriquí *see* Barú, Volcán
Volga 89 B7 *river* NW Russian Federation
Volga Uplands 59 G3 *Russ.* Privolzhskaya Vozvyshennost' *mountain range* W Russian Federation
Volgodonsk 89 B7 Rostovskaya Oblast', SW Russian Federation
Volgograd 89 B7 *prev.* Stalingrad, Tsaritsyn. Volgogradskaya Oblast', SW Russian Federation
Volkhov 88 B4 Leningradskaya Oblast', NW Russian Federation
Volnovakha 87 G3 Donets'ka Oblast', SE Ukraine
Volodymyr-Volyns'kyy 86 C1 *Pol.* Włodzimierz, *Rus.* Vladimir-Volynskiy. Volyns'ka Oblast', NW Ukraine
Vologda 88 B4 Vologodskaya Oblast', W Russian Federation
Vólos 83 B5 Thessalía, C Greece
Vol'sk 89 C6 Saratovskaya Oblast', W Russian Federation
Volta 53 E5 *river* SE Ghana
Volta Blanche *see* White Volta
Volta, Lake 53 E5 *reservoir* SE Ghana
Volta Noire *see* Black Volta
Volturno 75 D5 *river* S Italy
Volzhskiy 89 B6 Volgogradskaya Oblast', SW Russian Federation
Võnnu 84 E3 *Ger.* Wendau. Tartumaa, SE Estonia
Voorst 64 D3 Gelderland, E Netherlands
Voranava 85 C5 *Pol.* Werenów, *Rus.* Voronovo. Hrodzyenskaya Voblasts', W Belarus
Vorderrhein 73 B7 *river* SE Switzerland
Vóreioi Sporádes 83 C5 *var.* Vórioi Sporádhes, *Eng.* Northern Sporades. *Island group* E Greece
Vórioi Sporádhes *see* Vóreioi Sporádes
Vorkuta 92 C2 Respublika Komi, NW Russian Federation
Vormsi 84 C2 *var.* Vormsi Saar, *Ger.* Worms, Swed. Ormsö. *Island* W Estonia
Vormsi Saar *see* Vormsi
Voronezh 89 B6 Voronezhskaya Oblast', W Russian Federation
Võru 84 D3 *Ger.* Werro. Võrumaa, SE Estonia
Vosges 68 E4 *mountain range* NE France
Vostochno-Sibirskoye More 93 F1 *Eng.* East Siberian Sea. *Sea* Arctic Ocean
Vostock Island *see* Vostok Island
Vostok 132 C3 *Russian research station* Antarctica
Vostok Island 123 G3 *var.* Vostock Island; *prev.* Stavers Island. *Island* Line Islands, SE Kiribati
Voznesens'k 87 E3 *Rus.* Voznesensk. Mykolayivs'ka Oblast', S Ukraine
Vrangelya, Ostrov 93 F1 *Eng.* Wrangel Island. *Island* NE Russian Federation
Vranje 79 E5 Serbia, SE Yugoslavia
Vranov *see* Vranov nad Topl'ou
Vranov nad Topl'ou 77 D5 *var.* Vranov, *Hung.* Varannó. Prešovský Kraj, E Slovakia
Vratsa 82 C2 Vratsa, NW Bulgaria
Vrbas 78 C3 *river* N Bosnia and Herzegovina
Vrbas 78 C3 Serbia, NW Yugoslavia
Vsetín 77 C5 *Ger.* Wsetin. Zlínský Kraj, E Czech Republic
Vučitrn 79 D5 Serbia, S Yugoslavia
Vukovar 78 C3 *Hung.* Vukovár. Vukovar-Srijem, E Croatia
Vulcano, Isola 75 C7 *island* Isole Eolie, S Italy
Vung Tau 115 E6 *prev. Fr.* Cape Saint Jacques, Cap Saint-Jacques. Ba Ria-Vung Tau, S Vietnam
Vyatka 89 C5 *river* NW Russian Federation
Vyborg 88 B3 *Fin.* Viipuri. Leningradskaya Oblast', NW Russian Federation
Vyerkhnyadzvinsk 85 D5 *Rus.* Verkhnedvinsk. Vitsyebskaya Voblasts', N Belarus
Vyetryna 85 D5 *Rus.* Vetrino. Vitsyebskaya Voblasts', N Belarus
Vynohradiv 86 B3 *Cz.* Sevluš, *Hung.* Nagyszöllös, *Rus.* Vinogradov; *prev.* Sevlyush. Zakarpats'ka Oblast', W Ukraine

W

Wa 53 E4 NW Ghana
Waal 64 C4 *river* S Netherlands
Wabash 18 C4 Indiana, N USA
Wabash River 18 B5 *river* N USA
Waco 27 G3 Texas, SW USA
Waddān 49 F3 NW Libya
Waddeneilanden 64 C1 *Eng.* West Frisian Islands. *Island group* N Netherlands
Waddenzee 64 C1 *var.* Wadden Zee. *Sea* SE North Sea
Waddington, Mount 14 D5 *mountain* British Columbia, SW Canada
Wādī as Sīr 97 B6 *var.* Wadi es Sir. 'Ammān, NW Jordan
Wadi es Sir *see* Wādī as Sīr
Wadi Halfa 50 B3 *var.* Wādī Ḥalfā'. Northern, N Sudan
Wādī Mūsā 97 B7 *var.* Petra. Ma'ān, S Jordan
Wad Madanī *see* Wad Medani
Wad Medani 50 C4 *var.* Wad Madanī. Gezira, C Sudan
Waflia 117 F4 Pulau Buru, E Indonesia
Wagadugu *see* Ouagadougou
Wagga Wagga 127 C7 New South Wales, SE Australia
Wagin 125 B7 Western Australia
Wāh 112 C1 Punjab, NE Pakistan
Wahai 117 F4 Pulau Seram, E Indonesia
Wahiawa 25 A8 *Haw.* Wahiawā. Oahu, Hawaii, USA, C Pacific Ocean
Wahībah, Ramlat Āl 99 E5 *var.* Ramlat Ahl Wahībah, Ramlat Al Wahaybah, *Eng.* Wahibah Sands. *Desert* N Oman
Wahibah Sands *see* Wahībah, Ramlat Āl
Wahpeton 23 F2 North Dakota, N USA
Wahran *see* Oran
Waiau 129 A7 *river* South Island, NZ
Waigeo, Pulau 117 G4 *island* Maluku, E Indonesia
Waikaremoana, Lake 128 E4 *lake* North Island, NZ
Wailuku 25 B8 Maui, Hawaii, USA, C Pacific Ocean
Waimate 129 B6 Canterbury, South Island, NZ
Waiouru 128 D4 Manawatu-Wanganui, North Island, NZ
Waipara 129 C6 Canterbury, South Island, NZ
Waipawa 128 E4 Hawke's Bay, North Island, NZ
Waipukurau 128 D4 Hawke's Bay, North Island, NZ
Wairau 129 C5 *river* South Island, NZ
Wairoa 128 D2 *river* North Island, NZ
Wairoa 128 E4 Hawke's Bay, North Island, NZ
Waitaki 129 B6 *river* South Island, NZ
Waitara 128 D4 Taranaki, North Island, NZ
Waiuku 128 D3 Auckland, North Island, NZ
Wakasa-wan 109 C6 *bay* C Japan
Wakatipu, Lake 129 A7 *lake* South Island, NZ
Wakayama 109 C6 Wakayama, Honshū, SW Japan
Wake Island 120 D1 *atoll* NW Pacific Ocean
Wake Island 130 C2 *US unincorporated territory* NW Pacific Ocean
Wakkanai 108 C1 Hokkaidō, NE Japan
Walachei *see* Wallachia
Walachia *see* Wallachia
Wałbrzych 76 B4 *Ger.* Waldenburg, Waldenburg in Schlesien. Dolnośląskie, SW Poland
Walcourt 65 C7 Namur, S Belgium
Wałcz 76 B3 *Ger.* Deutsch Krone. Zachodniopomorskie, NW Poland
Waldia *see* Weldiya
Wales 67 C6 *Wel.* Cymru. *National region* UK
Wales 14 C2 Alaska, USA
Wales Island, Prince of *see* Pinang, Pulau
Walgett 127 D5 New South Wales, SE Australia
Walker Lake 25 C5 *lake* Nevada, W USA
Wallachia 86 B5 *var.* Walachia, *Ger.* Walachei, *Rom.* Valachia. *Cultural region* S Romania
Walla Walla 24 C2 Washington, NW USA
Wallis and Futuna 123 E4 *Fr.* Territoire de Wallis et Futuna. *French overseas territory* C Pacific Ocean
Walnut Ridge 20 B1 Arkansas, C USA
Walthamstow 67 B7 SE England, UK
Walvis Bay 56 A4 *Afr.* Walvisbaai. Erongo, NW Namibia
Walvish Ridge *see* Walvis Ridge
Walvis Ridge 47 B7 *var.* Walvish Ridge. *Undersea feature* E Atlantic Ocean
Wan *see* Anhui
Wanaka 129 B6 Otago, South Island, NZ
Wanaka, Lake 129 A6 *lake* South Island, NZ
Wanchuan *see* Zhangjiakou
Wandel Sea 61 E1 *sea* Arctic Ocean
Wandsworth 67 A8 SE England, UK
Wanganui 128 D4 Manawatu-Wanganui, North Island, NZ
Wangaratta 127 C7 Victoria, SE Australia
Wanki, Río *see* Coco, Río
Wanlaweyn 51 D6 *var.* Wanle Weyn, *It.* Uanle Uen. Shabeellaha Hoose, SW Somalia
Wanle Weyn *see* Wanlaweyn
Wanxian 106 B5 Chongqing, C China
Warangal 113 E5 Andhra Pradesh, C India
Warburg 72 B4 Nordrhein-Westfalen, W Germany
Ware 15 E4 British Columbia, W Canada
Waremme 65 C6 Liège, E Belgium
Waren 72 C3 Mecklenburg-Vorpommern, NE Germany
Wargla *see* Ouargla
Warkworth 128 D2 Auckland, North Island, NZ
Warnemünde 72 C2 Mecklenburg-Vorpommern, NE Germany
Warner 27 G1 Oklahoma, C USA
Warnes 39 G4 Santa Cruz, C Bolivia
Warrego River 127 C5 *seasonal river* New South Wales/Queensland, E Australia
Warren 18 D3 Michigan, N USA
Warren 18 D3 Ohio, N USA
Warren 19 E3 Pennsylvania, NE USA
Warri 53 F5 Delta, S Nigeria
Warrnambool 127 B7 Victoria, SE Australia
Warsaw *see* Mazowieckie
Warszawa 76 D3 *Eng.* Warsaw, *Ger.* Warschau, *Rus.* Varshava. *Country capital* (Poland) Mazowieckie, C Poland
Warta 76 B3 *Ger.* Warthe. *River* W Poland
Warwick 127 E5 Queensland, E Australia
Washington 22 A2 *off.* State of Washington; also known as Chinook State, Evergreen State. *State* NW USA
Washington DC 19 E4 *country capital* (USA) District of Columbia, NE USA
Washington, Mount 19 G2 *mountain* New Hampshire, NE USA
Wash, The 67 E6 *inlet* E England, UK
Waspam 31 E2 *var.* Waspán. Región Autónoma Atlántico Norte, NE Nicaragua
Waspán *see* Waspam
Watampone 117 E4 *var.* Bone. Sulawesi, C Indonesia
Waterbury 19 F3 Connecticut, NE USA
Waterford 67 B6 *Ir.* Port Láirge. S Ireland
Waterloo 23 G3 Iowa, C USA
Watertown 19 F2 New York, NE USA
Watertown 23 F2 South Dakota, N USA
Waterville 19 G2 Maine, NE USA
Watford 67 A7 SE England, UK
Watsa 55 E5 Orientale, NE Dem. Rep. Congo (Zaire)
Watts Bar Lake *reservoir* Tennessee, S USA
Wau 51 B5 *var.* Wāw. Western Bahr el Ghazal, S Sudan
Waukegan 18 B3 Illinois, N USA
Waukesha 18 B3 Wisconsin, N USA
Wausau 18 B2 Wisconsin, N USA
Waverly 23 G3 Iowa, C USA
Wavre 65 C6 Wallon Brabant, C Belgium
Wāw *see* Wau
Wawa 16 C4 Ontario, S Canada
Waycross 21 E3 Georgia, SE USA
Wearmouth *see* Sunderland
Webster City 23 F3 Iowa, C USA
Weddell Plain 132 A2 *undersea feature* SW Atlantic Ocean
Weddell Sea 132 A2 *sea* SW Atlantic Ocean
Weener 72 A3 Niedersachsen, NW Germany
Weert 65 D5 Limburg, SE Netherlands
Weesp 64 C3 Noord-Holland, C Netherlands
Węgorzewo 76 D2 *Ger.* Angerburg. Warmińsko-Mazurskie, NE Poland
Weimar 72 C4 Thüringen, C Germany
Weissenburg 73 C6 Bayern, SE Germany
Weiswampach 65 D7 Diekirch, N Luxembourg
Wejherowo 76 C2 Pomorskie, NW Poland
Welchman Hall 33 G1 C Barbados
Weldiya 50 C4 *var.* Waldia, *It.* Valdia. N Ethiopia
Welkom 56 D4 Free State, C South Africa
Welle *see* Uele
Wellesley Islands 126 B2 *island group* Queensland, N Australia
Wellington 129 D5 *country capital* (NZ) Wellington, North Island, NZ
Wellington *see* Wellington, Isla
Wellington 23 F5 Kansas, C USA
Wellington, Isla 43 A7 *var.* Wellington. *Island* S Chile
Wells 24 D4 Nevada, W USA
Wellsford 128 D2 Auckland, North Island, NZ
Wells, Lake 125 C5 *lake* Western Australia
Wels 73 D6 *anc.* Ovilava. Oberösterreich, N Austria
Wembley 67 A8 SE England, UK
Wemmel 65 B6 Vlaams Brabant, C Belgium
Wenatchee 24 B2 Washington, NW USA
Wenchi 53 E4 W Ghana
Wen-chou *see* Wenzhou
Wenchow *see* Wenzhou
Wenmen Island *see* Wolf, Isla
Wenzhou 106 D5 *var.* Wen-chou, Wenchow. Zhejiang, SE China
Werda 56 C4 Kgalagadi, S Botswana
Werkendam 64 C4 Noord-Brabant, S Netherlands
Weser 72 B3 *river* NW Germany
Wessel Islands 126 B1 *island group* Northern Territory, N Australia
West Antarctica *see* Lesser Antarctica
West Bank 97 A6 *disputed region* SW Asia
West Bend 18 B3 Wisconsin, N USA
West Bengal 113 F4 *state* NE India
West Cape 129 A7 *headland* South Island, NZ
West Des Moines 23 F3 Iowa, C USA
Westerland 72 B2 Schleswig-Holstein, N Germany
Western Australia 124 B4 *state* W Australia
Western Desert *see* Sahara el Gharbîya
Western Dvina 63 E7 *Bel.* Dzvina, *Ger.* Düna, *Latv.* Daugava, *Rus.* Zapadnaya Dvina. *River* W Europe
Western Ghats 112 C5 *mountain range* SW India
Western Isles *see* Outer Hebrides
Western Sahara 48 B3 *UK disputed territory* N Africa
Western Samoa *see* Samoa
Westerschelde 65 B5 *Eng.* Western Scheldt; *prev.* Honte. *Inlet* S North Sea
West Falkland 43 C7 *var.* Isla Gran Malvina. *Island* W Falkland Islands
West Fargo 23 F2 North Dakota, N USA
West Irian *see* Irian Jaya
West Mariana Basin 120 B1 *var.* Perece Vela Basin. *Undersea feature* W Pacific Ocean
West Memphis 20 B1 Arkansas, C USA
West New Guinea *see* Irian Jaya
West Papua *see* Irian Jaya
Weston-super-Mare 67 D7 SW England, UK
West Palm Beach 21 F4 Florida, SE USA
Westport 129 C5 West Coast, South Island, NZ
West River *see* Xi Jiang
West Siberian Plain *see* Zapadno-Sibirskaya Ravnina
West Virginia 18 D4 *off.* State of West Virginia; also known as The Mountain State. *State* NE USA
Wetar, Pulau 117 F5 *island* Kepulauan Damar, E Indonesia
Wetzlar 73 B5 Hessen, W Germany
Wevok 14 C2 *var.* Wewuk. Alaska, USA
Wewuk *see* Wevok
Wexford 67 B6 *Ir.* Loch Garman. SE Ireland
Weyburn 15 F5 Saskatchewan, S Canada
Weymouth 67 D7 S England, UK
Wezep 64 D3 Gelderland, E Netherlands
Whakatane 128 E3 Bay of Plenty, North Island, NZ
Whale Cove 15 G3 Nunavut, C Canada
Whangarei 128 D2 Northland, North Island, NZ
Wharton Basin 119 D5 *var.* West Australian Basin. *Undersea feature* E Indian Ocean
Whataroa 129 B6 West Coast, South Island, NZ
Wheatland 22 D3 Wyoming, C USA
Wheeler Peak 26 D1 *mountain* New Mexico, SW USA
Wheeling 18 D4 West Virginia, NE USA
Whitby 67 D5 N England, UK
Whitefish 22 B1 Montana, NW USA
Whitehaven 67 C5 NW England, UK
Whitehorse 14 D4 *territory capital* Yukon Territory, W Canada
White Nile 50 B4 *Ar.* Al Baḩr al Abyaḑ, An Nīl al Abyaḑ, Bahr el Jebel. *River* SE Sudan
White Nile 50 B4 *var.* Bahr el Jebel. *River* S Sudan
White River 22 D3 *river* South Dakota, N USA
White Sea *see* Beloye More
White Volta 53 E4 *var.* Nakambé, *Fr.* Volta Blanche. *River* Burkina faso/Ghana
Whitianga 128 D2 Waikato, North Island, NZ
Whitney, Mount 25 C6 *mountain* California, W USA
Whitsunday Group 126 D3 *island group* Queensland, E Australia
Whyalla 127 B6 South Australia
Wichita 23 F5 Kansas, C USA
Wichita Falls 27 F2 Texas, SW USA
Wichita River 27 F2 *river* Texas, SW USA
Wickenburg 26 B2 Arizona, SW USA
Wicklow 67 B6 *Ir.* Cill Mhantáin. *Cultural region* E Ireland
Wicklow Mountains 67 B6 *Ir.* Sléibhte Chill Mhantáin. *Mountain range* E Ireland

Wieliczka – Zavidovići

ieliczka 77 D5 Małopolskie, S Poland
eluń 76 C4 Łódzkie, C Poland
ien 73 E6 *Eng.* Vienna, *Hung.* Bécs, *Slvk.* Vídeň, *Slvn.* Dunaj; *anc.* Vindobona. *Country capital* (Austria) Wien, NE Austria
iener Neustadt 73 E6 Niederösterreich, E Austria
ierden 64 E3 Overijssel, E Netherlands
iesbaden 73 B5 Hessen, W Germany
ight, Isle of 67 D7 *island* S England, UK
ijchen 64 D4 Gelderland, SE Netherlands
ijk bij Duurstede 64 D4 Utrecht, C Netherlands
ilcannia 127 C6 New South Wales, SE Australia
ilhelm, Mount 122 B3 *mountain* C PNG
ilhelm-Pieck-Stadt *see* Guben
ilhelmshaven 72 B3 Niedersachsen, NW Germany
ilkes Barre 19 F3 Pennsylvania, NE USA
ilkes Land 132 C4 *physical region* Antarctica
illard 26 D2 New Mexico, SW USA
illcox 26 C3 Arizona, SW USA
illebroek 65 B5 Antwerpen, C Belgium
illemstad 33 E5 *dependent territory capital* (Netherlands Antilles) Curaçao, Netherlands Antilles
illiston 22 D1 North Dakota, N USA
ilmington 19 F4 Delaware, NE USA
ilmington 21 F2 North Carolina, SE USA
ilmington 18 C4 Ohio, N USA
ilrijk 65 C5 Antwerpen, N Belgium
inchester 67 D7 *hist.* Wintanceaster, *Lat.* Venta Belgarum. S England, UK
inchester 19 E4 Virginia, NE USA
indhoek 56 B3 *Ger.* Windhuk. *Country capital* (Namibia) Khomas, C Namibia
indorah 126 C4 Queensland, C Australia
indsor 19 G3 Connecticut, NE USA
indsor 126 D1 New South Wales, SE Australia
indsor 16 C5 Ontario, S Canada
indsor 67 D7 S England, UK
indward Islands 33 H4 *island group* E West Indies
indward Islands *see* Barlavento, Ilhas de
indward Passage 32 D3 *Sp.* Paso de los Vientos. *Channel* Cuba/Haiti
inisk 16 C2 *river* Ontario, S Canada
inisk 16 C2 Ontario, C Canada
innebago, Lake 18 B2 *lake* Wisconsin, N USA
innemucca 25 C5 Nevada, W USA
innipeg 15 G5 Manitoba, S Canada
innipeg, Lake 15 G5 *lake* Manitoba, C Canada
innipegosis, Lake 16 A3 *lake* Manitoba, C Canada
inona 23 G3 Minnesota, N USA
inschoten 64 E2 Groningen, NE Netherlands
insen 72 B3 Niedersachsen, N Germany
inston Salem 21 E1 North Carolina, SE USA
insum 64 D1 Groningen, NE Netherlands
interswijk 64 E4 Gelderland, E Netherlands
interthur 73 B7 Zürich, NE Switzerland
inton 126 C4 Queensland, E Australia
inton 129 A7 Southland, South Island, NZ
isconsin 18 A2 *off.* State of Wisconsin; also known as The Badger State. *State* N USA
isconsin Rapids 18 B2 Wisconsin, N USA
isconsin River 18 B3 *river* Wisconsin, N USA
isła 76 C2 *Eng.* Vistula, *Ger.* Weichsel. *River* Śląskie, S Poland
ismar 72 C2 Mecklenburg-Vorpommern, N Germany
ittenberge 72 C3 Brandenburg, N Germany
ittlich 73 A5 Rheinland-Pfalz, SW Germany
ittstock 72 C3 Brandenburg, NE Germany
.J. van Blommesteinmeer 37 G3 *reservoir* E Suriname
ładysławowo 76 C2 Pomorskie, N Poland
łocławek 76 C3 *Ger./Rus.* Vlotslavsk. Kujawsko-pomorskie, C Poland
łodawa 76 E4 *Rus.* Vlodava. Lubelskie, E Poland
lotzkasbaken 56 B3 Erongo, W Namibia
odonga 127 C7 Victoria, SE Australia
odzisław Śląski 77 C5 *Ger.* Loslau. Śląskie, S Poland
öjjä *see* Wotje Atoll
oking 67 D7 SE England, UK
olf, Isla 38 A4 *var.* Wenmen Island. *Island* W Ecuador
olfsberg 73 D7 Kärnten, SE Austria
olfsburg 72 C3 Niedersachsen, N Germany
olgast 72 D2 Mecklenburg-Vorpommern, NE Germany
ollaston Lake 15 F4 Saskatchewan, C Canada
ollongong 127 D6 New South Wales, SE Australia
olvega 64 D2 *Fris.* Wolvegea. Friesland, N Netherlands
olverhampton 67 D6 C England, UK
önsan 107 E3 SE North Korea
oodburn 24 B3 Oregon, NW USA
oodland 25 B5 California, W USA
oodruff 18 B2 Wisconsin, N USA
oods, Lake of the 16 A3 *Fr.* Lac des Bois. *Lake* Canada/USA
oodville 128 D4 Manawatu-Wanganui, North Island, NZ
oodward 27 F1 Oklahoma, C USA
orcester 67 D6 *hist.* Wigorna Ceaster. W England, UK
orcester 19 G3 Massachusetts, NE USA
orcester 56 C5 Western Cape, SW South Africa
Workington 67 C5 NW England, UK
Worland 22 C3 Wyoming, C USA
Worms 73 B5 *anc.* Augusta Vangionum, Borbetomagus, Wormatia. Rheinland-Pfalz, SW Germany
Worms *see* Vormsi
Worthington 23 F3 Minnesota, N USA
Wotje Atoll 122 D1 *var.* Wōjjā. *Atoll* Ratak Chain, E Marshall Islands
Woudrichem 64 C4 Noord-Brabant, S Netherlands
Wrangel Island *see* Vrangelya, Ostrov
Wrangel Plain 133 B2 *undersea feature* Arctic Ocean
Wrocław 76 C4 *Eng./Ger.* Breslau. Dolnośląskie, SW Poland
Września 76 C3 Wielkopolskie, C Poland
Wuchang *see* Wuhan
Wuday 'ah 99 C6 Najrān, S Saudi Arabia
Wuhai 105 E3 Nei Mongol Zizhiqu, N China
Wuhan 106 C5 *var.* Han-kou, Han-k'ou, Hanyang, Wuchang, Wu-han; *prev.* Hankow. Hubei, C China
Wuhsi *see* Wuxi
Wuhsien *see* Suzhou
Wuhu 106 D5 *var.* Wu-na-mu. Anhui, E China
Wujlān *see* Ujelang Atoll
Wukari 53 G4 Taraba, E Nigeria
Wuliang Shan 106 A6 *mountain range* SW China
Wu-lu-k'o-mu-shi *see* Ürümqi
Wu-lu-mu-ch'i *see* Ürümqi
Wu-na-mu *see* Wuhu
Wuppertal 72 A4 *prev.* Barmen-Elberfeld. Nordrhein-Westfalen, W Germany
Würzburg 73 B5 Bayern, SW Germany
Wusih *see* Wuxi
Wuxi 106 D5 *var.* Wuhsi, Wu-hsi, Wusih. Jiangsu, E China
Wuyi Shan 103 E3 *mountain range* SE China
Wye 67 C6 *Wel.* Gwy. *River* England/Wales, UK
Wyndham 124 D3 Western Australia
Wyoming 22 B3 *off.* State of Wyoming; also known as The Equality State. *State* C USA
Wyoming 18 C3 Michigan, N USA
Wyszków 76 D3 *Ger.* Probstberg. Mazowieckie, C Poland

X

Xaafuun, Raas 50 E4 *var.* Ras Hafun. *Headland* NE Somalia
Xaçmaz 95 H2 *Rus.* Khachmas. N Azerbaijan
Xaignabouli 114 C4 *prev.* Muang Xaignabouri, *Fr.* Sayaboury. Xaignabouli, N Laos
Xai-Xai 57 E4 *prev.* João Belo, Vila de João Bel. Gaza, S Mozambique
Xalapa 29 F4 *var.* Jalapa, Jalapa Enríquez. Veracruz-Llave, SE Mexico
Xam Nua 114 D3 *var.* Sam Neua. Houaphan, N Laos
Xankandi 95 G3 *Rus.* Khankendi; *prev.* Stepanakert. SW Azerbaijan
Xánthi 82 C3 Anatolikí Makedonía kai Thráki, NE Greece
Xátiva 71 F3 *var.* Jativa; *anc.* Setabis. País Valenciano, E Spain
Xauen *see* Chefchaouen
Xeres *see* Jeréz de la Frontera
Xiaguan *see* Dali
Xiamen 106 D6 *var.* Hsia-men; *prev.* Amoy. Fujian, SE China
Xi'an 106 C4 *var.* Changan, Sian, Signan, Siking, Singan, Xian. Shaanxi, C China
Xian *see* Xi'an
Xiangkhoang *see* Pèk
Xiangtan 106 C5 *var.* Hsiang-t'an, Siangtan. Hunan, S China
Xiao Hinggan Ling 106 D2 *Eng.* Lesser Khingan Range. *Mountain range* NE China
Xichang 106 B5 Sichuan, C China
Xieng Khouang *see* Pèk
Xieng Ngeun *see* Muong Xiang Ngeun
Xigaze *see* Xigazê
Xigazê 104 C5 *var.* Jih-k'a-tse, Shigatse, Xigaze. Xizang Zizhiqu, W China
Xi Jiang 102 D3 *var.* Hsi Chiang, *Eng.* West River. *River* S China
Xilinhot 105 F2 *var.* Silinhot. Nei Mongol Zizhiqu, N China
Xilokastro *see* Xylókastro
Xin *see* Xinjiang Uygur Zizhiqu
Xingkai Hu *see* Khanka, Lake
Xingu, Rio 41 E2 *river* C Brazil
Xingxingxia 104 D3 Xinjiang Uygur Zizhiqu, NW China
Xining 105 E4 *var.* Hsining, Hsi-ning, Sining. *Province capital* Qinghai, C China
Xinjiang *see* Xinjiang Uygur Zizhiqu
Xinjiang Uygur Zizhiqu 104 B3 *var.* Sinkiang, Sinkiang Uighur Autonomous Region, Xin, Xinjiang. Admin. region *autonomous region* NW China
Xinpu *see* Lianyungang
Xinxiang 106 C4 Henan, C China
Xinyang 106 C5 *var.* Hsin-yang, Sinyang. Henan, C China
Xinzo de Limia 70 C2 Galicia, NW Spain
Xiqing Shan 102 D2 *mountain range* C China
Xixón *see* Gijón
Xizang *see* Xizang Zizhiqu
Xizang Gaoyuan *see* Qingzang Gaoyuan
Xizang Zizhiqu 104 B4 *var.* Thibet, Tibetan Autonomous Region, Xizang, *Eng.* Tibet. Admin. region *autonomous region* W China
Xolotlán *see* Managua, Lago de
Xuddur 51 D5 *var.* Hudur, *It.* Oddur. Bakool, SW Somalia
Xuwen 106 C7 Guangdong, S China
Xuzhou 106 D4 *var.* Hsu-chou, Suchow, Tongshan; *prev.* T'ung-shan. Jiangsu, E China
Xylókastro 83 B5 *var.* Xilokastro. Pelopónnisos, S Greece

Y

Ya'an 106 B5 *var.* Yaan. Sichuan, C China
Yabēlo 51 C5 C Ethiopia
Yablis 31 E2 Región Autónoma Atlántico Norte, NE Nicaragua
Yablonovyy Khrebet 93 F4 *mountain range* S Russian Federation
Yabrai Shan 105 E3 *mountain range* NE China
Yafran 49 F2 NW Libya
Yaghan Basin 45 B7 *undersea feature* SE Pacific Ocean
Yahotyn 87 E2 *Rus.* Yagotin. Kyyivs'ka Oblast', N Ukraine
Yahualica 28 D4 Jalisco, SW Mexico
Yakima 24 B2 Washington, NW USA
Yakima River 24 B2 *river* Washington, NW USA
Yakoruda 82 C3 Blagoevgrad, SW Bulgaria
Yaku-shima 109 B8 *island* Nansei-shotō, SW Japan
Yakutat 14 D4 Alaska, USA
Yakutsk 93 F3 Respublika Sakha (Yakutiya), NE Russian Federation
Yala 115 C7 Yala, SW Thailand
Yalizava 85 D6 *Rus.* Yelizovo. Mahilyowskaya Voblasts', E Belarus
Yalong Jiang 106 A5 *river* C China
Yalova 94 B3 Yalova, NW Turkey
Yalpuh, Ozero 86 D4 *Rus.* Ozero Yalpug. *Lake* SW Ukraine
Yalta 87 F5 Respublika Krym, S Ukraine
Yalu 103 E2 *Chin.* Yalu Jiang, *Jap.* Oryokko, *Kor.* Amnok-kang. *River* China/North Korea
Yamaguchi 109 B7 *var.* Yamaguti. Yamaguchi, Honshū, SW Japan
Yamaguti *see* Yamaguchi
Yamal, Poluostrov 92 D2 *peninsula* N Russian Federation
Yambio 51 B5 *var.* Yambiyo. Western Equatoria, S Sudan
Yambiyo *see* Yambio
Yambol 82 D2 *Turk.* Yanboli. Yambol, E Bulgaria
Yamdena, Pulau 117 G5 *prev.* Jamdena. *Island* Kepulauan Tanimbar, E Indonesia
Yam HaMelah *see* Dead Sea
Yam Kinneret *see* Tiberias, Lake
Yamoussoukro 52 D5 *country capital* (Côte d'Ivoire) C Côte d'Ivoire
Yamuna 112 D3 *prev.* Jumna. *River* N India
Yana 93 F2 *river* NE Russian Federation
Yanbu 'al Baḩr 99 A5 Al Madīnah, W Saudi Arabia
Yangambi 55 D5 Orientale, N Dem. Rep. Congo (Zaire)
Yangchow *see* Yangzhou
Yangiyŭl 101 E2 *Rus.* Yangiyul'. Toshkent Wiloyati, E Uzbekistan
Yangon 114 B4 *Eng.* Rangoon. *Country capital* (Myanmar) Yangon, S Myanmar
Yangtze *see* Chang Jiang
Yangtze Kiang *see* Chang Jiang
Yangzhou 106 D5 *var.* Yangchow. Jiangsu, E China
Yankton 23 E3 South Dakota, N USA
Yannina *see* Ioánnina
Yanskiy Zaliv 91 F2 *bay* N Russian Federation
Yantai 106 D4 *var.* Yan-t'ai; *prev.* Chefoo, Chih-fu. Shandong, E China
Yan-t'ai *see* Yantai
Yaoundé 55 B5 *var.* Yaunde. *Country capital* (Cameroon) Centre, S Cameroon
Yap 122 A1 *island* Caroline Islands, W Micronesia
Yapanskoye More *see* Japan, Sea of
Yapen, Pulau 117 G4 *prev.* Japen. *Island* E Indonesia
Yap Trench 120 B2 *var.* Yap Trough. *Undersea feature* SE Philippine Sea
Yap Trough *see* Yap Trench
Yapurá *see* Caquetá, Río
Yapurá *see* Japurá, Rio
Yaqui, Río 28 C2 *river* NW Mexico
Yaransk 89 C5 Kirovskaya Oblast', NW Russian Federation
Yarega 88 D4 Respublika Komi, NW Russian Federation
Yarkant *see* Shache
Yarlung Zangbo Jiang *see* Brahmaputra
Yarmouth *see* Great Yarmouth
Yarmouth 17 F5 Nova Scotia, SE Canada
Yaroslavl' 88 B4 Yaroslavskaya Oblast', W Russian Federation
Yarumal 36 B2 Antioquia, NW Colombia
Yasyel'da 85 B7 *river* SW Belarus
Yatsushiro 109 A7 *var.* Yatusiro. Kumamoto, Kyūshū, SW Japan
Yatusiro *see* Yatsushiro
Yaunde *see* Yaoundé
Yavarí *see* Javari, Rio
Yaviza 31 H5 Darién, SE Panama
Yavoriv 86 B2 *Pol.* Jaworów, *Rus.* Yavorov. L'vivs'ka Oblast', NW Ukraine
Yazd 98 D3 *var.* Yezd. Yazd, C Iran
Yazoo City 20 B2 Mississippi, S USA
Yding Skovhøj 63 A7 *hill* C Denmark
Ýdra 83 C6 *var.* Ídhra. *Island* S Greece
Ye 115 B5 Mon State, S Myanmar
Yecheng 104 A3 *var.* Kargilik. Xinjiang Uygur Zizhiqu, NW China
Yefremov 89 B5 Tul'skaya Oblast', W Russian Federation
Yekaterinburg 92 C3 *prev.* Sverdlovsk. Sverdlovskaya Oblast', C Russian Federation
Yelets 89 B5 Lipetskaya Oblast', W Russian Federation
Yell 66 D1 *island* NE Scotland, UK
Yellowknife 15 E4 *territory capital* Northwest Territories, W Canada
Yellow River *see* Huang He
Yellow Sea 106 D4 *Chin.* Huang Hai, *Kor.* Hwang-Hae. *Sea* E Asia
Yellowstone River 22 C2 *river* Montana/Wyoming, NW USA
Yel'sk 85 C7 *Rus.* Yel'sk. Homyel'skaya Voblasts', SE Belarus
Yelwa 53 F4 Kebbi, W Nigeria
Yemen 99 C7 *off.* Republic of Yemen, *Ar.* Al Jumhūrīyah al Yamanīyah, Al Yaman. *Country* SW Asia
Yemva 88 D4 *prev.* Zheleznodorozhnyy. Respublika Komi, NW Russian Federation
Yenakiyeve 87 G3 *Rus.* Yenakiyevo; *prev.* Ordzhonikidze, Rykovo. Donets'ka Oblast', E Ukraine
Yenangyaung 114 A3 Magwe, W Myanmar
Yendi 53 E4 NE Ghana
Yengisar 104 A3 Xinjiang Uygur Zizhiqu, NW China
Yenierenköy *see* Agialoúsa
Yenisey 92 D3 *river* Mongolia/Russian Federation
Yenping *see* Nanping
Yeovil 67 D7 SW England, UK
Yeppoon 126 D4 Queensland, E Australia
Yerevan 95 F3 *var.* Erevan, *Eng.* Erivan. *Country capital* (Armenia) C Armenia
Yeriho *see* Jericho
Yerushalayim *see* Jerusalem
Yeu, Île d' 68 A4 *island* NW France
Yevlax 95 G2 *Rus.* Yevlakh. C Azerbaijan
Yevpatoriya 87 F5 Respublika Krym, S Ukraine
Yeya 87 H4 *river* SW Russian Federation
Yezd *see* Yazd
Yezyaryshcha 85 E5 *Rus.* Yezerishche. Vitsyebskaya Voblasts', NE Belarus
Yiannitsá *see* Giannitsá
Yichang 106 C5 Hubei, C China
Yıldızeli 94 D3 Sivas, N Turkey
Yinchuan 106 B4 *var.* Yinch'uan, Yin-ch'uan, Yinchwan. Ningxia, N China
Yinchwan *see* Yinchuan
Yin-hsien *see* Ningbo
Yining 104 B2 *var.* I-ning, *Uigh.* Gulja, Kuldja. Xinjiang Uygur Zizhiqu, NW China
Yíthion *see* Gýtheio
Yogyakarta 116 C5 *prev.* Djokjakarta, Jogjakarta, Jokyakarta. Jawa, C Indonesia
Yokohama 109 D5 Aomori, Honshū, C Japan
Yokohama 108 A2 Kanagawa, Honshū, S Japan
Yokote 108 D4 Akita, Honshū, C Japan
Yola 53 H4 Adamawa, E Nigeria
Yonago 109 B6 Tottori, Honshū, SW Japan
Yong'an 106 D6 *var.* Yongan. Fujian, SE China
Yonkers 19 F3 New York, NE USA
Yonne 68 C4 *river* C France
Yopal 36 C3 *var.* El Yopal. Casanare, C Colombia
York 67 D5 *anc.* Eboracum, Eburacum. N England, UK
York 23 E4 Nebraska, C USA
York, Cape 126 C1 *headland* Queensland, NE Australia
Yorkton 15 F5 Saskatchewan, S Canada
Yoro 30 C2 Yoro, C Honduras
Yoshkar-Ola 89 C5 Respublika Mariy El, W Russian Federation
Youngstown 18 D4 Ohio, N USA
Youth, Isle of *see* Juventud, Isla de la
Yreka 24 B4 California, W USA
Yssel *see* IJssel
Ysyk-Köl *see* Issyk-Kul', Ozero
Yu *see* Henan
Yuan *see* Red River
Yuan Jiang *see* Red River
Yuba City 25 B5 California, W USA
Yucatan Channel 29 H3 *Sp.* Canal de Yucatán. *Channel* Cuba/Mexico
Yucatan Peninsula 13 C7 *peninsula* Guatemala/Mexico
Yuci 106 C4 Shanxi, C China
Yue *see* Guangdong
Yueyang 106 C5 Hunan, S China
Yugoslavia 78 D4 *off.* Federal Republic of Yugoslavia, *SCr.* Jugoslavija, Savezna Republika Jugoslavija. *Country* SE Europe
Yukhavichy 85 D5 *Rus.* Yukhovichi. Vitsyebskaya Voblasts', N Belarus
Yukon 14 C2 *river* Canada/USA
Yukon *see* Yukon Territory
Yukon Territory 14 D3 *var.* Yukon, *Fr.* Territoire du Yukon. Admin. region *territory* NW Canada
Yulin 106 C6 Guangxi Zhuangzu Zizhiqu, S China
Yuma 26 A2 Arizona, SW USA
Yumen 106 A3 *var.* Laojunmiao, Yümen. Gansu, N China
Yun *see* Yunnan
Yungki *see* Jilin
Yung-ning *see* Nanning
Yunjinghong *see* Jinghong
Yunki *see* Jilin
Yunnan 106 A6 *var.* Yun, Yunnan Sheng, Yünnan, Yun-nan. Admin. region *province* SW China
Yunnan *see* Kunming
Yunnan Sheng *see* Yunnan
Yuruá, Río *see* Juruá, Rio
Yushu 104 D4 Qinghai, C China
Yuty 42 D3 Caazapá, S Paraguay
Yuzhno-Sakhalinsk 93 H4 *Jap.* Toyohara; *prev.* Vladimirovka. Ostrov Sakhalin, Sakhalinskaya Oblast', SE Russian Federation
Yuzhou *see* Chongqing
Ylanly *see* Il'yaly

Z

Zaanstad 64 C3 *prev.* Zaandam. Noord-Holland, C Netherlands
Zabaykal'sk 93 F5 Chitinskaya Oblast', S Russian Federation
Zabern *see* Saverne
Zabīd 99 B7 W Yemen
Ząbkowice *see* Ząbkowice Śląskie
Ząbkowice Śląskie 76 B4 *var.* Ząbkowice, *Ger.* Frankenstein, Frankenstein in Schlesien. Wałbrzych, SW Poland
Zábřeh 77 C5 *Ger.* Hohenstadt. Olomoucký Kraj, E Czech Republic
Zacapa 30 B2 Zacapa, E Guatemala
Zacatecas 28 D3 Zacatecas, C Mexico
Zacatepec 29 E4 Morelos, S Mexico
Zacháro 83 B6 *var.* Zaharo, Zakháro. Dytikí Elláș, S Greece
Zadar 78 A3 *It.* Zara; *anc.* Iader. Zadar, SW Croatia
Zadetkyi Kyun 115 B6 *var.* St. Matthew's Island. *Island* Mergui Archipelago, S Myanmar
Zafra 70 C4 Extremadura, W Spain
Żagań 76 B4 *var.* Zagań, Żegań; *Ger.* Sagan. Lubuskie, W Poland
Zagazig 50 B1 *var.* Az Zaqāzīq. N Egypt
Zágráb *see* Zagreb
Zagreb 78 B2 *Ger.* Agram, *Hung.* Zágráb. *Country capital* (Croatia) Zagreb, N Croatia
Zāgros, Kūhhā ye 98 C3 *Eng.* Zagros Mountains. *Mountain range* W Iran
Zagros Mountains *see* Zāgros, Kūhhā-ye
Zaharo *see* Zacháro
Zāhedān 98 E4 *var.* Zahidan; *prev.* Duzdab. Sīstān va Balūchestān, SE Iran
Zahidan *see* Zāhedān
Zaḩlah *see* Zahlé
Zahlé 96 B4 *var.* Zaḩlah. C Lebanon
Záhony 77 E6 Szabolcs-Szatmár-Bereg, NE Hungary
Zaire *see* Congo
Zaječar 78 E4 Serbia, E Yugoslavia
Zakháro *see* Zacháro
Zākhō 98 B2 *var.* Zākhū. N Iraq
Zākhū *see* Zākhō
Zákinthos *see* Zákynthos
Zakopane 77 D5 Małopolskie, S Poland
Zakota Pomorskiea *see* Danzig, Gulf of
Zákynthos 83 A6 *var.* Zákinthos, *It.* Zante. *Island* Iónioi Nísoi, Greece, C Mediterranean Sea
Zalaegerszeg 77 B7 Zala, W Hungary
Zalău 86 B3 *Ger.* Waltenberg, *Hung.* Zilah; *prev. Ger.* Zillenmarkt. Sălaj, NW Romania
Ẓalim 99 B5 Makkah, W Saudi Arabia
Zambesi *see* Zambezi
Zambeze *see* Zambezi
Zambezi 56 D2 *var.* Zambesi, *Port.* Zambeze. *River* S Africa
Zambezi 56 C2 North Western, W Zambia
Zambia 56 C2 *off.* Republic of Zambia; *prev.* Northern Rhodesia. *Country* S Africa
Zamboanga 117 E3 *off.* Zamboanga City. Mindanao, S Philippines
Zambrów 76 E3 Podlaskie, E Poland
Zamora 70 D2 Castilla-León, NW Spain
Zamora de Hidalgo 28 D4 Michoacán de Ocampo, SW Mexico
Zamość 76 E4 *Rus.* Zamoste. Lubelskie, E Poland
Zancle *see* Messina
Zanda 104 A4 Xizang Zizhiqu, W China
Zanesville 18 D4 Ohio, N USA
Zanjān 98 C2 *var.* Zenjan, Zinjan. Zanjān, NW Iran
Zante *see* Zákynthos
Zanthus 125 C6 Western Australia
Zanzibar 51 C7 *Swa.* Unguja. *Island* E Tanzania
Zanzibar 51 D7 Zanzibar, E Tanzania
Zaozhuang 106 D4 Shandong, E China
Zapadna Morava 78 D4 *Ger.* Westliche Morava. *River* C Yugoslavia
Zapadnaya Dvina 88 A4 Tverskaya Oblast', W Russian Federation
Zapadno-Sibirskaya Ravnina 92 C3 *Eng.* West Siberian Plain. *Plain* C Russian Federation
Zapadnyy Sayan 92 D4 *Eng.* Western Sayans. *Mountain range* S Russian Federation
Zapala 43 B5 Neuquén, W Argentina
Zapiola Ridge 45 B6 *undersea feature* SW Atlantic Ocean
Zapolyarnyy 88 C2 Murmanskaya Oblast', NW Russian Federation
Zaporizhzhya 87 F3 *Rus.* Zaporozh'ye; *prev.* Aleksandrovsk. Zaporiz'ka Oblast', SE Ukraine
Zapotiltic 28 D4 Jalisco, SW Mexico
Zaqatala 95 G2 *Rus.* Zakataly. NW Azerbaijan
Zara 94 D3 Sivas, C Turkey
Zarafshon 100 D2 *Rus.* Zarafshan. Nawoiy Wiloyati, N Uzbekistan
Zaragoza 71 F2 *Eng.* Saragossa; *anc.* Caesaraugusta, Salduba. Aragón, NE Spain
Zarand 98 D3 Kermān, C Iran
Zaranj 100 D5 Nīmrūz, SW Afghanistan
Zarasai 84 C4 Zarasai, E Lithuania
Zárate 42 D4 *prev.* General José F.Uriburu. Buenos Aires, E Argentina
Zarautz 71 E1 *var.* Zarauz. País Vasco, N Spain
Zarauz *see* Zarautz
Zaraza 37 E2 Guárico, N Venezuela
Zarghūn Shahr 101 E4 *var.* Katawaz. Paktīkā, SE Afghanistan
Zaria 53 G4 Kaduna, C Nigeria
Zarós 83 D8 Kríti, Greece, E Mediterranean Sea
Zarqa *see* Az Zarqā'
Żary 76 B4 *Ger.* Sorau, Sorau in der Niederlausitz. Lubuskie, W Poland
Zaunguzskiye Garagumy 100 C2 *Turkm.* Üngüz Angyrsyndaky Garagum. *Desert* N Turkmenistan
Zavet 82 D1 Razgrad, N Bulgaria
Zavidovići 78 C3 Federacija Bosna I Hercegovina, N Bosnia and Herzegovina

INDEX